Frommer's

New Zealand

by Adrienne Rewi

WILEY

John Wiley & Sons, Inc.

ABOUT THE AUTHOR

Photojournalist **Adrienne Rewi's** passion for words and writing has taken her throughout Asia and into almost every writing genre and every subject. When not organizing her next overseas trip, taking photographs, or writing her next book, she is based in Christchurch writing for numerous New Zealand and international magazines. She is the author of seven editions of the bestselling travel guide *Frommer's New Zealand, Frommer's New Zealand Day by Day,* and has published three other non-fiction titles and assorted short stories.

Published by:

JOHN WILEY & SONS, INC.

111 River St.
Hoboken, NJ 07030-5774

ISBN 978-1-118-08601-8 (paper); ISBN 978-1-118-22328-4 (ebk); ISBN 978-1-118-23668-0 (ebk); ISBN 978-1-118-25270-3 (ebk)

Editor: Lorraine Festa, with Christine Ryan
Production Editor: Erin Geile
Cartographer: Roberta Stockwell
Photo Editor: Richard Fox
Production by Wiley Indianapolis Composition Services
Front Cover Photo: Arch Point, in Abel Tasman National Park ©HP Canada / Alamy Images
Back Cover Photo: Vineyards near Blenheim, Marlborough ©Simon Browitt / Alamy Images

For information on our other products and services or to obtain technical support, please contact our Customer Care Department within the U.S. at 877/762-2974, outside the U.S. at 317/572-3993 or fax 317/572-4002.

Wiley also publishes its books in a variety of electronic formats. Some content that appears in print may not be available in electronic formats.

Manufactured in the United States of America

5   4   3   2   1

CONTENTS

LIST OF MAPS

HOW TO CONTACT US

In researching this book, we discovered many wonderful places—hotels, restaurants, shops, and more. We're sure you'll find others. Please tell us about them, so we can share the information with your fellow travelers in upcoming editions. If you were disappointed with a recommendation, we'd love to know that, too. Please write to:

Frommer's New Zealand, 7th Edition
John Wiley & Sons, Inc. • 111 River St. • Hoboken, NJ 07030-5774
frommersfeedback@wiley.com

ADVISORY & DISCLAIMER

Travel information can change quickly and unexpectedly, and we strongly advise you to confirm important details locally before traveling, including information on visas, health and safety, traffic and transport, accommodations, shopping, and eating out. We also encourage you to stay alert while traveling and to remain aware of your surroundings. Avoid civil disturbances, and keep a close eye on cameras, purses, wallets, and other valuables.

While we have endeavored to ensure that the information contained within this guide is accurate and up-to-date at the time of publication, we make no representations or warranties with respect to the accuracy or completeness of the contents of this work and specifically disclaim all warranties, including without limitation warranties of fitness for a particular purpose. We accept no responsibility or liability for any inaccuracy or errors or omissions, or for any inconvenience, loss, damage, costs, or expenses of any nature whatsoever incurred or suffered by anyone as a result of any advice or information contained in this guide.

The inclusion of a company, organization. or website in this guide as a service provider and/or potential source of further information does not mean that we endorse them or the information they provide. Be aware that information provided through some websites may be unreliable and can change without notice. Neither the publisher nor author shall be liable for any damages arising herefrom.

FROMMER'S STAR RATINGS, ICONS & ABBREVIATIONS

Every hotel, restaurant, and attraction listing in this guide has been ranked for quality, value, service, amenities, and special features using a star-rating system. In country, state, and regional guides, we also rate towns and regions to help you narrow down your choices and budget your time accordingly. Hotels and restaurants are rated on a scale of zero (recommended) to three stars (exceptional). Attractions, shopping, nightlife, towns, and regions are rated according to the following scale: zero stars (recommended), one star (highly recommended), two stars (very highly recommended), and three stars (must-see).

In addition to the star-rating system, we also use **seven feature icons** that point you to the great deals, in-the-know advice, and unique experiences that separate travelers from tourists. Throughout the book, look for:

special finds—those places only insiders know about

fun facts—details that make travelers more informed and their trips more fun

kids—best bets for kids and advice for the whole family

special moments—those experiences that memories are made of

overrated—places or experiences not worth your time or money

insider tips—great ways to save time and money

great values—where to get the best deals

The following abbreviations are used for credit cards:

AE   American Express   DISC   Discover   V   Visa

DC   Diners Club   MC   MasterCard

TRAVEL RESOURCES AT FROMMERS.COM

Frommer's travel resources don't end with this guide. Frommer's website, **www.frommers. com**, has travel information on more than 4,000 destinations. We update features regularly, giving you access to the most current trip-planning information and the best airfare, lodging, and car-rental bargains. You can also listen to podcasts, connect with other Frommers. com members through our active-reader forums, share your travel photos, read blogs from guidebook editors and fellow travelers, and much more.

THE BEST OF NEW ZEALAND

Back in 1979, New Zealand cartoonist and satirist Tom Scott, writing in *NZ Listener* magazine, had this to say about New Zealand: "Terrible tragedy in the South Seas. Three million people trapped alive."

The big news in 2003 was that we hit the four million population mark, and more than half of that increase was due to immigration. (By 2011, that number climbed to 4.5 million.) Given that we have around 44 million sheep, one New Zealander still equates to a whole lot of fresh lamb. But look beyond the farm gate and you'll find we've caught up with the rest of the world. We may bob about at the bottom of the Southern Hemisphere, but it would be unfair to consider the country a backwater.

New Zealand continues to notch up big gains in tourism, welcoming more than two million visitors a year, despite international upheavals like terrorist attacks and economic downturns. Tourism is our largest source of overseas income. International visitors contribute around NZ$8.3 billion to the economy each year and the tourism sector at large contributes NZ$19 billion to the country's economy annually. One in every ten New Zealanders now works in the tourism industry. And we're better equipped for tourists than ever. Efficient visitor centers abound, with accommodations ranging from budget to exclusive. You can shop 7 days a week, whoop it up at clubs and bars 24 hours a day, or savor a glass of internationally recognized New Zealand wine in an inexpensive cafe. You can get real coffee in as many variations as you can imagine, and New Zealand's fresh, innovative cuisine will leave you begging for more. Even provincial New Zealand has pulled up its socks without losing its heart. Small-town pride is beaming, and farmers are turning their hands to boutique tour operations and gorgeous restored B&Bs to supplement farm incomes, changing the whole nature of many backwater rural districts. Yet you'll still find, at its core, the very Kiwi hospitality that has made this country famous.

You may have heard that New Zealanders are born wearing wet suits and carrying paddles, such is their appetite for the outdoors and adventure. No part of the country is more than 128km (79 miles) from the sea, and a coastline spread with splendid beaches dishes up thousands of beautiful coastal walks and chances to surf and soak in the sun.

New Zealand is also a winter magnet for international skiers and is the white-knuckle capital of the world. This is where you can push it to the limits, pit yourself against your fears and limitations, take risk by the throat, and go for it—leaping off bridges into surging river gorges attached to a giant rubber band, or taking a stab at luging, Zorbing, sky diving, paragliding, kayaking, white-water rafting, and jet-boating. There's no lack of invention when it comes to adrenaline-pumping activities in this country.

But you don't have to be an extreme athlete to enjoy New Zealand. There are just as many ways to be laid-back and indulgent—tour wineries that have stampeded their way to the top of world ratings in record time; take in the wealth of Polynesian and Maori culture that forms the backbone of an increasingly multicultural society; or check out the strong historic and architectural reminders of a colonial past. There are lush gardens, art galleries, museums, and plenty of one-off reminders that New Zealand is like no other place.

I was born in New Zealand and despite frequent trips overseas, I can't shake off the inherent sense of belonging here. This book presents "my" New Zealand. After many months traveling thousands of miles, testing mattresses, comparing prices, leaping off cliff tops (well, almost), speeding up rivers, and eating and drinking in far too many restaurants, I am more convinced than ever that New Zealand is one of the quirkiest, quaintest, craziest places on earth. It's one of the most favored destinations of the new millennium, and before you've even left here, you'll want to come back. Dip into these pages, and you'll see why.

THE most UNFORGETTABLE TRAVEL EXPERIENCES

- **Swim with Sharks:** You've got to be keen, I admit, but this can be done in perfect safety. You can come face to face with *Jaws*'s South Seas cousins in a tough metal cage in a knuckle-biting thrill just north of Gisborne. See "Gisborne & the East Cape" in chapter 9.

- **Explore a Glacial Lake:** Few things are as mind-blowing as a boat trip on Tasman Lake, on Aoraki/Mount Cook, sailing between towering ice cliffs and floating icebergs in total, surreal silence. It's one of only three places in the world you can do a tour like this, so don't miss it. See "Mount Cook" on p. 408 in chapter 15.

- **Whale-Watch in Kaikoura:** When a mighty sperm whale flaps its tail at you, you won't forget it soon. These big sea monsters come to this particular stretch of water for a marine habitat rich in their kind of plankton. Don't be surprised to see dolphins aplenty, too. See "Marine Experiences in Kaikoura" on p. 369 in chapter 13.

- **Take the Train:** Rated one of the five most spectacular train journeys in the world, the TranzAlpine is an easy day trip that gives a dramatic introduction to the splendor of South Island landscapes. Tunnels, beech forests, viaducts, massive river gorges—they're all there for the taking. See "An Unforgettable Train Trip" on p. 355 in chapter 13.

- **Eat Bugs and Beetles at the Wildfoods Festival:** Prime yourself! You'll need culinary fortitude for this mind-boggling event—you could be served up anything from wriggling grubs to the unmentionable body parts of a number of wild and not-so-wild animals. This is the West Coast at its most rugged best. See the "Wildfoods Festival" box on p. 384 in chapter 14.

- **Stalk Kiwis at Night:** And I mean the birds! Prepare for surprises on this little southern adventure. It's the only place in the country where you can creep about lonely beaches at night with flashlights and not get arrested! At the same time, you'll be one of the lucky few who get to see a wild kiwi foraging for its supper among the seaweed. See "Making a Date with a Kiwi" on p. 487 in chapter 16.

o **Walk Around Sky Tower:** And I mean from the top, not at ground level. See how brave you really are when it comes to walking around the thin perimeter ring of one of the tallest towers in the Southern Hemisphere. The fearless will be rewarded with amazing views; the terrified can cower inside the viewing level. See "Sky Jump" on p. 112 in chapter 5.

o **Visit a Maori *Marae*:** Experience the *hongi* (the formal nose-to-nose Maori greeting), see deeply moving song-and-dance performances, and eat from a traditional underground *hangi* (oven). Do this in Rotorua as part of an organized tour experience, or seek permission to visit one of the dozens of East Cape *marae* (village commons). See "Rotorua" in chapter 8 and "Gisborne & the East Cape" in chapter 9.

THE best BEACHES

o **Waiheke Island's Onetangi Bay:** Stand on the bay's wide stretch of golden sand, and you can see for miles. On a clear day, throw yourself down into the sand and gaze at the steep pinnacles of Great Barrier Island and Little Barrier, off in the hazy distance. There might even be a few glimpses of the Coromandel in between deliciously warm swims. See "A Side Trip to Waiheke Island" in chapter 5.

o **Karikari Peninsula's Beaches:** This is the Far North at its subtropical best—endless sweeps of sparkling white sand lapped by crystal-clear, azure-blue waters. And from Tokerau Beach to Rangiputa to Matai Bay, you could have miles of it to yourself for beachcombing, sunbathing, and swimming (with care). See "Bay of Islands & the Far North" in chapter 6.

o **Coopers Beach:** Partly shaded by a bank of red-emblazoned pohutukawa trees, how could you not be content to stretch out here? Exercise? A walk to the water should do it! See "Bay of Islands & the Far North" in chapter 6.

o **Hot Water Beach:** Don't ask me why, or how, but if you get here 2 hours before or after low tide, you can hollow out a spot on the beach for yourself, and then wait for natural hot water to seep up through the sand. A natural spa experience without paying a cent! See "The Coromandel Peninsula" in chapter 6.

o **Mount Maunganui's Ocean Beach:** Surf, sand, and sun—some people never want more than that. Slather on a bit of suntan lotion, don a pair of sunglasses and a skimpy swimsuit, and you'll be able to mix in with the best of the bronzed bodies that make an annual pilgrimage to this perennial beach and surf favorite. See "Tauranga & Bay of Plenty" in chapter 7.

o **Kaiteriteri Beach:** Half of Canterbury makes a beeline for these blissful shores every summer. It's not expansive—in fact it's quite small, but perfectly formed nonetheless, and there's a busy vacation atmosphere with packed campgrounds and holiday houses. And with Nelson's endless hours of sunshine, who could complain about size? See "Nelson, Richmond & Motueka" in chapter 12.

o **Abel Tasman National Park's Beaches:** Bush-wrapped and locked between rocky headlands, these idyllic golden patches from Marahau north to Totaranui are accessible by sea only. That's what makes them so special. Gliding through the turquoise waters in your sea kayak, with curious seals to keep you company, you can take your pick of isolated havens. See "Abel Tasman National Park & Golden Bay" in chapter 12.

THE best ACTIVE VACATIONS

- **Scuba Diving in the Poor Knights:** Jacques Yves Cousteau rated this among the best diving spots in the world. This unique marine reserve has the best of tropical currents sweeping in to make it warm and inviting for a wide variety of tropical species that aren't found anywhere else in New Zealand's waters. See "Into the Deep Blue Sea" on p. 159 in chapter 6.
- **Blackwater Rafting in the Waitomo Glowworm Caves:** Daredevils can now go underground to leap off waterfalls; slink through dark, damp, underground waterways; rappel off Lost World rock faces; and do other things in the dark. See "Hamilton & the Waikato" in chapter 7.
- **Trout Fishing in Taupo:** They say the fish in Lake Taupo are so big that when you catch one, the lake level drops. The dozens of other rivers (especially world-renowned Tongariro) and streams in the region also have rich pickings for the fisherman. See "Taupo" in chapter 8.
- **Sea Kayaking in Abel Tasman National Park:** It takes a lot to beat this balmy little paddle into the best-preserved and most beautiful coastline of New Zealand. Keep company with nosy seal pups and dolphins; call into pristine, deserted beaches; and explore rocky headlands. See "Abel Tasman National Park & Golden Bay" in chapter 12.
- **Walking the Glaciers:** Dig out those snow boots and walking poles, add a dash of nerve and daring, and take the walk of a lifetime down Fox or Franz Josef glaciers in the deep south. And don't forget your camera so you can bring home those unforgettable views into the snow caves. See "Franz Josef & Fox Glaciers" in chapter 14.
- **Getting Wild in Queenstown:** This is New Zealand's adrenaline capital, where you get more than one chance to show how crazy you really are. There are more daredevil stunts per square inch here than anywhere else in the country. An international skiing mecca in winter, it readily transforms itself into summer madness as well. See "Queenstown" in chapter 15.
- **Walking the Fiordland Tracks:** If you fancy yourself as a multiday tramper, there's plenty to keep you out of mischief in Fiordland. This is where you get some of the best walks in the world—the Milford, the Hollyford, the Kepler, and the Routeburn tracks. See "Tramping" in chapter 4 and "Te Anau" in chapter 15.

THE best OF NATURAL NEW ZEALAND

- **Ninety Mile Beach and Cape Reinga:** From the spiritual tip of the North Island where, Maori say, the souls of the dead depart, to mountainous sand dunes, quicksand, and the broad flat stretch of Ninety Mile Beach, this is a must-see area filled with the unexpected. See "Bay of Islands & the Far North" in chapter 6.
- **Waiotapu Thermal Wonderland:** The earth's molten core hints at its artistic potential in a veritable rainbow of color and steamy chaos manifested in geysers, mud pools, hot bubbling lakes, steamy terraces, and more. A photographer's paradise, but tread carefully. See "Bubble, Bubble, Toil & Trouble: The Geothermal Attractions" on p. 194 in chapter 8.

- **Tongariro National Park:** Three major volcanoes dominate a rugged central plateau landscape: Ruapehu, Tongariro, and Ngauruhoe. An indomitable threesome, they're rife with Maori legend and rich in a few modern stories as well. Great for skiers, trampers, and anyone else wanting a physical challenge. See "Tongariro National Park" in chapter 8.
- **Fox and Franz Josef Glaciers:** This is one of the very few places on earth where you'll find full-fledged glaciers this close to the ocean. In a slow, ever-onward creep, they make their way from the heights of the Southern Alps down into untouched rainforest. See "Franz Josef & Fox Glaciers" in chapter 14.
- **Fiordland:** Come here on a wet day (and that's easy because this place gets the most rainfall in New Zealand), and you'll think you've stepped into the living set of *The Lord of the Rings*. This place defies all superlatives. It is the ultimate must-see. See "Te Anau" in chapter 15.
- **The Catlins Coast:** This is wild, natural New Zealand at its unspoiled best. From unique fossil forests to all manner of seabirds and mammals, native bush, waterfalls, wild beaches, unforgettable tangles of driftwood, and a frustratingly changeable climate—the area takes a lot of beating, but the resulting dramatic impact is unforgettable. See "Dunedin" in chapter 16.
- **Ulva Island:** Tucked into Stewart Island's Paterson Inlet, tiny Ulva Island will leave you speechless with its incredible native bird life. It's wall-to-wall feathers here—and what's more, they're not afraid of humans. Don't go without your camera; you'll need evidence once you start telling friends back home about it. See "Stewart Island" in chapter 16.

THE best TRAMPS

For details, see "Tramping" in chapter 4.

- **Tongariro Crossing:** Often described as one of the best 1-day walks in New Zealand, this high-altitude hike across volcanic terrain will give you cold mountain springs, lava flows, an active crater, emerald-colored crater lakes, and unforgettable views. Ideal for the fit and enthusiastic hiker. See "Tongariro National Park" in chapter 8.
- **The Abel Tasman Coastal Track:** This is an easy 3- to 5-day walk where the guided option gives you the choice of ditching those hefty packs. From start to finish, 52km (32 miles) later, it winds in and out of gorgeous sheltered coves, golden beaches, rocky headlands, and natural unspoiled bush. See "Abel Tasman National Park & Golden Bay" in chapter 12.
- **The Heaphy Track:** No softy guided options here: You go it alone for 4 to 6 days from the junction of the Brown and Aorere rivers, across tussock-covered flats to the wild seas of Karamea on the West Coast. See "Westport & Karamea" in chapter 14.
- **The Milford Track:** The mother of them all, the Milford is one of the world's best and most-loved multiday tramps. Stretching through the best of Fiordland, this 54km (33-mile) trail follows the Clinton and Arthur valleys and crosses McKinnon Pass with views you'll never forget. See "Te Anau" in chapter 15.
- **The Routeburn Track:** Like the Milford and the Hollyford before it, this track makes its way into virgin rainforest and the sort of wild fairyland scenery where you'd expect to see elves and gnomes prancing around. See "Queenstown" in chapter 15.

o **The North West Circuit:** This is a real test for experienced trampers who think they can face 10 to 12 days walking 125km (78 miles) through bird-filled native bush, big beaches, and long stretches knee-deep in mud. I'm told the rewards are plenty. See "Stewart Island" in chapter 16.

THE best DRIVES

o **Auckland City to Mission Bay:** This is the stuff of a weekend afternoon spin to see how the other half lives. Best done in a Ferrari, a BMW, an Audi, or an equally cool classic if you want to leave a lasting impression. Tight shorts and in-line skates do the trick just as well if you want a cheaper set of wheels. Do the cafe crawl; join the walkers, the runners, and the dog strollers; or just drool over million-dollar real estate. See "Orientation" in chapter 5.

o **Rotorua's Blue and Green Lakes:** From the stately redwood forest on the edge of town, all the way past the Blue and Green lakes to the Buried Village and Lake Tarawera and back again, you'll squeal with delight at a dozen different things. There are lots of picnic spots on the way, but the Landing Café at Lake Tarawera is a good bet if you forget the hamper. See "Rotorua" in chapter 8.

o **The Capital to Mellow Martinborough:** Once you've left the motorways behind, you'll be up and over the winding Rimutaka Hill Road in little more than 40 minutes. Then it's downhill all the way to Martinborough's enchanting pocket of prizewinning wineries. Surrender to hedonism and squander time in idyllic vineyard settings. Make the only exercise you do raising your glass, or at most a wee stroll through pretty little Martinborough Village, where cute shops await. See "A Side Trip to Wairarapa" in chapter 11.

o **Queen Charlotte Sound:** Take the scenic loop from Picton to the little fishing village of Havelock and back to Picton on the main highway. Stop and admire the bush-clad sounds and the boats, and indulge in fresh green-lipped mussels grown in these very waters at the Mussel Boys restaurant, in Havelock. It's a narrow winding road around the Sounds, so take it quietly. See "Picton & Blenheim" in chapter 12.

o **Greymouth to Westport:** Pretty, pretty, pretty! Nikau palms, native bush, tree ferns, jagged rocks, roaring surf, and the big blue Tasman Sea combine to make this a lovely half-day outing. Be sure to stop at the famous Punakaiki Pancake Rocks, where blowholes have a spectacular hissy fit as the ocean roars into, under, and around rocky caverns on the coast. See "Westport & Karamea" in chapter 14.

o **The Famous Milford Road:** Even the Wanaka–Haast Road can't match the splendor of this one. It's been called one of the best drives in the world, and no amount of raving can do it justice. You really have to experience it. Virgin rainforest, mirrorlike lakes, astounding waterfalls (especially during rain), beech forest, mountains of moss, bright orange lichens, and sheer mountain faces thousands of feet high contribute to the overall picture—not to mention the slightly daunting Homer Tunnel. See "Milford Sound" in chapter 15.

THE best MUSEUMS

o **Auckland Museum:** After a very significant internal revamp, this museum is everything you'd want in a city's storehouse of treasures: fun, interactive, attractive, informative, and filled with interesting collections. Its Maori and Polynesian section, the biggest in the world, sends shivers down your spine; if you've got kids, let them loose in the Discovery Centre, where they can legally stick their fingers into just about anything. See p. 109 in chapter 5.

o **New Zealand National Maritime Museum:** At the pinnacle of New Zealand's boating history—with the America's Cup Challenge right in our backyard—the Maritime Museum is booming. Look for *KZ 1* outside, and inside discover 1,000 years of the country's maritime history. See sail makers, boat builders, and wood-turners at work and take a cruise on one of the vessels. See p. 114 in chapter 5.

o **Museum of New Zealand—Te Papa Tongarewa:** One of the largest national museums in the world, this giant edifice on Wellington's waterfront is said to be years ahead of anything else like it. Truly bicultural, it's a magical place where art and artifacts meet technological brilliance, creating riveting displays and interactive playthings for all ages. Here you'll find everything from a whale skeleton and a working Maori marae to art collections and virtual-reality diversions. See p. 279 in chapter 11.

o **Canterbury Museum and the International Antarctic Centre:** Although these two museums are completely separate entities located miles apart, together they present a terrific overview of life and history in Antarctica. Nowhere else in the world will you find this much gathered information about the great icy continent. There's everything from wildlife displays to human exploration accounts and a real ice chamber so you can get the feel of life in subzero temperatures. See p. 348 and p. 349 in chapter 13.

THE best MAORI EXPERIENCES

o **Auckland Museum:** This is the perfect place for an early lesson in things Maori. The recently revamped museum has the largest collection of Maori artifacts in the world. Large war canoes, meetinghouses, greenstone weapons, and feather cloaks are here. On top of that, the Manaia Maori Performance Group puts on a stunning show three times a day. See p. 109.

o **Te Puia's Whakarewarewa Thermal Reserve and New Zealand Maori Arts & Crafts Institute:** Maori guides will lead you through the thermal reserve, explaining the significance of the area to the Maori people. There's also a live song-and-dance performance, a tour of a replica Maori village, and the chance to watch working weavers and carvers in the Arts & Crafts Institute, which was set up in 1963 to foster traditional craft skills. See p. 190.

o **Tamaki Maori Village:** This re-created ancient Maori village presents Maori life as it used to be pre-European settlement. You'll tour the village with a Maori elder, learn the ancient myths, watch a traditional performance, and eat from a traditional hangi. See "Rotorua" in chapter 8.

o **Whakarewarewa Thermal Village:** This small village of just 70 or so people has a 300-year history of settlement. It's probably the only place in the world where people live in such proximity to geothermal activity and still harness the natural forces of the earth for washing and cooking. See "Rotorua" in chapter 8.

o **East Cape:** This is a remote enclave of Maori culture—one of the last places in New Zealand where the Maori language is part of everyday life. You'll find more than 100 marae scattered along the length of the East Cape Road, and if you ask permission, in most cases you'll be allowed to enter. There are numerous Maori settlements and highly decorative Maori churches. See "Gisborne & the East Cape" in chapter 9.

THE best B&BS

o **A-Kahu** (Rotorua; ✆ 07/347-4148): I had one of the best B&B stays in New Zealand with Kiri Atkinson-Crean and her husband, Nigel Crean—a young, contemporary Maori couple, who will give you a real insight into what it means to be Maori in modern New Zealand. On top of that, their beds and rooms are divine, the food is fantastic, and there is laughter aplenty. See p. 201.

o **Booklovers Bed and Breakfast** (Wellington; ✆ 04/384-2714): Journalist and author Jane Tolerton is a woman with a passion for history and the astonishing book collection to prove it. Her charming city villa bulges with books and her rooms are large, comfortable, and close to town. See p. 272.

o **Glendinning House** (Dunedin; ✆ 03/477-8262): Sandy Black and Jocelyn Robinson live in an elegant brick mansion in the nicest part of town. Jocelyn, a former caterer, tempts guests with ongoing edible treats. Rooms are huge and are the perfect place to imagine life as a wealthy colonialist. See p. 467.

o **Pencarrow** (Queenstown; ✆ 03/442-8938): You'll have to completely revise your benchmark for service and value for money after staying with Bill and Kari Moers. They give a whole new meaning to guest comforts, and I think they should give lessons to B&Bs everywhere. See p. 430.

o **Waiorau Homestead** (Wanaka; ✆ 03/443-2225): Get a taste of the country in this beautifully restored homestead, where chef Blyth Adams and his wife, Ann Lockhart, will spoil you rotten. Modern comforts prevail against a backdrop of rural history and spectacular scenery. See p. 406.

o **Maison de la Mer** (Akaroa; ✆ 03/304-8907): If you want to know how a top B&B should be run, visit the experts. Bruce and Carol Hyland have hosted over 14,000 guests during their tenure in the hospitality industry, and their newest Akaroa venture is as luscious as their last. You'd be silly to miss it. See p. 363.

THE best LUXURY ACCOMMODATIONS

o **Kauri Cliffs** (Kerikeri; ✆ 09/407-0010): I could find no fault whatsoever with this sublime northern retreat. It is, as the saying goes, "heaven on a stick," and I'm not even a golfer! The staff here are some of the friendliest in the country and the rooms—especially the bathrooms—are my idea of true luxury. See p. 154.

o **Eagles Nest** (Russell; ✆ 09/403-8333): Combine the very best of international taste with the magic of Northland's subtropical environment and a rich vein of natural energy, and you get a luxury retreat quite unlike any other in New Zealand. Daniel and Sandie Biskind have created a world-class retreat worthy of anyone's prolonged attention. See p. 154.

o **Huka Lodge** (Taupo; ✆ 07/378-5791): Exclusivity reigns supreme at this Small Luxury Hotels of the World member. International awards bounce off the walls, and guests invariably comment on rooms fit for kings. It has a supreme location beside the Waikato River just above the Huka Falls and a reputation for quality and service that seems impossible to shake. See p. 211.

- **Treetops Lodge & Estate** (Rotorua; ✆ 07/333-2066): My expectations may never be the same again after staying at Treetops. Being spoiled with one of the most gorgeous suites in the country tends to have that effect. Set in a unique native bush environment, it's a true sanctuary that will lower your heart rate within minutes of arriving. See p. 199.
- **The Farm at Cape Kidnappers** (Hawke's Bay; ✆ 06/875-1900): Like its big sister, Kauri Cliffs, this stay richly deserves all the superlatives. It's a case of "your wish is our command" here and if you're a golfer, you'll love what's been rated the 10th best course in the world outside the U.S. The cliff-edge, rural setting is to die for. See p. 241.
- **Eichardt's Private Hotel** (Queenstown, ✆ 03/441-0450). This Small Luxury Hotels of the World member has received glowing accolades in Andrew Harper's *Hideaway Report,* and it's becoming the hotel of choice for discerning, upscale travelers. In a remodeled historic building in central Queenstown, it oozes first-class style and understated glamour. It remains one of my favorites. See p. 428.
- **Blanket Bay** (Queenstown; ✆ 03/442-9442): If you want luxury on a grand scale in a majestic setting to match, look no further. These gorgeous stone buildings marry so completely with the awesome landscape, it seems as if they were always here. Inside, you'll find an outstanding level of service and comfort. See p. 434.

THE best BOUTIQUE HOTELS & SMALL LODGES

- **Te Whau Lodge** (Waiheke Island; ✆ 09/372-2288): Every time I visit Te Whau I'm convinced all over again that Gene O'Neill and Liz Eglinton give you the best of everything—winning personalities, fabulous food, great rooms, and views you won't believe. There's something quintessentially Kiwi about the whole experience that I'm proud to recommend. See p. 136.
- **Ridge Country Retreat** (Tauranga; ✆ 07/542-1301): The generosity and style of rooms here leave many more expensive stays in the shade. Joanne O'Keeffe and Penny Oxnam are some of the best (and funniest) hosts I've met. I'm confident your expectations will be exceeded at every level. The food is divine! See p. 182.
- **Millar Road** (Hastings; ✆ 06/875-1977): Waking up to staggering views over vineyards, orchards, and rolling green hills is only part of the pleasure of this exquisite stay. Somewhere between lodge and B&B, these two modern, self-contained "cottages" are divine. I can't get the memory of them out of my head. It's a classy, unexpected gem filled with contemporary New Zealand art, and I know you'll want to stay at least a week! See p. 241.
- **Ohtel** (Wellington; ✆ 04/803-0600): I couldn't believe my luck when I found this small, chic, ecofriendly, waterfront hotel packed to the gills with collectible mid-century modern furniture. It's an unbeatable value, a total sensory experience, and one of my top picks for something unique and memorable. See p. 273.
- **Arrowtown House** (Arrowtown; ✆ 03/441-6008): This boutique hotel is the third brainchild of seasoned travelers and hosts alike, Steve and Jeanette Brough, who are two of the best hosts in the country. Located in a pretty, tree-lined residential street, it's an understated haven within a short walk of the village. See p. 434.

o **River Birches** (Turangi; ☎ **0800/102-025**): This is one of my favorite recent discoveries. Transplanted New Yorker Jason Bleibtreu and his wife, Rebecca—both former journalists covering the world's hot spots—have spent years living in hotels, so they know exactly what it takes to create a restful haven. They've imbued this special place with an extra level of professionalism that's hard to fault. And the location? Right beside one of the best trout-fishing rivers in the world! See p. 215.

o **Remarkables Lodge** (Queenstown; ☎ **03/442-2720**): Brian Savage and Colleen Ryan sailed the world for 10 years chartering their yacht. We can be thankful they came ashore in Queenstown and took this well-established lodge and shook it by the scruff of the neck. With new life and an understated level of class that puts it above many, it's a top retreat tucked into the foot of the very remarkable Remarkables mountains. See p. 433.

THE best RESTAURANTS

o **The French Café** (Auckland; ☎ **09/377-1911**): This is posh-plush (in an elegant, understated kind of way) and professionalism-plus. Consistently rated one of Auckland's best and most romantic restaurants, this little den will take your taste buds to new, dizzying heights. See p. 107.

o **DINE By Peter Gordon** (Auckland; ☎ **09/363-7030**): This sleek, dimly lit culinary "palace" is the playground of London/New Zealand celebrity chef Peter Gordon set in the SKYCITY Grand Hotel. It's fusion cuisine at its best. Just make sure you save a few good breaths for gasping at the bill. See p. 102.

o **Logan Brown** (Wellington; ☎ **04/801-5114**): Located in a restored bank building on the edge of the red-light district, this restaurant will exceed your expectations. Consistently voted one of the capital's best eateries—for its service and its delicious focus on top meat cuts and wild game—it shouldn't be bypassed. See p. 274.

o **Herzog** (Blenheim; ☎ **03/572-8770**): Expect the very best from this winery and restaurant that has been held up by New York's *Wine Spectator* for its impressive stock of around 3,200 of the world's best wines. It's a fine-dining experience you won't soon forget. See p. 307.

o **Rotherhams** (Christchurch; ☎ **03/341-5142**): Swiss-born chef Martin Weiss has mastered the art of stunning his hungry patrons. In an interior that's all about romance and special occasions, he presents meals that excel in both presentation and taste. Not to be missed—likewise the extensive wine list. See p. 345.

o **The Bunker** (Queenstown; ☎ **03/441-8030**): Don't start celebrating until you've actually found it and are sitting at one of its tables! Notoriously hard to find (that's part of its charm), and expensive when you get there, this hidden culinary jewel delivers on all the superlatives it receives. Make sure you hunt it down. See p. 436.

THE best SHOPPING

o **Auckland:** The whole city is a treasure-trove of shops. Try the chic fashion and design shops of High Street; international designers duty-free at DFS Galleria Customhouse; upmarket boutiques in Parnell; antiques on Manukau Road; mainstream fashion in Newmarket—plus the super-classy Nuffield Street and its top designer labels; big mall shopping at St. Luke's Shopping Centre; and fabulous specialty shops on K'Road and Ponsonby Road. See "Shopping" in chapter 5.

- **Rotorua:** A rich vein of New Zealand souvenirs runs right through the whole city, but for the best Maori arts and crafts, look to Tamaki Maori Village. See "Rotorua" in chapter 8.

- **Wellington:** The Old Bank Building on Lambton Quay has only added to the electric atmosphere of this capital shopping area. Wander the length of the Quay for fashion, books, shoes, and more; move up through Willis Street for more of the same, and into Cuba Mall for edgy design stores and off-the-wall retail surprises. Check out Tinakori Road for a handsome cluster of boutiques. See "Shopping" in chapter 11.

- **Nelson:** Long recognized as the best region for leisure crafts shopping, greater Nelson is dotted with hundreds of pottery, craft, and jewelry studios. Find international-quality art glass at Höglund Art Glass Studio and go from there. Many craftspeople are located out in the country, so you get a bonus look at the countryside as well. See "Nelson, Richmond & Motueka" in chapter 12.

- **Hokitika and Greymouth:** Jade/greenstone/*pounamu* and gold are found in abundance in these two West Coast towns. Stores specializing in both are found side by side in both Hokitika and Greymouth. See "Greymouth & Lake Brunner" and "Hokitika: Greenstone, Glowworms & Gold" in chapter 14.

- **Queenstown:** This is the home of expensive shopping. You'll find that most things have big price tags, but the quality is invariably tops. There are leading New Zealand and international clothing labels, sheepskin products, souvenirs, leather, original arts and crafts, and masses of jewelry. See "Queenstown" in chapter 15.

NEW ZEALAND IN DEPTH

Kia ora, welcome to New Zealand! Get used to this greeting because you're going to hear it a lot during your stay. Kia ora simply means hello in greeting, or go well as a farewell. The meaning will be obvious in context. (See below for more details on Maori terms you'll hear.)

Many people think we live in remote, watery isolation down here in New Zealand, and that we're overrun by 60 million sheep and rugby players as big as kauri trees. Well, for a start, sheep numbers have dropped. Current estimates are closer to 44 million, and while there are some big boys out there, they're not all 7 feet tall, wearing rugby boots and All Blacks jerseys.

New Zealand is no longer the sleepy little backwater it was back in the 1950s, although lingering pockets do exist, and you'll still find that, as incomprehensible as it seems, thousands of North Islanders have never been to the South Island and vice versa. That aside, a lot has been achieved here in a few short decades. We share in the rapid changes of the big, wide world and we celebrate the good things that progress has brought us. There have been downsides—like the brutal clearing of native forests and the lack of respect for a truly unique landscape—but we're wiser now, and we have 13 national parks protecting the most enviable slices of these little islands.

Although some still won't believe this, I'd like to clarify that New Zealand is not joined to the geographical hip of Australia. In fact, the 1,600km (990 miles) separating us account for some pretty significant differences. Australia, for instance, is vast; New Zealand is not. Australia has a very large red desert in its middle; New Zealand doesn't. And whereas Australia was settled by British convicts, we New Zealanders like to remind everyone that we started out as England's other pasture. The one irrefutable thing the two countries do share is a lively, generally good-spirited rivalry over just about everything, but especially sports.

NEW ZEALAND TODAY

Like any young country, New Zealand is growing rapidly and facing issues associated with progress. Urban drift accounts for 80% of the population living in towns and cities, most of which is north of Lake Taupo, with a full third of the population in the Auckland region alone. City infrastructures, transport systems, and housing developments are struggling in some cases to keep up with the pace.

Biculturalism has been the loudest catchphrase of the past decade. From the late 19th century until after World War II, there was a marked decline in the use of the Maori language because schools insisted that only English be taught. Since the 1960s, however, there has been a growing resurgence of interest in Maori identity, language, and tradition, and many Maori are now bilingual, thanks to extensive language programs in schools.

The Waitangi Tribunal, set up by the New Zealand government in 1987 to settle unresolved issues related to the Treaty of Waitangi, has brought Maori grievances to light. Many claim their ancestors were tricked out of much of their land. Today, a good portion of that land has been returned to Maori ownership and many tribes have established lucrative business and corporate entities in the seafood, forestry, farming, and tourism industries.

Today, a combination of farming practices, growing populations, urban spread, and increasing tourism numbers are putting pressure on the land. New Zealanders have always taken pride in their "clean, green" image, but as evidence suggests we may not be as clean and green as we had hoped, there are strong moves to take better care of our natural assets. Sustainability is a big issue, especially in industry and tourism.

In face of our passion for the great outdoors and our reputation for being crazy adventurers, you could be forgiven for thinking that the arts have been overlooked. Nothing could be further from the truth. The main cities—Auckland, Wellington, Christchurch, and Dunedin—all have vibrant cultural hearts; and New Zealand has given the world more than its fair share of talented artists, musicians, writers, filmmakers, and designers.

We've carved out an international reputation for much more than those hefty rugby players I mentioned earlier. Maybe it's because we have always been isolated. Maybe it's because, as a young country, we are still finding our way, still striving to prove we can foot it with the best of the Northern Hemisphere. Whatever the reason, New Zealanders are fiercely proud of their patch. Wherever else they go in the world, they invariably prove themselves as innovative, hardworking, passionate people, making their way in the wider world but always, somehow, still attached to their island roots.

LOOKING BACK: NEW ZEALAND HISTORY

EARLY MAORI SETTLEMENT There's more than one theory as to how New Zealand's first inhabitants settled here. The Maori legend tells of Kupe, who in A.D. 950 sailed from Hawaiiki, the traditional homeland of the Polynesians. The legend doesn't tell us exactly where Hawaiiki was located in the South Pacific, but present-day authorities believe it belonged to the Society Islands group that includes Tahiti.

It wasn't until the mid–14th century that Maori arrived in great numbers. These settlers found abundant supplies of seafood and berries, which they supplemented with tropical plants like taro, yams, and Kumara (sweet potato) that they'd brought along from Hawaiiki. Dogs and rats also made the voyage, and they were added to the protein source. The cultivation of these imported vegetables and animals gradually led to an agricultural society in which Maori lived in permanent villages based on a central *marae* (village common or courtyard) and *whare runanga* (meetinghouse). This is where the distinctive Maori art forms of woodcarving and tattooing evolved.

ABEL TASMAN & DUTCH DISCOVERY   The first recorded sighting of New Zealand by Europeans occurred in December 1642. Abel Tasman, who was scouting territory for the Dutch East India Company, spied the west coast of the South Island, entered Golden Bay, and met the Maori before even reaching land. As his two ships anchored, several Maori war canoes entered the water and paddlers shouted hostile challenges. The next day, Maori attacked a cockboat, killing four sailors. Tasman fired at the retreating canoes and departed. Bad weather forced him to proceed up the west coast of the North Island. Failing to find a suitable landing spot, he sailed on to Tonga and Fiji, and Golden Bay was known as Murderer's Bay for many years to come.

CAPTAIN COOK   When Captain James Cook left England in 1768 on the *Endeavour*, he carried orders from King George III to sail south in search of the "continent" reported by Abel Tasman. If he found it uninhabited, he was to plant the English flag and claim it for the king; if not, he was to take possession of "convenient situations," but only with the consent of the indigenous people.

On October 7, 1769, Nicholas Young, son of the ship's surgeon, spotted New Zealand from his perch in the mast. Naming the headland (in the Gisborne area) Young Nick's Head, Cook sailed into a crescent-shaped bay and anchored. With the help of a young Tahitian chief, Tupea, who had sailed with the crew as a guide and interpreter, Cook tried to make contact with the Maori, but to no avail. They remained hostile and would not accept Cook's gifts, nor let him take food and water to his men.

Disappointed, Cook claimed the country for King George, and named the bay Poverty Bay because, as he noted in his journal, "it afforded us not one thing we wanted." Sailing north, he rounded the tip of the North Island and went on to circumnavigate both islands. During the next 6 months, he accurately charted the country, and missed only the entrance to Milford Sound (which is virtually invisible from the open sea) and the fact that Stewart Island was not part of the mainland.

THE BRITISH ARRIVE   Sealers began arriving in 1792 and essentially stripped the South Island waters of its seal colonies. Whalers, too, discovered rich hunting grounds in New Zealand water. Oil vats soon dotted the Bay of Islands, which provided safe harbor.

Traders and merchants, attracted by the wealth of flax, the abundance of trees for shipbuilding, and the lucrative trading of muskets and other European goods with the Maori, were little better than the sealers and whalers in respecting the country's natural resources. Great forests were felled and luxuriant bushlands disappeared.

The immigration of Europeans, mostly from Great Britain, had a devastating impact on Maori culture. Most destructive was the introduction of liquor, muskets, and diseases against which the Maori had no immunity. Muskets intensified the fierce intertribal warfare, eventually becoming so common that no one tribe had superiority in terms of firepower. By 1830, Maori chiefs began to realize the weapon was destroying all their tribes.

Missionaries also began to come during this period. They were responsible for putting the Maori language in writing (largely for the purpose of translating and printing the Bible), establishing mission schools, and upgrading agricultural methods through the use of plows and windmills.

Lawlessness grew along with the number of British immigrants, and harm was inflicted on both Maori and the new settlers. The missionaries complained to the British government, which was by no means eager to recognize faraway New Zealand as a full-fledged colony, having already experienced problems with America and Canada. As an alternative, the Crown placed New Zealand under the jurisdiction of New South Wales in 1833, and dispatched James Busby as "British Resident" with full responsibilities to enforce law and order. Unfortunately, he was completely ineffective.

THE TREATY OF WAITANGI   Back in Britain, the newly formed New Zealand Company began sending ships to buy land from the Maori and establish permanent settlements. Their questionable methods caused increasing alarm in London. Between 1839 and 1843, the New Zealand Company sent out 57 ships carrying 19,000 settlers, the nucleus of the permanent British population.

In 1839, Captain William Hobson was sent by the government to sort out the concerns. By catering to the Maori sense of ceremony, he arranged an assembly of chiefs at the Busby residence in the Bay of Islands. There, on February 6, 1840, the Treaty of Waitangi was signed after lengthy debate. The treaty guaranteed Maori "all the rights and privileges of British subjects" in exchange for their acknowledgment of British sovereignty, while granting the Crown exclusive rights to buy land from the Maori. Many of the chiefs did not understand what they had signed. Nevertheless, 45 of them ultimately signed the treaty, and when it was circulated around the country, another 500 signed as well.

Instead of easing tensions, though, the Treaty of Waitangi ushered in one of the bloodiest periods in New Zealand's history. The British were eager to exercise their right to purchase Maori land, and while some chiefs were eager to sell, others were not. As pressures forced them to sell, the Maori revolted, and when Chief Hone Heke (the first to sign the treaty) hacked down the British flagpole at Kororareka (Russell) in 1844, it signaled the beginning of some 20 years of fierce battles. The British finally emerged the victors, but the seizure of that Maori land continues to be the subject of debate today.

FROM WAITANGI TO THE PRESENT   By the time the 1860s arrived, gold had been discovered on the South Island's West Coast. The Gold Rush opened up huge tracts of Central Otago, and Cobb & Co, a stagecoach company, extended their coaching operations to link the major towns from Christchurch south. They added to that in 1866, initiating a coach service across Arthur's Pass to the gold fields of Westland. By the end of the 1860s, Dunedin was by far the largest city in the country thanks to gold wealth. Advances in rail transport flourished during this period, and with waves of new immigrants keen to seek their golden fortune, New Zealand entered a period of lively economic activity that was to see it through the 1870s and 1880s.

Whaling, too, changed the face of New Zealand during this period. It was one of our first major industries and with the influx of international whalers came traders, missionaries, onshore whaling stations, and new housing settlements. Many whalers stayed on, leaving their ships to marry into Maori families—the fact that there are many Maori families today with Scandinavian names is part of that legacy.

In 1892, the introduction of the first refrigerated shipment of lamb to England heralded a new era in New Zealand beef and lamb exports. History was made in 1893 when New Zealand became the first country in the world to allow women to vote.

By 1914, thoughts had turned to war. One hundred thousand New Zealanders joined the Australia–New Zealand Army Corps to fight in World War I, and New Zealand lost more soldiers per capita than any other nation.

The 1930s were colored by the Great Depression, unemployment, riots, and, on a happier note, the beginning of air services across Cook Strait. Our soldiers returned to battle in 1939 with the advent of World War II, and in 1947 the Statute of Westminster was adopted by the government, giving New Zealand full independence from Britain.

For many, the 1950s were a golden era. The economy had long since settled, our men were back from war, and, for the first time, New Zealand's population hit two million. Life was easy in the '50s. Threats were few and achievements began piling up—Edmund Hillary became the first man to climb Mount Everest, we had our first royal visit when the newly crowned Queen Elizabeth arrived, and the Auckland Harbour Bridge heralded a new age of modernity when it opened in 1959.

It's hard to believe now, but New Zealand had to wait until the 1960s to get its first regional television—in Auckland. We didn't get color television until 1973, by which time the New Zealand population had hit three million and the Auckland International Airport had opened.

The country's economy has traditionally depended on the success of wool, dairy, and meat exports with protected, unlimited access to British markets. This changed when Britain entered the European Common Market in the 1970s. New Zealand was then forced to diversify and do business with many other countries. By the mid-1980s, meat, wool, and dairy products accounted for just under 50% of our export income.

The mid-1980s also heralded the complete deregulation of the domestic economy. It took a decade of struggle for many industries to come to terms with the changes. (This is the main reason our infamous sheep numbers dropped from 72 million in 1983 to the present low of around 44 million.) The stern belt-tightening ultimately bore fruit, however, and by 1993, the economy was flourishing. Today, forestry, horticulture, fishing, tourism, and manufacturing are the leading industries. Tourism is the country's largest single source of foreign exchange. Overall standards and the level of professionalism have improved tenfold in recent years, making New Zealand one of the ripest countries in the world for visitors.

ART & ARCHITECTURE

ART As a visitor viewing our museum collections and contemporary galleries, it will soon become obvious that our artistic roots are firmly embedded in a mix of European tradition and Pacific, especially Maori, influences. In some ways the two are quite different. The early European tradition favored an emblematic and literary pairing of image and poetic allusion with subject matter leaning toward the land and self-questioning. The Maori tradition of figurative imagery (traditionally expressed in carving) asserted a strong genealogical identity. While it's easy to generalize, that difference probably still holds true today for much of New Zealand's contemporary art. While Maori artists have borrowed from the European traditions (materially and stylistically), contemporary Maori art is still usually very strongly concerned with what it means to be Maori. There is often a strong reference to heritage, myths, and legends in Maori work, though figurative art has also been inspired by the land and nature.

That said, Pakeha artists (non-Maori artists) are also heavily inspired by the land and nature. Perhaps that goes back to our short history and our closeness to the land. It's not so long ago that we were clearing forest (150 years) and carving out new lives in these remote islands. I think most New Zealanders at some point in their lives are aware of that geographical isolation. Our country and our population are both small, so perhaps we are more keenly aware of everything that happens to the land here; and perhaps we have a subconscious awareness of just how much our survival depends on the land. It would be fair to say that New Zealand as a nation has also struggled to come to terms with its own sense of identity as it developed from a pioneering colony into a modern western nation. Nowhere is that more obvious than in our artistic expressions. Time and again, still, you will hear people here talking about "a New Zealand identity" as if it were some mythical aspiration; yet I am firmly of the view that we already have an established New Zealand identity—especially in our art.

Among the most collectible of our contemporary artists are names like Colin McCahon (1919–87), Len Lye (1901–80), Toss Woollaston (1910–98), Rita Angus (1908–70), Philip Clairmont (1949–84), Bill Hammond (b. 1947), and Maori artists Ralph Hotere (b. 1931), Shane Cotton (b. 1964), Michael Parekowhai (b. 1968), and Robyn Kahukiwa (b. 1938) to name just a tiny smattering. Other important artists to look out for include Philip Trusttum, Barry Cleavin, Andrew Drummond, Tony Fomison, Neil Dawson, Séraphine Pick, Peter Robinson, Richard Killeen, Dick Frizzell, Mark Braunias, Gretchen Albrecht, and others. No matter how many I list, someone equally important will be left out.

ARCHITECTURE When the first settlers arrived here, the only architecture in New Zealand was the Maori-built *raupo* (reed) *whare* (houses) and some ramshackle whalers' huts. It goes without saying that the British settlers quickly felled trees and began building little cottages (and later bigger houses and mansions) based on the British model. As wealth in the new colony increased, so did the stature and durability of the buildings. New Zealand's first substantial buildings were erected by missionaries in the Bay of Islands around 1814. You can still visit **Kemp House** and the **Stone Store,** both built in the Georgian style that set the tone for much that was to come.

Today in the wealthier suburbs of Auckland (Remuera, Parnell, Mount Eden, Devonport); Wellington (Thorndon, Mount Victoria); Christchurch (Fendalton, Merivale); and Dunedin (Maori Hill) you'll still find many fine large Georgian-style and Victorian homes. Christchurch and Dunedin in particular are known for their fine Victorian Gothic architecture. Sadly, many of these houses have been pulled down to make way for the new. Large sheep and cattle stations are spread throughout the country, but the South Island is blessed with huge homesteads from this period. If you're lucky, you may get to stay in some that have been converted into lodges or upmarket bed-and-breakfast accommodations. Canterbury's **Otahuna Lodge** is one example. It is one of the finest examples of Queen Anne architecture in Australasia and has been beautifully restored and converted into one of New Zealand's finest luxury lodges. I've tried to list a number of excellent B&Bs in fine old homes throughout the guide, so if you're interested in architecture, make sure you check each chapter.

You'll also find some splendid early architecture in our churches. Throughout the country, from tiny towns to large cities, there are hundreds of examples of excellent ecclesiastical architecture well worth visiting. In the more remote areas of Northland and East Cape, you'll also find many exquisite little Maori churches. The best examples of these are **St. Faith's Church** in Ohinemutu, Rotorua, and **St. Mary's** at Tikitiki on East Cape. Both are open to the public and both feature exquisite carving and tukutuku paneling that you won't see anywhere else in the world.

Architecture buffs should also seek out Napier and the wider Hawke's Bay for one of the finest collections of Art Deco and Spanish mission architecture outside of Miami. Central Napier was rebuilt almost entirely in Art Deco style after the massive 1931 earthquake that obliterated the city. And in Oamaru in the South Island (btw. Timaru and Dunedin), you'll find an impressive collection of classical and Renaissance buildings complete with Corinthian pillars that will make you wonder if you've landed in a remote outpost of Greece.

Contemporary architecture—both domestic and commercial—is increasingly finding "a New Zealand voice." Our architecture very much follows the path of art in that regard. Yet it is said that only around 2% of New Zealanders employ an architect to design their home—it being seen as the realm of the wealthy—and many of the finest examples of modern New Zealand residential architecture are tucked away down long driveways, well away from easy public view. There are, however, many fine public buildings. Some, like the **Museum of New Zealand Te Papa Tongarewa** in Wellington and the **Christchurch Art Gallery** in Christchurch, have not been without controversy and detractors. But we're a small nation and too often small minds rebel against the new. Perhaps that's the way of an isolated, island nation?

Wineries, too, are at the leading edge of New Zealand contemporary architecture as increasing numbers of vineyards realize the power of individualistic branding that includes a statement winery and (often) restaurant. Fine examples include Peregrine (Central Otago), Cable Bay (Waiheke Island), Craggy Range (Hawke's Bay), Elephant Hill (Hawke's Bay), and Villa Maria, Oyster Bay, and Spy Valley, all in Marlborough.

NEW ZEALAND IN POP CULTURE

Katherine Mansfield (1888–1923) put New Zealand on the literary map with her still-admired short stories set in New Zealand (though she spent most of her adult life in Europe). Among contemporary fiction writers, **Keri Hulme** won the prestigious Booker McConnell Prize for *The Bone People* in 1985; the late **Janet Frame** became famous for *Owls Do Cry, An Angel at My Table,* and several others; **Owen Marshall** is perhaps our finest living short-story writer; and the late **Barry Crump** is a legend of a completely unique, raw, backcountry style, having produced books like *A Good Keen Man* and *Hang On a Minute Mate.*

Top Maori writers include **Witi Ihimaera, Patricia Grace,** and **Alan Duff.** In addition, **Maurice Gee, Maurice Shadbolt, Fiona Kidman,** and **Lauris Edmond** all warrant attention.

Filmmaker **Jane Campion** attracted world attention with *The Piano* (1993), which was nominated for nine Academy Awards. (**Anna Paquin** of Wellington won best supporting actress.)

Director **Peter Jackson** grabbed headlines when he secured Hollywood funding for *The Lord of the Rings,* which was filmed in 2000 with the biggest film budget ever. His *Heavenly Creatures* (1994) was the winner of the Silver Lion at the Venice Film Festival; and of course the *Lord of the Rings* trilogy went on to win a cluster of Oscars. Jackson has since added to his success with *King Kong* and, at press time, was filming *The Hobbit.* The Weta Studios in Wellington are now a major tourism venture, and there are numerous location tours all over New Zealand.

Two of Maori author **Alan Duff's** novels have also been made into successful films; *Once Were Warriors* and *What Becomes of the Broken Hearted* shocked audiences with their true-to-life violent portrayal of Maori gang society. Niki Caro's *Whale Rider* in 2002 won international acclaim. Spurred on by Peter Jackson's success, we now have a thriving film industry.

The very fact that we have such diverse landscapes within a small country has also attracted international filmmakers keen to film here. Much of *The Chronicles of Narnia: The Lion, the Witch and the Wardrobe* was filmed in the South Island; and Tom Cruise filmed *Samurai* in the North Island's Taranaki district. Indian Bollywood film crews are also regular visitors.

We've also turned out our fair share of musicians, none more famous than internationally regarded opera singer **Dame Kiri Te Kanawa.** On the pop scene, **Crowded House** and **Tim Finn** had big international hits in the '80s and '90s; and today we have a slew of Auckland-based rap artists making it big. Finally, **Hayley Westenra** has won hearts worldwide with her pop-opera crossover albums.

EATING & DRINKING

Dining Customs

New Zealand has not "grown up" with a long tradition of service in restaurants, so there will be times when you wonder if we even know what the word "service" means. For many young people, being a waitress or waiter is a reluctantly sought holiday job to earn money for university studies—and sadly, it often shows. However, the competitive market is forcing restaurant owners to wake up to the importance of good, friendly, smiling service, and many polytechnics now offer proper training. It is heartening to see a gradual swing toward a belief that restaurant service can be a career option, not just a long-suffering ordeal.

Service glitches are more noticeable in smaller provincial centers; some of that can be attributed to a lack of suitable local employees. Areas such as the West Coast face the reality of young people moving out to the cities; and major tourist centers like Queenstown tend to have a very transient population of restaurant employees.

New Zealand restaurants are either licensed to serve alcohol or BYO (bring your own); some are both. BYO of course is cheaper, as you don't have to pay the restaurant's surcharge on the wine, though some BYO establishments charge a corkage fee (usually NZ$3–NZ$8) for opening the wine bottle. **Note:** BYO means wine only, not beer or any other alcoholic beverages.

New Zealand restaurants and cafes do not apply any surcharges to simply sitting at a restaurant table. You are only charged for what you purchase. However, where there are outdoor cafe tables, you must purchase from the restaurant/cafe they're owned by.

Most cafes and restaurants now have table service, but some smaller cafes still operate on a counter service policy, where you place your order at the counter and pay before receiving your meal.

Note: All eateries are now smoke-free. This is a government edict, with smoking banned across-the-board in all restaurants, nightclubs, and public buildings.

Tipping is not customary in New Zealand, although I've never met a New Zealander who doesn't like a show of appreciation for good service and value. But that's relative. My policy is *don't tip for the sake of it.* This does nothing to foster an improvement in our serving standards, which, let's face it, still need work.

Dining hours vary from one eatery to another. Many cafes and restaurants open for coffee from around 9 to 10am and serve lunch between noon and 2 or 3pm, reverting to coffee and snack service only after that, then serving dinner from 6pm on. Others open for dinner only and that is almost always from 6pm onward.

Food

New Zealand is a land of edible bounty—Canterbury lamb; Central Otago pinot noir; Bluff and Nelson oysters; Nelson scallops; Kaikoura crayfish (lobster); West Coast whitebait; South Island venison; Marlborough green-lipped mussels; Akaroa salmon; Stewart Island blue cod; Central Otago cherries and apricots—and you shouldn't miss any of it.

Within the restaurant scene itself, there has been a revolution in the last decade. Fine dining (silver service) still lingers in a few city pockets, but the upmarket trend is predominantly toward fine gourmet food in more relaxed, contemporary settings. Increasing numbers of restaurants are also sourcing fresh, local ingredients, often specific to their region and often organically grown. As farmers' markets spring up all around the country and increasing amounts of genuinely organic meat and produce become available (albeit at extra cost), chefs are able to secure the very best ingredients to ensure flavorsome, healthy menus. Most will state this on their in-house menus.

Pacific Rim has been the primary culinary influence for some time, and although many chefs have stopped using the term, preferring modern or contemporary New Zealand terminology instead, the end result is much the same—the combination of classic Pacific and Asian ingredients combined to perfection and presented elegantly. You'll be spoiled with all the choices in this category, especially in Auckland, Wellington, Christchurch, and Queenstown (in that order).

For moderately priced, casual meals, including lunches, there are now so many cafes, restaurants, and bars it seems silly to try to define what each delivers. In short, you will seldom be without a choice. Most prepare good soups, salads, and main courses based around beef, lamb, chicken, fish, and vegetarian choices. Many others specialize in counter food, rather than menu-based options, and include panini, pastries, pies, sandwiches, and salads. Just be aware that many of the more casual cafe/bar establishments offering lighter meals often turn into rowdy drinking holes after 11pm.

There are a huge number of ethnic restaurants in all the main cities—Indian, Thai, Vietnamese, Chinese, Japanese, and Korean are the most common, but you'll also come across Burmese, Afghani, Turkish, Mexican, Spanish, Italian, French, and Middle Eastern choices in Auckland, Wellington, and Christchurch. Thai, Chinese, Vietnamese, and Indian restaurants are usually the cheapest of the ethnic choices, and you'll be able to enjoy great meals for a very reasonable price.

On top of the usual restaurant and cafe experiences, you'd be doing yourself a disservice if you miss trying a few iconic Kiwi meals. **Fish and chips** for instance. The fish-and-chip shop is still one of the most popular takeaway choices in this country—despite the colonization of McDonald's, Pizza Hut, and other conglomerates—and you'll find a fish-and-chip shop in virtually every town and village in the country. It goes without saying that some are better than others. Many still offer the meal—deep-fried battered fish and fat potato fries—wrapped in newspaper, which is how most New Zealanders prefer them; but some have opted for fancier packaging.

The small **meat pie** is still a Kiwi favorite, too. Every dairy and service station in the country has a pie warmer and, I'm almost reluctant to report, the meat pie is famed as a hangover cure after a night of heavy drinking.

The **barbecue** is a summer favorite. Almost every family in New Zealand will probably have a barbecue at some point during the summer months. Our balmy evenings lend themselves to eating outdoors and there's nothing quite like it. It invariably includes sausages and steak—often wrapped in bread and smothered in tomato sauce—accompanied by salads. Like most things, though, the barbecue is also changing and many people now apply as much culinary invention to the once-humble barbecue as they do any meal. I have friends who stay at the beach every summer and they live off freshly barbecued fish, scallops, and crayfish (lobster) plucked straight from the ocean and enhanced with their own particular sauces and spices. It's as good as any restaurant meal.

Last but certainly not least, the traditional **Maori** *hangi,* where food is cooked underground, is a must-do experience while you're in New Zealand. Traditionally, it involves lighting a fire and putting large stones in the embers to heat. Simultaneously, a large pit is dug. The heated rocks are then transferred into the pit, covered with wet sacking and/or wet newspapers. Prepared lamb, chicken, pork, fish, shellfish, and vegetables (most commonly sweet potato, pumpkin, and cabbage) are wrapped in leaves, placed in flax baskets (now made of wire or mesh), and lowered into the cooking pit, covered with more newspaper and earth, and left to steam. The moist, tender, melt-in-your-mouth food is lifted a few hours later.

Hangi food is not to everyone's taste—certainly not initially. The distinctive smoky flavors are an acquired taste. If you'd like to try hangi food, ask at visitor centers for tour operators who include a hangi. You'll find this easiest in Rotorua, where a number of hotels offer hangi meals as part of a cultural performance package. Bear in mind, though, that because of modern health and safety regulations, many hotels now prepare their hangi meals using gas-fired ovens, so the meal will lack some of the unique traditional smoky flavors that, to my mind, make a hangi meal.

Other distinctly New Zealand culinary experiences include the sheer craziness of the annual Hokitika Wildfoods Festival, where the policy is "If it's not moving, it's edible" (p. 384); the numerous annual wine and food festivals; and farmers' markets held in individual provinces. All are always well publicized at information centers.

Price categories for eating in New Zealand are as follows: Inexpensive (up to NZ$150), Moderate (NZ$151–NZ$300), Expensive (NZ$301–$600), and Very Expensive (NZ$601 & up).

Drink

A decade ago New Zealand's **wine** exports totaled around NZ$100 million; soon they are expected to top NZ$1 billion. That's rapid growth by anyone's standards, and as you drive around New Zealand you'll probably wonder if there'll be any farmland left without flourishing vines in another 10 years. It was a very different story 20 to 30 years ago when our nation's vineyards and wineries were restricted to a few longstanding operations in West Auckland and Hawke's Bay. That all changed in the 1990s when a British wine critic tagged New Zealand sauvignon blanc as "arguably the best in the world." Since then, the growth in the wine industry has been unbelievable. We now have 10 major winegrowing regions spanning latitudes 36 to 45 and the entire length of the country. That makes for some diverse growing conditions and some very distinct wine styles. Turns out we can just about grow anything here, although it is our pinot noir and our sauvignon blancs that have made us famous internationally. There is also growing recognition of our chardonnay, *méthode traditionelle* sparkling wines, our Rieslings, cabernet sauvignon, and our merlot—all of which have cemented New Zealand's reputation as a producer of world-class wines. I have highlighted major wineries in all the wine regions throughout the guide; you'd do well to get yourself a copy of the *Classic New Zealand Wine Trail* when you arrive here. It's available from all visitor centers and is well worth your while if you enjoy wine and food.

To say that New Zealand is a nation of **beer** drinkers is an understatement. We don't use the phrase "rugby, racing, and beer" here for nothing. There was a time when the New Zealand beer scene was dominated by just one or two major breweries—Lion and DB for example—but in the last 10 years there has been a proliferation of small boutique breweries springing up all over the country. I may be wrong, but it seems to me that this has almost been in response to the astonishing growth of our wine industry; or maybe it was a backlash to the domination of the industry by a few big players. Whatever the reason, New Zealand beer drinkers are happier than they've ever been. You can travel from one end of the country to the other and never drink the same beer twice. To name just a few brewers there's Epic Beer in Auckland; Macs in Wellington; Founders Organic in Nelson; Dux de Lux in Christchurch and Queenstown; Monteith's in Greymouth; Twisted Hop in Christchurch; Speight's and Emerson's in Dunedin; and Wanaka Beerworks in Wanaka. You can do an excellent beer tour in Wellington and you can visit breweries in most major centers. I have included these in the appropriate chapters.

Vodka is also a word on many people's lips—specifically 42-Below Vodka, that multi-award-winning sensation that tackled the world head-on with its stunning advertising campaign. Based in Auckland, 42-Below hit the shelves around 2002 and it's been winning international awards ever since—or as their cheeky advertising campaign says, they've "had more awards for best vodka than you've had hot dates."

In the **soft drink** line (sometimes called fizzy drinks here), we've also had a flurry of recent activity. Our ever-popular Lemon & Paeroa, "World Famous in New Zealand," is part of contemporary New Zealand lore. Ever since therapeutic spring water was discovered in the little Thames Valley town of Paeroa in the 19th century, it's been a huge hit. Now we have many new players bringing us a whole range of new soft drink flavors—from elderberry to feijoa and guava. Most have sidestepped mass marketing and have targeted boutique delicatessen stores. That's where you'll find more new brands than I can possibly name here—all of them well worth sampling.

Coffee is the other revolution! In the last decade we have turned into a nation of caffeine addicts. There are numerous coffee grinding companies in most cities—Christchurch alone has close to 20—and cafes serving excellent espresso are springing up on every corner. You'll also find mobile espresso carts in all sorts of unexpected places, from sports grounds and farmers' markets to street corners and beaches. There's even one on Stewart Island. A number of national cafes have moved into franchising. Yes, we have Starbucks here, but you'll find their cafes are usually filled with tourists. Most New Zealanders prefer a different brew (more like the coffee of Melbourne and Italy) and if they're going to frequent a franchise, they're usually loyal to a New Zealand–based operation.

You'll also find some "interesting" interpretations of espresso in the provinces—not all of them drinkable—but at least they're trying. It all comes down to good espresso training and product knowledge; too bad not all cafes have learned how important it is to invest in these. But with increasing numbers of students pouring out of our hospitality schools, we can only hope to see improvement in this area.

Organic and fair trade coffee is readily available in all the larger cities and towns.

Dialing the Weather

In New Zealand, call **Metservice** at ℂ **0900/999** followed by your New Zealand area code to hear the current and expected weather conditions for the region you are in. Calls cost NZ$1.30 per minute including GST. You can also visit the Metservice website, www.met service.co.nz, for further details, or check their blog, http://blog.metservice.com/, for the latest updates. Check the website for details about receiving weather updates via SMS texting at a time to suit you. Daily updates cost NZ50¢; on-demand updates cost NZ99¢. For further information, call **Metservice** toll-free at ℂ **0800/932-843.**

WHEN TO GO

New Zealand is in the Southern Hemisphere; therefore, all seasons are the opposite of those in North America, Europe, and other Northern Hemisphere locations.

There really isn't a bad time to travel to New Zealand. Keep in mind, though, that most Kiwi families take their main annual holidays between mid-December and the end of January, which puts enormous pressure on accommodations in major summer beach destinations. During the Easter break and school holidays in April, June to July, and September to October (see "Holidays," below, for exact dates), it also pays to reserve well in advance.

Remember, too, that accommodations at ski destinations like Ohakune, National Park, Methven near Mount Hutt, Wanaka, and Queenstown fill up quickly—reserve early and be prepared to pay higher winter rates. In most other areas, though, you'll be paying lower rates during the winter months (Apr–Aug). In some summer-peak areas, the winter also means that tour, lodge, and adventure operators may take advantage of lower tourist numbers and take their own holiday breaks, closing their businesses for 1- to 3-month periods.

Weather

New Zealand's climate, especially by Northern Hemisphere standards, is pretty mellow for much of the year. You'll find a far greater seasonal difference in the South Island than in the subtropical North, and don't believe anyone who says it never gets cold here or that there are no extremes. In Central Otago, winter temperatures are often 14°F (–10°C) and sometimes as low as –4°F (–20°C), with summers up to 100°F to 104°F (38°C–40°C). By comparison, the northern part of the North Island is subtropical. That means *lots* of winter/spring rain, and often daily light showers.

The west coast of the South Island can get up to 100 inches or more of rain a year on its side of the Southern Alps, while just over the mountains to the east, rainfall is a moderate 20 to 30 inches annually. Rain is also heavier on the west coast of the North Island, averaging 40 to 70 inches annually. Milford Sound, though, beats the lot; it's the wettest place in the country, with a phenomenal 365 inches of rain a year.

THE SEASONS

SPRING (SEPT, OCT, NOV) This is a beautiful time to visit—the countryside is flush with new green grass, baby lambs, and blooming trees. Christchurch in the spring means blossoms, bluebells, and daffodils in abundance; Dunedin is a splurge of rhododendron color. The weather can still be very changeable right up to mid-October, so come prepared with light rain gear. In the South Island, it's still perfectly normal to get late snowfalls in September.

Average Seasonal Temperature & Precipitation

Temperatures reflected are daily average (°C/°F). Rainfall reflects the daily average in millimeters/inches (mm/in.) and is accurate within 1 millimeter.

		SUMMER	FALL	WINTER	SPRING			SUMMER	FALL	WINTER	SPRING
BAY OF ISLANDS	MAX. TEMP	25/77	21/70	16/61	19/66	WESTPORT	MAX. TEMP	22/72	17/63	13/55	15/59
	MIN. TEMP	14/57	11/52	7/45	9/48		MIN. TEMP	12/54	10/50	5/41	8/46
	RAINFALL	7/0.28	1/0.44	16/0.64	11/0.44		RAINFALL	12/0.48	14/0.56	15/0.6	16/0.64
AUCKLAND	MAX. TEMP	24/75	20/68	15/59	18/65	CHRISTCHURCH	MAX. TEMP	22/72	18/65	12/54	17/63
	MIN. TEMP	12/54	13/55	9/48	11/52		MIN. TEMP	12/54	8/46	3/37	7/45
	RAINFALL	8/0.32	11/0.44	15/0.6	12/0.48		RAINFALL	7/0.28	7/0.28	7/0.28	7/0.28
ROTORUA	MAX. TEMP	24/75	18/65	13/55	17/63	MOUNT COOK	MAX. TEMP	20/68	14/57	8/46	14/57
	MIN. TEMP	12/54	9/48	4/39	7/45		MIN. TEMP	9/48	4/39	-1/30	4/39
	RAINFALL	9/0.36	9/0.36	13/0.52	11/0.44		RAINFALL	12/0.48	13/0.52	13/0.52	14/0.56
WELLINGTON	MAX. TEMP	20/68	17/63	12/54	15/59	QUEENSTOWN	MAX. TEMP	22/72	16/61	10/50	16/61
	MIN. TEMP	13/55	11/52	6/43	9/48		MIN. TEMP	10/50	6/43	1/34	5/41
	RAINFALL	7/0.28	10/0.4	13/0.52	11/0.44		RAINFALL	8/0.32	8/0.32	7/0.28	9/0.36
NELSON	MAX. TEMP	22/72	18/65	13/55	17/63	INVERCARGILL	MAX. TEMP	18/65	15/59	11/52	15/59
	MIN. TEMP	13/55	8/46	3/37	7/45		MIN. TEMP	9/48	6/43	1/34	5/41
	RAINFALL	6/0.24	8/0.32	10/0.4	10/0.4		RAINFALL	13/0.52	14/0.56	12/0.48	13/0.52

SUMMER (DEC, JAN, FEB) This is peak tourist season, so you'll pay top dollar for accommodations and airfares. Book early to avoid disappointment—this also applies to the major walking tracks, such as Milford, for which you should make bookings 6 months ahead. The country's beaches come alive, and boaties flock to the water. Fresh fruit is falling off the trees. (You must try Central Otago cherries and apricots; the apple district is Hawke's Bay.) Everyone should see Central Otago when the lupines are flowering, with brilliant colors etched against blue skies and golden tussock.

AUTUMN (MAR, APR, MAY) I think the best time to visit is February through April. The temperatures are pleasant (still hot in Feb in most parts), and even in April you'll be wearing summer clothes in the upper North Island. The most spectacular autumn colors are found in Queenstown, Central Otago, and Christchurch. Keep Easter and April school holidays in mind, though, when lodgings may be tight in some areas.

WINTER (JUNE, JULY, AUG) If you're a skier, you'll be heading to Queenstown, Mount Hutt, Canterbury, or the Central Plateau in the North Island—and paying top dollar for the privilege. Otherwise, if you travel elsewhere during this period, you won't need to prebook much at all (except during the July school holidays). You'll find some excellent rates—just don't expect great things from the weather.

Holidays

National public holidays include New Year's Day (Jan 1), New Year's Holiday (Jan 2), Waitangi Day (Feb 6), Good Friday (varies), Easter and Easter Monday (varies), ANZAC Day (Apr 25), Queen's Birthday (first Mon in June), Labour Day (last Mon in Oct), Christmas Day (Dec 25), and Boxing Day (Dec 26).

Regional holidays include Wellington (Jan 22), Auckland (Jan 29), Northland (Jan 29), Nelson Region (Feb 1), Otago (Mar 23), Southland (Mar 23), Taranaki (Mar 31), Hawke's Bay (Nov 1), Marlborough (Nov 1), Westland (Dec 1), and Canterbury

(Dec 16). Regional holidays are always observed on a Monday. If the date lands on a Friday or weekend, the holiday is observed on the following Monday. If it falls earlier in the week, it is observed on the preceding Monday.

School holidays consist of three midterm breaks—in April, June to July, and September to October—that last for 2 weeks each, plus 6 weeks for the December holidays. Kiwi families do much of their traveling during these periods, so book early.

New Zealand Calendar of Events

More information can be found in the regional chapters that follow and by going to the Tourism New Zealand website at **www.newzealand.com**. For an exhaustive list of even more events beyond those listed here, check http://events.frommers.com, where you'll find a searchable, up-to-the-minute roster of what's happening in cities all over the world.

JANUARY

ASB Bank Tennis Classic, Auckland. International women's tennis tour event preceding the Australian Open. Attracts leading overseas players. Call ✆ **09/373-3623,** or check www.asbclassic.co.nz. First week of January.

Heineken Open, Auckland. International Men's ATP tour for leading international tennis players. Call ✆ **09/373-3623,** or check www.heinekenopen.co.nz. Early January.

Auckland Anniversary Day Regatta, Auckland. "The City of Sails" hosts this colorful annual sailing event, which attracts both local and international competitors and spectators. Call ✆ **0800/734-2882,** or check www.regatta.org.nz. Last Monday in January.

World Buskers Festival, Christchurch. A week of zany street entertainment provided by leading entertainers. Call ✆ **03/377-2365,** or visit www.worldbuskers festival.com. Mid- to late January.

Wellington Cup Race Meeting, Wellington. Leading horse-racing event (galloping), held in conjunction with the National Yearling Sales. Call ✆ **04/528-9611,** or check www.trentham.co.nz. Late January.

FEBRUARY

Hawke's Bay Wine and Food Festival, Hawke's Bay. A showcase of the region's world-class wines and good food. Call ✆ **0508/946-326** in New Zealand, or check www.harvesthawkesbay.co.nz. First week of February.

Speight's Coast to Coast, South Island. A major multisport endurance race from Kumara on the West Coast to Sumner, Christchurch, featuring a 33km (20-mile) mountain run followed by a 67km (42-mile) kayak race and a 142km (88-mile) cycle dash. Call ✆ **03/348-3282,** or check www. coasttocoast.co.nz. February 5–6.

Waitangi Day Celebrations, Bay of Islands. New Zealand's national day celebrating the signing of the Treaty of Waitangi. Call ✆ **09/402-7308.** February 6.

Garden City Festival of Flowers, Christchurch. Ten days of garden visits, floating gardens, and floral carpets in the "Garden City." Call ✆ **03/365-5403,** or visit www. festivalofflowers.co.nz. Mid-February.

Brebner Art Deco Weekend, Napier. A fun celebration of the city's Art Deco heritage that includes dancing, jazz, vintage cars, walks, and tours. Most participants dress in 1920s and 1930s fashions. Call ✆ **06/835-0022,** or check www.artdeconapier.com. Third weekend in February.

Devonport Food and Wine Festival, Devonport. Held near the Ferry Wharf in this picturesque Auckland village, the festival includes jazz, classical, and opera performances. Call ✆ **09/378-9030,** or visit www.devonportwinefestival.co.nz. Late February.

Auckland Arts Festival. A biennial extravaganza of national and international dance, music, theater, and visual arts. The next festival will be in 2013. Call ✆ **09/309-0101,** or check www.aucklandfestival.co.nz. Late February to March.

MARCH

Celebrate Pasifika Festival, Auckland. Auckland's Pacific Island communities celebrate the largest 1-day cultural festival in the South Pacific. Not to be missed. Check www.celebratepasifica.com for more info. First week of March.

New Zealand International Festival of Arts, Wellington. The largest and most prestigious event on the New Zealand arts calendar features top overseas and national artists and entertainers. A vibrant mix of all art forms, from contemporary dance to fine music and theater. Call ✆ **04/473-0149,** or visit www.nzfestival.nzpost.co.nz. Beginning of March.

Ellerslie International Flower Show Christchurch, Christchurch. New Zealand's premier garden event has shifted from Auckland to Christchurch. It showcases the best of garden design over 5 days in Hagley Park. Nurseries and garden retailers also participate. Call ✆ **03/941-8999,** or visit www.ellerslieflowershow.co.nz. Early March.

Hokitika Wildfoods Festival, Hokitika. A culinary adventure for the brave and curious, this 1-day event presents the weird and wonderful of New Zealand's wild foods, including wild pig, possum pâté, goat, various bugs and insects, honey, fish, and venison. Call ✆ **03/756-9048,** or check www.wildfoods.co.nz. Mid-March.

Arrowtown Autumn Festival, Arrowtown. A week of market days, music, and street entertainment celebrating the gold-mining era. Call ✆ **03/442-0809** or 027/210-1570, or visit www.arrowtownautumnfestival.org.nz. The week after Easter.

APRIL

Warbirds Over Wanaka, Wanaka. Now classified as one of the best Warbirds air shows in the world, it combines classic vintage and veteran aircraft, machinery, fire engines, and tractors with dynamic Air Force displays and aerobatic teams in the natural amphitheater of the Upper Clutha Basin. Call ✆ **03/443-8619,** or visit www.warbirdsoverwanaka.com. Easter weekend (in even-numbered years only).

Fletcher Challenge Forest Marathon, Rotorua. A full marathon around Lake Rotorua for serious competitors. Attracts over 500 runners. Call ✆ **07/348-3301,** or check www.rotoruamarathon.co.nz. Late April to early May.

MAY

Bay of Islands Country Music Festival, Bay of Islands. This festival draws musicians from all around New Zealand, and there's at least one international act each year. Call ✆ **09/404-1063,** or check www.countryrock.co.nz. Second weekend in May.

Matariki, nationwide. Matariki is the Maori New Year, which coincides with the time when the Pleiades constellation is visible. It is traditionally a time for planting new crops. Since 2000 there has been renewed interest in Matariki, and a diverse range of cultural celebrations are now held throughout the country. Visit www.matarikifestival.co.nz and www.matariki.net.nz for more information. Late May through June.

JUNE

National Agricultural Fieldays, Hamilton. One of the largest agricultural shows in the world, exhibiting the best of New Zealand agriculture, horticulture, floriculture, and forestry products. Call ✆ **07/843-4499,** or visit www.fieldays.co.nz. Mid-June.

JULY

Queenstown Winter Festival, Queenstown. Queenstown officially goes mad with a host of zany mountain events and street entertainment. Call ✆ **03/441-2453,** or check www.winterfestival.co.nz. Mid-July.

Christchurch Arts Festival. Biennially in July to August, this festival showcases the best of national and international dance, music, theater, and visual arts. For more information, visit www.artsfestival.co.nz.

AUGUST

Bay of Islands Jazz and Blues Festival, Bay of Islands. More than 50 jazz bands from New Zealand and overseas provide live entertainment at various places around Paihia and Russell, night and day. Call ✆ **09/404-1063** in New Zealand, or go to www.jazz-blues.co.nz. Early tomid-August.

SEPTEMBER

Montana World of Wearable Art Awards, Wellington. This creative extravaganza in Wellington should not be missed. Call ℂ **03/547-0863,** or go to www.world ofwearableart.com. Mid- to late September.

Alexandra Blossom Festival, Alexandra. An annual parade of floats and entertainment, celebrating the onset of spring. Call ℂ **03/377-2823,** or check www.blossom.co.nz. Late September to early October.

Gay Ski Week. A week of celebrations on and around the slopes. See www.gayski weeknz.com for more information. First week of September.

OCTOBER

Kaikoura Seafest, Kaikoura. An annual celebration of the best seafood and Marlborough and Canterbury wines, plus fun and entertainment for the entire family. Call ℂ **0800/473-2337** in New Zealand, or visit www.seafest.co.nz. Early October.

Dunedin Rhododendron Festival, Dunedin. Fun-filled days highlighted by garden tours and cultural events to celebrate the city's magnificent displays of rhododendron blooms. Call ℂ **03/477-1092,** or check www.rhododunedin.co.nz. Mid- to late October.

Nelson Arts Festival, Nelson. Twelve days of music, dance, theater, and street performances throughout the city. Call ℂ **03/545-8734,** or check www.nelsonartsfestival. co.nz. Mid-October.

Queenstown Jazz Festival, Queenstown. Over 200 musicians attend and play in bars and restaurants in a nonstop jam session with food and dancing. Call ℂ **03/441-2453,** or visit www.queenstownjazz.co.nz. Late October.

NOVEMBER

Toast Martinborough, Martinborough. An annual wine-and-food festival. Call ℂ **06/306-9183,** or go to www.toastmartin borough.co.nz. Mid- to late November.

Canterbury A&P Show, Christchurch. The South Island's largest agricultural and pastoral event, which includes thoroughbred and standard-bred racing and the New Zealand Cup. Call ℂ **03/343-3033,** or go to www.theshow.co.nz. Second week of November.

Southern Traverse, South Island. An adventure race for teams of three to five serious competitors through New Zealand's toughest terrain. The endurance events cover high ridges, lakes, and river crossings throughout Otago. Call ℂ **03/441-8215,** or check out www.southerntraverse.com. Late November.

DECEMBER

Nelson Jazz Festival, Nelson. A wide variety of local and national jazz bands perform in a weekend event, culminating in a special New Year's Eve concert. Call ℂ **03/547-2559,** or visit www.nelsonjazz. co.nz. Late December to early January.

LAY OF THE LAND

New Zealand is part of a fiery rim of volcanoes that encircle the Pacific Ocean. The last large eruption occurred in 1886—Mount Tarawera near Rotorua left an estimated 150 people dead. Our most recent showoff has been Mount Ruapehu, which did its best to ruin the central North Island ski season for several years in a row in the late '90s.

Today, New Zealand bears all the fascinating geographical hallmarks of a tumultuous geologic history. It may have a reputation for being "very green," but most visitors are astonished to discover a small country of incredible geographic diversity. There are 500-million-year-old marble outcrops on the top of the Takaka Hills in Nelson, and volcanic ash and pumice have created a barren, desertlike landscape in the central North Island. Franz Josef is one of the fastest-moving glaciers in the world, and the Marlborough Sounds are a labyrinth of islands and waterways. Parched tussock country and strange rocky outcrops cover Central Otago, and the Canterbury Plains spread wide and flat as evidence of pre-human glacial erosion.

Despite all this earthly fury, the land has been blessed with an endless coastline of stunning beaches—white or golden sand on the east coasts, black or gray on the west coasts. Craters have filled to create jewel-like lakes, and rivers and streams are the endless arteries and veins that feed lush flora.

Flora & Fauna

FAUNA

For 70 million years, New Zealand has been completely separate from all other land-masses. We've been left with a few pretty strange creatures as a result: four flightless birds—the kiwi, weka, kakapo, and takahe—along with an ancient reptile (the tua-tara), directly descended from the dinosaurs. The **kiwi,** of course, has been embraced as a national symbol, so much so that many New Zealanders are quite happy to be called Kiwis themselves. And that odd spiky "lizard," the **tuatara,** is being encouraged to breed itself silly in captivity to ensure it will be around for future generations to marvel at.

Apart from that, we don't have anything very exciting in the way of wildlife. New Zealand has no native mammals. It was the first Polynesian settlers who brought in both the dog and the rat. Captain Cook then arrived with pigs, goats, fowl, and probably more rats. As more foreign animals were introduced, it became necessary to bring in other animals to control those that had become pests. We now have more than 33 introduced species of mammals, 34 species of birds, 14 species of freshwater fish, at least 1,000 species of introduced insects, plus an Australian lizard and frog or two. Unfortunately, a good many of the above are pests, especially the opossum, which eats its way through frightening quantities of our forests every night. Oddly, while we in New Zealand are busy trying to eradicate this Australian native, in Australia they are busy protecting it.

The good news is, we have no nasties—no snakes, predatory animals, or deadly critters of any kind. The only one that comes close is the poisonous **katipo spider,** which you're unlikely to even see, unless you're on the western beaches of the North Island and spot a small black spider with a bright red stripe on its abdomen. There are sometimes **sharks** in the waters around New Zealand, though, so be sure to ask the locals about this, even though shark attacks are rare.

BIRD-WATCHING Our bird life is abundant and our native birds (around 250 species) in particular are a rich lot, attracting bird-watchers from all over the world. Because of New Zealand's isolation and the evolutionary patterns that have developed here as a result, many species are found nowhere else in the world. The **bellbird,** plain of feather and easily missed, is the songster supreme. The handsome inky **tui,** with his white-tufted neck, comes a close second. The flightless **weka** is rowdy rather than tuneful, and you'll see him in the bush or poking his nose into campsites. The green-and-orange **kea** is a cheeky mountain parrot with a reputation for mischief on the ski fields and in high-country camps. Make sure you don't leave any belongings about, as keas love to steal whatever is not locked away. This especially applies to anything shiny. They are notorious for damaging mirrors, aerials, and other attachments on vehicles; and their large, strong beaks will give you a nasty bite, so don't be tempted to feed them.

Seabirds of course abound and you'll be delighted by nesting **albatross** and **gannets,** elegant **white herons, penguins,** and many more. Keen bird-watchers have many choice spots to visit. The **Miranda Seabird Coast near Thames** on the Coromandel Peninsula is home to 8,500 hectares (21,000 acres) of tidal flats that attract millions of migratory species every year. **Farewell Spit northwest of Nelson** is another major migratory path, and **South Brighton Spit in Christchurch** attracts millions of godwits every year on their return from Siberia. You can enjoy seabird tours at **Kaikoura. Otago Peninsular** is home to both albatross and penguin colonies, which you can visit. Another not-to-be-missed bird-watching location is **Okarito in the South Westland,** home to the white heron nesting colonies. Keep in mind that the only access to these protected areas is via guided tours, which I've listed in the appropriate chapter. There are several tourism operators offering seabird tours around the peninsular coastline. **Stewart Island** is another superb destination for bird-watchers. Not only does it have a wealth of pelagic species which you can arrange to see by boat; it also has easy access to **Ulva Island,** a protected bird sanctuary that is home to several unique species. One of the delights here is the tiny native robins that are surprisingly tame and fearless. If you scratch the ground gently, they will hop right up to your feet, providing you with unforgettable photo opportunities. Stewart Island is also the only place in New Zealand where you can join nighttime kiwi-spotting tours that take you out into the wild to see this native icon. You'll be very lucky to see a kiwi in the wild on your own, as they tend to forage deep in the bush at night, or on remote, often inaccessible beaches.

Birds are easier to spot in clearings or secondary forests than they are in primary forests. Unless you have lots of experience bird-watching, your best hope for enjoying a walk through the forest lies in employing a trained and knowledgeable guide. (By the way, if it's been raining a lot and the trails are muddy, a good pair of rubber boots comes in handy.)

As with any form of bird or wildlife spotting, the standard rules apply. Here are a few helpful hints:

- **Listen.** Pay attention to rustling in the leaves; whether it's bellbirds up above or penguins on the ground, you're most likely to hear an animal before seeing one.
- **Keep quiet.** Noise will scare off animals and prevent you from hearing their movements and calls.
- **Don't try too hard.** Soften your focus and allow your peripheral vision to take over. This way you can catch glimpses of motion and then focus in on the prey.
- **Bring binoculars.** It's also a good idea to practice a little first to get the hang of them. It would be a shame to be fiddling around and staring into space while everyone else in your group oohs and aahs over a kiwi.
- **Dress appropriately.** You'll have a hard time focusing your binoculars if you're busy swatting flies. Light, long pants and long-sleeved shirts are your best bet. Comfortable hiking boots are a real boon, except where heavy rubber boots are necessary. Avoid loud colors; the better you blend in with your surroundings, the better your chances are of spotting birds.
- **Be patient.** The forest isn't on a schedule. However, your best shots at seeing birds (or other wildlife) are in the very early morning and late afternoon hours.
- **Read up.** Familiarize yourself with what you're most likely to see, and if you plan to study the birds, get a copy of *The Field Guide to the Birds of New Zealand* by Barrie Heather and Hugh Robertson. It's published by Penguin and is the only

guide endorsed by the Ornithological Society of New Zealand. The same authors also produce a smaller book, *The Hand Guide to the Birds of New Zealand*. If you'd like a more colorful reference, get *Know Your New Zealand Birds* by Lynette and Geoff Moon, published by New Holland. They also produce a small, handbag-size *Photographic Guide to New Zealand Birds*.

It is also important to remember that you put yourself at grave risk by wandering off into the bush alone. You will have a much safer and more satisfying bush bird-watching experience by joining a guide who knows exactly where and when to go to find specific species. Also check at information centers for the best local knowledge of key bird-watching areas, the species you are likely to see, and tour operators or guides who can take you there.

FLORA

When it comes to **flora,** we have diverse vegetation—everything from coastal grasses, moss-covered **rainforests,** and dense **primeval forests** of ancient podocarp trees to palms, lush ferns, orchids, Norfolk pines, bougainvillea, flame trees, and hibiscus. In the far north, the Waipoua Forest is home to our giant kauri trees, which are one of the oldest species in the world. Tane Mahuta, the largest of the kauri trees, is said to be over 2,000 years old. In the central North Island and throughout the mountainous regions of the South, there are tortured-looking alpine plants, brilliant lichens, beech forests, and gigantic tree ferns. Because of that same geographic isolation that shaped our bird life, 84% of New Zealand's flowering plants are found nowhere else in the world.

New Zealand is a highly productive agricultural country, and during early settlement, much of the land was developed at the expense of our unique native forests. Lush pastoral lowlands have been coaxed out of swampland; and many high country farmlands are littered with the rotting tree stumps that attest to once thriving forests.

That, inevitably, is the cost of human progress. In all, around one-third of the country's total land area has been cleared since the arrival of European settlers. In more recent decades, though, New Zealand has taken a very proactive stance toward the protection of what remains. We have 13 national parks that can never be destroyed, and these are the places you should explore to get a feel for New Zealand the way it once was. But as I will mention many times throughout this guide, treat native forest areas with great respect and never venture into them alone, or without being extremely well-equipped with food, water, warm clothing, and some sort of communication device. Many thousands of people have been lost in the bush; many have never been found again. Don't take the warnings lightly.

RESPONSIBLE TRAVEL

New Zealand has a long-established reputation for being "clean and green," and Tourism New Zealand's 100% Pure New Zealand brand campaign has reinforced that. It goes without saying that tourism in this country is largely shaped by the uniqueness of our environment and culture, and as the major contributor to the nation's economy, it is vital that all New Zealanders have a genuine desire to ensure its future.

No surprise, then, that ecotourism is now the fastest growing sector of New Zealand's tourism industry. Everyone is jumping on the sustainable tourism bandwagon, and while most are driven by genuine altruistic motives, the cynic in me suspects many are becoming "green-rated" as a marketing ploy, without backing up their claims of being ecofriendly with anything beyond tokenism.

SOME sustainable PROPERTIES IN NEW ZEALAND

Following is a selection of properties that have either attained Green Globe benchmarking, a Qualmark Enviro rating, or both. Throughout the book I have also noted the properties and tourism operators who have a commitment to sustainable practices.

Auckland
Bethells Beach Cottages (p. 101)
Braemar on Parliament Street (p. 96)
The Great Ponsonby Arthotel (p. 97)
Langham Hotel Auckland (p. 94)
SKYCITY Grand Hotel (p. 94)

Northland & Coromandel
Base Pipi Patch (p. 153)
Carrington Resort (p. 155)
Colleith Lodge (p. 168)
Villa Toscana (p. 168)

Waikato & Bay of Plenty
Kamahi Cottage (p. 177)
Novotel Tainui (p. 176)
Ridge Country Retreat (p. 182)

Rotorua & Tongariro National Park
Bayview Chateau Tongariro (p. 219)
Maruata Rotorua (p. 201)
Peppers on the Point (p. 198)
Treetops Lodge & Estate (p. 199)

Gisborne & Hawke's Bay
The County Hotel (p. 240)
Knapdale Eco Lodge (p. 280)

Wanganui
The Flying Fox (p. 258)

Wellington
Bolton Hotel (p. 270)
InterContinental Wellington (p. 270)
James Cook Hotel Grand Chancellor (p. 271)
Mount Victoria Homestay (p. 272)
Ohtel (p. 273)

Nelson
Abel Tasman Marahau Lodge (p. 325)
Abel Tasman Ocean View Chalets (p. 325)
Awaroa Lodge (p. 325)
Shelbourne Villa (p. 318)
39 Russell (p. 317)

Christchurch & Canterbury
The Classic Villa (p. 339)
The Marque Christchurch (p. 337)
Wilderness Lodge (p. 366)
The Worcester of Christchurch (p. 338)

West Coast
Breakers Boutique Accommodation (p. 379)
Chelsea Gateway Motor Lodge (p. 375)
Te Waonui Forest Retreat (p. 393)
Wilderness Lodge Lake Moeraki (p. 395)

Wanaka
Edgewater Resort (p. 405)
Lime Tree Lodge (p. 404)
Maple Lodge (p. 405)
Wanaka Springs (p. 406)
Whare Kea Lodge (p. 404)

Mount Cook
Hermitage Hotel (p. 411)

Queenstown
The Heritage (p. 431)
Queenstown Top 10 Holiday Park Creeksyde (p. 432)
The Rees Hotel & Luxury Apartments (p. 432)
Remarkables Lodge (p. 433)

Fiordland & Southland
Fiordland Lodge (p. 446)
The Lodge at Tikana (p. 481)

Stewart Island
Stewart Island Lodge (p. 488)

Dunedin
Nisbet Cottage (p. 468)

In light of the worldwide focus on sustainability issues, it is apt that New Zealand takes a second look at itself. Despite all those "clean and green" claims, the country has long been a poor performer in industrial and agricultural waste management and recycling. That is changing fast. Farmers are developing cutting-edge technology to improve dairy farm effluent management; industries are being forced to comply with new waste management regulations aimed to help clean up our waterways; and businesses across-the-board are taking a lively approach to pest and weed control, reforestation, and the restoration of prime ecological environments. Tourism operators and organizations are also working much more closely with central and local governments to address concerns about waste disposal associated with campers and motor homes, and tourists' accessibility to local recycling programs. In short, there has been a groundswell of interest in sustainability measures, and there is now an expectation that business operators will put their best foot forward—especially in the tourism arena.

Leading the charge is Tourism New Zealand, with its unique approach to sustainability based on the traditional Maori principles of *manaakitanga* (hospitality) and *kaitiakitanga* (guardianship)—welcoming visitors while protecting and managing our culture and environment. Its Tourism Strategy 2015 is based on a whole New Zealand approach that will see increasing numbers of sustainability initiatives put into action over the coming few years. This includes initiatives like the New Zealand Emissions Trading Scheme, which aims to encourage all sectors of the economy, including tourism, to find smart, efficient ways to cut back their emissions. A transport strategy will focus on creating a sustainable transport network throughout the country.

Already in place is the Qualmark Responsible Tourism Operations program, a partnership between Tourism New Zealand and the New Zealand Automobile Association. While the system does have its detractors (with negativity focused on the nature of its rating system), it has gone some way toward tidying up New Zealand's accommodations sector. In terms of sustainability and ecotourism, it must be said that some rating system is better than no rating system. You'll now find many tourism providers boasting about having a Qualmark Enviro-Gold, -Silver, or -Bronze rating—so many, in fact, that it's hard not to suspect some of the motives behind this huge rush to sign on. Businesses performing at the top level of this rating system, though, will be energy efficient and will have active waste management and water conservation practices, and will be taking part in conservation initiatives and community activities. It is largely thanks to this integrated quality and environmental tourism performance assurance system—the first of its kind in the world—that New Zealand was voted Overall Winner and Best Destination in the Virgin Holidays Responsible Tourism Awards in London in 2008. The judges recognized Qualmark Green as one of New Zealand's most important achievements in responsible tourism.

New Zealand's Environmentally Sustainable Tourism Project is another worthy of attention. Jointly run by the Ministry for the Environment and the Ministry of Tourism, it established six regional tourism charters committed to the sustainable practices laid down in Tourism New Zealand's sustainable strategy. Enterprise Northland, Destination Rotorua, Tourism Bay of Plenty, Latitude Nelson, Lake Wanaka Tourism, and Venture Southland/Destination Fiordland all work toward improving the environmental performance of participating tourism operators. You can find all members signed up to these charters by asking at the appropriate regional visitor centers.

Increasing numbers of New Zealand businesses are also becoming Green Globe Benchmarked or Green Globe Certified. Green Globe is based on Agenda 21, a comprehensive plan of action regarding sustainable development endorsed at the United Nations Earth Summit in 1992. There are currently Green Globe participants in more than 50 countries around the world. A tourism operation can only use a

Green Globe logo once it has been measured to be above the benchmarking base-line performance level. The Green Globe website (www.greenglobeint.com) lists New Zealand operations affiliated with the program.

Recycling generally has taken on a new impetus in New Zealand in the last 2 years. Every major city's rubbish collection program now has separate bins for paper and recyclable goods, organic waste and nonrecyclable matter; and national parks and public areas are well-equipped with rubbish bins. Recycling within hotels (for guests) is much less common. Many hotels have instituted sustainable practices but that doesn't usually extend to providing recycling bins within guest rooms. I suspect that will change as pressure on the environment continues. I've provided a separate box listing a number of accommodations and tourism providers that I think are approaching the matter of sustainability with commitment and integrity.

While sustainable tourism operations and community initiatives are increasingly common in New Zealand, there are very few restaurants totally committed to organic menus. That said, increasing numbers of chefs are sourcing organic meats and other ingredients to include in their menus. Organic produce is much more widely available in New Zealand now, but it is still more highly priced—sometimes ridiculously so. Even the huge groundswell of farmers' markets throughout the country has done little to lower the price of genuine organic produce. So if you order organic, expect to pay more.

One of the most exciting aspects of sustainability in New Zealand has been the huge growth in volunteer projects with a sustainability focus. I have detailed several of those in "Volunteering & Working in New Zealand" later in this chapter. In short, there are numerous opportunities to sign on for replanting programs, track and walkway building projects, native bird–breeding programs, pest trapping in national parks, working on organic farms, and more. This is an excellent way to give your holiday a meaningful edge that will be rewarding for both yourself and New Zealand's unique environment.

You can help even more by flying here with our national airline, **Air New Zealand.** Not only did they carry out the world's first commercial aviation test flight using a sustainable second-generation biofuel derived from the plant *Jatropha curcas,* they also have an active carbon offset program, which allows customers to make a donation to the Air New Zealand Environment Trust.

In addition to the resources for New Zealand listed above, see www.frommers.com/planning for more tips on responsible travel.

TOURS

Academic Trips & Language Classes

There are numerous English language schools in New Zealand, which allow international students of all ages to enjoy the natural beauty at the same time as studying. You can do short courses on a Visitor Visa (less than 3 months); study for 6 months on a Working Holiday Visa (limited to certain countries); or apply for a Student Visa, for fulltime study for 4 years. **English Schools New Zealand** (www.english-schools.co.nz) is a directory of schools offering ESL (English as a Second Language) in 15 locations around New Zealand. **Language Schools New Zealand** (www.languageschool.co.nz) offers courses in Christchurch and Queenstown, and accommodates students with New Zealand families.

If you'd like to get an insight into New Zealand's agricultural industry, **Agritour,** Palmerston North (℃ **06/354-9063;** fax 06/354-9064; www.agritour.co.nz), arranges technical study tours visiting agribusinesses, research stations, orchards, and forests to suit your needs. For those interested in nature, ecology, and sustainability issues, Dunedin-based **Nature Quest New Zealand** (℃ **03/489-8444;** www.nature-quest.co.nz) offers a range of adventures for students wishing to study here. The New Zealand landscape acts as an outdoor classroom and courses are designed to broaden participants intellectually, socially, and personally.

Clean Green Photo Tours, Wanaka (www.cleangreen.co.nz), can arrange anything from a 2-hour instructional course to multi-day photographic excursions to Stewart Island, Fiordland, and even the unforgettable Sub-Antarctic Islands on board the 18m (59-ft.) ketch *Talisker*. Photographer Gilbert van Reenen shares his most beautiful, off-the-beaten-track locations. **Travelling Light Photography** (www. tlphoto.co.nz) puts you in the very capable hands of accredited photojournalist and professional photographer Marcus Adams, who can tailor a photography tour to your needs. Finally, photographer and guide Phillip Bartlett of **Capture New Zealand** (www.capturenewzealand.co.nz) offers 7- to 12-day tours of the North and South Islands, wilderness or wildlife, or 4WD drive adventures that take you into places you'd never otherwise be able to photograph.

Fiordland Ecology Holidays, Manapouri (℃/fax **03/249-6600;** www.fiordland. gen.nz), can take you away on its oceangoing yacht for 3 to 7 days of low-impact natural-history adventure in the remote areas of Fiordland. A maximum of 12 people can swim with seals and dolphins, go snorkeling and diving, and set out on bush walks. There are also berths available on scientific research trips. **Navigator Tours ★★★**, Auckland (℃ **09/817-1191;** www.navigatortours.co.nz), specializes in high-end indigenous Maori experiences that focus on real people, living real lives in fresh, innovative ways. Whether it be learning to make a *hangi* (earth oven), meeting a Maori professor for coffee, taking a ride in a *waka* (war canoe), or enjoying a forest walk or a visit to a marae, a Navigator experience is one you will never forget.

Southern Discovery Holidays, Greymouth (℃ **03/768-6649;** fax 03/768-9149; www.nzholidayheaven.com), offers a 12-day Millionaires Tour, visiting the South Island's gold fields in search of gold; 14-day School Geography Study Tours on the South Island, which include adventure activities; Golden Age Holidays, which offer small groups of retired people a new approach to vacationing; plus a wide range of special-interest holidays, including photography, painting, gardens, farms, ornithology—you name it, the staff will prepare it for you.

The **Tourism New Zealand** website (www.newzealandtourism.co.nz) has a very good directory of other educational and specialized tours of New Zealand.

Adventure & Wellness Trips

ADVENTURE HOLIDAYS

New Zealand is an adventurer's paradise and whether you're a golfer, a surfer, a hunter, or a fisherman, you'll find tours geared specifically toward your needs. The variety is huge and covers most types of sports and adventures throughout the country.

Auckland-based **New Zealand Surf 'n' Snow Tours** (℃ **09/828-0426;** www. newzealandsurftours.com) offers surf tours within the Auckland region, plus 5-and 12-day ultimate kiwi surfing experiences in Auckland and Northland, that give you an insight into New Zealand's beach and surf culture. In winter (July–Oct), they switch to snow tours of the mid–North Island ski fields.

Several companies cater to hunters and fishermen, but be forewarned: New Zealand has strict laws governing fishing and hunting licenses, so make sure you study those. I've listed contacts for the applicable administrative bodies on p. 70 in chapter 4. **Backcountry NZ ★★★**, Christchurch (© **021/644-507**; fax 03/308-2665; www.backcountry.co.nz), is a leading group with great guides that offers a wide range of fishing and hunting tours with stays in luxury accommodations, all set against a dramatic South Island mountain landscape.

If historic homesteads and beautiful gardens are of interest, you'll be hard-pressed to beat the 6- to 7-day South Island tours offered by Belinda McKenzie of **Homestead Tours ★★★** (© **03/692-2824**; www.homesteadtours.co.nz). Escorted by Belinda and members of her family, the tour visits many of the South Island's grandest, historic homesteads on farming stations that you would otherwise never be able to see.

For a 12-day autumn grand tour of New Zealand led by horticulturalist and designer Kevin Walsh, contact **South Pacific Travellers' World** (www.southpacific travellers.co.nz). The tour starts in Auckland and travels south, arriving in Christchurch in time for the annual Ellerslie International Flower Show.

Tour companies related to other specific sports are listed in the appropriate section of chapter 4, "The Active Vacation Planner."

RETREATS

If you're looking to come to New Zealand to take time out and rejuvenate yourself, you'll find plenty of opportunities to do so. For a full list of spiritual and/or meditation retreats, check www.nzspiritualdirectory.net.nz, which details spiritual, healing, and meditation retreats and workshops throughout the country. The website www.retreatsonline.com/newzealand also refers you to a number of North and South Island retreats. The **Mahamudra Centre,** Main Road, Colville, Coromandel (www.mahamudra.org.nz; © **07/866-6851**), is a Tibetan Buddhist meditation center on 3.2 hectares (8 acres) in the peaceful Colville Valley in the Coromandel region. It hosts group or solo courses and retreats with visiting lamas and teachers. Accommodations are in camping grounds, dormitories, or self-contained cabins.

The **Auckland Buddhist Centre,** 381 Richmond Rd., Grey Lynn, Auckland (www.aucklandbuddhistcentre.org; © **09/378-1120**), is dedicated to the teaching and practice of Buddhism in a modern world. The center invites visitors for meditation, or to attend courses and retreats; check the website for regular updates.

Yoga enthusiasts will find great value at **Stillpoint,** 109 Kelling Rd., Upper Moutere, Nelson (www.stillpointyoga.co.nz; © **03/543-2218**), which is home to world-renowned Ashtanga Yoga teachers John and Lucy Scott.

HOTEL & DAY SPAS

Most major hotels in New Zealand now feature their own day spa, and there has been a proliferation of privately owned day spas opening throughout the country. I have detailed many of these in the body of the guide.

In my view, the most luscious of the Auckland hotel spas are as follows: **Chuan Spa,** Langham Hotel Auckland, 83 Symonds St. (www.chuanspa.co.nz; © **09/300-2960;** p. 117) and **East Day Spa,** SKYCITY Grand Hotel, 123 Albert St., Auckland (www.eastdayspa.com; © **09/363-7050**), which is another beautifully appointed den of indulgence offering the full array of restorative treatments (p. 117).

In the Bay of Islands, **Paihia Beach Resort & Spa,** 116 Marsden Rd., Paihia (www.paihiabeach.co.nz; © **0800/870-111** in NZ, or 09/402-0111), has a splendid spa facility, **La Spa Naturale** (p. 153), which has been voted one of the top 10 spas in Australasia and the South Pacific by *Condé Nast Traveller (UK).*

In the far south, the day spa at **Sofitel Queenstown,** 8 Duke St. (www.sofitel. com; © **03/450-0045**), also deserves a mention for its luxurious appointments and its delicious body treatments (p. 428).

Beyond hotels, you'll find numerous other day spa facilities, including Rotorua's multi-award-winning **Polynesian Spa,** Government Gardens (www.polynesianspa. co.nz; © **07/348-1328**), which is world renowned for its therapeutic hot mineral pools and its lakeside spa therapy rooms (p. 188); and the **Spa at Hanmer Springs,** 42 Amuri Ave., Hanmer Springs (www.hanmerspa.co.nz; © **03/315-0029**), judged Best Natural Bathing Spa in the inaugural Australasian Spa Association's Spa of Excellence Awards (p. 366).

FOOD & WINE TRIPS

A bounty of fresh ingredients, limitless supplies of fine wine, and a growing appreciation of both have meant a proliferation of small, boutique cooking schools in New Zealand. Daylong or weekend classes are the main focus. One of the best is **Ruth Pretty Cooking School ★★**, 41 School Rd., Te Horo, north of Wellington (© **06/364-3161;** www.ruthpretty.co.nz), which offers classes most weekends from February through December. Lessons from Ruth and invited top chefs culminate in long, outdoor lunches. Private classes are also available.

Auckland Seafood School, First Floor, Auckland Fish Market, 22 Jellicoe St., Freemans Bay, Auckland (© **09/379-1497;** www.afm.co.nz), holds regular short courses in its state-of-the-art facility that includes a 66-seat auditorium and a kitchen with eight self-contained cooking stations. From barbecue to traditional French, Vietnamese, or classical recipes, it's all about fish. Also in Auckland, **Main Course,** 20 Beaumont St., Auckland (© **09/302-1460;** www.maincourse.co.nz), offers courses in everything from seafood and vegetarian to gluten-free and Italian cooking.

In Christchurch, Celia Hay's **New Zealand School of Food & Wine ★★**, 63 Victoria St., Christchurch (© **03/379-7501;** www.foodandwine.co.nz), has a well-earned reputation for turning out accomplished hospitality graduates. The school runs full-time 16-week courses in cookery, restaurant and cafe management, and professional wine knowledge. It has an associated award-winning restaurant. Forty-five minutes northwest of Christchurch, in the tiny town of Oxford, you'll find consummate cookbook writer and chef Jo Seagar. **Seagars at Oxford** (www.joseagar. com) offer various 1-day cooking courses that cover several cooking styles and cuisines. There is also a superb kitchenware shop and Jo's very popular cafe.

In Queenstown, **Kia Toa Cuisine,** at Punatapu Lodge (© **03/442-6985;** www. cuisinequeenstown.com or www.punatapu.com), offers specialized, short-term classes in a luxury lodge environment. The focus is always on New Zealand produce. The courses may include foraging for wild foods or visits to farmers' markets, wineries, orchards, local restaurants, and high country sheep stations.

You'll find details of local wine tours in each regional chapter. In addition, you should arm yourself with the *Classic New Zealand Wine Trail Guide* and the *Jasons Taste Traveller* guide, both free from all i-SITE visitor centers around the country.

GUIDED TOURS

Package tours are simply a way to buy the airfare, accommodations, and other elements of your trip (such as car rentals, airport transfers, and sometimes even activities) at the same time and often at discounted prices. One good source of package deals to New Zealand is the airlines themselves. Most major airlines offer air/land packages, including **American Airlines Vacations** (✆ 800/321-2121; www.aavacations.com), **Delta Vacations** (✆ 800/654-6559; www.deltavacations.com), **Continental Airlines Vacations** (✆ 800/301-3800; www.covacations.com), and **United Vacations** (✆ 888/854-3899; www.unitedvacations.com). Several big **online travel agencies**—Expedia, Travelocity, Orbitz, Site59, and Lastminute.com—also do a brisk business in packages. **Qantas Vacations USA** (✆ 800/641-8772 in the U.S., or 310/322-6359; fax 310/535-1057) and **Qantas Vacations Canada** (✆ 800/268-7525 in Canada; fax 416/234-8569) offer good deals as well.

In the United States, **Artisans of Leisure,** 18 E. 16th St., Ste. 301, New York, NY 10003 (✆ **800/214-8144** in the U.S.; www.artisansofleisure.com), offers exclusive, highly personalized luxury tours for individuals and small groups, and New Zealand is one of their most popular destinations. Their tours run 7 to 19 days and combine top rooms in premium lodges with activities that can range from tasting wine and food to arts and cultural events and outdoor activities—your choice. **Active Downunder,** 1220 Rosecrans St., #911, San Diego, CA 92106 (✆ **800/425-9036** in the U.S.; www.activedownunder.com), is owned and operated by New Zealanders; their specialty is highly customized active, leisure, and luxury vacations in New Zealand. They are experts with insider knowledge, and their personalized itineraries include boutique and luxury accommodations, along with cultural and adventure activities. **Nature Expeditions International,** 7860 Peters Rd., Ste. F-103, Plantation, FL, 33324 (✆ **800/869-0639** in the U.S.; www.naturexp.com), offers 1- to 15-day guided cultural, wildlife, and "soft" adventure tours to New Zealand. They cater specifically to small groups.

In New Zealand, there are many companies offering escorted tour options. Some of the reputable operators include:

- **Contiki Holidays,** P.O. Box 68640, Newton, Auckland (✆ **0508/266-8454** in NZ; www.contiki.co.nz), offering 3- to 18-day coach tours for 18- to 35-year-olds throughout New Zealand.
- **Thrifty Tours,** P.O. Box 31257, Milford, Auckland (✆ **0800/803-550** in NZ, or 09/359-8380; www.thriftytours.co.nz), with well-planned 2- to 16-day tours.
- **Discover New Zealand,** 120 Albert St., Auckland (✆ **0800/330-188** in NZ, or 09/356-2190; www.discovernewzealand.com), offers a range of 3- to 16-day tours designed for travelers who want the value and security of pre-booked arrangements combined with the freedom and independence of doing their own thing.
- **Scenic Pacific Tours,** P.O. Box 14037, Christchurch (✆ **0800/500-388** in NZ, or 03/359-3999; www.scenicpacific.co.nz), offers a large range of day excursions, short tours, and independent holidays.
- **Navigator Tours,** 553 Richmond Rd., Grey Lynn, Auckland (✆ **09/817-1191;** www.navigatortours.co.nz), offers a diverse range of unique, personalized, guided tours throughout New Zealand, staying at high-end accommodations.
- **TIME Unlimited Tours** (✆ **09/446-6677;** www.newzealandtours.travel) is an award-winning company offering a range of Maori cultural, kayaking, fishing, and walking tours of regional New Zealand.

VOLUNTEERING & WORKING IN NEW ZEALAND

If you wish to work in New Zealand during your trip, you need to acquire a working holiday permit. Details of visa and work permit requirements can be found at the New Zealand Immigration website, www.immigration.govt.nz. There are usually plenty of short-term working opportunities, especially in the summer when orchards, market gardens, and vineyards often need casual workers. The New Zealand hospitality industry usually employs large numbers of working tourists as well. That said, the current global recession has impacted the availability of jobs, so make sure you do your research before landing here. Additional job sites include www.seek.co.nz, www.nzrecruitme.co.nz, www.anyworkanywhere.com, www.jobstuff.co.nz, and www.jobzone.co.nz. The New Zealand immigration website lists many more links to specialized agricultural, horticultural, ski, hospitality, or general jobs.

Personally, I think there are far more interesting jobs available in the volunteer arena. Admittedly, you don't earn money while you're working, but you will take home the intense satisfaction of knowing you have helped others while enjoying a rewarding, personal experience. Many organizations offer volunteer positions within New Zealand. The **Global Volunteer Network** operates in many countries, including New Zealand. Their comprehensive website, www.volunteer.org.nz, details their programs, which include assistance to conservation groups and conservation projects within New Zealand. Volunteers are involved in habitat restoration, predator control projects, tree planting, invasive weed removal, monitoring re-vegetation growth rates, and more. Working within a kiwi sanctuary to help preserve our national icon must be rated as a rare and privileged experience. This program is based in Wellington, and you need to be moderately fit, proficient in English, and 18 and over to participate.

Volunteering New Zealand (© 0800/865-268; www.volunteernow.org.nz) focuses on putting the age, wisdom, and acquired experience of those from age 55 to 65 to good use. Their website features an Opportunities Page that lists volunteer positions for these "young seniors" who may have retired from the workforce but still have much to give to community welfare. **Volunteer Abroad** (www.volunteerabroad.com) lists numerous opportunities to take part in interesting community projects, from conservation work to educational and outdoor leadership courses. Other good websites to check are www.conservationvolunteers.org.nz, www.transitionsabroad.com,

---

MAORI for beginners

Here's a list of the most commonly used prefixes and suffixes for place names:

Ao   Cloud
Ika   Fish
Nui   Big, or plenty of
Roto   Lake
Rua   Cave, or hollow, or two (Rotorua's two lakes)
Tahi   One, single
Te   The
Wai   Water
Whanga   Bay, inlet, or stretch of water

These are other frequently used words:

Ariki   Chief or priest
Atua   Supernatural being, such as a god or demon
Haka   Dance (war, funeral, and so on)
Hangi   An oven made by filling a hole with heated stones, and the feast roasted in it
Hongi   The pressing together of noses in traditional greeting
Karakia   Prayer or spell
Kaumatua   Elder

www.unitedplanet.org, www.geovisions.org, www.wwoof.co.nz, www.greenhearttravel.org, and www.partnershipvolunteers.org.

WALKING TOURS

Tramping (also known as hiking) is one of the best ways to explore the pristine forests, clear blue lakes, sparkling rivers, fern-filled valleys, and snowcapped peaks of New Zealand. The **Department of Conservation (DOC)**, P.O. Box 10-420, Wellington (✆ **04/471-0726;** fax 04/471-1082; www.doc.govt.nz), maintains more than 12,500km (about 7,700 miles) of tracks (trails) and 1,000 backcountry huts throughout New Zealand's 13 national parks and numerous scenic reserves.

Many companies offer combination tours of hiking, kayaking, and other adventures in one or more areas. The **New Zealand Guided Walks Network** (www.walknewzealand.com) was set up in conjunction with Tourism New Zealand to raise the profile of high-quality guided walking experiences available in New Zealand. The Walks Network is a group of independent companies that operate guided walks in our national parks, wilderness areas, and special reserves, providing the best available accommodations with meals, comfortable bedding, and bathroom facilities. Qualified guides provide comprehensive interpretation of natural and cultural history; walkers need only carry personal items—not including food or bedding.

Hiking New Zealand ★★, in Christchurch (✆ **03/384-3706;** fax 03/376-6483; www.hikingnewzealand.com) offers small group hiking/camping tours of 5 to 20 days throughout the national parks. They're designed for people wanting to participate in day hikes and a variety of other activities like cycling, kayaking, jet boating, caving, viewing wildlife, and glacier hiking in iconic New Zealand locations.

Bush and Beyond (✆/fax **03/528-9054;** www.bushandbeyond.co.nz) offers guided 1- to 8-day tramps in Kahurangi National Park; you can also add in photography and wildlife excursions. **Kahurangi Guided Walks** (✆ **03/525-7177;** www.kahurangiwalks.co.nz) also operates in this area, offering year-round small-group guided walks in the Abel Tasman and Kahurangi national parks.

New Zealand Wild Walks (✆ **03/443-9422;** www.wildwalks.co.nz) offers remote treks for fit, adventurous travelers in the backcountry of Mount Aspiring National Park. Small guided groups of five people maximum tackle everything from

Kereru Wood pigeon	**Poi** Bulrush ball with string attached, twirled in action song
Kia ora Hello, Go well	
Kumara Sweet potato	**Tangi** Funeral mourning or lamentation
Mana Authority, prestige, psychic force	
Marae Courtyard, village common	**Taonga** Treasure
Mere War club made of greenstone (jade)	**Tapu** Under religious or superstitious restriction (taboo)
Pa Stockade or fortified place	**Tiki** Human image, sometimes carved of greenstone
Pakeha Caucasian person; primarily used to refer to those of European descent	**Whare** House

picturesque beech forests and isolated valleys to alpine meadows and glacier trekking. **Canterbury Trails,** in Christchurch (*©* **03/337-1185;** fax 03/337-5085; www. canterburytrails.co.nz), offers easy to moderate 9-day Wilderness South Expeditions via minivan, which include guided walks and heritage and ecology experiences. It also offers 14-day Natural North'South New Zealand tours in conjunction with Kiwi Dundee Adventures in the Coromandel (see chapter 6). And in the far south, **Kiwi Wilderness Walks** (*©* 021/359-592; fax 03/442-8342; www.nzwalk.com) offers 3- to 5-day tramping, kayaking, and wildlife experiences in remote areas of Stewart Island, the Waitutu Track, and Dusky Sound.

Tuatara Tours ★★ (*©* **0800/377-378** in NZ, or 03/962-3280; www.tuatara tours.co.nz) specializes in fully guided outdoor walking adventures aimed at people with an average-to-excellent level of fitness. Four- to 14-day guided walks (and cycling tours) explore the South Island, with well-informed guides and a very comfortable level of accommodation. More excellent "moderate" hikes in the North Island are offered by **Walking Legends** (*©* **07/345-7363;** www.walkinglegends. com), which has 3- to 6-day packages around Lake Waikaremoana and in the remote regions of Te Urewera National Park.

MAORI LANGUAGE & CULTURE

The Maori language is a Polynesian dialect. It was first given a written form in the early 19th century by missionaries and British linguists. In the latter part of the 19th century, Maori were forced to adopt the English language in schools, and it wasn't until the 1960s that a strong Maori resurgence began. The **Maori Language Act** of 1987 really changed things. It made Maori an official New Zealand language along with English, and a Maori Language Commission was set up to create authentic Maori names for government departments and major organizations. Today, there are Maori radio stations and television channels, and Maori is taught in all levels of the education system.

When you visit New Zealand, you will be surrounded by things Maori: Words, place names, and many tourist ventures are all indications of this revitalized culture. No one expects you to be able to pronounce many Maori names—it's hard enough for those who have spent their lives here—but these tips might make it easier. Some Maori words are both singular and plural and require no *s*. *Maori, Pakeha,* and *kea* are

A Word on Cultural Protocol

If you want to visit a Maori marae, always make sure you ask permission first, but be aware that unless you are staying with a Maori family, or participating in a commercially run tour, you are unlikely to gain access. You must never eat, chew gum, or take food onto the premises. Some Maori will request that you take off your shoes, and some may have particular rules about visits by women during certain ceremonies.

And **never** take photographs inside a meetinghouse. If you are uncertain about whether or not photographs are appropriate, just ask. In short, behavior on the marae is governed by strict protocol and you **WILL** be challenged if you ignore these rules. To save yourself and others a great deal of embarrassment, please do not offend. But don't panic; you will be instructed on the proper behavior.

all good examples (like the English words *deer* and *fish*). There are 15 letters in the Maori alphabet: A, E, H, I, K, M, N, O, P, R, T, U, W, NG, and WH, and every syllable ends in a vowel. The vowel sounds are of great importance and when two vowels come together, each is given its proper sound. WH is usually pronounced as an F.

In the last decade or so, the inclusion of Maori words and phrases in everyday life has become increasingly common. As a visitor here, you'll come across a number of words that may seem incomprehensible. *Kia ora* is probably the simplest and the most common. *Kai* (food) is also in common usage, as are *whanau* (family), *iwi* (tribe), and *tangata whenua* (literally "people of the land"—in reference to Maori).

Tourism New Zealand and many tourism operators have also adopted a number of traditional Maori values as part of their contemporary business practice. These include *manaakitanga* (hospitality/nurturing), *kaitiakitanga* (guardianship), *rangatiratanga* (leadership), and *kotahitanga* (unity). The two that visitors will come across most often are *manaakitanga,* which is an all-encompassing sense of hospitality, sharing, and welcome; and *kaitiakitanga,* which is most used (in a tourism context) in relation to the guardianship of treasures *(taonga),* and the bounty of the land and its resources.

SUGGESTED NEW ZEALAND ITINERARIES

Making your way around New Zealand is simple, and many tourists find that renting a car is the cheapest and most flexible option. But if you're short on time, fly between major destinations and pick up a rental car for short journeys.

Many of you will find the roads "virtually empty" compared to those in your own countries. That said, don't be misled by the seemingly short distances between places. Most roads are only two lanes—except near bigger cities, where they become four-lane highways—and in some places they're steep, winding, and narrow as they negotiate river gorges and mountain tracts. Allow much more time than you would for a similar length journey at home.

THE REGIONS IN BRIEF
The North Island

AUCKLAND ★★★   Far too often overlooked as little more than a landing port, Auckland has first-rate attractions, quality accommodations, and diverse leisure opportunities. It is without doubt the most cosmopolitan of the cities, and its balmy climate has a special appeal. Waitemata Harbour and Hauraki Gulf offer some of the world's finest sailing, boating, and fishing, and in the aftermath of the 2002–03 America's Cup yachting challenge, many quality hotels, bars, and restaurants are thriving. Cultural offerings abound in museums, galleries, and performing arts centers; and shopping is the most diverse in the country. There are more than 1,000 restaurants and a wild nightlife scene, and if you're into a beach lifestyle, there are numerous choices within easy reach. You may think it's just another big city, but Auckland has a Polynesian backbone that makes it truly unique. If you're touring only the North Island, Auckland is a perfect base.

NORTHLAND ★ & COROMANDEL   Both are within easy reach of Auckland and can be tackled as a day trip if you're short on time. However, each warrants at least a couple of days' exploration; if you have to choose between the two, I'd definitely swing up to the far north.

Northland is served by a far better infrastructure in terms of transportation, hotels, and restaurants, and its beach attractions (on the east coast) are too numerous to itemize. That said, you'll find far more tourists here, too, at least in the Bay of Islands area. Head north, though, and a whole world of unpopulated beaches awaits. Fishing, diving, boating, and camping are all big draws. The area's rich Maori culture is also an excellent introduction to New Zealand's history.

The Coromandel Peninsula is a slightly more rugged version of Northland, to the south of Auckland. It has a craggier coastline, a more remote landscape, and sections with very poor roads. Accommodations are middling to say the least (with a few exceptions). Still, there's color and character here, and it's long been a favorite with New Zealand campers and beach bunnies—especially the eastern side of the peninsula, where you'll find some top surf beaches.

WAIKATO & BAY OF PLENTY ★   I spent my childhood in the Waikato region, but I find little to recommend for the visitor. Hamilton is trying its hardest, and it would be fair to say that it suffers from being in Auckland's shadow. The Waitomo Caves have traditionally been the area's biggest attraction, and although their natural splendor is undeniable, I find Waitomo a rather depressing place—a strange hive of tourist buses, darting in and out of otherwise undisturbed farmland.

The Bay of Plenty, on the other hand, has come of age. Tauranga and Mount Maunganui have always been hot spots. Again, the emphasis is on a beach lifestyle—boating, fishing, surfing, sunbathing, and golf are the main attractions—and some stunning accommodations are available. If you've been to Australia's Gold Coast, you'll sense a hint of that style here.

ROTORUA ★★★, TAUPO ★ & TONGARIRO NATIONAL PARK ★★
Rotorua is on almost every visitor's hit list. Some would say that makes the area objectionably touristy. I don't agree. Rotorua has spent millions refining its attractions and accommodations, of which there are many, and it offers a unique geographic and Maori cultural slice of New Zealand life. In terms of adventure tourism, it is biting at the heels of Queenstown.

Taupo and Tongariro National Park, in combination with Rotorua, make the whole central region an unbeatable value in terms of volcanic landscape and adventure variety. And the area is plenty big enough to avoid being bothered by others. (It's away from key attractions.) Come here for volcanic and Maori attractions, the world's best trout fishing, mountaineering, skiing (water and snow), mountain biking, and tramping.

GISBORNE & HAWKE'S BAY ★★★   This is one of the most underrated areas of the country. East Cape and Gisborne offer a rare insight into Maori culture, free of tourist hype. The area has amazing beaches and world-class surfing conditions, and, in combination with Hawke's Bay, is probably the country's most important wine-producing region. In terms of accommodations, Gisborne is definitely lacking, and its laid-back rural approach doesn't always find favor with visitors. Hawke's Bay, on the other hand, has the best range of boutique B&Bs and cottages in the country. Napier's Art Deco charms are legendary and definitely worthy of inspection.

TARANAKI & WANGANUI   Let's put it this way—if you want the best of small-town, provincial New Zealand, this is it. I'm most drawn to Taranaki. New Plymouth is surprisingly vibrant in its own right, and you can't help but feel that, stuck out here on its own western limb, it couldn't care less about the rest of the country. Mount Taranaki and the sea are big attractions for trampers and surfers, and the region's gardens are stunning. Tom Cruise seemed to like the area when he was filming *The Last Samurai*. Wanganui has a major asset in its river, but it needs to spruce up accommodations.

WELLINGTON ★★★ The capital has come alive in almost every aspect. The Museum of New Zealand–Te Papa Tongarewa is, of course, a major attraction and has been built with style and flair. Once you have explored it, you will understand more clearly much of what you have seen, or are about to see, throughout the country. Wellington is also home to several national cultural companies, so you'll find a rich performing arts program. In addition, its restaurant, nightlife, and shopping opportunities are many and varied.

And don't overlook the vineyard and craft delights of the **Wairarapa ★**, where you'll find the biggest selection of stunning rural cottages in New Zealand.

The South Island

NELSON ★★ & MARLBOROUGH ★ The best year-round climate in New Zealand can be found here. Characterized by three stunning national parks and gorgeous beaches, Nelson is often talked about with a mix of derision and envy for its alternative, slightly hippie/artsy communities, but this is a top region to visit if you're into arts and crafts and outdoor pursuits. And for oenophiles, there's a growing pocket of wineries that, in combination with the Marlborough wine region, make it a must-see destination. Both areas have some superb B&Bs, homestays, and backpacker accommodations.

CHRISTCHURCH & CANTERBURY ★★★ After Auckland, Christchurch is the second major destination for overseas tourists. Quite apart from the fact that it's the primary starting point for South Island exploration, Christchurch is loved for its fine Victorian-Gothic architecture, its hints of old England, and although it is more than a little bruised after recent earthquakes, there is still plenty to see and do here. It has several ski fields within a 2-hour drive, good surfing beaches, and over 40 wineries. Day trips to Hanmer, Kaikoura, Akaroa, South Canterbury, and Methven are all popular, but each of them warrants a longer stay.

WEST COAST ★ & THE GLACIERS ★★ The top of the West Coast, from Westport north to Karamea, and the south, from Haast to the glaciers, are quite remarkable. It's just a pity about the middle bit. Apart from greenstone shopping and the crazy Hokitika Wildfoods Festival, I can never find much to recommend in the central part of the West Coast. But I will concede that it has played a vigorous and important role in shaping New Zealand's history and economy, and you certainly won't find anything quite like it elsewhere.

QUEENSTOWN & ENVIRONS ★★★ For sheer physical impact, this southwestern portion of New Zealand is utterly unbeatable. It's easy to understand why everyone flocks here at least once. Don't be put off by this nonsense about Queenstown being "too touristy." It's a recognized international tourist resort, for goodness sake, so of course there will be lots of tourists! It has a long-standing reputation for being a work-hard, play-hard, party-hard sort of a place, and as far as I'm concerned, the more the merrier.

Milford Sound ★★★ is another matter entirely. It is simply stunning, but the excessive number of buses (over 50 a day) is quite disgusting and should be reduced to make it a better experience for everyone. It is a remote wilderness area, but it's hard to sense that with 3,000 other people standing around looking at the same mountain peak!

Wanaka ★ has a much more low-key personality than Queenstown. It makes a beautiful stopover between Queenstown and the West Coast. You'll find some stunning lodges and B&Bs here.

DUNEDIN ★, SOUTHLAND & STEWART ISLAND ★★ Invercargill and Southland are sleepy, slow, incredibly friendly, and very, very green, but not that well prepared for the visitor. Dunedin is simply gorgeous, very Gothic, and in winter, very grim. But as a summer destination, it's lovely and has lots to offer the wildlife lover. Get out onto Otago Peninsula and be prepared to have your breath taken away. It also has some handsome B&B and lodge-style accommodations in the most amazing old houses.

Farther south, the Catlins Coast and Stewart Island are remarkably unspoiled by anything—especially tourism. I'm almost loath to mention either for fear of instigating a mass influx of visitors, but good old Kiwi pride gets in the way, and I can't help boasting about these two truly magical destinations.

NEW ZEALAND IN 1 WEEK

I hear it all the time: "This is such a small country, but we never realized there would be so much to see; we wish we'd allowed more time." Seeing New Zealand in 1 week is possible, but it will require early starts and long days. Personally, I'd ditch the car idea and fly between four major stops—Auckland, Wellington, Christchurch, and Queenstown—to save time. There are regular internal flights between all major towns and cities, and if you shop around some of the smaller airlines, you can get good deals. Otherwise, you'll spend 90% of your time in a vehicle, suffering from jet lag, with little left over for the sights.

Day 1: Arrive in Auckland ★★★

Try to arrive early and focus your attention on **Viaduct Harbour** (p. 112), a great introduction to New Zealand's passion for boats. Go for a sail on *NZL 40* (p. 113), which is moored here. The **New Zealand National Maritime Museum** (p. 114) is also here and gives a great overview of our maritime history and short cruises on the historic scow *Ted Ashby*. In between, join the crowds lazing about over good coffee and fine food. There are at least a dozen restaurants to choose from. Stay at **Hilton Auckland** (p. 91), perched on the end of the wharf.

Day 2: Waiheke Island ★★★

Catch a ferry across to Waiheke Island for a day of laid-back wine tasting and beach walking. Factor in lunch at **Te Whau Vineyard** (p. 136), where you can gaze over staggering views and one of the best wine cellars in the country. Visit **Connells Bay Sculpture Park** (p. 132) with work by leading New Zealand artists, and swim in the clear warm waters of **Onetangi Bay** (p. 132). Return to Auckland in the late afternoon, visit **Auckland Museum** (p. 109), and eat at the **French Café** (p. 107).

Day 3: Wellington ★★★

Get up early and fly to Wellington. For the definitive overview of New Zealand, go straight to **Te Papa** (p. 279). Don't miss the Passports and Mana Whenua displays. Walk along the waterfront, down the Lambton Quay shopping precinct, and catch the **cable car** (p. 280) up to the **Botanic Garden** (p. 280). Go down the other side to Tinakori Village for lunch. Walk back down Bowen Street, past the **Beehive and Parliament** (p. 281). After unwinding at **Caffe Astoria** (p. 274), enjoy dinner at **Logan Brown** (p. 274).

Day 4: Christchurch ★★★

Take an early flight to Christchurch, hire a car at the airport, skip the city, and drive 1 hour to pretty Akaroa, admiring rural landscapes along the way. For interesting art and great coffee, stop at **Little River Gallery** (p. 362). Take another break at the hilltop for great camera shots. Over the hills, try tasty **Barry's Bay Cheese** (p. 363). In Akaroa, take a nature cruise with dolphin-watching, or saunter along the promenade, taking in quaint architecture and dinky shops. When you return to Christchurch, stay at **Clearwater Resort** (p. 342), which is close to the airport.

Day 5: Arrive in Queenstown ★★★

Sleep in and wake up to ducks floating on the lake outside your window. Ease yourself into a late breakfast before flying to Queenstown. Once there, at the airport, take a memorable helicopter ride with **Over The Top** (p. 423) and land high on a mountain peak for lunch in total solitude. You'll remember this forever. Back on the ground, spoil yourself at the **Sofitel** (p. 429).

Day 6: Queenstown Adventures

Rise early, meet the locals for breakfast at **Joe's Garage** (p. 438), and then have the quintessential adventure experience on **Shotover Jet** (p. 424). Move on to Arrowtown, explore the quaint old Chinese gold mining area, and have lunch at **Saffron** (p. 439). If you're ready for more action, do the **Kawarau Bungy** (p. 419), or watch others, and then visit **GVW Winery** (p. 421). Alternatively, use this day to enjoy **a scenic flight to Milford Sound,** a cruise, and return flight (p. 421).

Day 7: Back to Christchurch

Fly back to Christchurch to connect with your international flight. If you have time between flights, visit the nearby **International Antarctic Centre** (p. 349), **Orana Park** (p. 349), or **Willowbank Wildlife Reserve** (p. 349)—where you're sure to see a kiwi. Alternatively, unwind with a round of golf at **Clearwater Resort** (p. 342). If you decide you were silly to try and cram it all into a week, see the next itinerary.

NEW ZEALAND IN 2 WEEKS

Two weeks in New Zealand gives you more opportunities to drive between destinations and take in the color of the provinces. Still, don't underestimate the time your journey will take. New Zealand has good roads, but 20km (12 miles) in some parts of the country could be narrow, steep, and winding—which means it might take you twice as long to negotiate them as it would back home. In general, roads are

New Zealand 1- and 2-Week Itineraries

well maintained and all major roads are paved. Drive with care on narrow, unpaved roads if you venture into more remote areas. What I've suggested here gives you a taste of both main islands, sticking to main centers with the greatest concentration of activities.

Day 1: Arrive in Auckland ★★★

Arrive in Auckland and rest for a whole day, doing nothing more taxing than eating and drinking at **Viaduct Harbour** (p. 112). At night, go to the top of **Sky Tower** (p. 110) for the big daddy of views and a meal in the revolving restaurant.

Day 2: Auckland's Major Sights

Prepare to sightsee until you drop. Get on the **Explorer Bus** (p. 87)—the cheapest and easiest way to see as much as possible in 1 day. You'll set eyes on Mission Bay's pretty beach promenade, visit **Kelly Tarlton's Underwater World** (p. 111), and get a taste of Maori culture at **Auckland Museum** (p. 109). The bus drives through the leafy **Botanic Gardens** (p. 117) and through Parnell village. It stops at the **SKYCITY** complex (p. 94), the **Museum of Transport & Technology** (p. 113), and much more.

Day 3: Waiheke Island ★★★

Rise early and catch a ferry to **Waiheke Island** (p. 129). Hire a car and drive around the island, visiting wineries, olive groves, artists' studios, and unspoiled beaches. Some of the best surprises are in the little bays away from Oneroa township. Following visits to **Whittaker's Musical Museum** (p. 132) and **Te Whau Garden** (p. 132), have lunch at **Mudbrick Vineyard** (p. 137). Later in the day, sit on Onetangi Beach and watch the sunset. Stay at the **Boatshed** (p. 136).

Day 4: Rotorua ★★★

Arrive back in Auckland by midday and fly to Rotorua. Hire a car. If you want a day of complete rest and solitude in unabashed luxury, head for **Treetops Lodge** (p. 199). If you want to see the sights, go straight to **Rotorua Museum** (p. 188) for an excellent overview of geothermal and volcanic history. Spend the rest of the afternoon at **Te Puia** (p. 190) to see bubbling mud and Maori cultural performances. Watch the sun set over the lake and relax in a hot rock pool at **Polynesian Spa** (p. 188).

Day 5: The Thermal Attractions ★★

Drive 30 minutes south to see the wonders of **Waimangu** and **Waiotapu** (p. 194). Waimangu has shorter walks but fewer spectacular sights; I prefer Waiotapu. If you're back in town by early afternoon you could take a guided tour of **Ohinemutu** (p. 193), the original Maori village on the lakefront, followed by a walk among the **Whakarewarewa Forest** redwoods (p. 197). Finish the night with a tour and cultural performance at **Tamaki Maori Village** (p. 193).

Day 6: Drive to Wellington

Rise early for a day of driving, but *be careful*, as roads in the Rotorua region are busy with huge logging trucks. A 5-hour journey will take you around **Lake Taupo** (p. 208), where there are plenty of lake-edge stops for photographs, through the stark beauty of **Tongariro National Park** (p. 215), and through heartland farming provinces. You could stop off for a night in the **Wairarapa** (p. 292)—or at least stop to eat in one of **Greytown's cute cafes** (p. 297)—or drive the last taxing, winding, uphill leg over the Rimutaka Hills to Wellington. Alternatively, go the coastal route along the Kapiti Coast.

Day 7: Wellington ★★★

Te Papa (p. 279) is a must-visit. Spend 2 to 3 hours there and don't miss the gift shop for top-quality crafts. And you can't visit the capital without a ride up the **cable car** (p. 280), a wander through the **Botanic Garden** (p. 280) at the top, and a sit-in at a session of **Parliament** (p. 281). Art lovers should see **City Gallery Wellington** (p. 282), and if you like the funky side of life, wander up **Cuba Street** (p. 289). Late afternoon, amble around the waterfront to **Oriental Parade** (p. 282). Have dinner at **Logan Brown** (p. 274) or **Matterhorn** (p. 276).

Day 8: A Ferry Crossing

Rise early and catch one of the first ferries to **Picton** (p. 298) on the **Interislander** (p. 496). The 3-hour trip is an experience in its own right and if the weather's good you'll have a picturesque passage through **Queen Charlotte Sound** (p. 300). Catch the 1:40pm **TranzCoastal** (p. 367). This rail journey is a scenic feast through vineyards and along a rugged coastline hugged by steep mountains. You might want to get out at **Kaikoura** (p. 366) and go **whale-watching** (p. 369), or continue on to Christchurch, arriving around 7pm.

Day 9: Christchurch ★★★

Get up early and head up Dyers Pass Road (in a hired car) to the top of the **Port Hills** (p. 352). My favorite drive is along the top, heading east, stopping for the fabulous views down into **Lyttelton Harbour** (p. 335) on your right. Drop down into the trendy seaside village of **Sumner** (p. 334), have coffee at **Coffee Culture** (p. 346), and walk along the white sands of Sumner Beach. Back in town, the swanky new architectural wonder that is **Christchurch Art Gallery** (p. 348) is bound to impress—don't leave without visiting their shop and Form Gallery. Wander down the boulevard to **Canterbury Museum** (p. 348), past the **Arts Centre** (p. 347), and into the **Botanic Gardens** (p. 348).

Day 10: Drive to Queenstown

Prepare to be impressed by the landscapes on this 5- to 6-hour journey. You'll pass by the unbelievably turquoise Lake Tekapo—look out for the stop at the south end of the lake, which affords picture-perfect views of Mount Cook—and through the grand beauty of Lindis Pass. The lupines will be flowering along the summer roadsides of the Mackenzie Country and you won't be able to resist pulling out your camera. Stop on the Queenstown side of Cromwell at the **Big Picture** (p. 412) for refreshments, wine tastings, and an overview of the region's vineyards and wineries. Don't miss stops at the fresh summer fruit stalls along the way. Apricots are near perfect here.

Day 11: Queenstown ★★★

Sleep in and breakfast late at **Joe's Garage** (p. 438) before taking an early cruise across Lake Wakatipu on the vintage steamship **TSS *Earnslaw*** (p. 419). You'll be back in plenty of time to take the **gondola** (p. 416) up to **Bob's Peak** for breathtaking views over Queenstown. Leap off the **bungy** (p. 422) if you dare, or descend on the gondola and wander into the **Kiwi & Birdlife Park** (p. 416). Dine on seafood at **Boardwalk** (p. 435).

Day 12: The Wineries

Hire a car (or take a guided tour) and drive yourself around the best of Central Otago's wineries. The top four closest to Queenstown are **GVW Winery** (p. 421), **Peregrine** (p. 421), **Amisfield** (p. 438), and **Chard Farm** (p. 420). Don't miss Gibbston's wine cave, its cheesery, and its excellent lunches under a canopy of vines. Alternatively, wander around central Queenstown stores for excellent duty-free shopping and have lunch at **Eichardt's** (p. 436), or take in a round of golf at **Millbrook Resort** (p. 433) and eat in one of its restaurants, finishing off with a soothing massage in the splendid spa. Have dinner at the **Bunker** (p. 436).

Day 13: Fly to Milford Sound ★★★

Be up early for a memorable scenic flight or helicopter ride to **Milford Sound** (p. 421). Take a **boat cruise** (p. 448) and make sure you include the **Underwater Observatory** (p. 449). Flying is by far the best option if you're short on time, although it is weather dependent. Bus trips can take around 12 hours roundtrip. When you're back in Queenstown at the end of the day, dine at **Saffron** (p. 439) in **Arrowtown** (p. 418).

Day 14: Back to Christchurch

Enjoy a lazy morning in Queenstown before flying to Christchurch to connect with your international flight. If you have time between the two flights, go to the **International Antarctic Centre** (p. 349) near the airport, or, if you've yet to see a live kiwi, check out the nearby **Willowbank Wildlife Reserve** (p. 349). If you fancy big cats, visit the cheetahs at **Orana Park** (p. 349).

NEW ZEALAND FOR FAMILIES

Kids will love New Zealand. There are enough weird, wonderful, curious, funny, and interesting things on these islands to amuse the most inquiring child's mind. I'd recommend 3 weeks if you're traveling with a family (you can stretch out the 2-week itinerary below), so it's less taxing on everyone. And I'd either go "bush and beach" with a tent at a northern beach camping ground so the kids can run wild and free; or I'd stick to three major centers—Auckland, Rotorua, and Nelson—for the best concentration of kid-related activities. Much of the gut-busting excitement of Queenstown has age limits, but if your kids are old enough and you want a longer trip, tack on the "Ten Action-Packed Days in the South Island" tour, below.

Day 1: Arrive in Auckland ★★★

Start slowly with an easy day, checking out combo deals and family passes at the visitor center at **Viaduct Basin** (p. 112), where the kids can watch the boats and visit the **New Zealand Maritime Museum** (p. 114). Boys, especially, seem to get a real kick out of a ride on the historic scow, *Ted Ashby*. Give them a bird's-eye view of the city from the **Sky Tower** (p. 110), taking them up in the exterior glass lift and letting them walk over the glass floor. Dine in the revolving restaurant at the top.

Day 2: Auckland Sights

Impress the kids right from the start with **Kelly Tarlton's Antarctic Encounter & Underwater World** (p. 111)—where else can they see an underground colony of penguins? Drive around to **Mission Bay** (p. 86), rent rollerblades, swim at the beach, have a picnic lunch, and feed the sea gulls. Spend the afternoon at **Auckland Museum** (p. 109) and make sure you let the kids loose in the superb Discovery Centre, where they can open drawers and touch exhibits. The Wild Child display and the Maori Treasures are also good value.

Day 3: More of Auckland

Get off to an early start at **Auckland Zoo** (p. 114), which has heaps of great stuff for kids. Check out the daily animal encounters and view sea lions through underwater viewing windows. Or consider their Safari Night Sleepovers and guided night walks instead of a day outing. Drive to **Butterfly Creek** (p. 114), flirt with winged beauties, ride on the Red Admiral Express, and see animals at Buttermilk Farm. Drive north to **Snowplanet** (p. 114), where you have the unlikely pleasure of a midwinter snow experience in the midst of a subtropical summer.

Day 4: Drive to Rotorua

Hire a car and start the 3-hour drive to Rotorua early. Stop at **Hamilton** (p. 171) along the way and feed the ducks at **Hamilton Lake** (p. 174). In the afternoon, visit **Rotorua Museum** (p. 188) and "experience" a volcanic eruption in the theater there. Follow this with a leisurely drive around the Blue and Green Lakes to the **Buried Village** (p. 191), to see the remains of Te Wairoa village, which was buried by the eruption of Mount Tarawera in 1886.

Day 5: Rotorua ★★★

The kids will be screwing their noses up at the smell of sulfur in the air, so get out there and show them what it's all about. Drive down to **Waimangu** and **Waiotapu** (p. 194). Allow half a day for both, or, if you have to choose, 2 hours for Waiotapu. Back in town, feed the kids from one of the takeaway stands at the lakefront and then let them loose at **Skyline Skyrides** (p. 190), where they can plummet downhill on a luge, or better still, have an adventure in the **Zorb** (p. 198). The **Agrodome** (p. 190) is a hive of kids' activities—I'd plan to spend the afternoon here. Finish with a relaxing dip at **Polynesian Spa** (p. 188).

Day 6: Maori Experiences

Spend the morning investigating the wonders of **Te Puia** (p. 190), which includes the Whakarewarewa Thermal Reserve and the New Zealand Maori Arts & Crafts Institute. Stay and watch Pohutu Geyser blow its top. In the afternoon, take a guided tour of **Ohinemutu Maori Village** (p. 193) on the lakefront. Set the evening aside for a hangi meal and a Maori experience at **Tamaki Maori Village** (p. 193).

Day 7: Drive to Wellington

The drive south normally takes about 5 hours, but allow a day. Stop at **Lake Taupo** (p. 204) for a go at the **Hole-in-One Challenge** (p. 210). And visit **Huka Falls** (p. 206), just off the main highway north of Taupo. Have a picnic at one of the little beaches around the lake and then head into **Tongariro**

New Zealand for Families

Other Suggested New Zealand Itineraries

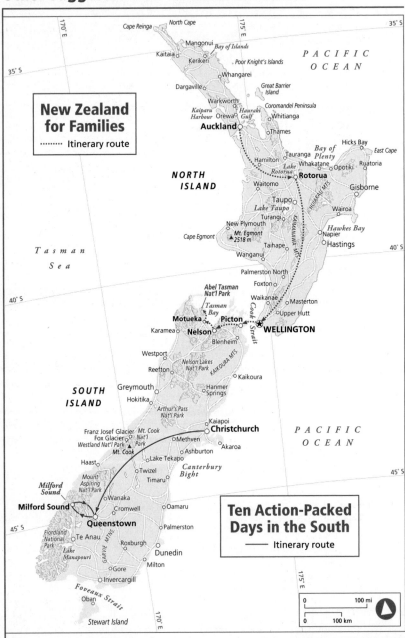

New Zealand for Families
.... Itinerary route

Ten Action-Packed Days in the South
— Itinerary route

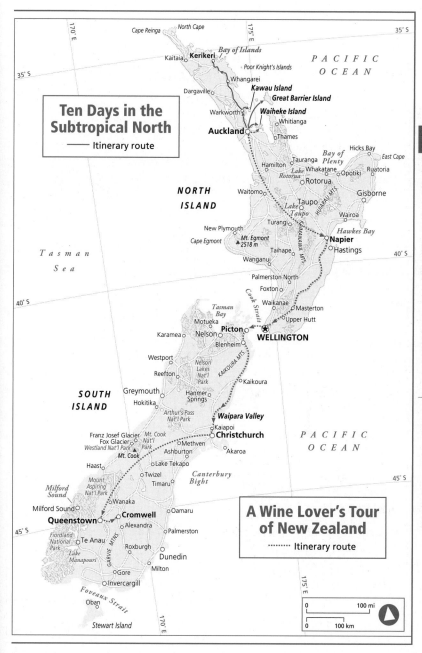

Ten Days in the Subtropical North
— Itinerary route

North Cape
Cape Reinga
Bay of Islands
Kaitaia
Kerikeri
Poor Knight's Islands
Whangarei
Dargaville
Kawau Island
Great Barrier Island
Warkworth
Waiheke Island
Whitianga
Auckland
Thames

PACIFIC OCEAN

Hicks Bay
Hamilton
Tauranga
Bay of Plenty
East Cape
Lake Rotorua
Whakatane
Opotiki
Ruatoria
Rotorua
Waitomo
Gisborne

NORTH ISLAND

Taupo
HUIARAU MTS
Lake Taupo
Wairoa
Turangi
New Plymouth
Hawkes Bay
Cape Egmont
Mt. Egmont ▲ 2518 m
Napier
Taihape
Hastings
TARARUA MTS
Wanganui
Palmerston North
Foxton
Tasman Sea
Waikanae
Masterton
Upper Hutt
Cook Strait
Tasman Bay
Motueka
Waikanae
Karamea
Picton
Nelson
Blenheim
★ **WELLINGTON**
Westport
Nelson Lakes Nat'l Park
Reefton
KAIKOURA MTS
Greymouth
Hokitika
Hanmer Springs
Kaikoura
Arthur's Pass Nat'l Park

SOUTH ISLAND

Franz Josef Glacier
Fox Glacier
Mt. Cook Nat'l Park
Waipara Valley
Westland Nat'l Park
Kaiapoi
Mt. Cook
Christchurch
Methven
Haast
Ashburton
Akaroa
Lake Tekapo
PACIFIC OCEAN
Mount Aspiring Nat'l Park
Twizel
Canterbury Bight
Timaru
Milford Sound
Wanaka
Milford Sound
Oamaru
Cromwell
Queenstown
Alexandra
Fiordland National Park
Te Anau
Palmerston
GARVIE MTS
Roxburgh
Dunedin
Lake Manapouri
Milton
Gore
Invercargill
Foveaux Strait
Oban
Stewart Island

A Wine Lover's Tour of New Zealand
········ Itinerary route

0 — 100 mi
0 — 100 km

National Park (p. 215) for beautiful mountain landscapes. The kids will be ready for another stop at **Pukaha Mount Bruce National Wildlife Centre** (p. 293)—keep your eyes open to spot a kiwi; and maybe there'll be time to squeeze in a snack stop at **Greytown** (p. 297) before you wind your way across the Rimutaka Ranges and down into Wellington by late afternoon.

Day 8: Wellington ★★★

Spend your first 3 hours exploring the **Museum of New Zealand—Te Papa Tongarewa** (p. 279) and allow extra time for the kids to experience the interactive displays on the ground floor. Let them run free along the waterfront after that—there'll be boats and people aplenty for them to watch. Head up the **cable car** (p. 280) next to the **Botanic Garden** (p. 280), where you should take them to the **Carter Observatory** (p. 281) for a bit of stargazing. If you never got to the zoo in Auckland, don't miss the **Wellington Zoo** (p. 281) and its interactive animal experiences. Wander down **Cuba Mall** (p. 266) late afternoon and let the kids get wet in the **Bucket Fountain** (p. 282).

Day 9: Ferry Ride to Picton

Catch the early **Interislander** (p. 496) across to Picton. The ferry has movie theaters and play areas for kids. Hire a car and drive to Nelson. Stop 10 minutes short of Nelson at **Happy Valley Adventures** (p. 315) for 4WD bike adventures and the sky swing. In Nelson, hunt out **Penguino** (p. 321) for a well-deserved specialty ice cream.

Day 10: Nelson ★★★

Start at the **World of Wearable Art & Classic Cars Museum** (p. 311) where everyone's eyes will pop out on stalks. Let the kids loose next at **Nelson Fun Park** and **Natureland Zoo** (p. 314). Enjoy a picnic at nearby **Tahunanui Beach** (p. 314) and then spend the afternoon swimming, making sand castles, and generally relaxing on one of the most popular beaches in the area. You'll probably want to visit Penguino again after that.

Day 11: Exploring the Area

Watch glass blowing at **Höglund Art Glass International Glass Centre** (p. 314), then drive to **Mapua** (p. 310), visiting pottery studios along the way. Stop at orchard stalls for a crisp apple snack. Dabble fingers in open displays at **Touch the Sea Aquarium** (p. 314) and have a yummy late lunch at the **Naked Bun Patisserie** (p. 322). Drive on through **Motueka** (p. 307) and turn right to **Kaiteriteri** (p. 315), one of the prettiest golden-sand beaches you'll ever see. Spend the afternoon playing and swimming, or take a water taxi around the gorgeous coast of **Abel Tasman National Park** (p. 323). Stay at Kaiteriteri or Motueka for the night.

Day 12: Abel Tasman National Park ★★★

Drive through Kaiteriteri and around to **Marahau** (p. 323) to get yourselves aboard one of the Abel Tasman kayaks (p. 72). This unbeatable experience amid clear waters will amaze you. Watch for seals and penguins and don't forget to take your swimming togs. Alternatively, take a guided day walk on the **Abel Tasman Coastal Track** (p. 64). Get back to Nelson in time for dinner—perhaps fish and chips on the beach as the sun sets.

Day 13: Outdoor Adventures

Wander around Nelson's pretty shopping streets in the morning, or go for a walk along the **Boulder Bank** (p. 316). In the afternoon hire **bikes** (p. 315), go swimming at the beach, or fish off the end of the Nelson wharves. Visit **Founder's Heritage Park** (p. 311).

Day 14: Return to Wellington

Rise early for the 2-hour drive to Picton. Allow time to wander along the shore, watching boats coming and going before getting back on the ferry to Wellington. Connect with your international flight home in the afternoon or early evening.

A WINE LOVER'S TOUR OF NEW ZEALAND

New Zealand has come of age as a producer of internationally acclaimed wines, and the great thing about the country's six major grape-growing regions is that they're packed into some of the most stunning landscapes. They're often close to gourmet food producers, many have terrific restaurants, some offer boutique lodgings, and impressive architecture is to the fore. In an ideal world, you could easily spend 2 to 3 weeks "soaking" in a New Zealand wine tour because it offers so much more than just wine and vineyards, but the following itinerary outlines a more realistic (for most travelers) 10-day tour of highlights.

Day 1: Arrive in Auckland ★★★

The greater Auckland region (including Waiheke Island) has over 100 vineyards and wineries. In the interest of early research, head for the **Glengarry Wines** (p. 118) in Central City to sample your first New Zealand wines and to pick up information about the country's wine tourism. Have dinner at **Vinnies Restaurant** (p. 105).

Day 2: Henderson Valley

Drive 30 minutes from the city to New Zealand's oldest grape-growing region, where there are a bundle of wineries along Henderson Valley Road and Lincoln Road. Seek out **Soljans Estate's winery and cafe** (p. 118) for lunch and then drive on to **Constellation New Zealand** (p. 118). If you don't want to drive yourself, take one of the wine tours listed on p. 120 to get a comprehensive overview in a short time. Stay at **Bethells Beach Cottages** (p. 101), which are set among sculptured gardens with views of the Tasman Sea. If you return to the city, dine at the **French Café** (p. 107).

Day 3: Waiheke Island ★★★

Catch the ferry to **Waiheke Island** (p. 129). Pick up a rental and visit some of the 45 vineyards on the island. **Fullers** (p. 130) and **Ananda Tours** (p. 130) both offer wine tours. If you'd rather be independent, make sure you visit **Te Whau Vineyard** (p. 133), which has more than 500 cellared wines. It's highly rated by *Wine Spectator* and has an impressive menu. You can't really get lost on this little paradise, and if you did, would you care? Splurge on a stay at **Te Whau Lodge** (p. 136), where you'll wine and dine in style overlooking vineyards.

Day 4: Fly to Hawke's Bay ★★★

Head back to the mainland (reluctantly, I'd guess) and fly to **Napier** (p. 232)—a twin heaven of endless grapes and oh-so-pretty **Art Deco architecture** (p. 235), not to mention gorgeous boutique vineyard accommodations, a dazzling array of restaurants, and some of the best wines in the country. Spend the afternoon at the **National Aquarium of New Zealand** (p. 234) for a change of pace and drink afternoon champagne at the **County Hotel's bar** (p. 244).

Day 5: The Wine Trail

Do a fun bicycle tour of a handful of vineyards with **On Yer Bike Winery Tours** (p. 237), passing olive groves, orchards, wineries, and ostrich farms. Take your camera, as well as bottled water, a hat, sunscreen, and sunglasses to protect against the hot sun. Switch back to your car in the evening and splash out on dinner at the unforgettable **Terroir** (p. 243) at **Craggy Range Winery** (p. 236) in the Havelock North area. Get there in daylight so you can look through the fabulous winery and tasting gallery. Try their classy vineyard stay, or plant yourself at nearby **Millar Road** (p. 241).

Day 6: More Tasting at Maraekakaho Road

If you haven't been there yet, head for the vineyards in the Maraekakaho Road area, finishing up at **Sileni Estates Winery & Epicurean Centre** (p. 237) in time for a drawn-out lunch at their classy restaurant. Head back into Napier for a 2-hour, self-guided afternoon **Art Deco Walk** (see "An Art Deco Amble", p. 235). Make sure you stop at **Ujazi** (p. 242) for coffee and cake, and right next door, loosen your purse strings on fabulous New Zealand arts and crafts at **Statements Gallery** (p. 234).

Day 7: The Marlborough Wine Region ★★★

Rise early and drive the 4 hours to Wellington, where you'll catch the **Interislander** (p. 496) to Picton. You'll find world-class vineyards here as far as the eye can see. Bring your camera and stamina, along with a wine map from the **visitor center** (p. 299), which lists all the wineries open for meals and tastings, plus the wines they produce. There are about 40 cellar doors open to you, so make a day of it. Splurge on dinner at **Herzog** (p. 307), an epicurean and wine lovers' heaven with top European chefs, and stay in the heart of the Renwick wine area at **Vintners Retreat** (p. 304).

Day 8: Waipara Valley ★★★

Hire a car and drive the 4 hours south to Waipara Valley. Call in at **Waipara Springs Winery** (p. 353) for coffee and save yourself for lunch at award-winning **Pegasus Bay** (p. 353) just down the road. Visit other local wineries and stop by **Athena Olive Groves** (p. 352) for a different taste sensation. Drive 45 minutes south to Christchurch and catch a flight to Queenstown.

Day 9: Queenstown ★★★

Hire a car, pick up a wine map from the visitor center, and head out to **Amisfield Winery** (p. 420) overlooking Lake Hayes. Be impressed by **Peregrine** (p. 421) unique architecture and make an extended stop at **GVW Winery** (p. 421). Explore their wine tunnel, the great gift shop, and the cheesery. When you get back, hunt down the **Bunker** (p. 436) for perfectly matched wine and gourmet food.

Day 10: Cromwell & Bannockburn

Take a scenic drive through Kawarau Gorge. Near Cromwell stop at fruit stalls and the **Big Picture** (p. 412) for an excellent film, a tasting auditorium, a selection of wines and gourmet foods, and a cafe. Set your sights on **Felton Road,** the **Mt. Difficulty Wines cafe,** and **Olssens Garden Vineyard.** If you'd rather take a tour of this area, contact **Queenstown Wine Trail** or **Appellation Central Wine Tours** (p. 421). Try the degustation menu at the **Rees True South** (p. 436) for dinner if you have time, or catch a late flight to Christchurch to meet your international connection.

TEN ACTION-PACKED DAYS IN THE SOUTH ISLAND

The title of this itinerary assumes you're a fun-loving, adventure-seeking, fear-proof adrenalin addict with tons of stamina. If that's the case, you might want to head straight for Queenstown and stay there. It has more crazy, pulse-quickening activities per square inch than anywhere else, and most are easily accessed without a vehicle. There's also an active hotel pickup plan at work. Make sure you check out the many money-saving combo deals available. I haven't listed late-night fun here because that's a whole other story; chapter 15 gives you the pointers you'll need to ensure your nights are as vigorous as your days.

Day 1: Arrive in Queenstown ★★★

Spend the day regaining preflight energy with a leisurely amble around the town's adventure suppliers. Get social at **Joe's Garage** (p. 438), the preferred hangout of local adventure types, and soak up the energetic hum of hundreds of fellow international adventure seekers. Do some research at the **i-SITE Visitor Centre** (p. 415) and have a few drinks at **Tatler** (p. 437), where local bar staff will fill you in on all the best nightspots.

Day 2: Up & About

Start with a gobsmackingly daring burst of speed through high rock canyons on the **Shotover Jet** (p. 424). Pick up your stomach and head back into town and take the **gondola** (p. 416) to the top of Bob's Peak. Pick up speed with a few **luge rides** (p. 424), scare yourself with a **bungy** (p. 422) overlooking the town, and float back down to Queenstown park via a **tandem parapente** (p. 424).

Day 3: The Ultimate Jump

Be the ultimate daredevil and tackle the full bungy package—yes, that means all four of them! Start with 43m (140 ft.) at the "original" **Kawarau Suspension Bridge** and work your way up (and down) from there. If you've already done the **Ledge** at the top of Bob's Peak, do the **Ledge Swing** instead—or try the bungy here again at night. Forget being squeamish, and take your camera because all four bungys are located in stunning landscapes. Make sure you get the T-shirt that attests to your courage!

Day 4: The Dart River ★★★

Imagine rivers wild and calm overhung with lush green ferns, the sound of native birdcall, and nothing else—except the excited squeals of your fellow adventurers. The Dart River deserves all the superlatives. Start with a 5-hour jet boat and a walk through unspoiled native bush with **Dart River Safaris** (p. 426). If you're short on daredevil confidence after all the bungy jumps, float the river with **Funyaks** (p. 426). A day to remember!

Day 5: Taking to the Air

Push your budget to the limits with a helicopter ride into the mountains and have the highest altitude picnic you're ever likely to enjoy. Choppy Paterson of **Over The Top** (p. 423) knows how to impress with remote mountaintop lake settings. Calm down after that adventure by taking a leisurely afternoon cruise on the *Earnslaw* (p. 419).

Day 6: Watersports

Fast-paced watersports are on today's agenda. Start with **Canyoning NZ** (p. 423), and find yourself slipping down river canyons in a wet suit and a helmet. **Serious Fun River Surfing** (p. 424) brings a new twist to an old sport—it's all washing-machine rapids and rapid slithering down rocky river gorges. In the afternoon, go **white-water rafting** (p. 425). There are several operators to choose from and river grades to suit your nerves, physical prowess, and stamina. The Shotover River is generally viewed as more challenging than the Kawarau.

Day 7: Milford Sound ★★★

Your toughest choice will be "fixed wing" or helicopter. Whichever you choose, be prepared to be impressed by jagged mountain peaks, lush green bush, unbelievably blue lakes, golden tussock, and azure blue skies. If a **Milford boat cruise** (p. 448) is not energetic enough for you, team up with **Rosco's Milford Sound Sea Kayaks** (p. 449) for a surreal paddling adventure. Take your camera and stay overnight at **Milford Sound Lodge** (p. 450).

Day 8: Milford Track ★★★

Join a 1-day guided walk on **Milford Track** (p. 68) with **Trips 'n' Tramps** (p. 68)—just 12 people getting a taste of this world-famous mountain route. Enjoy total silence, majestic mountain landscapes, remote passes, a wilderness tea break, photography stops, waterfalls, and rainforest glades. This may be the quietest of your adventures, but it may be the *pièce de résistance*.

Day 9: Back to Queenstown

Before you fly out of Milford, visit the **Underwater Observatory** (p. 449) for a unique glimpse of rare underwater life forms. Return to Queenstown by helicopter or plane (the 5- to 6-hr. bus trip is dead time) and spend the afternoon doing a mountain bike tour with **Gravity Action** (p. 422), which will give you an up-close and personal look at the landscapes you've just flown over.

Day 10: Back to Christchurch

Rise before dawn and join **Sunrise Balloons** (p. 424) for a last magical overview of this splendid place where mountains and lakes rise out of the early morning mists. It's the perfect memory to take away before you fly home.

TEN DAYS IN THE SUBTROPICAL NORTH

It always astounds me that so many overseas visitors arrive in Auckland and immediately drive or fly south—or that they avoid the North Island altogether in favor of the south. Sure, the South Island landscapes are more dramatic, but the top of the North, especially in summer, is a quintessential Kiwi experience: white-sand beaches, warm oceans, endless days of swimming and sunbathing, barbecues at the beach, campfires, parties, boats, surf, and sun. I've mapped out 10 days that include three of Auckland's nearby islands to give you a feel for the more laid-back side of New Zealand life. Waiheke Island is the most populated and the most popular and heaven for wine drinkers, while the much less-visited Great Barrier Island (many New Zealanders have never even been there) is an unspoiled treasure that operates on its own clock.

Day 1: Arrive in Auckland ★★★

Rest for a while before heading off to **Viaduct Harbour** (p. 112), which will give you an instant appreciation of New Zealanders' obsessions with boats. Sit in one of the stylish cafes and restaurants, and watch the boats come and go. Visit the **New Zealand National Maritime Museum** (p. 114) for an insight into what the ocean really means to northerners. In the afternoon, take the **Explorer Bus** (p. 87) to **Auckland Museum** (p. 109), where you can admire the views and the grassy green swathe of the **Botanic Gardens** (p. 117). Drive around to **Mission Bay's seaside promenade** (p. 86) and have a picnic dinner as you watch people swim at sunset.

Day 2: Take to the Water

Have a rare sailing experience on America's Cup yacht, **NZL 40** (p. 113), or join **Fullers Auckland** (p. 120) for an invigorating cruise of Waitemata Harbour. It's all sea spray, sunshine, and flapping sails out there, plus you'll have great views of the city skyline. Enjoy lunch wharf-side and then go up the **Sky Tower** (p. 110) for the best views in New Zealand.

Day 3: Waiheke Island ★★★

Rise early and take the ferry to **Waiheke Island** (p. 129). Save time and go straight into a guided tour of the island, or hire a car and drive around the beaches, wineries, and pretty, unpopulated bays. There's something intangible at work here and you'll quickly be seduced into the relaxed pace of island life. Have lunch at **Te Whau Vineyard** (p. 136) and dinner at **Mudbrick Vineyard** (p. 137), or eat fish and chips on **Onetangi Bay** (p. 132) after a late-afternoon swim.

Day 4: Matakana & Kawau Island

Head back to Auckland and then drive north to Warkworth and the **Matakana/ Sandspit** (p. 134) area. Catch a water taxi across to **Kawau Island** (p. 134) for a fun day out. New Zealand's early governor, Sir George Grey, built the historic Mansion House on the island; you'll find unexpected Australian "natives" here— eucalyptus trees, wallabies, kookaburras, and rosella parrots.

Day 5: The Bay of Islands ★★★

Back on the mainland, drive north to **Paihia** (p. 145). Base yourself here if you want to try all the attractions, or go to **Russell** (p. 147) if you're after a peaceful retreat. Visit **Waitangi Treaty Grounds** (p. 146) for a dose of Maori culture and some lovely boardwalks through native bush and mangrove swamps. Wander through the cool, green leafy grounds to find **Waikokopu Café** (p. 157) and the massive Maori *waka* (canoe) on display by the beach. Sit on the beach and enjoy the sun.

Day 6: Kerikeri

This is our northern fruit capital. Enjoy citrus, persimmons, kiwifruit, and macadamia nuts. Stop at **Kerikeri Bakehouse** (p. 157) for picture-perfect picnic food. Take your bounty down to the **Kerikeri Basin** and eat by the river before exploring the local sights. Spend the afternoon at **Marsden Estate Winery** (p. 148) or drive to a local beach and swim until the sun goes down.

Day 7: Drive to Auckland

Drive back to Auckland Airport and catch a plane to **Great Barrier Island** (p. 137). It's a 35-minute flight in a small plane, so don't go taking everything but the kitchen sink. Your fellow passengers are likely to be dogs, surfers with their boards, and other eccentric sorts who have made this charming island home. The flight is a worthwhile experience in its own right. Fly in over the beach and drop down onto the grass runway. Grab a hire car and make your way to **Earthsong Lodge** (p. 140) on the sandhills of Medlands Beach.

Day 8: The North of the Island

Drive north to **Glenfern Sanctuary** (p. 139) and take Tony Bouzaid's guided walk through native bush. Watch for dolphins leaping about in the deep green waters of Fitzroy Harbour. Drive farther north along unpaved roads to **Whangapoua Beach** (p. 139) and don't be surprised if you're the only person there. It's a surreal experience to feel like the last person left on earth as you stand on this perfect horseshoe of pristine white sand. Walk along the beach to the **S.S. Wairarapa** (p. 139) shipwreck graves.

Day 9: Tryphena & Okupu

Spend the morning at **Tryphena** (p. 138). Take a kayak trip and watch for the friendly dolphins that swim here. Drive back to **Claris** (p. 138) for lunch at **Claris Texas Café** (p. 140) and ask about the historic pigeon post at the postal agency next door. Follow the road over to Okupu, calling at **Christine Young's unique little museum** (p. 139). Drop down to the beach, park your car, and walk to the south end of Okupu Beach to meet with the little track that takes you around the headland and into Blind Bay.

Day 10: Fly Back to Auckland

You'll have fallen in love with "the Barrier" by now, so have a lazy morning on the beach, go for a swim, watch the surfers, or take a boat ride with Richard Lintott to see the **gannet colony** (p. 238). Fly back to **Auckland** in the late afternoon to connect with your flight.

THE ACTIVE VACATION PLANNER

From the northernmost tip to the last speck of land in the south, New Zealanders have found ways to tackle the great outdoors, and their enthusiasm for the whole adventure game has drawn millions of curious people to see just what it's all about.

Regardless of your fitness level, you'll find something to suit you. You can do almost anything in New Zealand—rock climbing, caving, horse trekking, paragliding, and much more. Following are details on the major activities, such as tramping, skiing, and biking; look to the regional chapters for additional information.

The **Tourism New Zealand** website (www.newzealand.com) will key you into wilderness and big thrills. Ask for the excellent *Naturally New Zealand Holidays* guide at a New Zealand Tourism Board office near you or from **Naturally New Zealand Holidays** (© **03/318-7540;** fax 03/318-7590; www.nzholidays.co.nz).

TRAMPING

Tramping (also known as hiking) is one of the best ways to explore the pristine forests, clear blue lakes, sparkling rivers, fern-filled valleys, and snowcapped peaks of New Zealand. The **Department of Conservation (DOC),** P.O. Box 10-420, Wellington (© **04/471-0726;** fax 04/471-1082; www.doc.govt.nz), maintains more than 12,500km (about 7,700 miles) of tracks (trails) and 1,000 backcountry huts throughout New Zealand's 13 national parks and numerous scenic reserves.

A series of short walks or one big multiday hike? Both are available, but much will depend on your fitness level and the amount of time you have. Consider whether you want to be a **freedom walker** (independent) or a **guided walker.** Independent walkers can sleep in huts with bunk beds, cooking facilities, and toilets, but they must carry their own food, bedding, and cooking utensils. These overnight huts are sometimes staffed, should you need any assistance or advice along the way.

Tramping in New Zealand is best tackled from late November to April, when temperatures are the most moderate. From May to October, alpine tracks can be difficult and often dangerous once snow falls. (See the

SAFETY IN THE GREAT outdoors

You won't find snakes and predatory animals here (at least not the four-legged kind), but anyone venturing out into wilderness areas ought to be prepared with a few common-sense safety hints.

o **Emergencies:** For emergencies anywhere in the country, dial ✆ **111.**

o **Getting lost:** Trampers must register their intended route and estimated time and date of return with the Department of Conservation (DOC) office closest to where they plan to trek. This is vitally important because, if no one knows you're out there, they're not going to start looking for you if you get lost or injured. Likewise, let DOC know as soon as you're finished so search parties are not set into action—and be aware that you can now be billed hundreds of thousands of dollars for an unnecessary search brought about by your actions and lack of consideration. Be very careful—if you hike alone and get lost or injure yourself, you are much more likely to become a statistic.

o **Weather:** Although New Zealand has a mild climate, the weather can change rapidly at any time of year, especially in the high country. *Always* tell people where you are going and when you are due back, and always go prepared with the right all-weather gear (at all times of the year), a sensible survival kit, and a good topographical map *that you can read!*

o **Hypothermia:** Hypothermia can kill—even in summer, and its signs and symptoms should never be ignored. Watch for early warning signs: feeling cold, shivering, tiredness or exhaustion, anxiety, lethargy, lack of interest, clumsiness, slurred speech, difficulty seeing, a sense of unreality, and irrational behavior. The later signs indicating a serious medical emergency are obvious distress, the cessation of shivering despite the cold, collapse and unconsciousness, and coma. The progress of hypothermia can be very fast, with as little as 30 minutes from the first symptoms to unconsciousness. It

weather and temperature information in chapter 2 before planning a hiking vacation.) Don't forget to bring broken-in boots, a day pack, water bottles, sunglasses, sunscreen, a flashlight (known as a "torch" in New Zealand), and a hat. **Remember:** You should never attempt any multiday hikes without first checking in, paying your fees, and giving DOC staff an idea of your plans; and always be aware of changeable weather conditions and the very real potential for hypothermia—even in summer. **The importance of this cannot be underestimated.** Every tourist season dozens of people ignore this sound advice and a good number end up being rescued by emergency services. Be warned that in some circumstances you will now have pay for the rescue services and that is never a cheap exercise. For more information see "Safety in the Great Outdoors," below.

SHORT WALKS   There are literally hundreds of fabulous short walks through all sorts of landscapes. From a leisurely stroll along a city promenade to deserted beaches, fern-lined bush walks, forest trails, volcanic wanders—you name it, and you can probably have it. Every region has its hidden treats. Check the regional chapters is imperative that you stop and find shelter, prevent further heat loss, assist in re-warming, get the victim into dry clothes, and seek help as quickly as possible.

Hypothermia is caused by cold, wind, wet clothing, lack of food, fatigue, injury and anxiety, and recent illness, especially the flu. Everyone is at risk, even the fit and healthy. It is always best to have four or more people in your party so one can stay with the victim and two can go for help.

o **Avalanches:** Skiers and snowboarders often start the avalanche that catches them. Most avalanches occur during and immediately after storms, and they are common on slopes steeper than 20 degrees.

o **Sun:** New Zealand's clear, unpolluted atmosphere produces strong sunlight and high ultraviolet levels. Wear brimmed hats, sunglasses, and lots of SPF 15+ sunscreen if you plan to be outdoors for longer than 15 minutes.

o **River levels:** Plan your trip around the use of bridges. Avoid river crossings and be aware of rising water levels during heavy rain.

o *Giardia:* In the bush, you should boil, filter, or chemically treat all water from lakes and rivers to avoid contracting this waterborne parasite, which causes diarrhea.

o **Sand flies:** Small in size, but big in nuisance value, sand flies are found in wet bush areas around rivers, lakes, and streams. They can be effectively controlled with regular use of strong insect repellents. If you get bitten, topical application of hydrocortisone ointment or tea-tree lotion should ease itching.

o **Safety brochures:** All of the above issues are dealt with in detail in a range of excellent free brochures produced by the **New Zealand Mountain Safety Council,** P.O. Box 6027, Te Aro, Wellington (© **04/385-7162;** fax 04/385-7366; www.mountain safety.org.nz), available at visitor information and DOC centers.

that follow for some popular choices and seek advice from any visitor center or Department of Conservation office, most of which have an extensive array of walking brochures.

Short walks tend to range from 45 minutes to a full day. Depending on your interests, don't forget to bring along binoculars, a camera, and a sketch pad or journal. If you're in doubt about the difficulty of a trail, always ask the visitor center staff, or be prepared to turn back if the going gets too tough. Hiking trails in New Zealand are generally very well maintained.

MULTIDAY WALKS New Zealand has some of the best multiday walks in the world. The trails are well maintained and take you through unforgettable scenery. Several can also be done as guided walks, which makes them accessible to people of all fitness levels.

Not everyone can agree on which one is the *best* walk, but the DOC has identified these tramping tracks as the "Great Walks" in New Zealand: the **Waikaremoana,** the **Tongariro Crossing,** and the **Ruapehu Circuit** on the North Island; the **Abel**

Tasman Coastal Track and the **Heaphy, Routeburn, Milford,** and **Kepler tracks** on the South Island; and the **Rakiura Track** on Stewart Island.

If you'd like to strike out on your own, contact the **Department of Conservation,** P.O. Box 10-420, Wellington (☎ **04/471-0726;** fax 04/471-1082; www.doc. govt.nz). It maintains visitor centers throughout the country. Freedom walkers (independent hikers) need to get hut passes or tickets and register their hiking plans (known as "intentions") before setting out. The Milford and the Routeburn are generally the only two tracks where freedom walkers need to make advance reservations. Facilities along other trails are on a first-come, first-served basis. The DOC advises against children 9 and under attempting any of the serious multiday hikes.

See the individual walks below for information on **guided walks.** Outfitters will arrange a guide, accommodations, meals, and the carrying of all gear except daypacks, which individual walkers carry themselves.

New Zealand's Best Tramps

MARLBOROUGH, NELSON & BEYOND

See the map "Marlborough, Nelson & Beyond," on p. 300, for the tramps in this area.

ABEL TASMAN COASTAL TRACK   Because of the enormous popularity of this stunning walkway through coastal forest and gorgeous beaches, the DOC introduced a booking system for overnight huts that is in effect from October through April each year. The four huts have bunks, heat, and water, but no cooking facilities. Access to Marahau, where you begin, is by road or boat. Water taxis make it convenient to do just 1 day of the walk if your time is short. Buses pick you up at the end of the trail.

Duration/Distance: 3 to 5 days/52km (32 miles)

Start: Marahau, Abel Tasman National Park

End: Wainui Bay, Abel Tasman National Park

Open: Year-round; guided walks available year-round

Contact Information: Independent walkers can contact the **Department of Conservation,** King Edward and High streets, P.O. Box 97, Motueka (☎ **03/528-1810;** fax 03/528-1811). Hut fees are NZ$36 to NZ$38 per night; camp fees are NZ$13 to NZ$15 per person per night; transport is extra. You can book online at the DOC website; purchase a Great Walks Ticket to ensure access to the huts.

For guided walks, contact **Wilson's Abel Tasman National Park** (☎ **03/528-2027;** fax 03/528-2029; www.abeltasman.co.nz). Its 5-day kayak-and-walk package costs NZ$2,030 for adults only. They also have a 3-day guided walk for NZ$1,350 for adults and NZ$945 for children over 12. **Kahurangi Guided Walks** (☎ **03/525-7177;** www.kahurangiwalks.co.nz), has 1-, 2-, and 3-day walks in the Abel Tasman and customizes trips to meet customer needs.

HEAPHY TRACK   This track is known for its beauty and diversity. It crosses a range of landscapes, from the junction of the Brown and Aorere rivers over expansive tussock downs to the lush forests and roaring sea of the West Coast. The seven huts on the track have bunks, heat, water, and cooking facilities (except at two huts), and although you need a hut and camp pass, this does not guarantee a bunk. There are accommodations and transport at each end of the track, but be sure to arrange this before setting out. For transport to the beginning of Heaphy Track, contact **The Heaphy Bus Co.** (☎ **0800/128-735** in NZ, or 03/540-2042; www.theheaphybus. co.nz) or **Golden Bay Coachlines** (☎ **03/525-8352;** www.gbcoachlines.co.nz). If you're planning to travel to Westport or return to Nelson at the end of the track, make

your transport reservations before you leave through the **Golden Bay Visitor Information Centre,** Willow Street, Takaka (© **03/525-9136;** gb.vin@nelsonnz.com).
Duration/Distance: 4 to 6 days/77km (48 miles)
Start: Brown Hut, Kahurangi National Park
End: Kohaihai River Mouth, north of Karamea, Kahurangi National Park
Open: Year-round; guided walks available year-round
Contact Information: For an independent walk, contact the **Department of Conservation,** 1 Commercial St., P.O. Box 53, Takaka (© **03/525-8026**). Hut fees are NZ$32 per night; camping fees are NZ$15 per night; transport is extra.

For guided walks, call **Kahurangi Guided Walks** (©/fax **03/525-7177;** www.kahurangiwalks.co.nz), **Bush and Beyond** (©/fax **03/528-9054;** www.naturetreks.co.nz), or **Southern Wilderness NZ** (© **03/520-3095;** fax 03/520-3096; www.southernwilderness.com).

QUEEN CHARLOTTE WALKWAY This 71km (44-mile) track passes through lush coastal forest, around coves and inlets, and along ridges offering spectacular views of the Queen Charlotte and Kenepuru sounds. (Boating is also popular here.) Stretching from historic Ship Cove to Anakiwa, the track can be walked in 3 to 5 days, and if you want a richer experience, you can add kayaking, mountain biking, diving, fishing, and bird-watching along the way. If you take a guided walk, you'll stay in cabins, rustic lodges, and homestays, and your pack will be carried by boat, meeting you at each overnight stop. If you'd rather not complete the whole 5-day venture, you can take a guided 1-day walk. Access to Ship Cove is by boat or floatplane, and you can start or finish the walk at any point.
Duration/Distance: 5 days/71km (44 miles)
Start: Ship Cove, Marlborough Sounds
End: Anakiwa, Marlborough Sounds
Open: Year-round; guided walks conducted November through May only
Contact Information: For an independent walk, contact the **Department of Conservation,** Picton Field Centre, Picton (© **03/575-7582;** fax 03/573-8262; www.qctrack.co.nz). Camping costs NZ$10 per night; lodging is available at various price levels. All adult unguided track visitors will also be asked to contribute NZ$5 to the Queen Charlotte Track Tribute Fund, a trust fund established to maintain the track as a place of rare beauty. QCT Tribute tickets can be purchased from the dedicated machine located at Picton Town Wharf prior to your departure, or paid to the water transport operator you use. *Note:* There are no rubbish facilities on the walk, so you must take out everything you take in. Transfers are available with the **Cougar Line** (© **0800/504-090** in NZ; fax 03/573-7926; www.queencharlottetrack.co.nz), which will drop you off, transfer your pack, and pick you up. Similar services are offered by **Endeavour Express** (© **03/573-5456;** fax 03/573-5434; www.boatrides.co.nz).

You can arrange a guided walk of Queen Charlotte Track with the **Marlborough Sounds Adventure Company** (© **0800/283-283** in NZ, or 03/573-6078; fax 03/573-8827; www.marlboroughsounds.co.nz). Its 3- to 5-day walks include boat transfers, a guide, meals, hot showers, and accommodations in three lodges for around NZ$1,595 to NZ$1,950. The Ultimate Sounds Adventure (3 days/2 nights) starts at NZ$755 with bunkroom accommodations, or NZ$970 twin-share en suite. It features 1 day of walking, 1 day sea kayaking, and 1 day of mountain biking. **Wilderness Guides Marlborough Sounds** (© **0800/266-266** in NZ, or 03/575-5432; fax 03/573-5430; www.wildernessguidesnz.com) organizes 1- to 5-day guided or independent walks including luggage transfers and hotel-style accommodations.

CANTERBURY

BANKS PENINSULA TRACK This private Canterbury track crosses farmland, Hinewai Reserve, and volcanic coastline. You'll experience sandy beaches, safe swimming, waterfalls, cliff faces, beech forest, penguins, seals, dolphins, and rich bird life. The track twice rises to over 600m (1,970 ft.) and features rugged exposed headlands, requiring a reasonable level of fitness. Children must be accompanied at all times. Accommodations are supplied in four farm cottages, two of which have a small shop for purchasing basics.

Duration/Distance: 4 days/35km (22 miles)
Start & End: Akaroa Village, 80km (50 miles) from Christchurch
Open: October 1 to April 30
Contact Information: Call **Banks Peninsula Track Ltd.** (✆ 03/304-7612; fax 03/304-7738; www.bankstrack.co.nz). The 4-day tramp costs NZ$255 per person; the 2-day tramps costs NZ$165.

KAIKOURA COAST TRACK This popular, dramatic coastal walk takes you through the best of New Zealand's high-country farming territory, with cottage accommodations at three farms along the way. You'll need a reasonable degree of fitness, as the track climbs from the sea to a height of 600m (1,970 ft.), with wonderful views over the Kaikoura Mountains. The track is also suitable for mountain biking. It's located a 1½-hour drive north of Christchurch and 45 minutes south of Kaikoura.

Duration/Distance: 3 days/43km (27 miles)
Start & End: "Hawkswood" historic sheep station, Kaikoura
Open: October through April
Contact Information: Contact Sally and David Handyside (✆ 03/319-2715; fax 03/319-2724; www.kaikouratrack.co.nz). The track costs NZ$215 per person; groups are limited to 10 people. A 2-day mountain-bike option is available for NZ$85 per person. Public transport is available in the form of shuttle buses and the InterCity coach service, both of which run between Christchurch, Kaikoura, and Blenheim. Shuttles depart the Christchurch visitor center, where you can get details about the service. The cost of a shuttle to the track beginning at the Staging Post (on St. Hwy. 1) is NZ$65.

QUEENSTOWN & FIORDLAND

Independent walkers must have a reservation for walking the Milford and Routeburn tracks discussed below. Contact the **Department of Conservation,** Great Walks Booking Desk, Fiordland National Park Visitor Centre, P.O. Box 29, Te Anau (✆ 03/249-8514 or fax 03/249-8515 outside NZ; 03/249-7924 or fax 03/249-7613 inside NZ; www.doc.govt.nz). The number of people allowed on the tracks is limited and the demand great, especially from mid-December through January, so reserve as early as possible—6 months ahead is sometimes necessary. Remember those safety rules and warnings about hypothermia (see "Safety in the Great Outdoors," above)—they hold particularly true here. In this region, unpredictable weather can occur at any time, in any season, and you should always carry appropriate clothing for the worst weather conditions.

THE GRAND TRAVERSE This 6-day excursion follows the Routeburn Track northbound for 3 days and then crosses into the Greenstone Valley Track for 3 days; it's available between November and April. The guided walk costs NZ$1,765 for adults, NZ$1,560 for children ages 10 to 15 (no children 9 and under permitted) and includes transport, meals, and accommodations. Make arrangements through

Ultimate Hikes (☎ 0800/659-255 in NZ, or 03/450-1940; fax 03/450-1941; www.ultimatehikes.co.nz).

GREENSTONE VALLEY TRACK   This walk follows an ancient Maori trail used by tribes to access the rich greenstone lodes near Lake Wakatipu. The trail you'll walk, however, was cut in the late 1800s by Europeans, who created a route between Lake Wakatipu and Martins Bay on the Fiordland coast. You'll pass Lake Howden and Lake McKellar, and follow the Greenstone River through deep gorges and open valley to Lake Wakatipu. Boat transfers are available to and from Elfin Bay. The Greenstone track can be walked in either direction, or can be linked to the Routeburn or Caples tracks for a 4- to 5-day round-trip (see "The Grand Traverse," above).
Duration/Distance: 2 days/40km (25 miles)
Start & End: Elfin Bay, Lake Wakatipu, 86km (53 miles) from Queenstown via Glenorchy
Alternative Start & End: Lake Howden near the Divide Shelter, 80km (50 miles) from Te Anau on the Milford Road
Open: November through April
Contact Information: For independent walks, contact the **Department of Conservation,** Fiordland National Park Visitor Centre, Lakefront Drive, P.O. Box 29, Te Anau (☎ 03/249-7924; fax 03/249-7613). The hut fee is NZ$30 per night, plus transport.

For guided walks, call **Ultimate Hikes** (☎ 0800/659-255 in NZ, or 03/450-1940; www.ultimatehikes.co.nz), which provides accommodations and knowledgeable guides.

HOLLYFORD TRACK   This relatively flat track follows the Hollyford River out to the coast at Martins Bay. You can walk it as a round-trip or as a one-way with a fly-out from Martins Bay. You can also jet-boat the Demon Trail section of the track. Because there are no alpine crossings, this is one of the few Fiordland tracks that can be done year-round.
Duration/Distance: 4 days/56km (35 miles) one-way
Start: Hollyford Camp, 9km (5½ miles) off Milford Road
End: Martins Bay (walk back or fly out)
Open: Year-round; guided walks available October through April only
Contact Information: For independent walks, contact the **Department of Conservation,** Fiordland National Park Visitor Centre, P.O. Box 29, Te Anau (☎ 03/249-7924; fax 03/249-7613). There is a hut fee of NZ$25 per night. The jet-boat, flight out, and bus transportation are extra.

For guided walks, contact **Hollyford Track** (☎ 0800/832-226 in NZ, or 03/442-7789; fax 03/442-7781; www.hollyfordtrack.co.nz), which offers stays in a comfortable lodge with hot showers. The 3- to 4-day package costs from NZ$1,695 for adults, NZ$1,295 for children ages 10 to 14, and includes pre-tour lodging in Te Anau.

KEPLER TRACK   This 4-day tramp starts and ends at the Lake Te Anau outlet control gates. You'll pass through beech forests and a U-shaped glacial valley, and walk along the edges of Lakes Te Anau and Manapouri. This is a challenging hike with a lot of altitude variations. The track zigzags up 800m (2,600 ft.) and drops 1,000m (3,300 ft.)—the single most useful thing you can take is a walking pole. Access is provided by shuttle bus and boat transfer.
Duration/Distance: 3 to 4 days/67km (42 miles)
Start & End: Te Anau Control Gates
Open: Late October to mid-April

Contact Information: For independent walks, contact the **Department of Conservation,** Fiordland National Park Visitor Centre, P.O. Box 29, Te Anau (✆ **03/249-7924;** fax 03/249-7613). Hut fees are NZ$52 per night; the night camping fee is NZ$16. Transport is extra. Early bookings are essential.

MILFORD TRACK ★ Many consider the famous Milford Track the finest anywhere in the world. Known for its glacially carved valleys, alpine flowers, and waterfalls, the 4-day walk is closely regulated by DOC staff, both for the safety of hikers and for the preservation of the wilderness region. You'll walk from Glade Jetty at Lake Te Anau's northern end to Sandfly Point on the western bank of Milford Sound. The track follows the Clinton and Arthur valleys and crosses MacKinnon Pass, the one steep and more difficult stretch that takes about 2 hours to ascend. From here, at 1,073m (3,519 ft.), it's all downhill to Sandfly Point, where you'll be ferried across Milford Sound. You can spend the night at Milford or return to Te Anau, but reservations must be made for either option.

Duration/Distance: 4 days/54km (33 miles)
Start: Lake Te Anau (Te Anau Downs)
End: Sandfly Point near Milford Sound
Open: Late October to mid-April

Contact Information: For independent walks, contact the **Department of Conservation,** Great Walks Booking Desk, Fiordland National Park Visitor Centre, P.O. Box 29, Te Anau (✆ **03/249-8514;** fax 03/249-8515; greatwalksbooking@doc.govt. nz). Reservations are accepted from early November to mid-April for the following tramping season, which runs from mid-October to mid-April. No more than 24 people can start the walk on any given day. The cost is NZ$155 for all three huts and about NZ$100 to NZ$125 extra for transport.

Milford Track Guided Walk (✆ 0800/659-255 in NZ, or 03/450-1940; fax 03/450-1941; www.ultimatehikes.co.nz) provides coach transport to Te Anau via Queenstown and allows walkers greater flexibility in making international flight connections. Prices include guides, meals at overnight lodges, and accommodations at each end of the trek. Walkers carry their own day packs. From December to March 13, fees for a 6-day package (beginning and ending in Te Anau) run from NZ$1,995 to NZ$3,020 for adults and NZ$1,790 for children ages 10 to 15, depending on the style of accommodation chosen. In November and from March 14 to April 4 (dates vary slightly each year), the package costs slightly less.

The highly rated **Trips 'n' Tramps** (✆ 03/249-7081; fax 03/249-7089; www. tripsandtramps.com) offers a 1-day option, with one guide for a maximum of 12 people. The package includes a scenic Lake Te Anau cruise, up to 5 hours on the Milford Track, easy walking (no hills), and a lunch stop (bring your own) at Clinton Hut. The cost is NZ$175; it's available November through March.

ROUTEBURN TRACK ★ The Routeburn is a moderate track that links Mount Aspiring and Fiordland national parks via the Harris Saddle. In summer, it is one of the most popular tracks, but in winter, it's extremely hazardous and impassable with high avalanche danger. It takes you into the heart of unspoiled forests, along river valleys, and across mountain passes, and requires a good level of fitness. Bus transfers are available to the start of the track and from the finish for about NZ$125 one-way from Queenstown; the DOC can furnish you with a list of all transport options. Remember that the Routeburn is not a circuit track and there are over 350km (220 miles) of road transport required between both ends of the track. Transport may cost you up to NZ$250 if you need to return to your starting point.

Duration/Distance: 2 to 3 days/39km (24 miles)

Start & End: The Routeburn Shelter, 75km (47 miles) from Queenstown via Glenorchy, or the Divide Shelter, 80km (50 miles) from Te Anau on the Milford Road. The Routeburn can be walked in either direction.

Open: Late October to mid-April

Contact Information: For independent walks, contact the **Department of Conservation,** Great Walks Booking Desk, Fiordland National Park Visitor Centre, P.O. Box 29, Te Anau (✆ **03/249-8514;** fax 03/249-8515; greatwalksbooking@doc.govt. nz). Hut fees are NZ$52 per night, camping fees NZ$16 per night. Transport costs are extra; advance track reservations are required.

For guided walks, call **Ultimate Hikes** (✆ **0800/659-255** in NZ, or 03/450-1940; www.ultimatehikes.co.nz), which offers a 3-day guided Routeburn Walk package that begins in Queenstown. A coach will take you to "The Divide" (on Milford Rd.); you'll walk to Lake McKenzie, across the Harris Saddle, and past the Routeburn Falls. A coach will return you to Queenstown. Comfortable lodges are provided. The cost is from NZ$1,270 for adults, NZ$1,065 for children ages 10 to 15. Rates include transport, meals, and accommodations. Tours depart regularly from November through April, but you should reserve as far in advance as possible. **Guided Walks New Zealand** (✆ **03/442-7126;** fax 03/442-7128; www.nzwalks.com) also offers a 1-day option on the Routeburn for NZ$245 for adults and NZ$140 for children under 14.

For a 6-day excursion, called the **Grand Traverse,** combine the Routeburn and Greenstone Valley tracks. See "The Grand Traverse," above, for details.

STEWART ISLAND

This is New Zealand's third-biggest island and a veritable nature paradise overlooked by most of the world—including the rest of New Zealand. But it is a spot for some astounding multiday treks and hundreds of delightful short walks. For information on the island, see chapter 16.

NORTH WEST CIRCUIT ★ This track is designed for well-equipped, experienced trampers who will take 10 to 12 days working their way around the island's northwest arm. Nature is at its best in clean beaches, birds, and bush, but mud is widespread and often knee-deep on the track. You'll get great views and complete solitude.

Duration/Distance: 8 to 12 days/125km (78 miles)

Start & End: Half Moon Bay, Oban

Open: Year-round

Contact Information: For independent walks, contact the **Department of Conservation,** P.O. Box 3, Stewart Island (✆ **03/219-0002;** fax 03/219-0003; stewartislandfc@doc.govt.nz). The North West Circuit Pass costs NZ$40 and allows 1 night in each hut on the North West Circuit Track, excluding the Great Walks huts at Port William and North Arm. A Great Walks Pass (NZ$15 per night) is required for Port William and North Arm huts, which are part of the Rakiura Track. This also applies to campgrounds at Port William, Maori Beach, and Sawdust Bay. All other huts require hut tickets. A NZ$99 Backcountry Pass may be used on the North West Circuit or Southern Circuit tracks. Huts are equipped with running water, mattresses, toilets, and wood-fired stoves. Before undertaking this walk, consider watching the excellent video of the track at the DOC office in Oban village, Half Moon Bay.

Kiwi Wilderness Walks, Queenstown (✆ **0800/733-549** in NZ, or 021/359-592; fax 03/442-8342; www.nzwalk.com), offers a 5-day tour in Stewart Island

National Park, which includes kiwi spotting at Mason Bay, a visit to Ulva Island, and sea kayaking in Paterson Inlet for NZ$1,695 adults. This walk is not recommended for children 9 and under. **Ruggedy Range** (✆ **03/219-1066;** www.ruggedyrange. com) has guided treks on part of the North West Circuit priced from NZ$455 to NZ$860 per person. These include kiwi-spotting trips.

RAKIURA TRACK This is one of New Zealand's Great Walks and is suitable for anyone of moderate fitness. It takes trampers through bush and along beaches and open coast, and much of it is boardwalked. There are two huts and three designated campsites.

Duration/Distance: 3 days/36km (22 miles)

Start & End: Half Moon Bay, Oban

Open: Year-round

Contact Information: For independent walks, contact the **Department of Conservation,** P.O. Box 3, Stewart Island (✆ **03/219-0002;** fax 03/219-0003; stewartislandfc@doc.govt.nz). You must purchase a date-stamped Great Walks Pass or campsite pass (NZ$20 per-night hut fee) before taking this walk. Conservation staff may be on the track, and they will impose a surcharge on trampers using accommodations facilities without a pass, which must be displayed on packs at all times. Nightly campsite fees are NZ$5.10 per person. **Ruggedy Range** (✆ **03/219-1066;** www. ruggedyrange.com) has a 3-day guided walk on Rakiura for NZ$895 per person.

FISHING

Any prospective fisherman in New Zealand should get a copy of *Sports Fishing Guide,* a free booklet produced by the **New Zealand Fish and Game Council** (✆ **04/499-4767;** fax 04/499-4768; www.fishandgame.org.nz). The guide supplies you with the myriad rules and regulations you need to know. It also gives details on major freshwater fishing spots. The **New Zealand Professional Fishing Guides Association** (✆ **06/868-4214;** www.nzpfga.com) may also be helpful. For an online directory of New Zealand fishing magazines, go to www.nzfishing.com. One of the best is *NZ Fishing World* (www.nzfishingworld.co.nz). For help in planning a New Zealand fishing holiday from North America, contact the **Best of New Zealand Adventure Travel,** 2817 Wilshire Blvd., Santa Monica, CA 90403 (✆ **800/528-6129** in the U.S., or 310/998-5880). This agency specializes in angler activities and has a 48-page brochure called *The Best of New Zealand Fly Fishing* (which also includes information on saltwater fishing). For more information visit www.bestofnz flyfishing.com.

Freshwater Fishing

New Zealand's reputation as a trout fisherman's paradise is well established internationally. It is the world's best place to fish for wild **brown trout** during the season, which lasts from the first Saturday in October to the end of April. During this time, all rivers and streams are open for brown and **rainbow trout,** but local restrictions may apply. There are several areas where you can fish year-round: the **Rotorua District** and **Lake Taupo** on the North Island, and **Lake Te Anau, Lake Brunner,** and **Lake Wakatipu** on the South Island.

The **Tongariro River,** near Turangi, is one of the prime trout-fishing rivers in the world. May through October are the best months to snag rainbow and brown trout, which average nearly 2 kilograms (over 4 lb.)! This period is also good for fishing in

Keeping New Zealand Waterways Clean

Sadly, many New Zealand waterways now carry the unwanted organism *Didymosphenia geminate (Didymo)*, also known as "rock snot," which is a freshwater diatom (type of alga) that was first reported on the Lower Waiau River in the South Island in 2004. Biosecurity New Zealand (www.biosecurity.govt.nz) has since declared the whole of the South Island a controlled area for *Didymo*. This means that fishermen, boat owners, and others using waterways for pleasure activities are legally required to do everything they can to prevent its spread. Unfortunately, *Didymo* is a microscopic pest that can be spread in a single drop of water. You therefore need to ensure that all watersports equipment, including boots, waders, fishing lines, boats, skis, and anything else used in the water is thoroughly clean and dry before moving from one waterway to another. As the name suggests, when *Didymo* takes over a waterway, it forms a slimy brown mass that attaches itself to everything. Please take extreme care not to aid in its spread.

Lakes Taupo and Rotorua. Lake Rotorua is not stocked, but it has one of the highest catch rates in the district.

The Eastern Fish and Game region has a huge range of fishing opportunities and diversity in both lake and river fishing. The bush-clad **lakes Waikaremoana** and **Waikareiti** provide spectacular boat and shoreline fishing for both brown and rainbow trout in untouched Te Urewera National Park.

Fishing is good in almost all areas of the South Island. In **Nelson,** you'll get rainbow trout and also quinnat salmon in many places, but it's the brown trout that's king of these mixed waters. **Canterbury** is best known for its prolific salmon runs that enter the large braided rivers such as the **Rakaia** and **Waimakariri,** and high-country rivers are known for small numbers of big fish.

In the West Coast region, **Lake Brunner** is the most popular angling water in the region, with brown trout averaging 1.1 kilograms (2½ lb.). Farther south, the **Waitaki** and **Rangitata rivers** have landed chinook salmon of 15 kilograms (33 lb.).

Fish and Game Otago has an excellent book, *Guide to Trout Fishing in Otago,* which covers 140 waters and gives information on access and methods. In **Southland,** dozens of rivers, streams, and lakes hold brown and rainbow trout, plus quinnat salmon. The waters of this region are widely known throughout New Zealand, but you have to be a competent fisherman and know your way around to be successful. **Southland Fish and Game,** P.O. Box 159, Invercargill (© **03/215-9117;** fishgame@southnet.co.nz), can supply maps, advice, information, and guides.

FISHING GUIDES If fishing is your passion, consider investing some cash in a good guide. Be warned, however, that freshwater fishing guides here are not cheap; some run as high as NZ$1,200 to NZ$1,800 per day for one or two people. Shop around for the best deals. I've listed a few outfitters in the regional chapters.

If you'd like to organize a fishing holiday, contact **South Island Fishing Tours** (©/fax **03/755-8032;** www.flyfishingnewzealand.co.nz). Tony and Marj Allan of Kawhaka Lodge in Hokitika offer 2- to 14-day fishing tours for one to two people, starting and finishing in Christchurch. **Chris Jolly Outdoors** (© **07/378-0623;** fax 07/378-9458; www.chrisjolly.co.nz) specializes in trout fishing on Lake Taupo (among other things) and can take you to the best trout rivers that flow into the lake. In

Wanaka, **Gerald Telford** (✆/fax **03/443-9257**; www.flyfishhunt.co.nz) offers a number of multiday fishing excursions that start at NZ$695 per person.

Saltwater & Big-Game Fishing

Deep-sea fishing is at its best along the magnificent 500km (310 miles) of Northland's coastline, slipping down into the Bay of Plenty. Waters less than an hour out from shore can yield **marlin, shark** (mako, thresher, hammerhead, tiger), five species of **tuna, broadbill,** and **yellowtail.** The season runs from mid-January to April, and you'll find well-equipped bases at the Bay of Islands in Northland, Whitianga on the Coromandel, and Tauranga and Whakatane in the Bay of Plenty. You can also fish for **kahawai, snapper,** and more anywhere along the New Zealand coast. Licenses are not required.

ALL SORTS OF WATERSPORTS

Boating

Whether it's cruising a secluded bay or inlet, exploring uninhabited islands, or sailing in harbors and on lakes, New Zealanders have got boating down to a fine art. Of course, Auckland is famous for its excessive boat tally, but you'll find this passion reflected everywhere (except perhaps on the South Island's West Coast). The Marlborough Sounds are another big boating haven, as are the Bay of Plenty and Northland. Anytime between December and April, you'll find Kiwis taking to the water in some kind of seaworthy vehicle.

CANOEING & KAYAKING The prime kayaking spot is Abel Tasman National Park, where boats appear to float in midair because the water is so clear. Sea kayaking is also popular in the Bay of Islands, in Hauraki Gulf, around Coromandel Peninsula, in Marlborough Sounds, in Milford Sound, and around Banks Peninsula and Otago Peninsula.

Try to book your adventures with members of **SKOANZ,** the **Sea Kayak Operators Association of New Zealand** (✆ **027/452-9255**; www.skoanz.org.nz), who must adhere to a code of practice covering safety, service, guides, and environment.

In Northland, you'll find reliable operators at **Coastal Kayakers,** Paihia (✆ **09/402-8105;** fax 09/403-8550; www.coastalkayakers.co.nz), which explores the outer islands with lagoons, rock caves, and sandy beaches. You can have canoe adventures with **Canoe Safaris,** Ohakune (✆ **06/385-9237;** fax 06/385-8758; www.canoesafaris.co.nz). It has 5-day expeditions in rugged Whanganui National Park from late October to mid-April.

In Abel Tasman National Park, **Abel Tasman Kayaks** (✆ **0800/732-529** in NZ; fax 03/527-8032; www.abeltasmankayaks.co.nz) has been guiding tours since 1986.

JET-BOATING For an adrenaline rush, try jet-boating—which is possible along most major rivers throughout the country. See regional chapters for more information.

SAILING Given the running of the 1999–2000 and the 2002–03 America's Cup Challenge in Auckland, it's a bit of an understatement to say that sailing is popular here. For the warmest, balmiest, most subtropical experiences, head for Northland, Auckland, and the Bay of Plenty; there's plenty of excellent sailing farther south, too.

For bareboat and skippered charters, contact **Moorings Rainbow Yacht Charters,** P.O. Box 8327, Symonds Street, Auckland (✆ **09/378-0719;** fax 09/378-0931; www.tongatapu.net) or **Royal Akarana Yacht Club,** Auckland (✆ **09/524-9945;**

fax 09/520-1380; www.rayc.org.nz), which charges from NZ$400 for various sailing courses. In Marlborough Sounds, try **Compass Charters,** 20 Beach Rd., Waikawa (© **03/573-8332;** fax 03/573-8587; www.compass-charters.co.nz), offering budget to luxury yacht and launch charters.

Pride of Auckland (© **09/359-5987;** www.prideofauckland.com) has four 15m (50-ft.) yachts available for daily scheduled and charter cruises for all ages and abilities (see chapter 5), and **tall ship** *Soren Larsen* (© **09/817-8799;** www.soren larsen.co.nz) is the tall ship that starred in the BBC's *The Onedin Line* television series in the late 1970s. It has a rich history and is available for day sailings and holiday cruises in New Zealand and the South Pacific (see chapter 5).

For general information on sailing, contact **Yachting New Zealand** (© **09/361-1471;** fax 09/360-2246; www.yachtingnz.org.nz).

WHITE-WATER RAFTING   The challenging Wairoa, Mohaka, and Kaituna rivers are popular on the North Island; in the south, you'll find action on the Shotover, Kawarau, and Rangitata rivers. You can do this year-round—wet suits and warm clothing are required in winter, though. Operators give instruction, supply equipment, and arrange transfers to and from launch points.

Rapid Sensations, Taupo (© **0800/353-435** in NZ; fax 07/378-7904; www. rapids.co.nz), takes 3-day trips on the upper Mohaka River. If you want an all-out 9 days of crazy fun, contact **Ultimate Descents,** Motueka (© **0800/748-377** in NZ; fax 03/523-9811; www.rivers.co.nz), which exposes you to the serious thrills of the Buller, Karamea, and Clarence rivers on the top of the South Island.

Scuba Diving & Surfing

SCUBA DIVING   With over 32,000km (20,000 miles) of coastline, New Zealand has no shortage of diving opportunities. The best diving seas in the land are around the **Poor Knights Islands** in Northland. This is where you'll find the wreck of the *Rainbow Warrior,* which is now covered quite nicely with reef formations. Visibility ranges from 20 to 69m (66–226 ft.) in the best months (Feb–June). Another excellent dive spot, renowned for its crystal-clear waters, is the much chillier **Stewart Island.** Brave divers can also immerse themselves in the murky, tannin-stained waters of **Milford Sound** for a truly unique experience.

No matter where you take the plunge, you must have evidence of your diving certification with you. For details, contact the **Dive Industry of New Zealand** (© **09/849-5897;** fax 09/849-3526). Good resources include *Dive New Zealand* magazine online (www.divenewzealand.com); the internationally renowned **Waikato Dive Centre** (© **07/849-1922;** fax 07/849-1942), which offers courses and dive trips; and Napier-based **Arlidge Adventures Dive Centre** (© **06/835-3005;** www.aadivecentre.co.nz) for courses and dive tours.

SURFING & WINDSURFING   When asked, every surfer will, of course, tell you his or her favorite beach is best, although it does seem unanimous that **Eastland** and **Gisborne** reliably turn out some of the best waves in the country. **Raglan,** west of Hamilton, is also popular; **Whangamata** and **Mount Maunganui,** in Bay of Plenty, and **Taylor's Mistake,** near Christchurch, are others to consider. For surfing tours of the Auckland-Northland region contact **New Zealand Surf Tours** (©/fax **09/832-9622;** www.newzealandsurftours.com).

Windsurfing is popular in many areas around Auckland: at Ferrymead in Christchurch; on Lyttelton Harbour, Christchurch; on Otago Peninsula; at Oakura near New Plymouth; and on Wellington Harbour.

All Sorts of Watersports

GOLF

New Zealand is a nation of golfers. There are approximately 400 private and public courses that offer myriad opportunities. And we're lucky to have some of the best, yet cheapest, golfing facilities you'll find anywhere. Greens fees are well below the world's average—you'll pay anything from NZ$10 to NZ$135 for 18 holes on a good course, and up to NZ$155 to NZ$475 for the country's top links. Clubs, equipment, and a motorized cart (trundler) can be rented.

Die-hards hit the courses year-round, but the best time to golf is from October to April, when temperatures range from 60°F to 70°F (16°C–21°C). Courses tend to be crowded on weekends, less so during the week.

There are 40 golf courses in the Auckland area alone. The **Gulf Harbour** and **Formosa Country Clubs** are the newest on the scene, and the former hosted the 1998 World Cup of Golf. In Rotorua, the **Arikikapakapa** course is dotted with geothermal activity, which makes the course tricky to play; near Taupo, you'll find one of the country's finest, the **Wairakei International Golf Course.** Wellington's **Paraparaumu Beach Golf Club** was rated one of the world's top 50 courses by *Golf Digest.* In Christchurch, both **Russley** and **Shirley** are well rated, along with **Balmacewan** and **St. Clair** in Dunedin.

For more information, contact the **New Zealand Golf Association** (© 09/485-3230; fax 09/486-6745; www.golf.co.nz).

For golf packages, contact **New Zealand Golf Excursions USA, Inc.,** 2141 Rosecrans Ave., no. 1199, El Segundo, CA 90245 (© **800/622-6606** in the U.S.; fax 310/322-4972), or **Kiwi Golf Tours** (© **800/873-6360**).

In New Zealand, try **Golf NZ** (© **06/870-8740;** fax 06/870-8749; www.golfnew zealand.co.nz), which offers multiday tours for 12 to 36 golfers and partners from NZ$1,600 per person including accommodations, travel, and golf; or **Big Boys Golf Tours** (© **06/858-4993;** www.bigboysgolf.co.nz or www.paradisegolf.co.nz), which offers tours of top golf courses in the Auckland region. Also check www.bestofgolf newzealand.com for golf holiday planning.

SKIING & SNOWBOARDING

When the sun warms up in the Northern Hemisphere, skiers and snowboarders come down to the Southern Hemisphere. The ski season generally runs from late June to September. The country has 13 conventional ski areas; as an added bonus at Mount Cook, you can fly by ski plane or helicopter to the 2,400m (7,900-ft.) head of the Tasman Glacier and ski down the 14km (8¾-mile) run. For up-to-the-minute South Island ski details, check out www.nzski.com.

Skiing

The two major ski fields on the North Island are Whakapapa and Turoa, on the slopes of **Mount Ruapehu** in Tongariro National Park, now both owned by a single company, Ruapehu Alpine Lifts. Ruapehu, with a simmering crater lake, is an active volcano and extends up some 2,760m (9,050 ft.), making it the North Island's highest peak. It erupted in 1995 and again in 1996, effectively ending all skiing activity for about 2 years. **Whakapapa** (© **07/892-3738;** fax 07/892-3732; www.mtruapehu.com) offers challenges for intermediate skiers and snowboarders and has good beginners' packages; for instruction contact **Whakapapa Ski & Snowboard School** (© **07/892-3410**). **Turoa** (© **06/385-8456;** fax 06/385-8992; info.turoa@mtruapehu.com) has great terrain for all levels of skiing, with good half-pipes for snowboarders, plus good beginning instruction packages for both sports.

On the South Island, **Mount Hutt Ski Field** (© **03/302-8811;** fax 03/302-8697; www.nzski.com) is 1¼ hours from Christchurch, with a good shuttle service operating from the city. Contact the **Mount Hutt Ski School** at © **03/308-5074** (www.mt hutt.co.nz). There are numerous club fields close to Christchurch, especially in the Porters Pass region. You'll find information on some of these fields at www.snow.co.nz, www.dobson.co.nz, www.skiporters.co.nz, www.mtlyford.co.nz, www.mtcheeseman. com, www.brokenriver.co.nz, www.craigieburn.co.nz, www.templebasin.co.nz, www. mtolympus.co.nz, www.foxpeak.co.nz, and www.skihanmer.co.nz.

Coronet Peak (© **03/442-4620;** www.nzski.com) is 18km (11 miles) from Queenstown with moderate to challenging fields. It's the oldest commercial field in the South Island and has several chairlifts including a six-seater high-speed lift, beginners' facilities, and good variety for experienced skiers. The **Remarkables** (© **03/442-4615**), 23km (14 miles) from Queenstown, has more diversity for experienced skiers. It's a smaller field with three chairlifts, one magic carpet, and a beginner handle tow, and is good for middle-ability skiers. It gets the afternoon sun, so it's slightly warmer in winter. There's a lot of heli-skiing on virgin snow in this area and an incredibly steep access road. **Cardrona Alpine Resort** (© **03/443-7411;** fax 03/443-8818; www.cardrona.com) is a middle-range field with good family facilities, including new social facilities, but it's a bit tame for experienced skiers. It lies 57km (35 miles) from Queenstown and 33km (20 miles) from Wanaka. Contact **Cardrona Development Centre** (© **03/443-7411;** www.cardrona.com) for lessons. **Treble Cone** (© **03/443-7443;** fax 03/443-8401; www.treblecone.co.nz) has the newest and biggest express chairlift in the country, which has improved the flow of skiers on the field. It's one of the more challenging fields and has a lot of variety, with very steep areas and narrow valleys. It also has a good base lodge and the best food facilities of all the southern ski areas. There's also heli-skiing in the Harris Mountains. For instruction, contact **Treble Cone Ski School** (© **03/443-7443;** www.treblecone.com).

Lift ticket prices in New Zealand range from NZ$95 to NZ$120; ski, boot, and pole rentals run from NZ$40 to NZ$60; and lessons are from NZ$110 for a half-day group class. Costs are lower for children and all ski fields offer a range of day and multiday passes, plus online specials.

For cross-country skiing, head for **Snow Farm,** located in the Pisa Range, near Wanaka (© **03/443-0300;** fax 03/443-9717; www.snowfarmnz.com), which is the only Nordic ski field of its kind in New Zealand. The area has ideal terrain for first-time cross-country skiers as well as good conditions for advanced skiers.

SKI PACKAGES & OUTFITTERS   In winter, you'll always find good ski deals from the three major cities—Auckland, Wellington, and Christchurch—that usually include cheap transport, accommodations, and a specified number of ski days. Check with the visitor centers in each city for the latest ski-package brochures.

Check out the highly recommended **Snowco** (www.snowco.co.nz), which features online ski and snowboarding packages, and **Ski New Zealand Online** (www.ski-newzealand.co.nz), which offers numerous ski package holidays at reasonable prices. The **NZ Super Pass** can be used at any time on any of the following South Island ski fields: Treble Cone, Mount Dobson, Mount Lyford, Ohau, Broken River, Mount Olympus, Craigieburn, and Temple Basin, or you can choose a day's skiing or snowboarding at Coronet Peak, the Remarkables, or Mount Hutt. You can also swap a day on the mountains with one of a huge range of other activities, including heli-skiing, ballooning, jet-boating, and many more. Coupons for the NZ Super Pass start from around NZ$275 for a 3-day pass. For information, contact **Coronet Peak** (✆ **03/450-1970;** www.nzski.com or www.nzsuperpass.com).

For heli-skiing in the Queenstown area, contact **HeliSki** (✆ **03/442-7733;** fax 03/442-3299; www.flynz.co.nz). Members of the Gardner family are all expert skiers, with one or two pilots among them, too. They have access to some of the most fantastic heli-ski terrain in New Zealand. Another contact is **Harris Mountain Heli-Skiing** (✆ **03/442-6722;** fax 03/442-2983; www.heliski.co.nz).

For more information on New Zealand skiing, check out the **New Zealand Snowsports Council** (✆ **04/977-1144;** www.gosnow.co.nz), **Snow Sport New Zealand** (✆ **03/443-4085;** www.snowsports.co.nz), or the websites www.goski.com and www.onthesnow.com.

Snowboarding

Treble Cone is "home to some of the best gully runs in New Zealand, which form into awesome quarter pipes, hips, and spines." So says one of the experts on www.boardtheworld.com, who rates Treble Cone eighth in the world for freeriding. Treble Cone is rated the top freeriding resort in Australasia and is best for experienced boarders. It has an active training program.

Cardona is better for beginner and intermediate boarders. It has undulating terrain, lots of gullies, and four half-pipes, and it offers a whole heap of support for snowboarders in general. It also has half-pipe camps throughout the season for all levels. **Coronet Peak** has lots of long groomed runs to tabletops, with quarter-pipes, kickers, and rollers. It's essentially a tourist field and is more expensive. The **Remarkables** offers pretty ho-hum snowboarding on the field itself, but the out-of-bounds territory offers extreme boarding for the daring. There's good stuff up in the backcountry if you're prepared to hike. Generally, though, the Remarkables is not a destination of choice for boarders.

Farther north, there's good snowboarding at **Temple Basin Ski Area,** in Arthur's Pass (✆ **03/377-7788**), and at **Turoa Ski Resort,** in Tongariro National Park (✆ **06/385-8456**).

SNOWBOARDING DEALS & TOURS New Zealand Surf 'n' Snow Tours (✆ **09/828-0426;** www.newzealandsnowtours.co.nz) has a wide range of North and South Island snowboard packages. **Mount Aspiring Guides,** in Wanaka (✆ **03/443-9422;** fax 03/443-9540; www.aspiringguides.com), offers a 5-day snowboarding tour in alpine wilderness areas, but snowboarders must be set up for backcountry travel. This is boarding in untracked areas, and you'll need an adventurous spirit, lots of experience, and the proper gear. Accommodations are in high mountain huts. (You get flown in.) This little venture will cost you in the vicinity of NZ$2,250 per person.

BICYCLING

Bicycle touring is a breathtakingly fresh way of seeing New Zealand, and it's an increasingly popular choice, especially on the South Island, where traffic densities are lower and the scenery is spectacular. There are numerous companies offering guided cycle tours—everything from short day tours through vineyards to more serious challenges like a month-long tour of the whole country.

The best news for many cyclists and tourism operators in May 2009 was Prime Minister John Key's announcement that the government, through the Ministry of Tourism, would spend NZ$50-million over 3 years to build a new national cycleway, running the length of New Zealand. Rather than being one direct north-south route, though, it is being designed as a network comprising existing cycleways with new sections to create a linked Great Rides passage through provincial New Zealand—similar in concept to the already-established Great Walks network. This means riders will get a much more comprehensive overview of New Zealand than they would by riding State Highway 1 from Kaitaia in the north to Bluff in the south.

The first stage of the development has identified seven key routes—five in the North Island and two in the South Island. These will build on existing cycleways, facilities, and tourism attractions. Track One will be in the Far North, linking the Hokianga on the West Coast to Opua and Russell on the east coast. Track Two will focus on the Hauraki Plains, linking Paeroa to Waihi and Thames. Track Three will be created around two Waikato River Trails near Hamilton and Lake Karapiro. Track Four will see the creation of the Central North Island Rail Trail linking Pureora to Taumarunui. Track Five, Mountains to Sea, will also be set in unique central North Island landscapes; and Track Six, the St James Great Trail, will focus on the very pretty Hanmer area in the South Island. Last but not least, Track Seven, in the Southland–Queenstown Lakes area, will take cyclists around the Mountain Rail Trail, through Walter Peak and Mount Nicholas Stations, along the Von Valley, and from Mosstown along the old railway line to Lumsden. At time of writing, the St James Trail was open and construction of 15 more sections was well underway. It is hoped that 2,000 kilometers (1,240 miles) of trails will be open by the end of 2011. Check the progress and find out much more about **Nga Haerenga, The New Zealand Cycle Trail** at www.nzcycletrail.com.

The new cycleways are expected to create many new jobs, both during the construction phase and in the resulting tourism operations that spring up in their wake. Those riding the trails will gain access to many remote landscapes and small towns and villages that would normally be bypassed on traditional tourist schedules; and for those who have always been nervous about cycling New Zealand on the main highways, the development of the Great Rides tracks will be welcome news. The tracks will also appeal to those who may only want to ride through one or two scenic sections.

SAFETY TIPS   Regardless of where you bike, always wear your helmet—they are mandatory in New Zealand, and you will be fined for not wearing one. Also, remember the following: Cyclists are not permitted on motorways (freeways); they must always ride on the left side of the road; and all traffic turning left gives way to everything on the right. At night, make sure you have a working white front light and a red rear light and reflector. It doesn't hurt to have pedal and jacket reflectors. A few cities—Christchurch is the standout in this regard—have designated cycle lanes within city limits, which makes pedaling safer.

RENTALS   If you're not interested in an organized tour and want to rent a bike when you get here, **Adventure Cycles,** in Auckland (✆ **09/940-2453;** www.adventure-auckland.co.nz), offers rentals throughout New Zealand and sales with a guaranteed buyback plan. It is also part of an association of 24 operators that can arrange organized activities. **Nelson Bike Rentals** (✆ **03/548-1666;** www.nelsonbikerentals.co.nz) has a huge range of road and mountain bikes available for short- or long-term rental. They also have a buyback scheme for long-term rentals, which is much more economical than bringing your own bike to New Zealand. **City Cycle Hire** in Christchurch (✆ **0800/343-848;** www.cyclehire-tours.co.nz) offers short- and long-term cycle hire, along with mountain biking riding adventures.

TOURS   There's an increasing number of organized bike-tour companies in New Zealand and I've listed many in "Outdoor Pursuits" in individual regional chapters.

New Zealand Pedaltours ★★★, in Parnell, Auckland (☎ 09/585-1338; fax 09/585-1339; www.pedaltours.co.nz), offers both North and South Island trips on 12 routes lasting from 2 to 37 days, on- and off-road. It creates customized tours of moderate exertion level, and a support van is always around to take the load off your pedals. Adventure South (☎ 03/942-1222; fax 03/942-4030; www.advsouth.co.nz) offers a range of 6- to 21-day cycle tours, mainly in the South Island, that may also include some walking excursions. They are geared to all fitness levels and are backed up by support vehicles. Tuatara Tours ★★, in Christchurch (☎ 0800/377-378 in NZ, or 03/962-3280; www.tuataratours.co.nz), has two excellent cycle tours for people who want to focus on fun and comfort. Their 4-day Hanmer Cycle Trail covers 170km (105 miles), taking you through the Waipara vineyard region to the alpine village of Hanmer, where you can end your journey in hot pools; and their Tekapo Canal Trail (140km/87 miles) introduces you to the South Island's dramatic landscapes. The Hanmer trail does have some small hills to cover; and you may have to battle against strong winds on both trails if you strike an infamous "Nor'wester."

OTHER SPORTS

Rock Climbing

Rock climbing and bouldering are alive and well in New Zealand, and the best place to start to get the lowdown on this activity is to go to www.climb.co.nz, which gives a regional overview of the country's best outdoor climbing locations, plus listings of the best rock climbing guidebooks and adventure operators. The Canterbury region is known to provide the most quality rock climbing locations in the country. If you want to join a rock climbing course, Wanaka Rock Climbing (☎ 03/443-6411; www.wanakarock.co.nz) offers 1-, 3-, and 5-day courses in the beautiful Matukituki Valley on the edge of Mount Aspiring National Park, near Wanaka. Auckland-based Cliffhanger Training & Tours (☎ 09/818-5451; www.cliffhanger.co.nz) caters to all skill levels with its 2-hour to full-day rock climbing coaching adventures, which are overseen by qualified instructors. I have detailed indoor rock climbing facilities in the "Outdoor Pursuits" section of regional chapters.

Horseback Riding

Horseback riding is a perfect way to get an up-close-and-personal view, rather than flashing through in a fast-moving vehicle. And most horseback riding operators will take you off the beaten track, into landscapes you would otherwise never see. I have detailed a number of horseback riding operations in "Outdoor Pursuits" in regional chapters. Most riding operations only offer short-term outings (1- to 4-hour treks) but they cater to a wide range of riding abilities. One of the best providers of longer treks is North Canterbury–based Alpine Horse Safaris ★★★ (☎ 03/314-4293; www.alpinehorse.co.nz), which offers 3- to 12-day treks covering up to 400km (more than 200 miles) of some of the most beautiful landscapes in the South Island. Plan to spend around 6 hours a day in the saddle. Accommodations are provided in mountain camps and musterers' huts. (Musterers are farm workers who gather livestock; their huts provide them with shelter when they're working in the high country.) Cape Farewell Horse Treks, 23 McGowan St., Puponga, Collingwood, Nelson (☎ 03/524-8031; www.horsetreksnz.com), has 1-hour to 7-day horse treks across the farmlands and beaches of the Abel Tasman region, near Nelson.

AUCKLAND

A uckland is as big, cosmopolitan, and hedonistic as any New Zealand city gets. History and future combine in this sprawling place, where you can walk above the harbor along the Auckland Harbour Bridge and the Sky Tower looms above a sea of skyscrapers. But while the sights are intriguing, it's the easy-going spirit of the Aucklanders and their impressive backyard that will really captivate you. Lush vineyards, sugar-white beaches, and island retreats are all just a hop away from the inner city bustle.

Things to Do   The grand, neoclassical **Auckland Museum** is a cavernous chest of Maori *taonga* (treasures); time your visit to catch tattooed Maori sticking their tongues out in the high-energy *haka* (war dance). Few big international cities are as outdoorsy as Auckland—locals flash past on rollerblades in **Cornwall Park** or at **Mission Bay,** kayak and sail on **Waitemata Harbour,** and kick back on **Waiheke Island**—join in the fun. Ride the glass elevator to the top of the space-age **Sky Tower** for giddying sunset views of the Auckland skyline.

Shopping   Auckland mixes shopping with sightseeing. You can tour **Waiheke Island's** gently sloping vineyards for spicy Syrahs and crisp Chardonnays or browse stores in seaside **Devonport's** historic streets. **High Street** is decidedly upmarket and harbors big-name designers; and you can browse other fashion-conscious boutiques of **Parnell** and **Ponsonby.** Hit colonial-era **Queen Street** for department stores and **Newmarket's** classy **Nuffield and Teed streets** for chic boutique shopping. Weekend is market time: Head for Pacific-flavored **Otara Market,** Parnell's **La Cigale French Market,** or Britomart's **City Farmers' Market.**

Nightlife & Entertainment   Bar-lined **Viaduct Harbour** is the place to watch Auckland strut its early-evening stuff. Sip frozen vodka with a too-cool crowd in the ice-carved **Minus 5 Bar.** Linger over champagne in one of the classy **Britomart bars,** or dance to the latest beats on **Ponsonby Road. Karangahape Road's** edgier nightlife kicks off around midnight in pumping bars, strip clubs, and live-music venues. For a more cultured evening, catch the revered **New Zealand Symphony Orchestra** at the **Auckland Town Hall.**

Hotels & Restaurants   Foodies can eat their way around the world in Auckland. Savor Pacific Rim cuisine with the in-crowd at one of **Viaduct Harbour's** see-and-be-seen restaurants. Dine alfresco on Spanish tapas or fresh fish at one of **Mission Bay's** beachfront cafes and bars. Or head to fashionable **Ponsonby Road** for relaxed fine dining.

Greater Auckland

NORTH ISLAND

Auckland

SOUTH ISLAND

Wellington

Christchurch

Dunedin

TE ATATU

Waitemata

16

Don Buck Rd.

Lincoln Rd.

HENDERSON

Great North Rd.

1

NEW LYNN

Godley Rd.

*Manukau
Harbour*

New North Rd.

2

MT. ALBERT

3

Blockhouse Bay Rd.

Richardson Rd.

Ridge Rd.

MT.
ROSKILL

0   2 mi

0   2 km

✈ Airport

- - - - - Ferry

**Auckland
International
Airport** ✈

Hauraki Gulf

TAKAPUNA Takapuna Beach

BIRKENHEAD
NORTHCOTE

Mokoia Rd.
Glenfield Rd.
Onewa Rd.
Lake Rd.

Harbour

RANGITOTO
ISLAND

Rangitoto Channel

HERNE BAY

PONSONBY

INNER CITY

Great North Rd.

Waitemata Harbour

See "Devonport" map

DEVONPORT Cheltenham Beach

North Head Historic Reserve

Ferry to Rangitoto, Waiheke, and Great Barrier Islands

4

5

6

PARNELL

See "Central Auckland" map

MT. EDEN DOMAIN

St. Lukes Rd.
Dominion Rd.
Mt. Eden Rd.
Remuera Rd.

7

Mission Bay

Kohimarama Beach

St. Heliers Bay

Tamaki Dr.

Kepa Rd.

REMUERA

ST. HELIER'S

EPSOM

Green Lane

Pah Rd.

Remuera Rd.

8

Ellerslie Panmure Hwy.

PANMURE

Church St.

Great South Rd.

Pakuranga Rd.

1

PAKURANGA

Bucklands Beach Dr.

20

OTAHUHU

Massey Rd.

MANGERE

East Tamaki Rd.

PAPATOETOE

9

ORIENTATION

Arriving

BY PLANE   The **Auckland International Airport** (℃ **0800/247-767** in NZ; www.aucklandairport.co.nz) is 21km (13 miles) south of the city, behind Manukau Harbour; a motorway makes it a swift 30- to 35-minute car trip into town. More than 25 international airlines serve the airport. The **Jean Batten International Terminal** opened in 1998 and after a NZ$100-million upgrade, completed in 2008, it now includes a new, environmentally friendly pier to accommodate the Airbus A380, plus it doubled its retail space, making it the largest arrivals duty-free store in the Asia-Pacific region. On arrival you'll be greeted by a large shopping zone, which includes almost 100 retail outlets, and that's *before* you even hit Customs and Immigration. Auckland is the only airport in the world with two competing duty-free agencies (DFS and Regency), so you'll get great deals on fashion, souvenirs, accessories, and New Zealand art and crafts.

If Auckland Airport is your departure point you can employ the **Collection Point** (℃ **09/256-8845**), which is the pick-up point for duty and tax-free goods purchased throughout New Zealand that have the Auckland Airport duty- and tax-free logo. Here, you can also purchase pharmacy, healthcare, and baby-care items. Temporary luggage storage (NZ$3 per bag; nothing left overnight) is available as is hairdryer rental (NZ$2) and towel rental with soap (NZ$10 with a NZ$5 refund) for use in the free showers and bathrooms near the chapel on this level. The collection point is open daily from 5:30am to 11pm. If you feel like pampering yourself, massage services are also available within the arrivals shopping zone. Nursery rooms with free cots and change tables are available on both the ground and first floor, and there is a children's playground on the first floor. There are numerous food outlets in both terminals.

The currency-exchange company **Travelex** (℃ **09/256-6457**; www.travelex.xo. nz) has 10 stores located in the international and domestic terminals, which are open daily for all arriving and departing flights. **ATMs** are located throughout both the international and domestic terminals. They accept Visa, MasterCard, American Express, Diner's Club, and all Plus cards.

From the shopping zone, you progress to the 44 Customs and Immigration counters. **Auckland i-SITE Visitor Centre** (℃ **0800/282-552** in New Zealand or 09/367-6009; www.aucklandnz.com), is located in the arrivals hall on the ground floor and is open daily from 7am to 9pm. A luggage wrapping service (for your departure) is available in the ground floor check-in area at Seal 'n' Secure (℃ **09/256-8769**), open Monday to Friday, 5am to 7pm and weekends, 5am to 9pm. For luggage storage, ask at the information center. Rental-car companies and currency exchange are also on the ground floor. **Internet kiosks** are located throughout the public and passenger-only areas in both terminals. A NZ$2 coin buys you 10 minutes online; credit cards are also accepted. **Wireless hotspots** in both terminals offer 1- or 4-hour time allocations; pay by Visa or MasterCard.

The **Domestic Terminal** is a 15-minute walk from the International Terminal. Simply follow the blue-and-white lines painted on the pavement. Alternatively, catch the free inter-terminal bus, which departs every 15 minutes between 5am and 10:30pm. It has been significantly improved after a NZ$42-million makeover, which enlarged retail and check-in areas and expanded security screening points. Another **i-SITE Visitor Centre** is in the arrivals hall of the Domestic Terminal (℃ **09/367-6009**). It's open daily 7am to 5pm. The **Airbus** (℃ **0800/103-080** in NZ;

www.airbus.co.nz) is the best value for transport between the airport and the city. Their bright blue bus runs 24 hours a day (every 15 min. from 6am–7:15pm, every 30 min. from 7:15pm–6am) from the airport to the city, calling at most major hotels and backpacker stops in the city. They run from the city to the airport (check the website for pickup points) every 15 minutes from 7am to 8pm and every 30 minutes from 8pm to 7am. The fare is NZ$16 one-way, NZ$25 round-trip for adults and NZ$6 one-way, and NZ$12 round-trip for children 5 to 15 years old. You buy tickets from the driver. If you're staying in a city hotel on the direct route, the driver will drop you off.

Taxis wait outside the arrivals area (door 8) at the international terminal and outside the luggage collection area (door 4) at the domestic terminal; the fare between the airport and city center is NZ$60 to NZ$80 on weekdays, more on weekends and at night. **Auckland Co-op Taxi** (℃ 09/300-3000) and **Corporate Cabs** (℃ 09/ 377-0773) are reliable choices but all of the companies licensed to service the airport offer a high standard of service.

Numerous shuttle companies will take you from the airport to your inner city lodging for around NZ$30 to NZ$40. **Super Shuttle** (℃ 0800/748-885 in New Zealand or 09/522-5100; www.supershuttle.co.nz) and **Auckland Airport Shuttle** (℃ 09/576-8904) both offer reliable service.

BY TRAIN & COACH (BUS)   The **Britomart Transport Centre** (℃ 09/366-6400; www.maxx.co.nz or www.veoliatransport.co.nz for local rail) has significantly streamlined all transport services. Located at the bottom of Queen Street near the waterfront, in the central business district, the transport exchange is close to ferry terminals and Central City bus stops. It features an underground rail transport center and it is the hub where intercity and commuter rail, buses, taxis, light rail, and ferry services all connect. Britomart has five train platforms, and trains depart from the same platform each day. It's open Monday to Thursday from 5am to 11pm, Friday from 5am to 1am, Saturday from 6:30am to 12:30am, and Sunday from 6:30am to 11pm.

In anticipation of the 2010 Rugby World Cup, Auckland significantly streamlined its bus and rail services. By the time this book hits the shelves, most of these upgrades should be in place, but check the Maxx website for the most up-to-the-minute status information; Britomart station information centers, including a Maxx Information Kiosk inside the Centre, also provide current information. The Maxx Kiosk is open Monday through Friday from 7:30am to 6:30pm, and from 8am to 3:30pm on weekends; it's closed Good Friday and Christmas Day. Most airport shuttles include Britomart in their circuits, and inner city bus services like The Link also travel via Britomart. For more information about current fares, see "Getting Around," below.

The Britomart Transport Centre is open daily. It has storage lockers; electronic visual displays of departure and arrival times; camera security; a cafe, sushi bar, florist, and convenience store; tour operators; toilets; currency exchange; and ATMs.

For information on the Tranz Scenic trains that serve Auckland, contact **TranzRail** (℃ 0800/802-802 in New Zealand or 09/366-6400). **InterCity Coachlines** (℃ 09/623-1503) and **Newmans** (℃ 09/623-1504; www.newmanscoach.co.nz) buses arrive and depart from the SKYCITY Travel Centre Coach Terminal, 102 Hobson St. (℃ 09/913-6100).

BY CAR   If you're driving, you will enter Auckland on **State Highway 1** from the south, on the major motorway system. I advise you to call ahead to your hotel and ask which motorway exit to take. Traffic congestion is an issue in Auckland, especially during morning and evening rush hours. If you don't have to drive in the city, avoid it. Parking is also increasingly expensive.

In Maori, Auckland is known as **Tamaki-Makau-Rau**—"the city of 100 lovers." The name is appropriate, for the area was desired by all and conquered by many. More than 18 Maori tribes have had claims to Auckland at one time or another. The first Maori settlers arrived in Hauraki Gulf about 1,000 years ago; the earliest Maori settlement, a site at Motutapu Island dating to the 1100s, was apparently buried under volcanic dust from the Rangitoto eruption. Of the 48 volcanic cones dotting Auckland's landscape, almost all wear the distinctive horizontal terracing that denotes a Maori *pa* site (essentially a fort built in a high place to defend the Maori).

Visitor Information

There are two centrally located Auckland visitor centers: **i-SITE Visitor Centre–Viaduct Basin,** Princes Wharf, Quay and Hobson streets, downtown; and **i-SITE Visitor Centre** at the Atrium, SKYCITY Auckland, Victoria and Federal streets. Both are open daily from 8am to 8pm. They share a phone number and website (✆ **09/367-6009;** www.aucklandnz.com).

The **Takapuna i-SITE Visitor Centre,** 49 Hurstmere Rd., Takapuna (✆ **09/486-8670;** www.northshorenz.com), is open Monday through Friday from 8:30am to 5pm; and Saturday, Sunday, and public holidays 10am to 3pm. The **Devonport i-SITE Visitor Centre,** 3 Victoria Rd., Devonport (✆ **09/446-0677;** www.northshorenz.com), is open daily from 8:30am to 5pm. All are closed December 25. Other useful resources include the **Department of Conservation Centre** (✆ **09/379-6476;** www.doc.govt.nz), which has information on walks, campgrounds, the gulf islands, and the national parks.

Online, you'll find endless amounts of information on Auckland at the following websites:

o **www.aucklandnz.com**: The home page of Tourism Auckland offers comprehensive listings of events in the Auckland region and helpful information for parents and families.

o **www.maxx.co.nz**: Auckland bus, ferry, and train information.

o **www.aucklandcitylibraries.com**: Information for parents and families.

o **www.akcity.govt.nz/whatson**: The Auckland City Council's guide to events in the city.

o **www.northshorenz.com**: Information on the North Shore.

o **www.destination-waitakere.com**: A source of information about the primary wine region of Auckland.

o **www.manukau.govt.nz**: Information on Manukau City.

o **www.greatbarrier.aucklandnz.com**: Information on Great Barrier Island.

o **www.doc.govt.nz**: The Department of Conservation's information on the national parks and marine reserves.

o **www.waiheke.aucklandnz.com**: Information on Waiheke Island.

Special Events

The annual **Auckland Anniversary Day Regatta ★★★** (✆ **0800/734-2882;** www.regatta.org.nz) attracts local and international entrants on the last Monday in

January. Held in Windsor Reserve in late February, the **Devonport Food & Wine Festival ★** (✆ **09/446-0688** or 445-3011; www.devonportwinefestival.co.nz) offers nonstop entertainment, samples from 20 wineries, and food galore. Jazz, classical music, and opera play a part. The biennial **Auckland Festival ★★★** (✆ **09/309-0101;** www.aucklandfestival.co.nz), a premier arts-and-cultural event held in the last week of September in odd-numbered years (2013, 2015, and so on), celebrates Auckland's distinct characteristics—especially its Pacific style. **New Zealand Fashion Week ★★★**, held in October, presents over 60 New Zealand designers to the world. International buyers and media arrive to check out fashion that is rapidly becoming a "must-see" on the global fashion map; visit www.nzfashionweek.com for details. The fun **Round the Bays Run ★★** (✆ **09/300-6200;** www.roundthebays. co.nz), held in late March, attracts runners from around the South Pacific who participate in the 8km (5-mile) run around the central bays. It ends with a barbecue in one of the city's parks. The **Royal Easter Show ★★** (✆ **09/638-9969;** www.royal eastershow.co.nz), held at the Epsom Showgrounds, focuses on excellence in agriculture and animal husbandry, with fresh produce stalls and the biggest carnival in New Zealand.

City Layout

Greater Auckland is actually a fusion of four cities—Auckland, Manukau, North Shore, and Waitakere. Each is on a motorway network, which crosses the harbor, rivers, creeks, and bays and carries thousands of commuters into the inner city to work. You can pick up a city map at the visitor center, but the **Automobile Association** (✆ **0800/500-213** in New Zealand) has a better one.

MAIN ARTERIES & STREETS The main street is **Queen Street,** which ends in Queen Elizabeth Square at **Customs Street. Quay Street** runs along the Waitemata Harbour. At the top end of Queen Street is **Karangahape Road** (usually called "K'Road"), a mere 2km (1¼ miles) from Quay Street. Within that area you'll find most of the inner city's shops, restaurants, nightspots, major hotels, and bus, rail, and air terminals. The most popular inner city suburbs with the best restaurants are **Parnell** and **Ponsonby. Newmarket** is favored for clothes and shoe shopping.

Neighborhoods in Brief

First, let's get a feel for the four cities. **North Shore City** is contemporary, casual, and cool, with, I'm told, a hint of California; **Central City** and East Auckland are much more cosmopolitan, with a growing Asian community in the wealthy eastern areas. To the west, **Waitakere City** is the principal winegrowing region; it retains strong evidence of early Eastern European settlement from the 1900s. To the south, **Manukau City** is a melting pot of Polynesian, Maori, and European lifestyles. Now on to the main areas:

Inner City It's hard to decide where the inner city begins and ends, but let's say it generally encompasses the central business district. This is where you'll find the major hotels and many attractions, including the boisterous and exciting Viaduct Harbour, home of the former America's Cup Village. It's also where you'll see the clearest evidence of New Zealand's increasingly multicultural society. The High Street/Vulcan Lane area is an "edgy" part of town if you're looking for a good time. Most water-based tours leave from the downtown Quay Street area. This is a great place to base yourself if you don't want to bother with a vehicle; everything is in walking distance.

Ponsonby/Herne Bay This is quintessential Auckland—bold, brazen, bohemian. It's where most of the best restaurants, bars, and cafes are; it's where the nouveau riche and the almost famous hang out; and you'll find some exquisite specialty shops and lots of divine old wooden houses. Some lovely B&Bs are here, and you won't need a car to have fun. Just off Ponsonby Road is **Karangahape Road,** famous for everything from off-the-wall nightclubs and sassy restaurants to ethnic stores and the whole gamut of sex shops, massage parlors, tattoo and body-piercing studios, and strip joints.

Mount Eden/Epsom These leafy, green hillside suburbs reek of old money. You'll find stunning mansions and villas aplenty—not all peopled by resident blue bloods, though, because the area also has a good number of student apartments. Both Mount Eden and Epsom have trendy little villages, where old shops and restaurants have been tarted up so the resident folk can feel they're living on the edge. There are some lovely B&Bs in the area, and it's a very pretty place to base yourself, close to One Tree Hill, Cornwall Park, and the inner city.

Parnell/Newmarket If you want plush, trendy, and sophisticated with an undercurrent of hedonism and excess, this is the suburb for you. Parnell Village is perfectly charming, with lots of super (and expensive) shops and restaurants (with nighttime bar action). It's close to the inner city, the Auckland Museum, and the beautiful Auckland Domain park. There are a few good B&Bs in this area, and in Newmarket, the fashion shopper's Saturday-morning paradise, you'll find heaps of good motels.

Remuera Known locally as "Remmers," this is Auckland's most affluent suburb. Stunning mansions, new high-rise apartments, some great upmarket B&Bs, and an easily accessed village full of specialty shops make it a good base. It's also close to the inner city.

Mission Bay/St. Heliers Wealthy seaside suburbs with big real estate price tags—if you have a Porsche or Ferrari, this is where you bring it to show off on a sunny weekend. Not such a good place to stay if you want to be within walking distance of the city, but it makes a delightful half-day outing. The area boasts lots of excellent restaurants and cafes, and it really buzzes on weekends, with people walking, running, and in-line skating along the waterfront.

Devonport/Takapuna These two neighborhoods lie over the Harbour Bridge, which can be a nightmarish drive in rush-hour traffic, but if you stay in Devonport you won't need a car at all. Simply lock it up, wander the cute village, and catch a ferry to the inner city when you want a faster pace. There are lots of excellent B&Bs here. Takapuna is the main shopping area of the North Shore, but it doesn't have as much character as Devonport.

The Eastern Suburbs Pretty to visit, all very well kept, but too far from inner city action—if that's what you're after. **Pakuranga, Howick,** and **Panmure** do, however, have a quiet beachside charm and are popular with boaties. To the south is **Otara,** home to Auckland's ever-growing Polynesian community.

Staying Safe

Personal safety is always a matter of common sense. Police cameras have been installed in several city areas to reduce crime, but it still pays to be vigilant. Much like public parks anywhere, the Auckland Domain is a place to avoid after dark. And it pays to take care at night in Albert Park and the Aotea Square area.

GETTING AROUND
By Bus

NZ Bus (✆ 09/373-9118; www.nzbus.co.nz), the intracity bus system, offers good service to most city highlights. Within Auckland, they run the North Star, Metrolink, Go West, Waka Pacific, The Link, and the new Inner City Service buses. At the time of writing, a number of significant changes planned to improve bus services around the central business district (CBD) and the suburbs of Parnell, Ponsonby, and Point Chevalier, had begun to roll out. Most should be in place by the time you arrive, but if in doubt, check the Maxx website, or ask for details at the Britomart Transport Centre. You can pick up timetables at Britomart Transport Centre and at the visitor centers listed above. For schedules, fares, and routes, call the company or pick up the free brochure *Auckland's Top Spots by Public Transport* from a visitor center. Fares depend on zones, running from NZ$1.80 to NZ$11. Children 5 to 15 pay half-price; those 4 and under ride free. Exact change is not required. If you intend to ride the bus frequently, spend NZ$12 and get a 1-day **Bus About Pass** for unlimited travel. The pass is good (after 9am) on The Link, Metrolink, North Star, Go West, and Waka Pacific buses. The 1-day **Discovery Pass** (NZ$16) is valid on the above buses, plus trains and Fullers North Shore ferries. There's also a NZ$25 **Family Bus About Pass** for one adult and five children, or two adults and four children traveling together (valid after 9am). Buy passes from the driver or at the terminals.

Warning: Auckland buses stop running around 11:30pm (earlier on some routes) Monday through Saturday, and 10pm on Sunday. If you're planning a night of revelry, count on taking a taxi home; or look out for NZ Bus's **NiteRider Bus** ★★ (✆ 09/366-6400; www.maxx.co.nz), which runs from 1 to 3am on Friday and Saturday. Fares are NZ$6 to NZ$8.

The Link bus service has also been streamlined to speed up the service. It runs both ways in a circuit around the attractions of the inner city rim. These distinctive, environmentally friendly green buses charge a NZ$1.80 fare. The whole circuit takes an hour and includes Quay Park, Downtown, the Britomart Transport Centre, Parnell, Newmarket, Karangahape Road, Ponsonby, SKYCITY, Queen Street, the University, and more. It operates every 10 minutes from 7am to 7pm Monday through Friday, and 7am to 11pm on Saturday; every 15 minutes from 7pm to 11:30pm Monday through Saturday, and 7am to 11pm on Sunday. NZ Bus's About and Discovery passes (see above) are good on The Link. For more information, call **NZ Bus** (see above).

The free **City Circuit bus** is scheduled for replacement by a new frequent **Inner City Service** operated by NZ Bus. It will link Karangahape Road with the waterfront Wynyard Quarter via Queen Street and Britomart Transport Centre. Buses will run every 5 minutes from Britomart up Queen Street from 7am to 7pm on weekdays and every 10 minutes at other times; and every 10 minutes to the Wynyard Quarter from 7am to 7pm, and every 20 minutes at other times. The service is expected to be in place in 2012; see the website for updates, including fees.

A new **Outer Loop Service** based on The Link but taking in a much wider circuit around the suburbs surrounding the CBD, will run every 15 minutes from Britomart Transport Centre. It connects to the main shopping centers of St. Lukes, Mount Eden, and Newmarket, and to MOTAT, Auckland Zoo, and Auckland Museum.

The double-decker **Auckland Explorer Bus** ★★ (✆ 0800/439-756 in NZ, or 09/524-7929; www.explorerbus.co.nz) departs from the Sky Tower or the Ferry Building on Quay Street every half-hour from 9am to 5pm daily in summer and 10am to

If you need help finding your way around the city, keep an eye out for the **Auckland City Ambassadors** (✆ 09/379-2020; www.aucklandcity.govt.nz).

They're decked out in bright yellow jackets and are in the downtown area daily from 9am to 6pm.

5pm in winter. It visits 14 major Auckland attractions; for NZ$40 adults, NZ$20 children 4 to 16, and NZ$90 family, you can hop on and off as many times as you want in a day. They accept Visa.

The other major innovation in the Auckland transport system is **HOP** (✆ 09/366-4467; www.myhop.co.nz), a new smartcard ticketing system that can be used to pay for public transport and lots of everyday items. The first stage of the HOP system was launched on North Star buses, to be followed by Waka Pacific, Go West, then Metrolink and Link bus services. At time of writing it was hoped that HOP would also be used on rail and ferry services by late 2011. Reusable HOP cards can be purchased from Britomart Transport Centre and cost NZ$10. The card can then be loaded with any value from NZ$10 to NZ$300 and the cost of your fare is deducted each time you make a trip. You can also buy a 10-trip pass but these do not allow you to buy everyday items. HOP is being rolled out in phases across Auckland and will eventually be accepted on all New Zealand bus routes. Check the HOP website for progress.

By Taxi

Typical rates start at NZ$5 and go up NZ$2 per kilometer (.62 mile). Cabs can be flagged down, ordered by phone, or picked up at taxi stands. Stands are at all terminals and on the corner of Customs Street West at Queen Street. Call **Auckland Taxi Co-Op** (✆ 09/300-3000; www.cooptaxi.co.nz) or **Corporate Cabs** (✆ 09/377-0773; www.corporatecabs.co.nz).

By Train

Veolia Transport runs between Auckland, Newmarket, Waitakere, Papakura, and Orakei, stopping at Remuera, Mount Eden, Mount Albert, and many other suburbs along the way. Fares range from NZ$1.80 to NZ$11. You can buy 10-trip passes, a **Day Rover Pass** (NZ$12 for adults, NZ$8 for children ages 5–15), or a Family Pass (NZ$24). Special passes are valid after 9am on weekdays and at all other times. Contact Maxx (✆ 09/366-6400; www.maxx.co.nz) for details and schedules.

By Ferry

The **Devonport Ferry** departs every half-hour daily from Pier 1 beside Queen's Wharf, Quay Street (✆ 09/367-9111; www.fullers.co.nz). The fare is NZ$11 round-trip for adults and NZ$5.50 for children ages 5 to 15. Fullers and SeaLink ferries serve Waiheke Island; for details, see "A Side Trip to Waiheke Island" (p. 129).

By Car

Driving in downtown Auckland can be problematic, and finding parking is difficult. Given the efficiency of the Explorer Bus, The Link, and the Inner City Service buses, it's a much better idea to explore the town without a car. However, if you insist, there are parking buildings operated by the City Council on Beresford Street just off Karangahape

Road; near the waterfront on Albert Street, west of Queen Street; on Victoria Street, slightly east of Queen Street; at Britomart off Customs Street, east of Queen Street; downtown to the east of Queen Street; downtown to the west of Queen Street, with an entrance from Customs Street West; Civic Underground on Mayoral Drive; and Victoria Street East. They're all open 24 hours daily; rates can be expensive. Metered car parking is also available. Expect to pay at least NZ$4 an hour in some areas.

By Bicycle

You need to be a competent and confident cyclist to weave through the inner city traffic but a bicycle is a great way to get around the suburbs. You can rent a bike from **Adventure Cycles,** 9 Premier Ave., Western Springs (© **09/940-2453;** www. adventure-auckland.co.nz). It's open Thursday through Monday from 7:30am to 7pm. Rates start at NZ$25 per day and include the mandatory helmet; a tandem rental starts at NZ$40 a day.

[FastFACTS] AUCKLAND

American Express Offices are at 105 Queen St. (© **09/379-8286**) and 67–69 Symonds St. (© **09/367-4422**). For credit card queries, call © **0800/656-660;** for traveler's check queries, © **0508/555-358.** Find them online at www.americanexpress.co.nz.

Area Code Auckland's area code (STD) is **09.**

Babysitters Most major hotels can furnish babysitters.

Currency Exchange Go to city center banks and most neighborhood branches for your banking needs. Banks are open Monday through Friday from 9am to 4:30pm. Hotels and restaurants usually convert traveler's checks, but you'll get a much better rate at banks. There is a dedicated currency exchange outlet at **Travelex NZ,** Brookfields House, Level 14/19, Victoria St. W. (© **0800/082-082;** www.travelex.co.nz; open normal business hours), and

at SKYCITY and at both the Auckland International Airport and the Domestic Airport (open daily during normal business hours).

Dentists For emergency and after-hours dental service, call **Emergency Dental Service,** on the corner of Greenlane East Road and Peach Parade, Remuera (© **09/523-3030;** www.dentistryforchickens.co.nz). It's open Monday through Friday from 8am to 11pm, Sunday until 10pm.

Doctors For emergency ambulance service, dial © **111.** For emergency medical services, call the **CityMed Medical Centre,** on the corner of Mills Lane and Albert Street, inner city (© **09/377-5525;** www.citymed.co.nz).

Embassies & Consulates Embassies are in Wellington (see "Fast Facts: Wellington," in chapter 11). For additional information on embassies in New Zealand, contact the **Ministry of Foreign Affairs & Trade**

in Wellington (© **04/494-8500;** www.mft.govt.nz; enquiries@mft.govt.nz).

Auckland has consulates of the **United States,** Level 3, 23 Customs St. E. (© **09/303-2724;** fax 09/366-0870); **Canada,** Level 9, 48 Emily Place (© **09/309-3690**); **Ireland,** Level 7, 23 Customs St. E. (© **09/977-2252**); and the **United Kingdom,** IAG House, 151 Queen St. (© **09/303-2973**).

Emergencies Dial © **111** to call the police, report a fire, or request an ambulance.

Hospitals Area hospitals include **Auckland City Hospital,** 2 Park Rd., Grafton (© **09/367-7000**), which incorporates the National Women's Hospital and the Starship Children's Hospital; and **Greenlane Clinical Centre,** 214 Greenlane West Rd., Epsom (© **09/367-0000**).

Internet Access Give either of these a go: **Cyber Max,** 291 Queen St. (© **09/979-2468**); or **Net Central**

Cyber Café, 5 Lorne St. ((C) **09/373-5408**).

Laundromat There is a 24-hour laundromat at 511 Great North Rd., Grey Lynn ((C) **09/376-6062**).

Lost Property Call the Central Police Station ((C) **09/379-4240**) or any local police station.

Luggage Storage & Lockers "Left luggage" facilities are at the Visitor Information Centre in the International Airport. The fee for 24 hours is about NZ$8 for hand luggage, NZ$15 for large items, and NZ$12 per suitcase. For more information, call (C) **09/256-8845.**

Newspapers & Magazines The *New Zealand Herald* is the daily paper. The *Sunday Star Times* and *Sunday News* are Sunday-morning publications.

Police For emergencies, dial (C) **111**. For other matters, call the Central Police Station ((C) **09/379-4240**).

Post Office Most post offices are open Monday through Friday from 9am to 5pm. The central city Post Shop is at 23 Customs St. E. ((C) **09/302-1059**); it's open Monday through Friday from 9am to 5pm, and Saturday from 9am to noon. For *poste restante* (held mail) pickup, go to the Post Shop in the Bledisloe Building on Wellesley Street ((C) **09/379-6714**).

There is also a Post Shop on the ground floor of Courier Post House, 151 Victoria St. W. ((C) **09/367-9617**); and others in suburban locations. For post office questions, call (C) **0800/501-501**; www.nzpost.co.nz.

Services for Travelers with Disabilities For information on ramps, toilets, parking lots, telephones, and an equipment showroom, contact the **Disability Resource Centre,** 14 Erson Ave., Royal Oak ((C) **09/625-8069**; www.disabilityresource.org.nz). Both The Link and City Circuit bus routes have wheelchair-accessible buses.

WHERE TO STAY

If your idea of a holiday is the best views, the best beds, the best food, and the last word in service, Auckland's luxury hotels won't disappoint. For longer stays, there are plenty of fully serviced apartments, which give you more flexibility and independence. Among the best options is **CityLife Auckland A Heritage Hotel ★**, 171 Queen St. (www.heritagehotels.co.nz; (C) **0800/368-888** in NZ, or 09/379-9222), with 210 one- to three-bedroom suites and hotel rooms from NZ$275 to NZ$989. Or treat yourself to their penthouse suite for NZ$1,818. It's located directly above central Queens Street and is a handy walk to all the main attractions.

You won't find many B&Bs in the central city, but they are plentiful a little further out in the suburbs.

Rates listed here include 15% GST (goods and services tax) and parking, unless stated otherwise; all accommodations are non-smoking.

In the Inner City

VERY EXPENSIVE

Hilton Auckland ★★★ There's no other Hilton in the world quite like this boutique-style property, which opened in 2001. It's almost completely surrounded by water, perched on the end of Princes Wharf like the giant ship that inspired it and like those that dock alongside it. Rooms are modern, sophisticated, stylish—not overly large in some cases, but always exquisitely furnished, with fabulous bathrooms and amazing sea views. For even better views, opt for 1 of the 12 deluxe corner rooms that feature two whole walls of glass. The suites are shaped like the bow of a ship and boast vast decks. Ask about the presidential suite for ultimate luxury. The hotel is right in the heart of Viaduct Harbour, amid the best restaurants and bars in Auckland.

Central Auckland

St. Marys Bay

Madden St.

Pakenham Rd.

Poore St.

Beaumont St.

Guant St.

Halsey St.

Freemans Bay

Western Viaduct

Viaduct Basin

Princes Wharf

Air New Zealand

Queen Elizabeth II Sq.

Customs St. West

Market Place

Wolfe St.

Swanson St.

St. Patrick's Sq.

Wyndham St.

Gorst Ln.

Kingston St.

Durham St. West

High St.

Fanshawe St.

Hardinge St.

Victoria St. West

Nelson St.

Victoria St. West

Durham St. East

Hobson St.

Federal St.

Albert St.

Elliot St.

Lorne St.

Kitchener St.

VICTORIA PARK

Drake St.

Sale St.

Wellesley St. West

Cook St.

Visitor Information Centre

Aotea Sq.

Rutland St.

St. Paul

Vincent St.

Mayoral Dr.

Greys Ave.

White St.

Airedale St.

MYERS PARK

Turner St.

Pitt St.

Liverpool St.

City Rd.

Karangahape Rd.

Upper Queen St.

CEMETERY

CEMETERY

Grafton Bridge

HOTELS ■

Abaco on Jervois **10**
Amora Hotel Auckland **17**
Ascott Parnell **34**
Auckland International Hostel-YHA **20**
Braemar on Parliament Street **29**
The Brown Kiwi Travellers Hostel **9**
CityLife Auckland **15**
The Elliott Hotel **16**
The Great Ponsonby Arthotel **18**
Heritage Auckland **8**
Hilton Auckland **3**
Hotel DeBrett **25**
Kiwi International Hotel **19**
Langham Hotel Auckland **23**
Mollies on Tweed **18**
Omahu Lodge **34**
Quest Parnell **31**
Remuera Motor Lodge & Inner City
   Camping Ground **34**
Scenic Hotel Auckland **22**
SKYCITY Grand Hotel **13**

RESTAURANTS ◆
Clooney **11**
DINE by Peter Gordon **13**
Eight **23**
Euro **4**
The French Café **30**
The Grove **7**
Harbourside Seafood Bar
& Grill **5**
O'Connell Street Bistro **26**
Orbit **12**
Pastis **14**
Pita Pit Britomart **27**
Smart Sushi **28**
Soul Bar & Bistro **6**
Takuki's Cave **21**

ATTRACTIONS ●
America's Cup Village **1**
Auckland Art Gallery **24**
Auckland Museum **33**
New Zealand National
Maritime Museum **2**
Parnell shops **32**
Sky Tower **12**

(i) **Information**
✉ **Post Office**

5

Princes Wharf, 137-147 Quay St. www.hilton.com. ⓒ **0800/448-002** in NZ, or 09/978-2000. Fax 09/978-2001. 165 units. NZ$710–NZ$880 guest and deluxe rooms; NZ$1,310–NZ$2,210 suite. Off-season and special rates available. AE, DC, MC, V. Valet parking NZ$40. **Amenities:** Restaurant; bar; babysitting; concierge; gym w/trainer; glass-fronted heated outdoor pool suspended from 4th-floor bridge; room service. *In room:* A/C, TV, fridge, hair dryer, minibar, Wi-Fi.

Langham Hotel Auckland ★★★ Fresh from a sumptuous multimillion-dollar makeover, this business favorite is now Auckland's plushest hotel. They have service down to a fine art and staff are the friendliest in the city. All rooms are opulent but the four floors of Club Rooms offer that little bit extra: king-size beds and lovely marble bathrooms, plus Club Lounge access and business facilities. The hotel has Green Globe Certification and was awarded Qualmark Enviro-Gold status in 2008. Treat yourself to dinner in **Barolo**—it's a feast for the eye and the stomach. Overall, the Langham is more traditional than the Hilton and much larger.

83 Symonds St. www.langhamhotels.com. ⓒ **0800/616-261** in NZ, or 09/379-5132. Fax 09/377-9367. 411 units. NZ$315–NZ$370 classic & executive; From NZ$495 Langham hotel club rooms; NZ$635–NZ$2,845 suite. Leisure packages and long-stay rates. AE, DC, MC, V. Valet parking NZ$30. **Amenities:** 3 restaurants; 2 bars; limousine airport transfers (NZ$75–NZ$90); babysitting; concierge; concierge-level rooms; health club w/fully equipped gym and trainer; Jacuzzi; heated rooftop lap pool; room service; 2 saunas; Chuan day spa; Wi-Fi in lobby. *In room:* A/C, TV/DVD, fridge, hair dryer, Wi-Fi & Internet, kitchenette in studio suites, minibar.

SKYCITY Grand Hotel ★★★ This is the five-star baby in the SKYCITY stable. Linked to the SKYCITY hotel and casino complex by a bridge, it offers the best of everything: smart rooms with good bathrooms, one of the best restaurants in Auckland (**DINE by Peter Gordon;** see p. 102), and a gorgeous lap pool and spa facility. It's a centrally located oasis of luxury offering very good deals and a wow-factor New Zealand contemporary art collection. It's close to the heart of SKYCITY activity, which is always a busy, happening hub. It's much bigger than the Hilton and less formal than the Langham. The hotel has a Qualmark Enviro-Gold rating.

90 Federal St. www.skycitygrand.co.nz. ⓒ **0800/759-2489** in NZ, or 09/363-6000. Fax 09/363-7010. 314 units. From NZ$619 luxury king or twin room; From NZ$1,130 suites. Long-stay, off-peak, and special rates. AE, DC, MC, V. Valet parking NZ$30. **Amenities:** 2 restaurants; 2 bars; Mercedes airport transfers from NZ$110 one-way; babysitting; concierge; gym; Jacuzzi; heated indoor lap pool; room service; sauna; East West Day Spa, specializing in Eastern-style holistic treatments; Wi-Fi and business center in lobby. *In room:* A/C, TV/DVD, fridge, hair dryer, Internet, minibar.

EXPENSIVE

The Elliot Hotel ★ Take a 145-year-old historic building and refurbish it for the modern age and you get this classic-styled boutique hotel right in the heart of the city. You couldn't wish for a better location, just a few steps off Queen Street and close to the Sky Tower. The self-contained apartments are equipped with everything you need, including a kitchen, washing machine, and dryer; high ceilings lend an air of graciousness and old world charm. Best of all, you're right on top of The Stables Epicurean Village and hotel guests can enjoy charge-back facilities at the numerous cafes, bars, and restaurants there.

15-31 Wellesley St. www.theelliothotel.com. ⓒ **0800/565-665** in NZ, or 09/308-9334. Fax 09/308-9344. 60 units. NZ$455 studio; NZ$515 1-bedroom suite; NZ$575 executive studio; NZ$750 2-bedroom suite. Long-stay and special deals. AE, DC, MC, V. Limited onsite parking NZ$20 per night. **Amenities:** Nearby restaurants and bars, many w/charge-back facility for guests. *In room:* A/C, TV/DVD, fridge, hair dryer, Internet, fully equipped kitchen, laundry, minibar.

Heritage Auckland ★★ The Heritage has size, location, and friendly service on its side. Just a short walk from main shopping and entertainment areas, the hotel

Devonport

HOTELS ◼
Admirals Landing **3**
The Captain's Landing **5**
Peace & Plenty Inn **4**

RESTAURANTS ◆
Monsoon **2**

ATTRACTIONS ●
Devonport Museum **1**
Devonport Naval
    Museum **6**

comprises two distinct parts—the Hotel wing in a restored, landmark Art Deco building; and the purpose-built contemporary Tower wing—completed in 1998 and 1999, respectively. All rooms are generous suite-style units with good-size bathrooms. A slight premium applies on the self-contained Tower suites, many of which boast great harbor views. The hotel attracts a wide range of visitors from international performers and sports teams to business and leisure travelers. It has a Qualmark Enviro-Gold rating.

Hotel Wing, 35 Hobson St.; Tower Wing, 22 Nelson St. www.heritagehotels.co.nz. © **0800/368-888** in NZ, or 09/379-8553. Fax 09/379-8554. 274 units. NZ$289 superior room; NZ$314–NZ$621 suite. Long-stay, off-peak, and special rates. AE, DC, MC, V. Valet parking NZ$35. **Amenities:** 2 restaurants; 2 bars; babysitting; concierge; 2 gyms; 2 Jacuzzis; rooftop heated outdoor pool; heated indoor lap pool; room service; sauna; all-weather outdoor lit tennis court; Wi-Fi throughout. *In room:* A/C, TV, fridge, hair dryer, kitchenette and full kitchen, Internet, minibar.

Hotel DeBrett ★★   Small, chic, and a great value, this boutique gem is nestled in the heart of High Street's fashion district. Set in a restored, historic building, the rooms are individually decorated in mid-century modern style, showcasing New Zealand arts and crafts. It's colorful, contemporary, and individual, and filled with various meeting spots. Not surprisingly, it's a favorite with business visitors and those who want to be in close contact with some of Auckland's classiest stores and restaurants.

Owners John Courtney and Michelle Deery have imbued the place with an exciting energy and they've set high standards in service. And if you like books, you'll love the drawing room, stocked with the couple's collection of art, books, music, and movies.

2 High St. www.hoteldebrett.com. ☎ **09/925-9000.** 25 units. NZ$300 classic room; NZ$400 boutique suite; NZ$500 O'Connell suites; NZ$600 loft suites. Special deals. Children under 16 free of charge. Rates include continental breakfast, pre-dinner drink, 24-hour room service, free Internet and Wi-Fi, and free local calls. AE, DC, MC, V. Valet parking NZ$20 per night. **Amenities:** Restaurant; bar; babysitting; concierge; nearby gym; massage; 24-hr room service. *In room:* A/C, TV/DVD, fridge, hairdryer, Wi-Fi, minibar.

MODERATE

Amora Hotel Auckland ★   There is something intangibly serene about the Amora (previously The Duxton). Maybe it's the location on a leafy, tree-lined street, or the green park the Amora overlooks. Either way, it's quieter and more intimate than some of the bigger hotels. Treat yourself to a special executive suite Jacuzzi package that includes breakfast and Internet access. Apartments with full laundry facilities and kitchens are also a big plus.

100 Greys Ave. www.auckland.amorahotels.com. ☎ **0800/155-555** in NZ, or 09/375-1800. Fax 09/375-1801. 149 units. NZ$185–NZ$275 deluxe; NZ$285–NZ$325 executive suite; NZ$385–NZ$425 penthouse suite. Long-stay, off-peak, and special rates. AE, DC, MC, V. Valet parking NZ$30 per day; self-parking NZ$15 per day. **Amenities:** Restaurant; bar; airport transfers (NZ$75 one-way); babysitting; concierge; guest access to small gym across road (NZ$15 day pass); Jacuzzi; outdoor heated pool; room service; Wi-Fi in lobby. *In room:* A/C, TV/DVD, fridge, hair dryer, Internet, kitchenette, minibar.

Braemar on Parliament Street   History and character are at the heart of this three-story Edwardian gentleman's town house (ca. 1901); you feel it as soon as you walk in. Four rooms—two with en-suite bathrooms, two with shared bathroom—are riddled with charm. The Batten Suite (once home to legendary pilot Jean Batten's father) is the best and biggest. John and Susan Sweetman have an astonishing collection of historic Auckland photographs, and the numerous Persian rugs and colonial antiques make this place a feast for the eye and a home away from home. It's the only upmarket B&B in the central business district and it's just a short walk from trendy High Street, downtown activities, restaurants, and transport systems. Braemar earned its Qualmark Enviro-Gold rating for its ecofriendly approach to hosting, energy conservation, and recycling.

7 Parliament St. www.aucklandbedandbreakfast.com. ☎ **0800/155-463** in NZ, or 09/377-5463. Fax 09/377-3056. 4 units. NZ$225–NZ$350. Long-stay rates. Rates include breakfast. AE, DC, MC, V. Free parking. **Amenities:** Babysitting; free bikes; nearby golf course, pool, and tennis courts. *In room:* TV, hair dryer, Wi-Fi.

INEXPENSIVE

For a sensibly priced stay in a landmark building right in the heart of the city, **Scenic Hotel Auckland,** 380 Queen St. (www.scenichotelgroup.co.nz; ☎ **0800/696-963** or 09/374-1741), offers 100 very comfortable rooms priced from NZ$230 to NZ$529. Ask for one of the eight rooms on the northwest face, which boast incredible views straight down Queen Street. It's a modest but perfectly situated option with a good cafe and bar at street level.

Budget travelers will find a clean, affordable spot right in the heart of the city at the 120-room **Kiwi International Hotel,** 411 Queen St. (www.kiwihotel.co.nz; ☎ **0800/100-411** in NZ, or 09/379-6487). Recently renovated, it offers en-suite (NZ$95), economy (NZ$65), or family rooms (NZ$139), plus a family apartment (NZ$149) that sleeps five. It's within walking distance to all major attractions, shops, and restaurants, and it has its own bar and restaurant and Internet access.

Auckland International Hostel-YHA   This hostel opened in mid-1999 in a large converted office block and it's now one of the best hostels in the country, serving over 50,000 guests each year. Everything is clean, modern, and comfortable, and security is tight. It's just a 5-minute walk to Central City. This is the flagship YHA hostel; its sister establishment, Auckland City YHA, is only 100m (330 ft.) away. This facility has a communal lounge, a smokers' room, bike and luggage storage, and large kitchens.

1-35 Turner St. (P.O. Box 68-149). www.yha.co.nz. © **0800/278-299** in NZ, or 09/302-8200. Fax 09/302-8205. 170 beds. NZ$24–NZ$30 dorm space; NZ$82–NZ$109 private room. NZ$3 extra per person per night for non-YHA members. AE, MC, V. Limited off-street parking NZ$10; reservation required. *In room:* No phone.

In Ponsonby
VERY EXPENSIVE
Mollies on Tweed ★★★   A member of the Small Luxury Hotels of the World, Mollies has accumulated plenty of international accolades, and its award-winning gourmet restaurant, **The Dining Room** (p. 104), complete with dining terrace, is definitely a must-have experience. The grand old 1870s home has been extensively renovated and expanded to provide 13 stylish suites and apartments. If you take the upstairs level, you'll have a balcony; downstairs rooms open onto the garden. Nothing has been spared to create gorgeous interiors filled with antiques and smart furniture. The location is handy to Ponsonby Road restaurants, bars, and boutique shopping. Mollies combines the comforts of home with the privacy of apartment living.

6 Tweed St., St. Mary's Bay. www.mollies.co.nz. © **09/376-3489.** Fax 09/378-6592. 13 units. NZ$690 junior suite; NZ$920 villa suite; NZ$1,150 premier villa suite. Off-season, long-stay, and weekend rates. Rates include breakfast. AE, DC, MC, V. Free off-street parking. Children 11 and under on request only. **Amenities:** Restaurant; bar; airport transfer (NZ$140 one-way); babysitting (NZ$35 per hour); concierge; day spa; 24-hr. room service. *In room:* A/C (apts. only), TV/DVD, fridge, hair dryer, minibar, Wi-Fi.

MODERATE
If you want an excellent motel close to Ponsonby action, look no further than **Abaco on Jervois,** 59 Jervois Rd. (www.abaco.co.nz; © **0800/220-066** in NZ, or 09/360-6850; fax 09/360-6869). They offer a range of immaculate, modern rooms priced from NZ$125 to NZ$205. Executive and premium suites on the middle and top levels are the best and biggest. Premium suites have a Jacuzzi, shower, separate lounge, desk, kitchen, and free Internet. The complex is directly across the road from popular restaurants, bars, and cafes.

The Great Ponsonby Arthotel ★   This restored villa, owned by hosts Sally James and Gerard Hill, will delight you with its quiet location within walking distance of the best of Ponsonby. Comfortable rooms reflect a colorful Pacific mood. Three suites have both bathtubs and showers. The lovely Dunedin Room has its own deck, while the upstairs penthouse has a sitting room and balcony. Don't overlook the Palm Garden studios if you want extra space and privacy; some of these come with kitchenette, minibar, and DVD player. There's a sunlit lounge bulging with books, lots of New Zealand art and magazines, verandas for unwinding, and breakfasts to linger over. The property has a Qualmark Enviro-Gold rating and participates in recycling and energy conservation programs.

30 Ponsonby Terrace. www.greatpons.co.nz. © **0800/766-792** in NZ, or 09/376-5989. Fax 09/376-6527. 11 units. NZ$245 villa rooms; NZ$265 courtyard studios; NZ$325 palm garden suite; NZ$400 penthouse. Off-peak rates. Rates include breakfast. AE, DC, MC, V. Free off-street parking. Children 11 and under in some rooms. **Amenities:** Fixed-price taxi airport transfers; babysitting; free use of bikes;

5

AUCKLAND | Where to Stay

nearby golf course and pool. *In room:* LCD TV/DVD, fridge (in some), hair dryer, kitchenette (in some), minibar (in some), MP3 docking station, free Wi-Fi.

INEXPENSIVE

The Brown Kiwi Travellers Hostel   This 100-year-old house is on a quiet street just a block from the main Ponsonby action. The best deals here are the two rooms in the lovely little garden house, a purpose-built corrugated-iron dwelling tucked among banana palms and ponds. It serves as a double or triple facility and is less sardinelike than the in-house rooms. Overall, this place offers a good atmosphere and a terrific garden courtyard in which to while away summer days and nights.

7 Prosford St. www.brownkiwi.co.nz. ✆/fax **09/378-0191.** 32 beds, all with shared bathroom. NZ$28–NZ$35 dorm per person; NZ$38–NZ$65 twin/double. Discount for BBH Club Card members. MC, V. **Amenities:** Bar. *In room:* Hair dryer.

In Mount Eden/Epsom

INEXPENSIVE

Bavaria Bed & Breakfast Hotel   You can immerse yourself in the quiet leafy suburbs here, at the same time feeling like part of some large international family. The hotel states FREE STATE OF BAVARIA on the gate, and Rudi and Ulrike Stephan get a lot of German guests. But it's a cosmopolitan establishment equally enjoyed by large numbers of Americans and Canadians. The three upstairs rooms are the sunniest, and all have doors leading out onto the balcony. All units have en-suite bathrooms. The big, old villa is close to Mount Eden village, where there are several restaurants and cafes, and you can catch buses on nearby Dominion Road heading into the city, which is 10 minutes away. You can feel good about your stay here, because Bavaria uses solar energy and environmentally friendly cleaning products.

> **One Tree Hill**
>
> A stroll in **Cornwall Park** in Epsom is a must. You'll find fields with grazing sheep, charming walks, and One Tree Hill, which is famous for its lone tree. Stop first at the **Cornwall Park Visitor Centre** (✆ 09/630-8485; www.cornwallpark.co.nz) for maps and information on self-guided walks.

83 Valley Rd., Mount Eden. www.bavariabandbhotel.co.nz. ✆ **09/638-9641.** Fax 09/638-9665. 11 units. NZ$180; NZ$50 each extra adult; NZ$25 children 2–12; free for children 1 and under. Off-season and long-stay rates. Rates include breakfast. MC, V. Free off-street parking. **Amenities:** Nearby golf course; nearby tennis courts. *In room:* Hair dryer on request, free Wi-Fi throughout.

In Parnell/Newmarket

MODERATE

Ascot Parnell   Experienced hosts Bart and Therese Blommaert will meet you in person at the airport and take you back to one of the beautiful, ecofriendly suites in their modern apartment complex. It's a lovely location down a long, private driveway and just a short walk up the street to Parnell Village. The Blommaerts have been welcoming guests in various locations for nearly 20 years so they know just how to make you feel at home.

32 St. Stephens Ave., Parnell. www.ascotparnell.com. ✆ **09/309-9012.** Fax 09/309-3729. 3 units. NZ$225–NZ$385. Long stay & off-peak rates. Rates include breakfast. AE, DC, MC, V. Children over 10 only. Free off-street parking. **Amenities:** Airport transfers (NZ$75); free Wi-Fi throughout; outdoor pool (summer only); nearby tennis courts. *In room:* A/C, fridge, hairdryer, minibar.

Scented Heaven

You don't have to be a rose lover to appreciate the intoxicating perfumes that rise from Parnell's beautiful rose gardens at **Dove-Myer Robinson Park.** The 5,000 rose bushes laid out in formal beds make the park the perfect picnic spot. And look out for the gorgeous and historic little **St. Stephen's Chapel,** one of the city's first churches. Access to both is off Gladstone Road and Judges Bay Road.

Quest Parnell ✦ This modern, serviced apartment complex has everything you need: great location, excellent-value special deals, a beautiful swimming pool, and clean, fresh rooms (studios, and one- and two-bedrooms apartments available). Popular with both corporate and leisure visitors, it's perfectly located at the bottom of Parnell Village. There's a bit of an uphill walk to the shops and restaurants but that's a small price to pay for such good value. Rooms are modest and very well maintained and come with kitchen and laundry facilities. There's also an onsite gym.

8 Heather St., Parnell. www.questparnell.co.nz. ℂ **0800/804-808** in NZ, or 09/337-0804. Fax 09/337-0805. 40 units. NZ$185–NZ$310. Long stay & special deals. AE, DC, MC, V. Parking NZ$12 per night. **Amenities:** Restaurant & cafe charge-back; concierge; gym; heated pool. *In room:* TV, kitchen, laundry, hairdryer, Wi-Fi.

In Remuera
MODERATE
Omahu Lodge ★ ✦ Ken and Robyn Booth completely refurbished their elegant suites in 2011 and you'll be hard-pressed to find better value in this pricey suburb. All rooms have lovely views—whether they be of leafy One Tree Hill or the Omahu's beautiful swimming complex. The Poolside Suite has French doors opening to the water, plus its own lounge and a fernery off the bathroom. The upstairs Omahu room is the largest. All are beautifully fitted out with antiques and large modern bathrooms.

33 Omahu Rd., Remuera. www.omahulodge.co.nz. ℂ/fax **09/524-5648.** 4 units. NZ$220–NZ$350. MC, V. Rates include breakfast. **Amenities:** Nearby golf course; solar heated swimming pool; sauna; Jacuzzi. *In room:* TV, hairdryer, Wi-Fi.

INEXPENSIVE
If you're traveling by camper, you'll find excellent facilities at **Remuera Motor Lodge & Inner City Camping Ground,** 16 Minto Rd., Remuera (remlodge@ihug.co.nz; ℂ **0508/244-244** in NZ, or 09/524-5126). Its parklike setting includes motel units; tent, caravan, and campervan sites; communal facilities; a swimming pool; and Wi-Fi access. Unpowered tent sites are NZ$17 per adult per night (NZ$10 children under 15); a powered site is NZ$20 per night per person; and motel units are NZ$75 per night per person (NZ$15 each extra adult, NZ$10 child).

In Devonport/Birkenhead
EXPENSIVE
Peace & Plenty Inn ★ 📷 Romantics will love this gorgeous old home, which Judy Machin has transformed into the ultimate sumptuous, floral-themed haven. Every room has an en-suite bathroom—two with tub and shower, the rest shower only. The downstairs Albert room is the smallest unit but has the best bathroom; the Windsor is the biggest. Three upstairs rooms are sunny, with views and balconies.

Sunset Views

Take a picnic basket and go up the easy 10-minute bush walk to the top of Mount Hobson in Remuera. Watch the sun go down over wonderful 360-degree views of the harbor and city. Access to Mount Hobson Reserve is signposted on Remuera Road, just before you reach the village.

The whole place oozes character and ambience. The garden suite overlooks the lush subtropical garden, and the property has a Qualmark Silver-Shield for Responsible Tourism.

6 Flagstaff Terrace, Devonport. www.peaceandplenty.co.nz. ☏ **09/445-2925.** Fax 09/445-2901. 7 units. NZ$375. Long-stay and off-peak rates. Rates include breakfast. MC, V. **Amenities:** Airport transfers (NZ$100); babysitting; bike rentals; nearby golf course and tennis courts; massage. *In room:* TV, fridge (in some), hair dryer, Wi-Fi.

Stafford Villa ★★ 🎁 Guests lavish praise upon the Stafford Villa's posh B&B experience. Once home to a missionary family, the old two-story home, set in a quaint and tranquil Victorian suburb, was transformed by the industrious Mark and Chris Windram. Chris spent many years marketing small luxury hotels and resorts around the world, so she has a pretty keen idea of what makes a good holiday experience. The two rooms are lush and indulgent—"just a little over the top," says Chris, who believes guests like something different. You can breakfast in the conservatory, tucking into local produce and homemade preserves from the garden; and then take a 5-minute walk to the ferry and end up in downtown Auckland just 10 minutes later.

2 Awanui St., Birkenhead Point. www.staffordvilla.co.nz. ☏ **09/418-3022.** Fax 09/419-8197. 2 units. NZ$450. Rates include full breakfast, pre-dinner aperitif, and canapés. Long-stay and special rates, and weekend packages. AE, DC, MC, V. Free off-street parking. **Amenities:** Airport transfers (NZ$110–NZ$125 one-way); babysitting (NZ$20 per hour); nearby golf course; Wi-Fi in library. *In room:* A/C, LCD TV/DVD/CD, hair dryer, Wi-Fi.

MODERATE

Admirals Landing This waterfront home owned by well-traveled Howard and Joy Mace is typical of all that's good about staying in Devonport. It's just a short walk to over 30 restaurants and cafes, village shops, a golf course, and some of Auckland's best beaches. Rooms are light and bright with everything you'll need for a comfortable stay; the Waterfront Room has a large balcony with excellent views. Howard served as a military dentist and in addition to operating in London's Harley Street, he and Joy have lived in Indonesia. They have good stories to share.

11 Queens Parade, Devonport. www.admiralslanding.co.nz. ☏ **09/445-4394.** 3 units. NZ$255–NZ$285. Rates include breakfast. AE, DC, MC, V. **Amenities:** Nearby golf course. In room: TV, fridge, hair dryer, Wi-Fi.

The Captain's Landing The Captain's Landing promises single party booking so you're guaranteed to get a beautifully appointed bedroom (two, if your party requires it) and your own sitting room in this modern home on Devonport's waterfront. It's a leisurely 2-minute walk to the village and just 5 minutes from the ferry terminal, and Captain Bo Ekman and his wife, Margaret, go out of their way to make your retreat a restful one. Glass doors open onto a big private deck area where you can enjoy the sun; and the sitting room is filled with comfortable chairs and plenty of books, including some of Bo's own memorabilia from his shipping experiences around the world.

22 King Edward Parade, Devonport. www.thecaptainslanding.co.nz. ℰ **09/445-4188.** 2 units. NZ$280. NZ$100 for each extra person. No credit cards. Long stay & off-peak rates. Rates include breakfast. Closed June–Aug. **Amenities:** Nearby golf course. In room: TV/DVD, fridge, hair dryer, Wi-Fi.

In the Western Suburbs

Beach lovers should consider **Bethells Beach Cottages,** 267 Bethells Rd., Bethells Beach, Waitakere (www.bethellsbeach.com; ℰ **09/810-9581;** 2-night minimum stay), where two sunny, self-contained holiday cottages and a self-contained apartment are set in lush, private gardens—the ultimate Kiwi getaway—for NZ$250 to NZ$355, plus NZ$35 to NZ$45 for each extra adult guest and NZ$18 to NZ$23 for each child. Owners John and Trude Bethell Paice are very ecoaware and their accommodation has Green Globe 21 status aligned with Waitakere City Eco Plan. The pair have extensive knowledge of the Auckland region and are happy to help their guests find the best places to visit. And let's not forget the free Scandinavian hot tub!

Near the Airport

If you have an early-morning flight or you're checking into Auckland at night and want a quick bed, you can now stay in one of two new hotels right beside the airport. **Hotel Novotel Auckland Airport,** Auckland International Airport, Ray Emery Drive (www.novotel.com; ℰ **09/365-0000;** fax 09/365-0011), opened in mid-2011 in time for the Rugby World Cup. It is physically attached to the International Airport. Rooms range from around NZ$165 to NZ$300, and they have excellent online special deals. For the budget-conscious traveler, there are even better deals just a couple of minutes from the airport, at the **Formule 1 Hotel** (www.hotelformule1.com or www.aucklandairport.co.nz; no phone at press time), at the intersection of Leonard Isitt and John Goulter drives, Auckland International Airport. The property, which opened in August 2011, offers simple, functional, comfortable rooms for an incredible NZ$65 a night; if you stay multiple nights, the deal gets even sweeter.

WHERE TO EAT

You get no points for finding a brilliant restaurant in Auckland; there are too many of them for that to be considered a feat. And a good number of them are offering world-class cuisine at very affordable prices. The predominant cuisines are ethnic and Pacific Rim or fusion, the latter being that variable trend of combining the freshest, high-quality ingredients with whatever cultural element (theoretically Pacific-based) grabs the chef's fancy. As you can imagine, the interpretations are endless.

Although restaurants are scattered all over the city, you'll find they rub shoulders with each other in the Viaduct Harbour area, in the Britomart Precinct, and along Ponsonby Road—still the trendiest areas and favorites with big spenders. There is also a good haul along the downtown waterfront, at Mission Bay, and in Devonport and Takapuna on the North Shore. You can take your pick from innumerable Italian/Mediterranean-style eateries with starched white tablecloths and timber floors, and fashionable California/New York–style brasseries and elegant bistros. If you're looking for cheap eats, they abound throughout the city. There are literally thousands of places to choose from and you're seldom far from any of them—Asian restaurants and sushi bars in particular.

If you've singled out a popular favorite, it's a good idea to make reservations, especially on weekends, but in many cases you can simply stroll and choose. Tipping is perfectly in order but is not a custom anywhere in New Zealand.

A word on wine: New Zealand restaurants are generally classified as **licensed** (to sell beer, wine, and spirits) or **BYO** (bring your own). Some stipulate wine only (and may charge a corkage fee), or are unlicensed.

In the Inner City

EXPENSIVE

Harbourside Seafood Bar & Grill ★, first floor, Ferry Building, Quay Street (*©* **09/307-0556;** www.harboursiderestaurant.co.nz), is a chic place with great views and seriously good seafood. Two others not to be missed are **O'Connell Street Bistro ★★**, O'Connell and Shortland streets (*©* **09/377-1884**), a tiny but perfect 28-seat restaurant that's big on international style and flavors—definitely a place for special moments; and **Soul Bar & Bistro ★★**, Hobson and Customs Street West (*©* **09/356-7249;** www.soulbar.co.nz), which is now an institution in a prime Viaduct Harbour location with fabulous people-watching potential. Top chefs, an open-air style, and the best New Zealand fish make it a winner with international travelers, the business crowd, and high-flyers in general.

Clooney ★★★ INTERNATIONAL   Once an industrial warehouse and now one of Auckland's top dining experiences, this highly ranked dining space is a complete night out. From its elegant main dining area to its private dining rooms and basement lounge, it's all about style and delicious tastes. Expect top flavors in fire-grilled and rotisserie meat and seafood dishes; venison with preserved cherries, black pudding, and licorice is just one innovative example. It's favored by Auckland's elite.

33 Sale St. *©* **09/358-1702.** www.clooney.co.nz. Reservations required. Main courses NZ$32–NZ$46. AE, DC, MC, V. Daily 11am–late.

DINE By Peter Gordon ★★★ INTERNATIONAL/FUSION   Founder of London's legendary Sugar Club restaurant, top New Zealand chef Peter Gordon is in charge of the menu at this chic upmarket eatery that's consistently voted one of the top hotel dining rooms. Floating circles of dimmed light, artwork, and an inventive menu make it worth seeking out. Kick off with Japanese-inspired starters or pan-fried scallops, leaving space for duck breast on smoked polenta with cumin-roasted baby carrots and rainbow chard with a truffle, olive, radicchio, and chestnut salad. Complement your meal with a selection from their fine New Zealand wine list.

In the SKYCITY Grand Hotel, 90 Federal St. *©* **09/363-7030.** www.skycityauckland.co.nz. Reservations required. Main courses NZ$33–NZ$45. AE, DC, MC, V. Fri 11:30am–2:30pm; daily 5:30pm–late. Dessert 10–11pm.

Euro ★★ NEW ZEALAND/EUROPEAN   Celebrity chef Simon Gault is passionate about food at every level and dishes in his flagship restaurant pay homage to quality ingredients, simple presentation, and mouthwatering flavors. His flair with modern cooking techniques is also apparent in dishes like *paua* (abalone) served with sake aioli, freeze-dried lemon peel, aniseed, and parsley. All of it is easily enjoyed in the elegant, waterside location.

 Do the Hokey Pokey

A blend of vanilla ice cream with pieces of honeycomb candy (aka sponge toffee), Hokey Pokey is a New Zealand original, first manufactured by the Meadowgold Ice Cream Company of Papatoetoe, Auckland, in the 1940s.

Enjoy seared scallops or smoked duck confit followed by roast filet of Angus beef at New Zealand's only revolving restaurant, **Orbit,** 190m (295 ft.) up in the Sky Tower, Victoria & Federal sts. (✆ **09/363-6355;** www.skytower.co.nz). In addition to award-winning a la carte cuisine, you get unforgettable, changing 360-degree views. The dining room rotates fully once every hour. Admission to the Observation deck and Sky Lounge Café & Bar is complimentary for Orbit guests 45 minutes prior to dining, or after you've finished your meal. Orbit is open for lunch Monday through Friday (11:30am–2:15pm); dinner daily (5:30–9:45pm); dessert daily (10–10:30pm); brunch Saturday and Sunday (10am–2:30pm); and high tea Saturday and Sunday (2:30–4:30pm). Main courses run from NZ$34 to NZ$42, with a NZ$30 per person minimum lunch and dinner. Bookings are essential and all credit cards are accepted.

Shed 22, Princes Wharf, Viaduct Harbour. ✆ **09/309-9866.** www.eurobar.co.nz. Reservations required. Main courses NZ$32–NZ$48. AE, DC, MC, V. Daily noon till late.

The Grove ★★★ MODERN NEW ZEALAND Always near the top of Auckland's Best Restaurant lists (it won in 2010 and 2011), this outstanding restaurant is a master at delivering one of the best food and wine experiences in New Zealand. Lamb rack is slow-cooked to perfection with Greek yogurt; and a butter-poached crayfish tail with Parma ham and rosemary will make you swoon. Desserts are a triumph, too. Don't miss the citrus pressé with mandarin sorbet and a jam doughnut, or the platter of homemade petit fours.

St Patrick's Square, Wyndham St. ✆ **09/368-4129.** www.thegroverestaurant.co.nz. Reservations required. Main courses NZ$40–NZ$50. AE, DC, MC, V. Mon–Fri noon–late; Sat 6pm–late.

MODERATE

Eight ★★ INTERNATIONAL This innovative concept in dining—eight themed kitchens, each with their own chef and a daily changing signature dish—gives you the chance to create your own menu. It's a culinary journey through Japan, India, the U.S., France, and New Zealand. Simply choose what you want from the finest produce, in any of the kitchens, and it is cooked to your liking. Dishes from the various kitchens can be matched with an extensive range of top wines—over 40 of them served by the glass, though the wine is not included in the set price. You can also select from an a la carte menu but it would be a pity to miss this exciting, great value style of dining.

Lobby Level, The Langham Hotel, 83 Symonds St. ✆ **09/300-2852.** www.eightrestaurant.co.nz. Reservations recommended. Breakfast (6–11am) NZ$37 per person; lunch (noon–2:30pm) NZ$37 per person; dinner (6–11pm) NZ$67 per person; Sunday brunch (11am–3:30pm) NZ$37 per person. Children 5–12 half price. AE, DC, MC, V. Open daily 24 hr. for a la carte dining.

Pastis ★★ FRENCH/BRASSERIE French/Kiwi couple Alex and Lyn Roux have a real winner in this all-French gem; checked tablecloths and a lively atmosphere make for a great night out. Classic French dishes like braised duck leg in port, snails served in the shell with garlic butter, and *mille-feuille* or crêpes suzette all make an appearance. The music, staff, and wine are also French.

128 Victoria St. ✆ **09/309-4264.** www.pastis.pierre.co.nz. Reservations recommended. Main courses NZ$30–NZ$35. AE, MC, V. Mon–Fri 11:30am–10:30pm, Sat 5:30–10:30pm.

5

AUCKLAND

Where to Eat

Throughout 2011 and into 2012, you'll find a host of new bars, cafes, restaurants, and excellent food to go in the Britomart Precinct, which covers a block between Queen Street (behind the Britomart Transport Centre), Quay Street, Customs Street East, and Britomart Place. We don't have the space to list all the new discoveries here, and half the fun of any meal is discovering something special for yourself, so head for Britomart and look out for French cafes, delis, upmarket grocers, espresso bars, classy clubs, and tucked-away bars. Check www.britomart.org to see what's coming next.

INEXPENSIVE

Pita Pit Britomart ★ HEALTHY   This is fast food that's actually healthy, too. Light pita shells are stuffed full with lean protein (meat or vegetarian) and plenty of crisp, fresh vegetables. Every order is prepared at lightning speed to your requirements and the meat is grilled right in front of you while you decide on sauces, salads, and dressings. Roast lamb, beef, pork, chicken, tuna, falafel, hummus, and baba ganouj are all on the menu; small versions are available for kids.

Atrium on Takutai, 7 Britomart Place. ✆ **09/357-0000.** www.pitapit.co.nz. Pita meals NZ$8–NZ$15. MC, V. Mon–Fri 7am–midnight, Sat–Sun 9am–9pm.

Smart Sushi JAPANESE/SUSHI BAR   This delightful little restaurant, housed in a charming "glass box," dispenses a wide range of sushi made from the freshest possible ingredients. That's fairly typical of a sushi bar, of course, but here, they also offer traditional Japanese treats like *asdon buri, katsu,* tempura, and udon noodle soup—often with a contemporary twist. Service is friendly, fast, and personal, and you can purchase your meal to dine in the covered atrium or take away.

Atrium on Takutai, 48 Te Ara Tahuhu Walking Street, Britomart Place. ✆ **09/369-1771.** NZ$8–NZ$15. V. Daily 8am–6pm.

Tanuki's Cave ★ 🍴 JAPANESE YAKITORI   This hugely popular dark den pulses most nights of the week and you have to get in early (like 6pm) to get a spot. People line up all the way back up the stairs to the street, but don't let their hungry looks make you rush through the delicious and incredibly well-priced menu. Choose a selection of skewers (chargrilled yakitori and deep-fried, breaded kushiage) or the delicious tofu salad.

319B Upper Queen St. ✆ **09/379-5151.** Reservations recommended. Main courses NZ$6–NZ$14. MC, V. Wed–Sat 6pm–late.

In Ponsonby/Herne Bay

EXPENSIVE

Also try the fine Italian cafe **Prego** ★★, 226 Ponsonby Rd. (✆ **09/376-3095;** www.prego.co.nz), which is open daily for lunch and dinner from noon until late. Lovers of fine food must try the culinary finesse of **Sidart** ★★★, Level 1, Three Lamps Plaza, 283 Ponsonby Rd. (✆ **09/360-2122;** www.sidart.co.nz), which sits among the top ranks of Auckland's restaurants and is open Tuesday through Saturday for dinner from 6pm and Thursday and Friday lunch from noon. **The Dining Room** ★★★, located in Mollies on Tweed, 6 Tweed St., St Marys Bay (✆ **09/376-3489;** www.mollies.co.nz), is the best romantic choice for anyone who believes dining should be a full sensual experience. It features neo-classical treasures, opera recitals, fine service, and food to match. Open daily from 6:30pm.

SPQR ★★ INTERNATIONAL   If you want to see trendy Ponsonby at its strutting best and most colorfully diverse, come to SPQR. The menu is just a few strides above average, but it's the atmosphere and the people-watching ops that make it a winner. In what was once a tire-retread shop, now stylishly spartan with stainless steel and concrete, the film and media crowd, the gay community, and your average run-of-the-mill Joe Bloggs all lean about looking supercool. SPQR serves up tasty morsels such as thin pizzas, and roasted snapper on saffron and lime risotto until well after midnight. (See "The Club & Bar Scene" under "Auckland After Dark," later in this chapter.)

150 Ponsonby Rd. ℰ **09/360-1710.** www.spqrnz.co.nz. Reservations recommended. Main courses NZ$25–NZ$35. AE, DC, MC, V. Daily noon–2am.

Vinnies Restaurant ★★★ 🖾 MODERN NEW ZEALAND   Vinnies invariably appears on any top-five list of Auckland restaurants. Its wall full of awards draws attention to the chef's culinary artistry and innovation, and the restaurant's superb professional service and outstanding wine list. The atmosphere is relaxed, intimate and art-filled, and it's the perfect special-occasion choice. There's plenty of game on the menu—try the farm-raised duck or the wild rabbit tart; or graze (elegantly) from the degustation menu. Desserts reach their pinnacle in lavender-infused crème brûlée served with milk chocolate and pineapple *mille-feuille*.

166 Jervois Rd., Herne Bay. ℰ **09/376-5597.** www.vinnies.co.nz. Reservations required. Main courses NZ$37–NZ$45. AE, DC, MC, V. Tues–Sun 5pm–late.

MODERATE

Bambina 🍴 CAFE   This is a lively, popular spot with delicious counter food presented under glass domes. There's a big blackboard menu for all-day breakfasts with all the conventional favorites—eggs any way you want them, ricotta hot cakes, muesli, and fruit. Lunch fare runs to Turkish sandwiches, bruschetta, and rare-grilled tuna with coriander and lime.

268 Ponsonby Rd. ℰ **09/360-4000.** Reservations not required. Main courses NZ$12–NZ$24. AE, DC, MC, V. Daily 7am–4pm.

Chapel ★★ BISTRO   This is favored by locals, who rave about its crazy, over-the-top wallpaper, its delicious thin-crust pizzas, and its generally hip vibe. The Chapel Platter is also worth trying and an a la carte menu deals out big rib-eye steaks. The excellent wine list and cocktails may help you appreciate the eclectic design even more.

147 Ponsonby Rd. ℰ **09/360-4528.** www.chapel.co.nz. Reservations recommended. Main courses NZ$25–NZ$34. AE, MC, V. Mon–Wed 3pm–late, Thurs–Sun noon–late. Takeaway pizza available.

Dizengoff ★★ CAFE   When Dizengoff opened several years ago, everyone wanted to be here—or, more precisely, to be seen here. The place is invariably filled with stylish types who like to pick delicately at their healthy bagels and sip strange health drinks without mussing their lip gloss. All that aside, the food is just as tasty as it is healthy, and if you can squeeze into this swirling den of style, you'll certainly relish the big brunchy breakfasts.

256 Ponsonby Rd. ℰ **09/360-0108.** Reservations recommended. Main courses NZ$16–NZ$25. AE, DC, MC, V. Daily Mon–Fri 6:30am–5pm, Sat–Sun 7am–5pm.

GPK ★ NEW ZEALAND/EUROPEAN   This Ponsonby haunt has been around for a long time, thanks to its reliably good pizzas, lively mood, fresh a la carte menu, and

A cheap feed AT THE FOOD HALLS

If you're after a dollar-stretching fill-up, the city has plenty of food courts, where even NZ$5 to NZ$15 will satisfy the hunger pangs. One of the most popular is in **Downtown Shopping Centre,** QEII Square on Quay Street. It's open Monday through Thursday from 7am to 6pm, Friday from 7am to 8pm, and Saturday and Sunday from 7am to 4pm. There is an international food boulevard at **SKYCITY Metro,** 291–297 Queen St., open daily from 9am until late.

At the **Atrium Food Gallery,** Atrium Shopping Centre, on Elliot Street between Victoria and Wellesley streets,

you'll find everything from McDonald's to pasta, kabobs, Chinese, sushi, and a bakery. It's open Monday through Thursday from 7am to 6pm, Friday from 7am to 9pm, Saturday from 7am to 6pm, and Sunday from 7:30am to 6pm. Also in this area and a few notches higher in style is **Elliott Stables,** 39–41 Elliott St. (✆ **09/308-9331;** www.elliottstables. co.nz), which is a little epicurean lane filled with over a dozen specialty food stores and restaurants. There are artisan wine suppliers, cheesemakers, sushi joints, a chocolate cake company, and French and Italian cafes.

good prices. It's what we call a stayer. It's a good stop for a quick lunch, a late afternoon snack with a glass of wine, or an all-night session at the bar.

262 Ponsonby Rd. ✆ **09/360-1113.** Reservations recommended. Main courses NZ$18–NZ$30. AE, MC, V. Mon–Fri 11:30am–late; Sat–Sun 9am–late.

INEXPENSIVE

Café Cezanne CAFE   Everyone seems to love this old favorite, especially on weekends. The food is good and the atmosphere terrific. There's a worn-but-loved quality and they do very good breakfasts—the mushroom and smoked chicken omelet is one of the best I've had—and the big, fattening cakes will tempt if you're just in for coffee. There's nothing "designery" about the place; it's slightly frayed at the edges, in fact, but it has genuine warmth that is very appealing.

296 Ponsonby Rd. ✆ **09/376-3338.** NZ$15–NZ$25. MC, V. Mon–Fri 7:30am–late; Sat–Sun 8:30am–late.

In Mount Eden/Eden Terrace/Epsom/ Grey Lynn

Try **One Tree Grill** ★, 9 Pah Rd., Greenwoods Corner, Epsom (✆ **09/625-6407;** www.onetreegrill.co.nz), a smart little restaurant with a cute-as-a-button bar upstairs. It's hugely popular with locals and has excellent service. Another highly recommended option is **Bowmans** ★★, 597 Mount Eden Rd., Mount Eden (✆ **09/638-9676;** www.bowmansrestaurant.co.nz), which puts many inner city establishments to shame with its top service and consistently good food. **Molten** ★★, 42 Mount Eden Rd., Mount Eden (✆ **09/638-7236;** www.molten.co.nz), is another suburban treasure producing great meals bound to impress.

Circus, Circus, 447 Mount Eden Rd., Mount Eden (✆ **09/623-3833;** www. circuscircus.co.nz), is a little gem of a cafe filled with circus memorabilia and show posters, along with food and staff that make it worth visiting. It's open for breakfast, lunch, and dinner. **Delicious** ★★, 472 Richmond Rd., Grey Lynn (✆ **09/360-7590;** www.delicious.co.nz), is a divine little Italian that's big on melt-in-the-mouth handmade pastas—the eggplant, walnut, and ricotta tortelloni with Taleggio cream is to die for. The tables are a bit close but you won't regret it. Make sure you reserve a table—and save room for their delicious tiramisu.

The French Café ★★★ CONTEMPORARY EUROPEAN   I've never heard a bad word about this perpetual award winner. Come here to savor sensational, finely crafted dishes in a sophisticated interior that you will remember forever. From the foie gras to the roast duckling, you'll be sighing with pleasure. Better yet, you don't have to take out a bank loan to dine in this elegant little gem, which sits proudly in one of the seedier parts of town.

210 Symonds St. ℂ **09/377-1911.** www.thefrenchcafe.co.nz. Reservations required. Main courses NZ$28–NZ$42. AE, DC, MC, V. Tues–Sat 6pm–late.

In Parnell/Newmarket

EXPENSIVE

In contrast to Ponsonby's artsiness, Parnell attracts a trendy corporate crowd—the work-hard, play-hard crew. The result is icons such as **Veranda Bar & Grill ★★**, or **VBG,** 279 Parnell Rd. (ℂ 09/309-6289), where expensive Pacific Rim cuisine and a party atmosphere reign supreme. For an elegant fine-dining experience, head for **Antoines ★★★**, 333 Parnell Rd. (ℂ 09/379-8756; www.antoinesrestaurant.co.nz), which attracts a well-heeled clientele with rich French cuisine and impeccable service.

Cibo ★★ MODERN NEW ZEALAND   Now over 20 years old, Cibo has proven that a restaurant with all the right ingredients will endure. Elegant, favored by the business crowd, and popular for special occasions, it serves up the likes of pepper-crusted lamb with mint potato cakes and venison loin with cauliflower couscous with an assurance that guarantees return visits. You might need a map or a friendly local to point you in the direction, but it's worth the hunt.

Axis Building, 91 St. Georges Bay Rd., Parnell. ℂ **03/303-9660.** www.cibo.co.nz. Reservations recommended. Main courses NZ$36–NZ$40. AE, MC, V. Mon–Fri noon–late.

MODERATE

In Newmarket, try **Tasca Newmarket ★**, 8/25 Nuffield St. (ℂ **09/522-4443**), for Spanish food; **Caffe Massimo ★**, 23–27 Nuffield St. (ℂ **09/522-6700**), has excellent counter food, a lively atmosphere, and big windows that open to the street.

Iguaçu Restaurant & Bar ★ PACIFIC RIM   Iguaçu (pronounced Ig-wa-*soo*) deserves full marks for its fabulous interior. Giant silver-framed mirrors lend a

The Healthy Stuff

Rocket Kitchen, 234A Ponsonby Rd. (ℂ 09/360-8834; www.rocketkitchen.co.nz), is a yummy little urban food store selling great deli and takeout food items. **Greys Ave Deli,** 108 Greys Ave. (ℂ 09/373-2908; www.greysavedeli.co.nz), provides all things kosher; and **Ripe Delicatessen ★**, 172 Richmond Rd., Grey Lynn (ℂ 09/360-6159; www.ripedeli.co.nz), offers a wide range of takeout meals, salads, and goodies in general. It's very easy to find—just turn into Richmond Road off Ponsonby Road and drive for about 3 minutes. It will be on a corner on your left. They make terrific treat-filled baskets and for a minimal cost they will courier them anywhere in central Auckland, so you don't ever have to leave your hotel.

5

AUCKLAND | Where to Eat

grandiose atmosphere to an environment made light and airy by a glazed ceiling. Food here is generally very good and it's a favorite spot for the lunching business crowd. There's also a comprehensive children's menu and they have live jazz every Sunday from noon to 4pm. See also "The Club & Bar Scene" under "Auckland After Dark," later in this chapter.

269 Parnell Rd., Parnell. ☏ **09/358-4804.** www.iguacu.co.nz. Reservations recommended. Main courses NZ$25–NZ$40. AE, DC, MC, V. Daily 11am–late. Closed Dec 25.

Non Solo Pizza ★★ ITALIAN BRASSERIE   This is the perfect place for a lazy afternoon in a sunny courtyard (or inside), sipping on the best wines and working your way through a feast of Italian favorites, whether it's pizzas, pastas, small plates to share; or a genuine big-table meal with friends or family. Two great choices include homemade chicken-and-spinach ravioli tossed in thyme, sage, basil, and vine-ripened mushrooms, and tiger prawns pan-fried in garlic. Luscious desserts are the ultimate finish for a terrific, relaxed dining experience.

259 Parnell Rd. ☏ **09/379-5358.** www.nonsolopizza.co.nz. Reservations recommended. Main courses NZ$20–NZ$40. AE, DC, MC, V. Daily noon–late

Portofino ★ 🍴 NORTHERN ITALIAN   When you're after something quick, easy, and tasty, Portofino obliges with delicious pastas, pizzas, and chicken and veal dishes. It's small, dark, cozy, and terribly popular, so get there early if you want a guaranteed spot. Watch the chefs cooking, enjoy the friendly staff, and leave without spending a fortune. Portofino has several other city locations—the best is in Viaduct Harbour—but the Parnell eatery still scores more for atmosphere.

156 Parnell Rd., Parnell. ☏ **09/373-3740.** www.portofino.co.nz. Reservations recommended. Main courses NZ$20–NZ$25. AE, MC, V. Daily 11am–late.

INEXPENSIVE

Dunk CAFE   If all you want is breakfast or a light lunch, Dunk will deliver. They offer a very tasty range of pies, flans, soups, and salads, plus yummy sweet things to go with coffee. It's a no-fuss sort of place and service can be patchy, but their central location makes them easy to find and they have gluten-free options.

297 Parnell Rd., Parnell. ☏ **09/377-2414.** No reservations. Main courses NZ$10–NZ$15. MC, V. Mon–Fri 7am–5pm.

Java Room ★ ASIAN PACIFIC RIM   Asian cuisine reaches new heights in this Parnell institution. Malaysian owner Hooi Hing takes a pan-Asian approach, serving up curries, stir-fries, and *laksas* from India, Malaya, Indonesia, and beyond. It's tucked away off the main street but well worth hunting down for the orange duck curry or the South Indian fish curry with tamarind and star anise. In summer, you can dine on a deck that overlooks the Auckland Domain, the city's oldest park.

317 Parnell Rd. ℂ **09/366-1606.** www.javaroom.co.nz. Reservations recommended. Main courses NZ$18–NZ$26. AE, DC, MC, V. Mon–Sat 6pm–late.

In Remuera

In Remuera the **Maple Room** ★, 93–95 Upland Rd., Benson Road Village (ℂ **09/522-1672;** www.themapleroom.co.nz), scores big points for its tapas-style dishes and main courses like duck risotto and mint-and-chili lamb rump. It's open Monday through Saturday from 5pm until late, and for lunch on Thursday and Friday from 11am. **Sierra Café,** 367 Remuera Rd. (ℂ **09/523-1527;** www.sierracoffee.co.nz), has good counter food, and their freshly baked pies, quiches, frittatas, and extravagant cakes make for an over-the-top picnic. Tucked behind the Remuera shops, the **Thai Village** ★★, 10/415 Remuera Rd. (ℂ **09/523-3005;** www.thaivillagerestaurant. co.nz), has a nice ambience and can always be trusted to deliver an excellent dining experience. For a traditional French lunch, or cake and coffee, make sure you go to **Le P'tit Pyrénées** ★, 371 Remuera Rd. (ℂ **09/520-2900;** www.pyreneesdeli. co.nz). Their French breads and pastries are worth traveling for. (See also Devonport, below.)

In Devonport/Birkenhead

Your best choices in this area include **The Engine Room** ★★, 115 Queen St., Northcote Point (ℂ **09/480-9502;** www.engineroom.net.nz), an award-winning bistro famous for its good food, personal service, and attention to detail. **Eight.Two** ★★, 82 Hinemoa St., Birkenhead (ℂ **09/419-9082;** www.eightpointtwo.co.nz), serves innovative New Zealand cuisine, and is frequently noted among Auckland's Top 50 list. In Devonport, **Monsoon** ★, 71 Victoria Rd. (ℂ **09/445-4263**), is a snappy little Thai/Malaysian place. Because it's so popular, either go early or reserve. **Devonport Deli Café,** Victoria Rd., Devonport (ℂ **09/445-7777**), is a good coffee stop that's popular with locals. It's open daily from 6:45am to 5:30pm. For a divine lunch or picnic food, seek out **Pyrénées, The French Deli** ★, 87A Vauxhall Rd., near Cheltenham Beach (ℂ **09/445-0021;** www.pyreneesdeli.co.nz), a traditional, rustic French den, that will tempt you in more ways than you can imagine.

EXPLORING AUCKLAND

If you're short on time, hop aboard the **Auckland Explorer Bus** ★★★ (see "Getting Around," earlier in this chapter) and take in as much as you can.

The Top Attractions

Auckland Museum ★★★ ☺ Auckland's imposing museum building stands in the Auckland Domain on the rim of an ancient volcano surrounded by parks and gardens. There are two entrances—the original harbor entrance has the stunning views, the newer rear dome entrance in the Atrium shows off contemporary New Zealand architecture. Get a shaky start at Volcanoes, a gallery that introduces you to Auckland's turbulent natural history. It's the only city in the world built on a volcano field, and the interactive movie room, simulating the birth of a new volcano, will set you to thinking we're slightly crazy for living here at all.

The museum has the largest collection of Maori and Polynesian artifacts in the world, and for this reason alone it's worth a visit. The extensive **Maori Treasures Gallery** is a must-see. Key attractions in this area include the impressive 25m (80-ft.) war canoe chiseled from one enormous totara trunk and covered with intricate carvings. That same artistry is reflected in the 26m (85-ft.) meetinghouse, with its carved and painted walls and rafters. Also on display are magnificent greenstone weapons, tools, and feather cloaks. Three times a day—at 11am, noon, and 1:30pm (plus an extra 2:30pm performance Jan–Apr)—concerts by the local Ngati Whatua *iwi* (tribe) bring the culture to life.

The museum is easy to negotiate. Just remember the first floor is about the people, the second is about the land, and the third is our war memorial.

Pacific Pathways is a moody area housing a world-renowned collection of Pacific artifacts; *New Zealand at War: Scars on the Heart* tells an emotional story of New Zealand in conflict, from the Land Wars of the 1840s to its present-day peacekeeping operations. The first-floor **Natural History Galleries** showcase everything from dinosaur skeletons to live seaside rock pools. It's a fascinating area well supported by the superb **Discovery Centre.**

This first-rate museum experience gives a marvelous introduction to New Zealand history and culture. To get the most from it, allow 2 to 3 hours minimum. An on-site cafe is open during museum hours, although the service can be patchy and the coffee isn't always the best. There are two very good shops worth a visit, and don't forget to ask about the free Family Trails tours and the Night at Auckland Museum—a school holiday treat that the kids will love. Booking ahead is essential or check the website for holiday activity timetables. Be sure to take a stroll around the magnificent sculpture walk featuring eight works by New Zealand artists. The museum supplies a map and has the models on display.

Auckland Domain. ☏ **09/309-0443** or 306-7067 for recorded Infoline. www.aucklandmuseum.com. Admission to permanent collection NZ$10 suggested donation; charges for special exhibitions may apply. Maori cultural performance NZ$35 adults, NZ$13 children 6–15, NZ$88 family. Cultural Performance and Maori Gallery Tour NZ$45 adults, NZ$18 children 6–15, NZ$108 family. Museum Highlights Tour (11:30am & 2pm daily), NZ$20 adults, NZ$5 children 6–15. Daily 10am–5pm. Closed Dec 25 and Apr 25. Wheelchair access throughout. Explorer Bus every 30 min.

Sky Tower ★★★ ☺ In the first 18 months after it opened in August 1997, Sky Tower drew over a million visitors, making it New Zealand's most popular paid attraction. At 328m (1,076 ft.), it is one of the tallest buildings in the Southern

Auckland Multipass

Get four of Auckland's leading attractions for one unbelievable price—a discount of over 25%. **Sky Tower, Kelly Tarlton's, Fullers Auckland,** and **Rainbow's End** have combined for this great offer, which can be used over a 2-week period and includes a pass to revisit whichever attraction you liked the best. Purchase the pass from any one of the included attractions, from an i-SITE Visitor Centre, or online at www.multipass.aucklandnz.com. It costs NZ$109 for adults and NZ$55 for children ages 5 to 15. Also pick up Tourism Auckland's **Hot Deals Auckland** brochure, which details a wide range of special packages. It's available from Auckland i-SITE Visitor Centres (☏ **0800/282-552** in NZ, or 09/367-6009; www.aucklandnz.com).

Hemisphere, affording unforgettable views over the sprawling mass of Auckland. It has three observation decks, including an outdoor area, a glass lift and glass floor panels, multilingual audio guides, and a revolving restaurant. Access to the observation decks is on three glass-fronted elevators, which can whiz up the building in a speedy 40 seconds. I'm petrified of heights but even I got a thrill out of going to the top. I just closed my eyes in the glass lift!

The Lower Observation level is accessible by stairs (for the very fit) and has two restaurants, Orbit (a revolving restaurant) and Observatory (buffet-style); reservations are suggested. The Main Observation level features the latest technology, with live weather feeds and touch-computer screens that give geographical information. The Outdoor Observation area holds high-powered binoculars and is open to the elements. The Sky Deck is the highest public viewing area, with 360-degree views through seamless glass.

SKYCITY, Victoria and Federal sts. ℂ **0800/759-2489** in NZ, or 09/363-6000. Fax 09/363-6378. www.skytower.co.nz. Admission NZ$28 adults, NZ$11 children 6–14, NZ$61 family. Admission to Sky Deck NZ$5 extra. AE, DC, MC, V. Daily 8:30am–late. Underground parking for small fee.

Kelly Tarlton's Antarctic Encounter & Underwater World ★★ ☺ In your wildest dreams, you might have imagined a live underground penguin colony; at Kelly Tarlton's **Penguin Encounter,** it's an amazing reality. For full insight into this unique self-sustaining population of king and gentoo penguins, make sure you pick up the free brochure, which details the establishment of a full simulated Antarctic environment, complete with saltwater pools, in the heart of subtropical Auckland. You'll be able to board heated, soundproof Snow Cats and enter the frozen landscape.

Just as awe-inspiring is **Underwater World,** the dream and final project of the late Kelly Tarlton, a famous New Zealand diver. At Underworld World, visitors travel on a moving walkway through an acrylic tunnel under the ocean. Surrounded by giant stingrays, eels, sharks, and over 1,500 fish, you're treated to a diver's view without having to wear the wet suit. **Stingray Bay** shows off the remarkable creatures at close quarters. This area also includes the adjacent NIWA Interactive Room for kids, a refreshment kiosk, and large educational touch screens. This is a special attraction for all ages; allow 45 minutes to 2 hours. Ring ahead for daily feeding times.

23 Tamaki Dr., Orakei. ℂ **0800/805-050** in NZ, or 09/531-5065. Fax 09/528-5175. www.kellytarltons.co.nz. Admission NZ$35 adults, NZ$12 children 3–14, free for children 2 and under. Special rates for families and seniors. Shark Cage Adventure NZ$69; Cage-Free Shark Survival NZ$99. AE, DC, MC, V. Daily 9:30am–5:30pm (last entry 4:30pm). Take Mission Bay city bus, Explorer Bus, or Fullers Harbour Explorer. Free Kelly Tarlton's shuttle calls at several inner city hotels 4 times daily 9:30am–5:30pm. Free parking.

Auckland Art Gallery ★ Recognized as the leading New Zealand art space, Auckland Art Gallery holds more than 10,000 New Zealand and European works. It

5

AUCKLAND Exploring Auckland

When we talk about special moments, this may not be what you had in mind, but one thing's for sure: You won't soon forget this experience! **Sky Jump** is one of New Zealand's wackiest adrenaline rushes—perhaps the ultimate! For details on this 192m (630-ft.) controlled free fall from the Southern Hemisphere's tallest tower, call ℂ **0800/759-586** in NZ, or 09/368-1835, or check www.skyjump.co.nz. It costs NZ$225 for adults, NZ$175 for children (ages 10–15), and NZ$700 for a family (two adults, two children). MasterCard and Visa are accepted. It operates daily from 10:15am to 5:15pm, weather permitting (closed Dec 25). Minimum age is 10 years with parental consent. Maximum weight is 120 kilograms (265 lb.).

And if that isn't thrill enough on its own, brace yourself for **Sky Walk** (ℂ **0800/759-925** in NZ, or 09/365-1464; www.skywalk.co.nz), operated by the same company, at the same location. Sign up for this daredevil adventure and you'll be attached to a harness and asked to walk around the pergola ring of Sky Tower, 192m (630 ft.) above the streets below. It requires far more courage than I could muster and costs NZ$145 adults, NZ$115 for children, and NZ$460 for a family. Sky Walk has eight daily departures at 10:15am, 10:45am, 11:45am, 12:15pm, 2:30pm, 3pm, 4pm, and 4:30pm. Closed December 25.

is the oldest and largest public art gallery in the country and fresh from a NZ$121-million Main Gallery upgrade, it has secured that reputation. Re-opened in mid-2011 with 50% more exhibition space and a bold new entrance on Kitchener Street, it now represents three distinct architectural periods: the late Victorian (Wellesley and Kitchener wings), the neo-Classical (East Gallery), and the 21st-century additions. At time of writing, all exhibitions were still being staged at the New Gallery, which opened across the street in 1995 and houses a magnificent contemporary collection of new ideas, new works, and new artists. This is where you'll find the McCahon Room, which displays works by the late Colin McCahon, New Zealand's most respected modernist artist. The gallery has an ongoing program of family days, tours, lectures, and holiday programs.

Main Gallery: Wellesley and Kitchener sts. ℂ **09/307-7700,** or 309-0831 for recorded information and 09/379-1349 24-hr. information on the new gallery. Fax 09/302-1096. www.aucklandartgallery.com. Free admission; fees for some touring shows. New Gallery: Wellesley and Lorne sts. ℂ **09/307-4540.** Free admission to downstairs galleries; NZ$12–NZ$20 for temporary and touring exhibitions. Both galleries: Daily 10am–5pm. Closed Dec 25.

The Viaduct Harbour

After a 152-year history of the America's Cup, this village was created to support syndicates, corporations, superyachts, and the public together in one venue. Auckland's Viaduct Basin, more commonly called "The Viaduct," is a glistening creation that includes new apartment blocks, hotels, restaurants, cafes, bars, shops, markets, and every facility an earnest yachtie could ever want.

Between October 1999 and March 2000, and again from October 2002 to March 2003, the village was the place to soak up the excitement of the America's Cup challenge. Millions of visitors crammed in over the two periods, along with more than 2,000 competitors and team personnel, plus 200 international media representatives during each challenge. In addition to the America's Cup action, the village played host to up to 80 **superyachts** on each occasion, the largest gatherings in the Southern Hemisphere, turning Auckland into a Pacific Monte Carlo. Superyachts are luxury motor and sailing vessels in excess of 30m (98 ft.) long, ranging in value from NZ$4 million to over NZ$40 million. Viaduct Harbour can accommodate 88 super-yachts of up to 50m (165 ft.).

Visitors can experience grand-prix sailing on an authentic America's Cup yacht, *NZL 40* or *NZL 41*, built for the 1995 San Diego Challenge. You can be as involved as you want in the crewing action, no sailing experience required. For information on the daily sailings from Viaduct Harbour, call **Explore NZ** (*✆* **0800/397-567** in NZ, or 09/359-5987; www.explorenz.co.nz). The price per person is NZ$160 for 2 hours of sailing, and NZ$210 for a 3-hour race. Lower rates available for children ages 10 to 15; children 9 and under are not permitted. Sailing usually begins at 2pm depending on tides.

The Viaduct Basin development has changed the face of Auckland forever, providing a fistful of fabulous restaurants, clubs, and bars that have endured—despite the fact that Team New Zealand relinquished the America's Cup in the 2002–03 challenge. It is a marvelous place to explore, and given that some of Auckland's best eateries are here, you'd be silly to miss it.

Viaduct Harbour has also been a stopover point in the epic Volvo Ocean Race (formerly the Whitbread Round-the-World Race).

Walking over Water

Bring on the nerves of steel for **Auckland Bungy & Bridge Climb** ★★★, 105 Curran St., Westhaven Reserve, Herne Bay (*✆* **09/360-7748**; www.bungy.co.nz). Based on a concept similar to the successful Sydney activity, walkers are guided underneath and over the top of Auckland Harbour Bridge. The 1½-hour adventure begins with a full briefing by a professional guide at the base complex. Guests are then fitted with overgarments, radio headsets, and safety harnesses. It's achievable for people of almost all ages and all fitness levels, but you must be age 8 and over and preferably not have a fear of heights. The walk costs NZ$120 for adults and NZ$80 for children 7 to 15, and NZ$305 for families. Discounts for seniors are available. A bungy jump is NZ$150 for adults, NZ$120 from children 10 to 15. See "Outdoor Activities & Spectator Sports," later in this chapter, for more details. You can take a bus or a short walk from city hotels; complimentary transport is available from outside the National Maritime Museum, Viaduct Harbour. There's limited parking at the site.

Other Museums, Monkeys & More

Museum of Transport & Technology (MOTAT) ★★ ☺ This is the largest museum of transport and technology in the country, covering 16 hectares (40 acres) in Western Springs, 5km (3 miles) from the city center. You'll find trams, trains, steam engines, aircraft, and more. The museum houses major collections of road transport, historical buildings, and medical and dental equipment displays. You can take a tram ride (every 20 min.) from the Great North Road entrance past the zoo to the **Sir Keith Park Memorial** (there's a small charge). Displays here include interesting military exhibits, rail memorabilia, and one of the most impressive collections of historical aircraft in Australasia, including the only Solent Mark IV flying boat in the world. There are some great hands-on exhibits to keep you amused. Allow 2 hours.

805 Great North Rd., Western Springs. *✆* **0800/668-286** in NZ, or 09/815-5800. www.motat.org.nz. Admission NZ$14 adults, NZ$8 children 5-16, NZ$35 families. Daily 10am–5pm. Closed Dec 25. Explorer Bus.

New Zealand National Maritime Museum ★★★ ☺ The National Maritime Museum is perfectly placed—right in the heart of the America's Cup action. Inside are intricate working displays and fascinating exhibitions documenting 1,000 years of New Zealand maritime history. Watch traditional craftsmen restoring historical vessels, wood turning, and working on sails. Of course there's an exhibit on America's Cup history. Plus, you get the chance to hit the high seas yourself: The historic scow *Ted Ashby* gives 45- to 60-minute rides Tuesday, Thursday, Saturday, and Sunday at noon and 2pm. It's definitely the cheapest cruise you'll find. I particularly like the 1950s beach shop and bach (holiday house) display, which sums up much of the quintessential Kiwi seaside holiday experience. The 14 galleries and interactive displays in this acclaimed museum will keep you busy for at least 2 hours.

Hobson Wharf, Viaduct Basin. ✆ **0800/725-897** in NZ, or 09/373-0800. Fax 09/377-6000. www.maritimemuseum.co.nz. Admission NZ$18 adults, NZ$10 children 5–15, free for children 4 and under, NZ$40 families. Museum Combo (museum entry plus *Ted Ashby* harbor cruise) NZ$28 adults, NZ$14 children 5–15, NZ$54 families. AE, DC, MC, V. Summer daily 9am–6pm; winter daily 9am–5pm. Closed Dec 25. Park in Downtown Carpark & purchase a NZ$4.50 discounted parking pass at the Museum ticket desk for 4 hours parking.

Auckland Zoo ★★ ☺ Within 5 minutes of city high-rises, you can watch and hear Sumatran tigers snarl, lions roar, and monkeys chatter. Over 1,000 birds and animals from every continent make their home in this outstanding parkland, recognized as one of Australasia's leading zoos. It is home to New Zealand's largest collection of native and exotic species. You can meet kiwi, tuatara, and other locals at the Daily Native Fauna Encounter. Or you can visit the beach and see shorebirds and little blue penguins. You can also watch sea lions through a spectacular underwater viewing window. At the McDonald's South American Rainforest, troops of spider monkeys, bonnet macaques, squirrel monkeys, and siamangs swing from branch to branch. Check out Pridelands for giraffes, zebras, lions, and rhinos. Ask about the special ZOOM tours, which take you behind the scenes, or treat the kids to a Safari Night sleepover and barbecue.

Motions Rd., Western Springs. ✆ **09/360-3805,** or 360-3819 for recorded information. Fax 09/360-3818. www.aucklandzoo.co.nz. Admission NZ$20 adults, NZ$16 students and seniors, NZ$10 children 4–15, family passes NZ$36–NZ$54. ZOOM Tours daily NZ$75 per person. AE, DC, MC, V. Daily 9:30am–5:30pm (last admission 4:15pm). Closed Dec 25. Explorer Bus or Pt. Chevalier 045, which departs from Downtown Centre, inner city. Free parking.

Butterfly Creek ★★ ☺ Just minutes from Auckland International Airport and built over a large wetland, Butterfly Creek delivers more than 800 free-flying tropical butterflies. The big butterfly house is a delight. Complete with waterfalls, ponds, lush foliage, turtles, fish, and exotic birds, it allows you to get up close to stunningly colorful butterflies. If you're lucky, you'll see the world's largest moth, which has a wingspan of up to 280 millimeters (11 in.); be on the lookout for tarantulas, lizards, and giant weta.

10 Tom Pearce Dr. ✆ **09/275-8880.** Fax 09/275-1110. www.butterflycreek.co.nz. Butterfly House NZ$14 adults, NZ$8 children 3–15. Red Admiral Express NZ$5. Buttermilk Farm NZ$9 adults, NZ$7 children. Combo Butterfly House, Bugs About, Pirates Below, and Buttermilk Farm NZ$20 adults, NZ$10 children. Family rates available. Daily 9am–5:30pm Nov–March, 9:30am–5pm April–Oct.

Snowplanet ★★ ☺ If you want to polish up your ski or snowboard skills before heading south, take a trip over the Harbour Bridge and let loose in one of the largest indoor snow resorts in the world and the first snowdome in Australasia. You can

Exploring Auckland

AUCKLAND

The Gallery Guide

The bimonthly booklet, *The Auckland Gallery Guide,* which includes information about leading galleries and their exhibitions, is available free from information centers and art galleries. Its user-friendly maps are a great help. For galleries and exhibitions, call ℂ **09/378-4070** or fax 09/378-4063.

guarantee snow here 365 days of the year, and young and old can have a ball. It features three lifts, a terrain park, and a separate learners' area.

91 Small Rd., Silverdale. ℂ **09/427-0044.** www.snowplanet.co.nz. Day Pass NZ$60 adults, NZ$44 children 11 and under, family NZ$150; Night Pass 6–10pm, NZ$42 adults, NZ$30 children. Rental equipment and clothing available for extra cost. Mon–Fri 10am–10pm; Sat–Sun 8am–10pm.

BeesOnline Honey Centre ★ It would be silly to call this a honey of an excursion, but I'm going to anyway. You'll love this beautifully designed attraction, which reveals the inner workings of a beehive. Set in picturesque countryside beside two small lakes, the modern, ecofriendly center showcases production, honey tastings, and bee-related products and gifts. It is a 2007 Sustainable Business award winner and produces a large range of certified organic honeys. After a visit, you can dine at the award-winning cafe. On weekends there is a free honey tasting and honey and bee talk.

791 St. Hwy. 16, RD3, Waimauku. ℂ **09/411-7953.** Fax 09/411-5216. www.beesonline.co.nz. Free admission. NZ$12 factory tour and tasting. Daily 9am–5pm.

Historic Houses

Alberton ★★, 100 Mount Albert Rd. (ℂ **09/846-7367;** fax 09/846-1919; www.alberton.co.nz), is perhaps the finest of all Auckland's historic homes that are open to the public. The once-simple farmhouse, built in 1863, grew into the fairy-tale mansion that stands today. Owned by the New Zealand Historic Places Trust, it provides an intimate glimpse into Victorian life. It's open Wednesday through Sunday, 10:30am to 4pm (closed Good Friday and Dec 25); admission is NZ$8.50 for adults, free for children. **Ewelme Cottage,** 14 Ayr St., Parnell (ℂ/fax **09/379-0202;** www.historic.org.nz), was built for the Rev. Vicesimus Lush from 1863 to 1864 and named for Ewelme Village in England. The roomy *kauri* cottage is authentically preserved, right down to its 19th-century wallpaper. It contains an important collection of more than 800 books. Admission is NZ$7.50 adults, free for accompanied children. It's open Sunday only, 10:30am to 4:30pm (closed Dec 25). **Highwic,** 40 Gillies Ave., Epsom. (ℂ **09/524-5729;** www.highwic.co.nz), is one of New Zealand's finest Gothic Revival houses. Built in 1862, it gained additions modeled from an American pattern book in 1873. Its distinctive architecture and gardens offer insight into the lives of the wealthy Victorian family who retained possession of it until 1978. Admission is NZ$8.50 adults, free for accompanied children. It's open Wednesday through Sunday 10:30am to 4:30pm (closed Good Friday and Dec 25).

Especially for Kids

Most of Auckland's major attractions—Kelly Tarlton's, the Discovery Centre at Auckland Museum, the Auckland Zoo, Sky Tower, Snowplanet, Butterfly Creek, and the Museum of Transport & Technology (all described above)—will give the kids hours of fun. Here's another chance for family fun.

Rainbow's End Theme Park ★★ ☺ 🍴   This is New Zealand's premier adventure playground, with 9 hectares (22 acres) devoted to crazy rides and attractions for children. For those under 10, there's a Dream Castle with its own miniature roller coaster, carousel, and Ferris wheel. Older kids will scream their lungs out on New Zealand's only double-loop roller coaster, and there's more fun to be had on the log flume and the pirate ship, in the Enchanted Forest, and in an abandoned mine. Add bumper boats, cars, and virtual theater, and the whole family will be entertained.

Great South and Wiri Station roads, Manukau City. ☏ **0800/438-672** in NZ, or 09/262-2030. Fax 09/262-1958. www.rainbowsend.co.nz. All-day Super Pass (includes unlimited rides) from NZ$48 adults (14 & up), NZ$38 children 2–13, NZ$18 Castle Pass (children 2–5), NZ$18 spectator pass. Family passes and combo deals available. AE, MC, V. Feb–Dec daily 10am–5pm; Jan daily 10am–10pm. Closed Dec 25. Take the Manukau motorway exit 15 min. south of Auckland and drive 400m (1,300 ft.) to the end of the Rainbow. Free parking.

Parks & Gardens

The Auckland area has 22 regional parks, covering 37,038 hectares (91,484 acres) and more than 500km (310 miles) of walking tracks. The **Auckland Domain** ★, the city's oldest park, is an imposing crown of green just minutes from the city center. Within it, the **Wintergarden,** the steamy **Tropical House,** and **Fernz Fernery** are botanical showcases for indigenous and exotic plant specimens. Admission is free. The Wintergarden is open daily from 10am to 4pm. There are also extensive formal gardens, sweeping lawns, statuary, duck ponds, sports grounds, and dozens of picnic spots. Summer Sundays bring free jazz and rock concerts in the band rotunda, chamber music in the Wintergarden, and megaconcerts on the sports fields. Call ☏ **09/379-2020** or fax 09/571-3757 for details. There are several well-signposted entrances to the Auckland Domain. Two of the busiest are on Stanley Street and Parnell Road. There are also entrances on Grafton Road and Park Road.

Cornwall Park is a true urban oasis; with **One Tree Hill Domain,** it forms the largest park in Auckland. The two parks fan out from the hill and are grazed by sheep and cattle. Stone walls, beautiful avenues of oak trees, and dozens of pretty walkways wind their way through this haven. Access is off Manukau Road at Royal Oak and Greenland West and Campbell roads. **Cornwall Park Visitor Centre** (☏ **09/630-8485;** www.cornwallpark.co.nz) has information on walks in the park.

Photo Ops

Of course you can't beat the 360-degree view from **Sky Tower** (p. 110), and once you've seen that, all other views seem to pale by comparison—with the exception perhaps of shots taken on your **Auckland Bridge Climb.** An old favorite is **One Tree Hill,** accessible through the very pretty **Cornwall Park.** The obelisk is visible from everywhere in the city. Like Mount Eden, it was once a Maori *pa* (fort) dating from the 14th century. The "one tree" that dominated its profile

was, sadly, damaged by a Maori activist in 1996; it has been replaced by a grove of small trees that have yet to reach a significant height. **Mount Eden** is an extinct volcano and Auckland's highest natural point. It boasts terrific views of the city, the harbor, and Hauraki Gulf. **North Head Maritime Park** in Devonport offers a different perspective—looking back at the city from North Shore. You'll get great photos of the cityscape from here.

Day Spa Delights

Nothing beats relaxing in a quiet, sweet-smelling day spa at the end of a long day exploring. You're spoiled for choice in Auckland, but queen of them all is **Chuan Day Spa ★★★** at the Langham Hotel, 83 Symonds St. (📞 09/300-2960; www.chuanspa.co.nz), where you can linger in herbal steam rooms, saunas, Jacuzzi, and ice pools, or perhaps a facial and a gentle massage and body treatment. **East Day Spa ★★**, SKYCITY Grand Hotel, 123 Albert St. (📞 09/363-7050; www.eastdayspa.com), focuses on Eastern-style holistic skin-care, massage, and beauty treatments. **Bliss,** Crowne Plaza Hotel, 128 Albert St. (📞 09/368-4698; www.blissreflexology.com), offers traditional Chinese reflexology in a stylish, relaxing inner city haven. **The Sanctuary at Mollies Day Spa,** Mollies on Tweed, 6 Tweed St., St Mary's Bay (📞 09/376-3489; www.mollies.co.nz), is a peaceful suburban haven at Mollies boutique hotel. The focus here is on massage, facials, and divine body treatments.

The **Parnell Rose Garden** and **Dove-Myer Robinson Park** (named after a popular former city mayor) are off Gladstone and Judges Bay roads in Parnell. One of the city's first churches, little St. Stephen's Chapel, is also here.

The **Auckland Botanic Gardens,** 102 Hill Rd., Manurewa (📞 09/267-1457; www.aucklandbotanicgardens.co.nz), cover 64 hectares (158 acres). It's home to more than 10,000 plants. The gardens are open daily from 8am to 8pm in summer and 8am to 6pm in winter. The Visitor Centre is open during the summer Monday through Friday from 8am to 4:30pm, Saturday and Sunday from 9am to 5pm; Monday through Friday 8am to 4pm, Saturday and Sunday 9am to 4pm in winter; the cafe is open daily from 8:30am to 4:30pm. Guides for organized groups are available Monday through Friday. Call 📞 09/266-3698, e-mail botanicgardens@arc.govt.nz, or ask at the visitor center. To get here from the city, travel south and take the Manurewa motorway exit, turn left onto Hill Road, and drive to the entrance.

Also worth a look are **Eden Gardens,** 24 Omana Ave., Mount Eden. (📞 09/638-8395; www.edengarden.co.nz). They're open daily 9am to 4:30pm (9am–4pm in winter); the on-site cafe is open from 9am to 4pm. Admission is NZ$8 adults, NZ$6 seniors and students, free for children. Once a quarry, it is now a showplace for an amazing collection of rhododendron, vireya, hibiscus, bromeliads, palms, and many other subtropical species.

Wine out West

Greater Auckland is home to more than 110 vineyards. Henderson Valley is the country's oldest grape-growing area, dating to the arrival of Croatian and other Northern Hemisphere immigrants in the early 1900s. Today, the western suburbs and areas north to Kumeu are a major grape-growing region. Cabernet sauvignon is the most commonly planted grape; merlot and pinot noir are also important. Chardonnay and sauvignon blanc are the main white varieties. Most West Auckland wineries also draw fruit from other regions, mostly Gisborne, Marlborough, and Hawke's Bay. The Henderson and Kumeu areas are the most accessible for a day's outing. They're about 30 minutes from Central City. Waiheke Island is about 30 to 40 minutes away by ferry; it's by far the prettiest region and worth the time.

5

AUCKLAND

Exploring Auckland

You'll find a good cluster of wineries along Lincoln and Henderson Valley roads, and nestled in the surrounding hills. The small townships of Kumeu, Huapai, and Waimauku also have good selections. For information on wine tours, see "Organized Tours & Cruises," below. For further details on the area, pick up the free vineyard brochures from a visitor center. Following are the notables.

Babich Wines, 10 Babich Rd., Henderson (✆ **09/833-7859;** www.babich wines.co.nz), is only 20 minutes from Central City and is open for tastings Monday through Friday from 9am to 5pm, Saturday from 9am to 6pm, and Sunday from 11am to 5pm. One of the most picturesque wineries, it has a pleasant picnic area near its shop and vintages going back to 1990. **Soljans Estate,** 366 St. Hwy. 16, Kumeu (✆ **09/412-5858;** www.soljans.co.nz), produces internationally competitive wines. It has cellar sales and tastings, a cafe, and winery complex. Daily winery tours (11:30am–2:30pm) followed by a tasting cost NZ$12 per person. The winery is open daily 9am to 5:30pm; the cafe is open Monday through Friday 11am to 3pm, weekends 9am to 3pm. **Constellation New Zealand,** 45 Station Rd., Huapai (✆ **09/ 412-6666;** www.constellationnz.com), is the country's second-largest winemaker. The winery is open daily from 10am to 5pm. Wine tastings cost NZ$3 per person; no tours are available. **Matua Valley Wines,** 307 Waikoukou Valley Rd., Waimauku (✆ **09/411-8301;** www.matua.co.nz), produced the first New Zealand sauvignon blanc over 25 years ago. The winery is open daily from 10am to 5pm and has a lovely picnic area. **Coopers Creek,** 601 St. Hwy. 16, Huapai (✆ **09/412-8560;** www. cooperscreek.co.nz), has wine tasting and summer jazz performances. It's open Monday through Friday 9:30am to 5:30pm and weekends from 10:30am to 5:30pm. **Awa Valley Vineyard,** 74 Awa Rd., Kumeu (✆ **09/412-6377;** www.awavalley.co.nz), is a lovely weekend stop, with free wine tasting, a sandpit for children's play, and a picnic area. They're open Saturday and Sunday 10am to 5pm, weekdays by appointment. Closer to the city and just 5 minutes north of the airport at Mangere Gateway, you'll find New Zealand's most awarded wine producer, **Villa Maria Estate,** 118 Montgomerie Rd., Mangere (✆ **09/255-0660;** www.villamaria.co.nz), a good place for beginners and experts alike to get an introduction to New Zealand wine. Their winery and cellar are built inside the crater of a 20,000-year-old volcano. Open Monday through Friday 9am to 6pm, and 10am to 5pm on weekends.

If you're short on time, call at **Glengarry Wines ★★**, Sale and Wellesley streets (✆ **0800/733-505** in NZ, or 09/308-8346; www.glengarry.co.nz), where you'll find an extensive range of varietals from most New Zealand regions. It offers tax-free wine sales, wine tastings, worldwide home delivery, and wine-tour information. They're open Monday through Saturday 9am to 8pm, Sunday 11am to 7pm. Glengarry has several stores throughout Auckland; another convenient location is at 139 Ponsonby Rd. (✆ **09/378-8252**).

For information on Waiheke Island wineries, see "A Side Trip to Waiheke Island," later in this chapter.

Doing Devonport

TAKING THE FERRY Catching the **Fullers Ferry ★★** to Devonport is one of the nicest day's outings you can have in Auckland. Make your way to Pier 1, Ferry Terminal at 99 Quay St. (✆ **09/367-9111;** www.fullers.co.nz), and take to the water. You'll get great views of the city, Viaduct Basin, and the America's Cup Village as you head out aboard the catamaran *Kea*. The ferry operates daily every half-hour from 7:15am to 8pm and every hour from 8 to 11pm, and the trip takes 12 minutes.

The round-trip fare is NZ$11 adults, NZ$5.50 children ages 5 to 15. If you're planning to base yourself in Devonport, buy a 10-trip or weekly ferry pass.

DEVONPORT VILLAGE ATTRACTIONS   The village of Devonport is all about atmosphere, charm, historic buildings, the arts, and cafes. It has a summer holiday feel, even in the middle of winter, and especially on weekends. Stop at the **Devonport i-SITE Visitor Centre,** 3 Victoria Rd. (*©* **09/446-0677;** www.aucklandnz.com or www.devonportnz.com), where you can find out about things to see and do. It's open daily from 8:30am to 5pm.

The two historic backbones of the village are Victoria and Church streets, now the main business area. Many of the buildings here date to the first European settlement; a brochure called *The Old Devonport Walk* gives you all the details as you wander.

There are three excellent white-sand beaches in close range—**Devonport,** a good swimming spot with a playground; **Cheltenham,** a safe tidal beach; and **Narrow Neck Beach,** with safe swimming and a playground. **Mount Victoria** sits near the business center and allows great harbor views, and **North Head** was a significant defense spot for both Maori and the Europeans. The volcanic hill was further developed during World War II, and it's honeycombed with underground tunnels, chambers, and gun emplacements. **Devonport Explorer Tours** (*©* **09/357-6366;** www.devonporttours.co.nz) can take you here on a 1-hour minibus tour (allow 2 hr. with ferry ride) for NZ$35 per adult (including ferry ride); booking ahead is essential. Tours run daily 10am to 3pm all year.

At the colorful **Art by the Sea,** King Edward Parade and Church St. (*©* **09/445-6665;** www.artbythesea.co.nz), you'll find top-quality work by New Zealand artists. It's right next door to cafes and across the road from the sea; hours are Sunday through Friday from 10am to 5pm, Saturday from 10am to 5:30pm. **Peter Raos Glass Gallery ★★**, Shop 5, 2 Queens Parade (*©* **09/445-4278;** www.peter-raos.com), is also worth checking out for handmade art glass by a local resident and master glass artist. It's open Monday through Friday from 10am to 4pm and weekends 10am to 3pm.

Two museums worth visiting are the **Devonport Museum,** 31A Vauxhall Rd. (*©* **09/445-2661;** www.devonportmuseum.org.nz), open Saturday and Sunday from 2 to 4pm with free admission; and the new **Devonport Naval Museum,** 64 King Edward Parade, Torpedo Bay, Devonport (*©* **09/445-5186;** www.navymuseum.mil.nz), open daily from 10am to 5pm, with free admission. The latter is housed in a 19th-century submarine mining station and showcases the story of the New Zealand Navy. If you decide to stay for dinner, there are numerous restaurants and cafes (see "Where to Eat," earlier in this chapter). For something completely different, check out **Devonport Chocolates ★**, 17 Wynyard St. (*©* **09/445-6001;** www.devonport chocolates.co.nz), where you can see chocolate being made. The shop is open Monday through Friday 9:30am to 5pm, and weekends 10am to 4pm. (If you don't get to Devonport, visit their second store at 177B Ponsonby Rd., Ponsonby.)

Organized Tours & Cruises

You can book several half- and full-day tours of the city and its environs at the visitor center. The half-day tours cover sightseeing highlights, while all-day tours usually include something of the east or west suburbs, the zoo, and the vineyards.

Mike's Garden Tours (*©* **09/846-5350;** www.mikesgardentours.co.nz) are the only ones that combine sightseeing with private garden visits. There are several options, ranging in price from NZ$110 to NZ$200 for adults, half-price for children ages 5 to 15.

Island Escape

If you feel like spoiling yourself, join **Island Escape Cruises ★★★**, 10/22 Princes Wharf (🕐 0800/581-717 in NZ, or 09/358-1717; www.islandescape.co.nz), for a 5-day luxury cruise of Hauraki Gulf islands. Make your home in 1 of the boat's 10 big cabins and enjoy fishing trips, picnics ashore, bush walks, and expeditions from the ship by helicopter or boat. The 42m (138-ft.)

Island Passage is stylish from start to finish, and this adventure guarantees memories to write home about. The 5-day cruise costs NZ$3,750 to NZ$6,250 for double or twin occupancy, and includes all meals, snorkel equipment, fishing gear, and boat tours. This is a particularly indulgent way to get to Great Barrier, Waiheke, Kawau, and Tiritiri Matangi islands.

Tamaki Hikoi ★★ (🕐 0800/282-552 in NZ, or 09/367-6009; www.aucklandnz.com) is a 3-hour Maori walking tour through Auckland. A guide from the Ngati Whatua tribe retells legends, beginning at the dormant volcano of Mount Eden. After a picnic lunch, you continue past local landmarks, finishing at the downtown waterfront. The tour costs NZ$95 per person. There is also a 1-hour tour of Mount Eden for around NZ$40. It's an easy to moderate walk, mainly on road surfaces, but wear sensible walking shoes.

Bush & Beach ★★ (🕐 09/837-4130; www.bushandbeach.co.nz) will take you out to the wild west coast to experience the elemental side of Auckland. Half- or full-day tours can include visits to a gannet colony, a winery, or a virgin rainforest. They cost NZ$140 to NZ$225 per person. They also offer an all-day tour to Great Barrier Island for NZ$695 per person. Children 11 and under pay half-price. Make sure you wear sensible walking shoes. Their Best of Both Worlds tour provides a good overview of Auckland's diversity, taking in the city in the morning and the bush and beaches of West Auckland in the afternoon.

For a range of tours with a Maori flavor, contact **Potiki Adventures ★★** (🕐 021/422-773; www.potikiadventures.co.nz). From an urban marae visit to gathering shellfish to learning about flax weaving and Maori plant medicine, the company can organize personalized itineraries or take you on a full-day tour for NZ$225 adults, or NZ$95 children 14 and under. They're the only company that offers tours to the Otara Markets—probably the largest Polynesian market you will ever get to see.

One of the best wine tours is with **Auckland Wine Trail Tours ★★** (🕐 09/630-1540; www.winetrailtours.co.nz), which specializes in bringing small groups to leading growers. Half- and full-day tours cost NZ$110 to NZ$245 per person. The full-day Matakana tour (NZ$245 per person) introduces you to the wines of one of the loveliest rural areas near the city. **Fine Wine Tours ★★** (🕐 0800/023-111 in NZ, or 021/626-529; www.finewinetours.co.nz) has a great choice of half- and full-day food and wine tours for NZ$179 to NZ$299. The Great Auckland Food & Wine Lovers Tour (Mon–Sat; NZ$299 per person, including cafe lunch) is especially good and introduces you to cheesemaking, ice cream, a busy fish market, delis, a chocolate boutique, a distillery, and a winery, all in Auckland.

ON THE WATER

With 96 boat charter companies, Auckland won't deprive you of an opportunity to get out on the waves. **Fullers Auckland,** Ferry Terminal, 99 Quay St. (🕐 09/367-9111;

www.fullers.co.nz), is one company that makes it easy. One of its best-value deals if you're on a tight itinerary is the **Harbour Cruise,** a 1½-hour sightseeing excursion that shows off Viaduct Harbour, Devonport Naval Base, and the Harbour Bridge, with coffee and commentary. Fares are NZ$38 for adults, NZ$19 for children ages 5 to 15. The cruise includes a round-trip ticket to Devonport so passengers can visit the sea-side village at their leisure, or on any scheduled Fullers sailing. Tours depart from Pier 2, Ferry Terminal, 99 Quay St., at 10:30am and 1:30pm. Fullers also has a Volcanic Explorer option that visits Rangitoto Island at a cost of NZ$59 for adults, NZ$30 for children ages 5 to 15, and several Waiheke Island Explorer options, including a **Taste of Waiheke Tour ★**, which visits three award-winning wineries and a top olive oil producer. It costs NZ$129 and includes a light lunch at Stonyridge.

After winning the America's Cup twice, New Zealand is big on yachting. **Explore NZ ★★★** (© **0800/397-567** in NZ, or 09/359-5987; www.explorenz.co.nz) has some very exciting ways to experience Auckland from the water. Its **Pride of Auckland** operates a fleet of purpose-built sailboats, which offer lunch, dinner, coffee, and half-day cruises. And their **Sail New Zealand** operation offers a variety of tours in both Auckland and the Bay of Islands. *NZL 40, NZL 41,* and *Lion New Zealand* are all available for sailing or match-race tours (see "The Viaduct Basin," earlier in this chapter).

The Maritime Museum's (p. 114) own cruises on heritage vessels are a little cheaper, but the luncheon cruise has a boxed lunch as opposed to a sit-down meal; it's also shorter and on an entirely different type of vessel. All are excellent experiences.

If you want tall ship sailing, the *Soren Larsen* (© **0800/767-365** in NZ, or 09/817-8799; www.sorenlarsen.co.nz), star of *The Onedin Line* television series, is your vessel. You can book day sails, coffee cruises, or holiday voyages, which include a 5-night sailing cruise between Auckland and the Bay of Islands. Auckland day trips start at NZ$150 per person, longer voyages are NZ$1,600, which includes all meals. The New Zealand season is December through February. Day trips leave from Princes Wharf West, adjacent to NZ National Maritime Museum. Boarding is at 9:45am.

OUTDOOR ACTIVITIES & SPECTATOR SPORTS

Outdoor Pursuits

AIR BUNGY   The **Sky Screamer** (© 09/377-1328), Albert and Victoria streets, just down from Sky Tower, will send you skyward with a maximum adrenaline rush at 200kmph (124 mph). Prices start at NZ$50 per person. Open 11am to late.

BUNGY JUMPING   A. J. Hackett Bungy Auckland, Westhaven Reserve (bottom of Curran St.), Herne Bay (© **0800/462-8649** in NZ, or 09/361-2000; www.bungy.co.nz), is the world's first harbor bridge bungy. For NZ$150 adults and NZ$120 children ages 10 to 15, you can leap out over Waitemata Harbour.

CANYONING   Canyonz (© **0800/422-696** in NZ, or 027/532-3244; www.canyonz.co.nz) offers a range of energetic rappelling adventures on Auckland's west coast and in the Coromandel Peninsula (see chapter 6). Costs range from NZ$195 for the Blue Canyon adventure (minimum age 12) to NZ$295 per person for a Coromandel excursion to Sleeping God Canyon (minimum age 16), where you can slither down a 300m (1,000-ft.) waterfall way off the beaten track.

FOUR-WHEEL-DRIVE BIKING   If "real" adventure in the country is your thing, call **4 Track Adventures,** Restall Road, Woodhill Forest (C **0800/487-225** in NZ, or 09/420-8104; www.4trackadventures.co.nz). Its quad bikes are easy to ride, and you don't need previous experience. Expect to pay NZ$155 per person for a 1-hour safari. Two- and 3-hour safaris are also available. Van pickup from central hotels and backpackers is available for NZ$50. Minimum age for riders is 14, and 5 years for pillion passengers.

GOLF   You'll find more than 40 golf courses in the Auckland region. For details call the **Auckland Golf Association** (C/fax **09/522-0491;** www.auckgolf.co.nz), Monday through Thursday between 9am and 5pm, and ask for the course nearest you and current greens fees.

HORSEBACK RIDING   The Auckland region is home to about 20 riding operations. Visitor centers can give you advice about the outfitter nearest you. One of the closest to the inner city is **Valley View Riding** (C **09/837-0525**), in Henderson.

JET BOATING   Auckland Adventure Jet (C **0800/255-538;** www.auckland adventurejet.co.nz) will whisk you out onto Waitemata Harbour for a thrilling 35-minute, high-speed ride for NZ$98. They depart hourly from Pier 3D at the ferry Terminal at 99 Quay Street, at the bottom of Queen Street.

KAYAKING   Ian Ferguson was one of New Zealand's top athletes; he competed in five Olympic games, won four gold medals and one silver, and in 1996 was named New Zealand Olympian of the century. He is also the man behind **Fergs Kayaks ★★**. Located at **Ian Ferguson Marine Sports Centre,** 12 Tamaki Dr., Okahu Bay (C **09/529-2230;** www.fergskayaks.co.nz), it offers several kayaking options; the most fun, perhaps, is the Rangitoto Night Trip, which involves a 75-minute paddle out to the island and a 45-minute walk to the top of Rangitoto for a spectacular night view of Auckland. The trip leaves at 6pm, returns by 11pm, and costs around NZ$150.

MOUNTAIN BIKING   Downhill mountain biking is what you get with **Auckland Adventures** (C **09/379-4545;** www.aucklandadventures.co.nz). It offers a number of mountain bike tours for groups of five people or more, taking in the best of West Auckland. Costs range from NZ$85 to NZ$135 per person, and biking time varies from 1 to 3 hours, depending on your level of fitness.

SAILING   You'll find numerous brochures about sailing charters at the visitor center, and the staff there can help you decide. See also "Organized Tours & Cruises," above. If you'd like to learn the basics, contact **Sailing Away School of Sailing ★★** (C **09/521-2387;** www.sailingaway.co.nz), and sailing master Suzanne Bourke will take you out on the *French Connection.*

SURFING   New Zealand Surf 'n' Snow Tours (C **0800/787-386** in NZ, or 09/828-0426; www.newzealandsurftours.com) offers 1- and 2-day surf tours for NZ$50 to NZ$199 and a 5-day surf tour at NZ$899 in the Auckland and Northland regions.

SWIMMING   Accessible from Tamaki Drive (where there's frequent bus service from Britomart), the beaches at Judges Bay, Okahu Bay, Mission Bay, Kohimarama, and St. Heliers Bay are popular inner-harbor swimming spots. If you want pool swimming, the visitor center has an excellent brochure, which details 10 major complexes.

WALKING   An easy, enjoyable walk is along the promenade of **Tamaki Drive ★★**, which takes you from the inner city around to the pleasant seaside suburbs of Mission Bay and Kohimarama. **One Tree Hill, Cornwall Park,** and **Mount Eden** all offer a bit of physical exertion. If you really want to explore, contact **Waitakere Wilderness Walks** ((C)/fax **09/838-9007**; www.wildwalks.co.nz), which offers 1- and 2-day walks and photographic excursions in the unspoiled west coast. An excellent self-guided trek is the **Coast to Coast Walk ★★★**, a 4- to 6-hour walk through the inner city and suburbs. A comprehensive map available from the visitor center shows the 15km (10-mile) route.

Spectator Sports

For information on current events, contact the **Auckland i-SITE Visitor Centre** ((C) **09/367-6009**; reservations@aucklandnz.com), or check out the events listings at www.aucklandnz.com.

HORSE RACING   Auckland Cup Week ((C) **09/524-4069**; www.ellerslierace days.co.nz) usually takes place over 3 party-filled days in late February to early March at Ellerslie Race Course. It's the biggest day in New Zealand thoroughbred racing, with over 30,000 spectators.

Alexandra Park Raceway, Greenlane West Road, Epsom ((C) **09/630-6164**; www. alexandrapark.co.nz), mounts the **Lion Red Auckland Trotting Cup Carnival,** an extravaganza that includes the NZ$100,000 Great Northern Derby for 3-year-olds and the NZ$250,000 Lion Red Trotting Cup. Regular **Night Trotting** meets are on Friday and Saturday nights.

For more information on horse racing, call the **Recorded Racing Information Service** ((C) **09/520-7507**).

RUGBY   Check with the visitor center for current schedules of **All Blacks** and fiercely fought provincial rugby games nationwide. The rugby season runs from April to September. For rugby and league match information, contact **New Zealand Rugby Football Union** ((C) **04/499-4995**; www.nzrugby.co.nz) or **New Zealand Rugby Football League, Inc.** ((C) **09/524-4013**; www.rugbyleague.co.nz).

RUNNING   The **Round the Bays** fun run ((C) **09/525-2166**; www.roundthebays. co.nz) follows the contours of Auckland's Waitemata harbor; an estimated 70,000 participants are attracted to the 8.4km (5-mile) run, held each March.

TENNIS   The **ASB Bank Classic** (www.asbclassic.co.nz), in January, attracts women tennis players from around the world; the **Heineken Open** (www.heinekenopen.co.nz), the men's event, generally follows the women's event, also in January. Call (C) **09/373-3623** or fax 09/373-3625 for details.

SHOPPING

Most shops are open Monday through Friday from 9am to 5:30pm, with many staying open late on Thursday and Friday. Saturday hours are normally 10am to 4pm, although some shops stay open all day. Many are also open on Sunday. Several free shopping guides are available at visitor centers.

Tip: If you have the store mail your purchases back home, you won't have to pay the 15% GST—and you won't have to lug them all around the country.

5

Antiques Hunting

The most popular concentrations of antiques stores are around the Epsom area and in Parnell, Remuera, Ponsonby, and the inner city. **Lord Ponsonby Antiques,** 86 Ponsonby Rd., Grey Lynn (℄ **09/376-6463**), is as good a place as any to start. **Piper Antiques,** 31A Sale St. (℄ **09/376-9000**), is another good hunting ground.

In Parnell, **Murdoch McLennan,** 377 Parnell Rd. (℄ **09/309-4757**), has a beautiful range of English antiques; and a few doors down, **Baran de Bordeaux,** 367 Parnell Rd. (℄ **09/307-1201**), is filled with exquisite imported from the 17th- through the 19th-century French antiques and decorative items.

Look for **John Stephens Antiques,** 15 Shore Rd., Epsom (℄ **09/529-1660**); and **Country Antiques,** 489 Manukau Rd. (℄ **09/630-5252**). In Remuera, look for **Antiquities,** 89 Great South Rd. (℄ **09/520-0353**); **Abbey Antiques,** 87 Great South Rd. (℄ **09/520-2045**); and several others on the same stretch of Great South Road. And if you like old china—especially English brands—you'll adore fossicking at **Babushka,** 156 Garnet Rd., Westmere (℄ **09/378-9226**).

Duty-Free Delights DFS Galleria Custom House, Customs and Albert streets (℄ **0800/388-937** in NZ, or 09/308-0700; www.dfsgalleria.com), is New Zealand's most luxurious duty- and tax-free department store. It offers complimentary shuttle service, free delivery of purchases to the airport, and currency exchange. It's open daily from 10am to 10pm. For a list of all New Zealand duty-free stores, pick up the free *Duty Free & GST Free Shopping Guide* at the airport or visitor centers. If you shop at an off-airport duty-free store, be sure you have your airline ticket with you.

Inner City

Shoppers seeking the latest in cutting-edge fashion and design can pick up the pocket-size *Auckland Fashion Guide* from visitor information centers and then head for the **High Street–Vulcan Lane–O'Connell Street areas ★★★** (www.hotcity.co.nz)—the place to go for the best in New Zealand fashion houses, accessories, art—not to mention coffee and interesting food. This is where you'll find international fashion hotshots **Karen Walker** (www.karenwalker.co.nz), **Zambesi** (www.zambesi.co.nz), and **World** (www.worldbrand.co.nz). Also here is the excellent bookstore **Unity** (℄ 09/307-0731; www.unitybooks.co.nz). The lovely and innovative **Pauanesia ★★**, 35 High St. (℄ **09/366-7282**; www.pauanesia.co.nz), sells the very best in contemporary New Zealand and Pacific homeware. The **Vault,** 13 High St. (℄ **09/377-7665**; www.thevaultnz.com), is the perfect place for reasonably priced New Zealand and international design items—everything from jewelry to stationery to small gifts. The new **Chancery shopping area** (℄ **09/368-1863**; www.chancery.net.nz) is also here. It's packed with international brand stores and exclusive fashion names. If you're a *Lord of the Rings* fan, check out the big range of movie collectibles and jewelry at **DMC,** 61 High St. (℄ **09/303-4757**; www.lotrshop.co.nz).

All manner of middle-of-the-road stores line **Queen Street** from top to bottom, but I think you find much better shops down the little side streets running off it; here you'll often find excellent specialty shops, such as **Compendium,** 5 Lorne St.

(✆ **09/300-3212;** www.compendium.co.nz), which has an impressive collection of quality New Zealand craft work. It schedules regular exhibitions of glass, jewelry, pottery, wood, sculpture, clothes, and furniture. **Fingers ★★,** 2 Kitchener St. (✆ **09/373-3974;** www.fingers.co.nz), is Auckland's most established New Zealand jewelry collective. **Kura Gallery,** 188 Quay St. (✆ **09/302-1151;** www.kuragallery. co.nz), has a great range of original New Zealand art and crafts. There are also a wide range of retail outlets and eateries under construction as part of the Britomart development behind the Britomart Transport Centre; visit www.britomart.org for more details.

Ponsonby/Herne Bay/K'Road

Although better known for its wealth of eateries, Ponsonby also has some terrific specialty design stores and boutiques, with an emphasis on housewares, fashion, and furniture. Karangahape Road is worth browsing for its diversity and cultural mix, but don't expect high-quality goods here; it's better known for art galleries, featuring both the quirky and the bizarre. Check out **www.ponsonbyroad.co.nz** and **www.kroad. com** for details.

Parnell/Newmarket

Shopping Parnell is a special experience, albeit an expensive one, with everything from Timberland to Cartier. You'll find all sorts of exclusive gifts in a rabbit's warren of little historic buildings, restored to picturesque splendor, that stretch along a mile of **Parnell Road.** Click on www.parnell.net.nz for more information about this area. Visit Newmarket's latest hot spots, **Nuffield and Teed streets ★★★,** for the high-end stores of iconic international and Kiwi fashion brands like Karen Walker, Trelise Cooper, Kate Sylvester, and Zambesi. There are a number of excellent cafes and restaurants here too—the ideal place to pause between parcels. I like to go here just to look at the beautifully designed stores and to watch "the pretty people." Altogether, Newmarket (www.newmarket.co.nz) has over 40 designer fashion stores and New Zealand's largest concentration of shoe stores—24 of them! In this area also look out for the **Poi Room,** 17 Osborne St., Newmarket (✆ **09/520-0399;** www.thepoiroom. co.nz), for high-quality New Zealand art, design, jewelry, prints, glass, and textiles.

 Great Tastes

To satisfy your gourmet tastes or choose tasty morsels for a picnic, head for **Kapiti Shop,** 136–142 Fanshawe St. (✆ **09/377-2473;** www.kapiticollection. co.nz), which has a huge selection of premium New Zealand cheeses. Make sure you try Kapiti's ice cream—it's divine! Zarbo, 24 Morrow St., Newmarket (✆ **09/520-2721;** www.zarbo.co. nz), carries an excellent range of gourmet items. **Pandoro Panetteria,** 427 Parnell Rd., Parnell (✆ **09/358-1962;** www.pandoro.co.nz), and 290 Dominion Rd., Mount Eden (✆ **09/631-7416),** is an authentic Italian bakery offering organic, additive-free products. And enjoy the sights and sounds of an authentic working fish market at **Auckland Fish Market,** Jellicoe Street, near Viaduct Harbour (✆ **09/379-1490;** www.aucklandfishmarket.co.nz). It has a daily early-morning auction and a seafood school.

GOING TO market

For an excellent Pacific experience, visit the **Otara Market ★★★**, Newbury Street, Otara (✆ **09/274-0830**), held Saturday from 6am to noon. It's the largest Polynesian market in the world, with larger-than-life personalities, exotic foods and smells, wonderful *tapa* cloth, flax mats and baskets, and bone carvings.

Avondale Market, Avondale Race-course, Ash Street (✆ **09/818-493;** www.avondalesundaymarkets.co.nz), is held on Sunday from 6am to noon and has a strong Polynesian and Asian influence. It features a mass of fruit, vegetables, new and used clothes, and bric-a-brac. The **Aotea Square Markets,** The Edge, Queen Street (✆ **09/309-2677**), take place Friday and Saturday from 10am to 6pm; they feature New Zealand fashion labels, retro gear, foods, fabric, jewelry, and furniture. There is an excellent **City Farmers' Market** held every Saturday morning from 8am to noon in the large courtyards behind the Britomart Transport Centre. The **French Style Market** is held every Saturday and Sunday from 8am to 1pm at La Cigale, 69 St. Georges Bay Rd., Parnell.

AUCKLAND AFTER DARK

Auckland has something for everyone—the adventurous, the sophisticated, the young, and the young at heart. From 24-hour casinos and live theater to cinema, clubs, pubs, bars, and dance spots, you can party all the way to breakfast time.

For information about current cultural and entertainment events in the city, contact **Ticketek,** Aotea Centre (✆ **09/307-5000;** www.ticketek.co.nz), which provides easy credit-card booking with next-day courier delivery. It also makes bookings around the country—a good way to save time and avoid disappointment. The free newspaper *Tourist Times* also lists current happenings.

The Performing Arts

The **Edge,** 50 Mayoral Dr. (✆ **09/309-2677;** www.the-edge.co.nz), is the cultural core of Auckland. Located in the central area bordered by Mayoral Drive and Albert, Wellesley, and Queen streets, it includes the modern Aotea Centre, the impressive Auckland Town Hall, and the refurbished Civic Theatre. The **Aotea Centre** (✆ **09/307-5060**), opened in 1990 by Dame Kiri Te Kanawa, features theater, ballet, dance, opera, major stage productions, art exhibitions, and lots of local drama. The **Auckland Town Hall** is the city's best-known building. The Great Hall seats over 1,600 and is modeled after the Gewandhaus Concert Hall in Leipzig, Germany, which was bombed during World War II. It is regarded as one of the finest acoustically tuned concert halls in the world, and it schedules regular performances by the Auckland Philharmonia and the New Zealand Symphony Orchestra. For listings of events at The Edge, call ✆ **09/307-5060,** visit its website, or go to www.akcity. govt.nz.

The **SKYCITY Theatre** is the newest addition to the city's performance venues. The 700-seat theater features state-of-the-art technology and major local and international performers in dance, theater, rock, pop, jazz, and cabaret. For details on events, call ✆ **0800/759-2489** or visit www.skycity.co.nz.

The **Maidment Theatre** at Auckland University (✆ **09/308-2383;** www.maidment.auckland.ac.nz) is well known for New Zealand drama and theater sports; the **Bruce Mason Centre,** in Takapuna (✆ **0800/005-959** in NZ, or 09/488-**2940;** www.bmcentre.co.nz), offers a little of everything.

The Live Music Scene

Pick up the free *Auckland What's On* guide from the visitor center for the latest on the music scene. You'll find jazz and rhythm-and-blues gigs at places such as **London Bar,** Wellesley and Queen streets (✆ **09/373-3864**); and **Deschlers,** High Street (✆ **09/379-958**), which is popular with the 20- to 30-something after-work crowd. The **Alto Casino & Bar** at SKYCITY (✆ **09/363-6368**) also has live jazz performances.

If Irish music is your thing, you'll find it at **Danny Doolan's ★**, Viaduct Basin (✆ **09/358-2554**), where there's live entertainment on Thursday, Friday, and Saturday nights.

Dogs Bollix ★★★, at the intersection of Karangahape and Newton roads, Newton (✆ **09/376-4600**), is one of the city's premium music venues. It's a pub environment showcasing the best homegrown talent and international rock, Celtic, folk, and blues talent. **Kings Arms ★★★**, 59 France St., Newton (✆ **09/373-3420;** www.kingsarms.co.nz), is another top live rock-and-roll venue featuring international and local favorites. It has a big garden bar and also stages live music on Sunday afternoons. The **Powerstation ★★★**, 33 Mount Eden Rd., Eden Terrace (no phone; www.powerstation.net.nz), has been the iconic starting point for many well known New Zealand groups including internationally recognized Shihad. They feature local talent and international names like Ben Harper and the Beastie Boys.

The Club & Bar Scene

No matter how many nightspots are listed here, somebody's favorite will always be overlooked. If you want a night with the work-hard, play-hard business crowd, head for Parnell; older, richer, devil-may-care types flock to Viaduct Harbour and its many nighttime haunts. A younger, funkier set hangs out in High Street/Vulcan Lane or at Britomart in the inner city; most of the all-night clubs, drag clubs, and gay bars are along Karangahape Road; and Ponsonby is a favored upmarket place for drinks, dinner, and a general wind-up before hitting the club scene.

Inner City If you want to check out the yachting scene, head for the **Loaded Hog,** Viaduct Harbour, Hobson and Quay streets (✆ **09/366-6491**), where the pace is fairly frisky after a day on the water. **Spy Bar,** 204 Quay St., Viaduct Harbour (✆ **09/377-7811;** www.spybar.co.nz), is Auckland's top after-hours bar for a sophisticated older crowd.

Minus 5 Ice Lounge, Princes Wharf (✆ **09/377-6702**), is the "coolest" experience in town. Everything from the walls to the glasses is made of ice, and the temperature is a constant –5°F (–21°C), so make the essential booking and don your warmest coat. **Crow Bar,** 26 Wyndham St. (✆ **09/366-0398**), is a classy little rich joint that's trendy in the wee small hours. **Honey,** 5 O'Connell St. (✆ **09/369-5639**), is a sophisticated spot offering over 30 varieties of champagne and New Zealand's very own vodka label, 42-Below—the cocktails are winners. **Opium,** 291–297 Queen St. (✆ **09/378-0888**), is a very sexy, dimly lit Asian-inspired restaurant and bar frequented by Auckland's aspiring cognoscenti. The restaurant's all-blue **Ming Bar** is quite the place to be seen. It's located within the Sky Metro Building on Aotea Square. Another popular hangout for the who's who is the meganight spot, **Sale Street,** 7 Sale St., Freemans Bay ((C) **09/307-8148;** www.salest.co.nz), where you'll find everything from a restaurant and Yakitori bar to live music stages, a microbrewery, private bars, and a huge outdoor deck. They stage everything from comedy nights to themed parties.

Coco Club, 3 Fort Lane, inner city ((C) **09/309-3848**), is an upmarket alley bar and hidden gem for sophisticates, offering vintage champagne by the glass and live jazz every night. **Khuja Lounge,** 536 Queen St. ((C) **09/377-3711;** www.khuja.co.nz), is an institution. Its Latin/hip-hop/funk DJ scene is ever popular with the 20s and 30s crowd. And don't miss chef Peter Gordon's latest inspiration, **Bellota,** 91 Federal St., opposite SKYCITY Grand Hotel. It's a supercool, dark, sensuously modern take on a Spanish tapas bar. **La Zeppa,** 33 Drake St., Freemans Bay ((C) **09/379-8167;** www.lazeppa.co.nz), is another popular tapas and wine bar in the Victoria market area. It's popular with the corporate crowd.

Ponsonby   SPQR, 150 Ponsonby Rd. ((C) **09/360-1710;** www.spqrnz.co.nz), is the staple of Ponsonby Road. It has a great bar scene late Friday and Saturday nights; you'll see all sorts, both gay and straight, indulging in cocktails with fanciful names such as Horny Monkey and the Slapper. **Lime,** 167 Ponsonby Rd. ((C) **09/360-7167;** www.worldsbestbars.com), is the smallest bar of all, and everyone, just everyone, is determined to be first or second here—after that, there's always a queue to get in.

Sponge, 198 Ponsonby Rd. ((C) **09/360-0098;** www.spongebar.co.nz), attracts a younger dance crowd; and **Whiskey,** 210 Ponsonby Rd. ((C) **09/361-2666;** www.whiskeybars.com), has a chic interior and is the best late-night scene on Friday and Saturday. The very popular **Malt,** 442 Richmond Rd., Grey Lynn ((C) **09/360-9537;** www.maltbar.co.nz), feels like a local corner pub, but with more warmth and style.

Parnell/Newmarket   Iguaçu, 269 Parnell Rd., Parnell ((C) **09/358-4804**), has established a reputation for hedonism. A business crowd tends to let loose here on

Friday and Saturday nights, and it's pretty much a case of anything goes—certainly lively, and certainly a pickup joint of the first degree. A younger hip crowd looking for good house music heads to **Denim,** 207 Parnell Rd., Parnell (© **09/337-0227**).

The Gay Scene

It's hard to keep up with Auckland's ever-changing gay scene—especially when you're not gay. But I have it on good authority that **Urge,** 490 Karangahape Rd. (© **09/307-2155;** www.urgebar.co.nz), is a good bar for the "more masculine" crowd. Just be sure to wear leather! **Kamo,** 382 Karangahape Rd. (© **09/377-2313**), is a gay-friendly scene. The **Family Bar,** 270 Karangahape Rd. (© **09/309-0213;** www.familybar. co.nz), attracts a colorful gay crowd. The **Den,** 348 Karangahape Rd. (© **09/307-9191**), is a men's safe-sex cruise club; and you'll find a gay (male) sauna at **Centurian Sauna,** 18 Beresford Sq. (© **09/377-5571;** www.centuriansauna.co.nz). For a night of food and fun, you can visit drag cabaret shows at **Caluzzi Cabaret & Restaurant,** 461 Karangahape Rd. (© **09/357-0778**), and **Finale Cabaret Restaurant,** 350 Karangahape Rd. (© **09/377-4820**). For more information on venues and activities, check www.rainbowtourism.co.nz.

A SIDE TRIP TO WAIHEKE ISLAND ★★★

This divine little paradise is just 35 minutes from downtown Auckland by ferry. Of its permanent population of about 8,000, nearly 1,500 commute to the city each day to work; in summer, the island's population swells to over 40,000 as visitors come to languish in the enchanting mix of white-sand beaches, lush native bush, green farmland, top wineries and vineyards, and swish little cafes and restaurants. I strongly recommend that you stay at least 1 or 2 nights.

Essentials

GETTING THERE   By Ferry   Fullers Ferries (© 09/367-9111; www.fullers. co.nz) offers hourly service (20 sailings daily) from downtown Auckland to Waiheke Island. Ferries depart from Pier 2, Quay Street, in Central City. Most sailings are met by buses, shuttles, and taxis at Matiatia, near the main township of Oneroa. The Fullers trip takes 35 minutes and costs NZ$35 round-trip for adults, NZ$18 for children ages 5 to 15.

The **SeaLink Travel Group** (© 0800/732-546 in NZ, or 09/300-5900; www. sealink.co.nz) passenger and vehicular ferry leaves from Half Moon Bay, Pakuranga, and arrives at the Kennedy Point Wharf farther east across the Surfdale Causeway. Ferries run every hour daily between 6am and 6pm. The fare is NZ$138 round-trip for a car and driver. Passengers without cars pay NZ$32 adults, NZ$18 children ages 5 to 15. Reservations are essential.

Pine Harbour Ferry, Jack Lachlan Drive, Pine Harbour, Auckland (© **09/536-4725;** www.pineharbour.co.nz), operates regular service to Waiheke, between 8:30am and 5:40pm, with extended hours between December 27 and January 31. The round-trip fare is NZ$26 adults, NZ$16 children, and NZ$64 for a family. It's a shorter, cheaper ferry trip, but you have to drive farther on the Auckland side if you're staying in the city.

By Tour   Fullers Waiheke Explorer Tour ★★ (② **09/367-9111**) gives you the option of being met on the island by a bus and taken on one of four tours, which last from 1½ hours to all day. It's an excellent option if you're short on time and it includes unlimited bus travel on the island for the rest of the day. It departs daily at 10am and noon and costs NZ$49 for adults, NZ$25 for children 5 to 15 years old.

By Air   In 2009, the air-charter service **Air Discovery** (② **0800/247-347** in NZ, or 09/372-4480; www.airdiscovery.co.nz) began operating flights between Auckland Airport and Waiheke Island; the service whisks you to the island in just 15 minutes (NZ$149 per person each way).

ORIENTATION   Waiheke Island is approximately 19km (12 miles) long and has 90km (56 miles) of coastline, 40km (25 miles) of which is white-sand beaches. **Oneroa,** the largest shopping village on Waiheke, is a 15- to 20-minute uphill walk from Matiatia Wharf, where the passenger ferries dock. It's a 10-minute drive from the Kennedy Point Wharf, where the vehicular ferry docks. This western end of the island has the most settlement around **Sandy** and **Enclosure Bays** and **Palm Beach. Ostend** and **Surfdale** also have shops and cafes. The best supermarket is at Surfdale.

GETTING AROUND   By Car   If you don't want to take a car to the island, hire a rental when you arrive. **Waiheke Auto Rentals,** Matiatia Wharf (② **09/372-8998;** www.waihekerentals.co.nz), has good hourly rates and offers pickup and key drop-off service. Four-wheel-drive vehicles, scooters, motorbikes, and mountain bikes are also available. For bicycle rental, contact **Waiheke Bike Hire,** Matiatia Wharf car park (② **09/372-7937;** www.waihekebikehire.co.nz), open daily from 9am (except Dec 25). Rates begin at NZ$35 per day and subsequent days are NZ$15 each (cash only).

By Bus   For information on Waiheke Island bus services visit **Maxx** (② **09/366-6400;** www.maxx.co.nz). Buses serve most bays and beaches at the west end of the island. Pick up a schedule from bus drivers. Inquire about the **All-Day Bus Pass,** which costs NZ$8.50 adults, NZ$5 children ages 5 to 15, and NZ$22 family.

By Tour   An excellent way to get a feel for Waiheke is to go with **Ananda Tours ★★** (② **09/372-7530** or 027/233-4565; www.ananda.co.nz). It offers art studio, gourmet food and wine, and ecowalking tours with knowledgeable guides; prices begin at NZ$105 per person.

VISITOR INFORMATION   The best place to get information is at **Waiheke i-SITE,** 118 Ocean View Rd., Oneroa (② **09/372-1234;** www.waiheke.aucklandnz. com), open daily from 9am to 5pm. Their staff has extensive knowledge of available accommodations on the island. There is also an information kiosk at Matiatia Wharf.

For more information on Waiheke Island, check out www.waihekeonline.com and www.gotowaiheke.co.nz.

SPECIAL EVENTS   The **Waiheke Island Wine Festival** (② **09/372-7676;** www.aucklandnz.com), in February, is a great chance to taste the island's terrific, award-winning wines. Tickets go on sale in October. **Headland Sculpture on the Gulf** (② **09/372-9907;** www.sculptureonthegulf.co.nz) is a must-see in late January and early February. It's held every 2 years (check website for 2013 dates) and is an unforgettable outdoor exhibition of large scale contemporary sculpture along Waiheke Island's coastal walkway.

HOTELS ■
The Boatshed **6**
Estate Church Bay **5**
Te Whau Lodge **10**

ATTRACTIONS ●
Connells Bay Sculpture Park **15**
Te Whau Garden **11**
Waiheke Community Art Gallery **1**
Waiheke Island Historic Village
& Museum **13**
Whittaker's Musical Museum **1**

RESTAURANTS ◆
Cable Bay Vineyard **3**
Mudbrick Vineyard
& Restaurant **4**
Nourish Café **8**
Passage Rock Wines
& Restaurant **14**
Stephano's **7**
Stonyridge Vineyard
& Veranda Café **12**
Te Whau Vineyard Café **9**
Vino Vino **2**

5

Exploring the Island

In Oneroa, visit the **Waiheke Community Art Gallery,** 2 Korora Rd. (© **09/372-9907;** www.waihekeartgallery.org.nz), where you'll find a wide range of works from the many resident artists and craftspeople on the island. It's open daily from 10am to 4pm. You can pick up a copy of the Waiheke Art Guide there (or at the Visitor Centre). It lists about 20 local artists, many of whom open their studios to visitors. The guide also marks the location of six large public sculptures acquired from previous Headland Sculpture on the Gulf events. Nearby is the fascinating **Whittaker's Musical Museum,** 2 Korora Rd. ★ (© **09/372-9627;** www.musical-museum.org; about NZ$12), where Lloyd and Joan Whittaker will hold you spellbound with their 90-minute live performances on a range of antique musical instruments, including organs, concertinas, pianolas, and mouth organs (Sat at 1:30pm). A screening of a recorded show is shown Sunday through Friday at 1:30pm. The museum is open daily, 1 to 4pm.

The **Waiheke Island Historic Village & Museum,** 165 Onetangi Rd. (© **09/372-7143** or 09/373-6861), is overlooked by a fortified Maori settlement site first inhabited some 700 years ago. There are old cottages with collections of furniture, books, documents, and photographs. It's open Wednesday, and weekends year-round, and daily during school holidays and in summer, from noon to 4pm. Catch the Onetangi Bus no. 1 to get there.

Be up early to experience a bit of local culture at the **Ostend Market** ★, Ostend Hall, on the corner of Ostend Road and Belgium Street (© **09/372-4475;** www.ostendmarket.co.nz). A parade of local pottery, island-made goods, fruit and vegetables, herbal remedies, massage, plants, herbs, and more, it's held every Saturday from 8:30am to 12:30pm. On Sunday between 10am and 2pm, visit the **Waiheke Island Farmers' Market** at 7 Belgium St., Ostend.

Another "must" activity is a drive to the glorious **Onetangi Bay** ★★—in my mind, one of the best beaches in New Zealand. Here you can swim and surf in crystal-clear water with views as far as the eye can see. If you want to feel the true spirit of freedom, take it all off at the western end of **Palm Beach,** a small bay used for nude swimming.

For a peek into a fabulous private garden, check out Lance and Kay Peterson's **Dead Dog Bay** (formerly Te Whau Garden), 31 Vintage Lane (© **09/372-6748;** www.deaddogbayco.nz), which features a stunning combination of art and native bush. Even better is **Connells Bay Sculpture Park** ★★★, Cowes Bay Road (© **09/372-8957;** www.connellsbay.co.nz), where you'll find a superb display of work by top New Zealand sculptors set into the magnificent native bush landscape. Admission is NZ$30 adults and NZ$15 children 14 and under. This outstanding guided experience is by appointment only from late October through April. If you're a real art fan you might consider their accommodations for one or two couples (see p. 136).

For additional, delightful walks pick up the excellent *Waiheke Island Walkways* ★ brochure from the visitor center. It outlines and maps out eight great island walks.

Another fabulous way to see the island is to **Drive the Loop** ★★, a 1-day self-drive tour that starts and finishes at Waiheke Auto Rentals on Matiatia Wharf (see "Getting Around," above). The company provides the rental vehicle and loop tour package, which includes maps with all the most interesting people and places highlighted. It takes 4 to 8 hours (65km/40 miles) to complete the loop, depending on how often you stop, and costs NZ$120 to NZ$175, depending on the vehicle category. For information, call ✆ **09/372-8998** or fax 09/372-9822.

Visiting Vineyards

To the surprise of many, more than 40 vineyards operate on Waiheke Island, where the Mediterranean-style climate is perfect for growing grapes (and olives). Some of the country's best red wines come from the island. Before you start exploring, pick up the free *Waiheke Winegrowers' Map,* or check out the Waiheke Winegrowers' Association website, www.waihekewine.co.nz. Plan your visits around eating time, because several growers have excellent restaurants.

One of the leaders among the Waiheke vineyards is undoubtedly **Stonyridge ★★★**, 80 Onetangi Rd. (✆ **09/372-8822;** www.stonyridge.com). In 1987, Stonyridge produced the first Larose vintage, which was immediately judged one of the world's top red wines by the *London World Guide to Cabernet.* It has the dreamiest vineyard, with an incredibly picturesque view from its restaurant, which is one of the nicest places on the island to dine (lunch only; see "Where to Eat," later in this chapter). Tours of their cellar, vineyard, and olive grove (with two wine tastings) begin at 11:30am on Saturday and Sunday; admission is NZ$12 per person.

Mudbrick Vineyard & Restaurant ★★, 126 Church Bay Rd., Oneroa (✆ **09/372-9050;** www.mudbrick.co.nz), is another magical setting for a meal. **Goldwater Estate,** 18 Causeway Rd., Ostend (✆ **09/372-7493;** www.goldwater wine.com), is a small premium winegrower producing top cabernet/merlots. It's open daily noon to 4pm from December through February with reduced hours for the rest of the year. It offers tasting sessions and tours by arrangement. **Cable Bay Vineyards ★★★**, 12 Nick Johnstone Dr., Oneroa (✆ **09/372-5889;** www.cable bayvineyards.co.nz), features a beautiful architecturally designed complex that includes the winery, tasting room, restaurant, bar, and an art gallery. Cable Bay boasts dramatic views over Motukaha Island. They are open for lunch daily from 11am, and offer dinner Thursday through Saturday from 6pm.

Kennedy Point Wines & Olive Oil ★, 44 Donald Bruce Rd., Kennedy Point (✆ **09/372-5600;** www.kennedypointvineyard.com), has a winery and tasting room in a beautiful setting. **Te Whau Vineyard & Cafe ★★★**, 218 Te Whau Dr. (✆ **09/372-7191;** www.tewhau.com), has a smart cafe that serves lunch daily in

The Good Oil

Waiheke is fast becoming known for its premium extra-virgin olive oils, with some 20,000 olive trees growing on the island. Harvest season is April through May or June, and there is no better place to start sampling than **Rangihoua Estate ★**, 1 Gordons Rd., Rocky Bay (✆ **09/372-6214;** www. rangihoua.co.nz). The Frantoio Room is open Monday through Saturday in January and February; otherwise, tours and tastings are held Saturdays from 11am until 4pm, or by appointment. You'll find more award-winning olive oils at **Azzuro Olives**, 152 Te Whau Dr. (✆ **09/372-2700;** www.azzurogroves. com). Their farm shop offers olive tastings and sales, and includes fine alpaca clothing made from the alpaca herd on their property.

meandering IN MATAKANA ★★

Approximately 1 hour north of Auckland is the village of **Warkworth,** at the heart of the Kowhai Coast. It gives access to the very pretty **Sandspit/Matakana/Leigh area,** where you can catch a ferry to Kawau Island or visit a range of excellent swimming beaches. It's not exactly off the beaten track, but the whole area offers some fine accommodations, wineries, and boutique food operations, and the chance to mellow out away from fellow tourists.

The **Warkworth i-SITE Centre,** 1 Baxter St., Warkworth (✆ **09/425-9081;** fax 09/425-7584; www.warkworth-information.co.nz), is open daily from 9am to 5:15pm year-round (closed Dec 25). For Matakana information, check www.matakanacoast.com or www.matakanavillage.co.nz.

You'll find a nice little cluster of activities in the Sandspit and Matakana areas just a few minutes out of Warkworth, including several crafts outlets, among them **Morris & James Country Pottery & Café,** 48 Tongue Farm Rd., Matakana (✆ **09/422-7116;** www.morrisandjames.co.nz), makers of quality terra-cotta and glazed goods. It's open daily from 9am to 5pm with guided pottery tours Monday through Friday at 11:30am. Ask about throwing and decorating your own pot or platter.

Don't miss **ZEALANDIA Sculpture Garden ★★★**, 138 Mahurangi West Rd., Warkworth (✆ **09/422-0099;** www.zealandiasculpturegarden.co.nz). Created by leading New Zealand sculptor Terry Stringer, it features a sculpture park surrounded by farmland. It's open by appointment from November through March; admission ranges from NZ$10 to NZ$15. **Brick Bay Wines & Sculpture Trail ★★★**, Arabella Lane, Snells Beach (✆ **09/425-4690;** www.brickbaysculpture.co.nz), is another fine choice for art lovers. Admission is NZ$12 and they're open daily from 10am to 5pm. The **Matakana Village Farmers' Market ★★**, 2 Matakana Valley Rd. (✆ **09/422-7503;** www.matakanavillage.co.nz), is held Saturdays from 8am to 1pm. You can also explore the trendy Matakana shopping complex adjacent to the market. Refresh yourself afterward at **Brookview Tea House ★**, 1335 Leigh Rd., Matakana (✆ **09/423-0390;** www.brookviewteahouse.co.nz); or pick up perfect bread and picnic foods from **Matakana Patisserie ★★**, 70 Matakana Valley Rd. (✆ **09/422-9896;** www.matakanapatisserie.co.nz), which is open daily from 7am.

No trip to this area is complete without a cruise or ferry ride from Sandspit Wharf to **Kawau Island ★★** (www.kawauisland.org.nz). Sir George Grey, an early governor of New Zealand, built the Mansion House 150 years ago. It's now restored and open for visits; on the grounds you'll find the descendants of his "Australian imports": wallabies, kookaburras, and rosellas. **Reubens Water Taxis** (✆ **0508-282-552** in NZ, or 09/425-8006; www.aucklandescape.co.nz), will take you to the island for

summer and dinner Thursday through Saturday, with reduced winter hours. Tours are NZ$12 per person. With more than 500 cellared wines, Te Whau houses the most diverse collection of New Zealand wine in the world. **Passage Rock Wines & Restaurant,** 438 Orapiu Rd. (✆ **09/372-7257;** www.passagerockwines.co.nz), is in a tranquil bay and has a cafe. Its award-winning wines have grabbed international attention—as have its wood-fired pizzas.

NZ$55 round-trip for adults, NZ$28 for kids 5 to 11 years. They also operate the excellent **Royal Mail Cruise,** which leaves Sandspit wharf each day at 10:30am and takes you to remote island stops. It costs NZ$68 for adults (NZ$90 with an on-board BBQ lunch), NZ$30 children 5 to 11 (NZ$41 with lunch), plus a small DOC entry fee (NZ$4 adults, NZ$2 kids 5–15) for Kawau Mansion House.

If you'd like to stay on Kawau Island, **Kawau Lodge** ★, North Cove (www.kawaulodge.co.nz; ✆ 09/422-8831), is an ecofriendly stay. Rooms cost NZ$210 to NZ$245 per night, or a weekend package for NZ$695, which includes 2 nights' accommodations, all meals, and transfers from Sandspit to the island. It's a good base for exploring the famous **Goat Island Marine Reserve** ★★★, 4km (2½ miles) northeast of Leigh and about 40 minutes from Warkworth, which was established in 1975 as New Zealand's first marine reserve and is a mecca for divers. You can also explore aboard the **Glass Bottom Boat** at Leigh (✆ 09/422-6334; www.glassbottomboat.co.nz) on one of two tours, which cost around NZ$25 for adults, NZ$13 for children 5 to 15 years, and NZ$70 for a family.

If you decide to spend a night here—and I strongly advise you do—you will be spoiled for choice. **Takatu Lodge & Vineyard** ★★★, 518 Whitmore Rd., Matakana (www.takatulodge.co.nz; ✆ 09/423-0299) has four gorgeous suites in a stunning, contemporary property set amid a working vineyard. Their own Takatu wine is also available, and you'll get a free vineyard wine-tasting session with antipasti. Rooms cost NZ$710, which includes a three-course breakfast.

The **Saltings Estate** ★★, 1210 Sandspit Rd., Warkworth (www.saltings.co.nz; ✆ 09/425-9670), is also a delight. Two self-contained apartments overlook a small biodynamic vineyard and winery. The upper two-bedroom apartment has the best views. It's idyllic, and apartments cost you NZ$295 to NZ$495. Set among 40 acres of vineyards and olive groves, **Riverside Matakana** ★★, 170 Green Rd., Matakana (www.riversidematakana.co.nz; ✆ 09/423-0353), has 17 luxurious self-contained cottages, each with two bathrooms, room for six, and an outdoor barbecue. There are tennis and *pétanque* courts, a large swimming pool, and a boat ramp for sharing. Doubles cost around NZ$290 to NZ$350 per night.

In Warkworth, stop by the visitor center for the brochure listing restaurants, attractions, and lodging. One to consider is **Mariposa Palm Café,** 253 Point Wells Rd., Matakana (✆ 09/422-7597), a delightful cafe destination set amid a subtropical garden and nursery. It's open daily 9am to 4pm. Matakana Village also has several cafes and restaurants in addition to those listed earlier in this section.

If you want to take a wine tour, contact **Waiheke Island Wine Tours** (✆ 09/372-2140; www.waihekeislandwinetours.co.nz). Wayne Eagleton will pick you up from the 10am ferry at 10:35am and your tour will be finished in time for the 4pm ferry. A shared tour costs NZ$99 person (over 18). A private exclusive tour can be tailored to your tastes and costs NZ$230 per person. Fullers and Ananda Tours also offer vineyard tours; see "Getting There," above, for more information.

Where to Stay

The island has plenty of good backpacker and hostel options, priced from NZ$22 to NZ$85 per night; or call ℭ **021/709-302** (www.visitwaiheke.co.nz) for a range of excellent self-contained holiday houses to rent. The i-SITE website (see below) also lists many moderately priced holiday homes for rent.

You'll find plenty to be pleased about at the **Estate Church Bay ★★**, 56 Church Bay Rd. (www.theestatechurchbay.com; ℭ **09/372-2637**). Four beautiful rooms overlook vineyards and country views and go for NZ$525 to NZ$725. You might also consider the beautiful self-contained, 2-bedroom stay at **Connells Bay Cottage ★★**, Cowes Bay Rd., Connells Bay (www.connellsbay.co.nz; ℭ **09/372-8957**), which costs NZ$400 a night and sleeps two couples.

The Boatshed Hotel ★★   There's a real feel of New Zealand about this gorgeous spot above the beach, overlooking little Oneroa. To call it "relaxed luxury" is a little undefined, but you'll love the clean-cut elegance of the marine-themed suites. The Boatshed offers terrific sea views from private balconies and every comfort, right down to heated bathroom floors. For something special, splurge for the three-story Lighthouse suite, which has a private top-floor lounge and a first-floor bedroom with commanding views and a balcony. Ground-floor rooms are more spacious. You may never want to leave.

Tawa and Huia sts., Oneroa. www.boatshed.co.nz. ℭ **09/372-3242.** Fax 09/372-3262. 7 units. NZ$630–NZ$955. Rates include breakfast. Off-season rates. AE, DC, MC, V. Children 11 and under not accepted. **Amenities:** Dining room; bar; free airport and ferry transport; free use of bikes; concierge; nearby golf course; room service; watersports equipment rentals. *In room:* TV/DVD, fridge, hair dryer, minibar, Wi-Fi.

Te Whau Lodge ★★★ 🔥   Gene O'Neill and Liz Eglinton have an unbeatable combination: awesome views, dynamite culinary skills, and relaxed, friendly personalities. Built to blend with the landscape, the lodge utilizes timber finishes and that intrinsic New Zealand building material, corrugated iron. Every spacious room has its own theme, its own bathroom, and its own fabulous balcony. Gene and Liz will take care of all your activity bookings. And just when you think it can't get any better, Gene will present you with one of his delectable two-course table d'hôte dinners, using vegetables fresh from the lodge garden. The lodge has its own sewage disposal and gray water treatment plant, too. Te Whau doesn't have some of the extras of the Boatshed, but in my view it's a more intimate, friendly experience.

36 Vintage Lane, Te Whau Point, Waiheke. www.tewhaulodge.co.nz. ℭ **09/372-2288.** Fax 09/372-2218. 4 units. NZ$585. Reduced rate for 2 or more nights. Off-peak rates. Rates include breakfast and predinner canapés. Dinner NZ$70–NZ$100. AE, DC, MC, V. Children 11 and under not accepted. **Amenities:** Bar; free airport and ferry transport; concierge; nearby golf course; outdoor Jacuzzi; massage; room service; Wi-Fi in main reception areas. *In room:* TV/DVD on request, hair dryer.

Where to Eat

One of the best Waiheke restaurants is **Te Whau Vineyard Café ★★★**, 218 Te Whau Dr. (ℭ **09/372-7191**). *Wine Spectator* rated it one of the top New Zealand restaurants for wine lovers, and it has an amazing collection of over 500 New Zealand wines. It offers daily lunch from 11am to 5pm, dinner Thursday through Saturday in summer, and Friday to Sunday in winter, from 6:30 to 11pm. Main courses average NZ$38.

At **Mudbrick Vineyard & Restaurant** ★★, Church Bay Road, Oneroa (✆ 09/ 372-9050), diners gaze out over rolling farmland to the waters of Hauraki Gulf while enjoying French rural cuisine; main courses are NZ$28 to NZ$38. Stonyridge Vineyard's **Veranda Café** ★★, 80 Onetangi Rd. (✆ 09/372-8822; www.stonyridge. co.nz), serves excellent Pacific Rim cuisine in a glorious romantic setting. It serves lunch only—daily in summer, and on Saturday and Sunday in winter. Main courses are NZ$25 to NZ$35; reservations are required. Also great for lunch (and dinner Fri–Sat nights from 6pm) is **Cable Bay Vineyard** ★★, 12 Nick Johnstone Dr., Oneroa (✆ 09/372-5889; www.cablebayvineyards.co.nz).

In Oneroa village, **Vino Vino** ★, behind Green Hills Wines & Spirits, Oneroa (✆ 09/372-9888; www.vinovino.co.nz), is a local favorite for its big Mediterranean platters and full a la carte dining on a huge deck with stunning views.

Nourish Café ★, 3 Belgium St., Ostend (✆ 09/372-3557; www.nourish.co.nz), has a fresh seasonal menu with main courses around NZ$26, plus great baked goods. It's open daily 8am to 4pm, with late nights on Friday and Saturday. If you're after a tasty pizza or a light pasta dish, **Stefano's**, located in Surfdale Village (✆ 09/372-5309), has takeaways and a delivery service (and gluten-free pizzas on request).

A SIDE TRIP TO GREAT BARRIER ISLAND ★★

Imagine pristine white-sand beaches empty of people, lush mountains, and a vast network of walking tracks. Add rare birds and plant life, a permanent population of less than 1,000, and a seductive, laid-back lifestyle, and you have New Zealand's fourth-largest landmass, Great Barrier Island. The Department of Conservation administers over 70% of the island, and locals like to say that there are more conservationists per square inch than anywhere else in New Zealand.

This seductive paradise is *the* place if you're looking for a unique New Zealand wilderness experience. It's New Zealand as it used to be—all 285 sq. km (111 sq. miles) of it. It's isolated, yet it's only a 35-minute plane ride from our biggest city. It's a place the locals call "the Barrier" and I call "heaven." Get yourself there and you'll remember it forever.

Essentials

GETTING THERE   By Plane   Great Barrier Airlines (✆ 0800/900-600 in NZ, or 09/275-9120; www.greatbarrierairlines.co.nz) runs daily flights to the island from Auckland International Airport and North Shore Aerodrome. You can only take 15kg (33 lbs.) of baggage, and flights cost NZ$99 to NZ$125 one-way. **Fly My Sky,** Domestic Terminal, Auckland International Airport (✆ 0800/222-123 in NZ, or 09/256-7026; www.flymysky.co.nz), also offers daily flights to the island. Most flights land at Claris Airfield in the center of the island; some land at Okiwi Airfield, 8km (5 miles) from Port Fitzroy. The 35-minute trip costs NZ$99 to NZ$120 one-way.

By Ferry   Ferries land at Tryphena, at the southern end of the island. **SeaLink,** 45 Jellicoe St., Auckland Viaduct (✆ 0800/732-546 in NZ, or 09/300-5900; www. sealink.co.nz), runs 4½- to 5-hour trips to the island daily in summer and 3 days a week in winter (timetables vary). The *Eco Islander* has two theaters with plasma screens showing movies and documentaries, a cafe, and a reading room on board. The long trip can be grueling when the sea is rough. Round-trip fares are NZ$127 adults, NZ$102 seniors and students, NZ$85 children ages 5 to 15, and NZ$370 for a car. I think it's far better to pay a bit more for the short flight. And don't worry about taking a car—it's easy to pick up a cheap rental at the Claris Airfield. **Fullers Ferry** (© 09/367-9111; www.fullers.co.nz) is a much faster (2½-hr.) trip, but its timetable service operates only in high season (roughly, Dec–Jan).

ORIENTATION Great Barrier Island is approximately 15km (9⅓ miles) wide and 30km (19 miles) long, with Mount Hobson (621m/2,037 ft.) rising in the center. The island landscape is rugged, and much of it is inaccessible by road. The west coast is characterized by steep, forested ranges that run down to the sea; the east coast offers sweeping, white-sand beaches and rolling hills. The main areas of settlement are **Port Fitzroy** in the north; **Claris, Whangaparapara,** and **Okupu** in the center; and **Tryphena** in the south. Good roads connect them all. Claris and Tryphena are the main villages, though neither is much more than a few shops, cafes, a pub, and a post office. Port Fitzroy boasts one store, a dive station, and a boat club. There are no banks or ATMs on the island (although many businesses accept credit cards). Be prepared to pay more for basic supplies than you would on the mainland.

GETTING AROUND **By Car** Reasonably priced rental options include **GBI Rent A Car,** 67 Hector Sanderson Rd., Claris (© 09/429-0062; www.gbirentacar. co.nz), which offers free delivery to Claris Airfield and Tryphena Wharf. Prices start at around NZ$50 per day. **Aotea Rentals** (© 0800/426-832 in NZ; www.aoteacar rentals.co.nz) offers a similar service and prices from around NZ$95 per day. It is important to remember that the island is far from a suburban destination. Roads are often narrow and unsealed, there are no streetlights, and cellphone coverage is limited.

By Bus and Shuttle You'll find limited scheduled public transport on the island, but regular bus services meet boats and planes. **Great Barrier Travel** (© 0800/426-832 in NZ, or 09/429-0474; www.greatbarriertravel.co.nz) has daily service to walking tracks, beaches, and Port Fitzroy. A 1-day pass costs around NZ$50. There are also several shuttle companies.

By Bike Rental mountain bikes are available from **GBI Rent A Car** (© 09/429-0062; www.gbirentacar.co.nz) for NZ$45 to NZ$60 per day. **Paradise Cycles,** Tryphena (© 09/429-0700), has multiday special deals.

VISITOR INFORMATION The **Great Barrier Island Information Centre,** Main Road outside Claris Airfield (© 09/429-0767; www.greatbarrierisland.co.nz), is open daily from 7am to 8pm in the summer and 8am to 7pm in the winter. Auckland i-SITE Visitor Centres also supply some Great Barrier Island information at www.greatbarrier.aucklandnz.com.

SPECIAL EVENTS In January, the **Port Fitzroy Mussel Fest** (© 09/429-0072) provides stalls, entertainment, and as many succulent mussels as you can eat. The annual **Santa Parade,** in December at the Claris Sports Club, has a legendary reputation for fun.

Exploring the Island

Great Barrier has a rich history. Maori have inhabited the island for over 1,000 years, and Europeans created a thriving timber industry, milling the huge stands of native kauri trees for the shipbuilding industry. The island was a whaling station until the 1960s, and the relics of old stamping batteries attest to a rich gold- and silver-mining history. The remains of the **Oreville Stamping Battery** are beside the road on the way to Whangaparapara. Also in this area is the very popular **Kaitoke Hot Springs Track,** which leads to natural hot springs in a creek. Use the roadside toilet—it's the last one you'll see for a while. The springs are 45 minutes in. Don't forget insect repellent.

Farther north, at Port Fitzroy, you must visit Tony Bouzaid's **Glenfern Sanctuary ★★★**, Glenfern Road (*©* 09/429-0091; www.glenfern.org.nz). Take his guided walk of the most wonderful native wildlife sanctuaries anywhere. Over 8,000 trees have been planted as part of an ongoing reforestation project; timber boardwalks make the walk easy. Tony also offers multiday tramp-sail packages. Even farther north, you'll find the **S.S. *Wairarapa* Walkway** at the very beautiful (and deserted) **Whangapoua Beach.** The steamer *Wairarapa* wrecked on cliffs near Miners Head on October 29, 1894, with the loss of around 130 lives. A little gravesite at the northern end of the beach serves as a reminder of one of New Zealand's worst shipping disasters.

A range of tracks crisscross **Mount Hobson,** a focal point for keen trampers. There are stunning views from the top on a clear day, and the summit is the main nesting ground for the rare black petrel. It's at least a 2-hour round-trip walk. A signposted side track will take you to **Kaiaraara Kauri Dam,** one of the tallest kauri dams, built over 70 years ago to transport logs out of the forests. If you feel like a steep climb, you'll find the remains of two more dams farther upstream.

In Okupu is a delightful surprise: **Young's Museum ★**, 212 Blind Bay Rd. (*©* 09/429-0388). Christine Young, spurred on by the memory of her father, has put together the cutest little museum you'll find anywhere. It's a real Kiwi experience, with Christine showing you through her father's astounding collection of old photographs that depict early life on the island. Phone ahead for an appointment.

A good number of **artists and sculptors** live on the island; the visitor center can furnish a brochure detailing their whereabouts.

Aotea Sea Kayaks, Mulberry Grove, Tryphena (*©* **09/429-0664;** aoteakayak@hotmail.com), offers night kayak trips, sunset paddles, and harbor kayak cruises. Prices range from NZ$55 to NZ$95. **Bush and Beach ★★** (*©* **0800/042-3224** in NZ, or 09/837-4130; www.bushandbeach.co.nz) offers a range of excellent ecowalks and tours on the island. Their 1-day adventure leaves Auckland Domestic Airport at 7:15am (returns at 5:30pm) and includes two scenic flights, breakfast, and a picnic lunch. Moderate walking ability is required. It costs NZ$675 per person.

Where to Stay & Eat

If you plan on traveling to Great Barrier Island during the summer months, book your accommodations well in advance. In Port Fitzroy, **Fitzroy House,** Glenfern Road (*©* **09/429-0091;** www.fitzroyhouse.co.nz), has a three-bedroom, self-contained cottage; rates start at NZ$200 but expect that to double during peak season from (Dec 24–Jan 15). **Aotea Lodge,** Tryphena (*©* **09/429-0628;** www.aotealodge.com), has both backpacker accommodation (NZ$40 per person) and self-contained units from NZ$120 per night. On a hill above Okupu Beach, you'll find an eco-friendly gem in self-contained **Bay Lodge Cottage ★**, Moana View Road, Okupu (*©* **07/843-2000** or 09/429-0927; www.gamesail.co.nz), for NZ$275. You'll be treated to chilled wine, fruit, cheese, and flowers. Breakfast is included and no children under 12 are accepted.

At the top end of the market, you won't regret a hilltop stay in one of the three rooms at **Earthsong Lodge ★★**, 38 Medland Rd., Tryphena (✆ **09/429-0030;** www.earthsong.co.nz), where Trevor and Carol Rendle cook amazing meals as part of the NZ$762 room rate. The property is totally self-sustaining for energy and water.

Don't get too excited about dining possibilities on the island—they're few and far between, and relatively expensive compared to the city. **Claris Texas Café,** Claris (✆ **09/429-0811**), is one of the best choices, serving hearty breakfast fare, tasty lunches, and good coffee daily. You can eat out in the courtyard overlooking fields and idly wonder what might have become of the rest of the world. **Earthsong Lodge** (see "Where to Stay," above), is open to casual diners, but bookings are essential; its menu specializes in French and nouvelle cuisine. Things are more modest at **Tipi and Bobs Waterfront Restaurant** in Tryphena. You can expect good-value meals, especially if you like fresh fish and chips.

OUT FROM AUCKLAND

For information about Northland and the Coromandel Peninsula, see chapter 6.

En Route to Northland: The Hibiscus Coast

Located 48km (30 miles) north of Auckland, the Hibiscus Coast comprises the communities of Silverdale, Whangaparaoa, Orewa, Waiwera, and Puhoi. The area is a 45-minute drive from Auckland, and InterCity coaches offer service that makes a day's outing a reasonable option.

The **Hibiscus Coast Information Centre,** 214A Hibiscus Coast Hwy. (next to KFC), Orewa (✆ **09/426-0076;** hbcvic@rodney.govt.nz), is open Monday through Friday from 9am to 5pm, Saturday and Sunday from 10am to 4pm.

On the drive north, stop at **Waiwera Thermal Resort ★★**, State Highway 1 (✆ **0800/924-937** in NZ, or 09/427-8800; www.waiwera.co.nz), open daily from 9am to 9pm. Nineteen indoor and outdoor pools are kept at 82°F to 113°F (28°C–45°C); there are both private and communal pools. They also have an Infinity Day Spa, which offers many excellent treatment packages online. Admission to the pools is NZ$26 for adults, NZ$15 for children 5 to 14, NZ$22 for students, and NZ$10 for seniors and spectators.

En Route to the Coromandel Peninsula: The Pacific Coast Highway

The Pacific Coast Highway is not exactly a highway, certainly not in the American sense of the word. Rather, it is a combination of roads that make up one of the best scenic routes in the country, following the coastline from Auckland all the way to Hawke's Bay. Along the way, it delivers you to Coromandel Peninsula via the very pretty **Seabird Coast ★**.

It's worth stopping here for the **Kaiaua Fisheries Licensed Seafood Restaurant & Takeaways,** 939 East Coast Rd., Kaiaua (✆ **09/232-2776**), open daily from 9am to 9pm, which serves some of the best fish and chips in the country. And once you've filled your empty stomach, check out the **Miranda Shorebird Centre ★**, East Coast Road (✆/fax **09/232-2781;** www.miranda-shorebird.org.nz), where you'll find information about the millions of migratory birds that swing by here on their way north. The 8,500 hectares (21,000 acres) of tidal flats are a big attraction for wading birds and bird-watchers alike.

You can also relax in one of the largest hot mineral pools in the Southern Hemisphere or unwind in a private Jacuzzi at **Miranda Hot Springs Thermal Pools** (© **07/867-3055;** www.mirandahotsprings.co.nz). It's open Monday through Thursday from 8am to 9pm, Friday and Saturday from 8am to 10:30pm. Admission is NZ$15 adults (14 and over) and NZ$7 for children.

6 NORTHLAND & COROMANDEL

Northland—Te Tai Tokerau, or "Birthplace of a Nation"—is one of nature's best playgrounds, but surprisingly, visitors often overlook it. The Bay of Islands is what most people know of Northland. This is home to the fabulous Waitangi National Reserve, where the Treaty of Waitangi was signed between Maori and European settlers in 1840; this is also where visitors are best catered to in Northland. Beyond that, the region offers an idyllic summer lifestyle that seems to last year-round.

Northland's peninsular shape offers two contrasting coastlines: white scenic beaches that curve around sheltered coves and harbors to the east, and long stretches of wild, dune-backed beaches and kauri forests pounded by the Tasman Sea to the west.

Northland is made up of five main areas: Whangarei and the east coast, the Bay of Islands, the Far North, Hokianga, and the Kauri Coast. The population is sparse—just 148,000 for the whole region and in the Far North area alone, there are 7,250 sq. km (2,800 sq. miles) of farmland and forest occupied by just 56,000 people. Only three towns—Kaitaia, Kaikohe, and Kerikeri—have more than 4,000 residents. Clearly, you'll have large patches all to yourself, so start exploring.

The Coromandel region, like Northland, has long been a haven for New Zealand holidaymakers. It's closer to Auckland than most of Northland, but it has less to offer in terms of accommodations and organized tourism. Certainly the scenery is just as dramatic, and you'll get that same surfeit of remote beaches and laid-back lifestyle. Leaving Auckland and following the Pacific Coast Highway will take you into Coromandel's quaint, sometimes tatty seaside townships, around endless beaches and bays, and over rugged hill country into the heart of an area made famous by logging, gold mining, gum digging, alternative lifestyles, and artists. There's a raw quality to the Coromandel Peninsula that even the fledging tourist industry hasn't yet tamed.

Northland was the first region to participate in New Zealand's Environmentally Sustainable Tourism pilot project in 2002. It continues to actively promote and facilitate regional sustainability through its Sustainable Tourism Charter. Check www.enterprisenorthland.co.nz for a list of participating tourism operators.

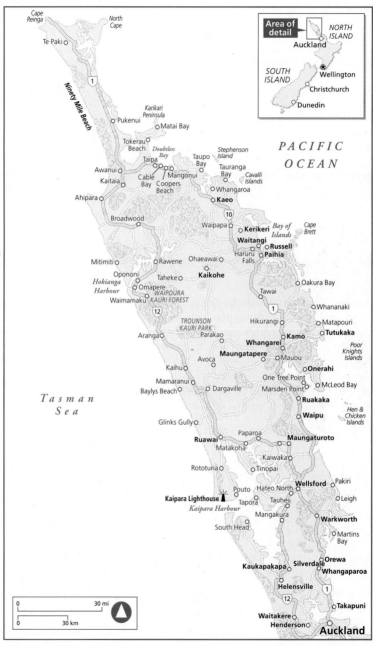

Cape Reinga
North Cape
Te Paki
Ninety Mile Beach
1
Pukenui
Karikari Peninsula
Matai Bay
Tokerau Beach
Doubtless Bay
Taipa
Awanui
Cable Bay
Mangonui
Coopers Beach
Kaitaia
Ahipara
Whangaroa
Broadwood
Kaeo
10
Waipapa
Kerikeri
Waitangi
Russell
Paihia
Mitimiti
Rawene
Ohaeawai
Haruru Falls
Opononi
Taheke
Kaikohe
Hokianga Harbour
Omapere
WAIPOUA KAURI FOREST
Waimamaku
12
Tawai
Oakura Bay
TROUNSON KAURI PARK
Hikurangi
Whananaki
Aranga
Parakao
Matapouri
Kamo
Tutukaka
Kaihu
Avoca
Whangarei
Maungatapere
Mauou
Poor Knights Islands
Mamaranui
Onerahi
Baylys Beach
Dargaville
One Tree Point
Marsden Point
McLeod Bay
Ruakaka
Hen & Chicken Islands
Glinks Gully
Waipu
Ruawai
Paparoa
Maungaturoto
Matakoha
Kaiwaka
Rototuna
Tinopai
Wellsford
Pakiri
Pouto
Hateo North
Tauhes
Leigh
Kaipara Lighthouse
Tapora
Kaipara Harbour
Mangakura
Warkworth
South Head
Martins Bay
Kaukapakapa
Silverdale
Orewa
Whangaparoa
Helensville
1
12
Takapuni
Waitakere
Henderson
Auckland

PACIFIC OCEAN

Stephenson Island
Taupo Bay
Tauranga Bay
Cavalli Islands
Bay of Islands
Cape Brett

Tasman Sea

Area of detail
NORTH ISLAND
Auckland
SOUTH ISLAND
Wellington
Christchurch
Dunedin

0   30 mi
0   30 km

BAY OF ISLANDS & THE FAR NORTH ★★★

Bay of Islands: 233km (144 miles) N of Auckland; Cape Reinga: 440km (273 miles) N of Auckland

The essential personal items for this area are swimsuit, sunglasses, and suntan lotion—perhaps a fishing rod or a wet suit if you're so inclined. With endless beaches, over 144 islands, and warm, clear blue waters to play in, you'll need little else. Recreation is king up here. There's great fishing, excellent diving, and a climate with average winter temperatures ranging from 45°F to 61°F (7°C–16°C) and summer days of 57°F to 77°F (14°C–25°C).

The Bay of Islands features three little townships: **Paihia/Waitangi, Russell,** and **Kerikeri.** In the Far North, the hot spots are **Doubtless Bay; Kaitaia,** the largest town; and up that last thin finger of land to **Cape Reinga,** believed to be the departing point for the spirits of the Maori dead.

Essentials

GETTING THERE & GETTING AROUND **By Plane** There are three Northland airports: Whangarei, Kerikeri, and Kaitaia. **Air New Zealand Link** (✆ **0800/737-000** in NZ, or 09/357-3000; www.airnewzealand.co.nz) offers daily service from Auckland to Kerikeri, with a shuttle bus to Paihia, and daily service from Auckland to Kaitaia. Charter flights are available with **Salt Air Bay of Islands** (✆ **0800/472-5824** in NZ, or 09/402-8338; www.saltair.co.nz) or **Skylink Air Charter** (✆ **09/422-7018;** www.skylink.co.nz).

By Coach (Bus) Both **InterCity** (✆ **09/623-1503;** www.intercity.co.nz) and **Northliner Express** (✆ **09/583-5780;** www.northliner.co.nz) have daily service between Auckland and Paihia, Kerikeri, and Kaitaia. Both offer discounts to VIP backpackers and seniors. There's no local bus service in the Bay of Islands, Doubtless Bay, or Kaitaia.

By Car If you plan to spend a few days in this area, pick up the free *Twin Coast Discovery Highway* map from any visitor center. It's an easy drive however you do it, with beautiful coastal views and rolling farmland all the way and usually very little traffic. Rather than going straight to the Bay of Islands (about a 3-hr. drive), you might want to explore the area known as Whangarei (p. 157). The drive from Auckland to Kaitaia via the east coast takes about 5 hours. Northland's west coast is also worth a visit if you have the time. The best plan is to go up the east side and drive back to Auckland via the west coast.

If you arrive via plane or bus, rental cars are available through **Pegasus Rental Cars** (✆ **0800/354-512** in NZ, or 09/402-8491; www.carrentalsbayofislands. co.nz). Help keep Northland roads clean by getting the official Northland visitor guide from information centers, which maps all recycling drop-off locations. Prepaid recycling bags are sold throughout Northland at service stations, supermarkets, camping grounds, and information centers for NZ$1.50 each.

By Ferry If you stay in Russell but want to eat in Paihia, you'll need to take the passenger ferry that connects the two. It's the only inexpensive means of getting from one shore to another, and it runs hourly beginning at 7am and ending at 7:30pm. In summer, crossings are extended to 10:30pm. Fares are NZ$7 each way or NZ$11 round-trip for adults, NZ$3.50 or NZ$5.50 round-trip for children 5 to 15. If you

Don't be like the majority of visitors who go only as far as the Bay of Islands. Some of the best beaches, natural landscapes, and tranquil retreats lie much farther north. It makes sense to travel up an extra day or 2, rather than staying in the Bay of Islands and, at best, taking a long 12-hour bus trip to Cape Reinga and back. Go the extra mile: You won't regret it.

miss the last boat, you can take the slightly more expensive water taxi. **Note:** The ferry from Paihia carries pedestrians only. If you're driving to Russell, take the car ferry at Opua. No reservations are needed; the ferry shuttles back and forth every 10 minutes, daily from 7am to 10pm, and costs NZ$12 one-way for a car and driver and NZ$1 per extra passenger. Campervans cost NZ$15 and motorcycles NZ$5 one-way. The car ferry lands at Okiato, which is about 10 minutes' drive from Russell township.

By Water Taxi   The **Island Water Taxi** (book at the visitor center) offers 24-hour service; fares depend on the time of day and the number of passengers.

By Tour   Several companies in Auckland offer 1-, 2-, and 3-day tours to the Bay of Islands and beyond. For good value and personal service, contact **Great Sights** (℃ 0800/653-339 in NZ; www.greatsights.co.nz). **Northliner Express** (℃ 09/307-5873; www.northliner.co.nz) also has a range of packages and good-value backpacker passes. **Kiwi Experience** (℃ 09/366-9830; www.kiwiexperience.com) offers well-priced 1-, 2-, and 3-day tours to the Bay of Islands and Cape Reinga. Tours to Cape Reinga operate from Bay of Islands, Doubtless Bay, and Kaitaia (see "To Cape Reinga," below).

ORIENTATION   **Paihia** and **Waitangi** basically form one settlement, which is the hub of the region's commercial and visitor action. All tours and cruises for the Bay of Islands start here. It's a short (1.5km/1-mile) walk to Waitangi, where the historic Treaty House is located. The main street is Marsden Road, which runs along the waterfront. Williams Road is a one-way street perpendicular to the coast; many of the shops are here.

   Russell is a tiny community across the water. The Strand runs along the waterfront. Most of the charter boats in the area are anchored here; access is by ferry.

   Kerikeri is a 20-minute drive north from Paihia. Once you turn off State Highway 10 onto Kerikeri Road, you'll find most of the main attractions and eateries.

   In **Doubtless Bay,** the little fishing village of **Mangonui** (82km/51 miles from Paihia) is the core settlement. **Coopers Beach, Cable Bay, Taipa,** and **Tokerau Beach** are all within a few minutes of Mangonui. From Cable Bay, the coast swings in a huge arc of fabulous remote beaches all the way up to **Karikari Peninsula.**

   Kaitaia is the major town of the Far North, 116km (72 miles) south of Cape Reinga. To the southwest lies the small town of **Ahipara** at the base of **Ninety Mile Beach,** which runs all the way up to the Cape.

VISITOR INFORMATION   You'll find the **Bay of Islands i-SITE Visitor Centre** at The Wharf, Marsden Road, Paihia (℃ 0800/363-463 in NZ, or 09/402-7345; www.visitfarnorthnz.com). Hours are 8am to 5pm in winter, 8am to 7pm in summer. Get your Kerikeri information here, too. Online, go to www.northlandnz.com, www. paihia.co.nz, www.russellnz.co.nz, or www.kerikeri.co.nz.

The **Far North i-SITE Visitor Centre** is at Centennial Park, South Road, Kaitaia (ⓒ **09/408-0879;** fax 09/408-2546; www.visitfarnorthnz.com). It's open daily from 8:30am to 5pm, closed only December 25. For information on Ahipara, Ninety Mile Beach, and Far North activities, see www.ahipara.co.nz or www.topofnz.co.nz.

SPECIAL EVENTS New Zealand's big, 3-day **Bay of Islands Sailing Week Regatta** starts off in late January. February 6 is **Waitangi Day,** a national holiday and cultural day and Paihia is center stage for the day's celebratory events. Dozens of *waka* (war canoes) and over 500 Maori warriors take part in the celebrations and are always a spectacular sight. The **Bay of Islands Jazz and Blues Festival** (ⓒ **09/402-7345**) runs day and night from early to mid-August at various venues around Paihia and Russell and the **Russell Spring Festival** is held in early September.

Exploring the Towns
IN PAIHIA/WAITANGI

Waitangi Treaty Grounds ★★★ Even if you're not interested in history, you'll love it here. This 506-hectare (1,250-acre) reserve has had a massive face-lift, and quite apart from its historical importance, there are fabulous boardwalks through beautiful parklike grounds and mangrove swamps. You can easily spend 2 hours here.

It was on the grounds of the small Georgian house that the Confederation of Chiefs signed the first treaty with the British government. The treaty granted to the Maori the rights of British subjects in exchange for recognition of British sovereignty. The home of James Busby from 1832 to 1880, its broad lawn was the scene of colorful meetings between Maori and Pakeha during the treaty negotiations on February 6, 1840. Inside, you'll see a facsimile of the treaty written in Maori, an exhibition of James Busby's family mementos, and rooms with period furnishings.

The reserve is also home to one of the most magnificent *whare runanga* (meetinghouses) in the country, complete with an inspiring sound-and-light show. The house contains elaborately carved panels from all the Maori tribes in New Zealand and it is one of the few meetinghouses in the country that allows you to photograph the interior. Just below the sweeping lawn, on Hobson's Beach, is an impressive 35m-long (115-ft.) Maori *waka* (war canoe) made for the treaty centennial celebrations from three giant kauri trees. The *waka* and the carved meetinghouse are the highlights of the grounds, in my view.

You'll get far more from your visit if you take one of the tours. I recommend Embrace Waitangi for a comprehensive overview; or Talk the Walk, which focuses on the natural environment and its relationship to Maori. (The more you see the more you save on entry). If your visit coincides with the February 6 celebration of **Waitangi Day,** you'll find the center of activity is the Waitangi National Trust Estate. There's lots of Maori song and dance, plus Pakeha officials in abundance, dressed to the nines in uniforms of then and now. Reserve far in advance, as it's a huge family day with crowds of vacationing Kiwis in attendance.

Waitangi Treaty Grounds, Tau Henare Dr., Waitangi. ⓒ **09/402-7437.** Fax 09/402-8303. www.waitangi. net.nz. Admission (valid for 2 consecutive days) NZ$25 adults, NZ$12 children 14 and under. Several packages include tours and activities. Maori cultural performances NZ$18 adult, NZ$10 children. Apr–Sept daily 9am–5pm; Oct–Mar daily 9am–7pm. Closed Dec 25.

Culture North ★★ Located in the Waitangi Estate grounds, this addition to the cultural program has been a finalist in the New Zealand Tourism Awards. It tells the 1,000-year story of the Maori people from the discovery of New Zealand through

For a truly unique, award-winning cultural experience, climb into a traditional *waka* (canoe) with Hone Mihaka of **Taiamai Tours Heritage Journeys ★★★** (*(C)* **0800/925-286** in NZ, or 09/405-9990; www.taiamaitours.co.nz). You'll be invited to paddle alongside members of the Ngapuhi tribe. They offer three options based on traditional experiences, which can include a marae welcome, a traditional *hangi* (meal), traditional prayers, speechmaking, and a soak in mineral hot springs with Ngapuhi elders. Tours depart from Horotutu Beach, beside the Waitangi Reserve Bridge at Paihia at 10am, 1, and 3pm (weather permitting) and cost from NZ$135 adults, NZ$105 children 6 to 10. No children under 6 years are permitted on the *waka*. For a truly unique Waitangi Day experience that will give you a far deeper and more intimate understanding of Maori culture, join Taiamai's **6-night marae and war canoe experience,** hosted by the Mihaka family. Starting 3 days before the major Waitangi Day celebrations, you'll be trained to crew and paddle a *waka* on the day. This rare opportunity is available only once a year to 32 lucky people, who need to be fit and healthy. Advance bookings are essential and will cost NZ$2,760 per person. See website for further itinerary details.

the present day. Combining drama with a stunning light-and-dance show, it's sure to please. It's a 2-hour program, and hotel pickup service is included. Culture North also provides guided tours of the treaty grounds, a marae visit, and other Maori cultural experiences.

Tau Henare Dr., Waitangi. *(C)*/fax **09/402-5990** or 401-9301. www.culturenorth.co.nz. Admission NZ$65 adults, NZ$33 children 3-15. Oct–Apr Mon, Wed, Thurs, and Sat 7:30–9:30pm. Closed Dec 24-26, Dec 31–Jan 2, and Feb 6. Open May–Sept by arrangement; call for information.

IN RUSSELL

Russell is a veritable minefield of historic sites. This is where the great Maori chief Hone Heke burned everything except the mission property, and chopped down the flagstaff (four times) in defiance of British rule.

If you plan to wander the historic sites, first visit the **Russell Museum,** 2 York St. (*(C)*/fax **09/403-7701;** www.russellmuseum.org.nz), open daily from 10am to 4pm (until 5pm in summer), closed December 25. Admission is NZ$7.50 for adults and NZ$2 for children. You can learn all about Maori-European contact and pick up heritage brochures pointing out other sites in the village. Behind the museum, check out the **Bay of Islands Maritime Park Headquarters and Visitors Centre,** The Strand (*(C)* **09/403-7685;** fax 09/403-7649). Its free 15-minute audiovisual *The Land is Enduring* gives an overview of Maori-European history in the area. It's open from 8:30am to 4:30pm (until 5pm in summer).

Farther down The Strand, you'll find **Pompallier Mission ★** (*(C)* **09/403-9015;** www.pompallier.co.nz). Built in 1841, this is New Zealand's oldest surviving Roman Catholic building. It housed a printing press used from 1842 to 1849 to print religious documents in the Maori language. Today, along with the press, there's a working tannery and bookbindery. Admission is NZ$10 for adults and free for accompanied children, students over 15 pay NZ$6. Prebooked tours cost NZ$7 per person. It's open from 10am to 4pm (until 5pm in summer).

For a look at the oldest wooden church in New Zealand, go to **Christ Church, Church Street** and Robertson Road. You can't miss the dear little building surrounded by colorful flowering hibiscus bushes. It's open daily from 9am to 5pm.

IN KERIKERI

The pretty town of Kerikeri has the most to offer in the Bay of Islands in the way of land-based attractions. Visiting the **Kerikeri Mission Station ★**, 246 Kerikeri Rd. (**© 0800/802-010** in NZ, or 09/407-9236; www.historic.org.nz or www.stonestore. co.nz), is essential if you want to continue the historic theme. It's home to New Zealand's oldest stone building, the **1835 Stone Store,** which has been open for business since 1836. Next door you'll see **Kemp House,** the first mission house and the oldest wooden house in the country. Entry to the ground floor of the store is free and you can shop for authentic heritage goods reminiscent of the store's golden era. You may opt for the full "Mission Experience," which includes an overview of the area's important early history, admission to the upstairs section of the Stone Store, and a tour of Kemp House; it costs NZ$10 per person and accompanied children ages 5 to 15 visit free. It's open daily, 10am to 5pm November through April and until 4pm the rest of the year. **Northern Steamship Company** (**© 0800/944-785** in NZ, or 09/407-9229; www.steamship.co.nz) offers 1-hour cruises of Kerikeri Inlet aboard SS *Eliza Hobson,* departing from the Stone Store Sunday through Friday at 2pm. The cost is NZ$30 for adults, NZ$15 for children ages 5 to 15, and NZ$85 for families.

Foraging for Fine Food

Pick up the *Northland Food and Wine Trail* brochure from the Bay of Islands Visitor Centre (see above) and discover the wealth of boutique food producers and wineries throughout the whole Northland region. You can tailor-make your own food trail, from their detailed descriptions and maps, to suit your own timetable.

Above the Basin is the well-preserved **Kororipo Pa,** a fort occupied by the fearsome chief Hongi Hika; across the river from the *pa* site is **Rewa's Village** (**© 09/407-6454**), a full-scale reconstruction of a *kainga* (fortified pre-European Maori fishing village). It's open daily 9am to 5pm (until 4pm in winter); admission is NZ$5 for adults and NZ$1 for children.

Garden enthusiasts will appreciate **Wharepuke Subtropical Garden,** 190 Kerikeri Rd., Stone Store Hill (**© 09/407-8933;** www.subtropicalgarden.co.nz), which is a growing "art gallery" of subtropical plants. It's open daily 8:30am to 6pm. Entry to the gardens and art gallery is free, but you need to make an appointment for the interactive subtropical garden tours and art courses. There is also a very good cafe here, which is open daily at 10am for lunch and from 5:30 to 10pm for dinner.

Kerikeri is also home to a thriving arts community. Pick up the excellent free brochure *The Kerikeri Art & Craft Trail,* which details 17 excellent outlets within a few kilometers of Kerikeri. A wide variety of top-quality Northland produce is showcased at the **Bay of Islands Farmers' Market ★★**, beside Take Note Bookshop, Hobson Avenue, Kerikeri (www.boifm.org.nz), which is held rain or shine every Sunday from 8:30am to noon.

To sample Northland wines, head for **Cottle Hill Winery,** 28 Cottle Hill Dr. (**© 09/407-5203;** www.cottlehill.co.nz), open Wednesday through Sunday 10am to 5pm with tastings for NZ$5; **Marsden Estate Winery,** 56 Wiroa Rd. (**© 09/407-9398;** www.marsdenestate.co.nz), open daily 10am to 5pm (till 4pm in winter), closed Good Friday, and December 25 and 26; or **Bishops Wood Estate,** 1329 St. Hwy. 10 (© **09/407-9628;** bishopswood@value.net.nz), open daily 10am until late.

For fine New Zealand–made skin-care products, free of all synthetic preservatives or synthetic parabens, check out the highly successful **Living Nature ★★★**, State Highway 10 (© **0508/548-464** in NZ, or 09/407-7895; www.livingnature.com).

IN THE FAR NORTH

In the Taipa area, **Matthews Vintage Collection,** 4365 State Highway 10, 5km (3 miles) north of Taipa (© **09/406-0203;** www.matthewsvintage.com), has an extensive array of restored vintage cars, tractors, and farm and domestic equipment. Admission is NZ$10 adults, NZ$5 children ages 5 to 15 years. **Far North Regional Museum,** 6 South Rd., Kaitaia (© **09/408-1403;** www.farnorthmuseum.co.nz), showcases the story of Maori and Dalmatian settlement, and the history of the kauri gum industry. They have a terrific photographic collection and some beautiful Maori *taonga* (treasures).

The **Ancient Kauri Kingdom ★★**, State Highway 1, Awanui (©/fax **09/406-7172;** www.ancientkauri.co.nz), is 7km (4⅓ miles) north of Kaitaia. You can view massive 30,000- to 50,000-year-old kauri logs that have been hauled from the Northland swamps, then see the fine furniture and crafts that are made from them. It's open daily, and admission is free. You can also see the remnants of ancient buried kauri forests, over 42,000 years old, at **Gumdiggers Buried Forest Park,** Heath Road, Waiharara (© **09/406-7166;** www.gumdiggerspark.co.nz). It's 25km (16 miles) north of Kaitaia and is open daily. It will also give you an insight into the tough lives of the early gum-digging pioneers.

Organized Tours & Cruises

There's no need to prebook before arriving in town, as there are plenty of operators; by shopping around, though, you'll get better deals. The only exception is between December 23 and January 15—if you're planning to visit then, you'll need to reserve ahead.

Dolphin Cruises & Tours, Maritime Building, Waterfront, Paihia (© **0800/653-339** in NZ, or 09/402-7421; www.dolphincruises.co.nz), offers several tours: Its most popular, the **Cream Trip—Day in the Bay ★**, includes swimming with dolphins, a trip to the Hole in the Rock (a large natural rock formation that rises up from the ocean with a hole in it, forming a tunnel that boats can pass through), and boom netting off the back of the boat so passengers can swim in the water behind the boat. It costs NZ$102 adults, NZ$51 children ages 5 to 15, and NZ$30 extra per person to swim with dolphins. The tour runs daily from 9:30am to 4:30pm, and includes an island stopover for lunch (bring your own). The **Swim with Dolphins Cruise ★★**, puts you in some of New Zealand's warmest waters. The purpose-built vessel *Orca II* has a large boom net so less confident swimmers also have the chance to enter the water to see these beautiful marine mammals. This trip costs NZ$89 for adults and NZ$45 for children. It's NZ$30 extra per person to swim with the dolphins.

Explore NZ ★★, Paihia (© **0800/397-567** in NZ, or 09/359-5987; www.explorenz.co.nz), will get your adrenalin pumping with an exhilarating sailing adventure on New Zealand's largest and fastest catamaran. Its 7-hour **On the Edge** daysail in the bay has daily departures from Paihia and Russell from October through April and costs NZ$125 adults, and NZ$89 children 5 to 15. It includes lunch on one of the gorgeous islands in the bay. And if you'd like to try an overnight cruise, step on board **Great Sights Bay of Islands ★★**, Paihia Waterfront (© **0800/653-339;**

www.overnightcruise.co.nz). Their NZ$12-million luxury vessel, *Ipipiri*, a 46m (151-ft.) catamaran, was launched in late 2009. Rates for the overnight cruise will range from NZ$366 to NZ$409 per person and include afternoon tea, a three-course dinner, and breakfast the next day. Cruises depart from Paihia daily from September through April at 1:30pm (returning 10:30am the following day).

TO CAPE REINGA

You'll be hard-pressed to find more dazzling seascapes than those on your way to **Cape Reinga ★★★**. The cape is situated at the top of Aupouri Peninsula, which features famous **Ninety Mile Beach** and three magnificent harbors: **Parengarenga,** with silica sand so white you need dark glasses; **Houhora;** and **Pukenui.** The **Cape Reinga Lighthouse** stands above the battling currents of the Tasman Sea and the Pacific Ocean.

Private cars are not allowed on Ninety Mile Beach, known as Te Oneroa a Tohe to Maori, which can be hazardous because of tidal sweeps, quicksand, runoff channels, sand holes, and plankton buildup. Leave the driving to the experts: Take one of the numerous coach tours to the cape, and you'll be able to make the return trip down the hard-packed sands, stopping first at the mountainous **Te Paki sand dunes ★★★** and **quicksand stream.**

Note: The round-trip from the Bay of Islands to Cape Reinga by private car takes about 7 hours—and that's not allowing for decent stops en route. A day tour from Kaitaia is a more reasonable alternative. I'd strongly advise you to spend an extra night and stay at Doubtless Bay or Kaitaia so you can do the area justice without feeling rushed.

FROM PAIHIA You can take the family-oriented 11-hour Cape Reinga day tour with **Fullers Great Sights Bay of Islands** (✆ **0800/653-339;** www.dolphin cruises.co.nz) for NZ$121 adults and NZ$61 children ages 5 to 15. A barbecue lunch costs around NZ$25 per person. **Awesome Adventures,** Maritime Building, Paihia (✆ **0800/653-339** in NZ, or 09/402-6985; www.awesomenz.com), is less formal, attracts a younger crowd, and stops to eat at a fish-and-chips shop. It costs NZ$118 for a full day and is less likely to have children on board. See "Organized Tours & Cruises," above, for more information.

FROM KAITAIA Go with a full-day excursion from **Sand Safaris Cape Reinga Tours,** 221 Commerce St., Kaitaia (✆ **0800/869-090** in NZ, or 09/408-1778; www. sandsafaris.co.nz), or **Harrisons Cape Runner Tours,** 123 North Rd., Kaitaia (✆ **0800/227-373** in NZ, or 09/408-1033; www.harrisonscapereingatours.co.nz). The cost is NZ$55 to NZ$60 for adults, NZ$25 to NZ$35 for children 14 and under.

FROM MANGONUI (DOUBTLESS BAY) You can do a 4×4 day tour with **Paradise Connexions Tours** (✆ **0800/494-392** in NZ, or 09/406-0460; www. paradisenz.co.nz). They offer a range of activities within their tailor-made tours, including winery visits.

Outdoor Pursuits

BEACHES The farther north you go, the better and more deserted the beaches get. Those on **Karikari Peninsula ★★★** have always been my favorites, but good swimming beaches dominate the whole northeast coast, from Auckland up.

FAST BOATING **Excitor,** Maritime Building, Paihia (✆ **09/402-6985;** www. dolphincruises.co.nz), can take you out to the Hole in the Rock aboard the *Excitor* for NZ$89 for adults, NZ$45 for children 14 and under. ***Mack Attack*** (✆ **09/402-8180;** www.mackattack.co.nz) charges NZ$85 for adults, NZ$45 for children.

FISHING   Light-line fishing is affordable; the visitor center in Paihia can furnish you with a list of fishing charters. Most supply rods and bait, and run 3- to 5-hour trips. Snapper fishing is especially popular; it ranges from NZ$60 to NZ$150 for a 4-hour boat trip. For game fishing contact **Wild Bill Sports Fishing Charters,** Opua Marina, Paihia (✆ **09/402-7085;** www.wildbill.co.nz), or **Earl Grey Fishing Charters,** Paihia and Russell Wharf (✆ **09/407-7165;** www.earlgreyfishing.co.nz). Both will arrange trips to suit individual preferences.

GOLF   You can arrange to play at the beautiful 18-hole waterfront **Waitangi Golf Club** (✆/fax **09/402-7713;** www.waitangigolf.co.nz). Greens fees are NZ$60 per person. Club, shoes, and cart hire are available.

KAYAKING   **Coastal Kayakers,** Paihia (✆ **09/402-8105;** www.coastalkayakers. co.nz), can take you to explore waterfalls, mangrove swamps, and a deserted island. No experience is necessary. A 4-hour trip costs NZ$75; a full-day trip is NZ$95. Farther north in the Tauranga Bay area, **Northland Sea Kayaking,** 305M Tauranga Bay Rd., Northland (✆ **09/405-0381;** www.northlandseakayaking.co.nz), is more of a wilderness experience, with accommodations provided on private beaches. Full-day tours are NZ$95 and half-day tours are NZ$75.

PARASAILING   For a bird's-eye view of the islands, soar with **Flying Kiwi Parasail,** Paihia Wharf (✆ **09/402-6078;** www.parasail-nz.co.nz), for NZ$99.

WALKING   Around the Bay of Islands, you can't go past the boardwalks and walkways in the **Waitangi National Trust Estate ★★★.** The visitor center in Paihia can furnish details of all the trails, as well as the very good booklet *Walking in the Bay of Islands Maritime and Historic Park* (NZ$5). The **Park Visitor Centre** in Russell,

---

 Sailing Away

You won't find any shortage of charter yachts and yacht tours. The Kiwi Experience (backpacker) crowd tends to favor **"She's a Lady" Island Sailing Adventures** (✆ 0800/724-584 in NZ, or 09/402-8119; www.bay-of-islands. com), which includes knee boarding, fishing, and two island stops in the full-day outing for NZ$97 (NZ$50 for children under 14). For the best value, consider **Gungha's Super Cruise ★** (✆ 0800/478-900 in NZ, or 09/407-7930; www.bayofislandssailing.co.nz), which has both the 14m (46-ft.) *Gungha* and a 20m (64-ft.) maxi yacht, *Gungha II.* It gets lots of repeat business for the full-day sailings, which include a scenic tour of the Bay of Islands with at least one island stopover and a yummy lunch for NZ$95. It has departures from Kerikeri, Paihia,

and Russell. For a 3-day sailing adventure, join the friendly crew of **Ecocruz,** The Wharf, Paihia (✆ 0800/432-627 in NZ, or 027/459-2153; www.ecocruz.co. nz), for NZ$595 to NZ$1,350. For a tall-ship adventure, step back in time with a voyage on the *R. Tucker Thompson,* Maritime Building, Paihia (✆ 0800/ 882-537 in NZ, or 09/402-8430; www. tucker.co.nz). It sails from October to the end of April and costs NZ$145 adults, NZ$73 children ages 5 to 15. If you want to try New Zealand's fastest commercial sailing catamaran, contact **Sail on the Edge,** Paihia (✆ 0800/724-569 in NZ, or 09/402-7900; www. explorenz.co.nz). Its 22m-long (72-ft.), 12m-wide (40-ft.) vessel is capable of speeds in excess of 30 knots. A day's outing costs NZ$160 adults, NZ$100 children ages 5 to 15.

P.O. Box 134 (© **09/403-7685;** fax 09/403-7649), or the **Ranger Station** in Kerik-eri (© **09/407-8474**), can help with trail maps and details. There are also some beautiful campsites, some on uninhabited islands in the bay, with nominal per-night fees. You must reserve with the park rangers in Russell. Try the **Kerikeri River Walk**—an easy 1-hour hike to **Rainbow Falls.**

Where to Stay

Remember one important fact if you want to stay in the Bay of Islands: From Decem-ber to January, the population swells from a mere 2,000 to over 30,000. Reserve well in advance.

Paihia has the biggest concentration of motels and hotels, while Russell and Kerik-eri offer more bed-and-breakfast options. Paihia is definitely the most convenient place to stay if you intend to take lots of tours and participate in organized activities. It also has the better food outlets, and you won't have to worry about missing the last ferry to Russell. Russell is the place to be if you want a quiet spot—for most of the time, there are far fewer people here, but I wouldn't go so far as to say that it's less touristy. Rates below include 15% GST and free parking; note that New Zealand has a no-smoking policy in all public buildings and most private accommodations.

If you want information about Department of Conservation campsites in North-land, contact the **Department of Conservation Visitor Centre,** 92 Otaika Rd., Whangarei (© **09/430-2007;** www.doc.govt.nz).

IN PAIHIA/OPUA

In addition to the options below, you might try the good-value contemporary comforts of **Scenic Hotel Bay of Islands ★**, on the corner of Seaview and MacMurray roads, Paihia (www.scenichotelgroup.co.nz; © **0800/696-963** in NZ, or 09/402-7826), where you'll find 114 renovated rooms. Standard and superior rooms run NZ$253 to NZ$299 but the new deluxe rooms (NZ$345) are best. They open onto private subtropical gardens. There's a solar-heated pool, and it's all within walking distance of the township. **Seaspray Suites Bay of Islands ★★**, 138 Marsden Rd., Paihia (www.heritagehotels.co.nz; © **0800/368-888** in NZ or 09/402-0013), has 30 very pleasant, new, one- and two-bedroom apartments overlooking Te Ti Beach. Prices range from NZ$250 to NZ$450 and some deals include breakfast.

Bay of Islands Lodge ★★ 🏨 This sophisticated custom-built gem is tucked into a bush-clad hillside with just native birds for company. Simply put, it's divine. From the French oak floors and the large, stylish living rooms to the big bedrooms with decks and state-of-the-art fittings, you'll want for nothing. It's beautifully done—a fabulous value and perfect for those wanting total privacy.

St. Hwy. 11, Paihia Rd., Opua. www.bayofislandslodge.co.nz. © **09/402-6074.** 4 units. NZ$595 double; NZ$50 extra person; NZ$2,150 for whole house. Rates include breakfast and open bar. Dinner by arrangement. Off-peak rates. AE, MC, V. 5 min. by car from Paihia. Well signposted on Paihia Rd., just after Opua Hill, before you enter the township. **Amenities:** Chef for in-house dining; airport transfers (NZ$70); nearby golf; heated outdoor pool; nearby tennis courts. In room: TV/DVD, hair dryer, Wi-Fi.

Copthorne Hotel & Resort 🏄 This is a standard-issue hotel, but it's in a unique and stunning location, right beside Waitangi National Trust, the sea, and a wealth of walking opportunities. Its peacefulness, sensible pricing, and one of the best outdoor swimming pool complexes in the country make up for the lack of glamour. Most of the modest rooms are king/splits with either sea views (premium) or garden views

BACKPACKERS IN paradise

Backpackers will think they've arrived in paradise: Paihia is the best-serviced backpacker town in the country. There are about 10 top-quality backpacker lodges, most of them cheek-by-jowl on Kings Road. **Base Pipi Patch,** 18 Kings Rd. (© **0800/227-369** in NZ, or 09/402-7111), attracts a lot of the Kiwi Experience buses and it has a Qualmark Enviro-Bronze rating for its efforts toward sustainability. It's just 50m (165 ft.) from the beach and has a pool set in a sunny courtyard; every room has its own bathroom. **Lodge Eleven Backpackers–YHA** ★, MacMurray and Kings roads (www.yha.co.nz; ©/fax **09/402-7487**), is highly rated; every room has its own shower and toilet. Located 100m (330 ft.) from the beach, the place is immaculate and offers personalized service.

Peppertree Lodge ★★, 15 Kings Rd. (www.peppertree.co.nz; © **0800/473-7737** in NZ or 09/402-6122), was built

for backpacker comfort and is seen by many as the best of the best. The **Pickled Parrot Backpackers Lodge,** 7 Grey's Lane (www.pickledparrot.co.nz; © **09/402-6222**), is the smallest backpacker lodge and offers free breakfast and free use of bikes. The **Mousetrap Backpackers,** 11 Kings Rd. (www.mousetrap.co.nz; © **09/402-8182**), is another small one (35 guests max) in a big, old house with sunny balconies.

Saltwater Lodge ★★, 14 Kings Rd. (www.saltwaterlodge.co.nz; © **0800/002-266** in NZ, or 09/402-7075), has top facilities and private bathrooms in every unit; and it is a member of the Northland Sustainable Tourism Charter. The well-equipped **Bay Adventurer Apartments & Backpacker Resort,** 28 Kings Rd. (www.bayadventurer.co.nz; © **0800/112-127** in NZ, or 09/402-5162); has its own tennis courts and Jacuzzi, which are big draws.

(standard). The ground-level Hibiscus wing overlooks the pool and every room in the Seaspray wing has a deck or balcony. Don't be put off by tour groups; there's room for everyone. I prefer Scenic Circle Bay of Islands Hotel for its smarter rooms, but Copthorne has a better pool and location, and a Qualmark Enviro-Gold Award.

Tau Henare Dr., Paihia. www.copthornebayofislands.co.nz. © **09/402-7411.** Fax 09/402-8200. 180 units. NZ$150–NZ$375. Long-stay and off-peak rates. AE, DC, MC, V. Located around the bay from Paihia township; 5 min. by car. **Amenities:** 2 restaurants; bar; babysitting; bike rentals; concierge; nearby golf course; Internet (20-min. free Wi-Fi in lobby); Jacuzzi; massage; outdoor heated pool; room service; outdoor tennis courts. *In room:* TV, fridge, hair dryer, minibar.

Paihia Beach Resort & Spa ★★   This waterfront resort has undergone a NZ$6-million revamp, and the spacious apartments here are sure to please, complete with everything you'll likely need for your stay; they are ideal for longer stays and for two couples or families traveling together. Modern, spacious, elegant, and well situated between the township and Waitangi, the resort also has the best and biggest day spa in Northland, where you can be pampered in every conceivable way, not to mention a fabulous restaurant, **Pure Tastes** (p. 156).

116 Marsden Rd., Paihia. www.paihiabeach.co.nz. © **09/402-0111.** Fax 09/402-6026. 21 units. NZ$445–NZ$675 double; NZ$62 extra person. Long-stay rates. Rates include breakfast. AE, DC, MC, V. Located just around the corner from township on way to Waitangi. **Amenities:** Restaurant; bar; babysitting; nearby golf course; Internet; 4 Jacuzzis; heated outdoor pool; room service; sauna rooms; large state-of-the-art La Spa Naturale day spa; watersports equipment. *In room:* TV/DVD, CD, hair dryer, Internet, kitchen.

Sanctuary Palms ★ 🔥   Four gorgeous, modern, self-contained apartments, each with their own character, sit high over Paihia township (which is just a 5-min. walk away); they offer style, luxury, and privacy at an incredibly reasonable price. The ground-floor room, Moulin Rouge, has a stunning bathroom and, like all the apartments here, truly feels like your home away from home. The upstairs Pasifika has a bigger lounge and a huge balcony with bush views; and the cool Waterfall room opens onto the garden waterfall.

31 Bayview Rd., Paihia. www.sanctuarypalms.co.nz. 🕿 **09/402-5428.** Fax 09/402-5427. 4 units. From NZ$350–NZ$480. Special packages, long-stay, and off-peak rates. MC, V. No children 17 and under. Rates include a welcome breakfast basket. **Amenities:** Nearby golf course; free Internet. *In room:* TV/DVD, hair dryer, free Internet, kitchen, minibar.

IN RUSSELL

A lot of the lodgings on this side of the water are high priced for what you get, so shop around. Personally, I think you get better value for your money in the Paihia-Opua area. For a budget-conscious stay, head for the **Top 10 Holiday Park,** 1 James St., Longbeach Road (www.russelltop10.co.nz; 🕿 **0800/148-671** in NZ, or 09/403-7826; fax 09/403-7221). They have a range of accommodations priced from NZ$95 to NZ$250. Tent and powered sites go for NZ$15 to NZ$22 per person.

   Russell Cottages ★, 16 Chapel St. (www.russellcottages.co.nz; 🕿 **09/403-7737;** fax 09/403-8002), are my pick for the independent traveler who likes a modern, self-contained stay. Sixteen one- to four-bedroom, two-level cottages sit in parklike gardens with a heated pool and Jacuzzi. They are priced from NZ$175 to NZ$395.

Eagles Nest ★★★ 🎁   It's hard to find the words to adequately describe this sublime eco-friendly retreat that is committed equally to luxury and environmental protection. Daniel and Sandie Biskind found the perfect place for their world-class sanctuary and spared no expense in creating something you'll remember forever. Sacred Space is the main house, which contains three luxury suites—the living room converts to an in-house theater at the flick of a switch. Across the gorgeous pool is the two-story honeymoon love nest known as First Light Villa, and on a far hill, the three-bedroom Eyrie, Eagle Spirit, and Tikitiki Ora offer a more low-key version of this sumptuous style. Rahimoana (the Presidential Villa), which comes with the use of a Porsche Cayenne Turbo and a personal concierge, is the ultimate in international luxury—and is priced accordingly. The core philosophy at Eagles Nest is to relax, regenerate, rejuvenate. It's an experience you'll relish and want to relive, over and over again—as long as you have a bottomless wallet.

60 Tapeka Rd., Russell. www.eaglesnest.co.nz. 🕿 **09/403-8333.** Fax 09/403-8880. 19 rooms in 6 self-contained units. From NZ$2,346–NZ$5,617 per villa; NZ$20,439 for Rahimoana. Rates include breakfast and airport transport. Long-stay, off-peak, and special deals. AE, DC, MC, V. Drive up and over Flagstaff Hill in Russell township; Tapeka Rd. is the 2nd left after the brow of the hill. **Amenities:** Exclusive dining room (spa cuisine) w/10,000-bottle wine cellar; airport transport from Kerikeri Airport (NZ$225); babysitting; free use of bikes; concierge; helicopter access to Kauri Cliffs luxury golf club; free use of off-site gym; massage; Jacuzzi in all villas; 5 villas have heated outdoor pool; room service; sauna in 3 villas; Wi-Fi in all villas. *In room:* A/C (in some units), TV/DVD, CD, Wi-Fi, hair dryer, kitchen, minibar, MP3 docking station.

IN KERIKERI

Kauri Cliffs ★★★ 📷   Set on 2,630 hectares (6,500 acres) of rolling coastal farmland, this golf club and lodge offers world-class facilities with an unforgettable view—not to mention the par-72 David Harman–designed golf course that sweeps along the cliff tops (and was voted 49th best in the world by *Golf* magazine). If you want premium pampering in a breathtaking setting, this is the place—luxury and comfort are a given, and every whim can be indulged. Rooms are spacious, bathrooms luxurious, and style greets you at every turn. It's much bigger and more extensively appointed than Eagle's Nest in Russell, but it has that same distinctive mark of quality that discerning international travelers expect. A world-class health spa completed in 2006 is just another reason to linger in "paradise."

Tepene Tablelands Rd., Matauri Bay, 25 min. northeast of Kerikeri. www.kauricliffs.com. © **09/407-0010.** Fax 09/407-0061. 22 units, one 2-bedroom cottage. NZ$1,426–NZ$10,063. Rates include full breakfast, pre-dinner drinks, a la carte dinner, use of all facilities except golf, spa, and airport transport. Off-season rates and special deals. Closed June. AE, DC, MC, V. 20 min. from Kerikeri Airport. **Amenities:** Restaurant (jacket required); bar; Kerikeri airport transport (NZ$140 one-way); babysitting (from NZ$25 per hour; min. 3-hr. charge); mountain bikes; concierge; world-class golf course; large gym; Internet; 2 outdoor Jacuzzis; outdoor heated pool, indoor heated lap pool; limited room service; sauna; full-service spa; 2 all-weather tennis courts. *In room:* TV/DVD, fridge, hair dryer, minibar, free Wi-Fi.

Stone Store Lodge ★ This elegant little stay is nestled into native bush just minutes from Kerikeri Inlet and a short drive from Kerikeri township. Each of the three well-appointed suites has its own bathroom (complete with heated floors and solar-heated water) and a balcony with pretty views across the Basin. It's a contemporary spot and host Richard Millar has a deft hand at preparing tasty wood-fired pizzas, should you wish to dine in. He also cares about his environment and has a Kiwi Green rating for his sustainable tourism efforts.

201 Kerikeri Rd. www.stonestorelodge.co.nz. © **09/407-6693.** 3 units. NZ$175–NZ$230 double; NZ$50 each extra person. Longer stay and off-peak rates available. Rates include breakfast. AE, DC, MC, V. No children 11 and under. **Amenities:** Nearby golf course; outdoor tub set in bush (NZ$22); massage. *In room:* A/C, TV/DVD/CD, fridge, hair dryer, minibar, Wi-Fi.

IN THE FAR NORTH

For a special treat, take yourself to the Karikari Peninsula, where you'll find some of the best beaches in New Zealand. You'll also find the superlative **Carrington Resort ★★★**, Maitai Bay Road, Karikari Peninsula (www.heritagehotels.co.nz; © **0800/368-888** in NZ, or 09/408-7222), set amid 3,000 hectares (7,410 acres) of rolling coastal land. It offers 10 spacious, modern lodge suites that open onto wide verandas with beach views. Fourteen separate villas set away from the main lodge provide three-bedroom comforts with golf-course views. A resort par excellence, it's well worth going the extra mile. Lodge rooms start at NZ$460, or NZ$640 with breakfast and dinner. The villas cost NZ$560. The lodge has a strong conservation and environmental policy in action and is responsible for the restoration of a large expanse of nearby wetlands.

In Doubtless Bay, one of the best spots is **Beach Lodge,** 121 St. Hwy. 10, Coopers Beach (www.beachlodge.co.nz; ©/fax **09/406-0068**). Its five delightful, two-bedroom, self-contained units are just a few paces from the white-sand beach; rates are NZ$400 to NZ$475, with lower rates off-peak. **Coopers Beachfront Suites,** 18 Bayside Dr., Coopers Beach (www.coopersbeach.net; © **09/406-1018**), has two light and bright suites overlooking the beach (one upstairs, one down), for NZ$175 to NZ$325, which includes breakfast provisions for the first morning. **Taipa Bay Resort ★★**, 22 Taipa Point Rd. (www.taipabay.co.nz; © **09/406-0656**), is 7km (4⅓ miles) north of Mangonui village. Their 32 suites and apartments allow you to enjoy sand and surf at your doorstep for NZ$185 to NZ$375.

In Kaitaia are several motel options and in nearby Ahipara you can enjoy three very nice self-contained, two-bedroom apartments at **Shippies ★**, Reef View Road, Shipwreck Bay (www.shippies.co.nz; ✆ 09/409-4729), for NZ$200 to NZ$300. Farther north at Houhora Heads, you'll find great waterfront camping at **Wagener Holiday Park & Backpacker Cabins** (www.northlandholiday.co.nz; ✆ 09/409-8511). Non-powered sites cost NZ$26; powered sites are NZ$30 per night; caravans NZ$56; cabin rooms NZ$44 to NZ$48. Farther south, near Dargaville and Waipoua Forest, check out **Waipoua Lodge ★★**, State Highway 12, Katui, Northland (www.waipoua lodge.co.nz; ✆ 09/439-0422). This very welcome addition to Northland's west coast features four stylish apartments set in gardens, separate from the 120-year-old main villa and dining room. I recommend you stay 2 or 3 days and take the guided night walk to see rare wild kiwi (an extra charge) and during the day, check out the remarkable kauri forests, or laze about on deserted golden sand beaches. The bed-and-breakfast rate is NZ$585 to NZ$625; if you include dinner it starts at NZ$830. A less expensive option is **Copthorne Hotel & Resort Hokianga,** SH12, Omapere South (www.copthornehokianga.co.nz; ✆ 09/405-8737; fax 09/405-8801), which has 33 guest rooms right on the water's edge of Hokianga Harbour, with regular rate packages available.

Where to Eat

The biggest and best concentration of restaurants and cafes is in Paihia, but there are some close rivals in nearby Kerikeri. As always in the provinces, service tends to wax and wane. The **Sugar Boat Restaurant,** Waitangi Bridge, Paihia (✆ 09/402-7018; www.sugarboat.co.nz), offers excellent meals in a unique ship setting. It's open daily in summer (mid-Nov through Mar) from 5pm to late with main courses around NZ$35. They also have a cocktail and tapas bar. A very pleasant new addition on the Paihia waterfront is **Island Life Restaurant ★★**, 78–94 Marsden Rd. (✆ 09/402-6199; www.islandlifepaihia.co.nz). Its a la carte menu presents a little of everything—Pacific rim, Asian, classic European; and the deli serves lovely breakfasts and lunches. It's open daily 8am until late and they feature live music on Friday and Saturday nights.

IN PAIHIA

Only Seafood ★★ SEAFOOD   The name says it all, as seafood takes center stage in a smart, white-walled, timber-floored interior. Start with delicious sushi and raw fish salads, then tuck into mains like a salmon filet stuffed with oysters, oven baked, and served with sauce Provençal, or marinated, char-grilled, and served with teriyaki sauce. If you're a seafood lover, you'll be in seventh heaven.

40 Marsden Rd. (upstairs), Paihia. ✆ **09/402-6066.** Main courses NZ$28–NZ$30. AE, DC, MC, V. Daily 5pm–late. Closed Dec 25–26.

Pure Tastes ★★ ASIAN/INTERNATIONAL   Don't miss this culinary gem. Chef Paul Jobin and his team have combined a cooking school, cafe, and restaurant in a winning format. The menu emphasizes seafood with strong Asian overtones—Penang fish curry, Asian wok toss, and Thai crispy beef are cases in point. It's bright and delicious, and the homemade ice creams are real winners. You can also choose a four- or five-course set menu, with or without wine pairings.

Paihia Beach Resort & Spa, 116 Marsden Rd., Paihia. ✆ **09/402-0003.** www.puretastes.co.nz. Main courses NZ$32–NZ$36. 4-course set menu NZ$75, with wine NZ$115; 5-course set menu NZ$90, with wine NZ$130. MC, V. Daily 7am–late.

Waikokopu Café ★ CAFE/LIGHT MEALS   Waikokopu wins with its dreamy lakeside, bush-enclosed location and its well-priced light meals. The menu changes regularly, but generally features delicious lunch goodies like Cajun chicken salad and corn and coriander fritters. If your wallet is feeling thin, pig out on the pancake pileup—a stack of wild-berry pancakes topped with Greek yogurt, drizzled with honey, or served with bacon, banana, and maple syrup. Vegetarians and children are attended to, and you can't beat sipping a good espresso while sitting out on the timber deck overlooking the water.

Treaty Grounds, Waitangi. ℂ **09/402-6275.** www.waikokopu.co.nz. Reservations required for dinner in summer. Main courses NZ$16–NZ$20. MC, V. Daily 9am–5pm (until 6pm in summer).

IN RUSSELL

The **Gables,** The Strand (ℂ **09/403-7618**), has previously won widespread praise, but it seems to have lost its gloss and is overpriced compared to some of the competition. The **Duke of Marlborough,** The Strand (ℂ **09/403-7829;** www.theduke. co.nz), gets good marks for sound pub-style food but variable service; and **Gannets** ★, on York Street (ℂ **09/403-7990**), scores the most points for tasty, good-value meals in a simple interior. The broadbill fish steaks are excellent. **Omata Estate** ★★, Aucks Road (ℂ **09/403-8007**), is part of a luxury lodge and winery on the water's edge, nearer the Opua Ferry Landing than Russell itself; it's recommended for its six-course degustation menu and dishes like confit of salmon and scallops with lime risotto; reservations are essential. **Kamakura** ★★★, 29 The Strand (ℂ **09/403-7771;** www.kamakura.co.nz), is my pick for the best on this side of the water. It's a sophisticated restaurant where "Pacific Rim cuisine meets Mediterranean with a touch of Japanese." You'll get the finest local produce and seafood, including fresh New Zealand crayfish blended into first-class meals with a high level of creativity. It's open daily, 8am until late (dinner only Thurs–Sat) with entrees around NZ$28 to NZ$34.

IN KERIKERI

Good cafes and restaurants come and go in Kerikeri, but worthy of mention are **Café Zest,** 73 Kerikeri Rd. (ℂ **09/407-7164**), which is a great spot for vegetarians; and **Marsden Estate Winery** ★, Wiroa Road (ℂ **09/407-9398**), which serves fabulous antipasto platters with estate-grown wine on a grape-covered courtyard overlooking lakes and vineyards. **Ake Ake Vineyard** ★★, 165 Waimate North Rd., Kerikeri (ℂ **09/407-8230;** www.akeakevineyard.co.nz), presents a delicious lunch Tuesday through Sunday in summer (Fri–Sun in winter) and dinner Thursday through Sunday all year-round. **Curry King,** Cobblestone Mall, Kerikeri Road, Kerikeri (ℂ **09/401-6172**), is a popular choice for traditional Indian meals from 11am to 2pm Tuesday through Friday for lunch, and daily for dinner from 5pm. If you're looking for the best picnic food in town, don't drive past **Kerikeri Bakehouse Café** ★★, 334 Kerikeri Rd. (ℂ **09/407-7266**); it's open daily from 7am to 4pm and supplies the most astounding range of edibles you'll find for hundreds of miles.

WHANGAREI ★★

169km (105 miles) NE of Auckland; 62km (38 miles) S of Paihia; 58km (36 miles) E of Dargaville

Like so many provincial New Zealand towns, Whangarei (pop. 52,000) has come a long way in the last decade. The development of its Town Basin has given it a fresh sparkle; international yachts moor quayside and a sprouting of cafes, galleries, and gift stores make it a pleasant place to wander. The city is also at the heart of a nature-lover's paradise: Pristine white-sand beaches abound up and down the nearby Whangarei Heads coastline and the Poor Knights Islands Marine Reserve is one of the world's best diving locations. Big-game fishing is the other star attraction.

Essentials

GETTING THERE & GETTING AROUND **By Plane** Whangarei is a 40-minute flight from Auckland with **Air New Zealand Link** (℃ 0800/737-000 in NZ), which provides service several times a day. **Great Barrier Airlines** (℃ 0800/900-600) flies to Whangarei from Auckland on Friday and Sunday. The **Airport Shuttle** (℃ 09/437-0666) offers passenger service to Whangarei.

By Coach (Bus) Both **InterCity** (℃ 09/623-1503) and **Northliner Express** (℃ 09/307-5873) pass through Warkworth and Whangarei several times a day.

By Car Warkworth is about 1 hour north of Auckland; Whangarei is 2 hours away. The highway between Auckland and Whangarei has a high incidence of accidents, so drive carefully. If you need a rental car, the major companies have offices at the airport.

VISITOR INFORMATION The **Whangarei i-SITE Visitor Centre,** 92 Otaika Rd., Whangarei (℃ 09/438-1079; fax 09/438-2943; www.whangareinz.com), is open daily from 8:30am to 5pm weekdays and 9:30am to 4:30pm on weekends and public holidays, with extended hours over summer. For information on beautiful Whangarei Heads area and the accommodation providers servicing the many secluded beaches there, visit www.whangareiheadstourism.co.nz.

Exploring the Town

I'd begin with a browse around the **Town Basin** ★★. This is where you'll find, among other things, the world's largest sundial and **Clapham's National Clock Museum** (℃ 09/438-3993; www.claphamsclocks.com), a rather zany collection of timepieces, clocks, and music boxes; an in-house Austrian clockmaker; and a gift store. It's open daily 9am to 5pm (closed Dec 25) and costs NZ$8 adults, NZ$4 children ages 5 to 15, and NZ$20 families.

Kiwi North ★ (℃ 09/438-9630; www.kiwinorth.co.nz), formerly the Whangarei Museum, now includes a Kiwi House (new in 2011) and a Gecko House, as well as the Heritage Park and Clarke Homestead. Located on State Highway 14 (the road to Dargaville), it's just 3 minutes from downtown. It's open daily from 10am to 4pm and costs NZ$10 for all attractions, NZ$9 for students, and NZ$5 for children over 3 years. The **Native Bird Recovery Centre** (beside the museum; ℃ 09/438-1457) is open Monday through Friday 10am to 4pm.

The **Whangarei Art Museum,** Cafler Park Rose Gardens, Water Street (until August 8, 2012) thereafter, The Hub, Whangarei Town Basin, Quayside, Dent Street (℃ 09/430-4240; www.whangareiartmuseum.co.nz), features local and national exhibitions and is open daily from 10am to 4pm. Entry is by donation. If you've ever wondered how paper is made, check out the **Paper Mill** ★, 300 Otaika Rd. (℃ 09/438-2652), which offers 40-minute papermaking tours (9:30am–2:30pm). The mill is open Monday through Friday, 10am to 3pm.

Gardeners will get a special joy out of the **Quarry Gardens** ★, Russell Road (℃ 09/437-7210; www.whangareiquarrygardens.org.nz), where an old quarry site

INTO THE deep blue SEA

Why stay on land when there's so much to see underwater? I've never fancied myself in a wet suit, but I can see the advantages if you plan to explore the magnificent marine environment off the Tutukaka Coast and the Poor Knights Islands (1 hr. offshore by boat). **Tutukaka,** 30 minutes from Whangarei, is the gateway to the **Poor Knights Island Marine Reserve ★★★**, where crystal-clear waters near the edge of the continental shelf are bathed in subtropical currents. Sheer cliff faces, sea caves, tunnels, and archways are teeming with a range of sea life, including subtropical fish not usually found in New Zealand waters.

The reserve was rated as one of the top 10 diving spots in the world by Jacques Yves Cousteau and is strictly controlled by the Department of Conservation with regard to fishing zones and restricted areas; make sure you go fishing or diving with a licensed operator. The main operator is **Dive! Tutukaka,** the Poor Knights Dive Centre, Marina Road, Tutukaka, Whangarei (© **0800/288-882** in NZ, or 09/434-3867; www.diving.co.nz), which offers a full range of snorkeling and diving options. Its staff members know all the best places—there are over 100 to choose from. Some of the team are also award-winning underwater photographers, so if that's what gets your heart ticking, you're in the right place. They have the largest dedicated dive charter fleet in New Zealand, accompanied by fully qualified dive guides and dive masters. They also offer a Twin Wrecks dive adventure on the scuttled ex-naval ships *Tui* and *Waikato,* which were prepared for adventure diving before being sunk to diver-friendly depths.

was converted into a lush subtropical display with numerous tracks linking to the Coronation Scenic Reserve. The **Quarry Arts Centre ★**, 21 Selwyn Rd. (© **09/438-1215;** www.quarryarts.org), is also nearby and is well worth a visit for its diverse range of artwork by members of the Northland Craft Trust, some of whom open their studios to the public.

If you're a keen photographer, you might want to join the thousands who have been captivated by **Whangarei Falls,** 5km (about 3 miles) from the town center on the road to Tutukaka Coast. The falls are easily accessed and make for some stunning images. Keen walkers, meanwhile, should consider **Bream Head Coast Walks ★★★** (© **09/434-0571;** www.coastwalks.co.nz), a beautiful 3-day self-guided wander along the Whangarei Heads on private farmland, beaches, rural roads, and recreational reserves. It costs NZ$435 per person, which covers 3 nights' lodging, all food, and daily transfers. A reasonable fitness level is required but you only carry a day pack. It's open from October 1 to May 31.

Get a glimpse of local life at the **Whangarei Growers' Market ★★**, held every Saturday morning in the carpark beside the Shell Service Station on Water Street, 6am until 10:30am.

Where to Stay

Whangarei has a good selection of motels; you can find out about them at the visitor center. Backpackers will find top-line comforts at **Bunkdown Lodge,** 23 Otaika Rd. (www.bunkdownlodge.co.nz; © **09/438-8886**), from NZ$26 to NZ$28 per person for dorm rooms, or NZ$55 to NZ$60 for twin or double rooms. If you prefer a boutique hotel atmosphere, check in to the 15-room **Lodge Bordeaux ★**, 361 Western Hills Dr., SH1 (www.lodgebordeaux.co.nz; ℂ 09/438-0404), where you can ease your travel stresses in a big double Jacuzzi for NZ$195 to NZ$300. There are two excellent new options just out of Whangarei. **Tahi Beach ★★**, 1980 Pataua North Rd., Pataua North (www.tahinz.com; ℂ 09/436-5495), offers two lovely self-contained, environmentally aware cottages (one two-bedroom, one four-bedroom), sitting in 296 hectares (740 acres) of beach, forest, and wetlands 30 minutes northeast of Whangarei. Rates are NZ$560 to NZ$650.

Where to Eat

Numerous new cafes and restaurants have sprung up in Whangarei, and you'll get a good overview by picking up the free brochure *Eating Out in Whangarei*. Making an impression is award-winning **A'Deco ★★★**, 70 Kamo Rd. (ℂ 09/459-4957; www.a-deco.co.nz), which is highly praised for its modern, fine dining in an elegant Art Deco residence. It's open Tuesday through Saturday for dinner and Wednesday through Friday for lunch. **Killer Prawn ★**, 26–28 Bank St. (ℂ 09/430-3333; www.killerprawn.co.nz), remains one of Whangarei's most popular dining establishments with its ultimate seafood, big steaks, chicken, and sizzling lamb dishes. I find it a little lacking in charm, without the class of A'Deco, but perfectly fine for a reasonable meal. It's open Monday through Saturday from 11am. Three cafes are worth noting: **Nectar Café,** 88 Bank St. (ℂ 09/438-8084; www.nectarcafe.co.nz), is well liked for its coffee and lively atmosphere; **Fresh ★★★**, 12 James St. (ℂ 09/438-2921), has an excellent all-day menu and is open Monday through Friday 8am to 5pm, and Saturday 8am to 2pm; and **Caffeine Espresso ★★**, 4 Water St. (ℂ 09/438-6925; www.caffienecafe.co.nz), has a lively, older, funkier atmosphere and is open Monday through Friday 7am to 3pm and weekends 7am to 2pm. **Vinyl Restaurant & Bar,** 14 Rust Ave., Whangarei (ℂ 09/438-8105; www.vinylrandb. co.nz), is tucked away down a lane off Rust Avenue (though it maintains a Rust Ave. address) but is worth hunting for. They have indoor and outdoor dining from a classic, contemporary menu that includes the likes of prime beef medallion with herb-roasted potatoes, braised red cabbage and horseradish cream. At Tutukaka, **Schnappa Rock**

 Meeting the Giants

Take home unforgettable memories by stepping into the spiritual environment of Waipoua Forest with **Footprints Waipoua ★★★**, 29 St. Hwy. 12, Opononi (ℂ 0800/687-836 in NZ, or 09/405-8207; www.footprintswaipoua.com). Local Maori guides will take you to meet *Tane Mahuta* (Lord of the Forest), the largest kauri tree in New Zealand. The night tour will make your spine tingle. **Crossings Hokianga ★★★**, 29 St. Hwy 12, Opononi (ℂ 0800/687-836 in NZ; www.crossingshokianga.co.nz), puts

you in the hands of quality Maori guides who will take you on an afternoon boat cruise, introducing you to local Maori legends and communities in historic Hokianga Harbour.

The **Kauri Museum,** 5 Church Rd., Matakohe (ℂ 09/431-7417; www.kauri-museum.com), is south of Dargaville and worth visiting for an insight into Northlands forestry history. It's open daily, 9am to 5pm (closed Dec 25). Admission is NZ$17 adults, NZ$4 children 5 to 15, and NZ$35 for families.

Restaurant and Bar ★, Marina Rd., Tutukaka (© **09/434-3774;** www. schnapparock.co.nz), is a very popular beach spot that's open daily from 8am till late.

En Route Back to Auckland, Via the West Coast

If you came up to the Far North from Auckland on Highway 1, you may want to return on a longer, less direct route that takes in the **Waipoua Kauri Forest ★★★** and the **Trounson Kauri Park.** If you do this, be sure to also enjoy the scenic beauty of **Hokianga Harbour.**

The kauri is the giant of the New Zealand native forest, and at Waipoua the largest trees are over 1,000 years old. Look for **Tane Mahuta (God of the Forest) ★★,** the largest known kauri in New Zealand, and **Te Matua Ngahere (Father of the Forest),** by volume the second-biggest known tree in the country. These and other special trees are signposted on the tourist drive through the forest. You'll find the **Kauri Coast i-SITE Information Centre** at 65 Normanby St., Dargaville (© **09/ 439-8360;** www.kauricoast.co.nz).

THE COROMANDEL PENINSULA ★★

119km (74 miles) E of Auckland

At the height of the gold rush in the late 1800s, the towns of the Coromandel Peninsula were heavily populated and thriving. Thames, now seen as the gateway to the peninsula, had a population of nearly 20,000 and between 80 and 90 pubs. Today, there are around 7,000 permanent residents and just four pubs, and it's still the biggest town on the peninsula. There's a sense of that more-colorful history all along the west coast, but as in Northland, most of the action is on the picturesque east coast.

This scenic finger of land, reaching into the sea between Auckland and the Bay of Plenty, is famous for its jagged western coastline and its balmy eastern beach recesses that provide endless opportunity for swimming, diving, boating, fishing, and general lazing about. Thousands of New Zealanders have been doing just that for decades. Big, bush-covered ranges divide the two coasts and offer the ultimate challenge for fit trampers, and there are quaint attractions scattered throughout.

You can comfortably reach the base of the Coromandel Peninsula from Auckland in just 1½ hours, and from Rotorua in 2¾ hours. While it's feasible to do most of the peninsula in a day trip, try to spend a couple of extra days in the area and explore more of what it has to offer. Keep in mind that it is a favorite summer holiday destination for New Zealanders, so book well ahead or you'll miss out on accommodations.

Essentials

GETTING THERE & GETTING AROUND **By Plane** **Air Coromandel/Great Barrier Airlines** (© **0800/900-600** in NZ, or 09/275-9120; www.greatbarrierairlines. co.nz) runs daily services and scheduled scenic flights between Whitianga and Auckland, Great Barrier Island, the Bay of Islands, Waiheke Island, Rotorua, and Tauranga.

By Ferry Operating between Auckland and Coromandel town is **360 Discovery Cruises** (© **0800/360-3472** in NZ; www.360discovery.co.nz). The trip takes 2 hours and costs NZ$112 round-trip for adults, NZ$68 children ages 5 to 15, which includes a transfer into town. They can also arrange for a rental car for you.

By Coach (Bus)   InterCity (✆ 09/623-1503) runs regular services between Auckland, Whitianga, and Coromandel.

By Car   If you're coming from Auckland: Drive south on State Highway 1 for about 50km (30 miles), then turn east on State Highway 2. About 34km (21 miles) later, you'll pick up State Highway 25 to Thames. If you want to head straight to the east coast beaches of Whitianga, Tairua, and Pauanui: Take the direct route, signposted EASTERN BEACHES, turning right at Kopu (St. Hwy. 26) away from Thames. Approximately 1km (½ mile) from this point, turn left onto State Highway 25a, which is the direct route. If you follow the Pacific Coast Highway through Thames and Coromandel town: Turn left at Kopu and follow the PCH "Hook" signs. This is a terrific trip, but if your destination is the east coast beaches, it will add at least 1 to 1½ hours to your journey. If you're traveling up the west side of the peninsula, then down the east coast through Whitianga to Pauanui, pass through Tairua township and continue south until you reach the service station on the left. This is where you turn off to Pauanui (there's a small sign) and travel north again.

The road from Colville village, north of Coromandel town, to the top of the peninsula is unpaved all the way and takes around 1½ hours. It's a stunning trip, but not recommended for the fainthearted. It is dirt only, very steep, narrow, and often a one-way lane with no room for passing—plus steep drops to the ocean. If you want to explore this area, I strongly advise you to join **Coromandel Discovery,** 316 Tiki Rd. (✆ 07/866-8175; www.coromandeldiscovery.co.nz).

By Taxi   Contact **Mercury Bay Taxi,** in Whitianga, at ✆ 07/866-5643.

VISITOR INFORMATION   The **Thames i-SITE Visitor Centre,** 206 Pollen St., Thames (✆ 07/868-7284; fax 07/868-7584; www.thamesinfo.co.nz), is open Monday through Friday from 8:30am to 5pm; Saturday, Sunday, and public holidays 9am to 4pm. The **Coromandel i-SITE Visitor Centre,** 355 Kapanga Rd., Coromandel (✆ 07/866-8598; www.coromandeltown.co.nz), is open in summer daily from 9am to 5pm; and in winter Monday through Saturday from 9am to 5pm, Sunday 10am to 2pm. The **Whitianga i-SITE Visitor Centre,** 66 Albert St., Whitianga (✆ 07/866-5555; fax 07/866-2205; www.whitianga.co.nz), is open Monday through Friday from 9am to 5pm, Saturday and Sunday from 9am to 4pm, and December 26

    A Word on Driving

Remember that getting to places on the peninsula often takes longer than you think. Many of the roads are narrow and winding and, off State Highway 25, generally unsealed (unpaved). Thames to Coromandel village takes almost 2 hours driving through numerous little coastal settlements. There are pretty beaches aplenty to stop at along the way, but *drive carefully!* North of Coromandel township, the roads become significantly worse. Rental-car companies previously forbade vehicles from traveling here, but if you stick to the Pacific Coast Highway path (St. Hwy. 25), you're generally okay. The route from Coromandel to Whitianga takes about 1 hour by State Highway 25 (recommended for rentals), and a similar length of time on the "infamous" 309 route, which has 24km (15 miles) of unpaved road and is narrow and winding. It may be scenic with some interesting stops along the way, but State Highway 25 is far less harrowing.

to January 31 from 8am to 6pm. Pick up the free 72-page *Coromandel Visitor's Guide* at any one of the above locations. **Waihi Visitor Centre,** Upper Seddon St., Waihi (© 07/868-6715; www.waihi.org.nz), is an excellent first stop if you'd like to discover Waihi's gold-mining history; it also provides accommodation information on Waihi Beach and Bowentown. For more on Bowentown, check www.bowentown.co.nz. **Whangamata i-SITE Visitor Centre,** 616 Port Rd., Whangamata (© 07/865-8340; www.whangamatainfo.co.nz), can help with its local activities and services.

The Thames office of the **Department of Conservation (DOC)** is on Kauaeranga Valley Road (© 07/867-9080; www.doc.govt.nz).

Coromandel Peninsula is well served with websites. You can find information on the region at any of the following: www.thecoromandel.com, www.mercurybay.co.nz, www.thepeninsula.co.nz, www.whitianga.co.nz, and www.pacificcoast.co.nz.

SPECIAL EVENTS For details of the colorful 2-week annual **Pohutukawa Festival,** held every November to December to celebrate the red-flowering native pohutukawa trees that line the coast, call © 07/868-0471, or check www.pohutukawafestival.co.nz. In late summer, Coromandel town celebrates with the **Homegrown Festival,** which focuses on food, art, and music. Contact the visitor center for details or check www.coromandelflavours.co.nz.

Exploring the Peninsula

Coromandel has an intangible, rustic quality that makes it rather alluring. Certainly, from a purely physical point of view, there's nothing quite like the sight of New Zealand's famous pohutukawa in full scarlet bloom (Dec–Jan), against black rock and white beach, for mile after endless mile.

There are good walks around Paeroa (near the Karangahake Gorge), Waihi, Whangamata, Tairua, Whitianga, Colville, Coromandel, and near Thames in the rugged Kauaeranga Valley. Information on the **Coromandel Forest Park** is available at the DOC office in Thames (see "Visitor Information," above). There's also a DOC office in Coromandel township at the i-SITE Visitor Centre.

In Thames, you'll find historic mining areas well signposted. For an intriguing insight into gold-mining in the Thames area, visit **Goldmine Experience,** Main Road, State Highway 25 (©/fax 07/868-8514; www.goldmine-experience.co.nz), which offers a 40-minute guided tour through an operational, 19th-century Stamper Battery and into one of the richest gold mines of the time. They're open daily from 10am to 4pm in summer (reduced hours in winter) and admission is NZ$15 for adults, NZ$5 for children ages 5 to 15.

From 1885 over 30 schools of mining provided practical training for gold miners; the largest of those, the **Thames School of Mines Museum ★★**, Brown and Cochrane streets (© 07/868-6227; www.historicplaces.org.nz), is open daily from 11am to 3pm in summer (reduced winter hours). In complete contrast, you can escape into the Tropics with over 400 butterflies at the **Butterfly and Orchid Garden,** Dickson Holiday Park, Victoria Street (© 07/868-8080; www.butterfly.co.nz). They're 3km (1¾ miles) north of the town and are open daily 9:30am to 4pm. Admission is NZ$12 adults, $7 children (3–15 years), and NZ$32 for families. If you feel like a wander, pick up the *Historic Grahamstown* brochure and check out the town's past. Add in a visit to **Thames Historical Museum,** corner of Pollen and Cochrane streets, Grahamstown (© 07/868-8509), which is open daily 1 to 4pm. Admission is NZ$6 adults and NZ$3 for children.

As you head north, just beyond Tapu, turn east off State Highway 25 and go 6.5km (4 miles) to the spectacular **Rapaura Watergardens** ★★, 586 Tapu-Coroglen Rd., Tapu, Thames Coast (© **07/868-4821;** www.rapaura.com). Numerous paths meander through the 26 hectares (64 acres) of gardens and 14 waterlily ponds, which are open daily from 9am to 5pm. Admission is NZ$15 for adults, NZ$6 for children ages 5 to 15, and NZ$36 per family. If you are in need of refreshment, the onsite cafe is a good stop. About 2.5km (1½ miles) past Rapaura Gardens, stop at Tapu and ask directions to one of nature's oddities, the **"square kauri,"** a 2,500-year-old kauri whose trunk is a perfect square. **Te Mata Beach** ★, also at Tapu, is a good hunting ground for specimens of carnelian-agate gemstones.

In Coromandel is the **Driving Creek Railway and Potteries** ★★★, 380 Driving Creek Rd. (© **07/866-8703;** www.drivingcreekrailway.co.nz). Barry Brickell, an accomplished potter, owns the country's only narrow-gauge mountain railway, which passes through replanted native forest. There are usually at least two departures daily (10:15am and 2pm), costing from NZ$25 adults, NZ$10 children ages 5 to 15, and NZ$55 for families. The station is 2.5km (1½ miles) from Coromandel town, and the 1-hour trip covers 3km (2 miles) of track, which took 27 years to build. A glass-blowing studio operates during summer and you can view working potteries and kilns.

Pick up the *Coromandel Craft Trail* brochure, which details over 30 of the peninsula's craftspeople, or visit **Weta Design** ★★, 46 Kapanga Rd., Coromandel Town (© **07/866-8823;** www.wetadesign.co.nz), which showcases work by New Zealand's top artists and craftspeople. It's open 10am to 5pm and organizes tax-free purchase and overseas mailing. **Waitati Gardens** ★, 485 Buffalo Rd., Coromandel Town (© **07/866-8659;** www.waitatigardens.co.nz), are a pleasant horticultural diversion (admission NZ$7; kids under 12 free); and make sure you visit the weird and whimsical at **Waiau Waterworks** ★★★, 309 Road, Coromandel (© **07/866-7191;** www.waiauwaterworks.co.nz). This haven of strange, water-based sculptures and gadgets is a great place for kids—as long as they're well supervised. It's open daily from 9am to 5pm; admission is NZ$12 for adults, NZ$6 for children ages 5 to 15.

On the east coast, Whitianga has the excellent **Mercury Bay Museum,** opposite the wharf (© **07/866-0730;** www.mercurybaymuseum.co.nz), open daily from 10am to 4pm (closed Dec 25), featuring exhibits dating from A.D. 800 to 950. Admission is NZ$5 for adults, NZ50¢ for children, and NZ$12 family. At **Bay Carving** ★★, 12 The Esplanade, Whitianga (© **07/866-4021;** www.baycarving.com), you can carve your own bone souvenir in 2 to 3 hours. They're open 10am to 4pm, daily in summer and closed winter Sundays. Carving costs from NZ$45 per person, per piece, depending on the design chosen.

 Waterfall Walk

The **Waiau Falls** are 11km (7 miles) east of Coromandel. A 5-minute walk from the **309 Road** ends at the foot of the falls. The **309 Kauris**, 1km (½ mile) farther east, are the finest, easily accessible stand of kauri trees on the peninsula. It's a delightful 10-minute bush walk to see them.

A fun activity is taking the **Whitianga Water Transport** (© **07/866-5472;** www.whitiangaferry.co.nz) passenger ferry to the Ferry Landing, the oldest hand-hewn stone wharf in Australasia, built in 1837. The ferry operates daily from 7:30am to 10:30pm (with extended hours from Christmas Day through Jan). Once at the Ferry Landing, you can wander a short distance to Front Beach to swim or have a

At **Hot Water Beach** ★★★, inquire about the time of the next low tide—thermal water heats parts of this beach for 2 hours on either side of low tide. That's when you can dig a hole in the sand, settle in, and soak in the hot salt water that comes up from underground springs. The underground volcanic fissures issue water as hot as 147°F (64°C) at a rate of 15 liters per minute. Sit back and chat with people from all around the world, who come to discover this rare phenomenon.

picnic, or a little further on (3km) to **Shakespeare Head Historic Reserve,** which is a popular lookout area featuring a memorial to Captain Cook's visit to the area. If you're energetic, you can walk on the pretty **Flaxmill Bay** (about 15–20 min from Ferry Landing) and stop for coffee at **Eggsentric Café & Gallery** (see p. 170). Alternatively, you can link up with **Cathedral Cove Shuttles,** Ferry Landing, Whitianga (© **027-422-5899;** www.cathedralcoveshuttles.co.nz), and go to Flaxmill Bay, Cooks Beach, Hahei, Hot Water Beach, Cathedral Cove, and other area attractions. It costs (one-way) NZ$10 to Cooks Beach, NZ$30 to Hahei, NZ$32 to Cathedral Cove, and NZ$38 to Hot Water Beach. If you're looking for a place to unwind at the end of the day, try the **Lost Spring** ★★★, 121A Cook Dr., Whitianga (© **07/866-0456;** www.thelostspring.co.nz), one man's passion come to reality. Alan Hopping began drilling for hot water in 1989. Twenty years and two failed attempts later, he finally hit the spring, and the luscious hot pools and day spa opened in 2008. They've been beautifully landscaped and are well worth a visit. It's open 11am to 9:30pm daily and it costs NZ$30 per hour, or NZ$65 for a day pass. Children must be 14 and over.

Organized Tours

The best tour companies are located at Pauanui, but their tours cover the whole peninsula. **Remote NZ Journeys** ★★★, 430 Hikuai Settlement Rd., Pauanui Beach (© **07/864-8731;** www.remotenzjourneys.co.nz), offers a wide range of hikes, nature treks, and guided and personalized tours. Their Night Glow Worm Experience is a lot of fun, and all tours include some history of the region, as well as information on Maori medicines and foods of the forest. Tours range in price, but start at NZ$120 per person. **Aotearoa Lodge & Tours,** 70 Racecourse Rd., Whitianga (© **0508/868-769** in NZ, or 07/866-2807; www.tournz.co.nz), specializes in multiday tours of Coromandel Peninsula, Rotorua, and East Cape, departing Auckland daily. Its 3-day A Touch of Coromandel tour is NZ$955 per person.

Kiwi Dundee Adventures ★★★, McBeth Road, Hikuai (©/fax **07/865-8809;** www.kiwidundee.co.nz), is the brainchild of passionate outdoors enthusiast Doug Johansen and his partner, Jan Poole. Doug is one of New Zealand's foremost nature guides, and he and Jan offer a range of full-day tours. Day tours are priced from NZ$230 per person, and include lunch. Several upmarket 3-day tours run between Auckland, Coromandel, and Rotorua, offering top-level accommodations for two to six people. These are priced on application and according to the accommodations used.

Take to the water with **Cathedral Cove Scenic Cruises** (© **0800/888-688** in NZ or 07/866-0329; www.cathedralcovesceniccruises.co.nz), who will take you exploring sea caves and islands. You can view fish via an underwater camera and snorkel in a marine reserve too. The 2½-hour excursion costs NZ$75 for adults, NZ$45 for children 5 to 15. The **Glass Bottom Boat ★★** (✆ 07/867-1962; www. glassbottomboatwhitianga.co.nz) is another excellent way to see a little of the area's amazing marine life. The excellent 2-hour ecotour to Cathedral Cove (snorkeling included), departs daily at 10:30am and 1:30pm (extended schedule in summer) for NZ$95 adults, NZ$55 children ages 3 to 15. Or join **Whitianga Adventures ★★** (✆ 0800/806-060 in NZ; www.whitianga-adventures.co.nz) to explore sea caves and islands for about 2 hours, for NZ$70 adults and NZ$45 children 5 to 16. All three boat operators depart from Whitianga Wharf daily at 10:30am and 1:30pm, with extra departures in summer.

Outdoor Pursuits

BEACHES **Whangamata** is a top surfing and swimming beach. **Cooks Beach** has safe swimming and lovely picnic areas, while **Buffalo Beach** is good for swimming and shellfish collecting—both are in the Mercury Bay area.

FISHING Numerous boat charters operate in Whitianga, Whangamata, and Waihi, and the visitor centers have masses of brochures. Tairua Beach offers excellent surf-casting. Coromandel's northern islands provide excellent snapper fishing. Try **Infinity Charters** (✆ 07/866-5936; infinitycharters@clear.net.nz), for an organized fishing experience, which offers competitively priced half- and full-day excursions.

Cathedral Cove

This gorgeous sheltered cove is part of the Hahei Marine Reserve and famous for its large sea cave. The beach and cave are accessible by walkway from Hahei.

GOLF The **Mercury Bay Golf & Country Club,** Golf Road, Whitianga (✆ 07/866-5479; www.mercury baygolf.co.nz), is an 18-hole course; greens fees are NZ$40. The **Dunes Golf Resort,** Matarangi Drive, Whitianga (✆ 07/866-5394; www. thedunesmatarangi.co.nz), is one of New Zealand's top 10 courses; fees are NZ$70 for 18 holes of casual play, or NZ$35 for 9 holes. **Coromandel Golf Club,** Hauraki Road, Coromandel (✆ 07/ 866-8539), is a scenic 9-hole course; fees are NZ$30 for nonmembers. And **Thames Golf Club,** State Highway 26, Kirikiri, Thames (✆ 07/868-9062), is a par-70, 18-hole course; greens fees are NZ$25 per person. Get an overview of Coromandel clubs at www.thecoromandel.com/golf.html.

HORSE TREKKING Riders with a sense of adventure might like to try the guided horse treks experience on an outback sheep station with **Twin Oaks Riding Ranch,** State Highway 25, 927 Kuaotunu Rd., Whitianga (✆ 07/866-5388; www.twinoaks ridingranch.co.nz), which charges NZ$60 for a 2-hour trek.

KAYAKING **Cathedral Cove Kayaks ★★★** (✆ 07/866-3877; www.seakayak tours.co.nz) operates from Hahei and offers daily tours from 7am to 9pm. It's a fabulous way to see beaches, islands, caves, and coves—no experience is necessary. They have a range of tours priced from NZ$95 to NZ$155.

MOUNTAIN BIKING North of Coromandel, you'll find a testing track between Stony Bay and Fletcher Bay, which takes about 2 hours each way. There are also good tracks in the Carter Holt Harvey (CHH) forests south of Tairua and at Whangamata.

To get into these areas, you need to register at the CHH office, just north of Whangamata (📞 **07/865-8473**), or at one of the visitor centers in the area.

SCUBA DIVING   Whitianga waters are ideal for diving. **Cathedral Cove Dive & Snorkel,** 48 Hahei Beach Rd., Hahei (📞 **09/866-3955**; www.hahei.co.nz/diving), has dive trips for certified divers, plus PADI dive courses for all levels, in the marine reserve or in the waters beyond. Snorkeling trips in divine locations are offered as well. Diving excursions range from NZ$75 to NZ$170; a PADI Open Water Course, including full gear (2 or more people), costs NZ$525 per person.

Where to Stay

North Islanders flock to Coromandel Peninsula December through February, so book well ahead. In the off season, you'll get motel beds at laughably good rates. Lodgings on the east coast are generally nicer than those on the Thames side.

Van and caravan sites in **Conservation Lands** are available on a first-come, first-served basis; camping fees are from NZ$10 per adult, and NZ$5 per child. For details, contact the **Department of Conservation,** P.O. Box 78, Thames (📞 **07/868-6381**), or the **Kauaeranga Visitor Centre** (📞 **07/867-9080;** www.doc.govt.nz).

The rates given below include the 15% GST.

IN OR NEAR THAMES

Tuscany on Thames ★★, Jellicoe Crescent, Thames (www.tuscanyonthames.co.nz; 📞 **07/868-5099**), is a smart motel complex with a swimming pool and 14 units with lovely bathrooms with big tubs. Rates start at NZ$145. Tararu is a great place for migratory seabirds and brilliant sunsets, and a chalet at **Coastal Motor Lodge** ★, 608 Tararu Rd. (Coromandel Coast Rd.), Thames (www.stayatcoastal.co.nz; 📞 **07/868-6843**), is just the place to enjoy them. The spacious A-frame chalets sleep two and have cute kitchenettes and balconies. The front unit near the road is particularly cozy. Motel rooms also available. Tariffs range from NZ$135 to NZ$190.

IN OR NEAR COROMANDEL

Coromandel Motel, Holiday Park & Backpackers, 636 Rings Rd., Coromandel (www.coromandelholidaypark.co.nz; 📞 **07/866-8830**), is an ideal budget choice for families. It's set in about 1.5 hectares (3½ acres) of grounds that are just a few minutes' walk from the shops. Choose from tent sites (from NZ$36), cabins (from NZ$80), and motel units (from NZ$155). **Driving Creek Villas** ★★, 4021a Colville Rd., Coromandel Town (www.drivingcreekvillas.com; 📞 **07/866-7755**) is a find, offering three boutique villas located in a private bush setting and fitted out with all the modern goodies. Each villa has two bedrooms, one bathroom, a big lounge, and a private garden. Tariff is NZ$275 to NZ$295; NZ$40 per extra person.

IN OR NEAR WHITIANGA

Marina Park Apartments ★★, 84 Albert St., Whitianga (www.marinapark.co.nz; 📞 **07/866-0599**), are convenient, uncluttered, and modern, and they overlook the marina in the heart of the village. Sixty bright, roomy one-, two-, and three-bedroom apartments are perfect for families and couples traveling together. There are the added bonuses of two heated Jacuzzis, swimming pool, and gym; and prices range from NZ$165 for one bedroom to NZ$450 for a three-bedroom apartment. **Oceans Resort** ★★, 18 Eyre St., Whitianga (www.oceansresort.co.nz; 📞 **07/869-5222**), has 20 spacious modern units in a quiet street close to Buffalo Beach and within walking distance of the town. There's a large swimming pool, tennis courts, and a children's playground. Rooms here range from NZ$150 to NZ$375. **Within the Bays,** 49 Tarapatiki Dr., Whitianga (www.withinthebays.co.nz; ℂ **07/866-2848**), has two very nice, modern guest rooms with great beach views for NZ$250 to NZ$295. They are very ecofriendly and operate a single-party booking system. At the **Beachfront Resort ★**, 113 Buffalo Beach Rd., Whitianga (www.beachfrontresort. co.nz; ℂ **07/866-5637**), you can walk from your clean, comfortable room to the sparkling sands of Buffalo Beach in a matter of seconds. Upstairs units have balconies; downstairs, a private patio opens onto the garden and beach. Rates ranges from NZ$150 to NZ$375; extra person NZ$25.

Villa Toscana ★★★ 📷 Giorgio and Margherita Allemano have replicated a Tuscan villa high on a hill overlooking native bush and the ocean, where they take great pleasure in welcoming guests from all over the world. Their Kiwi Green–certified, fully self-contained two-bedroom suite has its own entrance, deck, garden, barbecue, and outdoor Jacuzzi. You'll find no fault with the spacious, airy bedrooms. The decor is simple—lots of traditional Italian tiles and marble—plus a large bathroom with Italian fixtures, a granite kitchen, and a wide lounge for relaxing at the end of a busy touring day. Giorgio is happy to show you his underground wine cellar and, as a marine biologist and keen fisherman, he has plenty to talk about. Don't miss the genuine Italian gourmet dinners.

Ohuka Park, Whitianga. www.villatoscana.co.nz. ℂ **07/866-2293.** Fax 07/866-2269. One 2-bedroom suite. NZ$850; NZ$150 each extra person. Rates include breakfast and Whitianga Airport transport. NZ$180 per person for Italian gourmet dinner. Off-season rates. MC, V. Located 4km (2½ miles) north of Whitianga. **Amenities:** Dinner on request; bar; free airport transport; babysitting; free use of mountain bikes; nearby golf courses; Jacuzzi; 2 nearby outdoor tennis courts; 11m (35-ft.) Bertram game fishing launch for hire (NZ$1,100 per day); kayaks. *In room:* TV/DVD, hair dryer, kitchen, minibar, Wi-Fi.

IN PAUANUI/TAIRUA

Colleith Lodge ★★, 8 Rewa Rewa Valley Rd., Tairua (www.colleithlodge.co.nz; ℂ **07/864-7970**), has three very nice, modern B&B rooms with en-suite bathrooms overlooking a lap pool and Jacuzzi for NZ$525. They have a Qualmark Enviro-Silver rating and Wi-Fi throughout the property. No children under 15. **Harbourview Lodge ★**, 179 Main Rd., Tairua (www.harbourviewlodge.co.nz; ℂ **07/864-7040**), also has three en-suite rooms and a swimming pool and is more reasonably priced at NZ$175 to NZ$250 with an extra-person rate of NZ$25. Both make an ideal base for exploring the peninsula.

Grand Mercure Puka Park Resort ★★★ There's been a major upgrade at this idyllic hideaway and if you're a discerning traveler who expects nothing but the best, you'll love being spoiled—it has the premier upmarket accommodations on the peninsula. A series of exquisite "treehouses" climbs uphill, away from the main lodge, and is completely enclosed by native bush. But you won't have to walk or carry a thing; service is tops here and every scrap of luggage is attended to by the smiling (and incredibly fit) staff. Standard chalets contain a shower-only bathroom; superiors are larger with both tub and shower. Executive chalets have separate lounge/dining areas, while the luxurious Royal Puka Suite is a freestanding two-story, three-bedroom chalet with everything you're ever likely to need on an indulgent holiday.

Mount Ave., Pauanui Beach. www.pukapark.co.nz. ℂ **07/864-8088.** Fax 07/864-8112. 48 units. From NZ$350 standard room; NZ$1,600 suite. Long-stay and off-peak rates. AE, DC, MC, V. Drive into Pauanui with the Waterways Development on your left, go through the roundabout and onto a 2nd roundabout where Puka Park Resort is signposted. Make a hard right onto Pauanui Beach Rd.; turn right at the 2nd street onto Mount Ave. and follow this as far as you can. Turn left and go uphill to the resort. **Amenities:** Restaurant; bar; babysitting; free use of bikes; concierge; nearby golf course; gym; outdoor Jacuzzi; heated outdoor pool; room service; sauna; day spa beauty treatments; tennis court; watersports equipment rentals. *In room:* TV/DVD, fridge, hair dryer, minibar, Wi-Fi.

IN WHANGAMATA

Just about every town on the Coromandel has a camping ground; staying in one will give you a real feel for the iconic New Zealand camping holiday. **Whangamata Motor Camp,** Barbara Avenue, Whangamata (© 07/865-9128; fax 07/865-6512), is the closest camp to the beach and just a 2-minute walk to the main shopping street. The camp has powered and unpowered sites (NZ$15–NZ$25 per adult), plus self-contained cabins (NZ$50–NZ$95). You can stay at one of the region's most beautiful, unspoiled beaches at **Opoutere Coastal Camping ★★★**, 460 Ohui Rd., Opoutere (www.opouterebeach.co.nz; © 07/865-9152), where non-powered camp sites are NZ$18 per person, powered sites NZ$20, cabins NZ$110, and chalets NZ$150.

  Brenton Lodge ★, 2 Brenton Place, Whangamata (www.brentonlodge.co.nz; ©/fax **07/865-8400**), has a super location overlooking the whole of Whangamata town and beaches. Lovely gardens surround the delicious private suites, outfitted with kitchenettes. Lavender Cottage is the farthest from the main house and has the best view; Rose Cottage is all fresh and white with sloping ceilings; and the Garden Room above the main house is a haven overlooking the pool. Enjoy your gourmet breakfast in your room or alfresco on your private balcony. The tariff is NZ$390.

Where to Eat

IN THAMES

You won't find a lot of slick dining choices in Thames, but **Rocco Café,** 109 Sealey St. (© **07/868-8641**), in an old villa, offers light lunches and coffee, although **Waiomu Beach Café,** 622 Thames Coast Rd., Waiomu Bay (© **07/868-2554**), comes with higher recommendations. They're just across the road from the beach and have a good range of light food to enjoy with coffee. **Sola Café ★★**, 720B Pollen St. (© **07/868-8781**), is probably your best good-coffee choice in Thames itself. They have a small vegetarian menu and are open daily 9am to 4pm and for dinner on Friday nights.

IN COROMANDEL

Driving Creek Café ★★, 180 Driving Creek Rd. (© **07/866-7066**), just north of town in an old villa, serves delicious meals using local and organic produce. It's open daily from 9:30am to 4pm and is *the* place to get a feel for local culture—it's a laid-back venue set in the bush, with a piano planted in its center. **Umu Café ★★**, 22 Wharf Rd., Coromandel (© **0866-8618**), is a terrific casual spot for breakfast, lunch, or dinner. Meals range from fresh seafood dishes to pizzas, steaks, and salads with good vegetarian options and takeaway available. Check their cabinets for tasty picnic foods. Open daily 9am to 9pm.

  Peppertree Restaurant & Bar ★, 31 Kapanga Rd. (© **07/866-8211**; www. peppertreerestaurant.co.nz), is probably the best eatery in town, and its dinners present seafood, sushi, mussel fritters, local beef, and fresh vegetables in interesting combinations. It's open daily from 10:30am until late in summer, 11am to 9pm in winter. If you'd like a snack of fresh-smoked fish, mussels, scallops, salmon, or roe, then head for the **Coromandel Smoking Company ★★★**, 70 Tiki Rd. (© **07/866-8793**; www.corosmoke.co.nz), open daily from 8am until 6pm with reduced winter hours. **Coromandel Oyster Company** ★, 1611 SH25, Tiki Rd., Coromandel (📞 **07/866-8028;** corooysterco@xtra.co.nz), is another good spot to get fresh premium oysters, local mussels, prawns, scallops, chowders, sauces, and smoked seafood at wholesale prices—just the thing if you're considering a beach barbecue.

IN WHITIANGA

Whitianga has quite a range of fair-to-middling restaurants and cafes, so you won't go short of a meal. As in most provincial centers, service can be patchy. One of my favorite and most consistent spots is **Café Nina** ★, 20 Victoria St. (📞 **07/866-5440**), open daily, 8am to 5pm in summer, 9am to 4pm in winter. You'll get the best coffee and counter food in town at this 100-year-old miner's cottage tucked away in a small back street. It's very popular and always has a mixed, slightly alternative crowd.

The **Wild Hogs Bar & Restaurant,** 9 The Esplanade (📞 **07/866-4828**), is a great waterfront spot with a courtyard, good seafood, and wood-fired pizzas. They're open daily from 11am to late; be sure to make a reservation. The **Eggsentric Café** ★★, 1047 Purangi Rd., Flaxmill Bay (📞 **07/866-0307**), is near Cooks Beach and just a ferry ride from Whitianga itself. It has a great atmosphere and a chef who does inspiring and delicious things with fresh seafood. They're open Tuesday through Friday 10:30am till late, and weekends 9am until late. They'll even pick you up from the ferry if you wish. **Salt Bar and Restaurant** ★★, 1 Blacksmith Lane (📞 **07/866-5818;** www.whitiangahotel.co.nz), is one of the best spots for fine dining. It's open daily from 11am until late. For good seafood and tapas, try **Tuatua** ★, 45 Albert St. (📞 **07/866-0952**). Make sure you book ahead at night.

IN PAUANUI/TAIRUA

The one thing lacking in Pauanui is good eateries. You can go upmarket and have no regrets at **Grand Mercure Puka Park Resort** ★★★ (see above), or you can take the passenger ferry (NZ$5; hourly until 1am in summer) across to Tairua and dine at **Manaia** ★, 228 Main Rd. (📞 **07/864-9050**); or at the **Old Mill** ★, 1 The Esplanade (📞 **07/864-7884**), which is the more formal of the two.

IN WHANGAMATA

Café Onemana, Onemana Drive, Onemana (📞 **07/865-7200**), is open for lunch and dinner. They've got great ocean views and a friendly atmosphere. Bookings are recommended for evening dining.

En Route to Tauranga

Katikati, known locally as "The Mural Town," is south of Waihi on State Highway 2. In 1996, a festival was held to celebrate the painting of its 20th outdoor mural since 1991 and to reinforce its image as the mural town of New Zealand. For information on the town and surrounding Bay of Plenty area, call into the **Mural Town Visitor Centre,** 34 Main Rd. (📞 **07/549-1658;** katikatiinfo@wbopdc.govt.nz).

En Route to Hamilton

From Waihi, take State Highway 2 through the Karangahake Gorge and at Paeroa, turn onto State Highway 26. Follow this 76km (47 miles) to Hamilton.

WAIKATO & BAY OF PLENTY

Forty percent of New Zealand's total population—that's nearly 1.5 million people—lives within a 242km (150-mile) radius of the Waikato district. First settled by the Maori, who recognized its agricultural potential and appreciated its temperate climate, the Waikato is rich in natural resources and is a leading food producer. Its biggest natural asset is the Waikato River, the longest river in New Zealand.

The seaside townships of Tauranga, Te Puke, the mural town of Katikati, and Mount Maunganui (one of the country's most popular beach resorts) are the main components of the Bay of Plenty. Forget woolly sheep and start thinking fuzzy kiwifruit, because that's what this area is famous for. The area grows 80% of the country's export kiwifruit crop. It's also a place of mellow summers; great surf and beaches; big game fishing; long, lazy holidays; and the biggest retired population in the country. It literally is a bay of plenty. It is also one of the six pilot participants in the Environmentally Sustainable Tourism Project, dedicated to improving the environmental performance of local tourism operators.

HAMILTON & THE WAIKATO ★

127km (79 miles) S of Auckland; 107km (66 miles) NE of Rotorua; 107km (66 miles) E of Tauranga

Unfortunately for Hamilton, its proximity to Auckland (just a 1-hr. drive) means it's often overlooked as a sightseeing destination. Many travelers pass through the city heading south, usually to the famed Waitomo Caves in south Waikato or to Rotorua and Taupo.

If you want to linger awhile, though, you'll discover the hot springs and horse-racing world of Matamata township; the rich Maori culture of Ngaruawahia and more hot springs at Waingaro; the surf and beaches of Raglan; and the antiques and Kentucky-like thoroughbred world of Cambridge.

Hamilton—the country's largest inland city (urban pop. 145,000)—is a commercial and industrial center. There's something bland about the place despite its pretty face, but there's always a hint of change in the air.

Essentials

GETTING THERE & GETTING AROUND **By Plane** **Air New Zealand National & Link** (© 0800/767-767 in NZ) provides daily service to Hamilton Airport (www.hamiltonairport.co.nz). The airport is about 15 minutes south of the city. A shuttle service is provided by **Roadcat Transport** (© 07/823-2559; www.roadcat.co.nz) or **Super Shuttle** (© 0800/748-885; www.supershuttle.co.nz).

By Coach (Bus) Both **InterCity** (© 09/623-1503) and **Newmans** (© 09/623-1504) link Hamilton to other major centers. Within Hamilton, **Busit** (© 0800/428-7546; www.busit.co.nz), runs the free **CBD Shuttle,** which loops around the inner city; while the **Orbiter** connects the city's suburbs and main shopping areas. You'll find details of their departure times at the **Transport Centre,** corner of Bryce and Anglesea sts. (© 07/839-6650), which is the central transport hub for all local and regional buses, shuttles, taxis, and car hire services. It's open Monday through Thursday, 8:30am to 5pm, Friday until 7pm and weekends 9:30am to 3:30pm; and lockers are available for luggage storage.

By Train The **Tranz Scenic Overlander** route passes through Hamilton on the route between Auckland and Wellington. Call © 0800/872-467 or visit www.tranzscenic.co.nz for timetables and reservations.

By Car Hamilton is on State Highway 1, so you'll pass through it heading north or south. It's usually slightly over an hour's drive from Auckland, but the stretch of road between the two cities is notorious for bad accidents that result in fatalities. Please take particular notice of all yellow-line road markings, which designate no-passing sections of a highway. It's 1 to 1½ hours to Rotorua, Tauranga, or Taupo.

For rental cars call **Waikato Car Rentals,** Brooklyn Road, Hamilton (© 0800/154-444 in NZ, or 07/855-0094; www.waikatocarrentals.co.nz).

By Taxi **Hamilton Taxi Society** (© 0800/477-477 or 07/847-7477; www.hamiltontaxis.co.nz) operates a 24-hour service.

ORIENTATION Both State Highway 1 and the Waikato River run through the heart of Hamilton, although there is now a rather convoluted bypass through the suburbs if you want to avoid the inner city area altogether—just follow the signs as you approach either the north or south ends of the city. Victoria Street is the main street, and the main shopping area fills a compact area around it. The central area is easily negotiated on foot or by car.

VISITOR INFORMATION The **Hamilton i-SITE Visitor Centre** (© 0800/426-4586; www.visithamilton.co.nz) is at 5 Garden Place, Hamilton. It's open Monday through Friday from 9am to 5pm, Saturday 9:30am to 3:30pm; closed December 25. The **Waitomo Discovery Centre & i-SITE Visitor Information Centre,** 21 Waitomo Caves Rd., Waitomo (© 0800/474-839 in NZ, or 07/878-7640; www.waitomodiscovery.org), is open daily 8:45am to 7:30pm in summer, 8:45am to 5pm in winter. **Cambridge i-SITE Information Centre,** corner of Queen and Victoria streets, Cambridge (© 07/823-3456; fax 07/823-3457; www.cambridge.co.nz), is open Monday through Friday from 9am to 5pm and weekends 10am to 4pm. **Information Raglan** is at 2 Wainui Rd., Raglan (© 07/825-0556; fax 07/825-0557; www.raglan.org.nz), and is open Monday through Friday from 10am to 5pm, and Saturday, Sunday, and holidays from 9am to 4pm.

SPECIAL EVENTS The **Hamilton Gardens Arts Festival** (© 07/859-1317; www.hamiltongardensartsfestival.co.nz) is held in mid-February each year. **Balloons**

Over Waikato (☎ **07/849-5472;** www.balloonsoverwaikato.co.nz) is a spectacular event featuring over 30 hot-air balloons in mid-April. The **NZ National Agricultural Fieldays** (☎ **07/843-4499;** www.fieldays.co.nz) is a huge event staged at Mystery Creek in mid-June. It attracts nearly 150,000 national and international visitors. For further information on Waikato events, contact **Events Hamilton** (☎ **07/ 838-6679;** www.whatsonhamilton.co.nz or www.visithamilton.co.nz).

Exploring the Area

To learn about activities in the smaller rural towns of Morrinsville, Matamata, Ngaruawahia, Te Aroha, and Te Awamutu, pick up brochures from the Hamilton visitor center.

IN HAMILTON

Hamilton Gardens ★★, Cobham Drive (☎ **07/838-6782;** www.hamiltongardens. co.nz), is the region's most popular visitor destination. It consists of 58 hectares (143 acres) of specialty gardens along the banks of the Waikato River. You don't have to be a gardener to appreciate the serenity of the Japanese Garden, the beauty of the herb garden or the brilliance of the Indian Char Bagh and Italian renaissance gardens. The Gardens Terrace restaurant and the Gardens Café are both open daily from 10am to

5pm in summer and until 4pm in winter. The gardens themselves are open 7am to 6pm. An onsite information center is open daily 9am to 5pm. **Hamilton Lake** and its 56-hectare (138-acre) reserve is also a pleasant place for a quiet wander. You can do a delightful 45-minute circular walk around the lake, or relax at its lovely restaurant, while kids unwind in the large playground. It's just up the hill from the central business district, off Ruakiwi and Lake roads (two entrances).

The **Waikato Museum & Arts Post ★★★**, Victoria and Grantham streets (*℃* 07/838-6606; www.waikatomuseum.co.nz and www.artspost.co.nz), and **Exscite ★★★** (*℃* 07/838-6553; fax 07/838-6571) are especially good value and fun experiences for kids. The museum has a fine display of Maori art and carving from the area's Tainui people; Te Winika, a 200-year-old carved *waka taua* (war canoe), is a key attraction. Exscite is a madhouse of colorful fun designed as a learning environment for children. Museum admission is by donation (some exhibitions are charged); Exscite costs NZ$5 for adults, NZ$3 for kids, NZ$20 for a family. The museum, Exscite, and Arts Post are open daily from 10am to 4:30pm (closed Dec 25).

Hamilton Zoo and the FreeFlight Sanctuary ★★, Brymer Road (*℃* 07/838-6720; www.hamiltonzoo.co.nz), is a 25-hectare (62-acre) retreat for over 600 native and exotic animals and the largest walk-through bird aviary in Australasia. It's 5 minutes off State Highway 1, west of Hamilton, and is open daily from 9am to 5pm (last admission at 3:30pm). They also have late night openings (until 8pm) on Wednesdays and Saturdays in January and Saturdays in February. Guided tours and up-close animal encounters are also offered and must be booked (prices vary). Zoo entry is NZ$15 adults, NZ$7 children 2 to 16, and NZ$42 for a family. Onsite Flavours Café is open daily from 9am to 5pm. The Waikato River is an integral part of the city's character and there's no better way to get a feel for that than taking a leisurely trip with **Cruise Waikato ★★**, Memorial Park Jetty, Memorial Drive, near Victoria Bridge (*℃* 0508/426-458 in NZ; www.cruise-waikato.co.nz). They operate daily with sailings from Memorial Drive at 2pm; a general cruise costs NZ$25 for adults and NZ$12 for children 14 and under. There are a number of other history and food cruises priced around NZ$30 to NZ$$45. Bookings are essential.

When it turns dark, you might like to try your luck in Hamilton's casino complex, **SKYCITY Hamilton,** 346 Victoria St. (*℃* 07/834-4900; www.skycityhamilton.co.nz), which has 20 gaming tables, 300 gaming machines, plus bar and restaurant facilities. It's open daily 9am to 3am.

IN CAMBRIDGE

This pretty oak-filled town of 11,000 is the bright star of the Australasian bloodstock industry—sort of a miniature Kentucky, if you like. Its old homes and rolling green fields make it a delightful spot for a day visit from Hamilton, or a stopover on your journey south. In the last 2 years it has become more lively, and it deserves at least a 1-night stopover.

If you fancy **"A Night at the Trots,"** head to the **Cambridge Raceway,** Taylor Street (*℃* 07/827-5506; www.cambridgeraceway.co.nz), for the thrill and excitement of live harness and greyhound racing.

The town is also a treasure-trove of antiques. Antiques fairs are in September and April, and the Cambridge Information Centre has a good brochure that lists the best antiques dealers in Hamilton and Cambridge. If you're in the mood for a stroll, pick up the *Heritage Trail* brochure, which details heritage sites in town.

Nearby **Lake Karapiro**—8km (5 miles) from town—is also a pleasant outing for boating, sailing, water-skiing, swimming, and rowing. If you're lucky, you might even

RURAL discoveries

You don't have to go far from the city in any direction to find some unexpected treats. **Taitua Arboretum** ★, Taitua Rd., Whatawhata (© **07/847-5847**), is a stunning collection of mature trees (over 1,500 species) planted more than 3 decades ago by John and Bunny Mortimer. Admission is free and it's open daily from 8am until half an hour before sunset. **Te Aroha Mineral Spa Bath House** ★★, Domain Gardens, Boundary St., Te Aroha (© **07/884-9918;** www.tearohapools. co.nz), is a replica 1900-style bath house built in 2006, using the waters of a natural soda spa spring. The town has been a soothing stop for weary travelers for over a century and the new spa continues that tradition. It's open daily, 11am to 9pm Monday through Thursday, and 10:30am to 10pm Friday through Sunday. A private

spa costs NZ$18 for adults and NZ$11 for children 14 and under. They also have leisure pools (© **07/884-4499**) with an admission fee of NZ$6 adults, NZ$4 children under 14. **Hobbiton Movie Set & Farm Tours,** 501 Buckland Rd., Matamata (© **07/888-9913;** www.hobbitontours. com), combines a tour of a 506 hectare (1,250-acre) sheep farm with the piece of farmland that was transformed into The Shire from Middle Earth, used in the *Lord of the Rings* trilogy. It costs NZ$70 for adults, NZ$33 students, and NZ$6 children under 15. And the seaside town of **Raglan** (www.raglan.org.nz), is well worth a visit. It's a prime surfing spot, and has a large community of artists and some lovely cafes. To get there, leave Hamilton on State Highway 23. It's about a 45-minute drive.

---

spy one of New Zealand's Olympic rowing champions in training. Cambridge is home to the gold medal–winning Evers-Swindell twins, Georgina and Caroline.

IN WAITOMO: EXPERIENCING THE CAVES

The busy little pocket of tourist activity that is Waitomo is the exception in the otherwise quiet, cow-filled south Waikato pasture. The tiny village owes its existence to the remarkable limestone caves 70km (43 miles) south of Hamilton.

You can get to the area via the **Waitomo Shuttle** (© **0800/808-279** in NZ, or 07/873-8214), which connects to InterCity and Newmans coach services and Tranz Scenic trains in nearby Otorohanga. **Waitomo Wanderer Scenic Shuttle** (© **0508/ 926-337** in NZ, or 07/873-6108; www.waitomotours.co.nz) offers daily service between the caves and Rotorua. Kiwi Experience and Magic Travellers also run to the area. If you're driving from the north, take State Highway 1 south to State Highway 3, just south of Otorohanga, and turn west at the signpost for Waitomo Caves.

The **Waitomo Caves Discovery Centre & i-SITE Visitor Information Centre,** 21 Waitomo Caves Rd., Waitomo (© **0800/474-839** in NZ, or 07/878-7640; www.waitomodiscovery.org), is open daily (see hours above). Admission to the museum is NZ$5 for adults and free for children. You can save a lot of time by booking most of your underground activities right here.

The caves *are* what make Waitomo a visitor destination, and the best among them are the **Waitomo Glowworm Caves** ★★★, 39 Waitomo Caves Rd. (© **0800/456-922** in NZ, or 07/878-8227; www.waitomo.com), which opens daily at 9am. They've opened a brand new visitor center with spectacular Maori carvings that includes an exhibition center, theater, restaurant, cafe, and gift shop. The caves' most impressive feature is **"The Cathedral"** ★★★, which rises 14m (46 ft.) and is an acoustically perfect auditorium that has been the site of performances by the Vienna Boys' Choir and Dame Kiri Te Kanawa. Your tour takes you through 250m (820 ft.) of stunning underground scenery, culminating in the glowworm caves. A cafe and shop complex are also on-site.

If you have time, include **Aranui Cave ★★**—15 minutes down the road—which doesn't have glowworms, but does have the most spectacular natural formations; you're allowed to take photographs here. Tickets for both are sold at the Waitomo Glowworm Cave ticket office.

Tours in the Glowworm Cave include a magical boat ride through the **Glowworm Grotto.** These leave daily every half-hour from 9am to 5pm, and hourly in the Aranui Cave from 10am to 3pm. A two-cave combination ticket costs NZ$75 adults, NZ$35 children ages 4 to 14, and NZ$175 for a family. The best time to visit the Glowworm Grotto is mid- to late afternoon, when the crowds are smaller. Bring a sweater because it's cooler underground, and wear strong footwear for walking. The caves are easily accessible to those with reasonable mobility and there are good handrails and pathways. Don't forget to ask about their various combo cave deals.

After being closed to the public for 15 years, **Ruakuri** reopened in 2005. Laced with myth and legend, Ruakuri ("den of dogs") was first discovered by Maori almost 500 years ago. It takes its name from the pack of wild dogs that lived in the cave entrance. Tours of the cave now depart from the **Ruakuri Information Centre,** at the **Legendary Black Water Rafting Company,** 585 Waitomo Caves Rd. (✆ **0800/782-5874;** www.ruakuri.co.nz), daily (except Dec 25) at 9am, 10:30am, 11:30am, 12:30pm, 1:30pm, 2:30pm, and 3:30pm. Admission is NZ$75 adults, NZ$35 children ages 5 to 14.

Waitomo Adventures, 654 Waitomo Caves Rd. (✆ **0800/924-866** in NZ or 07/878-7788; www.waitomo.co.nz), is the other major player here. They have a wide range of underground daredevil adventures that include abseiling, rafting, swimming, and climbing. Most require a reasonable level of fitness and have a minimum age of 10, 12, or 15 years. Prices range from around $155 to NZ$425 and they offer several combo deals. **Spellbound Glowworm & Cave Tours ★★★**, Spellbound Tower, Waitomo Caves Rd. (beside Huhu Café; ✆ **0800/773-552** in NZ; www.glowworm. co.nz), have unbelievable glowworm concentrations and they're not as busy as the main Waitomo Caves. You head into the backcountry and the 3¼-hour tour includes two cave visits and short scenic walks. Wear comfortable shoes and take a camera. The tours costs about NZ$75 for adults, and NZ$30 for kids under 14.

If you'd rather stay aboveground, consider tackling the new **Dundle Hill Walk** (✆ **0800/924-866** in NZ, or 07/878-7788; fax 07/878-6266; www.waitomowalk. com). During this 2-day, clearly marked, self-guided walk through native bush, forest, and farmland, you'll walk about 12km (7½ miles) a day and stay at Dundle Hill hut. It requires moderate fitness and costs around NZ$75 adults, NZ$35 kids 15 and under.

Where to Stay

IN HAMILTON

If you want rural charm 20 minutes from Hamilton, ring Peter and Daphne Searle at **Uliveto Country Stay & Olive Grove ★**, 164 Finlayson Rd., Ngahinapouri (www. uliveto.co.nz; ✆ **07/825-2116**), which has two lovely rooms for NZ$140 to NZ$150; dinner is available on request. There are two beautiful suites in a separate guest wing at **Titoki Boutique Accommodation ★★**, 1846 C River Rd. North, Hamilton (www. titokiboutiqueaccommodation.co.nz; ✆ **07/854-4044**). It's perfect for two couples traveling together (no one under 15 years), and guest have their own lounge and dining room. Rooms are NZ$255 to NZ$275 and breakfast is included. The **Novotel**

Tainui ★★, 7 Alma St., Hamilton (www.novotel.co.nz/Hamilton; ⓒ **0800/450-050** in NZ, or 07/838-1366), is probably the most convenient and economic of the inner city hotels. New in 1999 (and refurbished in 2005), its large rooms have contemporary decor and overlook either the city or the river. The hotel is Qualmark Enviro-Gold certified and Green Globe benchmarked. Rates are NZ$160 to NZ$365.

IN CAMBRIDGE

There's lots of old-world charm at **Emanuels Lake Karapiro Lodge** ★★★, Karapiro Heights, 1829F State Highway 1, 20km (12 miles) south of Cambridge (www.karapirolodge.co.nz; ⓒ **07/823-7414;** fax 07/823-7219), where Ed and Ann Rompelberg have created a country retreat overlooking Lake Karapiro. The eight rooms are beautifully appointed and have private patios and en-suite bathrooms, and there are a gym, sauna, and Jacuzzi to unwind in. Rooms cost NZ$350 to NZ$800.

Huntington Stables Retreat ★★★ 🎁 They've done everything right in this luxury retreat in the middle of lush Waikato farmland, and their two stable suites skimp on nothing. The smartly furnished rooms are generous in size, plus there is a beautiful pool, Jacuzzi, and sauna right outside the back door. French doors open out from your private lounge to a deck overlooking farmland. From the wine cellar to the well-stocked pantry and fridge, you'll be exceedingly well looked after with every comfort at your fingertips. I was reluctant to leave.

106 Maungakawa Rd., RD4, Cambridge. www.huntington.co.nz. ⓒ/fax **07/823-4136.** 2 units. From NZ$400–NZ$495. Rates include breakfast. Long-stay and weekend packages. AE, MC, V. **Amenities:** Nearby golf course; Jacuzzi; outdoor pool; sauna; pétanque & croquet courts. *In room:* TV/VCR, hair dryer, kitchen, minibar, Wi-Fi.

Thornton House ★★ Christine Manson and David Cowley have opened the doors of their gorgeous 1902 villa, providing two beautifully decorated rooms that are bound to please. The Blue Room is smaller, cozy, and moody, with a shower-only en suite. The bigger Garden Room has a tub, an extra single bed, and a door to the veranda. The town center is just a 5-minute walk away.

2 Thornton St., Cambridge. www.thorntonhouse.co.nz. ⓒ **07/827-7567.** Fax 07/827-7568. 2 units. NZ$250–NZ$280. Rates include breakfast. Long-stay rates. AE, MC, V. **Amenities:** Hamilton Airport transfers (NZ$25); nearby golf and tennis. *In room:* TV/DVD, fridge, hair dryer, Wi-Fi.

IN WAITOMO

Given the nature of this place, I'm surprised no one has thought to build an underground hotel. Perhaps it would be better than some of the aboveground choices: The pickings are slim here. **Juno Hall Backpackers** ★★, 600 Waitomo Caves Rd. (www.junowaitomo.co.nz; ⓒ/fax **07/878-7649**), a new farmhouse-style hostel, has dorm rooms from NZ$27, and doubles from NZ$66 to NZ$95. A nice B&B in Waitomo, **Abseil Inn,** Waitomo Caves Village (www.abseilinn.co.nz; ⓒ **07/878-7815**), has four rooms from NZ$165 to NZ$185.

Kamahi Cottage ★★, 229 Barber Rd., RD5, Otorohanga (www.kamahi.co.nz; ⓒ/fax **07/873-0849**), is 30 minutes from Waitomo Caves and is the nicest B&B in the area. They have a charming self-contained, one-bedroom cottage for NZ$355 to NZ$475. They have an active recycling and conservation program operating on the family farm, with 200 hectares (500 acres) of native forest protected under legal covenant. Free Wi-Fi is available in the nearby homestead and dinners are available on request. As an alternative, you can try the **Waitomo Caves Hotel,** Lemon Point Road (www.waitomocaveshotel.co.nz; ⓒ **07/878-8204**), but I consider it overrated. It's a shame that this fabulous old building with its rich history and terrific location doesn't live up to its full potential but it's an adequate overnight stay if you've just come to see the caves. Rooms run from NZ$120 to NZ$295.

Where to Eat

IN HAMILTON

The visitor center has a helpful free *Dine Out* guide. You'll find the bulk of the best restaurants, cafes, bars, and nightspots in a tight cluster in and around the south end of Victoria Street.

Domaine ★★★, 575 Victoria St. (© 07/839-2100; www.domaine.co.nz), attracts a mixed business crowd during the day and has just enough flair to keep you coming back. Dine on delicious a la carte meals overlooking the river at the Novotel's **Cafe Alma** (see "Where to Stay," above). **Hindustan,** 10 Garden Place (© 07/838-3501; www.hindustan.co.nz), is an excellent Indian restaurant in central city. Also popular, especially for weekend brunch, is **River Kitchen ★★**, 237 Victoria St. (© 07/839-2906), where the atmosphere is always lively. For the best breakfasts and lunches, go to **Scott Epicurean Café ★★**, 181 Victoria St. (© 07/839-6680); it's open daily.

If you're in the mood for relaxing in a casual local cafe/bar, head for a large tasty meal at **The Cook Café,** 7 Cook St., Hamilton East (© 07/856-6088). **Iguana** (© 07/834-2280) deserves a mention for its sushi, gourmet pizzas, comfy booths, and fast-paced night scene; and **Barzurk,** 250 Victoria St. (© 07/834-2363; www.barzurk.co.nz), is sought out for its superb pizzas and laid-back atmosphere. The **Museum Café ★★**, 1 Grantham St. (© 07/839-7209), offers dinner Tuesday through Saturday and over-the-river cafe service throughout the day; and if you just feel like a quick takeout, **Burger Fuel,** 213 Victoria St. (© 07/838-2400; www.burgerfuel.com), has plenty of filling options.

IN CAMBRIDGE

At last! The Cambridge dining scene has something to boast about. **Onyx ★★**, 70 Alpha St. (© 07/827-7740), should be your first port of call. Here you'll find fabulous wood-fired pizzas, great salads, and tasty seafood platters. **In Stone Café ★**, 85 Victoria St. (© 07/827-8590), is open for great coffee and snacks daily 7am to 7pm; and there's a hidden rural gem called the **Boatshed Café ★★**, RD2, Amber Lane (© 07/827-8286), which overlooks Lake Karapiro and also runs a rental kayak operation that takes you through a canyon sparkling with glowworms.

IN WAITOMO

About the best you'll find in these parts is **Huhu Café ★**, 10 Waitomo Caves Rd., Waitomo (© 07/878-6674; www.huhucafe.co.nz), where a tasty all-day breakfast will set you up for a day of underground fun. They serve delicious evening meals (reservations recommended) that feature dishes like braised lamb medallions. They're open daily from 8:30am to 8:30pm. Blackwater Rafting's **Long Black Café,** Main Road (© 07/878-7361), where the counter food includes good vegetarian fare, is a good coffee stop too.

TAURANGA & BAY OF PLENTY ★★★

208km (129 miles) SE of Auckland; 86km (53 miles) NW of Rotorua

Once-sleepy Tauranga is New Zealand's second-fastest-growing area after Queenstown, and has one of the largest natural harbors in the country, with over 1,000 yachts and launches moored in two marinas. The Port of Tauranga is also a popular stop for cruise ships. It has an urban population of about 120,000 and boasts 2,400 hours of sunshine per year. Tauranga and its nearby beachfront neighbor, Mount Maunganui, are thriving urban centers, and no matter what time of year you visit, you'll be spoiled with choices for anything related to outdoor beach-driven activity.

Essentials

GETTING THERE **By Plane** **Air New Zealand** (✆ 0800/767-767 in NZ), operates daily flights from Tauranga and Whakatane to Auckland, Wellington, and Christchurch. The airport is located in Mount Maunganui, 5km (about 3 miles) from Tauranga city.

By Coach (Bus) **InterCity** (✆ 09/623-1503) and **Newmans** (✆ 09/623-1504) both operate daily services between Tauranga and Auckland, Napier, Rotorua, Taupo, Thames, and Wellington. The **Magic Travellers** (✆ 09/358-5600) buses also stop in Tauranga en route to Rotorua.

By Car Drive south from Auckland on State Highway 1, then go east on State Highway 2; the trip takes around 3 hours. From the Coromandel Peninsula, take Highway 25 or 26 to Waihi and pick up Highway 2; this route takes about 1½ hours. If you're coming from Hamilton, the trip takes 1½ hours, and from Rotorua, around 1 hour.

ORIENTATION Once you get used to the frequent roundabouts, you'll find this an easy city to navigate. **Edgewater** is the beautifully paved product of multimillion-dollar inner city redevelopment. It's one of the prettiest downtown areas in the country. **Cameron Road** is the main arterial route. The main bridge offers a shortcut to **Mount Maunganui,** where you'll find that Project Phoenix has converted the downtown shopping area into a palm-filled promenade that's hard to beat. **Ocean Beach** features great stretches of sand and a growing number of high-rise apartments and holiday homes. More than 60km (37 miles) of continuous white-sand beach runs from Mount Maunganui to Whakatane.

GETTING AROUND Some distance out from Tauranga, expect to share the road with a scary number of huge trucks, all bound for the port. The traffic flow is fast and often congested. Public transport is limited within Tauranga itself. Walk if you can.

VISITOR INFORMATION The **Tauranga i-SITE Visitor Centre,** Civic Centre, 95 Willow St. (✆ 07/578-8103; fax 07/578-7020), is open 9am to 5pm daily. Pick up a free copy of the excellent *Bay of Plenty Visitor Guide*. The **Mount Maunganui i-SITE Visitor Centre** is on Salisbury Avenue (✆ 07/578-8103; fax 07/578-7020). The **Katikati Information Centre** is at 36 Main Rd. (✆ 07/549-1658; fax 07/549-1798). For more information on the area, check out www.bayof plentynz.com, www.cityoftauranga.co.nz, and www.tauranga.co.nz.

SPECIAL EVENTS Tauranga and Mount Maunganui offer a profusion of summer events that cover everything from ironman competitions and yachting regattas to beauty pageants and jazz festivals. Pick up the free *Oceanfest* guide to summer events at the visitor center, call ✆ 07/577-7209, or visit www.bayofplentynz.com/events for more information.

Exploring the Area
IN & NEAR TAURANGA

Sun, sea, and surf rule here. But before you take to the water, take a look at **Kiwi360,** 35 Young Rd., Te Puke (✆ 07/573-6340; www.kiwi360.com), 5km (3 miles) south of Te Puke. It's definitely different, and if you want insight into the multimillion-dollar kiwifruit industry, this is the place—and it's great for kids, too. There are daily kiwi cart tours every hour through orchards and theme parks (NZ$25 adults; NZ$10 children ages 5–15), a kiwifruit souvenir shop, and a restaurant. It's open daily 9am to 5pm, except December 25.

The mural town of **Katikati** is worth a brief stopover. Ask at the visitor center for the location of some of the town's many professionally painted street murals—there are over 40. And take a dip in the thermal **Sapphire Springs,** 274 Hot Springs Rd. (© **07/549-0768;** www.sapphiresprings.net.nz), set on 31 hectares (78 acres) of native bush. They're open daily 8am to 7pm.

In Tauranga, the **Elms Mission House,** Mission and Chapel streets (© **07/577-9772;** www.theelms.org.nz), is one of the finest examples of colonial architecture of its time (1847). The house is open Wednesday, Saturday, Sunday, and public holidays from 2 to 4pm and costs NZ$5. If you're interested in more of the town's history, pick up the excellent brochure *Historic Tauranga* from the information center.

Tauranga Art Gallery ★★, corner of Wharf & Willow streets (© **07/578-7933;** www.artgallery.org.nz), is well worth a look. It's a beautifully designed space showcasing historic and contemporary art, both local and national. It's across the road from the i-SITE Visitor Centre and open daily from 10am to 4:30pm; free admission.

Garden enthusiasts can pick up the *Garden Trail* brochure at the visitor center. **McLaren Falls Park** ★★, McLaren Falls Road, Tauranga (© **07/577-7000**), is another lovely stop. It consists of 170 hectares (420 acres) of lake-land park set amid pastoral farming and horticulture, containing one of the best botanical tree collections in the North Island. If you have a license you can fish for trout, or simply enjoy the arboretum and numerous walking tracks.

The most spectacular of Tauranga's attractions is nearby **White Island** ★★★, New Zealand's only active marine volcano. Known as Whakaari to Maori, this active volcano sits 48km (29 miles) off the Bay of Plenty coast. It is privately owned and was declared a scenic reserve in 1953. Visitors cannot land on the island without permission and its spectacular sights are best seen via a guided tour.

Given its easy accessibility, White Island is something of a mecca for the world's volcanologists and scientists, who come to study its lava flows and explosive ash eruptions. Attempts to mine sulfur on the island in 1914 ended when a lahar killed 10 workers; and a major eruption here from 1981 to 1983 completely altered the island's landscape and destroyed an entire pohutukawa forest. Another eruption in 2000 covered the island in mud and scoria.

Despite its fiery reputation, though, White Island remains a highlight for many visitors. If you're considering a visit, rest assured that the island's volcanic activity is constantly monitored by surveillance cameras, seismographic equipment, and sensors within the crater walls. You won't be allowed on the island if there is even the slightest risk of increased activity. Fishermen might like to know that the waters around White Island are home to an abundance of fish—everything from marlin to tuna. Fishing excursions operate out of both Whakatane and Tauranga.

Among the operators offering aerial excursions are **Vulcan Helicopters** (© **0800/804-354** in NZ, or 07/308-4188; www.vulcanheli.co.nz), which operates out of Whakatane and costs around NZ$550 per person. **White Island Tours** ★★★, 15 Strand St. E., Whakatane (© **0800/733-529** in NZ, or 07/308-9588; www.white island.co.nz), will put you on a luxury launch and give you a 6-hour guided tour with lunch and safety gear included. This is an award-winning eco-experience that you won't forget in a hurry. It costs NZ$185 per person and you need to be reasonably agile to negotiate the inflatable boat that takes you ashore from the main launch. Tracks on the island can be uneven and you'll be on your feet for around 2 hours. No open-toed footwear or sandals are permitted, and it is not recommended for children 7 and under. They operate from 6:30am to 10pm in summer (9pm winter). Don't despair if you don't make it to White Island from here, as there are several Rotorua operators, which also offer great flights.

IN MOUNT MAUNGANUI

The town is named after the small mountain known to Maori as **Mauao,** which is a place of cultural and legendary significance to the local Maori tribes. The biggest attraction here has always been **Ocean Beach ★★★**, famed for its surf and great swimming. The **Mount ★★** itself has a network of lovely walkways. The full 3.5km (2-mile) walk around the Mount takes about an hour. You can also climb to its 252m (827-ft.) summit, which takes about 2 hours. Pick up the free *Walker's Guide to Mauao* from the visitor center. The Mount is also home to New Zealand's first artificial surf reef, which is located just offshore on Marine Parade.

At the base of the Mount, on Adams Avenue, the **Mount Hot Pools ★★★** (© 07/ **575-0868;** www.tcal.co.nz) are in a modern complex where you can soak away all your aches and pains in water warmed to 102°F (39°C); the active and children's pools are 90°F (32°C). Private pools and massage services are available. Hours are Monday through Saturday 6am to 10pm, and Sunday 8am to 10pm. Admission is NZ$12 for adults and NZ$8 for children ages 5 to 14, NZ$6 for children 2 to 4. Private pools go for NZ$12 per person for 30 minutes.

Outdoor Pursuits

DOLPHIN SWIMMING   Several companies offer the opportunity to get in the water with the common dolphins that live in the bay. Try **Butler's Swim With Dolphins,** Pier C, Berth C60, Tauranga Bridge Marina (© **0508/288-537** in NZ, or 07/ 578-0821; www.swimwithdolphins.co.nz). Expeditions depart Tauranga daily at 8:45am and the Mount at 9:15am for a full-day outing; and cost around NZ$145 for adults, NZ$110 for kids. For more on the ethics of swimming with dolphins, see p. 34.

FISHING   Blue Ocean Charters, Tauranga Bridge Marina, Tauranga (© **0800/ 224-278;** www.blueocean.co.nz), offers half- and full-day reef fishing, day and overnight hapuka fishing, and ecotrips to Mayor Island. Prices range from NZ$75 to NZ$100 per person depending on the trip type; kids under 13 cost NZ$50.

FOUR-WHEEL-DRIVE ADVENTURES   Springloaded Fun Park (© 0800/ 867-386 in NZ, or 07/533-1515; www.springloadedfun.co.nz) is at Paengaroa on State Highway 33, a half-hour south of Tauranga. Open daily from 9am (closed Dec 25–26 and Mon–Tues in winter), they have self-drive 4WD cars from NZ$60 for adults and NZ$35 for children ages 14 and under for 3km (2 miles) of fun.

JET-BOATING   Reliable thrills can be had with **Springloaded Jet** (© 0800/867-386 in NZ, or 07/533-1515; www.springloadedfun.co.nz). Prices start at NZ$95 per adult, NZ$45 for children 15 and over; children 14 and under are not allowed.

KAYAKING   Combine gentle kayaking with a lovely glow worm experience on Lake McLaren with **Waimarino.com,** by the Wairoa River, 36 Taniwha Place, Bethlehem (© **07/576-4233;** www.waimarino.com). It's New Zealand's only glowworm kayak tour. It costs NZ$125 for a standard tour with refreshments. They also offer a range of more lively options including ocean kayaking.

SKY DIVING   **Tauranga Tandem Skydiving** at 2 Kittyhawk Way, Tauranga Airport (✆ **07/576-7990;** www.tandemskydive.co.nz) is your best bet. A basic jump will cost NZ$255 to NZ$345.

SURFING   **Hibiscus Surf School,** Mount Maunganui (✆ **07/575-3792;** www. surfschool.co.nz), offers exclusive personal tuition with surf instructor Rebecca Taylor, who will quickly bring you up to speed on local surf and ocean conditions.

WHITE-WATER RAFTING   There's no shortage of rafting operators. **Wet 'n' Wild Rafting ★,** 2 White St., Rotorua (✆ **0800/462-723** in NZ, or 07/348-3191; www.wetnwildrafting.co.nz), operates on five rivers in this region, offering a wide range of adventures depending on your level of experience. You can add more fun by combining rafting with jet-boating, a helicopter ride, and mountain biking. Prices start at NZ$99 to NZ$110 per person.

Where to Stay

Every summer, more than 60,000 New Zealanders make their annual holiday pilgrimage to Tauranga and Mount Maunganui. If you plan to come here between December and February, book well in advance. All rates below include 15% GST and free parking.

IN & NEAR TAURANGA

You'll find most motels on Waihi Road and 15th Avenue. The **Tauranga YHA** is at 171 Elizabeth St. (www.yha.co.nz; ✆ **0800/278-299** in NZ, or 07/578-5064). For a great-value bed and breakfast, head straight for **Casa del Mare ★★,** 35 Monticello Key, Palm Springs Estate, Papamoa, Tauranga (www.casadelmare.co.nz; ✆ **07/542-2996**), where two beautifully appointed rooms opening onto the garden go for NZ$150 to NZ$250. The **Hotel on Devonport ★★,** 72 Devonport Rd. (www.hotelondevonport.net.nz; ✆ **0800/322-856** in NZ, or 07/578-2668), is a smart boutique establishment with big, modern rooms, that's well-located in the center of the city. Rates run from NZ$255 for a standard to NZ$325 for a suite. The gorgeous **Ridge Country Retreat ★★★,** 300 Rocky Cutting Rd., Welcome Bay, Tauranga (www.rcr.co.nz; ✆ **07/542-1301**), is a real find—a boutique lodge and spa that provides just about anything you could wish for in a smart, contemporary environment on 14 hectares (35 acres) of sloping hills and native bush just out of the city. Rooms are big and sumptuous, and it's all about understated luxury. Six spacious villas feature a private deck and individual outdoor geothermal tubs. Suites go for NZ$755 to NZ$980, while a villa will set you back NZ$1,175.

IN MOUNT MAUNGANUI

Pacific Coast Backpackers, 432 Maunganui Rd. (www.pacificcoastlodge.co.nz; ✆ **0800/666-622** in NZ, or 07/574-9601), is just a few hundred meters from the beach and downtown. Dorm beds are NZ$24 to NZ$32 per person and doubles NZ$68 to NZ$85 per room. At the top end, you'll be well looked after with 60 gorgeous seaside apartments at **Oceanside Resort & Twin Towers ★★,** 1 Maunganui Rd., Mount Maunganui (www.oceanside.co.nz; ✆ **0800/466-868** in NZ, or 07/575-5371). The high-rise complex also features a heated lap pool, gym and sauna, and secure underground parking. Rates range from NZ$185 for a studio to NZ$410 for a two-bedroom suite. A selection of restaurants and cafes are available inside the complex and within walking distance.

Where to Eat

IN TAURANGA

The dining scene in this area has taken off, and you'll probably miss restaurants and cafes every time you blink. There's a cluster of very good ones on The Strand, in the Wharf Street area, and on Devonport Road between Spring and Elizabeth streets. Pick up the free *Dine Out* guide from the visitor center.

Try **Spinnakers Restaurant & Bar,** Tauranga Bridge Marina (© **07/574-4147**), on the water's edge, for fabulous seafood and a wide range of breakfast, lunch, and dinner offerings; or **Cafe Bravo ★★**, Red Square, Tauranga (© **07/578-4700;** www.cafebravo.co.nz), a consistent award-winner serving up delicious meals, gourmet pizzas, and good coffee. It's open daily from 9am; dinner is served Tuesday through Saturday. **Café Versailles ★★**, 107 Grey St., Tauranga (© **07/571-1480;** www.cafe-versailles.co.nz), is a romantic spot for an authentic French meal. It's open Monday through Saturday 3:30pm until late. **Gold Mela ★★**, 350 Cameron Rd., Tauranga (© **07/578-1197**), is an excellent Italian restaurant that's big on atmosphere and ideal for families. It's open Monday through Saturday, 5pm till late.

Tucked away in the Old Yacht Club Building, at the south end of The Strand, **Harbourside Brasserie & Bar ★★★** (© **07/571-0520**) is eternally popular. It's open daily from 10:30am until late; there's a strong seafood slant to its menu and the views are unmatched. **Collar & Thai ★★**, Upstairs, Goddards Centre, 21 Devonport Rd. (© **07/577-6655;** www.collarandthai.co.nz), is a popular haunt serving the best Thai curries. It's open for lunch Monday to Saturday from 11:30am, and for dinner daily from 5pm. Try **Mills Reef Winery ★★**, 143 Moffats Rd., Bethlehem, Tauranga (© **07/576-8800;** www.millsreef.co.nz), for a fabulous winery lunch. It's open daily for lunch and Thursday for dinner. All meals are teamed with Mills Reef wines.

IN MOUNT MAUNGANUI

The favorite for Thai meals is **Thai-phoon Restaurant ★★**, 14a Pacific Ave. (© **07/572-3545**), open daily from 6pm. **Astrolabe Café & Bar ★★**, 82 Maunganui Rd. (© **07/574-8155**), is big on space and style and serves delicious salads. It's open daily from 10am till late. You'll get very good Italian meals at **ViVo,** 14 Pacific Ave., Mount Maunganui (© **07/575-8245**), which has a terrific family atmosphere. It's open Tuesday through Sunday from 6pm till late, also open for weekend lunch.

En Route to Rotorua

As you head south to Rotorua on State Highway 2, you'll pass through **Te Puke,** the "Kiwifruit Capital of the World." Here's where you'll find **Kiwi360** (see "Exploring the Area," earlier). The road is good for the hour-long journey, but it gets crowded with lots of heavy logging trucks headed for the port in Tauranga—drive with extreme care!

ROTORUA, TAUPO & TONGARIRO NATIONAL PARK

Rotorua sits on the edge of one of the most awesome and concentrated volcanic areas in the world. In every direction is tangible evidence of a riotous geological past extending back millions of years. The Te Arawa people settled the area in the mid–14th century, and their descendants began tourism in the area in the 19th century, guiding visitors to the famous Pink and White terraces. The 1886 eruption of Mount Tarawera destroyed the terraces, but the legendary Maori hospitality lives on. Coupled with enough daredevil activities to rival Queenstown's reputation as New Zealand's adventure capital, the famous welcome continues to draw international visitors at a rate of 1.6 million a year.

Volcanic activity was also responsible for the formation of Lake Taupo. In A.D. 186, an enormous eruption—estimated to have been 100 times greater than that of Mount St. Helens in 1980—tore a savage hole 30km (20 miles) wide, 40km (25 miles) across, and 180m (600 ft.) deep. Today, we're thankful for that. Where would New Zealand holidaymakers be without the cool blue waters that provide ideal conditions for fishing, water-skiing, and boating?

South of Taupo lies Tongariro National Park, home to three volcanoes. Tongariro was New Zealand's first national park (the world's second after Yellowstone), and today it is a winter playground for skiers and a perfect place for summer tramping.

ROTORUA ★★★

221km (137 miles) SE of Auckland; 86km (53 miles) S of Tauranga

You'll smell Rotorua long before you see it. The sulfuric aroma in the air is an unmistakable prelude to geothermal things to come. This natural wonderland and the 16 major lakes in the area are the draw for visitors. In fact, Rotorua has long had a reputation for being too touristy, but recent

Rotorua & Environs

Buried Village of
Te Wairoa **3**

Hell's Gate & Wai Ora Spa **1**

Lady Knox Geyser **6**

Tamaki Maori Village **4**

Waimangu Volcanic
Valley **5**

Waiotapu Thermal
Wonderland **6**

Whakarewarewa
Thermal Village **2**

city beautification and heaps of new adventures, accommodations, and attractions have given it a whole new lease on life.

If you're interested in Maori culture, this is the most accessible place to find it. A third of the population of 68,000 is Maori; that's the highest percentage of any city in the country. Rotorua may attract a lot of visitors (2.9 million annually), but unlike Queenstown, its attractions are spread wide and you seldom have to jostle with others. There's plenty of room for everyone. And if you're keen to support sustainable initiatives, the Rotorua Sustainable Tourism Charter (www.sustainablenz.com) has identified a group of tourism operators committed to protecting and enhancing the natural environment. Members are assessed and their operations carry the charter logo. You can find out who they are and what role they are playing at the Rotorua i-SITE Visitor Centre & Travel Office.

Essentials

GETTING THERE   By Plane   Air New Zealand National and Link (© 0800/767-767 in NZ; www.airnewzealand.co.nz) provides daily service to all other major centers. **Super Shuttle** (© 07/349-3444) provides daily transport to and from the airport, 15 minutes out of town, for NZ$25 to NZ$30.

By Coach (Bus)   InterCity, Newmans, Magic Travellers, and **Kiwi Experience** all provide service to Rotorua. Contact the **Bus Stop,** 67 Fenton St. (© 07/348-179; fax 07/348-6044), for coach and ferry bookings throughout New Zealand.

By Car   Centrally located Rotorua is only a 1-hour drive from the cities of Taupo, Hamilton, and Tauranga; a 3-hour drive from Auckland; and a 5-hour drive from Wellington. Roads in the area are excellent, but Rotorua is in the heart of the forestry industry, which means a heavy volume of large, fast-traveling logging trucks. Take care at all times.

ORIENTATION   Rotorua sits in the curve of Lake Rotorua's southwestern shore, spreading inland in a neat pattern. **Fenton Street** is the main drag and the home of the area's souvenir shops. It runs from the lake for 3.5km (2 miles) south to **Whakarewarewa Village** (just call it "Whaka," as the locals do), the area's most accessible thermal reserve. The center of town is not large. **Tutanekai Street** is the main shopping street; **City Focus,** under the sail-like structure, is in the middle of it all.

Note: Don't wander in Kuirau Park after dark. Make sure to remove all valuables from cars, and lock those cars, too.

GETTING AROUND   City and suburban buses run approximately every hour on weekdays, less frequently on weekends. You'll find taxis at the visitor center and on Fenton Street, or you can call © 07/348-5079. If you need a car, call **Pegasus Rental Cars,** 274 Te Ngae Rd. (© 0800/803-580 in NZ, or 07/345-8455).

VISITOR INFORMATION   **Rotorua i-SITE Visitor Centre & Travel Office,** 1167 Fenton St. (© 0800/768-678 in NZ, or 07/348-5179; fax 07/348-6044; www.rotoruanz.com), is open daily from 8am to 5:30pm (closed Dec 25). It provides travel

 Sore Feet?

A sheltered seat and a free, hot, thermal footbath are right outside the main entrance to the visitor center and bus stop. Go ahead and take your shoes off and soak your weary feet for a few minutes.

and sightseeing reservations, currency exchange, luggage storage, a cafe and restaurant, an excellent souvenir shop, and showers and toilets. The visitor center's guide booklets are an excellent value.

Travel information is also available at **AA Travel Centre,** 1121 Eruera St. (📞 07/348-3069; fax 07/346-2034). The **Redwoods Visitor Centre, Whakarewarewa Forest,** Long Mile Road (📞 07/350-0110; www.redwoods.co.nz), provides information on the extensive walking tracks in Whakarewarewa Forest and Redwood Grove. It's open weekdays 8:30am to 5:30pm (until 4:30pm in winter), and weekends 10am to 5pm (until 4pm in winter). For more information on the area, check www.rotoruanz.com and www.rdc.govt.nz. The Redwoods is located 5km (about 3 miles) southeast of the city and you can be there in 5 minutes by car.

Pick up a free copy of *Thermal Air,* an excellent little publication listing activities, attractions, eateries, and events. The local newspaper, the *Daily Post,* also has listings.

[FastFACTS] ROTORUA

The **post office,** Hinemoa Street (📞 **07/347-7851**), is open Monday through Friday 7:30am to 5pm, Saturday 8am to 4pm, and Sunday 10am to 3pm. **Thomas Cook,** Fenton and Hinemoa streets (📞 **07/348-0640**), is open Monday through Friday 9am to 5pm and Saturday 9:30am to 12:30pm. For Internet access, try **Cyber World,** 1174 Haupapa St. (📞 **07/348-0088**), or **Cybershed,** 1176 Pukuatua St. (📞 **07/349-4965**).

SPECIAL EVENTS The route of the **Rotorua Marathon** (📞/fax **07/348-3301;** www.rotoruamarathon.co.nz) goes around Lake Rotorua. This very serious competition takes place in late April or early May. In April, fishermen compete in the **Tagged Trout Tournament** (📞 07/348-5179; www.taggedtrout.co.nz), which presents 2 days of fishing with great prizes. The **Rotorua Festival of Arts Te Ihi Te Wehi** (📞 07/348-9134; www.rotoruaartsfestival.co.nz) provides 16 days of creative events in early March. In late January, the biennial **Opera in the Pa** (📞 07/348-9047) features New Zealand's best young Maori, European, and Polynesian opera voices at a different location each time. Check www.rotoruanz.com/events closer to time for the 2013 venue.

> **Sacred Lake**
>
> Of the 16 major lakes in the area, most are ideal for swimming and watersports—except Lake Rotokakahi, the Green Lake. This lake is *tapu* (sacred) to the Maori and, therefore, off-limits for swimming, boating, and fishing.

Exploring Rotorua

Although the major thermal areas and Maori culture remain very popular, **Mount Tarawera** ★★★ now plays a big part in Rotorua tourism. It has a strong mystical history for the Maori, and I keep hearing rave reports about four-wheel-drive and fly-over crater tours. If your time is short, the top must-see/must-do attractions are the **Te Puia; Rotorua Museum;** either of the geothermal reserves, **Waiotapu** or **Waimangu;** and a scenic flight over **Mount Tarawera.** This is easy to manage in 2 days. Visit the museum first or last for a comprehensive overview of Mount Tarawera's role. And pick up the *Passport to Rotorua's Finest Attractions* brochure from the visitor center—it details the bus service that frequents 18 leading attractions.

THE MAJOR SIGHTS & ATTRACTIONS
In the City Area

Rotorua Museum ★★★ Set in the world-famous Bath House, the Rotorua Museum has a new lease on life. The new Don Stafford Wing opened with 50% more gallery space in August 2011, and includes eight new galleries dedicated to the stories of the local Te Arawa people and the history of Mount Tarawera. There is also an excellent exhibition of Te Arawa *taonga* (treasures) set off against state-of-the-art technology and modern lighting. A fabulous, high-tech cinema experience is well worth a visit, especially if you want insight into the Mount Tarawera eruption of 1886. The new extension also includes two new art galleries that showcase some of the museum's collection, along with significant touring art exhibitions. The restored section of the Great South Seas Spa is equally fascinating. People came from all over the world to visit the spa and were encouraged to take "electric baths," a rather bizarre practice that saw electric currents fed into the bath water. And don't forget to go down into the basement and up onto the roof. This will give you a unique insight into the makeup of this stunning building, not to mention great lake and city views.

Queen's Dr., Government Gardens. ✆ **07/350-1814.** www.rotoruamuseum.co.nz. Admission NZ$18 adults, NZ$7 children 5–18, NZ$23–NZ$40 family. Summer daily 9am–8pm; winter daily 9am–5pm. Free tours daily on the hour from 10am. Rotorua Stories Cinema every 20 min. from 9am; Maori Battalion Cinema every 30 min. from 9:30am. Closed Dec 25.

Polynesian Spa ★★★ 📷 Don't leave town without indulging in this divinely soothing experience—voted by U.K. *Condé Nast Traveller* readers as being among the top 10 thermal spas in the world in 2009. The jewel in this watery crown is the **Lake Spa** complex, with four Japanese rotenburo pools at different temperatures, set among rocks and waterfalls beside the lake. Add to that the **Lake Spa Retreat,** where you can lie back and have delicious things done to your body in the name of stress release and relaxation. (I highly recommended the mud body wrap.) This is the swanky section of the complex: You get extra service, a private bar, and a lounge—it's well worth the cost. The **Family Spa** is another top addition. It has a warm freshwater pool with a toddlers' pool and a mini–water slide; adults can enjoy two adjacent hot mineral pools while they supervise the brood. The complex has 27 bathing pools in total, including 13 beautiful new private pools, refurbished in 2007. Ask for one of the four private lake-view pools and lie back and savor the magic.

Adults have the use of a large hot mineral pool, plus the three adjacent Priest Spa acidic pools, famous for their curative effects on ailments such as arthritis and rheumatism. The water in these pools comes from acidic springs, and the temperature

Saving on the Sights

Check the visitor center or its website (www.rotoruanz.com) for the latest **Rotorua Hot Deals** (www.rotoruahotdeals.com). New packages and deals are added regularly throughout the year, but typically include Tamaki Tours, Polynesian Spa, Agrodome, Skyline Skyrides, and many other star attractions and activities. **Rotorua Adventure**

Combos (✆ **0800/338-786** in NZ, or 07/357-2236; www.rotoruacombos.com) also combines many of the city's leading attractions in well-priced packages; and **Rotorua 5 Star Super Pass** (✆ **07/348-5179**; www.rotorua5star.co.nz) gives you good deals on access to Polynesian Spa, Skyline Skyrides, and Te Puia.

HOTELS ■
A-Kahu **2**
Amora Lake Resort **20**
Base Hot Rock **9**
Koura Lodge **2**
Maruata Rotorua **4**
Millennium Hotel Rotorua **17**
Novotel Lakeside **6**
Peppers on the Point **2**
Quest Rotorua **29**
Regal Palms **26**
Regent of Rotorua **7**
Rotorua top 190 Holiday Park **8**
Silver Fern Rotorua **23**
The Springs **24**
Solitaire Lodge **21**
Treetops Lodge & Estate **30**
Wai Ora Lakeside Spa Resort **20**
Wylie Court Motor Lodge **25**

RESTAURANTS ◆
Abracadabra Café **11**
Aorangi Peak Restaurant **1**
Capers Epicurean **12**
Fat Dog Café **10**
Lime Caffeteria **16**
Relish **14**
Seismic Gastrobar **13**
Triple 1 Five **15**
Urbano **22**

ATTRACTIONS ●
Agrodome **1**
Government Gardens **19**
Ohinemutu Maori Village **5**
Polynesian Spa **18**
Rainbow Springs Kiwi Wildlife
    Park & Kiwi Encounter **3**
Rotorua Museum **19**
Te Puia **27**
Whakarewarewa Thermal
    Village **28**

varies from 102°F to 108°F (39°C–42°C). The water in all other pools is quite different. It's soft alkaline water, which flows from a boiling spring 100m (330 ft.) from the complex and is cooled by the addition of the town's water. The Polynesian Spa is incredibly popular, so you'll seldom be alone unless you opt for a private pool or Luxury Spa experience, but it's worth it nonetheless—especially if you have aching muscles.

Government Gardens, lakefront end of Hinemoa St. ✆ **0508/765-977** in NZ, or 07/348-1328. www.polynesianspa.co.nz. Admission adults-only pool and Priest Spa NZ$22; Lake Spa NZ$44 adults, NZ$16 children 5–14; Family Spa bathing NZ$14 adults, NZ$7 children, NZ$36 family; private pools NZ$22 adults, NZ$28 children 5–14, NZ$28 deluxe lake view. Spa therapies NZ$90 for 30 min., NZ$160 for 1 hr. AE, MC, V. Daily 8am–11pm.

Te Puia ★★★ Te Puia encompasses the Geothermal Valley, the Maori Cultural Experience, and the New Zealand Maori Arts & Crafts Institute; and it is one of Rotorua's top attractions. It boasts two excellent interactive galleries (no photographs allowed) and both the weaving and carvings schools let you watch artworks evolve. The highlight of the thermal reserve is definitely the effusive **Pohutu Geyser.** It usually erupts 10 to 25 times a day to a height of 16 to 20m (53–66 ft.). This steamy little valley is also known for its mud pools, which average 194°F to 203°F (90°C–95°C). The 1½-hour guided tour is a good option, allowing you a chance to learn about the culture and the thermal activity. It includes a look through a replica of a Maori village (as opposed to the real living Maori village of nearby Whakarewarewa), and the New Zealand Maori Arts & Crafts Institute, established in 1963 to foster traditional Maori carving and weaving skills. If this is your first experience with Maori culture, I'd spend about 2 to 3 hours here minimum—if only to get value from the rather exorbitant entry fee—and see one of the live performances as well—either the midday concert or the Te Po performance at 6pm, which includes a full *hangi* (earth oven) meal. Don't miss the excellent gift shop.

Hemo Rd. ✆ **0800/837-842** in NZ, or 07/348-9047. Fax 07/348-9045. www.tepuia.com. Admission NZ$46 adults, NZ$23 children 5–15, NZ$125 family; with cultural performance NZ$58 adult, NZ$29 children, NZ$155 family. Te Po performance NZ$115 adults, NZ$60 children 5–15, NZ$310 family. AE, MC, V. Daily 8am–6pm (winter until 5pm). Guided tours hourly 9am–5pm. 3 Maori concerts daily at 10:15am, 12:15pm, and 3:15pm.

In & Around Nearby Ngongotaha

Skyline Skyrides ★ ☺ Skyline Skyrides is one of the most popular Rotorua attractions, and for the panoramic views from Mount Ngongotaha alone, the ride is worth it. Entertain the whole family with crazy ways to descend—the regular scenic luge, intermediate and advanced luge tracks, or the chairlift. The scenic track has viewing bays so you can stop and take photographs of the terrific views. The Sky Swing is also based here; it hoists three passengers to over 36m (120 ft.) before swinging them out over Mount Ngongotaha at speeds up to 140kmph (90 mph). A restaurant (with an excellent buffet) and cafe provide for the peckish.

Fairy Springs Rd. ✆ **07/347-0027.** Fax 07/348-2163. www.skyline.co.nz. Gondola NZ$25 adults, NZ$13 children 5–14, NZ$62 family; luge ride NZ$10. Packages available for gondola plus multiple luge rides. Sky Swing NZ$30 adults, NZ$25 children 5–14. Daily 9am–late. 4.5km (3 miles) north of town on St. Hwy. 5.

Agrodome ★ ☺ Not everyone wants to come face-to-face with 19 different sheep breeds in one place at one time, but if you do, this is your chance. You can also see a shearing display and a working sheepdog demonstration, tour the 160-hectare (395-acre) farm, or find yourself something satisfyingly woolly in the souvenir shop. Sheep aside, there's a range of adventure activities here, too—helicopters, jet-skiing, bungy jumping, Swoop, Zorb, and Freefall Xtreme (see "Outdoor Pursuits," later in this chapter, for details)—plus a cafe, restaurant, and a woolen mill. You pay individually for these. Agrodome is a great one-stop show that should keep the kids happy. And don't forget to ask about the wide range of adventure packages, which provide multiple activities at a reduced rate. Combo packages for the Agrodome and *Lakeland Queen* (p. 196) are also available here; combos range in price from NZ$71 to NZ$105 for adults and NZ$30 to NZ$52 for children 5 to 15.

Western Rd. ☏ **0800/339-400** in NZ, or 07/357-1050. Fax 07/357-5307. www.agrodome.co.nz. Admission to Agrodome show NZ$29 adults, NZ$15 children 5–15; Agrodome show and organic farm tour combo NZ$56 adults, NZ$28 children 5–15, NZ$110 families. AE, MC, V. Daily 8:30am–5pm. Shows daily 9:30am, 11am, and 2:30pm.

Paradise Valley Springs ★ ☺ You can go from sheep to trout in a few easy minutes, with an unexpected bonus: lions! This very pretty place has delightful bush walks through a wildlife sanctuary, trout-filled streams, and a wetlands area. There is also an underwater viewing cave and a spawning stream where you can hand-feed the trout. When there are suitably sized lion cubs in-house, you can pet them—something the kids will love. Even the farmyard animals seem utterly content, no doubt from living in such idyllic surrounds. The bush walk is bigger and better than that at Rainbow Springs (below) and you have a lovely country drive on the way out.

467 Paradise Valley Rd. ☏ **07/348-9667.** Fax 07/349-3359. www.paradisevalleysprings.co.nz. Admission NZ$30 adults, NZ$15 children 5–15, family pass NZ$75. AE, MC, V. Daily 8am–dark (last entry 5pm). Lion feeding daily 2:30pm; cub petting 10:40am–4:30pm.

Rainbow Springs Kiwi Wildlife Park & Kiwi Encounter ★★ ☺ As at Paradise Valley Springs (above), you'll find water teeming with trout. But instead of lions, you'll get kiwi and tuatara. Kiwi Encounter is unique in that it presents "conservation in action"—the raising of kiwi chicks from eggs for release into the wild. It's the only purpose-built Operation Nest Egg Project open to the public. The excellent tour will give you insight into these rare birds and how they are being saved from extinction. Watching a kiwi hatch on video is a special experience. At time of writing, a NZ$10-million expansion program was underway for Rainbow Springs. This will include a complete makeover and the building of a new reptile encounter and a children's playground that features a high-tech, interactive water slide ride. The revamped park is slated to open in early 2012.

Fairy Springs Rd. ☏ **0800/724-626** in NZ, or 07/350-0440. Fax 07/350-0441. www.rainbowsprings. co.nz and www.kiwiencounter.co.nz. Admission NZ$26 adults, NZ$15 children 5–15; Kiwi Encounter tour NZ$32 adults, NZ$20 children 5–15; combo NZ$50 adults, NZ$30 children 5–15. AE, MC, V. Daily 8am–10pm (9pm in winter). Shows daily 10:30am, 11:45am, 1pm, 2:30pm, and 4pm. Guided springs tours 11:45am and 1pm. Ask about their night tours.

Just Outside Rotorua

Buried Village of Te Wairoa ★ ✋ The Buried Village has an excellent little museum that details the eruption of Mount Tarawera and its aftermath. It displays many of the objects unearthed after the Mount Tarawera eruption buried the small village of Te Wairoa in 1886. A meandering pathway set among trees and meadows by the Te Wairoa Stream connects the Buried Village's excavated dwellings. You'll see remains of a flour mill, Maori *whare* (house), stores, the Rotomahana Hotel, and more. Thirty-minute guided tours (included in the admission price) begin at various times. If you're fit and agile, make sure you include the steep path to view the pretty waterfall—to my mind it's the best thing about the place. It's certainly a pretty spot with an interesting story, but I can't help feeling it's a little overpriced for what you get.

1180 Tarawera Rd., RD5. ✆/fax **07/362-8287**. www.buriedvillage.co.nz. Admission from NZ$32 adults, NZ$8 children 5–15, NZ$64 families. AE, DC, MC, V. Daily 9am–5pm (winter until 4:30pm). Closed Dec 25. 15 min. from the city on a scenic drive past the Blue and Green lakes.

MAORI CULTURAL EXPERIENCES

It's easy to be completely confused by the number of Maori cultural experiences available in Rotorua. Basically, they all offer a *hangi* (earth oven feast) and a song-and-dance performance, and they're all similarly priced. The hangi is the traditional Maori method of cooking. A large pit is filled by a wood fire topped by stones; when the stones are heated through, baskets of food are placed on top and covered with damp cloths. Earth is then shoveled over to create a natural oven. After about 3 hours, dinner is unveiled, with intermingling flavors of various foods lightly touched by wood smoke. Not all hangi are this authentic—indeed, many hotel hangi are now steamed for health and safety requirements.

The prize for the best concert and hangi is a tossup between three leading players, **Tamaki Maori Village** (see below), **Te Puia** (see above), and **Mitai Village** ★★★, 196 Fairy Springs Rd., Rotorua (✆ **07/343-9132;** www.mitai.co.nz), which is open daily with a concert and hangi performance from 6:30 to 9:45pm (NZ$122 adults, NZ$63 children 10–15, NZ$33 children 5–9, NZ$333 family). The Tamaki evening has become more commercial and has lost a little of its shine, but it gives a good rundown of Maori history and is in a re-created village out of town. Mitai scores big with its stunning arrival by *waka* (war canoe) and guests get taken into the bush to see glowworms afterward. It's a more authentic performance and the food is better. Both will get you home around 10:30 or 11pm. A singalong in the homeward bound Tamaki bus may better suit a younger crowd.

Te Po ★★★ at Te Puia is also a terrific performance with smaller numbers and it will have you home by around 8:30pm. If you choose to do their combo, you are picked up at 4:30pm and do the last guided walk of the Whakarewarewa Thermal Valley before the cultural event and hangi. Their hangi food—which includes mussels, shrimp, and their famous steam pudding—wins hands down.

All the major hotels have nightly hangi and concerts, which run about NZ$85 to NZ$125 per person. Of these, the **Royal Lakeside Novotel,** Tutanekai Street (✆ **0508/446-244** or 07/346-3888; www.novotel.co.nz; 6:30 to 9pm), is one of the best and cheapest. The show presents a good balance between old and new. The steamed hangi (not as smoky or tasty as the earth-cooked version) is beautifully presented and has lots of extras. While you eat, a contemporary Maori guitarist performs and traces the development of Maori tourism. Although you don't get the feel of a marae here, a strong and consistently good performance group sings in several languages.

A visit to **Whakarewarewa Thermal Village** ★★★, 17 Tyron St., Rotorua (✆ **07/349-3463;** www.whakarewarewa.com), provides insight into the workings of a modern, real-life Maori village set among geothermal activity. It may be a little over-rated in terms of actual geothermal activity, but this is the only place in New Zealand—perhaps in the world—where people continue the 300-year-old tradition of using natural geothermal energy as part of their everyday cooking and washing practices. You can also see Pohutu Geyser from here for half the price you pay to see it at Te Puia; and in the summer it's fun to watch the kids diving for coins in the river below the bridge. It's open daily from 8:30am to 5pm, with guided tours between 9am and 4pm and cultural performances with hangi (NZ$62 adults, NZ$32 children 5–12) daily at 11:15am and 2pm. Admission is NZ$30 for adults, NZ$13 for children 5–12, and NZ$75 for families.

Keep in mind that Maori land claims currently under negotiation may see the adjacent government-owned Te Puia land returned to the Ngati Wahiao people of Whakarewarewa in coming years. This is unlikely to impact on your visitor experience, but we'll keep you posted.

You can also make your own way to **Ohinemutu Maori Village ★**, on Rotorua's lakefront. Follow the lake road past the Royal Lakeside Novotel and turn onto Houkotuku Street, which is just past the first little group of shops. Turn right onto Ariariterangi Street and drive to the historic Tamatekapua meetinghouse, cemetery, and the very beautiful St. Faith's Church. (Always ask permission before entering, and respect the fact that photographs are not allowed inside the church.) You'll see tons of natural thermal activity in the area, much of it steaming up in people's gardens. Be warned that the streets are extremely narrow—drive slowly because kids often play in the streets here. Also look out for **Ohinemutu Maori Handcrafts,** just past the church on Mataiawhea Street (© **07/350-3378**). It's open daily 8am to 6:30pm in summer and from 9am to 5pm in winter.

If learning the traditional Maori *haka* (war dance) appeals, visit **Haka World,** Kiwi Paka, 60 Tarewa Rd. (© **07/347-1717;** www.hakaworld.com), and let Tiki Edwards put you through the paces for NZ$35 to NZ$40. He runs two sessions—9 to 11am and 1 to 3pm.

Tamaki Maori Village & The Chronicles of Uitara—Journey of Ages ★★
This family company has taken numerous honors in the New Zealand Tourism Awards. The re-created, pre-settlement Maori village, 20 minutes from the city, presents tribal life as it used to be. Carving, weaving, *moko* (tattooing), singing, dancing, chanting, and cooking are all part of the living-village experience. At night, you can enjoy one of the best Maori performances and genuine hangi meals in Rotorua. The "Chronicles of Uitara," in Rotorua itself, is a blend of guided tour, character theater, and storytelling on a series of indoor sets. You get to experience the lifestyle and warrior traditions of pre-European times, as well as the story of Uitara IV's campaign for a place within a rebel warrior cult, destined to change Aotearoa forever. It is an ideal scene setter or follow-up to the village experience, and this is where the evening tours begin. The Tamaki operation is now very large and commercial, which may not appeal to some, but they're still very professional; and if you miss them in Rotorua, you can visit Tamaki Heritage Village in Christchurch, which opened in 2007 and features a different part of the early Maori story.

1220 Hinemaru St. © **0508/826-254** in NZ, or 07/349-2999. Fax 07/347-2913. www.tamakimaorivillage.co.nz. Hangi and concert NZ$105 adults, NZ$60 children 5–15; NZ$305 family pass. Prices include evening pickup from your hotel. Combo deals. AE, DC, MC, V. Daily 5:30pm. Closed Dec 25. The village is on St. Hwy. 5, 20 min. north of Taupo.

Organized Tours

You'll find heaps of brochures for half- and full-day tours at the visitor center. Most of the tours take in the main geothermal attractions and are similarly priced.

Walking Legends Guided Walks (© **0800/925-569** in NZ, or 021/545-068; www.walkinglegends.co.nz) operates fully guided 4-day treks from Rotorua, in the **Lake Waikaremoana Track ★★** in Te Urewera National Park, 150km (93 miles) southeast of Rotorua. It has its own launch to transport passengers and luggage to and from the start and finish of the track. You'll get into real outback country with this one; the 4-day experience costs NZ$1,310 adults and NZ$1,000 children 12 and under. Moderate fitness is required. They also offer 1-day guided walks in Whirinaki Forest and the Tongariro Crossing from NZ$190 for adults and NZ$130 for children.

BUBBLE, BUBBLE, TOIL & TROUBLE:
geothermal ATTRACTIONS

When you enter this region, you quickly realize there's something hard at work underfoot. Steam rises out of gutters and along roadsides, and you can never be entirely sure where the next hiss and roar will come from. Volcanic and geothermal activity has always played a major role in the landscape here, so be sure to experience it for yourself. The visitor center has information on shuttle services to the main geothermal areas. These usually cost NZ$25 to NZ$45; in some cases, prices include admission to the chosen area.

Twenty minutes south of Rotorua, you'll find **Waimangu Volcanic Valley ★★**, 587 Waimangu Rd. (© 07/366-6137; www.waimangu.com). Created on June 10, 1886, by Mount Tarawera's impressive blowout, Waimangu is the only hydrothermal system in the world wholly formed in historic times as a result of a volcanic eruption. Today, you can walk through the valley and look at the many features, the best of which fall during the first 45 minutes of the 1½-hour walk. These include **Frying Pan Lake,** the world's largest hot-water spring, and the impossibly turquoise **Inferno Crater ★★**—a mysterious lake where the level rises and falls on a regular 38-day cycle. The valley is open daily from 8:30am to 5pm (last admission 3:30pm). The walk costs NZ$35 for adults, NZ$13 for children ages 6 to 16, and NZ$85 for a family. You can get a package that includes a boat cruise, a total of 3 hours. If you include the 2-hour hiking trail you'll see more craters, but make sure you're fit as the trail takes you up and over a mountain.

Personally, I'd do just the first 45 minutes of the above walk, skip the boat cruise altogether, and head 10 minutes farther south to **Waiotapu Thermal Wonderland ★★★** (© 07/366-6333; www.waiotapu.co.nz). Waiotapu is a much more intensive and colorful geothermal exhibition. It's open daily from 8:30am to 5pm (last admission 3:45pm), and you'll want to allow 1 to 1½ hours. You can go it alone or with a guided tour, and once again, the bulk of the best attractions are within the shorter (30- to 40-min.) walk. The best features here are the reliable **Lady Knox Geyser ★★**, which performs around 10:15am daily. It's in a separate park nearby, but you get in on the same ticket price. If you want to see the geyser, I strongly advise you to get tickets no later than 9:45am in peak season. My favorite highlights are the spectacular **Champagne Pool ★★★**; New Zealand's largest bubbling **mud pool;** and the vivid green **Devil's Bath.** Admission is NZ$35 for adults, NZ$12 for children 5 to 15, and NZ$90 for families. Just prior to arriving at Waiotapu, look out for the signpost to the mud pool—it's big and it's free.

Forty-five minutes south of Rotorua, you'll find the **Orakei Korako Cave &**

Outdoor Pursuits

Rotorua is teeming with fast-paced opportunity, and everything is within easy reach. Ten minutes in one direction and you get jet-skiing, Zorbing (see below), luging, bungy jumping, four-wheel-drive safaris, off-roading, and horseback riding. Just 20 minutes from Rotorua on the Tauranga Highway, you can raft the highest Grade V waterfall in the Southern Hemisphere, leap on a jet boat, or go mountain biking, walking, or off-roading.

Thermal Park ★★, 494 Orakei Korako Rd. (☏ **07/378-3131;** www.orakeikorako. co.nz), a pocket wonderland of geysers, hot springs, boiling mud, and the majestic Aladdin's Cave on the shores of Lake Ohakuri. This little valley of incredible beauty is preserved by its isolation and inaccessibility—it can be reached only by boat (no extra charge). Boats don't run on a timetable; you can cross at any time. You might want to save this for the journey south—Taupo is just 25 minutes away. Allow at least an hour for a good look around. As in any geothermal area, stay on the formed pathways to avoid danger. The resort is open daily from 8am to 4:30pm (4pm in winter). Admission is NZ$36 for adults, NZ$15 for children 15 and under, NZ$92 for families. To get there, turn off on State Highway 5, just after Golden Springs at Mihi Bridge.

Hell's Gate & Wai Ora Lakeside Spa ★★ (☏ **07/345-3151;** www. hellsgate.co.nz) is 15km (9⅓ miles) northeast of Rotorua on State Highway 30 to Whakatane. This Maori-owned reserve is steeped in culture, and its 8 hectares (20 acres) of thermal activity are different every day—and magnificent in the rain. Reputedly the fiercest of the thermal valleys, it has hot-water lakes, sulfur formations, Rotorua's only mud volcano, and the largest boiling whirlpool in New Zealand. It also offers a range of spa experiences, including massage and semi-private outdoor mud baths. Don't forget to ask about cheaper combo packages. The thermal walk is pretty but not as spectacular as Waiotapu's, and while the soak in thermal mud is sensual, it's a little uninspired and the mud is hard to wash out of your swimsuit. It's open daily from 8:30am to 8:30pm (closed Dec 25). Admission is NZ$35 for adults, NZ$20 for children under 16, and NZ$80 for families—you pay extra for the spa experiences. It's a fun experience to try but I think you get a better mud experience at the Mud Room at **Spa at QE** ★, Whakaue Street, Rotorua (☏ **07/348-0189;** www.qe health.co.nz), which is open Monday to Friday 8am to 10pm and weekends from 9am to 10pm. It costs NZ$55 to NZ$85 and you'll sleep well after it. Or enjoy beautiful mineral spas and mud wraps at **Wai Ora Day Spa,** 77 Robinson Ave., Holdens Bay, Rotorua (☏ **07/343-5152;** www.waioraresort.co.nz), which couples Maori healing and wellness practices with natural spa products.

If you want to get a glimpse of geothermal action in the city free of charge, head for **Kuirau Park,** off Pukuatua and Ranolf streets. This is the site of the huge eruption in 2000, and you can still see the dead trees and white ash in the cordoned-off area. There are steaming vents everywhere, and it is vital that you stay on formed pathways. Please heed this warning as people have perished after climbing the barrier fences and falling into the scalding pools. Stay out of the park at night.

BUNGY JUMPING At **Rotorua Bungy and Swoop** (☏ **07/357-4259;** www. rotoruabungy.co.nz or www.agroventures.co.nz), you can leap from a 43m (141-ft.) tower; but just when you thought things couldn't get any more insane, they go and invent New Zealand's first **Swoop.** You'll be strapped into a hang-gliding harness with two others and lifted 40m (131 ft.) in the air. Pull the rip cord and experience the feeling of flying at 130kmph (81 mph) with a G-force factor of 3. You must be at least 1m (3 ft., 3 in.) tall to swoop. For NZ$120 you can do the bungy plus either the Swoop, the Agrojet (jet-boating), or the Freefall Extreme (sky diving). The bungy alone

The *Lakeland Queen,* Lakefront (© 07/348-0265; www.lakelandqueen.com), underwent a major makeover in 2006 and emerged 10m (33 ft.) longer and able to carry 300 guests. You can take a breakfast, lunch, or dinner cruise, or a 1-hour afternoon tea cruise (2:30pm). Breakfast cruises (NZ$45 for adults, NZ$23 for children ages 5–12) depart at 8am; the 1-hour Express Lunch Cruise (NZ$54 for adults, NZ$27 for children ages 5–12) departs at 1pm. The 2-hour dinner cruise, departing 7pm, includes a four-course menu and costs NZ$70 for adults, NZ$35 for children ages 5 to 12. *Note:* The *Lakeland Queen* does not land on Mokoia Island, the lake's sanctuary for endangered native birds. If you'd like to explore Mokoia Island, contact

Mokoia Island Experiences ★★, Rotorua Lakefront (© 07/349-0976; www.mokoiaisland.co.nz). The company offers a number of excellent tours from a Maori perspective, including their Island Experience Tour—a 2½-hour guided tour that includes a fast catamaran ride, a traditional Maori welcome, an exploration of the island's flora and fauna, a soak in a hot pool, plus tastes of indigenous foods. This costs NZ$75 for adults, NZ$38 for children ages 5 to 15. This is a great place to go if you're interested in conservation and bird life. The Wairua Package (NZ$170 adults, NZ$95 children), includes a visit to Mokoia Island, Hell's Gate (p. 195), a hangi, and time at Wai Ora Lakeside Spa Resort. It's a 6½-hour experience, starting at 9:30am.

is NZ$95 for adults, NZ$80 for children 15 and under; jumpers must be at least 10 years old (parental consent required for all under 16) and weight at least 35kg (77 lbs.).

FISHING   Within minutes of the city, you can be in the thick of some of the best wild trout fishing in the country. Lakes Tarawera, Okataina, and Rotoiti offer the best chance of catching a trophy fish. They're open for fishing from October to the end of June and hold both wild and stocked trout. The greatest trout population per acre is in Lake Rotorua, where wild fighting rainbow trout average 2 to 4 pounds and brown trout 5 to 7 pounds. Make sure you get your Rotorua fishing license before you start.

Bryan Colman Trout Fishing ★★, 32 Kiwi St., Rotorua (© 07/348-7766; www.troutfishingrotorua.com), is run by a top guide—the longest-serving in Rotorua—who offers light tackle trolling and fly- and spin-fishing for rainbow trout for NZ$120 per hour, minimum 2 hours (this can be shared by four people). A fishing license is NZ$25 per person.

FLIGHTSEEING   Volcanic Air Safaris, Memorial Drive (© 0800/800-848 in NZ, or 07/348-9984; www.volcanicair.co.nz), offers a range of helicopter and float-plane tours, from a 6-minute floatplane or helicopter spin over the city (NZ$80) to 3-hour volcanic tours all the way out to **White Island ★★** in the Bay of Plenty (NZ$762 per person by helicopter, NZ$535 by floatplane). A tour of Orakei Korako Hidden Valley with a landing, by helicopter or floatplane, is a popular choice for NZ$445 to NZ$515.

FOUR-WHEEL-DRIVE ADVENTURES   Test your nerve at **Off Road NZ ★★**, 193 Amoore Rd. (© 07/332-5748; www.offroadnz.co.nz), 20 minutes north of the city off State Highway 5. The four-wheel-drive bush safari departs daily, every hour from 9am to 5pm, and costs NZ$95 for adults and NZ$15 for children up to 16. You'll find yourself in tunnels, waterfalls, mud, and more mud. Otherwise, try out the Monster 4×4 Thrill Ride designed to test the best at NZ$50 per driver.

GOLF The Arikikapakapa course at the **Rotorua Golf Club,** 399 Fenton St. (© 07/348-4051; www.rotoruagolfclub.co.nz), is a gently undulating, all-weather course with an international reputation. Greens fees are NZ$70 for international visitors, and club hire is NZ$30. **Government Gardens Golf,** Government Gardens (© 07/348-9126; www.governmentgardensgolf.co.nz), has a 21-bay driving range and is open daily from 8am to 8pm; greens fees run NZ$16. Miniputt is NZ$11 per player and the driving range charges NZ$9 for 50 balls, NZ$14 for 110 balls.

HORSEBACK RIDING The **Farmhouse,** 55 Sunnex Rd. (© 07/332-3771; www.thefarmhouse.co.nz), is the largest horse-trekking facility in New Zealand, with over 100 horses for all ages and abilities. It's a working farm and homestay as well, and all gear is provided. It's open daily 9am to 7pm in summer (4pm in winter), and riding starts at NZ$26 per person for a 30-minute ride, or NZ$42 for 1 hour.

JET-BOATING You can spin out on the **Agrojet,** available through Agroventures (© 07/357-4259; www.agrojet.co.nz or www.agroventures.co.nz) on a special man-made watercourse that will see you reach speeds of 100kmph (62 mph) in 4.5 seconds. Don't forget to check out the Agrodome combo packages. A single Agrojet ride is a good value at NZ$49.

KAYAKING Take it easy on Rotorua's lovely lakes with **Adventure Kayaking** (© 07/348-9451; www.adventurekayaking.co.nz). Half-day paddles with a thermal pool swim cost NZ$85; full-day tours are NZ$120; and individual kayak hire goes for NZ$45 per seat per day.

LUGING See the "Exploring Rotorua" section, earlier in this chapter, for information about the endlessly popular **Skyline Skyrides luge ★★** (© 07/347-0027; fax 07/348-2163).

MOUNTAIN BIKING Rotorua is a mecca for mountain bikers. Visit www.ride rotorua.com for every last detail on trail updates, maps, and activities. Go it alone on rented bikes from **Kiwi Bikes,** 1128 Hinemoa St. (© 07/348-2929; www.kiwi bikes.co.nz), and head for the trails at Redwoods Forest, Whakarewarewa. You'll pay NZ$55 for a half-day rental, NZ$70 for a full day. Or team up with the crew at **Planet Bike ★★**, Whakarewarewa Forest (© 07/346-1717; www.planetbike.co. nz), which caters to all levels. Prices start at NZ$45 per person for 2 hours. Half-day tours and full-day adventure combos are available.

SKY DIVING Leap out over Rotorua at around 2,850m (9,348 ft.) with **NZONE– The Ultimate Jump** (© 0800/376-796; www.nzone.biz), and be prepared to drop around NZ$299. Courtesy transport from the city is provided.

WALKING Apart from numerous strolls around the various lakes, the **Whakare-warewa Forest ★★★** offers six well-marked walking tracks for all ages and levels of fitness. You can spend half an hour or a whole day making your way through the forest. The beautiful **Redwood Memorial Grove Track ★★★** is the most popular. It meanders through giant 60m (200-ft.) California coastal redwoods and takes 30 minutes from the forest visitor center on Long Mile Road. Also popular is the **Motut-ara Walkway ★★**, which wanders around the lakefront to Sulphur Bay. The 1½-hour walk passes through unusual "moonscape" outcrops of sulfur along the way. **Lake Okareka Walkway ★★**, located 12km (7 miles) southeast of Rotorua, is a pretty walk that takes you 2.5km (about 1½ miles) around the lake shore. The roundtrip takes around 1½ hours and you'll see plenty of bird life. The walkway and composting toilets (at Silver Beach) are stroller and wheelchair accessible.

Whirinaki Rainforest Guided Walks ★★★, Whirinaki Forest (© 0800/869-255 in NZ, or 07/377-2363; www.rainforest-treks.co.nz), offers 1- to 3-day fully catered treks led by professional Maori guides, starting at Rotorua or Taupo. You'll pay NZ$175 for a 1-day ecocultural walk; NZ$375 for a 1-day private guided walk; or NZ$775 for the 3-day Rainforest Trek.

WHITE-WATER RAFTING If you want world-rated championship rafting guides, head for **Kaituna Cascades Raft & Kayak Expeditions,** Trout Pool Road, Okere Falls, Rotorua (© 07/345-4199; www.kaitunacascades.co.nz). It'll give you the best time you've ever had, including a 7m (23-ft.) drop over the Southern Hemisphere's highest commercially rafted waterfall. The company operates on the Kaituna, Rangitaiki, and Wairoa rivers. Prices range from NZ$82 to NZ$120, depending on the river you choose. **River Rats Raft & Kayak** (© 0800/333-900 in NZ, or 07/345-6543; www.riverrats.co.nz) is another excellent company. It operates on the above rivers, plus the Tongariro; trips cost NZ$99 to NZ$130, depending on the river. Also dependent on the river is the minimum-age requirement (usually 10 or 13).

ZORBING Where else can you find yourself inside a giant plastic bubble, with the option of being wet or dry as you roll 250m (820 ft.) down a steep, slippery slope? It's like nothing you've ever done before. A wet or dry ride costs from NZ$45 per person. Ask about combo deals. The **Zorb** is at Agrodome, Western Road, Ngongotaha (© 0800/227-474 in NZ, or 07/357-5100; www.zorb.co.nz), and it's great fun to watch even if you don't want to participate.

Where to Stay

There are at least 14,000 visitor beds in Rotorua, so you shouldn't have any trouble finding one to suit you. Hotels and motels abound—Fenton Street is a veritable motel mile—and many motels in Rotorua provide private heated Jacuzzis in each unit. Be warned, though: These are not all thermal pools. New motel complexes are not allowed to draw off the city's geothermal reserves, so check first if you want a thermal pool. If you're interested in a personalized hospitality experience, pick up the *Rotorua Farm and Homestay* brochure at the visitor center.

Rates below include 15% GST and parking.

VERY EXPENSIVE

Solitaire Lodge ★★, 16 Ronald Rd., Lake Tarawera (www.solitairelodge.co.nz; © 07/362-8208; fax 07/362-8445), has 10 rooms in an unbeatable tranquil location 20 minutes out of the city. They're priced from NZ$1,690 to NZ$2,035, which includes pre-dinner drink with canapés, a 4-course dinner, full breakfast the following morning, and use of all lodge facilities including kayaks, motorized dinghies, and trout fishing equipment. All rooms are large and private, and graced with beautiful lake views.

Peppers on the Point ★★ 🎁 Opened in 2004, this grand 1930s home has been remodeled into a stylish nine-suite lodge with fabulous lake views plus a modern four-bedroom villa. Set on 2 hectares (5 acres), it has retained a character-filled charm and elegance that surpasses others in the Kawaha Point area. The main suite is one of the best bedrooms in Rotorua, complete with a huge deck and large bathroom. All suites here are large and unlike many in the area, the lodge is family friendly. The cottages are my favorite hide-outs. Like the villa, they are for single-party bookings only. They even have a small chapel on-site, and the property is a member of the Rotorua Sustainable Charter.

214 Kawaha Point Rd., Rotorua. www.peppers.co.nz. © **07/348-4868.** Fax 07/348-1868. 9 units (including 2 cottages), one 4-bedroom villa. NZ$1,675 premier suite; NZ$1,212–NZ$1,473 lodge and cottage suite; lake villa, price on application. Long-stay, off-peak, and special deals. Rates include breakfast, pre-dinner drinks and canapés, and dinner. AE, DC, MC, V. Take St. Hwy. 5 from Central City; after 5 min., turn right onto Kawaha Point Rd., just before Skyline Skyrides. Turn left at shops, then take 1st right. **Amenities:** In-house chef, bar, and wine cellar; babysitting (NZ$25 per hour); concierge; 3 nearby golf courses; small gym; 3 Jacuzzis in lake cottages and villa; limited room service; sauna; outdoor tennis court; Wi-Fi in main lodge building. *In room:* A/C, TV/DVD, fridge, hair dryer, Internet.

Treetops Lodge & Estate ★★★   The sublime Treetops Lodge is Rotorua's top stay, perfect for nature lovers and those who appreciate the finer things in life. The lodge has a proactive stance when it comes to conservation and sustainability too. Set on 1,000 hectares (2,470 acres) of wilderness game reserve, which includes an 800-year-old forest, and surrounded by 24,300 hectares (60,000 acres) of Department of Conservation land, Treetops opened in January 2000, a half-hour outside Rotorua. It is a true sanctuary that specializes in big-game hunting, as well as a peaceful retreat, but you don't have to do either; feel free to simply take in the world-class luxury. Once nestled into your big, stylish suite, savoring the valley or lake vistas, you'll think you're in paradise. Every suite is appointed with top-quality furnishings in the best of taste. Rooms and huge bathrooms are exquisite in every detail. Guests in lodge suites have exclusive use of a kitchen; villas have kitchenettes.

351 Kearoa Rd., RD1, Horohoro. www.treetops.co.nz. © **07/333-2066.** Fax 07/333-2065. 12 units. NZ$1,666 lodge suite; NZ$2,454 villa. NZ$6,664 exclusive use of owner's retreat for up to 8 guests. Extra person NZ$478. Rates include breakfast, pre-dinner cocktails, dinner, selected lodge activities, and airport transport. Long-stay rates and special deals. AE, DC, MC, V. 30 min. from Central City. **Amenities:** Bar; babysitting; bike rentals; concierge; nearby golf course; room service; watersports equipment rentals. *In room:* TV/DVD/VCR, fridge, hair dryer, kitchenette (villas), minibar, Wi-Fi.

EXPENSIVE

Novotel Lakeside ★★, lake end of Tutanekai St. (www.accorhotels.com; © **0800/ 776-677** in NZ, or 07/346-3888; fax 07/347-1888), is definitely one of the better Rotorua hotels, and the closest one to Central City and the main restaurant beat. The lake-view superior rooms are the most popular, but parkside units are generally quieter. Eight king suites have Jacuzzis in the bathrooms, and two executive suites are split-level, with mezzanine bedrooms. Prices range from NZ$165 to NZ$650; you'll pay more for the royal suite. Another good choice is **Millennium Hotel Rotorua ★★**, corner of Eruera and Hinemaru streets (www.millenniumrotorua. co.nz; © **0800/654-685** in NZ, or 07/347-1234; fax 07/348-1234), perfectly located across the road from the internationally acclaimed Polynesian Spa. Its 227 guest rooms are priced NZ$190 to NZ$550 and it has a friendlier vibe than the Novotel.

Koura Lodge ★★   David and Gina Wells have created a beautiful retreat tucked into a bush setting on the edge of the lake. Four rooms are located close to the lake in the main building and open onto the lawn; and larger rooms with private balconies and lake views are in the upper building. The upper level 2-bedroom apartment (with its own billiard table) is ideal for a family or two couples traveling together.

209 Kawaha Point Rd. www.kouralodge.co.nz. © **07/348-5868.** Fax 07/348-5869. 10 units. NZ$345– NZ$990. Rates include breakfast. Long-stay rates. MC, V. **Amenities:** Concierge; nearby golf course; Jacuzzi; massage; sauna. *In room:* TV/DVD, fridge, hairdryer, Wi-Fi.

The Springs ★★   Guests have a choice of four sumptuous rooms with king-size beds, fine linens, walk-in wardrobes, lovely en-suite bathrooms, and doors to a private terrace. Murray and Colleen Ward treat you well, and the tall hedges give this central residential property a sense of privacy. This stay is hospitality-plus.

16 Devon St., Rotorua. www.thesprings.co.nz. ✆ **07/348-9922.** Fax 07/348-9964. 4 units. NZ$360–NZ$400. Rate includes breakfast. Long-stay rates. DC, MC, V. Closed July–Aug. Children 14 and under not accepted. **Amenities:** Nearby golf course. *In room:* TV, hair dryer, Wi-Fi.

MODERATE

Wai Ora Lakeside Spa Resort, 77 Robinson Ave., Holdens Bay, Rotorua (www.waiorarresort.co.nz; ✆ **0800/345-318** in NZ, or 07/343-5100), is 10 minutes out of the city but you get silence, a good restaurant, a lovely pool, free Internet, gorgeous day spa treatments, and the choice of 30 rooms priced from NZ$199 to NZ$495. It's a little overpriced compared to the Amora (below), but it does have the spa facility on its side. If you favor the peace and quiet of an out-of-town lakeside location, then the relatively small **Amora Lake Resort,** 366 St. Hwy. 33, Okawa Bay, Rotorua (www.amorahotels.com; ✆ **0800/655-555** in NZ, or 07/362-4599), is for you. Rooms look out to lake and garden views. Some have indoor Jacuzzis with shutters that fold open to the bedroom, and all are roomy and nicely furnished. It's just 15 minutes out of town and is incredibly good value for money with rooms from NZ$145.

Regal Palms ★★★   This stay is a cut above the average motel. The multi-award-winning property is better equipped than many hotels and you'll get generous apartment-style rooms and friendly service as well. It's outfitted with a host of leisure amenities that will make it very attractive to traveling families, but it's equally popular with the business crowd and those after a romantic getaway.

350 Fenton St., Rotorua. www.regalpalms.co.nz. ✆ **0800/743-000** in NZ, or 07/350-3232. Fax 07/350-3233. 44 units. NZ$190–NZ$400. AE, DC, MC, V. **Amenities:** Bar; nearby golf course; heated outdoor pool; sauna; day spa; gym; tennis courts; minigolf; kids' playgrounds; free barbecue areas. *In room:* A/C, TV/DVD, kitchen minibar, hairdryer, Internet.

Regent of Rotorua ★★   This glamorous spot will appeal to travelers who prefer a small, intimate, boutique hotel experience. Once a 1960s motel complex, the Regent has been reborn as a sophisticated, inner city stay that everyone falls in love with. Its handy location in the city, just up from the lake, is another plus. It has a Qualmark Enviro-Bronze rating and water and heating are geothermally powered.

1191 Pukaki St., Rotorua. www.regentrotorua.co.nz. ✆ **0508/734-368** in NZ, or 07/348-4079. Fax 07/348-4032. 23 units. NZ$179–NZ$349. Special deals. AE, MC, V. **Amenities:** Bar, The Regent Room Restaurant; airport transfers on request; babysitting; concierge; nearby golf course; mini-gym; 24-hr. room service; heated outdoor pool & thermal indoor pool. *In room:* A/C, TV/DVD, kitchenette, fridge, hairdryer, minibar, free Wi-Fi.

Silver Fern Rotorua ★   Service at this modern complex is reliably friendly and owners Allan and Shirley enjoy sharing their local knowledge and experiences. All rooms either have spa pools (ground floor), or spa baths; all upstairs rooms have large balconies. Two-bedroom apartments and interconnecting rooms are ideal for families and couples traveling together. Allan's own photography throughout is a nice touch.

326 Fenton St., Rotorua. www.silverfernrotorua.co.nz. ✆ **0800/118-808** in NZ, or 07/346-3849. Fax 07/346-2765. 25 units. NZ$155–NZ$355. Special deals & packages. AE, DC, MC, V. **Amenities:** Free airport & city transfers; babysitting; nearby golf course; free use of bikes; day spa; limited room service; barbecue area. *In room:* TV/DVD, kitchenette, fridge, hairdryer, minibar, Wi-Fi.

INEXPENSIVE

There are several excellent camping grounds in the Rotorua area; the closest to central city is **Rotorua Top 10 Holiday Park,** 1495 Pukuatua St. (www.rotoruatop10.co.nz; ✆ **0800/223-267** in NZ, or 07/348-1886), which is a short walk from town. It has camping sites, cabin accommodations, and excellent new shared facilities for

Treat yourself to a firsthand experience of contemporary Maori hospitality at either of two drop-dead gorgeous B&Bs run by young professional Maori couples and their families. The very classy **A-Kahu ★★**, 155 Kawaha Point Rd. (www.akahu.co.nz; ℂ 07/347-4148), has four sumptuous en-suite bedrooms set apart from main living areas. Kiri Atkinson-Crean and her husband, Nigel, share their strong tribal links, and their modern home is filled with contemporary Maori art. It's a big-hearted, family-oriented experience that I loved. Rooms are great value at around NZ$380. Across town, Oscar and Renee Nathan have established a very chic, self-contained experience at **Maruata Rotorua ★★**, 2 Kuirau St. (www.maruata.co.nz; ℂ 021/801-559), where you'll be able to connect with Maori culture at all levels—through art, music, videos, books, wine, and food. It features changing displays of contemporary Maori art (for sale), and I love the central locality (close to mud pools) and the serenity of the little cottage. It costs from NZ$325 per couple and gets cheaper the more nights you stay. They are members of the Rotorua Sustainable Charter and there is free Wi-Fi throughout.

NZ$40 to NZ$180. Another good budget option is **Quest Rotorua ★**, 7 Tryon St. (www.questrotorua.co.nz; ℂ **0800/355-575** in NZ, or 07/347-3333), which is very close to Whakarewarewa Thermal Village and has rooms from NZ$110, and always offers good special deals. **Wylie Court Motor Lodge,** 345 Fenton St. (www.wyliecourt.co.nz; ℂ **07/347-7879;** fax 07/346-1494), is my pick for a sensibly priced, fun option, especially for families. Rooms at the 22-year-old property aren't flashy, but they're comfortable and every unit has its own thermally heated outdoor Jacuzzi; plus, the whole place is set amid beautiful gardens with two playgrounds. Rooms cost NZ$145 to NZ$185. Backpackers, meanwhile, have many choices in Rotorua. One of the best is **Base Hot Rock,** 1286 Arawa St. (www.stayatbase.com; ℂ **0800/223-363** in NZ, or 07/348-8636; fax 07/348-8616), which is centrally located and has dorm beds at NZ$28 and doubles at NZ$70.

Where to Eat

Not so long ago, finding even a decent cup of coffee here was a struggle. Things have improved a little, but the selection is still limited and there is a fairly flexible interpretation of the word "service." There's a growing cafe scene, much of it concentrated at the lake end of Tutanekai Street, known as "The Streat," although I've always found most of the eateries in this area overrated. Rotorua also has around 50 restaurants—everything from Turkish to Korean, Indonesian to Italian—so you'll certainly never want for inexpensive fare. For a family dining experience with great views, feast 600m (2,000 ft.) up at **Aorangi Peak Restaurant ★**, Mountain Road, Ngongotaha (ℂ **07/347-0046;** www.aorangipeak.co.nz). It pays to reserve a table. And don't forget to try the traditional **Maori hangi** while you're in Rotorua (see "Maori Cultural Experiences" under "Exploring Rotorua," earlier in this chapter). Pick up the free dining guide and *The Streat* cafe brochure at the visitor center.

MODERATE

In addition to those listed below, **Urbano,** 289 Fenton St. (ℂ **07/349-3770;** www.urbanobistro.co.nz), is a pleasant suburban bistro that's especially popular for weekend brunch. They're open daily 9am until late. **Triple 1 Five ★**, 1115 Tutanekai St (℃ **07/347-1115;** www.triple1five.co.nz), gets top marks for its healthy stone-grilled focus, and it's open for breakfast, lunch, and dinner. They also offer vegetarian and gluten-free options. The oddly named **Seismic Gastrobar,** 1158 Whakaue St. (℃ **07/348-2082**), is a good stop for drinks and pizza. They have live music on Friday nights, roast dinners on Sunday nights, and other assorted theme nights that may inject a little fun into your culinary travels.

Abracadabra Café ★ ⏚ CAFE/LIGHT MEALS   There's a lively mood in this colorful joint and its Moroccan-themed rooms give it the pizzazz other places lack. Big verandas and a beer garden are great summer options. The owners have spent time in Morocco, which is obvious in the menu choices—North African chicken kabobs, couscous salad, and star anise vegetable tagine. In addition, they have excellent baked goods and counter choices to enjoy with fair trade coffee. Or opt for late afternoon tapas with wine.

1263 Amohia St. ℃ **07/348-3883.** www.abracadabracafe.com. Main courses NZ$16–NZ$30. V. Tues-Sat 8:30am–11pm; Sun-Mon 9am–3pm.

Capers Epicurean ★★ ⏚ CAFE/DELI   This modest little place has almost no street appeal, but once you're inside it's a culinary heaven. Their cabinets bulge with a huge array of eat-in or takeout delicacies, and an all-day menu has another good range of choices—everything from soups, omelets, pancakes, and pastas to salads and fresh fish and chicken dishes. It's also a terrific place for picnic goodies and gift boxes of New Zealand food products. Come dinnertime, dishes like prime sirloin steak, roasted tuna loin, and lemon risotto with smoked salmon round out the menu.

1181 Eruera St. ℃ **07/348-8818.** www.capers.co.nz. Dinner reservations recommended. Main courses NZ$15–NZ$26. AE, MC, V. Daily from 7:30am; dinner 6–9pm.

Lime Caffeteria ★★★ CAFE/LIGHT MEALS   This is my favorite Rotorua haunt. It's light, bright, fresh as a squeezed lime, and the food is divine. You haven't lived until you've sampled the amazing blueberry and custard brioche! But there's more to Lime than small, tasty snacks and good coffee. It also turns out a delectable range of lunch options, like chicken and chorizo salad; and blue brie, fig, and pine nut phyllo parcels with green-grape salad; or Thai green curry risotto. Don't forget to buy a few picnic treats to munch while you're out walking.

1096 Whakaue St. ℃ **07/350-2033.** Reservations recommended. Main courses NZ$18–NZ$25. MC, V. Daily 7:30am–4:30pm.

Relish ★★ CAFE/PIZZERIA   Drop in for coffee or a light lunch, linger over one of the delicious pizzas turned out on the wood-fired oven, or choose from the a la carte menu. You'll be glad you indulged. Chicken teriyaki pizza gets my vote, but you might prefer an evening meal of Middle Eastern spiced duck breast. It's a casual dining environment, ideal after a busy day of sightseeing, and possibly the best option in The Streat zone.

1149 Tutanekai St. ℃ **07/343-9195.** www.relishcafe.co.nz. Reservations required for dinner. Main courses NZ$16–NZ$24, pizzas NZ$20–NZ$24. MC, V. Mon-Tues 7am–4pm; Wed-Sat 7am–9pm; Sun 8am–4pm.

INEXPENSIVE

Fat Dog Café ★★ ⏚ CAFE/LIGHT MEALS   This place is tops for atmosphere, a fact that people of all ages seem to have discovered. You'll find them here draped over old chairs and sofas—everyone from a whole herd of mountain bikers to someone who could be your granny. Food is not only cheap, it's also incredibly tasty and, dare I say it, healthy! There's a fabulous selection of counter food and a simple blackboard menu that lists the old adolescent favorites such as nachos and pies. Vegetable bakes, lasagnas, bagels, and salads can all be followed by something sweet and delicious, washed down with the best espresso in Rotorua. A funky little dive that's all color and charming chaos.

1161 Arawa St. © **07/347-7586.** Main courses NZ$12–NZ$25. AE, DC, MC, V. Daily 8am–late.

Shopping

Pick up the excellent *Rotorua Arts Trail* brochure from the visitor center. It gives names and contact details of many of the city's best artists, jewelers, and craftspeople. The best places to shop for Maori arts and crafts are **Te Puia,** at Whakarewarewa Thermal Reserve (© 07/348-9047), where you'll find superb carvings; and **Tamaki Maori Village,** State Highway 5 (© 07/346-2823), which has excellent displays of indigenous work at their replica village but you need to be part of their tours to access the shops.

   Simply New Zealand, Tourism Rotorua Centre, 1161 Fenton St. (© 07/348-8273; www.simplynewzealand.com), has an excellent range of New Zealand–made merino wool knitwear, delightful toiletries, and a host of souvenirs. **Rainbow Springs** and **Agrodome** (see "The Major Sights & Attractions," earlier in this chapter) have good shops for wool products. At **Mountain Jade,** 1288 Fenton St. (© 07/349-3968; www.mountainjade.co.nz), you can watch the creative process of carving jade as it happens. Their carving studio is open to the public daily from 9am.

Rotorua After Dark

Rest assured, there is more to Rotorua's nightlife than Maori hangi and concert performances. For a start, pick up a free copy of *Thermal Air,* which will point you in the direction of some of the best places to go.

   There's an Irish pub in every town; in Rotorua that's **O'Malley's Irish Bar,** 1287 Eruera St. (© 07/347-6410), which features live music most Friday and Saturday nights. A good hotel nightspot is the **Mezz Bar ★** in Rydges on Fenton Street.

   Backpackers will invariably have a good time at **Base Hot Rock Lava Bar,** 1286 Arawa St. The **Pig & Whistle City Bar,** 1182 Tutanekai St. (© 07/347-3025), has a boutique brewery and hearty pub-style meals, with live music on Friday and Saturday. **Fuze City Bar ★★**, Lake End, Tutanekai Street (© 07/349-6306), is open from 3pm until late Tuesday through Saturday and offers a smart environment for evening drinks, tapas, and gourmet pizza.

En Route to Taupo

It's a short drive to Taupo, just 84km (52 miles) over excellent roads. Throughout this area, watch out for logging trucks. If you haven't already done so, this could be a good time to call at one of the three main geothermal reserves, especially the **Hidden Valley Orakei Korako Geyserland Resort,** which is closer to Taupo than to Rotorua. Eight kilometers (5 miles) before you reach Taupo, look for the steamy **Wairakei Geothermal Power Station,** which harnesses all that underground energy to furnish electric power.

TAUPO ★

287km (178 miles) SE of Auckland; 84km (52 miles) S of Rotorua; 155km (96 miles) NW of Napier

I've always found Taupo somewhat disappointing, but many New Zealanders practically worship this little lakeside town. Certainly, from a visitor's point of view, it makes a perfect central base from which to take in the area attractions. It's within half a day's drive of the Hawke's Bay wine region, the mountains and ski fields of Tongariro National Park, the thermal wonderland of Rotorua, the white-sand surf beaches of Bay of Plenty, and the glowworms of Waitomo.

Taupo itself also has its merits—the vast sparkling waters of Lake Taupo are perfect for boating, water-skiing, and fishing; there are thermal pools; plenty of accommodations; some good, fast-paced outdoor activities; and a small permanent population of 30,000, which more than doubles in summer. There are also a number of new attractions and accommodations that make it a worthy stop. Make sure you take warm clothes because if it's not midsummer you're likely to freeze.

Essentials

GETTING THERE & GETTING AROUND **By Plane** **Air New Zealand Link** ((C) 0800/737-000; www.airnewzealand.co.nz) flies to Taupo from Auckland and Wellington five times a day, with connections to other destinations. In winter, **Mountain Air** ((C) 0800/922-812; www.mountainair.co.nz) has daily flights between Auckland and Turangi airports. For a taxi or airport shuttle, call (C) 07/378-5100.

By Coach (Bus) **InterCity** and **Newmans** buses arrive and depart from the Taupo Travel Centre on Gascoigne Street ((C) 07/378-9032). **Magic Travellers** and **Kiwi Experience** also serve Taupo. **Guthreys Express** ((C) 0800/759-999 in NZ, or 07/376-0027) has daily services from Taupo to Auckland, Rotorua, and National Park village, which is in Tongariro National Park. There is no local bus service but look out for the **Tongariro Taupo Hot Bus** ((C) 0508/468-287 in NZ; www.hotbus.co.nz), which provides return transport to most attractions. It departs from the i-SITE Visitor Centre on the hour from 10am to 3pm daily. One attraction costs NZ$20 and you pay NZ$5 for each subsequent attraction visited. You can spend as much time as you like at each attraction.

By Taxi For service in and around Taupo, call **Taupo Taxis** ((C) 07/378-5100).

By Car State highways 1 and 5 pass through Taupo. All roads in the area are excellent but drive with care in winter (when they're icy) and when there's a heavy flow of logging trucks. The drive to Rotorua is 1 hour; to Waitomo or Napier, 2 hours; to Hamilton or Tauranga, 2 hours; to Auckland, 4 hours; and to Wellington, 5½ hours.

By Bicycle To rent a mountain bike, contact **The Corner Shop (Avanti Centre),** 47 Horomatangi St. ((C) 07/378-7381; www.avantiplus.co.nz/taupo); the shop rents adult-size bikes only, NZ$30 per half-day and NZ$50 for a full day. You can also rent bikes from **Rainbow Lodge,** 99 Titiraupenga St. ((C) 07/378-5754; www.rainbow lodge.co.nz), who have bikes for NZ$25 a half day for guests and non-guests. Taupo is particularly geared for cyclists, with dedicated lanes, shared paths, and numerous recreational off-road rides. For more information check www.biketaupo.org.nz.

ORIENTATION Taupo spreads along the northeastern tip of the lake, where the Waikato River, New Zealand's longest, flows out of Lake Taupo's Tapuaeharuru Bay. The main road is **Tongariro Street.** Perpendicular to that are **Heu Heu** and **Horomatangi streets,** two of several that form the main shopping area. Tongariro Street

Lake Taupo Region

runs into **Lake Terrace,** the continuation of State Highway 1 that runs around the lake and takes you to most of the motels. The settlements of **Acacia Bay** and **Jerusalem Bay** are just across on the western shore of the lake.

VISITOR INFORMATION   The **Taupo i-SITE Visitor Centre** (✆ **07/376-0027;** www.greatlaketauponz.com) is easy to find—it's on Tongariro Street, the main road through Taupo. It has a wide selection of brochures and can arrange fishing guides and licenses, tours, and activities. It also sells stamps, phone cards, and souvenirs. Hours are 8:30am to 5pm daily. **Experience Taupo,** 29 Tongariro St.

  A Word on Parking Security

The carparks at Huka Falls Lookout, Craters of the Moon, and Spa Park are very prone to theft. Volunteers do patrol some carparks but make sure you remove all valuables from your vehicle and lock all doors. Lock other possessions in the trunk where they cannot be seen, and report anyone acting suspiciously in carparks to **Taupo Police** (✆ **07/378-6060**). The good news about parking in Taupo township is that it is generally free.

(℡ **0800/368-775** in NZ, or 07/377-0705; www.experiencetaupo.co.nz), is another good source of information. They stay open later than the visitor center (till 7pm in summer, 6pm winter), and they can organize all your adventures in the region with no booking fees.

[Fast FACTS] TAUPO

The **post office** is at the corner of Ruapehu and Horomatangi streets; it's open Monday through Friday from 8:30am to 5pm. Internet access is available at **CyberGate Internet Cafe,** 12 Gascoigne St. (opposite the bus station; ℡ **07/377-8118**). It's open daily 9:30am to 11pm. The first 3 minutes are free.

SPECIAL EVENTS The last Saturday in November is the **Lake Taupo Cycle Challenge** (℡ 07/378-1546; www.cyclechallenge.com). In October, more than 3,000 cyclists gather for the **PowerAde Day-Night Thriller** (℡ 07/378-0455; www.eventpromotions.co.nz or www.daynightthriller.co.nz), the largest mountain-bike event of its kind in the world. The annual **Taupo Half Marathon** (℡ 07/378-1546; www.taupohalfmarathon.org.nz) takes place in August. Check www.greatlake tauponz.com or www.eventscapital.co.nz for a full events calendar.

Exploring Taupo

Most of Taupo's interesting attractions are just north of the town in a cluster around the Wairakei Tourist Park. The visitor center has a good brochure on this area. At the top of the hill as you leave town heading north, turn right onto Huka Falls Road and stop first at the **Huka Falls Lookout ★★★**. The falls themselves aren't huge, but they are impressive for the speed at which the blue-green water of the Waikato River moves over the 24m (79-ft.) drop. You can walk alongside the gorge on a path and across the rushing water on a footbridge, which provides a safe but thrilling way to enjoy the falls. It's a dramatic spot to get photographs of the jet boats and cruise vessels as they come right up to the foot of the falls. You can also walk to the falls from Taupo (see "Outdoor Pursuits," below).

After you visit the other attractions in this area, divert down Aratiatia Road on your way back into town to see the **Aratiatia Rapids.** The gates of the dam above the rapids open every day at 10am, noon, 2pm, and 4pm from October to March. In less than 10 minutes, the dry riverbed goes from an empty basin of boulders to a raging river. After about half an hour, the gates close, the released water flows downstream, and the dry bed reappears. It's fascinating to watch. The best view is about 5 minutes' walk downstream, but you can also observe from the lookout.

The **Taupo Museum,** Story Place, Tongariro Domain, Taupo (℡ 07/376-0414; www.taupomuseum.org.nz), is open daily from 10am to 4:30pm (closed Good Friday and Dec 25). Galleries display Maori art and culture, and a wide selection of exhibits related to fishing, the timber industry, geology, and the lake. Check out the unique New Zealand garden that was a gold medal winner at England's Chelsea Flower Show in 2004; and their caravan and New Zealand camping holiday display is delightful. Admission is NZ$5 for adults, free for children 17 and under. They offer a free guided heritage walk on Sundays at 2pm.

Honey Hive ★ ☺ After your stop at the Huka Falls Lookout, get back on the Huka Falls Road Tourist Loop and continue to the Honey Hive. Dare I say it? The place is buzzing with activity, and you don't need to be a bee enthusiast to appreciate

Hot Dip

If you're walking the very pleasant Huka Falls Track, test out the hot stream that runs into the Waikato River at the Spa Park end of the track—but as in all geothermal pools, *don't* put your head under! Just after the start of the track, you'll cross a bridge over the stream. Access to the pool is below that. It's popular with Magic Traveller and Kiwi Experience types, so don't expect to always be alone.

the astounding array of bee-related products inside. You'll see an excellent range of gifts, from cosmetics and fruit wines to chocolate bees and woolly bees. Suffice to say that this makes a pleasant change from sheep. Also on-site is the Bees Knees Café, but don't go getting too excited about that—it definitely needs a revamp. The delicious honey ice cream is worth the stop.

Huka Falls Loop Rd. © **07/374-8553.** www.hukahoneyhive.com. Free admission. Daily 9am–5pm. Closed Good Friday and Dec 25–26.

Volcanic Activity Centre ★★★ The Taupo volcanic region is one of the world's largest, spanning 282km (175 miles), and this is the best place in the country to get an understanding of what's bubbling underfoot. Along with 3D maps of the area, there are touchscreen computers, a working model of a geyser, a tornado machine, an earthquake simulator, interactive volcanoes, and fabulous short films on all aspects of volcanic and geothermal activity. Allow at least an hour for a worthwhile visit.

Huka Falls Rd. © **07/374-8375.** Fax 07/374-8370. www.volcanoes.co.nz. Admission NZ$10 adults, NZ$6 children 5-15, NZ$26 families. AE, MC, V. Mon–Fri 9am–5pm; Sat–Sun 10am–4pm. Closed Good Friday, Dec 25, and till noon Apr 25.

Huka Prawn Park ★★ ☺ This is the place to see Malaysian river prawns happily getting fat in Wairakei's geothermally heated prawn farm. Interesting 30-minute tours run hourly between 11am and 4pm. You can feed the prawns by hand, then end your visit at the Prawn Works Bar 'n' Grill, where you can eat the ones that grew the fattest. It's a lovely setting overlooking the Waikato River. You can also jet-boat from here (see "Outdoor Pursuits," below). The restaurant has a kids' menu and play areas; for an extra charge, you can play Killer Prawn Golf after eating.

Huka Falls Rd. © **07/374-8474.** Fax 07/374-8063. www.hukaprawnpark.co.nz. Admission & All Day Fishing Pass: NZ$20 adults, NZ$15 children 5-15, NZ$50 families; Super Fun Pass All Day access to fishing, 10-min. fishing lesson, and guided tour of nursery & hatchery: NZ$24 adults, NZ$14 children 5-15, NZ$60 family. Hole-in-One Golf Challenge NZ$10 for 20 golf balls, NZ$20 for 45 balls. Daily 9am–4pm. Closed Dec 25.

Wairakei Natural Thermal Valley ★★ This attraction is worth visiting if you enjoy geysers, mud pools, and other strange geothermal phenomena. Call first at the Wairakei Geothermal Visitor Centre for guided steam-field and historical tours that will give you insight into geothermal power generation. Check out **Wairakei Terraces ★★**, next to Wairakei Steamfield (© **07/378-0913;** www.wairakeiterraces. co.nz), where, in a mysterious, steamy setting, you'll learn about Maori legends and history. They've done a good job of replicating the original Wairakei silica terraces that disappeared with the development of the geothermal power plant in the 1950s. There are also an evening concert, hangi, and a Maori village tour.

Just for Kids

Lilliput Farm, 136 Link Rd. (📞 07/378-2114; www.lilliput-farm-park.co.nz), is a 4-hectare (10-acre) treat for kids who like animals. They can hand-feed 20 different species and enjoy pony and donkey rides. The farm is open Monday to Friday 10am to 2pm, weekends 10am to 4pm. Admission is NZ$12 adults, NZ$6 children 5 to 12, NZ$30 families. Follow St. Hwy. 1 to Hamilton. Link Road is the first left, 4.5km (2 miles) from the Wairakei turnoff. Watch for signs.

Just off St. Hwy. 1. 📞 **07/374-8004.** Fax 07/374-8656. Geothermal tours NZ$20 adults, NZ$10 children 5–12; the Terraces NZ$20 adults, NZ$10 children, NZ$60 family. Maori cultural experience NZ$95 adults, NZ$48 children. Daily 9am–5pm in summer, 9am–4:30pm in winter. Closed Jan 1, Good Friday, and Dec 25–26.

SOAKING IN TAUPO HOT SPRINGS

Set in the unique natural Onekeneke Thermal Valley, **Taupo De Bretts Resort, Hot Springs & Spa ★★**, Napier/Taupo Road, State Highway 5 (📞 07/378-8559; www.taupodebretts.com), has been a favorite bathing spot for over 120 years. The water here is said to be the ultimate in providing therapeutic relief for muscular, bone, and skin ailments. Pools are filtered, drained, and cleaned every night. The pool complex is not as big, as modern, or as attractive as Rotorua's **Polynesian Spa** (p. 188), but it's definitely cheaper and feels just as good, and there is no sulfur in the water here. Facilities include 12 private pools, a children's pool, two Jacuzzis, a hydroslide, a volleyball court, *pétanque,* and a barbecue area. Admission to the public pools costs NZ$15 for adults, NZ$4 for children ages 3 to 12; NZ$5 for the giant dragon slide; barbecue rental from NZ$10. Private pools cost from NZ$18 for adults, and spa treatments range from NZ$60 to NZ$160. The complex is open daily from 8:30am to 9:30pm.

If you don't have time for a soak in Taupo, you can stop at the **Tokaanu Thermal Pools,** at the south end of Lake Taupo (see "En Route to Tongariro National Park," later in this chapter).

CRUISING THE LAKE

Taupo is New Zealand's biggest lake, with three excellent options for heading out on the water: the replica steamboat *Ernest Kemp,* the motor launch *Cruise Cat,* and the old yacht *Barbary.* The first two follow a similar path and pass the **Maori rock carvings ★★**, which are accessible only by boat. **Ernest Kemp Cruises** (📞 07/378-9222; adiwalker@reap. org.nz) operates 2-hour cruises daily for NZ$42 adults, NZ$12 children ages 5 to 15. It is essential to book through the visitor center or the Taupo Boat Harbour office. Cruises run three times daily at 10:30am, 2pm, and 5pm. The

Fun Savings

If you plan on making the rounds of adventure activities, check out the savings that package deals represent. The visitor center and Experience Taupo (above) will point you in the direction of seasonal savings.

Cruise Cat Experience (📞 07/378-0623; www.chrisjolly.co.nz) covers a longer distance than the *Ernest Kemp* in a shorter time. The tour operates daily from 11:30am to 1pm and costs NZ$40 for adults, NZ$16 for school-age children. The *Barbary*

The weekly Riverside Market is held every Saturday morning at Riverside Park, on Redoubt Road (beside the Waikato River). It features a wide range of goods from secondhand books and clothing to jewelry, fresh fruit, and Maori potatoes. It's set in a sunny hollow surrounded by large trees and is a pleasant place for a quick breakfast or lunch surrounded by local activity. It starts around 8am and continues into the afternoon.

Carvings Cruise (☎ **07/378-3444;** www.sailbarbary.com) departs at 10:30am, 2pm, and 5pm, and costs NZ$45 for adults, NZ$12 for children ages 5 to 15.

Organized Tours

Paradise Tours (☎ **07/378-9955;** www.paradisetours.co.nz) has a range of half-day excursions to local attractions from NZ$99 adults, NZ$45 for children 5 to 12, free for children 4 and under, plus full-day tours to Rotorua, Napier, and Waitomo. Their popular Taupo Sights tour includes a visit to the thermal wonders of Orakei Korako, Huka Falls, Honey Hive, Aratiatia Rapids, the marina, and the geothermal borefield. It's a good way to see the best of Taupo if you're short on time.

One of the best new tour options in the Taupo area is **pureORAwalks ★★★** (☎ **021/042-2722;** www.pureorawalks.com), which has a range of excellent walks from 3 hours to 3 days in duration in Tongariro National Park, Pureora Forest Park, and Whirinaki Forest Park. They also take guided walks over the magnificent Tongariro Alpine Crossing, and all their walks are led by local Maori guides. If you're short on time, their **Nature-Culture Walk** (3–6 hr.) is a good choice. It costs NZ$95 for adults and NZ$74 for children. Their 8-hour guided hike over the Tongariro Alpine Crossing costs NZ$315 for adults and NZ$210 for children, but you need to be very fit for this excursion and *always* take lots of warm clothing, even in midsummer.

Outdoor Pursuits

BIKING   Bike tours and rentals can be arranged through **Rapid Sensations,** 413 Huka Falls Rd. (☎ **0800/353-435** in NZ, or 07/374-8117; www.rapids.co.nz). Its tours go to the Craters of the Moon thermal area, a 2½-hour ride that costs NZ$75 per person. Rentals are NZ$55 per day. In Taupo, you can also rent bikes from **Cycle World,** 30 Spa Rd. (☎ **07/378-6117**). For more information, including tours, suppliers, and recommended cycle tracks, pick up the excellent brochure *Cycling Around Lake Taupo.*

BUNGY JUMPING   You don't even have to jump to be impressed by the scenery that surrounds the 47m (154-ft.) bungy platform cantilevered out over the Waikato River. Call **Taupo Bungy,** 202 Spa Rd. (☎ **0800/888-408** in NZ, or 07/377-1135; www.taupobungy.com). You'll pay from NZ$149 for a solo jump or NZ$298 to go tandem. The company offers free pickup from accommodations for jumpers and they have free Internet onsite. The bungy operates 9am until 7pm in summer (closed Dec 25). They also have the Taupo Cliffhanger swing onsite (www.taupocliffhanger.com), which costs NZ$99 for a solo swing and NZ$180 to go tandem. You can get a break on the price if you do both activities.

CLIMBING   Try something a bit different at **Rock 'n' Ropes,** Karetoto Rd., Wairakei Park, Wairakei (☎ **0800/244-508** in NZ, or 07/374-8111; www.rocknropes.co.nz). If you've ever dreamed of being part of a circus act, this is your chance to polish up on rope walking, trapezing, rock climbing, and assorted other airborne fun. Courtesy transport to the site is available. Adventures here are reasonably priced from NZ$20 to NZ$65. It's open daily 10am until 5pm.

FISHING   More than 100 years have passed since the first trout fry were released into the Lake Taupo region. Today, their plump descendants are one of the main draws. It's the best of New Zealand's trout fishing. You'll need a special Taupo-issued fishing license, which can be good for a day to a full season. Remember that the minimum legal size is 45 centimeters (18 in.) and the daily limit is three fish. The best river fishing is during the winter spawning runs (June–Sept) but lake fishing is good all year. The visitor center can give you a list of the dozens of fishing guides in the area. Two I recommend are **Chris Jolly Outdoors** (© 07/378-0623; www.chrisjolly.co.nz), which is great for large groups; and **Go Fish Taupo** (© 07/378-9395; www.gofishtaupo.co.nz), which offers guides for beginners and experienced fishermen alike for NZ$300 a half-day and NZ$550 for a full day.

FLIGHTSEEING   Scenic rides in **Taupo's Floatplane ★★** (© 07/378-7500; www.tauposfloatplane.co.nz) leave from the lakefront near Taupo Boat Harbour; they range from a 10-minute flight to a 2-hour White Island excursion for NZ$675. Ask about the 10-minute backpacker special for four people, at NZ$100 per person. **Mountain Air ★★★** (© 0800/922-812 in NZ, or 07/892-2812; www.mountainair.co.nz) offers breathtaking flights over the Volcanic Plateau. Helicopter fans will love a spin with **Clark & Jolly Helicopters ★★**, Taupo Airport (© 0800/424-677 in NZ, or 07/377-8805; www.helinz.com), which can put a package together to suit your whims and budget, starting at a quick 10-minute buzz over Taupo from NZ$100 per adult.

FOUR-BY-FOUR BIKING   Quad bikes are all the rage, and **Taupo Quad Adventures,** 24km (15 miles) north of Taupo on State Highway 1 (© 07/377-6404; www.taupoquads.co.nz), offers rides through native bush, farms, and forest trails that cost from NZ$95 to NZ$300.

GOLF   **Wairakei International Golf Course ★★★**, State Highway 1 (© 07/374-8152; www.wairakeigolfcourse.co.nz), is rated among the top 20 golf courses in the world outside the United States. Book well ahead; greens fees are NZ$150 for affiliated and NZ$200 for nonaffiliated members. The **Taupo Golf Club,** 32 Centennial Dr. (© 07/378-6933; www.taupogolf.co.nz), is one of only two New Zealand clubs to have two 18-hole courses. You have the choice of the Centennial Championship Course or

---

 Lakeside Hole-in-One ★★

If it feels like your lucky day, or perhaps you've given up on Lotto, try Taupo's crazy **"Great Lake Hole-in-One" Challenge** (© 07/378-8117). It's addictive, fun, and, to my mind, impossible. The truth is, it's not. Apparently, more than 200 people have managed to make it, winning fabulous prizes, including trips to Europe, bungy jumps, and dinners. The object is to stand on the shoreline and whack a golf ball 115m (378 ft.) over the water in the hope that it will fall directly into the tiny hole in the middle of a floating pontoon. Balls cost NZ$1 each, NZ$15 for 18, and NZ$20 for 25. A red hole-in-one wins NZ$5,000; an ace-in-one of the 12-inch-wide blue-and-white holes will earn you local lodgings, attractions, products, adventure packages, or dinners. And can you believe it? There's about one winner per week! You can take a shot daily from 9am to 9pm, depending on weather conditions, with reduced hours in winter.

the Tauhara Course. Greens fees are NZ$40 for affiliated and NZ$60 for nonaffiliated members.

JET-BOATING Two operators work two completely different areas of the Waikato River. **Hukafalls Jet ★★★,** Wairakei Tourist Park (✆ **0800/485-253** in NZ, or 07/374-8572; www.hukafallsjet.co.nz), specializes in impressive 360-degree spins and close-ups of Huka Falls. It charges NZ$105 for adults, NZ$59 for children 15 and under for a 30-minute adventure. **Rapids Jet,** Rapids Road, Aratiatia (✆ **0800/727-437** in NZ, or 07/378-5828; www.rapidsjet.com), runs farther upstream in the fast waters of the Aratiatia Rapids; prices are NZ$95 adults, NZ$55 children 5 to 15. Riders must be 5 and older, and taller than 1m (3 ft., 4 in.).

KAYAKING Paddle over the turquoise-blue waters of the Waikato River with **Canoe & Kayak** (✆ **0800/529-256** in NZ; www.canoeandkayak.co.nz). A 2-hour guided trip includes a soak in hot springs and costs NZ$75. For lake kayaking, call **Kayaking Kiwi** (✆ **0800/353-435** in NZ, or 07/374-8117; www.kayakingkiwi.co.nz); it offers rock drawing and volcanic kayaking trips (around 4–5 hr.) priced from NZ$99.

SWIMMING The completely revamped and extended **AC Baths,** top end of Spa Road (✆ **07/376-0350;** www.taupovenues.co.nz), opened in 2003, and it features indoor and outdoor pools, nine private pools, two hydroslides, a Jacuzzi, a sauna, and a cafe make it well worth a visit in summer, when Taupo gets fiercely hot. A rock climbing wall is a fun addition for all ages.

WALKING The visitor center's excellent *Taupo Walkways* brochure outlines the area's 10 most popular tracks. They range from 15 minutes to 1½ hours in length. One option is the 3km (2-mile) walk from Spa Park, in Taupo, along the riverbank to Huka Falls (2 hr. round-trip). You can carry on to Aratiatia Rapids, which takes another 2 hours.

WHITE-WATER RAFTING The guides with **Kiwi River Safaris** (✆ **0800/723-8577** in NZ, or 07/377-6597; www.krs.co.nz) know their stuff. They've had a minimum of 5 years' full-time experience and are qualified swift-water rescue technicians, with first aid and CPR certification updated annually. Options include daily Grade III to IV trips on Rangitaiki River and float trips on the Waikato River. The Grade IV to V trips on Wairoa River are for serious thrill seekers and happen only 26 days a year, when the hydro waters are released. Prices start at NZ$120 per person.

Where to Stay

All rates below include 15% GST and parking.

VERY EXPENSIVE

Huka Lodge ★★★ When an upmarket lodge has been around as long and won as many awards as Huka, you might be inclined to approach it with reverence and trepidation. That would be a mistake. They're all human here, and the key to enjoying

Huka is to cast aside preconceptions and simply wallow. It's hard to find fault with the 17-acre setting, the facilities, or the rooms. Guest rooms want for nothing, and the public spaces, especially the wine cellar and the Trophy Room, are divine. Once all alone in this price bracket in New Zealand, Huka faces increasing competition from new players in the field and can't afford to be complacent; yet it still has a certain something that few others can match. If you have a fat budget, opt for the sublime four-suite Owner's Cottage—it's been so popular they've added the gorgeous two-suite Alan Pye Cottage. Both provide an added level of privacy and service and have their own infinity swimming pools and Jacuzzis.

271 Huka Falls Rd., Taupo. www.thehukaretreats.com or www.hukalodge.co.nz. ℂ **07/378-5791.** Fax 07/378-0427. 19 units, 2 cottages. NZ$1,930–NZ$2,550 lodge suites; NZ$9,240–NZ$13,575 1 double room in cottages. NZ$475 per person Christmas Day/New Year's Eve surcharge. Minimum 3-night stay Dec 22–Jan 5. Rates include breakfast, cocktails, 5-course dinner, Taupo airport transport, and use of lodge facilities. Off-peak rates. AE, DC, MC, V. From St. Hwy. 1, turn onto Huka Falls Rd. and follow signs; lodge is 300m (1,000 ft.) upstream from Huka Falls. **Amenities:** Dining room; bar and wine cellar w/ biggest private collection in New Zealand (more than 30,000 bottles); babysitting; free use of bikes; concierge; nearby golf course; 2 Jacuzzis in cottages; massage; outdoor heated pool; room service; all-weather tennis court. *In room:* A/C, TV/DVD, fridge, hair dryer, kitchen in 2 cottages, minibar, Wi-Fi.

MODERATE

There are over 70 motels in Taupo alone, but they fill up fast on weekends and during summer holidays, so book ahead. In addition to the listings below, **Bayview Wairakei Resort** ★★, State Highway 1, Wairakei (www.wairakei.co.nz; ℂ 07/374-8021), is a good base; it's just 7km (4⅓ miles) out of town and in the heart of most of the attractions. The bulk of its 187 rooms go for NZ$150 to NZ$350, with some of the larger suites up to NZ$720. There are swimming pools, two restaurants, two bars, a gym, a 9-hole golf course, six Jacuzzis, and saunas at your disposal. It's a terrific spot for families (with children's programs), and an excellent value for longer stays. If you stay in the 1 of more than 500 rooms, you'll be just across the lawn from the pool. **Baycrest Lodge** ★, 79 Mere Rd., Taupo (www.baycrest.co.nz; ℂ **0800/229-273** in NZ, or 07/378-3838), has 16 units, which cost NZ$175 to NZ$225. Upstairs units all have spacious bathrooms with Jacuzzis, plus balconies overlooking the lake; downstairs units have their own private courtyard, each with a private thermal tub. **Quest Taupo,** 9 Tui St., Taupo (www.questtaupo.co.nz; ℂ **0800/350-005** in NZ or 07/378-7487), has 32 very good value rooms priced from NZ$120 to NZ$400.

Hilton Lake Taupo ★★ 🎖 The Hilton has colonized a heritage building above the Onekeneke Thermal Valley and turned it into a sophisticated complex where big rooms have thermal or lake views. The new suites and apartments are the best. They have big bathrooms, and private terraces (ground-floor units) or balconies, where you can relax on a hot day. The apartments have full kitchens and laundries and are incredibly good family value. As an added bonus, the property is home to Taupo's best restaurant, **Bistro Lago** (p. 214).

80–100 Napier/Taupo Hwy., Taupo. www.hilton.com. ℂ **07/378-7080.** Fax 07/376-2352. 113 units. From NZ$325. AE, DC, MC, V. **Amenities:** Restaurant, bar, concierge, nearby golf course, outdoor heated pool, sauna, gym, tennis court, 24-hr. room service. *In room:* A/C, TV/DVD, fridge, hairdryer, kitchen & laundry (in apartments), Internet.

Kauri Point Homestay ★ 🎖 Robert and Gail Corfe have a beautiful home set in 6 acres of gardens and their three big suites, each with its own sitting room area, are an unbelievable value. All beautifully appointed, the rooms open onto a large deck, which is just the spot to enjoy Gail's breakfast, of a late afternoon glass of wine.

4 Mark Wynd, Bonshaw Park, Taupo. www.kauripoint.co.nz. ℭ/fax **07/378-8355.** 3 units. NZ$220. Long-stay & off-peak rates. Rates include breakfast, drinks & canapés, morning & afternoon tea. No children under 12. AE, DC, MC, V. **Amenities:** Dinner on request; airport transfers; nearby golf courses; outdoor Jacuzzi. *In room:* TV/DVD, fridge, hairdryer, Wi-Fi.

INEXPENSIVE

For something more modest, go for backpacker accommodations at the **Rainbow Lodge,** 99 Titiraupenga St. (ℭ **07/378-5754;** www.rainbowlodge.co.nz), where beds go for NZ$25 to NZ$75. Backpackers will find useful information on www.backpacklaketaupo.com. There are also plenty of reasonably priced camping grounds in the area, although you'll need to book well ahead for a summer stay if you intend to beat New Zealanders on holiday.

Where to Eat

I'm told there are around 60 restaurants in Taupo, and I'd like to know where they're all hiding. Although there's no shortage of places to eat, "shining stars of cuisine" are a bit thin on the ground. As is the case anywhere in New Zealand, restaurants and cafes keep reinventing themselves and changing their names, styles, and menus. The good news is there are plenty of reasonably priced ethnic restaurants to choose from. A delicious lunch or summer evening meal at **Huka Prawn Park ★★** (p. 207), Huka Falls Road (ℭ **07/374-8474**), is worth your attention. It's the world's only geothermally heated prawn farm, and the prawn platter need not make you feel guilty. **Huka Vineyard Restaurant ★★**, Wishart Estate Vineyard, 56 Huka Falls Rd. (ℭ **07/377-2326**), is open for lunch daily from 10am. It's in a 100-year-old barn and specializes in wine and food matches. **Portofino Italian Café ★★**, 28 Tuwharetoa St. (ℭ **07/377-6293;** www.portofino.co.nz), is a very pleasant, casual place that serves up a big range of Italian favorites including a host of pasta dishes and pizzas.

Flax ★, 5 Horomatangi St. (ℭ **07/377-8052**), is a great little cafe with local color. Sporty types should head for **Hub Mountain Bike Café ★★**, 415 Huka Falls Rd. (ℭ **07/374-8409;** www.hubcafe.co.nz). It's where the mountain bikers hang out and they don't mind you turning up in your cycling gear. Bike racks are available. **L'Arte Mosaic Café & Sculpture Garden ★**, 255 Mapara Rd., Acacia Bay, Taupo (ℭ **07/378-2962;** www.larte.co.nz), is where you'll find resident ceramic artist, Judi Brennan, who has created this crazy, creative place. The food, the colorful environment, and the good service make it a little winner. If you want "coffee on the run" swing by **Streetwise Coffee,** a tiny hole-in-the-wall located at 30 Heu Heu St. (ℭ **07/377-0624**); it sells fair trade coffee and juices. **Volcanic Coffee ★**, 38 Tui St. (ℭ **07/377-4644;** www.volcaniccoffee.co.nz), is a boutique family-run roastery

 Say Cheese

The **Merchant of Taupo ★**, 111 Spa Rd. (ℭ **07/378-4626;** www.themerchant.co.nz), stocks a wide variety of imported and New Zealand cheeses, salamis, oils, sauces, wines, and other specialty items that you might like to take home as gifts—or personal treats!

Scenic Cellars ★★, 32 Roberts St. (ℭ **07/378-5704;** www.sceniccellars.co.nz), stocks over 3,000 wine labels—32 available for tasting in the store every day—in New Zealand's largest underground wine cellar.

serving delicious freshly ground coffee. For the best ice cream in town head straight for **Kaffe Eis ★★**, 13 Tongariro St. (✆ **07/378-8535**).

Bistro Lago ★★★ CONTEMPORARY NEW ZEALAND   Top Auckland chef Simon Gault is responsible for the exciting menu at this innovative restaurant. It's Taupo's best, no question. The interior is understated, leaving all the drama to culinary treats like wood-roasted market fish with carrot and ginger butter, perhaps followed by quince and chestnut clafouti with goat-cheese ice cream and caramelized quince.

Lake Taupo Hilton, 80–100 Napier/Taupo Hwy. ✆ **07/376-2310.** www.bistrolago.co.nz. Reservations required. Main courses NZ$33–NZ$38. AE, DC, MC, V. Daily 7am–11pm.

The Brantry Restaurant ★★ CONTEMPORARY NEW ZEALAND   Tucked into a two-story 1950s house, the Brantry gets rave reviews from the locals for its moody interior and good food. It's one of the pricier options in town, but dishes like stuffed lamb rump will leave you pleased to have made the effort.

45 Rifle Range Rd. ✆ **07/378-0484.** Reservations recommended. Main courses NZ$32–NZ$38. AE, MC, V. Tues–Sat 6pm–late.

Replete Café ★ DELI/CAFE   Trying to get lunch at Replete is like queuing for tickets to a sold-out show; everyone wants a piece of the action. The service can be flustered, but the food does tend to be good—great salads and pies. Replete appears to be Taupo's favorite daytime haunt for all ages, especially 30- to 40-something business types. They also have a superb cookery supplies store in an adjacent area.

45 Heu Heu St. ✆ **07/377-3011.** www.replete.co.nz. Lunch main courses NZ$15–NZ$25. AE, DC, MC, V. Mon–Fri 7:45am–5pm; Sat–Sun 8:30am–late afternoon.

Taupo After Dark

The core of Taupo's nightlife is geared toward backpackers. If you want to make a quiet start to the evening, head for **19th Hole,** at Wairakei International Golf Course, State Highway 1 (✆ **07/374-8152**), where you can enjoy a drink and chat. **Holy Cow,** upstairs at Tongariro and Tuwharetoa streets (✆ **07/378-0040**), is definitely the happening place for the young crowd. If you feel like a good beer followed by a quieter dining experience, head for **Plateau ★**, 64 Tuwharetoa St. (✆ **07/377-2425;** www.plateautaupo.co.nz), which celebrates Kiwi music and a range of Monteith's craft beers. For a touch of the Irish, head to **Finn MacCuhal's Irish Pub,** Tongariro and Tuwharetoa streets (✆ **07/378-6165;** www.finns.co.nz), where you can enjoy a Guinness and rowdy music. **The Shed Bar,** 18 Tuwharetoa St. (✆ **07/376-5393;** www.theshedbar.co.nz), is the quintessential New Zealand sports bar, complete with giant TV screens for watching the latest games. They also have live bands and DJs and a good range of beers.

En Route to Tongariro National Park

The 94km (58-mile) drive from Taupo to Tongariro National Park is an easy one along the eastern shore of Lake Taupo. At the southern end of the lake, stop at **Turangi** if trout fishing is your passion. The **Tongariro River** is one of the best-known trout-fishing sites in the world (see chapter 5). If you have time, also detour to **Tokaanu Thermal Pools.** Even if you don't swim, there's a nice nature walk. Or call in at the **National Trout Centre ★★**, south of Turangi (✆ **07/386-9243;** www.doc.govt.nz), which features interactive displays and an award-winning underwater viewing chamber that allows you to observe trout in their natural habitat.

If you didn't fancy stopping in Taupo, let me introduce you to a hidden gem—
River Birches Lodge ★★★, 19 Koura St., Turangi (✆ **0800/102-025** in NZ, or
07/386-0445; www.riverbirches.co.nz), which is a serene hideaway on the banks of the
Tongariro River, with three beautiful suites and a separate 3-bedroom cottage. Cedar
tubs, big decks, lovely gardens, fine cuisine and, should you be a fisherman, a webcam
that monitors the river's best fishing spots, make this an almost perfect stay. It's an
incredible value at NZ$460 to NZ$665, or NZ$1,400 for the whole house. Rates for
the separate cottage vary from NZ$385 to NZ$995, depending on the number of
people staying. Rates include breakfast; long stay rates and special deals are available.

State Highway 47 cuts off from State Highway 1 to lead you through plateau tussock land to State Highway 48 and the entrance to park headquarters. It's clearly
signposted. As you leave Lake Taupo behind, you enter a world dominated by the
grand volcanic landscape. Drive with great care on the Desert Road in winter, when
ice and snow cause major traffic hazards.

TONGARIRO NATIONAL PARK ★★

99km (61 miles) SW of Taupo; 141km (87 miles) NE of Wanganui

Tongariro National Park is New Zealand's oldest national park and, as of 1990, a World
Heritage Area, recognized for its outstanding natural and cultural features. It is a place
of extremes and surprises that will make you ponder your own diminutive reality.

The park can be explored from one of two main areas—**National Park** and
Whakapapa villages on the western side of the mountains, or **Turoa Ski Resort**
and **Ohakune township** to the south.

The core of the park consists of the sacred peaks Tongariro, Ngauruhoe, and Ruapehu, which were presented to the people of New Zealand in 1887 by Te Heuheu
Tukino IV, Paramount Chief of the Tuwharetoa tribe. At 2,797m (9,174 ft.), **Mount
Ruapehu** is the highest mountain on the North Island and is the principal skiing spot
in the region. Its **Crater Lake,** filled with acidic tepid water, has a bottom layer of
6m (20 ft.) of sulfur mud, which acts as a barrier between the water and the molten
rock below. In June 1996, this active volcano erupted, surprising scientists monitoring
its activity. A few days earlier, they had downgraded its danger rating after 8 months
of relative inactivity following the spectacular eruptions of September and October
1995. Before that, Ruapehu had been quiet for 8 years. There was a major lahar in
2007 when the crater-lake overflowed. Up-to-date information on Ruapehu is at
www.geonet.org.nz, or call Eastern Ruapehu Lahar and Warning System (✆ **0508/
452-427** in NZ; www.horizons.govt.nz).

Mount Ngauruhoe rises 2,290m (7,513 ft.), smolders constantly, and from time
to time (the last in 1975) sends showers of ash and lava from its crater.

Mount Tongariro is the lowest and northernmost of the three, measuring 1,968m
(6,455 ft.). It is also the focus of Maori legends. The peaks are at the end of a volcanic
chain that extends all the way to the islands of Tonga, 1,610km (1,000 miles) away.
Their origin is fairly recent in geological terms, dating back only about 2 million years.

The weather in Tongariro National Park is always changeable and can be savage
regardless of the season. Trampers and skiers should always seek the latest track and
weather details before venturing into the park.

Essentials

GETTING THERE & GETTING AROUND By Plane Mountain Air (☏ 0800/922-812 in NZ; www.mountainair.co.nz) has daily service linking Auckland with Mount Ruapehu. It also has a range of ski-flight packages.

By Train The **TranzRail** (☏ 0800/802-802; www.tranzscenic.co.nz) *Overlander* trains stop at National Park and Ohakune.

By Coach (Bus) InterCity (☏ 07/378-9032) provides service to the national park. **Whakapapa Express** (☏ 0800/828-763 in NZ, or 07/377-0435) offers daily ski and mountain transport between Taupo, Ohakune, and Whakapapa. **Ruapehu Ski Shuttle** (☏ 0800/331-995 in NZ, or 09/379-8886; fax 09/379-8151) serves National Park village, Whakapapa, and Ohakune from Auckland Sunday through Wednesday and on Friday.

By Car Highway 1 runs along the eastern side of the park; Highway 4 goes through National Park Village on the western side; highways 47 and 48 bring travelers from the south shore of Lake Taupo into the heart of the park; and Highway 49 turns off State Highway 1 at Waiouru at the south end of the park and travels to Ohakune. Mount Ruapehu is a 4-hour drive from either Auckland or Wellington.

VISITOR INFORMATION The **Whakapapa Visitor Centre** is in the village of Whakapapa at the end of State Highway 48 (☏ 07/892-3729; fax 07/892-3814; www.doc.govt.nz). It's open daily from 8am to 6pm in summer, 8am to 5pm in winter (closed Dec 25). It provides current volcanic, weather, and track information, as well as hut and camping passes, maps and brochures, hunting permits, and other items. The center has exhibits on the natural and human history of the park along with two excellent audiovisual displays, *The Sacred Gift of Tongariro* and *The Ring of Fire*. Information about the Whakapapa Ski Field, 7km (4⅓ miles) above the village, is also available.

Movie Mountain

A digitally altered representation of Mount Ngauruhoe appears as Mount Doom in *The Lord of the Rings* trilogy.

The **Ruapehu Visitor Centre,** 54 Clyde St., Ohakune (☏ 0800/782-734 in NZ, or 06/385-8427; fax 06/385-8527; www.visitruapehu.com), is open weekdays from 9am to 5pm, weekends from 9am to 3:30pm. You can reach the Ohakune **Department of Conservation** office at ☏ 06/385-0010. The **Turangi i-SITE Visitor Centre,** Ngawaka Place, Turangi (☏ 0800/288-726 in NZ, or 07/386-8999; fax 07/386-0074; www.greatlaketauponz.com), is another useful stop. It's open daily from 8:30am to 5pm. For information on National Park Village, go to www.nationalpark.co.nz.

Exploring the Park
ON THE SLOPES

Skiing is *the* activity in season (June–Oct), when the weather and Mount Ruapehu permit. The 1996 eruption closed the two main fields—Whakapapa and Turoa—for 2 years, and a mild winter in 1999 didn't improve things, but the situation appears to have recovered. Combined, these two fields offer over 700 hectares (1,730 acres) of patrolled, skiable terrain (and almost the same amount off-trail), with facilities and geographical variety to satisfy any skier. Whakapapa and Turoa will always be the names of the two ski areas, but since 2001, they've been united under one brand, Mount Ruapehu—New Zealand's largest ski area. You can get seamless lift passes to ski on either field; the company operates bus service between the two.

The **Whakapapa Ski Area** (© 07/892-4000; www.mtruapehu.com), above the Grand Chateau, is heavily populated compared to South Island fields, which is its biggest disadvantage. There's something for everyone in terms of skiing, but be careful that you don't sail over bluffs. A lot of skiers stay in the club huts on the field. Whakapapa's sister resort is Copper Mountain, in Colorado, with which it shares some reciprocal privileges. Ski lifts operate daily from 8:30am to 3:45pm. An All Mountain All Day Pass costs NZ$95 for adults, and NZ$57 for children 5 to 18. A Sightseeing Pass costs NZ$26 for adults, NZ$16 for children 5 to 18, and NZ$66 for a family. Rental of skis, boots, and poles cost NZ$39 for adults, NZ$33 for children 13 to 18, and NZ$29 for children 5 to 12.

The Whakapapa summer operation (Dec–Apr, daily 9am–4pm) includes guided Crater Lake walks from NZ$145 for adults, NZ$95 for children ages 5 to 18, and NZ$290 for a family; scenic chairlift rides go for NZ$25 adults, NZ$15 children 5 to 18, and NZ$61 for a family.

Whakapapa Shuttle (© 07/892-3716) offers the best transport to the mountain, which costs NZ$35 round-trip from National Park Village.

Many prefer **Turoa Ski Resort** (© 06/385-8456; www.mtruapehu.com), above Ohakune, because it draws fewer people. It boasts the longest vertical drop of any ski area in Australasia, plus an abundance of gullies for snowboarders. Ski lifts operate daily from 9am to 3:45pm and cost the same as at Whakapapa (above). Turoa is open only in winter (late June to early Nov). **Snow Express** (© 06/385-9280) offers the best transport, which departs from Ohakune's Junction Ski Shop every half-hour and costs NZ$30 round-trip.

Skiers and snowboarders can find more information on these ski fields and others in chapter 4. For the latest snow conditions and ski information, call **Snowphone** (© 083/222-180 in Turoa, or 083-222-182 in Whakapapa), or check www.snow. co.nz.

ON TRACK: A TRAMPER'S PARADISE

Walking in Tongariro National Park is spectacular, to say the least, and there are plenty of possible routes. Pick up the Department of Conservation's brochure *Whakapapa Walks* for an introduction to some of the best. **Taranaki Falls** ★ is a 2-hour, 6km (4-mile) circular track that starts above Whakapapa Village and takes in both native bush and stark tussock vegetation. Taranaki Falls plunges 20m (66 ft.) over the edge of a large lava flow, which erupted from Ruapehu 15,000 years ago. **Silica Rapids Walk** is a 2- to 3-hour loop track that also starts above Whakapapa Village. It takes you through a beech forest, past streams and rapids, and through subalpine plants and swamp as it returns to Bruce Road, 2km (1 mile) above the starting point.

The best walk of all is also the toughest—the famous **Tongariro Crossing** ★★★. Regarded as New Zealand's greatest 1-day walk, it takes you between Tongariro and Ngauruhoe, over the most stunning volcanic landscapes in the country. It involves an 800m (2,600-ft.) altitude gain and a couple of very sharp but short stretches. People of all fitness levels can generally cope, but many underestimate the climate at that altitude and almost every year visitors, who think they know better than the local experts, have to be rescued. Forget the fact that it is summer and take plenty

Men at War

There are dozens of stories of courage, compassion, and comradeship at the hefty **National Army Museum ★★★**, State Highway 1, Waiouru (② 0800/ 369-999 in NZ; www.armymuseum. co.nz). Children especially will love the chance to climb on old military vehicles. Others will want to remember the sacrifices made by so many in war time. There is a cafe, research center, kids' area, and gift shop; the complex is open daily from 9am to 4:30pm (closed Dec 25).

of warm woolen clothing (cotton is useless), as conditions change fast and furiously. The walking season is usually November to May. If you plan a winter walk take a guide, crampons, and an ice axe. It is important to organize transport at both ends of the walk. Contact the **Tongariro Track Transport** (② 07/892-3716; www. tongarirotrack.co.nz), or **Howard's Lodge Transport,** Carroll Street, National Park Village (② 07/892-2827; www.howardslodge.co.nz). For more details on the Tongariro Crossing, see the "Tramping" section in chapter 4.

BY BICYCLE

An essential information source for mountain bikers in this area is the pocketsize publication *Volcanic Plateau Mountain Bike Rides,* written and published by Kennett Brothers in association with the Department of Conservation and printed on waterproof paper. It details a host of rides in the area, including the highly regarded 42nd Traverse. The booklet is for sale at visitor centers and bike stores in the area.

The **42nd Traverse ★★★** is one of the most popular bike rides on the North Island. It covers old logging tracks through remote native bush and has an overall descent of 570m (1,870 ft.) through spectacular scenery. Depending on your enthusiasm for the task, it takes anywhere from 3 to 7 hours to complete. You'll need to organize transport to and from your vehicle; **Howard's Lodge,** Carroll Street, National Park Village (②/fax 07/892-2827; www.howardslodge.co.nz), or **Ski Haus,** Carroll Street, National Park Village (② 07/892-2854; www.skihaus.co.nz), can arrange that for you. Howard's Lodge also offers guided rides, but the best mountain bike company in this area is **Tongariro Mountain Bikes ★★**, the Rafting Centre, Atirau Road, Turangi (② 0800/101-024 in NZ or 07/386-6445; www.trr. co.nz), which has exclusive access to 3,800 hectares (9,400 acres) of backcountry trails and offers shuttle and hire service.

Where to Stay

Ohakune and National Park villages offer a good range of winter accommodations, but Whakapapa Village has fewer choices. You'll need to book well ahead to beat New Zealand skiers to the best beds—and even the best are fairly mediocre. In summer, the area is popular with trampers and mountain bikers, and because some properties close after the ski season, it's still wise to reserve ahead. Rates below include 15% GST.

IN OHAKUNE

This is where you'll find the greatest variety of accommodations, and it's only about an hour to Whakapapa, making it a good base. **Powderhorn Chateau ★★**, bottom of Mountain Road (www.powderhorn.co.nz; ℂ 06/385-8888), has the closest accommodations to the mountain on the Turoa side. It's definitely the best the town has to offer and it has two in-house restaurants—convenient when it's freezing outside. It was built in 1995 and has 30 well-appointed rooms with private bathrooms for NZ$215 to NZ$250. Luxury apartments that sleep six go for NZ$750 to NZ$850 per night, with significantly lower off-peak rates. **Ossie's Chalets & Apartments,** 59 Tainui St. (www.ossies-ohakune.co.nz; ℂ 06/385-8088), offers 14 two-story chalets with lovely Scandinavian-style timber interiors. Prices start at NZ$175, a good value for the money and cheaper again in summer.

IN NATIONAL PARK VILLAGE

Centrally located just west of Whakapapa Ski Area, National Park Village has a nice selection of good-value, low-cost accommodations. It's also the only place that offers a view of all three mountains. **Howard's Lodge ★**, Carroll Street (www.howards lodge.co.nz; ℂ/fax 07/892-2827), is a friendly budget spot with backpacker dorm beds and simple twins, doubles, and quads with shared facilities, plus deluxe rooms with en-suite bathrooms. Their prices range from NZ$110 to NZ$130. **National Park Backpackers ★**, Finlay Street (www.npbp.co.nz; ℂ/fax 07/892-2870), is a new complex that's drawing a big crowd to its indoor climbing wall. Dorm beds are around NZ$21 to NZ$35; doubles with en-suite bathrooms are NZ$65 to NZ$75. Camping there costs NZ$14 per person.

IN WHAKAPAPA VILLAGE

This small alpine village has limited accommodations, unless you take a Whakapapa On-Snow package deal and stay in one of the on-field ski clubs. **Whakapapa Holiday Park** (www.whakapapa.net.nz; ℂ 07/892-3897) has cabins, a self-contained lodge that sleeps 32, caravan and tent sites, and a fully stocked store. Prices start at NZ$25 per person for the lodge, NZ$19 per person for caravan and tent sites, and NZ$69 to NZ$79 for cabins. It's the cheapest and closest accommodations to the ski field and they offer transport to the ski area and for the Tongariro Alpine Crossing. **Skotel Alpine Resort** (www.skotel.co.nz; ℂ 0800/756-835 in NZ, or 07/892-3719) has everything from backpacker rooms to smart deluxe units and self-contained chalets. There's a restaurant, a good sauna and Jacuzzis, and a fun-filled bar during ski season. Superior rooms and chalets are priced from NZ$175 to NZ$225. Backpackers pay NZ$97 to NZ$133. Cheaper summer rates are available and they offer ski and equipment hire in winter.

The **Bayview Chateau Tongariro ★★** (www.chateau.co.nz; ℂ 0800/242-832 in NZ, or 07/892-3809), is the grande dame of the area. Built in 1929, the glorious old building has a New Zealand Historic Places Trust category I classification. Most guest rooms have been refurbished, and 40 newer rooms are now available (these are nicest options). The junior suites are an especially good value; but if you feel like splashing out, go for the gorgeous, big Te Heu Heu suite (NZ$1,000) and enjoy your own fireplace, Jacuzzi, and telescope. You pay top dollar in winter—NZ$195 to NZ$480—and get a much better rate in summer. Guests enjoy access to a heated indoor pool, sauna, gym, bars, restaurants, and New Zealand's highest 9-hole golf course.

Where to Eat

IN OHAKUNE

Don't hold your breath for fine dining in Ohakune, National Park, or the Whakapapa villages. I can only assume that skiers and trekkers get so hungry they'll eat anything. Most of the time the offerings are fair to middling; but if it's any comfort, you won't starve. Ohakune has the best range of eateries, but be aware that some of them close in summer. **Powderkeg Restaurant and Bar ★★**, at Powderhorn Chateau (© 06/ 385-8888), is a good winter bet for hearty meals and heaps of partying. It offers brasserie-style food. A more subdued, semi-fine-dining atmosphere characterizes Powderhorn's other year-round restaurant, the **Matterhorn**. There's always good food at the **Fat Pigeon Cafe ★★**, bottom of Mountain Road (© 06/385-9423), where you can relax in a charming garden setting. At the **Mountain Rocks Café & Bar,** Clyde and Goldfinch streets (© 06/385-8295), you can enjoy everything from big breakfasts to hearty dinners. It has a nice courtyard for outdoor summer dining. And last but not least, **Utopia Café,** 47 Clyde St. (© 06/385-9120), is very popular. It's opposite the Information Centre and is invariably filled with hungry, puffy-jacketed people in winter. Service can be a bit slow when it's busy but it has a lively atmosphere and it's a good place to hear about what's happening on the ski slopes.

IN NATIONAL PARK VILLAGE

The dining scene is finally improving here, although it is still rather limited, and open hours are unpredictable at best. **Ski Haus Restaurant & Bar,** Carroll Street (© 07/ 892-2854), is open year-round for breakfast and dinner, serving filling fare such as steaks, chicken dishes, and a few vegetarian offerings. **Basekamp Gourmet Burger Bar,** also on Carroll Street (© 07/892-2872), is good for pizzas and chunky burgers—try the venison and lamb burgers. The **Station Café,** National Park Railway Station, Station Road (© 07/892-2881), is popular, but often closed during the day.

IN WHAKAPAPA VILLAGE

Your best meals here will be at the **Ruapehu Restaurant ★★** (© 07/892-3809) at the Bayview Chateau Tongariro (see "Where to Stay," above). The Chateau's **Pihanga Cafe** is open daily from 11:30am until late, and although it's long overdue for a decor revamp, the reasonably priced meals, all under NZ$25, will fend off hunger pangs. That's the best I can say about it. Across the road, **Fergussons Café** has counter food, light meals, and good coffee daily from 8:30am to 5pm, but it won't be winning prizes anytime soon, either. **Skotel** (© 07/892-3719; see "Where to Stay," above) has a restaurant open to casual diners for breakfast and dinner. Once again, food is of the no-fuss, filling variety, but you'll find a great party atmosphere here in winter.

En Route to Gisborne

There are two ways of getting to Gisborne from Rotorua. You can drive along the Bay of Plenty route past Whakatane to Opotiki, and then cut through the Waioeka Gorge (St. Hwy. 2), or you can allow much more time and follow the East Cape Road (St. Hwy. 35), which takes in stunning scenery on the easternmost point of New Zealand.

The Cape drive will take 7 to 8 hours minimum—more if you stop to take photographs. This is probably the least-visited part of the country. Take great care on this road; there is often wandering stock, and locals don't always obey the road rules. For information on the East Cape Road and its attractions, see chapter 10.

The short route from Opotiki to Gisborne on State Highway 2 will take just 3 hours, but much of it is steep and winding through the Waioeka Gorge. It's faster, but it's boring compared to the East Cape Road.

En Route to Hawke's Bay

Head back to Taupo, where you'll turn onto the Napier-Taupo Highway, State Highway 5. The journey follows excellent roads and takes around 1½ hours. That said, take care, as this stretch of road is notorious for fatal accidents.

GISBORNE & HAWKE'S BAY

Gisborne and the East Cape epitomize all that's special about New Zealand—stunning unspoiled scenery, rich culture and history, white-sand beaches, fabulous wines, and friendly, hospitable people. Gisborne, the most isolated city in the country, lies just south of the sparsely populated East Cape in Poverty Bay and is separated by mountain ranges from both Bay of Plenty and Hawke's Bay.

Nearby Mount Hikurangi, the tallest nonvolcanic mountain on the North Island at 1,839m (6,032 ft.), is the first point on mainland New Zealand the sun touches each day, and Gisborne the first city in the world to see the light.

It is the place where both Maori and European voyagers first set foot on land. The *waka* (canoe) *Horouta* brought the first Maori settlers of the Great Migration from Hawaiiki over 1,000 years ago, and Captain James Cook stepped ashore at Kaiti Beach in Gisborne in 1769.

The Hawke's Bay region, 215km (134 miles) to the southwest, shares many of the same alluring natural features and has more than 30% of the country's finest vineyards. The adjacent cities of Napier and Hastings and the smaller community of Havelock North curve along the coast.

Both Gisborne and Hawke's Bay are blessed with mild climates, long hours of sunshine, and fertile soil—the perfect combination for horticulture. The landscape is a patchwork of orchards, market gardens, pasture, and vineyards.

GISBORNE & THE EAST CAPE ★★

293km (182 miles) NE of Rotorua; 298km (185 miles) SE of Tauranga; 504km (312 miles) SE of Auckland

Gisborne (pop. 46,600) had its big moment when it welcomed in the first light of the new century. There were hopes back then that the NZ$9.5-million revamp of the city would signal a bright, rich future for the area, but I think things have pretty much reverted to the same old quiet, provincial atmosphere that always prevailed. Mind you, the beautification was much needed, and it's good to see the place looking tidier and slightly more alive.

However, the small-town atmosphere is part of Gisborne's charm, and we shouldn't overlook the fact that it is a prosperous river port city and

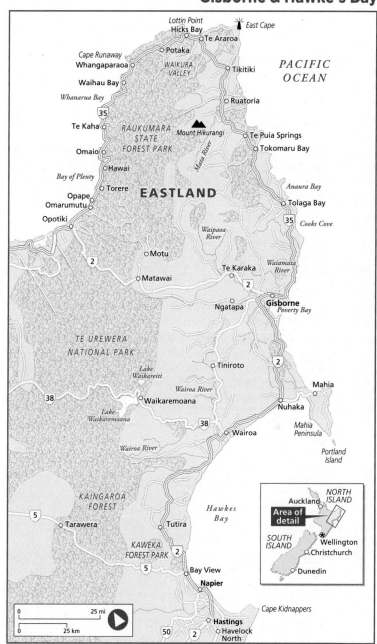

Lottin Point
Hicks Bay
East Cape
Te Araroa
Cape Runaway
Potaka
Whangaparaoa
WAIKURA
VALLEY
PACIFIC
OCEAN
Tikitiki
Waihau Bay
Whanarua Bay
Ruatoria
35
Te Kaha
RAUKUMARA
STATE
FOREST PARK
Mount Hikurangi
Te Puia Springs
Omaio
Tokomaru Bay
Hawai
Bay of Plenty
Torere
Anaura Bay
EASTLAND
Opape
Omarumutu
Tolaga Bay
Opotiki
35
Cooks Cove
Waipaoa
River
Motu
Waiamata
River
Te Karaka
Matawai
2
Ngatapa
Gisborne
Poverty Bay
TE UREWERA
NATIONAL PARK
Tiniroto
2
Lake
Waikareiti
Mahia
Wairoa River
38
Waikaremoana
Nuhaka
Lake
Waikaremoana
38
Mahia
Peninsula
Wairoa
Wairoa River
Portland
Island
KAINGAROA
FOREST
Hawkes
Bay
5
Tarawera
Tutira
KAWEKA
FOREST PARK
2
5
Bay View
Napier
Maia River
Maia River

NORTH
ISLAND
Auckland
Area of
detail
SOUTH
ISLAND
Wellington
Christchurch
Dunedin

0   25 mi
0   25 km

Cape Kidnappers
Hastings
Havelock
North
50   2

9

GISBORNE & HAWKE'S BAY

Gisborne & the East Cape

commercial center. It moves at a relaxed pace (and some days that's an understatement) and enjoys 2,200 hours of sunshine annually with summer temperatures consistently above 77°F (25°C), often rising above 95°F (35°C).

Apart from being the country's second-largest grape-growing district and the self-appointed Chardonnay Capital, this area is also the last genuine bastion of bicultural society largely unaffected by tourism. That bicultural heritage is evident everywhere, in the use of the Maori language in everyday life and in the fact that 45% of the population is Maori—the highest proportion of people of Maori descent anywhere in New Zealand.

If you'd like to experience an isolated part of the country that is more like New Zealand "used to be," then come to Gisborne and the East Cape.

Essentials

GETTING THERE & GETTING AROUND **By Plane** **Air New Zealand Link** (② 06/867-1608; www.airnewzealand.co.nz) operates daily flights from major New Zealand cities. For airport transport, call **Link Shuttles** (② 06/867-4765).

By Coach (Bus) **InterCity** (② 09/623-1503) offers daily bus service to Gisborne from Auckland, Wellington, and Rotorua. **Coachrite** (② 06/868-9969) travels to Hastings Monday through Friday. City buses operate Monday through Friday only, but Gisborne is better explored by car or taxi.

By Shuttle Shuttle buses provide transportation around East Cape between Opotiki and Gisborne. They leave daily from the visitor centers in both towns, which can provide information on schedules and fares.

By Taxi Call the **Gisborne Taxi Society** (② 06/867-2222).

By Car No matter which route you take to Gisborne—via East Cape, via Waioeka Gorge, or via Napier—you're in for a long and winding drive. The most interesting way, via East Cape, is also by far the longest. To make the most of the rich culture and stunning scenery in this area, you really need to stop overnight halfway (at Te Kaha or Hicks Bay, perhaps). Otherwise, be prepared to be on the road for 8 to 10 hours once you leave Opotiki. Also be very alert to stray animals and horsemen on these roads; and make sure you pick up the very informative *Pacific Coast Highway* guide from visitor centers. It's free, and it gives a good introduction to all the settlements you pass through.

ORIENTATION Gisborne is on the northern shore of Poverty Bay, where the Waimata and Taruheru come together to form the Turanganui River, the country's shortest river at just 1,200m (3,900 ft.). The city center is compact. **Gladstone Road** is the main thoroughfare. **Centennial Marine Drive** runs from the bustling port area around the bay to the mouth of the Waipaoa River. Most of the best restaurants are around the port area at the north end of Gladstone Road.

Opotiki lies at the eastern end of Bay of Plenty. It is the gateway to the **East Cape Road,** which is the final leg of the Pacific Coast Highway (St. Hwy. 35).

Wairoa, 99km (61 miles) south of Gisborne at the mouth of the Wairoa River, is the gateway to the wilderness areas of Urewera National Park and Lake Waikaremoana. The 3-day tramp around the lake is one of the Department of Conservation's Great Walks of New Zealand (see chapter 4).

VISITOR INFORMATION The **Gisborne i-SITE Visitor Centre,** 209 Grey St., across from Pizza Hut (② 06/868-6139; fax 06/868-6138; www.gisbornenz.com), is open daily from 8:30am to 5pm (closed Dec 25). For more information visit www.eastlandnz.com, www.destinationgisborne.co.nz, and www.pacificcoast.co.nz.

The **Wairoa i-SITE Visitor Centre** is at the corner of State Highway 2 and Queen Street, Wairoa (✆ **06/838-7440;** fax 06/838-3901; www.wairoadc.govt.nz); it's open weekdays 8am to 5pm, and weekends 9:45am to 10:45am and 3:15pm to 4pm. The **Opotiki i-SITE Visitor Centre,** at Elliot and St. John streets, Opotiki (✆ **07/315-3031;** fax 07/315-3032; www.opotikinz.com), is open in summer 9am to 4:30pm daily, and in winter, Monday to Friday 9am to 4:30pm, weekends 9am to 1:30pm.

[Fast FACTS] GISBORNE

The Gisborne **post office** is at 166 Gladstone Rd. (✆ **06/867-8220**). It's open Monday through Friday from 9am to 5pm. For **Internet access,** inquire at visitor centers (see above), though keep in mind that the Gisborne Library (www.gpl.govt.nz) on Peel Street has free wireless Internet.

SPECIAL EVENTS The **Gisborne Wine & Food Festival ★** is on Labour Weekend in October. For information, call ✆ **0800/447-667** in New Zealand; or check www.gisbornewine.co.nz. For details on all Eastland area events, contact local visitor centers.

Exploring Gisborne

To get a panoramic view of Poverty Bay, the city, and the harbor and rivers, head for **Kaiti Hill Lookout.** It's signposted at the northern end of Gladstone Bridge, and you can drive all the way to the brick semicircular lookout point. A statue of Captain Cook looks out to Young Nick's Head, at the opposite end of the bay. At the foot of Kaiti Hill is one of New Zealand's largest carved Maori meetinghouses, **Te Poho-o-Rawiri Marae ★★** (✆ **06/868-5364**). Visits can be arranged by appointment, providing an opportunity to see a living gallery of Maori art in the exceptionally detailed *tukutuku* (woven wall panels) and *kowhaiwhai* (painted scroll ornamentation) on the rafters.

The **Tairawhiti Museum ★★**, 18–22 Stout St. (✆ **06/867-3832;** www. tairawhitimuseum.org.nz), is one of the best small provincial museums in the country. It has displays on the Maori and European history of the area as well as geological and natural history, decorative arts, and maritime history. Admission is NZ$5 for adults and NZ$2 for children. It's open Monday through Saturday from 10am to 4pm and Sunday from 1:30 to 4pm (closed Good Friday and Dec 25). The **East Coast Museum of Technology,** Main Road, Makaraka (✆ **06/868-8254;** www. ecmot.8m.com), is 6km (4 miles) from the city. Its huge collection of vintage farm machinery, fire engines, and general equipment from a bygone era is open daily from 9:30am to 4:30pm. Admission is NZ$5 for adults, NZ$2 for children.

The internationally renowned **Eastwoodhill Arboretum ★★★**, 2392 Wharekopae Rd., Ngatapa (✆ **06/863-9003;** www.eastwoodhill.org.nz), lies 35km (22 miles) and 20 minutes west of Gisborne. It is an extraordinary testament to one man's passion for trees. This magnificent 70-hectare (173-acre) woodland park was the life's work of William Douglas Cook, who began planting the bare site in 1910. Today, it holds more than 3,500 species of 750 tree genera, making it the largest arboretum in

New Zealand. The arboretum is a haven for scientists, photographers, and garden enthusiasts alike—especially in autumn when the colors are lush and extravagant. It features over 25km of marked walking tracks, so allow at least 1½ hours and plan to have a picnic under the maples. It's open year-round daily from 9am to 5pm (closed Good Friday and Dec 25); admission is NZ$15 for adults and NZ$10 for seniors. Children 14 and under are admitted free. The 1-hour **Curator's Botanical Tour** costs an additional NZ$15. **Hackfalls Arboretum,** 187 Berry Rd., Tiniroto, 1 hour from Gisborne (⌀ **06/863-7083;** www.hackfalls.org.nz), has one of the biggest collections of maples and oaks in New Zealand. It's open daily; admission is NZ$5 per person. **Gisborne Botanical Gardens,** Aberdeen Road, is a pleasant distraction on the banks of the Taruheru River in the heart of town. Admission is free. Pick up the *Gardens to Visit* brochure from the Gisborne visitor center if you're interested in even more greenery.

A DROP OF WINE

Gisborne is New Zealand's second-largest producer of chardonnay grapes (after Marlborough), growing over a third of the national crop. The area also produces significant quantities of award-winning Riesling and a wide range of other varieties. Pick up the *Winery Guide* at the visitor center, fix yourself a picnic, and head out to explore. ***Note:*** Not all wineries are open to the public all the time, so it pays to phone ahead for hours. You'll find additional information at www.gisbornewine.co.nz.

The **Millton Vineyard ★★**, 119 Papatu Rd., Manutuke (⌀ **06/862-8680;** www.millton.co.nz), was established in 1984 as New Zealand's first commercial, fully certified organic winery. It's known for its Riesling, chenin blanc, and late-harvest dessert wines. It's set in a superb garden with a picnic area and is open daily from 10am to 5pm in summer, or by appointment year-round. **Montana Wines ★★**, Lytton Road, Gisborne (⌀ **06/867-9819;** www.montana.co.nz), was established in 1934 and is New Zealand's leading winemaker and wine exporter. The company has wineries in Auckland, Marlborough, Hawke's Bay, and Gisborne. The Gisborne winery produces the Ormond Estate, Patutahi Estate, Saints, and Montana labels—some of the country's best chardonnay. And check out the newest addition, the **Lindauer Cellars,** Solander Street (⌀ **06/868-2757;** www.montana.co.nz), which is open daily December through February, and Tuesday through Saturday from March to November.

The **Works & Longbush Wines ★★**, the Works, Esplanade, Inner Harbour, Gisborne (⌀ **06/863-1285;** www.longbush.com), is where the Thorpe family has worked its vineyards for more than 35 years and now produces three ranges of Gisborne-made wines under the Woodlands, Longbush, and Nick's Head labels. It focuses on chardonnay and merlot. You can taste the production at the Works, a restaurant and wine bar, from 10am to 6pm daily.

In addition to the above, you can also visit **Waiohika Estate,** 75 Waimata Valley Rd. (⌀ **06/867-4670**), for wine tastings and garden visits; **Amor-Bendall,** 24 Moana Rd., Wainui Beach (⌀ **021/859-435;** www.amor-bendall.co.nz), for chardonnay and pinot gris; and **TW Chardonnay ★★**, Back Ormond Road (⌀ **021/864-818;** call for an appointment; www.twwines.co.nz), for very good vineyard tours and tastings. If you'd like to learn the secrets of cider making, visit the **Cidery,** 91 Customhouse St. (⌀ **06/868-8300**), home to New Zealand's leading cider producer, Bulmer Harvest. It's open weekdays 9am to 5pm, weekends 10am until 3pm.

A SPOT OF CULTURE

Rotorua may have the most accessible concentration of Maori culture in the country, but Eastland is one of the few places in New Zealand where strong cultural and tribal affiliations are obviously evident in day-to-day activities. The Maori language is part of everyday life here.

The area is home to more than 100 working *marae* (village commons), which still form a focal point for most Maori communities. They are used regularly for meetings, celebrations, funerals, and family and tribal functions. Many can be viewed by arrangement, but there are two important rules to remember: You must not take photographs inside *marae* anywhere in New Zealand, and you must not smoke or take food inside. In many, you will also have to remove your shoes.

The remnants of ancient *pa* sites (Maori fortresses) abound throughout the region. Among the most notable are the one at Ngatapa near Gisborne and another in the hills to the north of Waikohu. The district also has a large number of *kohanga reo* (early-childhood education centers) and *kura kaupapa* (primary schools) where only Maori is spoken. Most other schools in the region have bilingual units.

You can see Maori culture at work and play in the many small communities around the East Cape Road. Just remember that these are ordinary New Zealanders, not museum exhibits, so be respectful of their privacy.

Two very good Maori-owned-and-operated tour companies will offer you a unique insight into Maori culture. **Tipuna Tours,** P.O. Box 19, Tolaga Bay (✆ **06/862-6118,** or 027-240-4493; www.tipunatours.com), can take you to the *Whale Rider* film location at very pretty Whangara, just north of Gisborne (NZ$80 per person); or they will customize half- and full-day tours that include *marae* visits, ancient *pa* sites, beautiful bays, and possibly a marine reserve. **Waka Toa,** 36 Potae Ave., Gisborne (✆ **06/868-5425;** www.wakatoa.com), has 1½- to 2½-hour tours that will give you an insight into Maori history and culture. The 2½-hour tour includes a cultural performance and light refreshments. It costs NZ$131 for adults and NZ$72 for children age 5 to 15. They operate daily on demand (closed Dec 25 & Jan 1).

Exploring the East Cape ★★★

State Highway 35 between Opotiki and Gisborne is a memorable 334km (207-mile) journey. The road is etched into the coastline, rewarding the traveler with an ever-changing vista of the South Pacific. In summer, scarlet pohutukawa trees border the bright blue bays, and all along the way you'll see deserted white-sand beaches that afford innumerable opportunities for walking and fishing.

Make sure you get a copy of *Jasons Pacific Coast Highway Touring Guide* (www.jasons.com), free from visitor centers throughout the North Island. As well as providing a detailed, very readable map, it illustrates highlights along the way.

The route is also a genuine cultural experience. Many of the larger bays are centers of Maori settlements, usually surrounding their home *marae*. At **Te Kaha,** the Tukaki meetinghouse in the marae has an elaborately carved lintel, which you can view by asking permission. **Whangaparaoa** is where the great migration canoe *Tainui* landed, and Potaka is the northern boundary of the Ngati Porou tribe. Hicks Bay, not quite midway, has marvelous views and the **Tuwhakairiora meetinghouse ★★,** one of the finest examples of carving on the cape. The carving was carried out in 1872 and is dedicated to local members of Ngati Porou who died in overseas wars. Turn left at the general store to reach the meetinghouse.

Sunrise at Mount Hikurangi

At 1,839m (6,032 ft.), Mount Hikurangi is the first point on mainland New Zealand to see the sunrise each day. At the summit are nine carved sculptures. A walking track to the top crosses private property, but because it is sacred to the Maori, you must gain permission from **Te Runanga o Ngati Porou,** who have offices in Ruatoria (✆ **06/864-8660;** www.ngatiporou.com). An excellent alpine hut on the higher reaches allows early-morning climbs to see the sunrise. Hut fees are NZ$5 per person; bookings are essential. It's best to take the Ngati Porou 4WD tour with tourism coordinator, Paora Brooking, to see the magnificent carvings on top of the mountain. He will give you a unique perspective into this mystical place.

Not far from Hicks Bay, the road descends to sea level and follows a narrow bay to **Te Araroa.** Here you'll find the country's oldest (600 years) and largest pohutukawa tree and a wealth of Maori history. A 20-minute side trip from here will bring you to the picture-book vista of the historic **East Cape Lighthouse ★★**. The track to the 1906 lighthouse must be covered on foot; it leads up 700 steps.

The next settlement is Tikitiki, where the historic **St. Mary's Church ★★★**, stands like a sentinel above the road. Built as a memorial to Ngati Porou soldiers who died in World War I, it is one of New Zealand's most ornate Maori churches. It should not be missed—the interior craftsmanship is breathtaking.

Next stop, just a short diversion off the main road, is **Ruatoria,** the center of Ngati Porou. Although scattered around the country, they compose New Zealand's second-largest Maori tribe. For more information on the local Ngati Porou tribe, check out the website www.ngatiporou.com. It lists a network of indigenous tour operators on the east coast, from Gisborne north to Potaka, who are committed to providing authentic, culturally appropriate experiences, which can include stays at a *marae.*

There are four *marae* at **Tokomaru Bay ★★**, plus a glorious sweep of beach and a selection of interesting old buildings. Take care when swimming in the ocean here.

The road then leads to **Tolaga Bay ★**, which has one of the longest free-standing jetties in New Zealand, plus, rather unexpectedly, the **Tolaga Bay Cashmere Company ★★**, 31 Solander St. (✆ **06/862-6746;** www.cashmere.co.nz), which produces fine merino, cashmere, and silk knitwear. The company's high-fashion garments are renowned throughout Australasia. This shop, which specializes in wholesale prices and seconds, is open in summer Monday through Friday from 9am to 4pm, and Saturday from 10am to 3pm. It is closed on winter weekends. Tolaga Bay is 54km (33 miles) north of Gisborne.

The **Ernest Reeve Walkway ★**, at the northern end of Tolaga Bay, leads to a lookout on the cliffs, overlooking the bay. The stunning views are worth capturing on film. Allow an hour for the roundtrip walk.

Outdoor Pursuits

BEACHES Gisborne has three major swimming beaches, **Midway, Waikanae,** and **Wainui.** Lifeguards patrol all three in season. **Kaiaua Beach,** 60km (37 miles) north of Gisborne and 6km (3¾ miles) off State Highway 35, is good for fishing, swimming, and picnicking. **Anaura Bay,** 77km (48 miles) north of Gisborne and 6km (3¾ miles) off State Highway 35, was Captain Cook's second landing spot in

New Zealand. It has a beautiful beach of unspoiled golden sand, offering safe swimming and good fishing. A 3.5km (2-mile) bush walk gives lovely scenic views; allow 2½ hours. You can make *marae* visits here; there is also a motor camp.

FISHING   In this area, you can do anything from freshwater fly-fishing for brown trout to game fishing for marlin in the Pacific. For the independent angler, the Pacific Coast Highway is the ultimate route for surf-casting, game fishing, and diving. Local knowledge is plentiful, and visitors can take a shortcut to success by contacting local fishing clubs or taking advantage of guides and charter services. Saltwater fishing does not require a license. The Motu, Waioeka, Hangaroa, and Ruakituri rivers offer some of the finest freshwater fishing. Licenses are required for all freshwater fisheries. **Surfit Enterprises,** 48 Awapuni Rd., Gisborne (✆ 06/867-2970; www.surfit. co.nz), offers a 7-hour fishing trip for NZ$150 per person. Their saltwater fly-fishing excursions are priced on request. For more information, call **Fish & Game New Zealand's Trout Line** (✆ 0800/876-885 in NZ; www.fishandgame.org.nz), the **Gisborne Fishery Office** (call ✆ 06/868-7160), or visit the New Zealand Ministry of Fishes online at www.fish.govt.nz.

GOLF   **Poverty Bay Golf Club,** Awapuni and Lytton roads, Gisborne (✆ 06/867-4402; www.gisbornegolf.co.nz), is one of the top 10 18-hole courses in the country. Fees are NZ$45 for 18 holes, NZ$30 for 9 holes; there's a pro shop on-site.

HORSE TREKKING   One of the best horse-trekking operations around is **Eastender Horse Treks,** 876A Rangitukia Rd., Tikitiki (✆/fax 06/864-3033; www. eastenderhorsetreks.co.nz), located near the top of East Cape. Their treks take you over beaches and through native bush and farmland and cost NZ$85 per person. They also offer backpacker accommodations (✆ 06/864-3820) for NZ$25 per person, cabins for NZ$60 double, and camping sites for NZ$10 per person per night.

SNORKELING WITH SHARKS   Get face to face with mako sharks—from the safety of a cage, of course. **Surfit Shark Cage Experience ★★★**, 48 Awapuni Rd., Gisborne (✆ 06/867-2970; www.surfit.co.nz), will take you out into reef waters teeming with the marine predators from November to April. The 5-hour experience costs NZ$310, which seems like a lot of money to terrify yourself—but think of the stories you can tell afterward. Spectators pay NZ$150. **Dive Tatapouri ★★★**, State Highway 35, Tatapouri (✆ 06/868-5153; www.divetatapouri.com), offers shark cage diving for NZ$300, and if you join their Reef Experience (NZ$40 adults, NZ$20 ages 5–15), you can see guides feeding and interacting with wild stingrays, eagle rays, and other reef dwellers. Waders are provided.

SURFING   The popular surf beaches are **Makorori Point ★★**, **Pouawa, Sponge Bay,** and **Kaiaua. Midway Beach** has the famous Gisborne pipe, known for its deep barrel rides, and **Waikanae** and **Wainui beaches** are also good for surfing and bodyboarding. **Kaiti Beach,** around the Gisborne Port and harbor area, offers excellent sailboarding and yachting. The visitor center staff will point you in the direction of numerous other surf breaks.

SWIMMING   **Gisborne Olympic Pool Complex,** Centennial Marine Drive (✆ 06/867-6220; fax 06/867-4953), is open daily from 6am to 8pm. It has indoor and outdoor pools, a dive pool, a Jacuzzi and therapy pool, a 98m (320-ft.) hydroslide, and a toddlers' pool.

WALKING   Good walking abounds in this area. For an easy amble, pick up the free brochure *Gisborne, An Historic Walk,* which leads around the inner city on a 1- to

3-hour wander. *Walks of the Eastland Region* (available at the visitor center), is a more comprehensive appraisal of excellent walks in the whole region. Serious trampers who want to investigate the wilderness areas of the remote **Te Urewera National Park** should contact the Department of Conservation, Aniwaniwa Visitor Centre, Private Bag, Wairoa (✆ **06/837-3803**). Apart from the famous multiday Lake Waikaremoana Great Walk, there are at least 15 short and day walks in this area.

Where to Stay

IN GISBORNE

Knapdale Eco Lodge ★★, 114 Snowsill Rd., Waihirere, Gisborne (www.knapdale. co.nz; ✆ **06/862-5444**), puts the emphasis on tranquillity and environmentalism. Set on a farm with a wide variety of animals and a farm forestry project, Kees and Kay Weytmans have two rooms priced at NZ$398 to NZ$472. The property has a Qualmark Enviro-Gold rating and along with solar heating, they grow all their own produce and also supply Gisborne Farmers' Market. If you'd like a beachfront stay, **Absolute Wainui B&B ★**, 69 Wairere Rd., Wainui Beach (www.absolutewainui. com; ✆ **06/867-0386**), has two very nice rooms (single-party bookings only) just 5 minutes' drive from Gisborne; they cost NZ$260 to NZ$400. If you prefer a more traditional inner city stay, head for **Te Kura B&B,** 14 Cheeseman Rd. (www.tekura. co.nz; ✆ **06/863-3497**), where Paul and Bronwyn Fenwick have two modest rooms in a lovely Arts and Crafts house for NZ$120 to NZ$140. One room is en suite and one has a private bathroom. Budget beds can be found at **Gisborne YHA Hostel,** 32 Harris St. (yha.gisborne@clear.net.nz; ✆ **06/867-3269**), which is close to town and offers 41 dorm beds for NZ$25 to NZ$30. All rates here and below include 15% GST and parking.

Portside Hotel ★★ 🍽 The Portside brings a new level of smart and much-needed apartment-style accommodations to Gisborne. Studio rooms are a little on the small side, but if you opt for the one-bedroom suite, you'll be more than happy. They have bigger kitchens, laundry facilities, and a big corner tub and shower. Two-bedroom suites sleep four, and connecting rooms mean flexibility. Prices are unbelievably good. The only downside is the lack of a restaurant, but there are plenty of choices close by.

2 Reads Quay, Gisborne. www.portsidegisborne.co.nz. ✆ **0800/767-874** in NZ, or 06/869-1000. Fax 06/869-1020. 58 units. NZ$270 guest room; NZ$310 1-bedroom suite; NZ$450 penthouse. Long-stay rates and special breakfast packages. AE, DC, MC, V. Closed Dec 28–Jan 2. **Amenities:** Airport transport (NZ$30); concierge; nearby golf course; very small gym; outdoor lit pool; Wi-Fi in lobby. *In room:* A/C, TV/DVD, fridge, hair dryer, kitchen or kitchenette, minibar, Internet.

AROUND EAST CAPE

I'm happy to report that the availability of accommodations around East Cape has improved greatly in recent years, which means you no longer have to rush around this spectacular knob of land in 1 day. At Te Kaha, 70km (43 miles) from Opotiki, you'll find the new **Te Kaha Beach Resort ★★**, State Highway 35, Te Kaha (www. tekahabeachresort.co.nz; ✆ **07/325-2830**), which has 24 rooms on a spectacular site overlooking the bay, for NZ$160 to NZ$325. They have a pool and a restaurant on-site. Thirty kilometers farther on, you'll find **Stollies ★**, State Highway 35, Waihau Bay (www.holidayhomes.co.nz; ✆ **07/325-3603**), which is a very nice new home with two guest rooms in a seaside suite and meals by arrangement. At the top of the Cape you'll find the much more modest **Hicks Bay Motor Lodge,** State Highway 35, Hicks Bay (www.hicksbaymotel.co.nz; ✆ **06/864-4880**), which has 40 very dated rooms in need of work from NZ$120 to NZ$150. Its singular advantage is that it is cheap and almost exactly halfway between Opotiki and Gisborne. And, saving the best till last—don't go past **Rangimarie Beachstay ★★**, 930 Anaura Rd., Anaura Bay (www.anaura-stay.co.nz; **✆ 021/633-372**), which is situated above one of the cape's loveliest golden sand beaches. They have a romantic self-contained cottage for NZ$220 a night, a suite for NZ$200, a loft bedroom with private bathroom for NZ$200, and a fourth room (with private bathroom) for NZ$175. There are no restaurants in the bay (which is 67km/42 miles north of Gisborne), but hosts David and Judy Newell are happy to provide meals by arrangement.

Where to Eat

Gisborne eateries in general could do with a little service shake-up but it is often difficult to get well-trained staff in a faraway place like Gisborne. You certainly won't go hungry—it just may lack a little finesse. That said, there are one or two gems. **La Quay,** 6 Reads Quay (**✆ 06/868-7578**), is slightly voluminous and lacking character, but I mention it here because this new cafe with a small delicatessen is handily located beside Portside Hotel. I enjoyed very good coffee here. And you'll seldom leave **The Fettuccine Brothers,** 12–14 Peel St. (**✆ 06/868-5700**), hungry. They're a reliable Italian-inspired local favorite and they have an extensive pasta takeaway menu too. They're open Monday through Saturday from 4:30pm.

Bookshop Café ★★★ CAFE   The place's own billing says it all—"Serious food and serious coffee." Located above Muir's Bookshop, with plenty of good books and magazines to browse, it has fabulous counter food, a delightful little balcony overlooking the main street, and the best coffee in Gisborne. Perfect for a light lunch.

62 Gladstone Rd. **✆ 06/869-0653.** Main courses NZ$12–NZ$20. AE, MC, V. Mon–Fri 8:30am–4pm; Sat–Sun 9:30am–3pm.

The Marina Restaurant ★★★ INTERNATIONAL   This is Gisborne's top dining experience. Located in the historic Lysnar Ballroom in a wonderful old colonial building on the waterfront, it boasts an elegant interior and a menu that includes culinary treats like seafood tagliatelle: sautéed prawns, fish, and calamari flambéed in Cognac and served with homemade pasta.

1 Vogel St., Marine Parade. **✆ 06/868-5919.** www.marinarestaurant.co.nz. Main courses NZ$30–NZ$38. AE, DC, MC, V. Reservations required. Thurs–Sat noon–3pm; Tues–Sat 6pm–late.

Ruba ★★ CAFE   In the grand old Union Steamship Company building, this hidden-away treat is worth seeking out. It serves terrific breakfasts, excellent coffee, and a lunch menu that's more creative and adventurous than what you'll find at some of the town's bigger eateries. A long pine table covered in magazines sets the casual mood. You won't regret a visit.

14 Childers Rd. **✆ 06/868-6516.** Main courses NZ$15–NZ$22. AE, MC, V. Mon–Sat 7am–4pm; Sun 9am–3pm.

Soho Restaurant & Bar ★ PACIFIC RIM   You'll find a little of the big city mood at this relaxed restaurant and bar but if you're in for dinner, keep in mind that live music or DJs kick into action after 9pm. It's a good place to sample local wine with tapas, or a light meal. The dinner menu also features big Asian or seafood platters for two, along with more standard mains centered on lamb, beef, chicken, and seafood.

2 Crawford Rd., Wharfside. **✆ 06/868-3888.** www.sohobar.co.nz. Main courses NZ$30–NZ$34, tapas NZ$18–NZ$20, platters NZ$35–NZ$55. Reservations recommended. Wed–Sun 11am–late.

Verve Café ★ CAFE/INTERNATIONAL Not only is this one of those refreshingly scruffy local haunts that abounds in personality, but it's also a three-time winner of the Regional Best Café award. It comes minus pretensions, and you'll find an incredibly mixed crowd enjoying the excellent coffee and simple food. It's especially popular with backpackers and surfers, but all ages congregate here. The menu includes everything from antipasto platters and nachos to pastas, curries, salads, and preparations of fish, lamb, beef, and chicken. This is Gisborne at its laid-back best. You won't leave hungry, and you will have tasted the local culture. They also have live music every Friday night and Internet service.

121 Gladstone Rd. © **06/868-9095.** Reservations recommended for dinner. Main courses NZ$12–NZ$26. AE, MC, V. Mon–Sat 8:30am–10pm; Sun 8:30am–3pm.

The Wharf Café, Bar & Restaurant PACIFIC RIM The location is unbeatable, but sadly, the food and service don't always live up to the hype. The menu reads well—braised lamb shank, beef and lentil curry, salmon with lemon-scented rice—so I think it's worth a shot. If you don't stay for dinner, it is a perfect spot for a quiet drink and a snack beside the water.

60 The Esplanade, Shed No. 1, The Wharf. © **06/868-4876.** www.wharfbar.co.nz. Reservations recommended. Main courses NZ$29–NZ$35. AE, DC, MC, V. Mon–Sat 8am–late, Sun 9am–3pm. Closed Dec 25–26.

En Route to Napier

The 216km (134-mile) drive along State Highway 2 from Gisborne to Napier passes through a wealth of picturesque natural scenery: rugged high-country sheep stations, lush native bush, Lake Tutira, and a breathtaking view of Poverty Bay from the top of the Wharerata Hills, 37km (23 miles) outside the city. Between Poverty and Hawke's bays, **Morere Hot Springs Scenic Reserve ★** (© **06/837-8856;** www.morere hotsprings.com) is signposted on the highway. It makes a nice stop-off point for a bush walk—there are six tracks, which take from 10 minutes to 2½ hours round-trip—a picnic, or a soak in the pools (both thermal and cold). Admission to the public pools is NZ$6 for adults, NZ$3 for children; private pools cost NZ$3 extra per person for a 30-minute soak. The bush walk costs NZ$6 for adults, NZ$3 for kids. The Reserve is open daily 10am to 9pm (till 5pm in winter); there's a cafe onsite.

HAWKE'S BAY ★★★

216km (134 miles) SW of Gisborne; 423km (262 miles) SE of Auckland; 228km (141 miles) SE of Rotorua

Napier is bursting at the seams with pride, and so it should be: It is the prettiest little city in New Zealand. It boasts an unbeatable combination of fabulous climate, elegant Art Deco architecture, as much award-winning wine as anyone could want, plus sea, surf, and pretty vineyards—and, combined with Hastings and Havelock North, the best selection of unique boutique accommodations in the country. A wealth of unexpected surprises awaits—it's one of my favorite places.

It hasn't always been this good. In 1931, a massive earthquake demolished the whole of Napier and nearby Hastings, killing hundreds of people. But like the phoenix, Napier rose again, this time on new ground lifted out of the harbor by the force of the earthquake. Rebuilt during the Depression, the town opted for the Art Deco and Spanish mission architecture so popular at the time. As a result, Napier (pop. 58,600) easily claims one of the world's largest collections of buildings in these styles.

Hastings (pop. 67,428) is something of a nonentity by comparison, though it does have some fine Spanish mission architecture, plus Te Mata Peak, with the best views in the district, and it's closest to the famous gannet colonies. It also has excellent wineries and some great accommodations.

Havelock North (pop. 8,507) is a genteel community surrounded by wineries, farms, and fruit orchards. It boasts some of the best-regarded private schools and some of the oldest commercial wine cellars in the country.

Essentials

GETTING THERE & GETTING AROUND **By Plane** **Air New Zealand** (✆ **06/833-5400**) provides daily service between Napier/Hastings and Auckland, Wellington, and Christchurch, with connections to other key centers. The airport is a 5-minute drive from Napier City and a 20-minute drive from Hastings. Shuttle service (✆ **06/879-9766**) into Napier costs NZ$30.

By Coach (Bus) **InterCity** (✆ **09/623-1503**) and **Newmans** (✆ **09/623-1504**) provide daily bus service between Napier/Hastings and Auckland, Gisborne, Rotorua, Taupo, Tauranga, and Wellington. **Magic Travellers** (✆ **09/358-5600**) and **Kiwi Experience** (✆ **09/366-9830**) both include Napier/Hastings on their routes. There is no bus terminal but most national services like InterCity depart from either the i-SITE Visitor Centre, or 120 Dalton St., near the Police Station. **GoBus** (✆ **06/833-8032;** www.gobus.co.nz or www.hbrc.govt.nz) operates the urban **goBay** services. A goBay Smartcard can be purchased on the bus for NZ$17 and topped up in lots of NZ$10. Most standard fares range from NZ$3 to NZ$4.50 for adults, NZ$1.50 to NZ$2.50 for children ages 5 to 14.

By Car An extensive highway system links the region to key North Island cities: Wellington on State Highway 2; Rotorua/Taupo on State Highway 5; Gisborne on State Highway 2; and Auckland via Taupo on State Highway 1 and State Highway 5. The drive from Auckland is 5 hours; from Wellington, 4 hours; from Rotorua, 2½ hours; from Gisborne, 2 hours; and from Taupo, 1½ hours. Three excellent, free touring guides cover this area: *Pacific Coast Highway* (www.pacificcoast.co.nz), *Thermal Explorer Highway,* and the *Classic New Zealand Wine Trail* (www.classicwinetrail. co.nz). Pick up copies at any visitor center.

By Taxi A **Napier Taxis** (✆ **06/835-7777**) stand is at 29 Clive Square East.

ORIENTATION The pride of Napier is **Marine Parade,** a beautiful stretch of waterfront lined with stately Norfolk pines. **Kennedy Road,** the main thoroughfare, diagonally bisects the town. The fishing wharf suburb of **Ahuriri,** around **Bluff Hill,** is home to nice shops and restaurants. The best beach is **Westshore Beach** in Westshore Domain, part of the new-land legacy of the 1931 disaster.

Hastings lies 20 minutes south of Napier, and Havelock North is 5 minutes southeast of Hastings.

VISITOR INFORMATION The **Napier i-SITE Visitor Centre,** 100 Marine Parade, Napier (✆ **0800/847-488** in NZ, or 06/834-1911; fax 06/835-7219; www. visitus.co.nz), is open daily 9am to 5pm (closed Dec 25), with extended hours from December 26 to March 31.

The **Hastings i-SITE Visitor Centre,** Russell Street South & Heretaunga Street East, Hastings (✆ **0800/427-846** in NZ, or 06/873-0080; fax 06/873-5529; www. visithastings.co.nz), is open Monday through Friday from 8:30am to 5pm, Saturday and Sunday from 9am to 3pm, with extended summer hours (closed Dec 25).

For a calendar of events in the area, check www.hawkesbaynz.com.

[FastFACTS] HAWKE'S BAY

The chief **post office** is on Dickens Street, Napier (✆ **06/835-3725**). For Internet access, try **Cybers Internet Café**, 98 Dickens St., Napier (✆ **06/835-0125**), open daily 8:30am to midnight. The **Chemist Shop Napier,** 32 Munroe St. (✆ **06/835-0438**), is open daily 8am to 9pm.

SPECIAL EVENTS   The **Harvest Hawke's Bay Wine and Food Festival** ★★★ (✆ **0508/946-326**; www.harvesthawkesbay.co.nz), during the first week of February, provides an opportunity to sample a wealth of food and wine in one location. The **Art Deco Weekend** ★★★, on the third weekend in February, draws up to 18,000 people for wining, dining, dancing, jazz, vintage cars, and special walks and tours. Most participants dress in 1920s and 1930s fashions. For details, contact the **Art Deco Trust** in Napier (✆ **06/835-0022**; www.artdeconapier.com).

Exploring Hawke's Bay

Napier is the focus of most of the bay's paid attractions, but you'll find the bulk of the wineries in the Hastings/Havelock North area. *Tip:* Get a **4 in 1 Pass** from the visitor center. This gives you entry to four Marine Parade attractions including the National Aquarium, Hawke's Bay Museum & Art Gallery, Ocean Spa, and Par 2 Mini Golf. The pass is also available from any one of the participating attractions.

IN NAPIER

The **National Aquarium of New Zealand** ★★★, Marine Parade (✆ **06/834-1404**; www.nationalaquarium.co.nz), opened in 2002, includes a huge ocean tank with an acrylic tunnel, plus themed exhibits. Napier opened the first public aquarium in New Zealand in 1956, and it now holds the most comprehensive collection. It's as close to the ocean as you can get without getting your feet wet, and the themed sleepovers for children and the interactive displays are a big hit.

The aquarium's magnificent architecture imitates the form of a stingray. Exhibits include tuatara, kiwi, piranha, crocodile, and every sea creature you could imagine. Kids have lots of hands-on activities, and feeding times (the reef tank at 10am, the ocean tank at 2pm) are always exciting. Allow 1 to 2 hours for a good visit. Admission costs NZ$17 for adults, NZ$8.70 for children 3 to 14, and NZ$44 for families. Swimming with Sharks (9am, 11am, and 3pm) costs NZ$60 per person and children under 15 must be accompanied by a paying adult. The Behind the Scenes Tour runs twice daily at 9am and 1pm and costs NZ$35 for adults, NZ$18 for children ages 3 to 14, and includes the price of aquarium admission. The aquarium is open daily 9am until 5pm (till 7pm Dec 26–31); closed on Christmas Day.

 Classy Crafts

Statements Gallery ★★★, Tennyson and Hastings streets, Napier (✆ **06/834-1331**; www.statementsgallery.co.nz), is one of my favorite places for finding that extra-special piece of colorful New Zealand art glass, beautiful handcrafted New Zealand jewelry, and ceramics you'll want to take home. It also stocks paintings, prints, and sculptures.

Outdoor Movies

Black Barn Vineyards Amphitheatre ★★★, Black Barn Road, Havelock North (📞 **06/877-7985;** www.blackbarn.com), is one of the best outdoor venues in the country; if you time it right (ring for the program), you could enjoy a fabulous live concert or an evening of open-air cinema. Sit on grass terraces surrounded by grapevines and enjoy one of your most memorable New Zealand nights. Book *early.*

The Museums   Chief among local museum attractions is **Hawke's Bay Museum & Art Gallery ★★**, 65 Marine Parade (📞 **06/835-7781;** www.hbmag.co.nz), a museum focused on the stories, heritage, art, and artifacts of New Zealand. At press time, however, the museum was closed for an NZ$80-million redevelopment; it is expected to reopen in 2013. You can check progress on their website.

For something a bit different, look into the **British Car Museum,** 63 East Rd., Haumoana (📞 **06/875-0561** or 025/231-3916; www.britishcarmuseum.co.nz), which parades more than 300 cars, trucks, petrol pumps, and other motoring memorabilia. It's open daily from 9am to 4pm and by appointment. Admission is NZ$10 for adults, NZ$3 for children under 13; credit cards not accepted.

Not quite a museum, but almost, is **Trainworld and Lilliput,** 88 Dickens St., Napier (📞 **06/835-8045**). Up to 37 miniature trains operate on 800m (2,625 ft.) of track in one of the world's largest 00-gauge model railways. It's open daily in summer from 10am to 4pm with reduced winter hours; admission is NZ$10 for adults, NZ$5 for children, and NZ$25 for families.

An Art Deco Amble   The city of Napier is virtually a museum of Art Deco and Spanish mission architecture, built from 1931 to 1933, after the earthquake. Some 80 years later, the buildings are remarkably unchanged. A map outlining a 1½- to 2-hour self-guided walk through the downtown area and another showing a more extensive scenic drive are available for NZ$5 each at the visitor center and at the **Art Deco Shop ★★**, 163 Tennyson St. (📞 **06/835-0022;** www.artdeconapier.com), which is open daily from 9am to 5pm (closed Dec 25), and is stocked with a wide range of brochures and terrific Art Deco gifts.

Guided walking tours ★★ run all year. Bookings are not necessary; just go to the Art Deco Shop and inquire about the next tour. The 1-hour **Morning Walk** leaves from the visitor center daily at 10am (except Dec 25). It includes an Art Deco booklet and ends at the Art Deco Shop, where you can watch a video. This walk is NZ$16 for adults, free for children ages 5 to 15. The **Afternoon Walk** begins at the Art Deco Shop at 2pm, daily from October through June and on Wednesday, Saturday, and Sunday from July to September. The 2-hour program includes an introductory slide presentation, an Art Deco booklet, and a 1½-hour walk. The cost is NZ$21 for adults. A 1-hour vintage car tour of Art Deco landmarks in a 1934 Buick costs NZ$140, maximum three people. Ask about the **Evening Walk** (NZ$20) and the **Deco Bus Tour** (NZ$40). You'll find more Art Deco and a whole cluster of boutique stores, restaurants, cafes, and accommodations over at the portside village of Ahuriri (www.ahuriri.co.nz). Just follow Marine Parade around past the port and follow the signs. The visitor center also has an Ahuriri brochure detailing businesses and attractions. If you'd like to explore the Spanish Mission architecture of Hastings, take the

9

GISBORNE & HAWKE'S BAY

Hawke's Bay

A TASTE OF THE wineries

Hawke's Bay is home to New Zealand's oldest winemaking establishments, and with over 40 wineries to choose from, you're bound to find a glass of something pleasing. The conditions are ideal for late-maturing varieties such as cabernet sauvignon and Riesling. Chardonnay, sauvignon blanc, and sweet dessert wines from this area are also prized. Most wineries are open daily, with free tours, tastings, and sales. At least 10 also feature restaurants. Make sure you pick up the free *Hawke's Bay Winery Guide* and map from the visitor center. New vineyards and wineries are opening all the time; or carry a copy of the *Classic New Zealand Wine Trail.*

Craggy Range Winery ★★★, 253 Waimarama Rd., Havelock North (✆ **06/873-7126;** www.craggyrange. com), opened in 2003. It's the brainchild of Americans Terry and Mary Peabody and is already producing excellent chardonnay, sauvignon blanc, and merlot. **Te Mata Estate,** 349 Te Mata Rd., Havelock North (✆ **06/877-4399;** www.temata. co.nz), has been erected in stages since 1870. It's been voted New Zealand's top winery. **Trinity Hill ★**, 2396 Hwy. 50, Hastings (✆ **06/879-7778;** www.trinity hill.com), is a modern winery with picnic hamper–style food available during the summer. It has a bent toward chardonnay and bordeaux-style reds. **Te Awa Winery ★★**, 2375 Hwy. 50, Hastings (✆ **06/879-7602;** www.teawa.com), produces bordeaux-style reds and top-label chardonnay and has one of the best winery restaurants, serving great lunches daily.

Vidal Wines ★★★, 913 St. Aubyn St. E., Hastings (✆ **06/876-8105;**

www.vidal.co.nz), was founded in 1905 and produces many prizewinning wines. Its popular restaurant is open for lunch and dinner daily and is consistently rated one of the best. **Alpha Domus ★★**, 1829 Maraekakaho Rd., Hastings (✆ **06/879-6752;** www.alphadomus.co.nz), is a tiny boutique operation that makes outstanding bordeaux-style reds. **Clearview Estate ★★**, 194 Clifton Rd., Te Awanga, RD2, Hastings (✆ **06/875-0150;** www. clearviewestate.co.nz), has a very pretty lunch restaurant. Its blissful seaside location among grapevines and olive and avocado trees makes it a winner. **Brookfields Vineyards & Restaurant,** Brookfields Road, Meeanee, Taradale, Napier (✆ **06/834-4615;** www.brook fieldsvineyards.co.nz), is another popular restaurant and vineyard setting closer to town. Brookfields' wines are fruit driven and age well.

Mission Estate Winery, 198 Church Rd., Taradale, Napier (✆ **06/845-9350;** www.missionestate.co.nz), was founded by the Catholic Society of Mary in 1851. You can dine in the historic seminary building Monday through Saturday nights. **Church Road Winery ★**, 150 Church Rd., Taradale, Napier (✆ **06/ 845-9137;** www.churchroad.co.nz), is another of the older wineries. Established in the late 1890s, it contains the first wine museum in New Zealand. It also stages summer concerts; a restaurant serves daily lunches. **Sacred Hill Winery ★★**, 1033 Dartmoor Rd., Puket-apu, Napier (✆ **06/844-0138;** www. sacredhill.com), occupies a divine hilltop setting and serves outdoor summer lunches on weekends from November to

1-hour guided walking tour that leaves from the Hastings i-SITE Visitor Centre every Saturday at 11am from October through May (or by appointment). It costs NZ$12 per person. You can book at the visitor center, or just show up on the day.

Easter. **Elephant Hill Estate & Winery** ★★★, 86 Clifton Hill, Te Awanga (ⓒ 06/873-0400; www.elephanthill.co.nz), produces premium single-estate wine and has a remarkable, architecturally designed winery building in copper and glass that includes a world-class restaurant.

A TOTAL WINE & FOOD DESTINATION If you have a weakness for fine food and fine wines, you must visit **Sileni Estates Winery & Epicurean Centre** ★★★, Maraekakaho Road, Hastings (ⓒ 06/879-8768; www.sileni.co.nz). You'll find a divine little gourmet-food store, the wine cellar, and more, all in a striking piece of architecture set among vineyards. The center is open daily from 10am to 5pm (4pm in winter). A 1-hour Vineyard & Winery Tour & Tasting operates daily at 11am and 2pm by appointment only, and costs NZ$15 to NZ$17 per person. They have additional tours that include cheese tasting and a tour of the Village Press Olive Oil press house and Sileni's own olive groves. If you don't have time to visit the wineries, check out the shelves at **Advintage,** 4 Donnelly St., Havelock North (ⓒ 0800/111-660; www.advintage.co.nz), where they are bursting with a huge range of New Zealand and international wines, with special deals galore. The shop is open Monday through Friday from 9am to 6pm, and Saturday 10am to 5pm.

WINE TOURS One of the most down-to-earth and personalized tours is with **Grant Petherick Exclusive Wine Tours** ★★, 805 Fitzroy Ave., Hastings (ⓒ/fax 06/876-7467; www.flyfishingwinetours.co.nz). He takes two to six people at a time, and everyone raves about him. Tours cost NZ$120 per person per hour. **Grape Escape** (ⓒ 0800/100-489 in NZ; www.grapeescape.co.nz) puts you in the capable and experienced hands of Greg Beachen. His afternoon wine tour (1–5pm) takes in four to five wineries and costs NZ$85. His Foodie Tour is NZ$95 per person.

If you feel like exercising, call **On Yer Bike Winery Tours** ★★★, 121 Rosser Rd., Hastings (ⓒ 06/879-8735; www.onyerbikehb.co.nz). Its flat-terrain tours are suitable for anyone and cycle past olive groves, orchards, ostrich farms, and horse studs (in addition to seven of the better Hastings wineries), giving you a back-road view of this charming region. You have a choice of rickshaws, tandem cycles, or mountain bikes; the tour team will collect any wine you purchase along the way. Tours are NZ$60 per person (some wineries may charge an additional tasting fee), and you should allow up to 5 hours. If you don't have time for a winery tour, head downtown to the **New Zealand Wine Centre** ★★, AMP Building, 1 Shakespeare Rd., Napier (ⓒ 06/835-5326; www.nzwinecentre.co.nz), which features red and white aroma awareness rooms, cellar door wine sales, and the Big Picture Wine Theatre, where you can meet six local winemakers (on film) and taste their wines. It's open daily from 10am to 8pm and the full wine experience with tasting costs NZ$29 per person (NZ$15 for nondrinkers).

IN HASTINGS

The **Hawke's Bay Exhibition Centre,** 201 Eastbourne St. East (ⓒ/fax 06/876-2077; hbec@inhb.co.nz), is the region's major venue for touring exhibits of paintings, sculpture, crafts, and historical material. It has a cafe and a shop specializing in local crafts. The center is open Monday through Friday from 10am to 4:30pm; Saturday, Sunday, and holidays from 11am to 4pm (closed Dec 25). Be sure to pick up the **Public Artworks** brochure ★★, which details the large number of public sculptures (over a dozen) that have been installed in Hastings and Havelock North as part of an award-winning revitalization program.

Driving to the top of **Te Mata Peak** ★★★, about 11km (7 miles) from Hastings, is a must-do activity. Take Havelock Road to Te Mata Peak, then to Simla Avenue to Te Mata Peak Road, and ascend the 393m (1,289-ft.) peak. On a clear day, the grand limestone ridge between beach and city offers panoramic views across the Ruahine, Kaweka, and Maungaharuru ranges, with the volcano Ruapehu visible in the distance. There are also walking tracks in the forest as you ascend.

Gannet Gazing Australian gannets have been nesting at **Cape Kidnappers** ★★★ since the 1870s, with numbers steadily increasing to around 6,500 pairs. This makes it the largest and most accessible mainland gannet colony in the world. The sanctuary affords stunning views and is open to the public from October to April. The best time to view the birds is from early November to late February. If you want to go it alone, drive 21km (13 miles) south to Clifton Domain; then it's a 2-hour walk along 8km (5 miles) of sandy beach. **Note:** The walk *must* be done at low tide because the high tide rides all the way up to the base of steep cliffs. Be sure to check with the Napier or Hastings visitor centers or with the **Department of Conservation** (✆ **06/834-3111**) about tide times.

There are two main organized tours, which basically differ in the form of transport. **Gannet Safaris Overland,** 396 Clifton Rd., Te Awanga (✆ **0800/427-232** in NZ, or 06/875-0888; www.gannetsafaris.co.nz), offers half-day tours in an air-conditioned coach from September to May; no walking is required. The 3½-hour trip departs daily at 9:30am and 1:30pm and costs NZ$65 for adults, NZ$35 for children age 5 to 15. **Gannet Beach Adventures,** 495 Clifton Rd., Te Awanga (✆ **0800/426-638** in NZ, or 06/875-0898; www.gannets.com), transports you by tractor and trailer for NZ$39 adults, NZ$24 kids 2 to 14. It includes 20 to 30 minutes of walking and lasts 4 hours. Tours operate from October through early May. Bookings are essential for both.

Outdoor Pursuits

BALLOONING   Waft skyward from Hastings with **Early Morning Balloons** (✆/fax **06/879-4229;** www.hotair.co.nz). Flight time is around 1 hour, but allow 4 hours total. Adults fly for NZ$360, kids 10 to 12 for NZ$325; breakfast is included.

CANOEING   **Sail 'n Surf,** Pandora Road and Humber Street, Ahuriri, Napier (✆/fax **06/835-0684**), rents canoes and windsurfers for use in a safe tidal waterway. A single canoe costs NZ$25 for 1 hour.

FISHING   **Grant Petherick Fly Fishing,** 805 Fitzroy Ave., Hastings (✆/fax **06/ 876-7467;** www.flyfishingwinetours.co.nz), caters to anglers of all abilities and offers full- and half-day trips for nymph and dry fly-fishing. He charges NZ$120 per person per hour.

GOLF   The **Napier Golf Club,** Waiohiki, State Highway 50, Taradale, Napier (✆ **06/844-7913**), is an excellent 18-hole course just minutes from the city. Greens fees are NZ$65 for nonaffiliated players. **Cape Kidnappers Golf Course ★★★,** 446 Clifton Rd., Te Awanga (✆ **06/873-1018;** www.capekidnappers.com), is one of the finest courses in the world. You'll pay around NZ$375 for a round.

Where to Stay

Stylish accommodations abound in Hawke's Bay, as a stop at the visitor center will attest. Endless choices include dozens of gorgeous little self-contained cottages, many of them in association with vineyards. Rates below include 15% GST and parking.

IN NAPIER

Summer visitors may well fancy camping in this balmy climate. If so, head straight for **Kennedy Park Top 10 Park ★,** Storkey Street, off Kennedy Road (www. kennedypark.co.nz; ✆ **0800/457-275** in NZ, or 06/843-9126), which has a grand history of treating generations of New Zealanders to a fabulous stay. Set on 2.8 hectares (7 acres) with a pool and a playground, it's a great place for kids. Backpackers will find good digs at **Napier YHA,** 277 Marine Parade (www.yha.co.nz; ✆ **06/835-7039**), just across the road from major attractions and close to town; and you'll find B&B lodgings at **Mon Logis,** 415 Marine Parade, Napier (www.babs.co.nz/monlogis; ✆ **06/835-2125**), which has four upstairs rooms a few minutes' walk from town for

---

 Going Behind Bars

Visit New Zealand's oldest prison with **Napier Prison Tours ★,** 55 Coote Rd., Bluff Hill, Napier (✆ **06/835-9933;** www.napierprison.com), and learn about its 1993 decommissioning and tales of the infamous characters who called it home. Look out for the ghosts and stand in the hanging yard, where people once paid a shilling to watch a hanging take place. Guided tours run daily from 9:30am to 3pm and cost NZ$22 adults, NZ$12 children 12 and under, and NZ$50 to NZ$65 for a family. They also have night tours and self-guided audio tours.

☺ CALLING ALL kids

Treat yourself to a moment's rest by letting the kids loose at **Splash Planet ★★**, Grove Road, Hastings (✆ **06/876-9856;** www.splashplanet.co.nz). The park has everything from go-carts, bumper boats, a pirate ship, and a train to castles, a continuous river-raft ride, an activity pool, a safe toddlers' pool, miniature golf, and more. It's open daily October to April from 10am to 6pm (closed May–Sept). Day Super Pass Admission is NZ$28 for adults, NZ$18 for children for 4 to 13, NZ$95 for families, NZ$5 for spectators, and kids under 3 and seniors free.

In Napier, you'll find lots of fun at **Napier Aquatic Centre,** Maadi Road, Onekawa (✆ **06/834-4150;** www.napier aquatic.co.nz). As well as swimming, you can play volleyball, miniature golf, touch rugby, and basketball. It's open daily from 6am to 9pm. For more watery fun, visit **Ocean Spa Napier ★★★**, 42 Marine Parade, Napier (✆ **06/835-8553**); it features toddler pools, lap pools, sauna and massage facilities, beauty therapy, and a cafe. It's open Monday through Saturday from 6am to 10pm, Sunday 8am to 10pm. Admission starts at NZ$10 for adults, NZ$8 for kids 14 and under, NZ$30 for families. Just down the road, beside the

i-SITE Visitor Centre, is **Par 2 Marine Parade Mini Golf** (✆ **06/834-0248;** www.par2golf.co.nz), where the whole family can join the fun. Admission is NZ$9 adults, NZ$6 kids ages 5 to 15, and NZ$26 for a family. It's open daily in summer from 9am to 7:30pm (9:30am–4:30pm in winter).

Another great place to burn off energy is **Kiwi Adventure Trust ★★★**, 58 West Quay, Ahuriri, Napier (✆ **06/ 834-3500;** www.kiwi-adventure.co.nz). It has climbing walls for beginners to experts and also offers kayak lessons and rentals, plus custom-made adventure trips. It's open Tuesday through Friday from 3 to 9pm, Saturday and Sunday 10am to 6pm. Indoor climbing costs NZ$17 for ages 12 and up, NZ$14 for kids age 7 to 11, and NZ$8 for under 7s. **Haumoana Farmyard Zoo,** 32 East Rd., Haumoana, Hastings (✆ **06/875-0244;** www.farmyardzoo.co.nz), lets kid interact with alpacas, turtles, ostriches, and common farm animals, or take a pony ride. Zoo entry is NZ$10 for adults, NZ$7 for children, and NZ$30 for a family. It's open daily from October through February, from 10am to 5pm weather permitting.

NZ$180 to NZ$240. You'll find bright, airy rooms (NZ$280–NZ$670) at **Scenic Hotel Te Pania,** 45 Marine Parade (www.scenichotels.co.nz; ✆ **0800/696-963** in NZ, or 06/833-7733), which is within walking distance of most shopping.

The County Hotel, 12 Browning St. (www.countyhotel.co.nz; ✆ **0800/843-468** in NZ, or 06/835-7800), is a very English-style boutique hotel in a faithfully restored Edwardian building right in the heart of Napier. It's not especially modern, but there's old-world charm and history here that many enjoy—it's one of only two major buildings that survived that 1931 earthquake. Service is attentive, rooms are good size, there's a library filled with over 1,000 books, and town is just footsteps away. Rates are NZ$375 queen or Jacuzzi room; NZ$395 to NZ$925 suite.

The Master's Lodge ★★ 🏨, 10 Elizabeth Rd., Bluff Hill (www.masterslodge.co.nz; ✆ **06/834-1946**), is a real find, with just two units (NZ$908 includes breakfast). Once owned by tobacco baron Gerhard Husheer (the master), the gracious home has been restored to its original splendor and is now under the ownership of

Larry and Joan Blume—ex–New Yorkers who are among the best hosts I have encountered. The large suites have million-dollar views over the city and bay, and their elegant appointments are faultless. One has a private bathroom, the other an unbelievably stylish en-suite bathroom with an elevated tub. No kids 12 and under.

IN HASTINGS

Glen Aros Country Estate, 1549 Raukawa Rd., Hastings (www.glenaros.com; ℂ **06/874-8885**), is a beautifully restored 1914 country homestead with six big, modern bedrooms for NZ$1,000, breakfast, predinner drinks, and canapés included. It has a peaceful garden setting and four-course meals (NZ$115) which showcase the best Hawke's Bay produce.

The Farm at Cape Kidnappers ★★★ 📷 Like its sister property Kauri Cliffs in Northland, this immaculate property leaves no stone unturned when it comes to comfort, service, and luxury. Every suite opens onto a private porch with panoramic views. If you want everything at your fingertips, opt for a lodge suite. Ridge suites—a short walk from the main lodge—are best if you want more privacy. The Owner's Cottage can be rented as a two-bedroom or four-bedroom cottage. The overall mood is one of chic rural elegance. Golfers will love the Tom Doak–designed golf course, rated the world's 10th best outside the U.S. by *Golf Digest*.

446–448 Clifton Rd., Te Awanga, Cape Kidnappers. www.capekidnappers.com. ℂ **06/875-1900.** Fax 06/875-1901. 22 suites, 1 cottage. Hilltop suite NZ$1,995; lodge or ridge suite NZ$2,775; 4-bedroom owner's cottage NZ$14,375. Off-peak rates. Rates include predinner drinks, gourmet dinner, full breakfast, complimentary minibar (excluding wine and liquor), and full use of lodge facilities excluding golf course. AE, DC, MC, V. Closed June. **Amenities:** Restaurant; bar at clubhouse; airport transport (NZ$150 each way); babysitting (NZ$35 per hour); free use of mountain bikes; concierge; 18-hole golf course; health club and spa; outdoor Jacuzzi in pool complex and 1 at owner's cottage; outdoor heated pool; room service. *In room:* A/C, TV/DVD, fridge, hair dryer, minibar, Wi-Fi.

Millar Road ★★ 👖 Millar Road is the quintessential Hawke's Bay experience, and a glorious hideaway. Perched high above a small vineyard and an adjacent persimmon orchard with views to die for, one large modern home and two plush cottages feature outstanding New Zealand art and design, and hosts Ginny and Jeremy Collinge have a wealth of local knowledge. I fell in love with this peaceful spot, with a pool on site and cottages that provide everything—including fabulous bathrooms.

83 Millar Rd., Hastings. www.millarroad.co.nz. ℂ **06/875-1977.** Fax 06/875-1927. 2 cottages. Haumoana House NZ$950 for 4 people; NZ$600 per cottage; NZ$75 per extra person per night. 2-night minimum. Rates include breakfast provisions. Long-stay and off-peak rates. AE, MC, V. **Amenities:** Bar; babysitting on request; nearby golf course; outdoor pool. *In room:* TV/DVD, CD, fridge, hair dryer, Wi-Fi.

IN HAVELOCK NORTH

This is where you'll find the biggest concentration of fabulous cottage, B&B, and new apartment accommodations. **Black Barn Vineyards ★★★**, Black Barn Road (ℂ **06/877-7985;** www.blackbarn.com), offers the best among them. They include **Summerlee** from NZ$1,650 for three couples; **Rush Cottage** for NZ$400; the **Black Barn** for NZ$675, which sleeps four; and the **River Houses** for NZ$675 to NZ$1,650. All are seriously classy.

Where to Eat

Including the wineries (see "A Taste of the Wineries," p. 236), Hawke's Bay has a number of good restaurants and cafes, but consistency of food and service is often an issue. Wineries are, in the main, concentrated around the Hastings/Havelock North area, while most good restaurants and cafes are in Napier. Of the wineries, **Sileni**

Estate, Clearview, Elephant Hill, and Vidal Estate have excellent restaurants, and Craggy Range Winery's **Terroir** (p. 243) is not to be missed.

IN NAPIER

In addition to the establishments below, you'll eat well at **Provedore ★★**, 60 West Quay, Ahuriri (*© 06/834-0189*), which offers modern New Zealand cuisine with Asian and Mediterranean influences. It's open for lunch and dinner Tuesday through Friday, and from 10am until late on weekends, and is a popular meeting place for artistic locals. For good light meals at reasonable prices, try **Soak ★**, at Ocean Spa Napier, Marine Parade (*© 06/835-7888*), which is open daily from 9am to 9pm. It's a super place overlooking the pools, to enjoy a long, lazy brunch from the casual cafe-style menu, or an evening meal with a great choice of Hawke's Bay wines. **Groove Kitchen Espresso ★★**, 112 Tennyson St., Napier (*© 06/835-8530*; www.groove kitchen.co.nz), is one of the town's better cafes and it's open daily 8am until 2pm Monday through Friday, and 8:30am to 3pm on weekends. It also opens for dinner on Friday and Saturday from 6:30pm until late. Loveable **Ujazi ★★★**, 28 Tennyson St. (*© 06/835-1490*), is all about shabby chic, great food, and excellent value for the money. It's considered *the* place for a hearty brunch, with tables spilling out onto the pavement. It's open daily 8am to 5pm (varies seasonally).

IN HASTINGS

Your best bets in this area are the winery restaurants (see "A Taste of the Wineries," p. 236). **Sileni Estates Restaurant ★★**, 2016 Maraekakaho Rd. (*© 06/879-8768*), is one of the most popular, although it's getting a run for its money from the

---

 Foodie Heaven

A wealth of local gourmet-food producers joined forces to create the **Hawke's Bay Wine Country Food Trail ★★★**. Pick up the free map at the visitor center and make your way to some of the tastiest spots in these parts. The choices are endless—handmade chocolates, breads, olives, wine, ice cream, honey, and more. It all culminates in the **HB Food Group Farmers' Market ★★★**, held at the Hawke's Bay Showgrounds, Kenilworth Road, Hastings (*© 06/877-1001*; www.savour hawkesbay.co.nz), Sundays from 8:30am to 12:30pm, and behind the Daily Telegraph Building, Tennyson Street, Napier, Saturdays from 8:30am to 12:30pm.

The **Village Growers' Market ★★★**, held at the Sun Dial, Black Barn Vineyards, off Te Mata Road, Havelock North (*© 06/877-7985*; www.black barn.com), is a colorful extravaganza of local food products in an idyllic vineyard setting. It's held Saturday mornings from early November through March from 9am to noon. Finish off the morning with a fabulous brunch at Black Barn Bistro (see below).

At **Te Mata Cheese**, 393 Te Mata Rd., Havelock North (*© 06/875-8282*; www.tematacheese.co.nz), you can see how cheese is made and sample their sheep-, cow-, and goat-milk cheeses. Stay on for a glass of wine and a delicious antipasto platter at their Cheese cafe, which is open daily from 10am to 4:30pm.

Finally, ice cream fans shouldn't miss **Rush Munro's Ice Cream Gardens**, 704 Heretaunga St. West, Hastings (*© 06/878-9634*; www.rushmunro.co.nz), which is open in summer Monday through Friday from 11am to 7:30pm, Saturday and Sunday 10am to 7:30pm, and reduced hours in winter.

new and very, very chic **Elephant Hill Estate Winery** ★★★, 86 Clifton Rd., Te Awanga (📞 **06/872-6060;** www.elephanthill.co.nz), which is open daily from 11am to 10pm. Its menu is inspired by contemporary European cuisine using the finest local products. **Vidal Winery Restaurant** ★★, 913 St. Aubyn St. E. (📞 **06/876-8105;** www.vidal.co.nz), gets top votes among the locals for consistently good lunches and dinners. It's open daily from 11:30am to 3pm for lunch and from 6pm for dinner. **Clifton Bay Café** ★★, 468 Clifton Rd. (📞 **06/875-0096**), is out of town on the way to Cape Kidnappers, but it's worth the trip for terrific breakfast and lunch, daily in summer from 10am to 4pm. Another great find is **River Bar Restaurant** ★★, Main Road, State Highway 2, Clive (📞 **06/870-0533;** www.clivehotel.co.nz), which is bound to surprise with the quality of its food and its warm, lively atmosphere. It sits 10 minutes between Hastings and Napier and has a great local wine list. **Opera Kitchen** ★★, 312 Eastbourne St., Hastings (📞 **06/870-6020;** www.operakitchen.co.nz), is a great spot with local food and wine. It's one of the most popular cafes in all of Hawke's Bay—and for good reason—so expect a crowd. It's open 7am to 5pm Monday through Friday and 7am to 4pm on weekends. Coffee fiends will do well to stop at **Bay Espresso,** 141 Karamu Rd., Hastings (📞 **06/876-5682;** www.bayespresso.co.nz), which is just out of the main town. They roast organic and Fair Trade coffee beans and their busy cafe is open from 7am to 4pm Monday through Friday and from 8am to 4pm on weekends.

IN HAVELOCK NORTH
Black Barn Bistro ★★★, Black Barn Road (📞 **06/877-7985;** www.blackbarn.com), is my absolute favorite place—a stylish bistro set among vines, with a gorgeous outdoor courtyard sheltered by overhead vines. It's open for lunch Wednesday through Sunday noon to 3pm. There's no better place to admire the scenery and sample the fruit of the land. **Terroir** ★★★, Craggy Range Winery, 253 Waimarama Rd. (📞 **06/873-0143**), is a big culinary adventure, and the high point of Hawke's Bay dining. Rated one of the top 13 winery restaurants in the world in 2004 by *UK Wine Spectator,* its French-style rustic menu is guaranteed to impress. It's open daily from noon; express dining 3 to 6pm; and dinner from 6pm to late (closed Mon Easter to Labour Weekend [Oct]). The good-value food and lively atmosphere at the **Rose and Shamrock Village Inn,** Napier Road and Porter Drive (📞 **06/877-2999;** www.roseandshamrock.co.nz), styled after an authentic Irish bar, also gets the thumbs up. The nearby **Olive Tree Café,** 7 Joll Rd. (📞 **06/877-0222**), is a simple spot that serves excellent light lunches and delicious counter food daily. **Diva Bar & Bistro,** Village Court, Napier Road (📞 **06/877-5149;** www.divavar.co.nz), serves lunch, light evening meals, and big bar platters with wine sold by the glass. They're open for lunch Tuesday through Friday and dinner Monday through Saturday (from 5:30pm).

Napier After Dark
Shed 2, West Quay, Ahuriri (📞 **06/835-2202;** www.shed2.co.nz), has lots of loud music, a big-screen TV, and good food. It's popular with a young crowd. Next door, there's a more sedate atmosphere in the lounge bar **Caution** ★★ (📞 **06/835-0028;** www.shed2.co.nz), serving cocktails and vintage Hawke's Bay wines. **O'Flaherty's Irish Pub,** Hastings Street, has regular live Irish music and big screens for sports fans. More Irish fun is at **Rosie O'Grady's Irish Bar,** Hastings Street (📞 **06/835-8689;** www.rosieogradys.co.nz). **Churchill's Champagne & Snug**

Bar, in the County Hotel, 12 Browning St. (© **06/835-7800;** www.countyhotel. co.nz), is a small corner bar with over 100 wines and champagnes to choose from.

En Route to New Plymouth

Contrary to expectations you might have of simply driving east to west from Napier to New Plymouth, by far the quickest way is to drive *south* from Napier. Pass through Waipukurau and Dannevirke on State Highway 2, connecting with State Highway 3 at Woodville and traveling on to Palmerston North. Continue on State Highway 3 to Wanganui, and then up to New Plymouth. This 412km (255-mile) trip should take about 5 hours without stops. The roads are excellent, and you'll be driving through prime farmland for most of the journey.

TARANAKI & WANGANUI

Situated between Auckland and Wellington, Taranaki is the westernmost province of the North Island. Its major city is New Plymouth, a busy port on the coast of the Tasman Sea. Taranaki is a leading dairy-farming region, an energy center with major reserves of natural gas and oil, and home to Mount Taranaki. The region is also famous for its lush gardens, beautiful parks, and world-class surf breaks. In 2008, the United Nations–endorsed Liveable Communities Award named New Plymouth the best city of its size in the world, and the city's Coastal Walkway the world's best environmental project.

Southeast of Taranaki is Wanganui, one of the major towns of the area now known as the River Region, which includes the provinces of Manawatu, Horowhenua, Tararua, Whanganui, and Rangitikei. Until recently, Wanganui did not play a significant part in overseas visitors' itineraries, but its leading light—the broody Whanganui River, the longest navigable river in New Zealand—is worth exploring. A number of good outdoor activities center on the river, and the town will give you an idea of the workings of small-town New Zealand.

NEW PLYMOUTH: GATEWAY TO EGMONT NATIONAL PARK

412km (255 miles) W of Napier; 164km (102 miles) NW of Wanganui; 369km (229 miles) SW of Auckland

You get the feeling that being left out on the western tip of the North Island has had benefits for New Plymouth. As if to compensate, residents have surrounded themselves with excellent cultural amenities, stunning gardens, and fabulous nature walks.

Then there are the cows, the milk, the cheese, and the world's biggest dairy factory at nearby Hawera, and some of the prettiest rolling green pasture you'll see anywhere in the country. Above all, literally, is Mount Taranaki, the Fuji-like jewel in the Egmont National Park crown, which attracts hundreds of trampers, mountaineers, rock climbers, and casual walkers. Be prepared to be surprised by this buzzy little city of 72,000 people.

Essentials

GETTING THERE & GETTING AROUND **By Plane** **Air New Zealand Link** provides daily flights from Auckland, Wellington, and Wanganui, with connecting service to other cities. Call ☎ **06/755-2250** for flight information. The New Plymouth Airport is approximately 8km (5 miles) from the city, a 10- to 15-minute drive. **Withers Coachlines** (☎ **06/751-1777**; www.withers.co.nz) provides shuttle service to and from the airport and they're much cheaper than taxis.

By Coach (Bus) **InterCity** (☎ **09/623-1503**) and **Newmans** (☎ **09/623-1504**) provide daily coach service. **Tranzit Coachlines** (☎ **06/765-7127**; www. trc.govt.nz/bus-routes) operates local city buses. Average city fares are NZ$3.50 to NZ$5.50 for adults and NZ$2 to NZ$3.50 for children ages 5 to 15.

By Shuttle A number of different companies, including Withers Coachlines (above), depart New Plymouth daily for the North Egmont Visitor Centre at Egmont National Park, returning to the city in the afternoon. Reservations are essential; the trip costs around NZ$55 to NZ$65 round-trip. **Taranaki Tours** (☎ **0800/886-877**; www.taranakitours.com) charges NZ$55 per person for this service.

By Car New Plymouth is reached on State Highway 3 from Wanganui via Stratford and from the north via Waitara; or on State Highway 45, the coastal highway (commonly called the Surf Highway), via Opunake. If you have plenty of time, enjoy history, and want to see a remote slice of "old New Zealand," take the **Forgotten World Highway 43 ★★★**, which runs between Stratford in Taranaki to Taumarunui in the Ruapehu region. It's about a 3-hour trip. Most i-SITE visitor centers carry the detailed, pictorial brochure of the trip, which includes all highlights along the way. Note that 12km (7½ miles) of the road are still unsealed and there are no petrol stations along the 155km (96-mile) route.

By Taxi Call **New Plymouth Taxis** (☎ **06/757-3000**) or **Energy City Cabs** (☎ **06/757-5580**).

ORIENTATION **Devon Street East** and **Devon Street West** are the main thoroughfares. Running parallel and to the north are the one-way streets **Powderham** and **Courtenay,** and to the west, **Vivian** and **Leach streets.** The main road into the city from the south is **Eliot Street.** Once you've memorized the one-way pattern, it's very easy to find your way around. The small towns of Stratford and Hawera lie to the south of New Plymouth.

VISITOR INFORMATION The **New Plymouth i-SITE Visitor Centre,** Puke Ariki, 65 St. Aubyn St. (☎ **0800/639-759** in NZ, or 06/759-6060; fax 06/759-6073; www.newplymouthnz.com), is open Monday through Friday from 9am to 6pm (Wed until 9pm), and Saturday, Sunday, and holidays from 9am to 5pm (closed Dec 25).

South Taranaki i-SITE Visitor Centre, 55 High St., Hawera (☎ **0800/111-323** in NZ, or 06/278-8599; fax 06/278-6599; www.southtaranaki.com), is open Monday through Friday from 8:30am to 5:15pm, and weekends 9:30am to 4pm, December through April (closed Dec 25); and 10am to 3pm May to November.

SPECIAL EVENTS During October's **Taranaki Rhododendron Festival** (☎ **0800/746-363**; www.rhodo.co.nz), more than 100 private and public gardens open their gates. The **TSB Bank Festival of Lights ★★** (☎ **06/759-6060**; www.festivaloflights.co.nz) takes place in Pukekura Park, nightly from mid-December through early February, weather permitting. **WOMAD** (www.womad.co.nz) is a massive 3-day

Taranaki & the River Region

multicultural festival of world music and dance held in March at Brooklands Park. **Parihaka** (www.parihaka.com) is a 3-day International Peace Festival featuring arts, music, and culture staged on the historic Parihaka Pa in January. Call the visitor center for more events, or check the events calendar on the website.

Exploring the Towns
IN NEW PLYMOUTH

For thought-provoking contemporary art, head for **Govett-Brewster Art Gallery ★★★**, Queen and King streets (© **06/759-6060;** www.govettbrewster. com). You'll find major works by world-renowned, Christchurch-born kinetic artist Len Lye (who spent most of his life in New York), accompanied by an ongoing program of changing exhibitions. They also have a small but excellent gift shop and a very good cafe. The gallery is open daily from 10am to 5pm. Entry is by donation.

The Taranaki Museum underwent massive renovations during 2001–02 and reopened in 2003 as **Puke Ariki ★★★**, 1 Ariki St. (© **06/759-6060;** www.puke ariki.com). The impressive two-wing complex rises up in the heart of the city, a groundbreaking knowledge center that houses the full public library, the museum, and the visitor information center. An air bridge connects the two wings. The museum showcases a major repository of Taranaki history, including many Maori treasures associated with the Taranaki tribes. "Treasures" is the name that encompasses all gallery spaces, each one focusing on different components of the Taranaki experience. Make sure you check out **Taranaki Stories,** which details the region's tumultuous Maori land wars, pioneer history, and current Taranaki life. The complex has two cafes (see "Where to Eat," below) and a large grass park. The museum is open Monday through Friday from 9am to 6pm (Wed until 9pm), and Saturday, Sunday, and holidays from 9am to 5pm (closed Dec 25). Admission is free.

The **TSB Bank Bowls New Zealand Museum,** Dean Park, Brooklands Road (© **06/758-0284;** bowlsnzmuseum@xtra.co.nz), has the well-deserved distinction of being the only lawn-bowling museum in the world—over 8,000 entries on lawn bowling's history. The museum is open by appointment only; call first.

Three beautifully restored historic buildings you can visit are **Richmond Cottage,** Ariki Street; **Te Henui Vicarage,** 290 Courtenay St.; and the **Gables Colonial Hospital,** Brooklands Park Drive. The visitor center can supply details on their hours.

Outdoorsy types might like to cruise the **Sugar Loaf Islands Marine Park,** off the coast of New Plymouth. **Chaddy's Charters,** Ocean View Parade, Moturoa (© **06/758-9133;** fax 06/759-9095; www.chaddyscharters.co.nz), will accommodate you on an English lifeboat. The 1-hour cruise takes you to the cluster of small islands, home to an astoundingly rich plant, bird, and wildlife population. The trip costs NZ$40 for adults, NZ$15 for kids ages 5 to 12. Fishing trips cost NZ$85 per person and require a minimum of six people.

And if you want to explore a quaint slice of rural life, pick up the detailed brochure and map from the visitor center and drive around the little knob of coast, formally State Highway 45, otherwise known as **Surf Highway.** As well as the premier surf spots, you'll find many small towns, access to Egmont National Park walking tracks, and more. The area has suddenly taken off, and a number of excellent new attractions have sprung up. Make sure you pick up the **Oakura Arts Trail** brochure from an information center, if you like to explore local arts and crafts.

IN HAWERA

In Hawera, a 50-minute drive south of New Plymouth, you'll find what is widely acclaimed as the best private museum in New Zealand. The **Tawhiti Museum ★★★**, 401 Ohangai Rd. (℃ **0800/921-921** in NZ; www.tawhiti museum.co.nz), is the brainchild of Nigel and Teresa Ogle. It uses life-size exhibits and scale models—all made by Nigel—to capture the history of South Taranaki. The Tawhiti Bush Railway operates on the first Sunday of each month, weather permitting. The museum, once a cheese factory, is open December 26 through January daily 10am to 4pm; June through August Sunday only 10am to 4pm; the rest of the year Friday through Monday 10am to 4pm. Admission is NZ$12 for adults, NZ$3 for children 5 to 15, and free for children 4 and under. The railway costs NZ$6 for adults, NZ$3 children. The wonderful Traders and Whalers display, showcasing the Taranaki coast from 1820–40, costs NZ$12 for adults and NZ$6 for children. This amazing labor of love has won many separate tourism awards and is definitely worth seeing. You'll find another quirky stop at **KD's Elvis Memorial Record Room,** 51 Argyle St., Hawera (℃ **027/498-2942;** www.digitalus.co.nz/elvis). This is where avid Elvis fan Kevin Wasley displays the astonishing collection of Elvis records and memorabilia that he has been gathering since 1959. It's open by appointment only, so phone first.

Visiting Gardens Galore

The *Taranaki Visitor's Guide,* available free from any of the region's visitor centers, lists 25 public and private gardens that are open to the public. That's just the beginning. **Pukekura Park & Brooklands ★★★**, accessible from Fillis Street, Brooklands Road, or Victoria Road, is a double hit of exquisite parkland that includes walkways, the Brooklands Zoo (daily 9am–5pm), playgrounds, a beautiful fernery (daily 8am–4pm), lakes, fountains, waterfalls, and specialist gardens. It's a free must-visit spot in any season. Between Christmas and February, try to visit the park at night to see the stunning **TSB Bank Festival of Lights ★★**. Also in New Plymouth, the private native garden paradise **Te Kainga Marire,** 15 Spencer Place, New Plymouth (℃ **06/758-8693;** www.tekaingamarire.co.nz), is open daily September through April 9am to 5pm, and costs NZ$10 per person.

The **Pukeiti Rhododendron Trust ★★**, 2290 Carrington Rd., RD4 (℃ **06/765-7127;** www.pukeiti.org.nz), has a world-class collection of rhododendron, azalea, and viraya set in centuries-old rainforest. It's a 30-minute drive from New Plymouth on Carrington Road; open daily 9am to 5pm (closed Dec 25). There is a cafe, shop, and display center, and admission is free. Two more must-see gardens offer free admission. **Tupare,** 487 Mangorei Rd. (℃ **06/765-7127;** www.tupare.info), is open daily from 9am to 8pm in summer and 9am to 5pm in winter. **Hollard Gardens,** 1686 Upper Manaia Rd., Kaponga (℃ **06/765-7127;** www.hollardgardens.info), is open daily from 9am to 8pm in summer, 9am to 5pm in winter. Kaponga, a small rural village, is about 1 hour from New Plymouth. From New Plymouth, head south on State Highway 3 to Stratford and turn right toward Dawson Falls. Turn left just past the village of Mahoe to get to Kaponga. The best time to visit is September through March.

Exploring Egmont National Park

The 33,534-hectare (82,829-acre) area surrounding Mount Taranaki/Mount Egmont was established as Egmont National Park in 1900. Centered on the volcanic cone of Mount Taranaki, with more than 140km (87 miles) of walks and tracks, the area is

New Plymouth & Egmont National Park

made up of subalpine forest, volcanic landforms, mountain streams and waterfalls, rainforest, and alpine herb fields. There are panoramic views of Taranaki province from the summit of the mountain, which is just 30km (19 miles) from New Plymouth.

The North Egmont entrance to the park is a 25-minute drive from New Plymouth; for shuttle transport, see "Essentials," above. The **North Egmont Visitor Centre,** 2879 Egmont Rd., Egmont Village (✆ **06/756-0990;** www.doc.govt.nz), displays geologic and botanic exhibits related to the park. It's open daily in summer from 8am to 4:30pm, and late March to late September Wednesday through Sunday from 9am to 4pm; and there is a small cafe onsite. *Warning:* Mountain weather can be harsh and changeable; care is needed above the tree line at all times. Mount Taranaki may be pretty but it has accounted for more deaths than any other mountain in New Zealand. Always check conditions with the Department of Conservation, Stratford (✆ **06/765-5144**), before a climb or hike.

Major attractions in the park include walking tracks, rock-climbing areas, delightful picnic spots, and waterfalls. The **Maunganui Ski Fields** (✆ **06/756-5493**) are on the Stratford side of the park in the area known as East Egmont. Follow the signs off Pembroke Road in Stratford. The ski area has T-bar and rope tows, a canteen, ski patrol, and instructors. For conditions, call **Snowphone** (✆ **06/767-7669**) or **Metphone** (✆ **0900/999-06;** NZ$1 per minute).

Mt. Taranaki Guided Tours (✆ **027/441-7042,** or 06/765-6234 after hours; www.mttaranakiguidedtours.co.nz), offers 1- to 4-day guided hiking trips up the mountain, with prices starting at NZ$350 per person. If you'd like the local Maori perspective on Mount Taranaki, seek out **Taranaki Tours ★★**, 48 Buller St. (✆ **0800/886-877** in NZ, or 06/757-9888; www.taranakitours.com), whose staff will talk about the spiritual significance of the mountain and the Taranaki Maori land wars. Their 7-hour "Around Mt. Taranaki" tour costs NZ$160 per person and requires a minimum of two people. Make sure you take plenty of warm, waterproof clothing—even in summer!

dawson FALLS

Dawson Falls, off Manaia Road, Kaponga, is well worth a visit. The 17m (54-ft.) falls are just 20 minutes from the parking lot, along a safe and attractive path in the bush. The **Dawson Falls Visitor Centre** (✆ **027/443-0248**) has a public exhibit with information on the history of the mountain and its flora and fauna. The visitor center is open in summer daily from 8:30am to 4:30pm; winter Wednesday through Sunday from 8:30am to 4:30pm. You'll also find a lodge, a waterfall lookout, many walking trails, and picnic areas. The falls are a 1-hour drive from New Plymouth. Head south on State Highway 3 to Stratford and take the signposted right-hand turn to the falls.

If you want to stay on Mount Taranaki, **Rahiri Cottage,** Egmont Road, Inglewood (rahiri@taranaki-bakpak.co. nz; ✆ **06/756-9093;** fax 06/278-6541), is a modest three-bedroom cottage set in Egmont National Park surrounded by native bush. It has two double rooms and one single room for NZ$225, and breakfast costs NZ$25 per person. Part of your rate goes toward kiwi conservation within the national park.

Outdoor Pursuits

FISHING   Ultimate Fishing Adventures (✆ **027/224-9992** or 06/759-2345) will take you game fishing, fresh- or saltwater fly-fishing, bottom fishing, or sea fishing. In summer it also has evening fishing packages. Or try **Taranaki Outdoor Adventures** (✆ **0800/200-625;** www.toa.co.nz), to organize a fishing charter.

GOLF   Taranaki is home to 20 courses, including the **New Plymouth Golf Club Ngamotu Links,** Devon Road, Bell Block (✆ **06/755-1349;** www.newplymouth golf.co.nz). The 18-hole, par-72 championship course is on magnificent parklike grounds and has a pro shop, bar, and restaurant. Greens fees are NZ$60 for nonaffiliated players.

KAYAKING   Canoe and Kayak Taranaki, 631 Devon Rd., New Plymouth (✆ **06/769-5506;** www.canoeandkayak.co.nz), will take you out to the Sugar Loaf Marine Reserve for a close-up look at seals and other marine life; or if you're of a more adventurous bent, they'll lead you to Grade II rapids on the Waitara River.

SURFING   Tara Wave Surf School (✆ **06/752-7474;** tarawave@xtra.co.nz) offers lessons at Oakura, one of the region's safest beaches. All gear is provided. In New Plymouth itself, **Beach Street Surf Shop,** 39 Beach St. (✆ **06/758-0400;** www.taranakisurf.com), is an institution. They'll point you in all the right directions for the best breaks and the best lessons.

SWIMMING   The **New Plymouth Aquatic Centre,** Kawaroa Park (✆ **06/759-6060**), is open Monday through Friday from 6am to 8:30pm, weekends and public holidays from 7am to 7pm (closed Dec 25). It offers a range of heated indoor and outdoor pools, hydroslides, and a steam room. **Taranaki Thermal Spa,** 8 Bonithon Ave. (✆ **06/759-1666;** www.windwand.co.nz/mineralpools), was established in 1914 and now provides a host of modern massage and beauty treatments to follow a hot soak in one of the private or group pools. They are open in summer Monday and Tuesday 9am to 5pm; Wednesday through Friday 9am to 9pm; Saturday noon to 9pm; and Sunday 2 to 8pm (winter hours vary slightly). Private pools cost NZ$40 per couple.

WALKING   A wide range of walks, from easy to energetic, crisscross the New Plymouth area. The visitor center produces an excellent series of foldout pamphlets and maps that highlight the best walks, including a very good *Walk Taranaki* guidebook. Do try and experience at least some of the multi-award-winning **Coastal Walkway ★★★**, which runs 7km (4⅓ miles) from the mouth of the Waiwhakaiho River in the east to Port Taranaki in the west. You'll pass world-class surf beaches, public art, and great seascapes along the way. You can book a mobility scooter (reservations and bond required), which is free between 8am and noon and 1 and 5pm. Contact ✆ **06/759-6060** or www.newplymouthnz.com for details. If you start the walk in the city, look out for Len Lye's magnificent, bending red sculpture, *Wind Wand,* which is clearly visible across the road from Puke Ariki.

Where to Stay

A lot of pleasant things have happened to the Taranaki accommodations scene in recent years, chief among them the addition of the smart offerings described below. **Taranaki Country Lodge ★★**, 169 Hursthouse Rd. (www.taranakicountrylodge. co.nz; ✆ **0800/395-863** in NZ, or 06/755-0274), has two suites set amid rolling Taranaki farmland; you'll pay NZ$200 to NZ$350 per night. Dinner is available on request and Jim and Robyn Hutchinson offer free airport transport and Wi-Fi. Next door to Pukekura Park, you'll find a very nice bed and breakfast stay at **Issey Manor** ★, 32 Carrington St., New Plymouth (www.isseymanor.co.nz; ② **06/758-2375**). Here, four quiet, stylish rooms (two with spa baths) go for NZ$145 to NZ$185; guests have the use of a separate lounge and kitchen and it's just a 5-minute walk to the city.

All rates here and below include the 15% GST and parking.

Nice Hotel & Bistro ★★★   New Plymouth's only small luxury hotel offers stylish rooms with individual charm. You'll find feather duvets, contemporary artwork, and generous bathrooms with double Jacuzzis or massage showers. The hotel is right in the heart of the city and it has a popular restaurant downstairs. The main suite is divine, with its own private lounge, fireplace, and grand piano. It's a cut above the usual hotel room. Its four longer-term "Best Suites" are located next door in an adjacent building; they are self-catering units but guests may also use the restaurant in the main lodge.

71 Brougham St., New Plymouth. www.nicehotel.co.nz. ② **06/758-6423.** Fax 06/758-6433. 8 units. NZ$250 double; NZ$350 suite. Long-stay rates and special deals. AE, DC, MC, V. Head onto Leach St. and turn right onto Brougham. No children 11 and under. **Amenities:** Restaurant and private dining rooms; bar; free use of bikes; several nearby golf courses; gym across the street. *In room:* TV, fridge, hair dryer, minibar, Wi-Fi.

The Waterfront Hotel ★ ✔   Location, location, location—this place has it, right beside the Puke Ariki museum and bustling inner city developments overlooking the ocean. Just 5 years old, the Waterfront has smart, uncluttered rooms (some connecting). Ocean-view units are the most sought after. The three big, one-bedroom apartments have roomy bathrooms, Jacuzzis, leather furniture, modern kitchens, and laundry facilities—and yes, they overlook the ocean. Units on the top two floors of the three-story building have air-conditioning. Crisp design and unbeatable value make the hotel popular with corporate and international travelers.

1 Egmont St., New Plymouth. www.waterfront.co.nz. ② **0508/843-928** in NZ, or 06/769-5301. Fax 06/769 5302. 42 units. NZ$170–NZ$600. MC, V. Long-stay and off-peak rates. **Amenities:** Restaurant; bar; airport transport; babysitting; free membership to town gym; nearby golf courses and tennis courts; room service. *In room:* TV/DVD, fridge, hair dryer, minibar, Wi-Fi.

Where to Eat

Prepare to be surprised by the standard of cuisine in this provincial outback. For a town of its size, it has an unbelievable number of very good eateries. **Andre L'Escargot Restaurant & Bar** ★★, 37–43 Brougham St. (② **06/758-4812;** www.andres.co.nz), is an elegant New Plymouth institution; it's still good dining, but it's now facing some local competition. It's open Monday through Saturday from 5pm until late and offers reliable classics like filet mignon, confit of duck, and venison rump.

   Tables Bistro ★★ at the **Nice Hotel** (② **06/758-6423;** www.nicehotel.co.nz), also gets lots of votes (see "Where to Stay," above). **Café Arborio** ★★, in Puke Ariki (② **06/758-4544**), is an Italian cafe that gets my vote as one of the best in town. It's on the first floor on the North Wing of the museum and library complex and is open 8am to 5pm Monday through Friday and 9am to 4pm in weekends. In the South Wing you'll find a great spot for coffee at **Daily News Café** (② **06/758-4544**), an espresso bar with a great stack of newspapers and magazines to read.

   Another top-quality spot is **Pankawalla** ★★★, 85 Devon St. W. (② **06/758-4444;** www.pankawalla.co.nz), a classy Indian restaurant that you wouldn't normally expect to find in the provinces. It's reasonably priced and is open daily from 6pm. For the best coffee, head straight for **Ozone Bean Store** ★★, 47A King St. (© **06/757-5404;** www.ozonecoffee.co.nz), open daily 8am to 5pm. Another good coffee and light lunch stop is **Chaos Cafe** ★, 36 Brougham St. (© **06/759-8080**), which is enormously popular with locals and always has a lively atmosphere. It's open Monday through Friday from 7:30am to 3:30pm, Saturday 9am to 3pm, Sunday 9:30am until 2pm. **Petit Paris** ★★, 34 Currie St. (© **06/759-0398;** www.petitparis.co.nz), meanwhile, has some of the most decadent French pastries and cakes you'll find anywhere. Red walls and Parisian accents set the mood for a tasty light lunch that can include freshly baked baguettes, quiche, salads, and croissant.

MacFarlanes Caffe, 1 Kelly St., Inglewood (© **06/756-6665**), 20 minutes southeast of New Plymouth, is popular for brunch. It has excellent coffee and a lively nighttime atmosphere on weekends. It's open Sunday through Thursday from 9am to 5pm, Friday and Saturday from 9am to late. To the southwest, **Lahar** ★, 64 Carthew St., Okato (© **06/752-4864**), is a local favorite known for superb coffee and service. It's well worth the 30- to 40-minute drive.

For those in a nocturnal party mood, the moody, contemporary timber interior at **Montrose Wine Bar** ★★, 49–51 Liardet St. (© **06/788-6596**), should set the mood. And **Frederic's** ★, 34 Egmont St. (© **06/759-1227;** www.frederics.co.nz), is a popular haunt for locals. It serves light meals—curries, salads, and the like—and is open daily from 11am until late.

En Route to Wanganui

The 2½-hour drive from New Plymouth to Wanganui goes through some of the best dairy farmland in New Zealand. Regardless of the time of year, the rolling landscape is generally green and lush. You'll pass through the rural towns of Inglewood, Stratford, Hawera, and Waverley before reaching Wanganui.

WANGANUI ★

164km (102 miles) SE of New Plymouth; 141km (87 miles) SW of Tongariro National Park; 193km (120 miles) N of Wellington; 252km (156 miles) SW of Napier

There's tourism potential in Wanganui, and the town has finally become aware of it. In the past few years it has transformed itself from a rather grubby little river town to something much prettier. Now that the inner city has a smart face, attention is turning to the long-awaited beautification of the town's major beach suburb, Castlecliff.

The single-biggest draw in the area is the history-rich **Whanganui River,** a moody snake of a river that's the second longest in the North Island and the longest navigable waterway in the country. It flows 290km (180 miles) from the upper reaches of Tongariro National Park to the Tasman Sea, where, at its mouth, you find **Wanganui township.** The river has always had a special place in Maori history. A long history of discontent between Maori and Pakeha over its use and ownership hopefully was settled with the mid-1999 Waitangi Tribunal decision to hand the river back to the Maori people. Local Maori won the argument to have the district and river spelling reverted to Whanganui (*whanga*=bay, *nui*=big) in 1991, but, despite a ruling by the New Zealand Geographic Board in 2009 that the name of the town should also be Whanganui, the people are still split. Hence it was made optional, so you'll see both spellings, regardless of the fact that "wanga" (as in Wanganui) has no meaning in Maori. The Whanganui River flows through **Whanganui National Park,** most of which is accessible only by boat or on foot. The population of the greater Whanganui District is around 48,000, and the area is blessed with 2,084 hours of sunshine annually.

Essentials

GETTING THERE & GETTING AROUND   **By Plane**   Wanganui Airport, 10 minutes outside the town center, is served daily by **Air New Zealand** (✆ 0800/737-000 in NZ; www.airnewzealand.co.nz).

By Coach (Bus)   **InterCity** (✆ 09/623-1503) and **Newmans** (✆ 09/623-1504) provide service between Wanganui and Auckland, New Plymouth, National Park Village (in Tongariro National Park), and Wellington. For information on Wanganui urban buses, check www.horizons.govt.nz. The city has four looped bus routes with buses traveling in both directions. Fares range from NZ$2 for adults and NZ$1.20 for children age 5 to 15. You can travel more cheaply by purchasing a reloadable GoCard (NZ$10), from the bus driver.

By Car   Wanganui is on state highways 3 and 4. It is 2½ hours from New Plymouth or Wellington, 3 hours from Taupo, and 4 hours from Rotorua.

By Taxi   Call **Wanganui Taxis** (✆ 0800/500-000 in NZ, or 06/343-5555).

VISITOR INFORMATION   The **i-SITE Wanganui Visitor Centre,** 31 Taupo Quay (✆ 0800/926-426 in NZ, or 06/349-0508; www.wanganui.com), is open Labour Weekend (Oct) to Easter, Monday to Friday 8:30am to 5pm and weekends and public holidays 9am to 4pm; January, Monday to Friday 8:30am to 5:30pm, weekends and public holidays 9am to 4:30pm; and Easter until Labour weekend Monday to Friday 8:30am to 5pm and weekends and public holidays 9am to 3pm.

SPECIAL EVENTS   The **Billy Webb Regatta** (www.billywebbchallenge.co.nz), held every December, features dozens of rowers on the Whanganui River. Art lovers are sure to enjoy the **Festival of Glass** in September (www.wanganuiglass.co.nz), which brings together the very best of the town's glass studios with workshops, demonstrations, and stunning glassworks for sale. **Celebrating Opera Week** (www.wow.gen.nz) occurs each January, with recitals, classes, and performances at the Royal Wanganui Opera House. The **Universal College of Learning (UCOL) School of the Arts** is held in January each year. A wide range of renowned artists and tutors lead workshops in glass, painting, photography, and writing (www.ucol.ac.nz).

Exploring Wanganui
THE MAIN ATTRACTIONS

The **Sarjeant Gallery ★★★**, Queen's Park (✆ 06/349-0506; www.sarjeant.org. nz), is one of the finest provincial galleries in the country. It boasts a large contemporary photographic collection and stunning architecture. It's open daily 10:30am to 4:30pm, holidays from 1 to 4:30pm (closed Dec 25 and Good Friday), and admission is free.

  Studio Arts

In late March to early April, the town's many artists open their studios to visitors. It's a great chance to see artists in their working environments and you might even pick up some excellent original artworks—prints, paintings, ceramics, glassware, sculpture—at bargain prices. Visit www.whanganuiopen studios.org.nz for details.

A Traditional Marae Visit

If you would like to meet local Maori at the **Koriniti Marae,** Whanganui River Road, Wanganui (© **06/342-8198;** fax 06/348-0398; www.koriniti.com), call first to make sure you do not interrupt private events like *tangi* (funerals).

Visitors are welcome to take photographs at the marae and to look through the Whare Taonga (museum). There is no charge, but a *koha* (donation) is welcome.

Nearby you'll find the **Whanganui Regional Museum ★★**, Watt Street (© **06/ 345-7443;** www.wanganui-museum.org.nz), which is renowned as New Zealand's finest provincial museum. It has rare collections of Maori canoes, artifacts, and moa bones. Before heading up the Whanganui River, make sure you see their excellent display and videos on the importance of the river. Kids will love the Bug Room and the moa skeletons. It's open daily 10am to 4:30pm (closed Dec 25 and Good Friday). Admission is NZ$6 for adults, and children 14 and under are free.

Ohorere Gardens, 1778 Papaiti Rd. (©/fax **06/342-5848**), is a private garden on the banks of the Whanganui River, 4km (2½ miles) from the city center. You'll see camellias, rhododendrons, more than 100 varieties of old roses, and ponds. It's open September through April on Wednesday and Sunday from 10am to 4pm. The entry fee of NZ$10 includes tea and coffee but personally, I think you get better value at the free Virginia Lake (see below) and **Bason Botanic Gardens ★★**, 552 Rapanui Rd. (www.basonbotanicgardens.org.nz), 11km (7 miles) out of town (pick up the brochure at the visitor center for directions), which is also free and is open daily from 8am until dusk, with the conservatories open daily 9am until 4:30pm. Bason boasts picnic spots aplenty and a glorious rare orchid display.

If you feel up to climbing hundreds of steps, cross the river to **Durie Hill Elevator and Tower.** Located opposite the Wanganui City Bridge at the bottom of Victoria Avenue, it begins with a pedestrian tunnel that takes you to the historic elevator, which in turn rises 66m (216 ft.) through the hill to the summit. You can then take the 191 narrow spiraling steps up the Memorial Tower for unparalleled views. Check with the visitor center for hours. For a lovely, quiet wander close to town, it takes a lot to beat **Virginia Lake ★**, on Great North Road on St. John's Hill (© **06/349- 0001;** www.wanganui.govt.nz). The lake is bordered by pleasant bush walks, hundreds of ducks waiting to be fed, a free-flying bird aviary that you can walk through, and a coin-operated fountain that impresses with brilliant colored displays at night. Walking around the lake takes approximately 30 minutes.

If you are interested in the arts, you'll be pleased to hear that some of New Zealand's top artists live in the area. Pick up the *Arts & Cultural Trail, Arts Guide,* and *Whanganui Artists Open Studios* brochures from the information center. They cover a wealth of painters, printmakers, sculptors, jewelers, potters, and glass artists. **Chronicle Glass Studio & Tours,** 2 Rutland St. (© **06/347-1921;** www.chronicleglass. co.nz), is a collective of local glass blowers worth checking out.

A SCENIC DRIVE TO PIPIRIKI

River Road, the only road that leads into Whanganui National Park from Wanganui, is narrow and winding but very scenic. Staying on River Road for approximately 1½ hours will lead you to the tiny settlement of Pipiriki, 79km (49 miles) upstream from Wanganui. Many marae lie along the river, and you'll pass the historic Maori mission of Jerusalem, once home to the famous New Zealand poet James K. Baxter.

EXPLORING WHANGANUI RIVER & WHANGANUI NATIONAL PARK

The Whanganui River has its origins high on Mount Tongariro. There the river is a mere alpine stream, but it gathers water from Mount Ngauruhoe and Mount Ruapehu as it descends through the Central Volcanic Plateau, toward Taumarunui, Wanganui, and finally the Tasman Sea.

There are 239 listed rapids along the Whanganui, but it is a Grade II river and therefore popular with canoeists of all levels. Many begin their river adventures at the Taumarunui end, making their way south to Wanganui. This trip can take 5 to 6 days, and the Department of Conservation maintains huts along the way for overnight stays.

In 1987, the huge, largely inaccessible, and remote bush areas surrounding the middle reaches of the Whanganui River were designated a national park, becoming the second-largest tract of native bush on the North Island. Several of the original routes for the early Maori and European inhabitants have been cleared, providing some of the country's most isolated wilderness tramping—the 3-day **Mangapurua** and **Matemateaonga tracks** (see "On Foot," below) are accessible only by canoe or jet boat.

One of the most popular spots in the park is the **Bridge to Nowhere,** which was built in 1935 deep in the bush across the Mangapurua Gorge to give access to the last pioneering settlement of the New Zealand government. The isolated settlement failed in 1942, but the bridge remains. You'll need to travel upstream (see "By Jet Boat," below) and then walk 40 minutes along some steep sections and narrow tracks to reach the bridge.

If you'd like to spend the day picnicking, head to **Hipango Park Reserve,** 26km (16 miles) upriver from Wanganui. The .8-hectare (2-acre) native bush reserve with recently upgraded barbecue pits and toilets is a popular destination for boat tours (see "By Riverboat," below). For details of **Journeys on the Whanganui,** a collection of river packages, visit www.whanganuiriver.co.nz.

There are a number of exciting ways to experience the Whanganui River and Whanganui National Park. Following are a few examples.

BY AERIAL CABLEWAY The Flying Fox ★★ (✆/fax **06/342-8160;** www. theflyingfox.co.nz) is a unique river experience 45 minutes from Wanganui. A little patch of civilization in the middle of nowhere is accessible by an aerial cableway, or "flying fox." Once you've negotiated this awesome swing across the river, you can enjoy charming cottage accommodations or bush campsites (see "Where to Stay," below). To reach it, take a jet-boat tour or drive up River Road and cross the river on the aerial cableway. Several tours stop here (see "By Bus," below). They offer a half-day canoe journey for NZ$90 per person and a half-day jet boat trip for NZ$120.

BY BUS If a 14-seat air-conditioned bus is your style, you can join the popular **Whanganui River Road Mail Tour ★★.** Call **Whanganui Tours** (✆ **06/347-7534;** www.whanganuitours.co.nz). The tour runs from 7:30am to 2:30pm and covers 190km (118 miles), delivering mail to remote farms, schools, and marae. The mail tour costs NZ$75. You can also meet up with the **Bridge To Nowhere Jet Boat Tour** (✆ **0800/480-308;** www.bridgetonowhere.co.nz) and you can stay overnight at the Bridge to Nowhere Lodge, the Flying Fox, or at Jerusalem Backpackers, where Catholic nuns put you up for the night.

BY CANOE Wades **Landing Outdoors,** RD2, Owhango (☎/fax **07/895-5995;** www.whanganui.co.nz), offers a number of 3-, 4-, or 5-day trips canoeing the river from Taumarunui to Pipiriki. They're based at the Taumarunui end of the river. Bridge to Nowhere Jet Boat & Canoe Tours (see below) also offers canoe trips.

BY JET BOAT **Bridge to Nowhere Jet Boat & Canoe Tours,** Ramanui Landing, Whanganui River (☎ **0800/480-308** in NZ, or 06/385-4622; www.bridgeto nowhere.co.nz), operates in the most beautiful part of the river. Its most popular 4-hour tour to the Bridge to Nowhere costs NZ$120 per person and is suitable for all ages. There is also a jet boat/canoe option, which allows you to enjoy a leisurely paddle downstream. **Whanganui River Adventures,** 2513 RD6, Pipiriki (☎ **0800/862-743** in NZ, or 06/385-3246; www.whanganuiriveradventures.co.nz), also runs Bridge to Nowhere jet-boat rides for NZ$120 per person. Its 45-minute ride through deep, moss-covered ravines to the home of the endangered native blue duck costs NZ$125 for adults and NZ$63 for children 4 to 15.

BY RIVERBOAT The Waimarie Paddle Steamer was built in 1890, sank in 1952, and was salvaged in 1993. Since then, it has been painstakingly rebuilt at the **Whanganui Riverboat Centre & Museum,** 1A Taupo Quay (☎/fax **06/347-1863;** www.riverboats.co.nz). Daily cruises (summer at 2pm, with reduced cruises in winter) travel 13km (8 miles) up the Whanganui River to Upokongaro, then return to the city. The cost is NZ$40 for adults and NZ$15 for children 5 to 15. They also offer lunch and barbecue packages. The center is open Monday through Friday from 10am to 4pm, and weekends 10am to 2pm (free admission). Call for winter sailing times.

ON FOOT Contact the **Department of Conservation,** Whanganui Area Office, 74 Ingestre St. (☎ **06/345-2402;** www.doc.govt.nz), for information on a range of walks. In brief, the **Skyline Walk** requires 6 to 8 hours and affords views of Mount Ruapehu and Mount Taranaki. The **Matemateaonga Track** takes 3 to 4 days; the 3-day **Mangapurua Valley Walk** includes the Bridge to Nowhere. **Whanganui River Jet,** Wades Landing Outdoors, RD2, Owhango (☎ **07/895-5995;** www.whanganui.co.nz), offers a complete charter service for trampers wanting to use either of these tracks. It will drop you off and pick you up at prearranged times on the riverbanks. Costs vary depending on which track you choose. Bridge to Nowhere Jet Boat & Canoe Tours (see above) also offers a track transport service.

Outdoor Pursuits

BEACHES **Castlecliff Beach,** 9km (5½ miles) from the city center, is a typical West Coast beach with black-iron sand and lots of driftwood. It's good for swimming and surfing and is patrolled by professional lifeguards in summer. Wild **South Beach,** obviously to the south of the city, is great for long beachcombing walks, while **Mowhanau** is a pretty swimming beach surrounded by *papa* cliffs (a soft and slippery cross btw. a mudstone and sandstone formation). It has a playground and good picnicking areas. Head north on the highway to New Plymouth and turn left onto Rapanui Road; continue another 9km (5½ miles).

BIKING **Lismore Forest,** just minutes from central Wanganui, has some of the best mountain bike tracks in the region. You can rent bikes from **Wanganui Pro-Cycle Centre,** 199 Victoria Ave. (☎ **06/368-5459**), for around NZ$50 per day.

GOLF   The **Wanganui Golf Club,** Belmont Links, Clarkson Avenue (☎ **06/344-4481**), is an 18-hole championship course. Greens fees are NZ$40 for 18 holes.

Where to Stay

Accommodations are not Wanganui's strong point. There are no major hotels and nothing truly upmarket, probably no more than 30 motel complexes, around 30 homestays or farmstays, and fewer than half a dozen backpacker establishments.

If remote is what you're after, try the **Flying Fox ★**, P.O. Box 333, Wanganui (www.theflyingfox.co.nz; ☎ **0800/483-292** in NZ, or 06/342-8160), with five units, including two self-contained cottages and a gypsy cart (carriage). The cottages go for NZ$200 a night, plus NZ$40 for an additional person. The gypsy cart accommodation costs NZ$100 (plus NZ$40 per additional person). All rates include breakfast. Everything sits under old walnut trees, and hosts Annette and John make natural beers and organic meals. *Note:* You'll have to cross the river on a flying fox (see "By Aerial Cableway," above), and it's 45 minutes upriver from Wanganui.

Even more remote, for those who truly do want to get away from it all, is **Bridge to Nowhere Lodge ★**, Ramanui Landing, Whanganui River (www.bridgeto nowhere.co.nz; ☎ **0800/480-308** in NZ; fax 06/348-7133), where rooms, breakfast, and dinner go for NZ$275, or self-catering with your own bedding (ideal for canoeists and trampers) for NZ$50 to NZ$75 per person. **Rutland Arms Inn,** 48–50 Ridgway St. (www.rutland-arms.co.nz; ☎ **0800/788-5263**), is an old-fashioned stay in an old pub that's right in the heart of the city. The eight big rooms here go for NZ$140 to NZ$185. **Riverwoods ★★**, 234–237 Kaiwhaiki Rd., Wanganui (www.riverwoods. co.nz; ☎ **06/342-5501**), is a beautifully restored, self-contained villa a short drive from the city on the banks of the Whanganui River. It sleeps six people and costs NZ$235 for two people and NZ$290 to NZ$455 for three to six guests. The **Tamara Backpackers Lodge ★**, 24 Somme Parade, Wanganui (www.tamaralodge.com; ☎ **06/347-6300**), is clean and comfortable, with a good kitchen and a friendly atmosphere. The house, once a maternity hospital and then a hotel, overlooks the river and is an easy walk to town. The fabulous rear garden has hammocks under giant palm trees. It's NZ$28 for a dorm bed, NZ$52 single, and NZ$66 to NZ$80 double.

All rates listed include the 15% GST and parking.

Where to Eat

Indigo ★★, Majestic Square (☎ **06/348-7459**; www.indigocafe.co.nz), is one of the few cafes in town that hints at city style; it's been judged Best Cafe in Wanganui. It has a great setting in the heart of town and very nice outdoor areas. It's open daily from 8am until late. Service can be patchy, but that's not uncommon in the provinces, where good staff are hard to find. **Big Orange/Ceramic Wine Bar ★**, 51 Victoria St. (☎ **06/348-4449**), operates as a lively cafe by day and a restaurant and bar by night. The lunch menu includes some excellent light meals, but the service can be slow. They're open Monday through Friday 7:30am to 5pm, and weekends from 9:30am to 5pm. **Jolt Coffee ★**, 19 Victoria Ave. (*©* **06/345-8840**), has good coffee and a laidback mood that makes it a favorite with locals. It's open Monday through Friday 7:30am to 5:30pm and Sunday 1 to 5pm.

More popular with the over-35s is **Legends,** 25 Somme Parade (*©* **06/345-7575**), overlooking the river. Although the meals are tasty and the surroundings pleasant, I prefer the grittiness of Jolt. Legends is open Wednesday through Friday 9am until late, weekends from 10am. **Vega ★**, Taupo Quay and Victoria Avenue (*©* **06/345-1082**), is a popular Italian restaurant that many consider the best in town. **Stellar,** 2 Victoria St. (*©* **06/345-7278**; www.stellarwanganui.co.nz), offers tasty meals for a good price (especially pizzas and desserts) Monday 3pm until late and Tuesday through Sunday 9am until late. **The Yellow House Café ★★**, Pitt & Dublin streets (*©* **06/345-0083**), is worth seeking out in its residential location just up from the Pitt Street bridge. Food here is healthy, wholesome, and delicious. They're open Sunday through Wednesday for breakfast and lunch from 8:30am until 5pm and stay open for dinner Thursday through Saturday until 10pm. Dinner reservations are essential.

En Route to Wellington

You can get to Wellington in two ways—on State Highway 1 down the coast via Levin, Waikanae, and Paraparaumu (the better road), or via Palmerston North, the Wairarapa, through Masterton, Carterton, Greytown, and Featherston. Both trips take about 2½ hours, but the Wairarapa journey begs for a few stop-offs that may well eat up some of your time. If you go this way, I strongly suggest you spend a night in the area (see "Where to Stay" in the "A Side Trip to Wairarapa" section in chapter 11). The **i-SITE Palmerston North Visitor Centre,** 52 The Square, Palmerston North (*©* **06/350-1922;** fax 06/350-1929; www.manawatunz.co.nz), can help with accommodations and local highlights.

If you travel down the coast road, be sure to drop by the **Southward Car Museum ★★**, near Paraparaumu, 45 minutes north of Wellington (*©* **04/297-1221;** www.thecarmuseum.co.nz). Even if you're not auto-inclined, I think you'll find it interesting as it contains much more than just cars. The museum is open daily from 9am to 4:30pm and costs NZ$12 for adults and NZ$3 for children ages 5 to 15. The **Kapiti Coast Visitor Information Centre,** Centennial Park, State Highway 1, Otaki (*©* **06/364-7620;** www.kapiticoast.govt.nz), can provide accommodations and adventure details for this increasingly popular holiday area. It's open Monday through Friday 8:30am to 5pm, weekends 9am to 4pm.

WELLINGTON

Wellington is a vibrant, sophisticated capital city bursting with suited bureaucrats and culture-buffs. A central fist of high-rises forms an intimate heart beside a harbor surrounded by hillsides dotted with quaint wooden houses, **Botanic Gardens,** and **ZEALANDIA** wildlife sanctuary. It's home to New Zealand's **movie industry,** the **New Zealand Ballet Company,** and the **National Museum of New Zealand—Te Papa Tongarewa,** where you can experience simulated earthquakes or gaze in awe at giant squid. The reclaimed **Waterfront** is alive with walkers, cyclists, skaters, cafes, and sculpture; and **Courtenay Place** neighborhood has one of the best bar/cafe/restaurant scenes in the country. And all of this, just an hour away from the **Wairarapa,** one of the country's top **wine-growing regions.**

Things to Do   **Te Papa Museum** is your best introduction to wider New Zealand and you'll be charmed by its unique interactive displays and collected treasures. Peer into black holes at **Carter Observatory,** or watch vets operating on huge animals at **The Nest, at Wellington Zoo.** Wander the **Waterfront** and **Civic Square** taking in public sculptures and the lunch crowd eating by the sea, or jogging the walkways. Ride the **Cable Car** for unforgettable harbor views, and take a tour of **Parliament House.**

Eating & Drinking   Wellington's dining scene is a reflection of its diverse, cosmopolitan population. You can eat your way around Asia, the Mediterranean, and the Middle East in fine tapas bars, French bistros, Italian pizzerias, bakeries and delis, Indian curry houses, Greek *tavernas,* or Japanese noodle bars. Or try fine dining at one (or all) of the city's top four: **Logan Brown, The White House, Boulcott Street Bistro,** and **Martin Bosley's Yacht Club Restaurant.** And just across the hills, the **Wairarapa Wine Region** is awash with small, boutique wineries where you can sample the fine red wines the region is famous for.

Shopping   Amble along **Lambton Quay** where department stores vie for attention; or try on high fashion in **The Old Bank Arcade. Cuba Mall** is home to the capital's Bohemian quarter and there's no better place to mix shopping with dining; it's riddled with shabby-chic boutiques and popular bars and cafes. But don't overlook the side streets, where top fashion houses, design stores, and art galleries have set up home.

Nightlife & Entertainment   You're seldom far from a cafe, bar, pub, or restaurant in this city. Head for **Courtenay Place, Allen Street,** and **Blair Street** to sip on cocktails in sophisticated themed bars; or sample a local craft beer at one of the prime **Waterfront** bars and pubs. That's also where you'll find **Circa** and **Bats** theaters for original New Zealand productions. Visit the **Embassy Theatre** where **Sir Peter Jackson** premiered *The Lord of the Rings,* or watch the **New Zealand Ballet** perform at **Westpac St James Theatre.**

ORIENTATION
Arriving

BY PLANE **Wellington International Airport** (www.wellingtonairport.co.nz) is 8km (5 miles) southeast of the city. The quickest route to the city from here passes through Mount Victoria via a two-lane tunnel. A more circuitous, but more scenic, route travels via Oriental Parade. The trip usually takes 15 to 20 minutes, although it can exceed 30 minutes at peak traffic times.

Wellington Airport operates both international and domestic business from the same building. It is served by the following international airlines: **Air New Zealand** (✆ 0800/737-000 in NZ, or 04/336-2400; www.airnewzealand.co.nz), **British Airways** (✆ 09/966-9777; www.ba.com), **Lufthansa** (✆ 0800/945-220 in NZ; www.lufthansa.com), **Qantas Airways** (✆ 0800/808-767; www.qantas.com), **Singapore Airlines** (✆ 0800/808-909; www.singaporeair.com), and **Pacific Blue** (✆ 0800/670-000; www.flypacificblue.com).

The leading domestic airlines that fly into Wellington are **Air New Zealand** (✆ 0800/737-000; www.airnz.com), **Jetstar** (✆ 0800/800-995; www.jetstar.com), and **Sounds Air Ltd.** (✆ 0800/505-505; www.soundsair.com). For **arrival and departure information,** call ✆ 04/388-9900.

The **Wellington Airport Visitor Information Centre** (✆ **04/385-5123;** fax 04/385-5137; www.wellingtonairport.co.nz) is on level one of the main terminal building. Staff members can assist with booking accommodations, TranzRail, Inter-islander ferries, and long-distance coaches. It's open daily from 7am to 8pm.

The terminal has nine cafes and restaurants in a large food hall that offer everything from pizza and pasta to wine and tapas. There are also car-rental desks, duty-free stores, gift shops, a Travelex Foreign Exchange service open during all international flight times, Internet stations, and ATMs. Coin-operated lockers can be found on the ground floor. Most retail outlets are open 6:30am to 8pm, some later. Duty-free stores are open for every international flight.

Super Shuttle (✆ **0800/748-885** in NZ, or 04/472-9552; www.supershuttle.co.nz) operates between the airport, the city, and the railway station Monday through Friday. It costs NZ$25 per person. Several shuttle operators provide door-to-door service at higher fares.

The **Airport Flyer,** the GO Wellington airport express bus **Metlink** (✆ **04/569-2933;** www.airportflyer.co.nz), goes right into the inner city and then on to Waterloo Interchange in Lower Hutt. It operates every 15 minutes, 365 days a year from 6:30am to 9:30pm. A Metlink Explorer Pass costs NZ$20 per person and gives unlimited all-day travel (after 9am), on all Flyer, GO Wellington, and Valley Flyer services. It's available from bus drivers. Single-ride tickets are also available. The trip from the airport to central-city stops takes about 45 minutes and costs around NZ$10 for adults and NZ$6 for children. A new fleet of buses complies with the latest European emission standard, Euro 5, which means exhaust emissions are up to 90% lower than the older buses. The buses also have air-conditioning, free Wi-Fi, and lowered floors for wheelchair access. The Airport Flyer departs from the southern end of the terminal on Level 0; exit the baggage claim area and turn right.

ATTRACTIONS ●

City Gallery Wellington **34**
The Dowse Art Museum **45**
Katherine Mansfield Birthplace **44**
Kelburn Cable Car Top Station **37**
Museum of New Zealand—Te Papa Tongarewa **31**
Museum of Wellington **50**
Parliament Buildings **58**
Pataka **45**
Te Raukura/ Te Wharewaka O Poneke **33**
Wellington Botanic Gardens **38**
Wellington Zoo **14**
ZEALANDIA: The Karori Sanctuary Experience **39**

NORTH ISLAND
Auckland

Wellington

SOUTH ISLAND
Christchurch

Dunedin

Wellington Information Centre

Town Hall

Civic Square

Mount Cook Terminal

Overseas Terminal

ⓘ Information
✉ Post Office
||||| Pedestrian Mall

0   0.2 mi
0   0.2 km

New Zealand Astronomy Centre

BOTANIC GARDENS

KELBURN PARK

The Dell

Anderson Park

Kelburn Cable Car

Parliament and Beehive

Wellington Cathedral

FRANK KITTS PARK

Trust Bank Ferry

City Bus Terminal

Railway Station/ Bus Depot

Wellington Harbour

Queens Wharf

Street labels: Upland, Rawhiti, Salamanca, Clermont, Talavera, Clifton, The Terrrace, Athol, Gilmer, Willis, Willeston, Hunter, Grey, Panama, Brandon, Johnston, Waring Taylor, Maginnity, Jervois Quay, Customhouse Quay, Lambton Quay, Stout, Ballance, Whitmore, Featherston, Waterloo Quay, Bunny, Thorndon Quay, Mulgrave, Aitken, Sydney St. East, Molesworth, Hill, Motorway, Parliament, Bowen, Easdale, Kinross, Bolton, Aurora, Wesley, Glenmore, Patanga, St. Mary, Lewisville, Barton, Ascot, Sydney St. West, Glenbervie, Tinakori, Everton, Glenbervie, Waterloo Quay

A **taxi** between the city center and the airport costs around NZ$35, depending on the destination. The fare to Lower Hutt is approximately NZ$65 to NZ$80. Taxi stands are directly outside the main terminal. **Eco Taxis** (© 04/387-4000; www.ecotaxis.co.nz) have a fixed fare of NZ$20 into the city (for cash). If you use a credit card it will cost NZ$25. If you have any problems with your taxi driver, call **Wellington Airport Operation** (© 04/385-5124).

BY TRAIN & COACH (BUS)   Most long-distance trains depart from the **Wellington Railway Station,** on Waterloo Quay. For long-distance rail information, call © 0800/802-802 in New Zealand or 04/495-0775, or visit www.tranzscenic.co.nz. Most major hostels and hotels are within a short taxi ride of the station.

For coach information, call **InterCity** (© 09/623-1503; www.intercity.co.nz) or **Newmans** (© 09/623-1504; www.newmanscoach.co.nz). Both lines operate out of the railway station. **Kiwi Experience** (© 09/366-1665) and the **Magic Travellers Network** (© 09/358-5600) also stop in Wellington.

BY CAR   Wellington is reached via highways 1 and 2. It's 195km (121 miles) from Wanganui (approx. 2 hr.); 460km (285 miles) from Rotorua (approx. 5 hr.); and 655km (406 miles) from Auckland (approx. 8 hr.). The motorway terminates right in the city.

BY FERRY   For information on the **Interislander** Wellington-Picton ferry, call © 0800/802-802 or check www.interislander.co.nz. Be aware that there are two ferry operators working between Wellington and Picton. The three Interislander ferries operate all year and take 3 hours to cross the strait. **Strait Shipping Ltd.,** Waterloo Quay (© 0800/844-844 in NZ; www.bluebridge.co.nz), operates **Bluebridge Cook Strait Ferry,** which offers three sailings most days going both ways between Wellington and Picton; call or check the website for times. The Bluebridge trip is cheapest but it takes 3 hours 20 minutes. If you book either online you get the best fares—especially if you book well ahead. Cook Strait can be notoriously rough in bad weather, so if you get seasick, take your medication.

Visitor Information

The **Wellington i-SITE Visitor Centre,** 101 Wakefield St., Civic Square (© 04/802-4860; fax 04/802-4863; www.wellingtonnz.com), is open Monday through Friday from 8:30am to 5:30pm (Tues till 5pm) and Saturday and Sunday from 9:30am to 4:30pm. It provides details of regional attractions and has the best range of free guides in the country. It also has a range of tiny pocket-size leaflets and cards on everything from transport systems to shopping, art, fashion, and free walking tours. Staff members can book accommodations and attractions, arrange transport, and sell stamps and phone cards. It also has an e-mail center and cafe. You'll also find good information at www.wellingtonwaterfront.co.nz.

For information on Lower and Upper Hutt areas, contact **Hutt City i-SITE Visitor Centre,** 25 Laings Rd., Lower Hutt (© 04/560-4715; fax 04/570-3374; www.huttvalleynz.com), or **Upper Hutt i-SITE Visitor Centre,** 84–90 Main St., Upper Hutt (© 04/527-2141; fax 04/527-9818; www.upperhuttcity.com). Both are open Monday through Friday from 9am to 5pm and weekends and public holidays from 9:30am to 2:30pm (closed Dec 25).

The free weekly publications *Capital Times* and *City Voice* are available at the visitor centers and leading hotels and cafes. Both have details on local happenings. If you're a keen follower of the performing arts, check at the visitor center for availability of discounted day-of-performance tickets.

Public Relief

Free public toilets are at 69 sites throughout the city. Staffed facilities are at the ANZ Building (at the corner of Lambton Quay and Featherston St.).

You'll also find restrooms at all major attractions and several department stores.

Special Events

Wellington is home to the country's biggest cultural event, the biennial **New Zealand International Arts Festival ★★★** (© 04/473-0149; www.nzfestival. nzpost.co.nz). It features international works and the best of New Zealand talent in everything from opera to jazz, dance to comedy. The next festival will be staged in February and March 2012. A major, growing spin-off from the festival is the **Wellington Fringe Festival ★★** (© 04/582-8015; www.fringe.org.nz); it's a separate event, which celebrates offbeat productions and innovative art forms, but that event is now held annually.

Summer City Festival (© 04/801-3500; www.wellington.govt.nz), staged during January and February each year, launches Wellington's events calendar with more than 70 free activities such as the Teddy Bears' Picnic, the Rock Barge Concert on Oriental Parade, a Pacific Islands Festival, and Summer Shakespeare in the Botanic Garden Dell. **Montana World of Wearable Art ★★★** (© 03/548-9299; www. worldofwearableart.com) is a theatrical costume spectacle not to be missed, now staged annually at the Events Centre Wellington in mid-September and early October. This 2-hour visual extravaganza attracts international entrants and sell-out audiences of over 22,000—not bad considering it started in Nelson in 1987 in a leaky tent with just 200 spectators. **Montana Wellington International Jazz Festival** (© 04/473-0149; www.jazzfestival.co.nz) features a superb roster of national and international jazz musicians performing modern jazz through the classics (mid- to late Oct at various city locations).

Martinborough Country Fair ★★ (© 06/304-9933; www.martinboroughfair. org.nz) is a popular gathering of crafts artisans from around the country. Held the first Saturday in February and the first Saturday in March, it attracts about 30,000 visitors. Martinborough is about an hour's drive northeast of Wellington. **Golden Shears** (© 06/378-8008; www.goldenshears.co.nz) is a 3-day international shearing contest that includes wool handling and sheep and goat shearing. It's held in late February or early March in Masterton, 103km (64 miles) northeast of Wellington. In November, catch a special 50-minute festival train from Wellington to the **Toast Martinborough Wine, Food & Music Festival ★★★** (© 06/306-9183; www.toastmartin borough.co.nz). Shuttles run a continuous circuit within a 10km (6-mile) area of Martinborough's town square to Martinborough vineyards, where tastings take place with the winemakers.

City Layout

The main focal point of the **inner city** is the harbor. The new Te Papa national museum fronts this water, as does the Queen's Wharf dining and shopping complex. Unlike the rest of the city, the central business district (CBD) is generally flat and easily negotiable. The best **shopping** is along Lambton Quay and Willis Street;

Manners Street and Cuba Mall also have plenty of stores. They are less upmarket, but **Cuba Mall** especially is one of the hippest areas, known for its edgy boutiques, design stores, and excellent eateries. This is my favorite part of Wellington because it's always busy and interesting. The inner area of Lambton Quay, Willis Street, and The Terrace is home to many of the nation's **corporate headquarters** and thus is second home to "the suits." Several leading hotels and apartment complexes are also in this area, so if you base yourself here, you won't need a car to see most of the major attractions and shops—but you will need earplugs for a sound sleep.

The heaviest concentration of **bars** and **eateries** is between Courtenay Place and Wakefield Street and the lanes running between them, especially Blair and Allen streets. Most of the inner city is safe, but I wouldn't go lurking around Cuba Mall after closing time, especially the top end, which has always been seen as the heart of the seedier side of the sex industry. Manners Mall is no more appealing late at night. Courtenay Place on Thursday, Friday, and Saturday nights is the center of nightlife, but there are often numerous people about who have consumed more than their fair share of alcohol and who may not be entirely open to reason. Generally, though, personal safety rules are the same as in any other international city—use common sense and don't wander about dark places alone in the middle of the night. Many inner city areas are now under security camera surveillance.

The Neighborhoods in Brief

Thorndon This neighborhood sits right on the fault line, but that hasn't detracted from real estate values here. It's seen as one of the premier suburbs in Wellington because of its beautiful historic buildings, its views, and its proximity to the inner city. There are some excellent bed-and-breakfasts within walking distance of Parliament Buildings, the city, the Botanic Garden, and Tinakori Village, a fashionable little spot for shopping and eating. The area's only downsides are the noise from the motorway, the heavy traffic on Tinakori Road, and the lack of both off- and on-street parking.

Mount Victoria This is where I would live if I thought I could afford anything bigger than a letter box. It's very close to the Courtenay Place end of town, everything is within walking distance, and it's filled with gorgeous (slightly less perfect) wooden houses. It's also quieter. Parking is generally earmarked for residents only during business hours, but you'll be fine after 6pm.

Kelburn Kelburn is easily accessed via the cable car from Lambton Quay, which runs up to the Botanic Garden and Victoria University. Homes in this area are sought after for their especially good harbor and city views.

Oriental Bay This part of town offers prime real estate just 800m (about ½ mile) around the water's edge from the inner city and Mount Victoria. Again, it's a great place to stay, with several hotels and private high-rise apartments stretched out along Oriental Parade, which is a favorite playground for in-line skaters, walkers, and runners. There are hints of San Francisco here, I'm told, plus a few excellent cafes and restaurants and beautiful city and harbor views.

Evans Bay This area is far less inspiring. It's farther out, around the point, and its prime attraction is its proximity to the airport.

Lower Hutt A city within a city—Lower Hutt is the ninth largest in New Zealand. It's across the harbor from Wellington proper and accessed via a short motorway drive, usually about 15 minutes in good traffic. This is where you'll find the fabulous New Dowse Art Museum.

GETTING AROUND

Wellington is blessed with an excellent public transport system, and you can easily see the best attractions without a car.

BY BUS   Call **GO Wellington** (✆ **04/387-8700;** www.gowellingtonbus.co.nz) for information on all urban services. Buses operate daily 7am to 11pm on most routes and the visitor center can give you a comprehensive city map that shows major bus routes and timetables. Timetables are also available from newsstands. The main city bus terminal, **Lambton Interchange,** is adjacent to the main railway station on the corner of Bunny and Featherston streets. The easiest places to catch buses in the inner city are Lambton Quay, Willis Street, Dixon Street, Cuba Mall, Courtenay Place, and the railway station.

The NZ$10 **BusAbout Day Pass** gives you unlimited 1-day travel (after 9am) on the GO Wellington and Valley Flyer services. The **Family BusAbout Pass** (NZ$22) gives you unlimited travel for one adult and five children, or two adults and four children, after 9am weekdays and all day on weekends, on Go Wellington and Valley Flyer Services. The **Metlink Explorer Pass** (NZ$22) gives you a full day of unlimited travel after 9am on a wide range of train and bus services in and around Wellington, Hutt Valley, and the Kapiti Coast. If you'd like to travel more cheaply and efficiently, buy the NZ$10 **Snapper Card** (✆ **0800/555-345;** www.snapper.co.nz), which stores NZ$300 and can be used for bus fares and everyday items, and can be reloaded. You simply swipe the card as you get on *and* off the bus and your fare is deducted. Children ages 1 to 8 use a green Snapper Card and kids 9 to 13, a red card. All the above passes can be purchased from your bus driver. Snapper Cards can also be purchased from participating retailers. Normal urban bus fares range from NZ$2.50 to NZ$5.

Newlands Coach Service (✆ **04/478-8315;** www.newlands.co.nz) operates bus routes 50 to 59 from central Wellington to the northern suburbs. Purchase tickets from the driver; these buses arrive on Featherston Street and leave from Lambton Exchange.

BY TAXI   There are taxi stands in front of the railway station; in the Lambton Quay shopping area between Grey and Hunter streets; on Bond Street just off Willis Street; on Dixon Street between Cuba and Victoria streets; and on Cambridge Terrace near Courtenay Place. For service, call **Gold & Black Taxis** (✆ **04/388-8888**) or **Wellington Combined Taxis** (✆ **04/384-4444;** www.taxis.co.nz). You'll pay a NZ$1 surcharge if you phone for a taxi. Wellington Combined Taxis recently became the first taxi company in New Zealand to receive carboNZero certification, which means they are committed to reducing their greenhouse gas emissions. They use only hybrid, diesel, or LPG cars for their 442-strong fleet.

BY TRAIN   **Tranz Metro** operates daily electric train service from Wellington to its outer suburbs. Trains arrive at the railway station on Bunny Street; everything is an easy walk or bus ride from there. You can save money with the purchase of a **Group Rover Pass** (NZ$35), which gives unlimited travel for a day for up to four people traveling together. A **Day Rover Pass** costs NZ$14, and both passes are a cheaper way to travel between central and Lower Hutt, Upper Hutt, Johnsonville, Kapiti, Porirua, and the Wairarapa. Call ✆ **0800/801-700** in New Zealand, or check www.metlink.org.nz or www.tranzmetro.co.nz for timetable information and discount fares.

Have Scooter, Will Travel

If you have limited mobility, you can enjoy central Wellington and the waterfront on a free mobility scooter. Book it for 4 hours and pick it up from one of four locations—**Freyberg Pool**, Oriental Parade (© **04/499-4444**); **Wellington City Council**, 101 Wakefield St. (© **04/499-4444**); **Fergs Kayaks**, Shed 6, Queens Wharf (© **04/499-8898**); or **Wellington Botanic Garden**, Tinakori Rd. (© **04/499-1400**).

BY CAR   If you can avoid using a car in downtown Wellington, do so; you'll save yourself a lot of hassles and steep parking fees. Traffic congestion is significant during the week and parking can be a problem. If you do drive, there are 10 major parking buildings in the inner city. All are well signposted and are open 24 hours. Rates range from NZ$4 to NZ$15 per hour. There are also pay-and-display parking areas, where a machine dispenses a ticket to be displayed in your car window. *Note:* If you don't display a ticket, you will receive a significant fine. On Saturday and Sunday, parking is free in all metered pay-and-display areas and in council parking buildings, but the time limits still apply. If you exceed them, you can also expect a fine. Parking in resident parking zones is also a costly business if you get caught. *Tip:* If you park in the Te Papa carpark, you pay NZ$3.50 per hour up to a daily maximum of NZ$28, so it works out cheaper to leave your car there all day and walk to your chosen spots. They also offer an evening special of NZ$6 if you park after 5pm and leave by 2am.

BY CABLE CAR   The cable car takes you from Lambton Quay straight up to the Botanic Garden, with a Victoria University stop on the way. It runs daily every 10 minutes from 7am to 10pm Monday through Friday, 8:30am to 10pm Saturday, 9am to 10pm Sunday and public holidays (closed Dec 25). A round-trip ticket costs NZ$6 for adults, NZ$2 for children 5 to 15. Family and senior discounts are available. For information, call © **04/472-2199.** Please note that the Cable Car will be closed in April 2012 for its next safety survey; normal services will resume May 2012.

BY FERRY   The **Dominion Post Ferry** runs daily between Queen's Wharf, Somes Island, Eastbourne, and Days Bay Wharf. The trip to Days Bay takes 30 minutes one-way, and Eastbourne Village is a good 10- to 15-minute trip from Days Bay. The one-way fare costs NZ$12 for adults and NZ$6 for children; a family pass is NZ$50. Call © **04/494-3339** or 499-1282, or check www.eastbywest.co.nz for timetable information.

[FastFACTS] WELLINGTON

American Express
The **foreign exchange bureau** is in the Cable Car complex, 280–292 Lambton Quay (© **04/473-7766**; fax 04/473-7765). It's open Monday through Friday from 8:30am to 5pm.

Area Code   Wellington's telephone area code (STD) is **04.**

Babysitters   Most hotels and B&Bs can arrange babysitters, or you can call **Wellington Nannies College** at © **04/384-5888** or visit www.wnc.co.nz.

Dentist   For 24-hour service, phone © **04/801-5551.**

Doctor   For emergency doctor referrals, call © **04/472-2999.**

Embassies & Consulates   The **U.S. Embassy** is at 29 Fitzherbert Terrace,

Thorndon (☎ **04/462-6000**); the **Canadian High Commission** is at Level 11, 125 The Terrace (☎ **04/473-9577**); and the **British High Commission** is at 44 Hill St. (☎ **04/924-2888**).

Emergencies Dial ☎ **111** to call the police, report a fire, or request an ambulance.

Hospitals **Wellington Hospital** is on Riddiford Street, Newtown (☎ **04/385-5999**).

Internet Access The **Email Shop,** 101 Wakefield St. (☎ **04/917-8860**), has a full range of Internet and computer services; it's open daily from 9am to 10pm. It also has outlets at the

Wellington i-SITE Visitor Information Centre (see "Visitor Information," above). For other options, try **Cybernomad,** 43 Courtenay Place (☎ **04/801-5964**), which offers high-speed Internet service, or **Cyber Spot Internet,** 180 Lambton Quay (☎ **04/473-0098**).

Newspapers Wellington's morning newspaper, the *Dominion,* and evening paper, the *Evening Post,* are both published Monday through Saturday. On Sundays, get the best paper in the country, the *Sunday Star Times.* Overseas newspapers are sometimes available at newsstands and in

the reading room of the National Library, Molesworth Street (☎ **04/474-3000**).

Pharmacies There are late-night pharmacies at 17 Adelaide Rd., Wellington (☎ **04/385-8810**), and 729 High St., Lower Hutt (☎ **04/939-6669**).

Police See "Emergencies," above.

Post Office The main post office is at 7 Waterloo Quay (☎ **0800/501-501;** www.nzpost.co.nz). Collect *poste restante* mail at **NZ Post,** 43 Manners St. (☎ **04/473-5922**). Post shops are open Monday through Friday, 9am to 5pm.

WHERE TO STAY

Everything in Wellington is geared for the corporate market. Hotel and motel rates are significantly higher Monday through Thursday, but you can pick up exceptionally good deals on the weekends, especially during the off-season. There has been a big increase in inner city apartment developments, and some exceptional values rise right off the heart of Lambton Quay and The Terrace, placing you perfectly in the heart of everything. Although there is a wide range of homestay options farther out, I'm always disappointed to discover that there are not as many upmarket B&Bs in the inner suburbs as there are in, say, Christchurch or Auckland.

All rates include 15% GST and free off-street parking unless otherwise stated.

In the Inner City
EXPENSIVE

You'll find **CityLife Wellington ★★**, 300 Lambton Quay (www.heritagehotels. co.nz; ☎ **0800/368-888** in NZ, or 04/922-2800), right above the city's best shopping district. They have 70 modern, self-contained apartments with all the mod-cons from NZ$265 to NZ$305 for a one-bedroom suite, and NZ$360 to NZ$485 for two- and three-bedroom suites. Valet parking is NZ$35 per night.

Amora Hotel Wellington ★★ After a NZ$4.3-million refit and rebrand, the 24-year-old Duxton hotel is now the Amora—a place of style, service, award-winning cuisine (at **The Grill**), and a great location all wrapped up in one. Ideally located across the street from Te Papa and the Michael Fowler Centre, it offers nine levels of comfort and attracts everyone from leisure and corporate travelers to international dignitaries. All rooms are large and have either harbor or city views. The club-level suites go up another notch in comfort and are well worth the extra price—especially if you get a weekend deal.

170 Wakefield St., Wellington. www.wellington.amorahotels.com. ✆ **0800/655-555** in NZ, or 04/473-3900. Fax 04/473-3929. 192 units. NZ$450 deluxe; NZ$500 club; NZ$550 club suite; extra person NZ$35. Off-peak rates and special deals. AE, MC, V. Valet parking NZ$25. **Amenities:** Restaurant; bar; babysitting on request; concierge; well-equipped gym; 24-hr room service. *In room:* A/C, TV w/pay movies, fridge, hair dryer, minibar, Wi-Fi.

InterContinental Wellington ★★★ Seen as Wellington's most luxurious hotel, this is the sort of place where you might rub shoulders with the rich and famous—or at least the cosmopolitan and corporate. Just over 20 years old, it's right in the heart of the central business district, and if you give in to indulgence, you'll love the top service and classy environment. The higher the price, the better it gets—and the top-floor Club rooms are the best. These have divine bathrooms with huge Jacuzzis and lots of other perks, including access to the Club Lounge. I like staying here because my favorite cafe, **Arabica** (p. 274), is right across the street and it's close to the best shopping. The hotel has a Qualmark Enviro-Gold rating and participates actively in water- and energy-saving measures and recycling.

Grey and Featherston sts., Wellington. www.intercontinental.com/wellington. ✆ **0800/154-181** in NZ, or 04/472-2722. Fax 04/472-4724. 231 units. NZ$250 classic queen; NZ$290 superior; NZ$375 club king; NZ$575 club executive; from NZ$1,900 presidential suite. Extra person NZ$35. Children 15 and under stay free in parent's room. Long-stay, off-peak, and special deals. AE, DC, MC, V. Valet parking NZ$30. **Amenities:** 2 restaurants; 2 bars; charged airport transfers; babysitting; concierge; well-equipped gym; Jacuzzi; high-rise heated indoor pool; room service; sauna; day spa and beauty treatments; Wi-Fi in public areas. *In room:* A/C, TV, fridge, hair dryer, Internet, minibar, Wi-Fi.

Museum Hotel ★ Perfectly located on the waterfront, across the road from Te Papa and close to dozens of restaurants, Museum Hotel offers both modern apartments and hotel rooms in two separate wings. You'll enjoy the opulent mood and the big, slightly eccentric New Zealand art collection, which gives it a funkier character than the nearby classic Duxton. The two-bedroom apartments are a good option for families and couples traveling together. Staff is very friendly.

90 Cable St., Wellington. www.museumhotel.co.nz. ✆ **0800/994-335** in NZ, or 04/802-8900. Fax 04/802-8909. 165 units. NZ$495 classic deluxe; NZ$615 harbor; NZ$650 premier studio; NZ$675 twin studio; NZ$735 1-bedroom suite; NZ$855 2-bedroom suite. Long-stay and special deals. AE, DC, MC, V. Valet parking NZ$20. **Amenities:** Restaurant; 2 bars; babysitting; concierge; free Wi-Fi in lobby; well-equipped gym; Jacuzzi; heated indoor lap pool; room service; sauna. *In room:* A/C in most, TV/pay movies, DVD in some, fridge, hair dryer, kitchen in some, minibar, charged Wi-Fi.

MODERATE

Close to bus, train, and ferry terminals, **Quest on Johnston ★**, 35 Johnston St. (www.questonjohnston.co.nz; ✆ **0800/508-021**), is a perfectly located 18-level apartment complex where there's always a great deal to be had. Its 67 studios and 1-, 2-, and 3-bedroom apartments are definitely worth a look. They go for NZ$105 to NZ$225. **Wellesley Boutique Hotel ★**, 2–8 Maginnity St. (www.wellesley boutiquehotel.co.nz; ✆ **04/474-1308**), is a former gentlemen's club that's been converted into a stylish stay in a heritage building. The 13 rooms are individually decorated—the 4 luxury rooms are the most spacious—and rates range from NZ$200 to NZ$450.

Bolton Hotel ★★ 🎁 New in 2005, this multistory, apartment-style hotel has an elegance and style that exceeds some of its bigger capital city cousins. The hotel was built with energy and water conservation in mind, and its Qualmark Enviro-Gold rating indicates a commitment to all avenues of sustainable tourism. Owners have paid meticulous attention to guest preferences, and rooms abound with luscious textural fabrics and unexpected extra touches—a comprehensive minibar, for instance, that includes an umbrella and disposable raincoat, the importance of which can't be overestimated in Wellington. It's colorful, crisp, modern, and close to the heart of the city. Above all, its rates are enticing. Ask about their classy Bolton suite if you want to indulge; it's very reasonably priced and ideal for families or couples traveling together.

Corner of Bolton and Mowbray sts., Wellington. www.boltonhotel.co.nz. ℂ **0800/996-622** in NZ, or 04/472-9966. Fax 04/472-9955. 142 units. NZ$180–NZ$325 studio; NZ$385–NZ$445 1-bedroom suite; NZ$500 2-bedroom suite. Long-stay, off-peak, and special deals. AE, DC, MC, V. Valet parking NZ$25 per night. **Amenities:** Restaurant; tiny lobby cafe; bar; airport transfer (NZ$70); babysitting; concierge; excellent gym; Jacuzzi; heated indoor lap pool; sauna. *In room:* A/C, TV/DVD/pay movies, fridge, hair dryer, kitchen (in most), minibar, free Wi-Fi throughout.

James Cook Hotel Grand Chancellor ★ 🖋 This hotel has earned its reputation for great rates in a prime location with friendly staff. Some locals aren't enamored of it, but I have a real soft spot for this hotel's liveliness and great value. Club Rooms on Level 26 provide complimentary breakfast and extra amenities in the Club Lounge. For the little extra you pay, these 17 slick rooms are the pick of the bunch. With its views of the bustling city, direct access to shopping on Lambton Quay, and commerce on The Terrace, this hotel is the perfect base for business or pleasure—and don't forget to ask about the cheaper weekend rates. The hotel runs recycling and power-saving programs, and has a Qualmark Enviro-Silver award.

147 The Terrace, Wellington. www.ghihotels.com. ℂ **0800/699-500** in NZ, or 04/499-9500. Fax 04/499-9800. 260 units. NZ$185–NZ$450. Long-stay, off-peak, and special deals. AE, DC, MC, V. Valet parking NZ$18. **Amenities:** 2 restaurants; 2 bars; babysitting; concierge; limited gym on-site w/use of full-size off-site gym; day spa and beauty treatments. *In room:* A/C, TV/DVD/pay movies, fridge, hair dryer, minibar, Wi-Fi throughout.

Victoria Court Motor Lodge ★ 🛍 Stay in this tidy, convenient complex and you can forget all about driving your car. It's just a hop, skip, and jump from central shopping and restaurants. What's more, the 25 units have much to offer in terms of value and comfort. The two-bedroom units especially are a gift for families or two couples traveling together, and when you see the smart kitchens, you might even feel inclined to cook. Best of all, it's just behind my favorite part of town—Cuba Mall.

201 Victoria St., Wellington. www.victoriacourt.co.nz. ℂ **0800/282-850** in NZ, or 04/472-4297. Fax 04/385-7949. 25 units. NZ$150–NZ$205. Extra person NZ$20. AE, DC, MC, V. Long-stay, off-peak, and weekend rates. Victoria St. is one-way heading west so enter it off Vivian or Dixon sts. **Amenities:** Babysitting. *In room:* TV, fridge, hair dryer, kitchenette or kitchen, Wi-Fi throughout.

INEXPENSIVE

Those traveling in campervans will be delighted to hear there is now a new, centrally located, campervan park within 3 minutes of the Interislander Ferry terminal and right next to many of Wellington's top attractions. **Wellington Waterfront Motorhome Park** (www.wwmp.co.nz) is well signposted on Waterloo Quay and has room for 39 vans. There is onsite power, an ablutions block, and a daily onsite manager (available 7am to 7pm). It costs NZ$50 per vehicle per day.

Wellington City YHA This is without doubt the best backpacker establishment in Wellington. It hums with activity as guests of all ages settle into crisp, colorful rooms—private or bunk style—and the international staff seems to know everything there is to know about the city. Location is a prime attraction, and rooms are well situated for sunshine and harbor views. Internet and postal services are available, and a lounge acts as a great social spot. There is a well-equipped kitchen, plenty of quiet intimate spaces, and a supermarket just across the road. All transport and other YHA bookings can be made on the premises.

Cambridge Terrace and Wakefield St., Wellington. www.yha.co.nz. (C) **04/801-7280.** Fax 04/801-7278. 320 beds. NZ$28–NZ$32 multi-share; NZ$80–NZ$120 double with en-suite bathroom; NZ$85–NZ$95 double with shared bathrooms. Nonmembers pay additional NZ$3 per person per night. Off-peak rates. MC, V. Carpark building nearby. **Amenities:** Dining room; Internet room. *In room:* Hair dryer on request.

In Thorndon/Kelburn

Lovers of heritage homes and a good view will enjoy the comforts of three lovely rooms at **Lambton Heights ★**, 20 Talavera Terrace, Kelburn (www.lambtonheights. co.nz; (C) **04/472-4710;** fax 04/472-4715), priced from NZ$195 to NZ$300. It's just 5 minutes from the inner city. If you prefer your privacy, head for **Ascot Cottage,** Ascot St., Thorndon ((C) **04/479-3721;** fax 04/479-3701), where you'll find a delightful 1-bedroom self-contained stay that sleeps four for NZ$200 to NZ$275. Breakfast provisions are supplied and it's just a short walk from Tinakori Village.

Gardens Homestay ★   Neil Harrap and Sally Guinness like to say that guests are simply friends they haven't met yet. As the inventor of New Zealand's Fly By Wire ride, Neil has an extensive knowledge of tourism, which he delights in sharing with those lucky enough to score a bed in this grand 1892 Victorian home filled with antiques. The large two-bedroom, upstairs suite (with one smallish bathroom) is ideal for two couples or family members traveling together. It's quiet and private, and has lovely views over one of Wellington's premier residential areas.

11 St. Mary St., Thorndon, Wellington. www.gardenshomestay.co.nz. (C) **04/499-1212.** One 2-bedroom suite. NZ$285. Long-stay and off-peak rates. Rates include breakfast. MC, V. **Amenities:** Free bikes; heated outdoor pool. *In room:* A/C, hair dryer, Wi-Fi.

In Mount Victoria/Oriental Parade

The **Copthorne Oriental Bay ★**, 100 Oriental Parade and 73 Roxburgh St., Mt. Victoria (www.millenniumhotels.co.nz; (C) **0800/808-228** in NZ, or 04/385-0279), is fresh from a major makeover and has 118 beautifully appointed rooms, each with a private balcony affording some of the best views in Wellington. Rates range from NZ$175 to NZ$225.

Booklovers Bed and Breakfast ★★ 🎒   Journalist and author Jane Tolerton offers four large rooms in her two-story Victorian home, and she's a terrific and knowledgeable hostess who knows just when to leave you alone. My pick is the downstairs room, but all are lovely. The whole place heaves with books—if you dabble in the bookshelves you may never want to leave! It's just a short walk from Courtenay Place, or hop on one of the buses that stop right outside the gate.

123 Pirie St., Mount Victoria. www.booklovers.co.nz. (C) **04/384-2714.** 4 units. NZ$195–NZ$250. Long-stay and off-peak rates. Rates include breakfast. MC, V. **Amenities:** Babysitting. *In room:* A/C, TV/DVD, guest fridge, hair dryer, free Wi-Fi throughout.

Mount Victoria Homestay   The visitors' book at Bill and Coral Aitchison's inner city home is filled with glowing reports on their hospitality and generosity—"hosts from heaven," they're called. Their 1920s villa was completely restored in 2002 and everything—from the Wedgwood and Spode dinnerware to hearty breakfasts to the tranquil garden courtyard where guests enjoy evening drinks—illustrates Coral's attention to detail. Two upstairs guest rooms are quiet and private, yet just a few minutes' walk from some of the capital's best restaurants and nightlife. Guests can participate in the Aitchisons' voluntary carbon-offset program to benefit a 100-acre conservation reserve.

11 Lipman St., Mount Victoria, Wellington. www.mountvictoria.co.nz. *©* **04/802-4886.** Fax 04/802-4877. 2 units. NZ$315. Rates include breakfast, canapés, and pre-dinner drinks. MC, V. **Amenities:** Babysitting. *In room:* TV/DVD, fridge, Wi-Fi.

Ohtel ★★★ *✦* I love this small, new, chic boutique hotel for its great location, its striking individuality, and its total commitment to sustainability. Stylishly furnished throughout with the owner's collection of mid-century modern furniture and German ceramics, it is perfectly placed, overlooking Te Papa and Oriental Parade. All rooms are large, but the six front-facing are the best for views. You get all the mod-cons here and they take a proactive ecofriendly stance with solar-powered showers and recycling within rooms. Best of all, the intimate scale makes it feel like home. It's a full sensory experience; I still dream about their gorgeous big bathrooms.

66 Oriental Parade, Mount Victoria. www.ohtel.com. *©* **04/803-0600.** Fax 04/803-0611. 10 units. NZ$495 studio; NZ$535 deluxe; NZ$595 suite; NZ$55 each extra person. Long-stay and off-peak rates. AE, MC, V. Valet parking NZ$28. **Amenities:** Lobby cafe for breakfast and cabinet food; bar; airport transfers NZ$48; babysitting; concierge; small cardio/weights gym and full-size gym nearby; nearby pool; limited room service; infra-red sauna; Wi-Fi in lobby. *In room:* A/C, LCD TV/digital movies, fridge, hair dryer, free Internet, minibar.

Near the Airport

Brentwood Hotel, 16–20 Kemp St., Kilbirnie, Wellington (www.brentwoodhotel.co.nz; *©* **0508/273-689** in NZ, or 04/920-0400; fax 04/920-0401), is a modest yet practical airport choice if all you want is a bed before an early departure. Rooms range from NZ$210 to NZ$230. **Villa Melina B&B,** 89 Ludlam St., Seatoun (www.villamelina.co.nz; *©* **0800/635-462** in NZ or 04/972-1205), offers three very nice ensuite rooms with breathtaking harbor views (NZ$185–NZ$375).

WHERE TO EAT

Wellington used to have the best concentration of restaurants and cafes of any city in New Zealand, but Auckland has edged it out. However, it's still crammed with a variety that reflects its cosmopolitan population. Everything is within walking distance and priced for all budgets. The visitor center's *Wine & Food Guide* gives an excellent introduction to many of the leading lights. Ethnic restaurants—Turkish, Greek, Indian, Thai, Mongolian, Japanese, Malaysian, Chinese, Korean, and more—abound and are found in the biggest concentration around Cuba Street and Courtenay Place. Cuba Street has become one of the hippest places to eat and a number of excellent restaurants and cafes there have loyal followers among locals. You'll also find a cluster of newer eateries in pockets along the waterfront, near Te Papa. And don't forget the suburbs: Thorndon, Mount Victoria, Oriental Parade, and Eastbourne, just for starters, have little pockets of culinary magic.

Situated strategically between the ever-expanding winegrowing regions of Marlborough and Wairarapa, Wellington couldn't be better placed to introduce you to the sublime delights of New Zealand's finest wines. It's wall-to-wall food and wine out here—go for it!

In the Inner City

EXPENSIVE

Boulcott Street Bistro ★★★ CONTINENTAL   A French-inspired menu will please lovers of classic cuisine with a contemporary twist—served to perfection in a cute little Victorian house right in the heart of the city. Small, intimate, and formal, it's elegance par excellence, and classic dishes like lamb shank, filet béarnaise, and crème brûlée will delight the testiest palate. It's popular so you may not get in the first time. Keep trying—if only for the lobster ravioli!

99 Boulcott St. ⓒ **04/499-4199.** www.boulcottstbistro.co.nz. No reservations. Main courses NZ$37–NZ$45. AE, DC, MC, V. Mon–Fri noon–2pm; Mon–Sat 6pm–late.

Logan Brown ★★★ INTERNATIONAL   Ask about Wellington's best restaurant, and the name Logan Brown will be mentioned consistently. It's all leather-upholstered booths, white-clothed tables, Corinthian pillars, and chandeliers big enough to swing on in what was once a banking chamber. The food is billed as "honest and simple" and focuses on fish and game. The wine list is lengthy with an uneven balance between French (they win) and New Zealand offerings. Funnily enough, you'll find this culinary star cast adrift in what was the city's red-light area—not that that should affect your decision to try the epicurean offerings of the most splendid a la carte restaurant in town. Service is impeccable. If you want to sample Logan Brown without emptying your wallet, go for the bistro lunch.

Cuba and Vivian sts. ⓒ **04/801-5114.** www.loganbrown.co.nz. Reservations recommended. Main courses NZ$40–NZ$45. AE, DC, MC, V. Mon–Fri noon–2pm; daily 5:30pm–late.

MODERATE

If you enjoy Indian food, **Great India Restaurant** ★, 141 Manners St. (ⓒ **04/384-5755**), comes highly recommended; it's open for lunch Monday through Friday midday to 2pm, and for dinner daily 5pm until late. Reservations are advised. I recommend **Ernesto** ★, 132 Cuba St. (ⓒ **04/801-6878**), if you want a relaxed, sunny cafe to read the morning paper. It's a little more relaxed than nearby Floriditas (see below), but the service can be patchy.

Caffe Astoria ★ MODERN CAFE/LIGHT FARE   This upmarket cafe has a prime setting in the center of Lambton Quay's little green space, and it's well patronized by businesspeople and earnest-looking Wellingtonians with a slightly professorial image about them. It's a great place to unwind with a bottle of wine, a good coffee, or a delicious snack. Its big interior is always full and buzzing, and it's a popular

---

 Quick Caffeine Fixes

Apart from the other cafes reviewed in this section, you'll find excellent coffee and good atmosphere at **One Red Dog,** 9–11 Blair St. (ⓒ **04/384-9777**); **Caffe L'affare** ★, 27 College St. (ⓒ **04/385-9748**), which has a fabulous humming atmosphere; and **Starbucks** (ⓒ **04/472-4861**), now firmly ensconced in several city locations, including the Old Bank Arcade & Chambers, on Lambton Quay (ⓒ **04/922-0624**), and also on The Terrace and on Willis Street. And for constant reliability, you can't beat my busy little favorite, **Arabica** ★ (ⓒ **04/473-7697**), opposite the Inter-Continental hotel on Grey Street, where people pour in like ants to a new food source.

Deli Fixings

Whether you want to stock up on picnic food or just sit and enjoy coffee with a fine range of edibles, don't miss these inner city delis and bakeries. **Dixon Street Gourmet Deli,** 45 Dixon St. (✆ **04/384-2436**), has a glowing reputation as long as my arm; and **Smith the Grocer,** in the Old Bank Arcade, Lambton Quay (✆ **04/473-8591**), is a surprise tucked in between leading fashion stores. Both have a wide range of specialty items to take home, plus delicious ready-to-eat treats for the moment. **Bordeaux Bakery,** 220 Thorndon Quay (✆ **04/499-8334**), and **Le Moulin,** 248 Willis St. (✆ **04/382-8118**), are two superlative French bakeries; and for Italian-style breads, try **Pandoro,** 2 Allen St. (✆ **04/385-4478; www.pandoro.co.nz**).

---

brunch spot on weekends. There's something quintessentially Wellington about it that shouldn't be missed. It's always my first stop when I arrive in the capital.

159 Lambton Quay. ✆ **04/473-8500.** Main courses NZ$15–NZ$26. MC, V. Mon–Thurs 7am–7:15pm; Fri 7am–8:15pm; Sat–Sun 9am–4pm.

Chow ★★ SOUTHEAST ASIAN   The fact that Chow has two inner city locations is an indication of its popularity. It has a casual, modern interior and its extensive range of noodles, grills, steamed dishes, and salads combined with wine, sake, cocktails, or teas, have made it a winner with busy professionals. Servings are tapas style, so order two or three menu choices. It's the sort of place I keep going back to because I know I'll always leave happy.

45 Tory St. and 11 Woodward St. ✆ **04/382-8585** or 04/473-4474. www.chow.co.nz. Main courses NZ$16–NZ$26. AE, MC, V. Daily noon–midnight.

Floriditas ★ EUROPEAN   A simple one-page menu makes for easy choices in this paisley-embellished corner retreat. European-inspired dishes like vegetable and ricotta lasagna and polenta-dusted calamari make a delicious lunch or light dinner, and the generally friendly staff is knowledgeable about their good wine list. It's also an excellent coffee stop, and daily sweet treats lining the countertop are there to be eaten. Don't resist the urge. I like the buzzy atmosphere here and it's a favorite with all ages, but it's enormously popular, especially in weekends, so be prepared to wait for a table.

161 Cuba St. ✆ **04/381-2212.** www.floriditas.co.nz. Reservations recommended for dinner. Main courses NZ$18–NZ$25. AE, MC, V. Mon–Sat 7am–11pm; Sun 8am–5pm.

Fratelli ★ ITALIAN   This is the place to come for fresh, 100% homemade pasta, gnocchi, risotto, and pizza. Chefs here blend traditional Italian cooking styles with new ideas to create great value meals like risotto with slow-cooked rabbit, button mushrooms, mascarpone, and preserved lemon. Traditional Italian desserts like tiramisu, *panforte,* and gelato should round off a very fulfilling evening.

15 Blair St. ✆ **04/801-6615.** www.fratelli.net.nz. Reservations recommended. Main courses NZ$22–NZ$30. AE, MC, V. Mon–Sat 5:30pm–late.

Lido Café ✦ CAFE   No matter what time of day you come here, you'll find a decent smattering of people to make things interesting. Lido has always been popular for its tasty meals, and its location opposite the City Council makes it a favorite lunch spot with the working crowd. This is a laid-back place, far from formal, and you can sit inside or out—see and be seen. The interior is looking a little tatty, but the place still tickles my taste buds with a menu that scans the continents.

Wakefield and Victoria sts. © **04/499-6666.** Main courses NZ$15–NZ$26. AE, DC, MC, V. Mon–Fri 7:30am–late; Sat–Sun 9am–late.

Monsoon Poon ★★ 🍴 SOUTHEAST ASIAN Sit and watch Southeast Asian chefs whisk up a myriad of divine dishes from Vietnam, India, Malaysia, China, Thailand, and Indonesia. You'll be spoilt for choice. Firecracker chicken rubbed in Malay chili paste and wok-fried is just one tongue-tingling example; or consider Bangkok street noodles, wok-fried with chicken, chili, tamarind, vegetables, and spiced cashew nuts. Either way you'll leave content after a great-value dinner.

12 Blair St. © **04/803-3555.** www.monsoonpoon.co.nz. Main courses NZ$18–NZ$22. AE, MC, V. Daily noon–midnight.

Osteria del Toro ★★ ITALIAN/MEDITERRANEAN There's a slightly over-the-top glamour to this restaurant and tapas bar that fits so perfectly with fine food. Whether it's a thin-crust Italian pizza, Spanish paella, Moroccan tagines, or the famous Greek saganaki cheese flamed with ouzo, you'll have a culinary night to remember here. And save space for mouthwatering desserts like tiramisu, baklava, or Spain's churros con chocolate.

60 Tory St. © **04/381-2299.** www.osteriadeltoro.co.nz. Main courses NZ$20–NZ$42. AE, DC, MC, V. Reservations recommended. Mon–Sat 6pm–late.

Pravda ★ CONTEMPORARY EUROPEAN The name, the pictures of Lenin, the sparkling chandeliers, the dark-wood paneling, and the long, dining hall all suggest something Russian, but the big brasserie menu takes a broader leap. Expect quality mid-price dishes like seared salmon or grouper with fennel and potato purée, confit of duck, or spiced lamb. It's sophisticated and doubles as a terrific cafe.

107 Customhouse Quay. © **04/801-8858.** www.pravdacafe.co.nz. Main courses NZ$24–NZ$28. AE, MC, V. Mon–Fri 11:30am–5pm; Sat 9am–3pm.

Shed 5 ★★ CONTEMPORARY SEAFOOD As the name implies, this is a huge restaurant, but its popularity and award-winning status are such that, even on a quiet

---

Cuba Character

This is my favorite bohemian part of Wellington with great food joints that shouldn't be missed. Top of the list is **Midnight Espresso** ★, 178 Cuba St. (© **04/384-7014**), an iconic, slightly scruffy melting pot of people and color. Quintessentially Cuba Street, it serves fabulous counter food and espresso late into the night. **Simply Paris** ★, 181 Cuba St. (© **04/801-5486**), is a French-owned cafe and patisserie with cakes to die for; I can never walk past it. **Caffe Italiano,** 229 Cuba St. (© **04/385-2703**), has an excellent deli and a lively weekend brunch scene that often includes the Italian community; and farther down, the French-owned bistro, **Le Metropolitain,** 146 Cuba St. (© **04/801-8007**; www.lemetropolitain.co.nz), has legions of fans that love the authentic provincial dishes and noisy atmosphere. **Matterhorn Bar & Restaurant** ★★★, 106 Cuba St. (© **04/384-3359**; www.matterhorn.co.nz), is a popular, award-winning choice—a dark, moody place where both the food and the service are superb. It turns into a classy nightspot after dinner and is also open for lunch.

The best of Wellington's worthwhile food courts is **Gourmet Lane,** in the BNZ Centre, 1 Willis St. This place is a dream for dollar-wise travelers, as even NZ$10 will fill the gaps. The choices include Chinese, burgers, gourmet pies, barbecue, and more. It's open Monday through Thursday from 8am to 5pm, Friday from 8am to 8pm, and Saturday from 10am to 3pm. Another popular choice is the **Reading Food Court** at Reading Cinema, Courtenay Place Central (✆ **04/801-4601**).

night, there is a decent crowd. If you like good seafood, this is the place to find it—right on the edge of the wharf. The menu also includes lamb, beef, venison, and chicken, and the service is friendly and unobtrusive.

Shed 5, Queen's Wharf. ✆ **04/499-9069.** www.shed5.co.nz. Reservations recommended. Main courses NZ$32–NZ$38. AE, DC, MC, V. Daily 11am–late.

Zico Cucina & Bar ★ 🍴 ITALIAN CAFE   Franco Zanotto left his role as executive chef at the famous Il Casino restaurant to start up this divine little cafe, and for that we can all be truly thankful. He's created just the right mix of relaxed informality, great-tasting food, and fun service. It's a family affair—his wife and sons also attend to your culinary needs—and the menu is so vast I had forgotten the first offerings before I read through to the last. Pizzas, seafood and veal dishes, and numerous pastas all deserve sampling. It's very popular, so be prepared to queue.

8 Courtenay Place. ✆ **04/802-5585.** Reservations required. Main courses NZ$22–NZ$32. AE, DC, MC, V. Mon–Fri 10:30am–late; Sat–Sun 5:30pm–late. Closed Dec 25–26 and Jan 1–3.

INEXPENSIVE

New Dynasty, 25 Tory St. (✆ **04/384-3288**), is a great place for traditional Chinese *yum cha* lunch—fat little dumplings and the like. The **Green Parrot,** Taranaki and Wakefield streets (✆ **04/384-6080**), is a backpacker regular that's been serving up big, old-fashioned meals for over 30 years. On Courtenay Place are numerous **kabob houses** that stay open late. **One Red Dog,** 9–11 Blair St. (✆ **04/384-9777**), has cheap wood-fired pizzas and good service.

In Thorndon/Kelburn

For a laid-back spot to put a smile on your face, head for **Backbencher Pub & Café,** 34 Molesworth St. (opposite Parliament; ✆ **04/472-3065**), where you'll find a great pub atmosphere that lightheartedly mocks the local parliamentarians. It's best summed up as cheap and cheerful. In Kelburn, seek out the pocket-size delights of **Kelburn Café,** 87–89 Upland Rd., Kelburn (✆ **04/475-8381**), which is open daily 9am to 5pm, serving great coffee and fabulous cakes.

Maria Pia's Trattoria ★★ ITALIAN COUNTRY   This gorgeous little family-owned and -operated trattoria was an instant success from the minute it opened its doors. Set in an old building, it has a warm, low-key interior that doesn't distract you in any way from the divine fresh pasta that is made, by hand, by Italian-born Maria every day. Located close to Parliament, it's invariably busy and the food is wholesome and authentic. The minestrone is a must and lemon sorbet a great way to finish.

55-57 Mulgrave St., Thorndon. ✆ **04/499-5590.** Reservations required. Main courses NZ$25–NZ$35. AE, MC, V. Tues–Fri 11:30am–2:30pm; Mon–Sat 6–11pm.

A Taste of France

La Cloche ★★, 134 Hutt Rd., Kaiwharawhara, Wellington (✆ 04/473-4892; www.lacloche.co.nz), sits at the bottom of the Ngaio Gorge beside a BMW showroom. It's there that you'll find the two Francois's—French business partners who have Wellingtonians lining up for all things French and edible in a former warehouse jammed with goodies to eat in or take away—over 40 French cheeses for a start, and their fresh breads are scrumptious. Open Monday to Friday 9am to 5pm; weekends 9am to 3pm.

Tinakori Bistro ★ MODERN NEW ZEALAND   This cute restaurant, right in the heart of Tinakori Village, is a delightful place for an evening meal, and it's been getting good reviews for years. You probably won't have a wild time here—the mood is generally pretty restrained—but the food is very good. I favor their fish of the day baked in an olive crust with fennel bulb tomato jus, but they also do a very good chargrilled beef filet with béarnaise sauce.

328 Tinakori Rd. ✆ **04/499-0567.** www.tinakoribistro.co.nz. Reservations recommended. Main courses NZ$25–NZ$34. AE, DC, MC, V. Tues–Fri noon–2pm; daily 6–10:30pm.

In Mount Victoria/Oriental Parade

Martin Bosley's Yacht Club Restaurant ★★★ MODERN NEW ZEALAND Previously reserved as the exclusive dining domain of members of the Royal Port Nicholson Yacht Club, this bright and classy spot has opened its doors to the wider public—and for that we can be truly thankful. You'll get some of the best dishes in Wellington here—luscious seafood served in myriad ways from an all-around creative menu. Try the smoked eel mousse or the oyster broth. Service is pleasant and confident and the waterside location is almost unbeatable. The menu changes daily, so there are always pleasant surprises.

Royal Port Nicholson Yacht Club, 103 Oriental Parade, Oriental Bay. ✆ **04/385-6963.** www.martin-bosley.com. Reservations recommended. Main courses NZ$35–NZ$45; degustation NZ$100–NZ$170. AE, DC, MC, V. Mon–Fri noon–3pm; Tues–Sat 6pm–late.

Ortega's Fish Shack ★★ SEAFOOD   Well known Wellington chef, Marc Limacher has created a wee gem that seems almost as cozy as a small, family dining room. Fish is the star of the menu—think Marlborough salmon, tuna steaks, and pan-roasted gurnard. Gruyere soufflé with basil cream should appeal to vegetarians.

16 Marjoribanks St., Mount Victoria. ✆ **04/382-9559.** www.ortega.co.nz. Reservation not accepted. Main courses NZ$30–NZ$37. AE, DC, MC, V. Mon–Sat 5:30pm–late.

The White House Restaurant ★★★ MODERN NEW ZEALAND   This is a top-priced option you'll hear recommended time and again. It draws the corporate crowd and the romancers and serves fine New Zealand food with great sea views. Flavors are mixed to perfection here and taste-teasers like spinach and oyster soup will leave you begging for more—grilled venison with mushrooms perhaps. They have excellent options for vegetarians and the fish is always perfect.

232 Oriental Parade (upstairs), Oriental Bay. ✆ **04/385-8555.** www.whr.co.nz. Reservations essential. Main courses NZ$39–NZ$45. AE, DC, MC, V. Daily 6pm–late; Fri noon–3pm.

Near the Airport

To call this area a culinary backwater is an understatement, and restaurants here seem to change like the weather. If you're staying in this area, consult with the locals. The best option is **Maranui Café,** the Parade, Lyall Bay (✆ **04/387-2829**), which is a quirky joint located in the distinctive Maranui Surf Life Saving Club building on the windy waterfront. It's a terrific place for coffee, big cakes, and light lunches, and with gulls soaring just outside the upstairs windows at table level, you'll soon forget all about the rush of the city. It's open daily 7:30am to 5pm. Make sure you check out the historic surf club photos in the stairwell. **Soi Café & Bar,** 305 Evans Bay Parade, Haitaitai (✆ **04/386-3830;** www.soicafebar.co.nz), is a new addition to Great Point Wharf. It's light, bright, and contemporary, and a lovely place to unwind over fish and salad or risotto before hitting the airport 5 minutes away. As the name suggests, there's an Asian undertone to the menu.

EXPLORING WELLINGTON
The Top Attractions

Museum of New Zealand—Te Papa Tongarewa ★★★ ☺ New Zealand's largest cultural investment and Wellington's most exciting attraction, Te Papa opened in 1998. It has since played a major role in increasing visitor numbers to the capital city. One of the largest national museums in the world, Te Papa is redefining the word *museum.* Built at a cost of NZ$317 million, it has attracted over 18 million visitors by combining interactive technology with stunning world-class displays that tell the story of New Zealand—its culture, history, art, and natural environment.

Te Papa is also a partnership between Pakeha (the majority culture of European descent) and Maori culture. It includes a range of magnificent exhibitions featuring **Mana Whenua ★★**, some of the country's most significant Maori treasures, as well as **Te Marae ★★**, a unique 21st-century carved meetinghouse.

The second level contains **Mountains to Sea,** which puts the spotlight on the natural world. From minuscule insects to a slightly creepy colossal squid specimen, with computer-generated interactive displays and 3D animation to keep people of all ages amused, it presents both the familiar and the bizarre of New Zealand's natural inhabitants. Head outdoors to **Bush City,** a living, growing exhibition of the natural environment, from native bush to volcanic landscapes. Cross a swing-bridge, visit a glowworm cave or a wetland, climb a lava flow, or dig for fossils. The story of New Zealand's dramatic landscape and the part that earthquakes, volcanic eruptions, and the weather play in its shaping, is told in **Awesome Forces.** This is also where you can see a carved figure of Ruaumoko, the Maori god of earthquakes, and where you can visit the earthquake house to experience a simulated aftershock of the Edgecumbe earthquake of 1987.

The part I love best, though, is **OurSpace ★★★**, a spectacular multimedia adventure. It includes **The Map,** a walk-on satellite map of New Zealand that triggers images; and **The Wall,** a fabulous interactive space where you can upload your own images to the Te Papa database and create works of art that merge with everyone else's. Two motion simulator rides add to the excitement. **The High Ride** takes you on an adrenalin-filled adventure through the thrill of adventure sports to a bungy jump off Auckland's Sky Tower. **The Deep Ride** explores an underwater volcano and creatures 2,000 meters (965,616 ft.) under the sea.

On Level 4, **Tangata o le Moana: The Story of Pacific People of New Zealand** explores how Pacific Island cultures have influenced and affected New Zealand—and kids will love the hologram movie of their early exploration. **Golden Days** is a captivating animated junk shop that comes alive, and **Passports ★★** explores the migrant story of New Zealand in a fantastic exhibition and audiovisual presentation that is one of the highlights of the museum. **Slice of Heaven/20th Century Aotearoa** explores the stories, people, and events that changed the 20th century.

Spread over six levels, the museum includes much more and warrants at least half a day's exploration. It's playful, imaginative, bold, and more than impressive. It is an essential destination if you're keen to learn more about New Zealand. Few people leave unmoved. It's stunningly high-tech and loads of fun. On top of that, the architecture isn't bad, either.

The 60-minute **Introducing Te Papa Tour** is an excellent choice if you're short on time. It runs hourly from 10am to 3pm November through March, and twice daily at 10:15am and 2pm in winter, with a 7pm Thursday tour year-round. The tour costs NZ$12 for adults and NZ$6 for children 15 and under. Request foreign-language guides at the time of booking. An excellent self-guided tour booklet is available at the information desk for NZ$3, and audio guides in several languages are also available.

Te Papa has two eateries: Te Papa Café (Level 1), serving excellent New Zealand fare; and Espresso Bar (Level 4), for coffee and snacks. It also has superb gift shops, **Te Papa Store,** featuring original crafts and top Maori designs, and **Te Papa Kids' Store,** chockfull of educational, fun, and distinctively New Zealand books and toys.

55 Cable St., on the Waterfront. © **04/381-7000.** Fax 04/381-7070. www.tepapa.govt.nz. Free admission; fees for some activities, tours, and short-term exhibitions. OurSpace rides NZ$10 adults, NZ$5 children 5-15. Daily 10am-6pm (Thurs till 9pm). Parking NZ$3.50 per hour up to daily maximum of NZ$28, or NZ$6 for evening if you arrive after 5pm.

Wellington Cable Car ★ ◙ This splendid little 4½-minute trip takes you to some of the best views you'll see anywhere. Pray for fine weather, as Wellington city and the harbor look spectacular from up here on a cloudless day. It's also the best way to access the Wellington Botanic Garden (see below); and there is a fine little **Cable Car Museum (© 04/475-3578;** www.cablecarmuseum.co.nz) at the top, detailing the 100-year history of the service. The museum has free admission and is open daily in summer from 9:30am to 5:30pm and in winter from 9:30am to 5pm (closed Dec 25). Please note that the Cable Car will be closed in April 2012 for its next safety survey; normal services will resume May 2012.

Cable Car Lane, 280 Lambton Quay (next to McDonald's) and Upland Rd., Kelburn, Wellington. © **04/472-2199.** www.wellingtonnz.com/cablecar. Round-trip fare NZ$6 adults, NZ$2 children, NZ$12 families. Mon-Fri 7am-10pm; Sat 8:30am-10pm; Sun and holidays 9am-10pm. Car runs every 10 min.

Wellington Botanic Garden ★ The Botanic Garden brochure and map, available at the Wellington visitor center or Treehouse Visitor Centre within the gardens, will help you make the most of your time in this leafy enclave. Established in 1868, the gardens have been managed by the Wellington City Council since 1891. They cover 25 hectares (62 acres), presenting a mix of protected native forest, conifer varieties, and plant collections with seasonal floral displays. The Lady Norwood Rose Garden is a colorful spectacle from November to May, with blooms flourishing in 106 formal beds. The Begonia House shows off tropical and temperate plants, including orchids and waterlilies, with a gift shop and Picnic Café adjacent. The Bolton Street Memorial Park includes a heritage rose collection and a historic cemetery. The chapel is open daily from 10am to 4pm.

The **Carter Observatory** ★★★, 40 Salamander Rd., Kelburn (✆ **04/910-3140;** www.carterobservatory.org), is another key attraction within the gardens. This is your chance to see the wonders of the Southern Hemisphere's night sky. It is a world-class attraction and kids will love the chance to spot black holes, the Milky Way, and other star groups through state-of-the-art digital technology. They also have excellent interactive displays. It's open daily November through April from 10am to 5pm, until 10:30pm on Saturday (closed Dec 25–26); May through October it's open daily from 10am to 5pm, and until 9:30pm on Tuesday and Saturday. Admission is NZ$18 for adults, NZ$8 for children 4 to 16. It's a 2-minute walk from the top of the Cable Car.

Access to the gardens is from the Cable Car or Centennial entrance on Glenmore St., Thorndon. ✆ **04/499-1400** for Treehouse Visitor Centre. www.wellington.govt.nz. Free admission. Daily dawn–dusk. Treehouse Visitor Centre Mon–Fri 9am–4pm; Begonia House Gift Shop & Cafe Oct–March 9am–5pm, Apr–Sept 9am–4pm. Shop closed Dec 25-26, Jan 1-2 and Good Friday. Karori Bus 3 from Lambton Quay stops outside Founders entrance on Glenmore St. Parking available along Glenmore St. and in the public lot adjacent to the Lady Norwood Rose Garden (limit 2 hours).

Wellington Zoo ★★ ☺ Wellington Zoo is renowned for its work with endangered species, such as the Sumatran tiger, chimpanzee, white-cheeked gibbon, and Malayan sun bear. It's also the only place in the capital to see the famous brown kiwi (the Kiwi House is open daily 9:30am–5pm) and the tuatara. The Tropical River Trail highlights a rainforest habitat, bird life, and several species of primates. An intriguing new feature is the zoo's NZ$6-million state-of-the-art animal hospital, **The Nest,** where a glassed-in gallery allows you to observe the surgical rooms. Zoo staff give a running commentary during animal check-ups and operations (10am–4pm daily). In February and March, look out for **Wild Summer Nights** ★★, when you can spend an evening at the zoo with a picnic (food outlets are available on the grounds) and listen to jazz or blues among the animals. Another interactive feature is the **Close Encounters** program ★★★, which offers the chance to hand-feed a red panda (must be 6 and over), a giraffe (6 and over), or the big cats (14 and over). All proceeds from Close Encounters go toward conservation projects.

200 Daniell St., Newtown. ✆ **04/389-3692** or 04/381-6755. Fax 04/389-4577. www.wellingtonzoo. com. Admission NZ$22 adults, NZ$10 children 3-16, NZ$40–NZ$55 family; NZ$75–NZ$200 for Close Encounters, bookings required. Daily 9:30am–5pm. Closed Dec 25. Bus: 10 or 23 to Newton Park from the railway station.

The Parliament Buildings ★★ New Zealand's Parliament Buildings are on Molesworth Street in the city center and include the distinctive beehive-shaped building that is the administrative headquarters. You can visit Parliament daily free of charge. The 1-hour tours include the Edwardian neoclassical **Parliament House,** the Victorian-Gothic **Parliamentary Library,** and, if the group is not too large, the 1970s-style **Beehive.** If you want to see history in the making, call first to check when the House is sitting. The Debating Chamber makes for fascinating spectator sport.

The refurbished buildings also present outstanding examples of New Zealand art. The most impressive of all is the spectacular work by Malcolm Harrison, which occupies the three-story height of the new Galleria. The Maori Affairs Select Committee Room, at the front of Parliament House, is another interesting feature, worth visiting for the remarkable carvings and weavings specially commissioned for it.

Across the road, the **Old Government Building** is also worth a look. It's the second-largest wooden building in the world and now houses the University Law Faculty. And since you're in the vicinity, you could also check out the **National**

WELLINGTON FOR free

Following are several chances to appreciate Wellington absolutely free:

- **Take in the Scenery from Mount Victoria:** Take a leisurely drive to the top and enjoy the spectacular views in all directions, or allow an hour or so to walk up the well-marked tracks, enjoy the sights, and return down a different route.
- **Savor Botanic Beauty:** Enjoy the lush greenbelt in the heart of the city. Check out the Carter Observatory and the sculptures in the gardens.
- **Explore Te Papa:** Don't overlook the possibility that one visit to the stunning Te Papa National Museum of New Zealand simply may not be enough!

- **Tour the Beehive:** Hope that a Parliamentary session coincides with your visit and stay and listen to the debates. Enjoy the artwork, too.
- **Wander Along Oriental Parade:** Amble along the waterfront, enjoying the architecture, the cafes, the views, and the buzz of activity as Wellingtonians race past on in-line skates and bikes.
- **Get Wet in the Bucket Fountain:** A popular city landmark since 1969 when it was unveiled as the centerpiece of the new Cuba Mall, the fountain surprises, soaks, and delights adults, children, and dogs alike.

Library of New Zealand, 70 Molesworth St. (✆ **04/474-3000;** www.natlib.govt. nz). The ground-floor National Library Gallery showcases the art and history collections of the Alexander Turnbull Library and is open Monday through Friday from 9am to 5pm, Saturday from 9am to 4:30pm, and Sunday from 1 to 4:30pm. The **Alexander Turnbull Library,** in the same building, is the research wing of the National Library, specializing in New Zealand and the Pacific. Books, serials, recordings, manuscripts, and archives are on the first floor and newspapers on the lower ground floor. On the second floor, visitors can peruse files of photographs. Drawings, paintings, and maps are available for research by appointment.

Parliament Buildings, Molesworth St. ✆ **04/817-9503.** www.parliament.nz. Free admission. Tours given hourly Mon–Fri 10am–4pm; Sat 10am–3pm; Sun 11am–3pm. Closed Jan 1–2, Waitangi Day (Feb 6), Good Friday, Dec 25–26. City Circular Bus stops at gates of Parliament.

More Attractions

City Gallery Wellington ★ City Gallery has a reputation for challenging viewers with the best of contemporary visual art—everything from painting, sculpture, film, and video to industrial and graphic design and architecture. It's not everyone's cup of tea, but if you want to know what's happening in the New Zealand world of contemporary art, it's a great place to start. A cafe, bar, and restaurant are also onsite.

Civic Sq., 101 Wakefield St. ✆ **04/801-3021.** Fax 04/801-3950. www.citygallery.org.nz. Admission by donation; some international exhibitions may carry an entry charge. Daily 10am–5pm. Free exhibition tours Sat–Sun at noon. Closed Dec 25.

The Dowse Art Museum ★★ If you found City Gallery a bit too intellectual (and some do), it will be well worth your while taking a trip out to The Dowse Art Museum, which has the best collection of New Zealand craft art in the country. They have regularly changing shows in a lively, colorful environment, generally with a broader appeal than those at the City Gallery. Exhibitions feature contemporary ceramics, jewelry, glass, textiles, wood, sculpture, and photography, most of it exceedingly pleasing to the eye.

45 Laings Rd., Lower Hutt. © **04/570-6500.** Fax 04/569-5877. www.newdowse.org.nz. Free admission; fees for some special exhibitions. Mon–Fri 10am–4:30pm; Sat–Sun and holidays 10am–5pm. Closed Dec 25. Situated 20km (12 miles) from Wellington city. Take the train to Waterloo Station and walk down Knights Rd. to the museum, or catch the Eastbourne/Big Red bus, which departs hourly from Courtenay Place to Queensgate.

Katherine Mansfield Birthplace ★ Anyone of a literary bent will get a great deal of pleasure from a visit to Katherine Mansfield's restored birthplace. New Zealand's most distinguished author and a short-story writer of world renown, Mansfield was born into the Beauchamp family in 1888. She left Wellington at age 19 for Europe, where she kept company with the likes of Virginia Woolf, T. S. Eliot, and D. H. Lawrence. The Beauchamp house has been meticulously restored. If you're familiar with Mansfield's stories, you'll get a sense of what inspired them as you walk about the family home.

25 Tinakori Rd., Thorndon. ©/fax **04/473-7268.** www.katherinemansfield.com. Admission NZ$8 adults, NZ$5 seniors and students, NZ$2 children under 12. Victorian teas by arrangement. Tues–Sun 10am–4pm. Closed Dec 25 and Good Friday. Bus: 14 Wilton (stops at nearby Park St.).

Museum of Wellington ★★ ☺ Housed in a historic icon, the 1892 Bond Store, this excellent, small museum presents the history of the area in six galleries with audiovisual displays, cinema screens, and traditional exhibitions of memorabilia and photographs. Make sure you see **Wahine Gallery,** which is a memorial to the 1968 marine tragedy in Cook Strait; and **A Millennium Ago,** where Maori legends are combined with special effects. If you want an intense glimpse into Wellington's past, this is the place to get it. Holograms and interactive displays are great for kids and there are free kids' activities every day.

The Bond Store, Queens Wharf. © **04/472-8904.** Fax 04/496-1949. www.museumofwellington.org.nz. Free admission. Short tours NZ$10; free at 2pm on Sun. Specialized tours NZ$35–NZ$45. Daily 10am–5pm. Closed Dec 25. City Circular bus.

☺ ESPECIALLY FOR kids

If you're ready to let the kids loose, head for **Capital E,** Civic Square, Victoria Street (© **04/913-3740;** www.capitale. org.nz), open Monday through Friday from 9am to 5pm and weekends 10am to 4pm. This wonderful place combines a varied program of exhibitions, events, and theater especially designed for families. It's all about fun, entertainment, and education. Call for current programs and admission prices.

Story Place, at Te Papa, Cable Street (© **04/381-7000;** www.tepapa.govt. nz), is a magical world of dress-ups,

storytelling, songs, and art activities for children 5 years and under. There are daily 45-minute sessions from 10:15am to 4:30pm and admission is NZ$5. Tickets can be purchased at Te Papa's Information Desk on Level 2 of the museum.

Older kids will get a buzz out of **Wet & Wild,** Frank Kitts Park, the Waterfront (© **04/235-9796**), where they can let loose on in-line skates, in paddleboats, or on water bikes. It's open daily December through February, weather permitting.

Pataka ★★   This modern gallery, 15 minutes north of the city, in Porirua, celebrates the cultural diversity of the region. It showcases the very best of Maori, Pacific Island, and New Zealand art, all of which gives you excellent insight into the region's heritage. If you're interested, there's also a chance to buy a piece of New Zealand art from their very good sales gallery.

Corner of Norrie and Parumoana sts., Porirua City. © **04/237-1511.** Fax 04/237-4527. www.pataka.org. nz. Free admission. Mon–Sat 10am–4:30pm; Sun 11am–4:30pm. Take the motorway heading north and exit at Porirua. Free parking.

Te Raukura/Te Wharewaka o Poneke ★   Opened in February 2011, this NZ$12.5-million purpose-built center on Wellington's gorgeous waterfront area, houses two ceremonial *waka taua* (war canoes) and *waka ama* (outrigger canoes). Built on the site of the old Te Aro Pa, one of Wellington's largest Maori communities until the late 1880s, the museum tells the story of the local Maori people and other significant *pa* around the harbor. The upper levels are fully equipped as a conference venue and it was a centerpiece of the October 2010 Rugby World Cup fan zone. The ground floor houses Karaka Café.

15 Jervois Quay, Taranaki St., Wharf. © **027/451-2196.** www.culturalvenues.co.nz or www.wharewakao poneke.co.nz. Free admission. Mon–Wed 7am–4pm, Thurs–Sat 7am–9pm, Sun 8am–6pm.

The Weta Cave ★ ☺   When Weta Workshop created the special effects for the *Lord of the Rings* trilogy (and many other movies), they initiated an enduring phenomenon. People still flock to the movie's locations and now, for the first time, they can get an inside look at the multi–Academy Award–winning Weta operation in this cavelike minimuseum. Close encounters with characters, props, and displays from the movies will give you a unique perspective on Middle Earth and other well-known movies like *King Kong* and *Narnia*—and like everything Weta does, it's memorable. Kids will love it, but so will Mum and Dad. There's also a terrific concept store where you can buy a range of pop culture and collectible items, including limited editions and hard-to-find miniatures.

Corner of Camperdown Rd. and Weka St., Miramar. © **04/380-9361.** www.wetanz.com. Free admission. Daily 9am–5:30pm. Closed Jan 1, Apr 25, Dec 25–26. Take bus route 2 toward Miramar and get off at Camperdown Rd.

ZEALANDIA: The Karori Sanctuary Experience ★★   Opened to the public in late 2002, this 252-hectare (623-acre) reservoir catchment was the world's first urban sanctuary. Only minutes from the inner city, it is home to rare native wildlife such as kiwi, saddlebacks, and tuatara, which were reintroduced after all pests and predators had been removed from the valley. Enjoy a self-guided bush walk and learn about the history of the area as well as plans for the continuing development of this unique urban greenbelt. Tracks range from flat and sealed to steep and muddy, requiring moderate fitness and sensible shoes, but you can take your time. The Sanctuary by Night tours are a real treat, and they depart daily 30 minutes before sunset. The new visitor center exhibit, opened in 2010, details the story of New Zealand's remarkable natural history and successful ecological restoration in the heart of the nation's capital. An excellent 5-minute film shows every half hour and between screenings you can check out the giant Haast eagle, native birdsong, giant snails, and the pests that play havoc with our forest environments. Allow half a day at least to get the most from the sanctuary.

31 Waiapu Rd., Karori. © **04/920-9200.** Fax 04/920-9000. www.visitzealandia.com. Admission Sanctuary only NZ$19 adults, NZ$9 children 5–14, NZ$46 family; Exhibition and Sanctuary NZ$29 adults,

AWAY FROM THE CROWDS: EXPLORING

hutt valley

Located just 15 minutes north of Wellington and easily accessed via the motorway, Hutt Valley is a scenic area made up of two separate cities, Upper Hutt and the larger Lower Hutt. Weaving alongside is the Hutt River, where you'll find some excellent walking and cycling tracks. The Hutt City and Upper Hutt i-SITE Visitor Centres (p. 264), have detailed walking trail maps. **Wellington Adventure Quad Bike Expeditions** (**(C)** **0800/948-6386;** www. wellingtonadventures.co.nz) offers several fun outings from a 1½-hour expedition for NZ$169 per person, to a 2-day exploration of the Hutt region for NZ$399 per person. The **Dowse Art Museum** (p. 282), is a key attraction in Lower Hutt; and **Jackson Street** in Petone is considered a place of national significance as the whole street is listed with NZ Historic Places Trust and the old shops are now home to many boutique stores and cafes.

Excellent beaches wrap around the upmarket seaside villages of **Eastbourne** and **Days Bay,** which are a short drive around the coast. Both are also accessible via the **Dominion Post Ferry** (p. 268). Regular bus and train services also run to Hutt Valley (p. 267). If you'd like to stay on this side of the harbor, **Guthrie Beachfront Cottage ★★**, 221 Marine Parade, Eastbourne (www. guthriecottage.co.nz; **(C)** **04/582-6221**), is a 2-bedroom cottage that would suit a small family or two couples traveling together. It's NZ$300 per couple and breakfast is included; each additional person costs NZ$40. **Boulcott Lodge ★★**, 615 High St., Boulcott, Lower Hutt (www.boulcottlodge.co.nz; **(C)** **0800/782-928** in NZ, or 04/586-1558), is an excellent, 17-room motel complex with rooms and apartments from NZ$145 to NZ$200. It has a Qualmark Enviro-Gold rating and Wi-Fi is available throughout. The visitor centers can put you in touch with some excellent **camping grounds.**

NZ$15 children, NZ$72. Daily 10am–5pm. Closed Dec 25. Access is from Waiapu Rd.; turn left when emerging from the Karori side of the Karori Tunnel. Bus: 12, 17, 18, 21, 22, or 23; travel past the entrance to Waiapu Rd. and disembark at the 1st stop after Karori Tunnel; the Sanctuary is an easy 5-min. walk at the end of Waiapu Rd.

Organized Tours & Cruises

The **Wellington City Sights Circuit Bus ★★** (**(C)** **09/583-5756;** www.citysights. co.nz) is a convenient and fun way to see the best of the capital's attractions. It departs daily every hour from Wellington i-SITE starting at 9:30am, with the last departure at 4:30pm. Each loop takes an hour and you can hop on and off at any of the 11 stops: Te Papa and the Waterfront, Courtenay Place, Basin Reserve, Wellington Zoo, Willis Street, Carter Observatory and Cable Car Museum, ZEALANDIA, Botanic Gardens, Parliament Precinct, and Lambton Quay. It costs NZ$30 for adults and children are free with a paying adult.

Hammond's Scenic Tours (**(C)** **04/472-0869;** www.wellingtonsightseeingtours. com) offers another comprehensive tour of Wellington. Their 2½-hour **Wellington City Tour** covers the financial and commercial area, Parliament buildings, and Botanic Garden; they also head up to Mount Victoria lookout and then around the

ISLAND sanctuary ★★★

Kapiti Island is a conservation lover's paradise. Managed by the New Zealand government as a nature reserve for over 100 years, it is known for its well-protected native flora and fauna. The island has always been important to a number of different Maori tribes, and of the total 1,965 hectares (4,854 acres), 13 hectares (32 acres) at Waiorua Bay are still designated Maori land. This is where you'll find **Kapiti Nature Lodge** and **Kapiti Island Nature Tours** (© 06/362-6606; www.kapitiislandnaturetours.co.nz), owned by John and Susan Barrett and John's sister, Amo Clark. John's *whanau* (family) has lived on Kapiti since the 1820s, and they have a wealth of historical and conservation knowledge about the island, which you'll discover if you take one of their guided walks. Their lodge offers cabins (each with four bunks) set in native bush, plus some oceanview accommodations with en suites; the dining room is in the central lodge. There's also a wealth of activities from nature and history walks to weaving weekends, amazing photo opportunities, night kiwi spotting, and the chance to swim, snorkel, or scuba dive in Kapiti Marine Reserve. The lodge has a capacity for just 10 overnight guests and 24 day visitors.

Every person visiting Kapiti Island must have a permit, and extra permits are required to enter the Department of Conservation land on either side of Kapiti Nature Lodge. These can be acquired through the Wellington DOC office (www.doc.govt.nz) and cost NZ$12 for adults, NZ$6 for children. Ferries to the island, departing from Kapiti Boating Club at Paraparaumu just north of Wellington, depart each day at 9am and 2:30pm, and cost NZ$65 for adults and NZ$40 for children. The trip takes 15 minutes, and because Kapiti is a strictly controlled conservation area, you will be asked for a bag check to eliminate the possibility of pests and predators getting onto the island. The team at Kapiti Island Nature Tours can help you organize permits. They also offer a day tour to the island if you're short on time. The day tour includes the ferry trip, a guided walk, and lunch, and costs NZ$358 per person. The Overnight Stay and Kiwi Spotting Experience includes all meals, a guided walk, and the tour, and costs NZ$567 per person.

coastal bays, returning to the city via View Road. It costs NZ$55 for adults and NZ$25 for children ages 4 to 14; tours depart daily at 10am and 2pm.

Flat Earth ★★ (© **0800/775-805** in NZ, or 04/977-5805; www.flatearth.co.nz) offers a range of excellent specialty tours, including very interesting **Maori Treasures** tours priced from NZ$229 per person for a half-day, and excellent half-day **Capital Arts Tours** that immerse you in the city's art and architecture for NZ$159 per person.

Zest Food Tours ★★ (© **04/801-9198;** www.zestfoodtours.co.nz) is a real hit with foodies. Its **Walking Gourmet** (daily 9:30am–1:30pm) costs NZ$255 per person and introduces you to the capital's lively food scene and hard-to-find places. **Taste Wellington** (daily 9:30am–3pm) costs NZ$399 per person and includes coffee roasting, top specialty food stores, a wine-matched lunch at an award-winning restaurant, and a visit to the home of a local food writer. **Chocolate Espresso** (9:30am–noon) is a behind-the-scenes look into Wellington's chocolate hot spots for NZ$135 for adults and NZ$99 for children under 12. Custom tours can be tailored to specific interests.

Wild About Wellington ★★ (© 027/441-9010 in NZ; www.wildabout wellington.co.nz) has a fabulous **Boutique Beer Tasting Tour,** which is hosted by local beer expert/writer Neil Miller. The private 1-hour walking day tour for one or two guests is great value at NZ$190 (NZ$225 for two guests); and a 3-hour evening tour is NZ$190 per person. Fashion lovers should ask about their terrific **City of Style Tour,** which takes you to meet local fashion designers for NZ$125 per person.

Seal Coast Safari ★ (© 0800/732-527 in NZ, or 04/801-6040; www.sealcoast. com) offers a completely different outing that departs daily from the visitor center at 10am and 1:30pm. For NZ$99 for adults (children 14 and under half-price), you'll spend 2¾ hours taking the coastal road to the seals at Red Rocks. **Walk Wellington** (© 04/385-1675; www.walkwellington.org.nz), on the other hand, gives you a fabulous value introduction to the city. The Essential Wellington tour is NZ$20 per person and departs from the visitor center daily, rain, hail, or shine, at 10am. Additional afternoon walks are offered in summer at 5:30pm Monday, Wednesday, and Friday. **Wellington Movie Tours** (© 027/419-3077 in NZ; www.movietours.co.nz) will give you a comprehensive overview of the Wellington movie scene, including visits to *The Lord of the Rings* locations, the Weta Cave (p. 284), and a look at on-site movie clips, and movie props. Tours range from NZ$40 to NZ$120 per person.

Finally, **Wellington Rover Tours** (© 0800/426-211 in NZ, or 04/471-0044; www.wellingtonrover.co.nz) is another excellent company offering a wide range of interesting area tours. Their half-day **Rover Ring Tour** will take you to seven of the best *Lord of the Rings* locations in the greater Wellington area. It departs at 8:30am and 1:30pm and costs NZ$95 for adults and NZ$50 for children 12 and under. Their full-day **Adventure Wairarapa** outing includes a choice of horse-trekking, mountain biking, or high ropes (an exploration of risk-taking, trust, and coaching that involves harnesses, helmets, cables, ropes, and wooden beams strung 6–15m/20–50-ft. high among trees and poles) in the morning, followed by a hearty homestead lunch; in the afternoon you visit Martinborough village and nearby vineyards. It costs NZ$240 for adults and NZ$140 for children under 12.

ON THE WATER

Take a Somes Island excursion with the **Dominion Post Ferry** (see "Getting Around," earlier in this chapter). Simply take the ferry and stop off on the island, picking up a return ferry a few hours later. The island recently reopened to the public after 100 years of restricted access. In recent times, it has served as a quarantine station and before that as a prisoner-of-war camp. It has been replanted and developed as a wildlife refuge and has walking tracks and great views.

OUTDOOR PURSUITS

GOLF There are a number of courses within 25 minutes of Wellington city. **Paraparaumu Beach Golf Club,** 376 Kapiti Rd., Paraparaumu Beach (© 04/298-4561; www.paraparaumubeachgolfclub.co.nz), is an 18-hole, par-71 course rated 1 of the top 50 courses in the world by *Golf Digest.* Greens fees are NZ$140, club rental is NZ$45, and carts are NZ$40. Reserve well in advance. **Hutt Golf Club,** Military Road, Lower Hutt (© 04/567-4722; www.huttgolfclub.co.nz), is an 18-hole, par-70 course where you'll pay NZ$75 for a round. **Karori Golf Club,** South Makara Road, Wellington (© 04/476-7337; www.karorigolf.co.nz), is an 18-hole, par-70 course; a round costs NZ$40 during the week and NZ$50 on weekends.

IN-LINE SKATING This is a great way to explore Oriental Parade. Skates can be hired from **Fergs Kayaks,** Queens Wharf (© **04/499-8898;** www.fergskayaks.co. nz), for NZ$8 per half-day. Daily rates available.

KAYAKING **Fergs Kayaks** (see above) is owned by New Zealand's legendary canoeist and Olympic gold medalist Ian Ferguson. You can do the self-paddle thing for NZ$15 to NZ$40 per hour, or join a guided group. Try the night harbor tour, NZ$80 to NZ$105 per person for 2½ hours of paddling, with soup and snacks at the end. **Tamarillo Sea Kayaking,** Kapiti (© **025/244-1616;** fax 04/239-9789), offers a more remote, nature-based sea-kayak experience around Kapiti Island, one of New Zealand's most famous conservation reserves. Instruction is given to those with no previous experience. The all-day adventure includes a chartered launch trip to and from the island and costs NZ$195. Birders will love this one.

MOUNTAIN BIKING This is one group that truly celebrates Wellington's hilly terrain. You have the choice of everything from a leisurely ride around the bays to a spine-chilling route that includes a vertical cliff face. For bike information, contact **Penny Farthing Cycles,** 89 Courtenay Place (© **04/385-2279;** www.pennyfarthing.co.nz). **Mud Cycles,** 338 Karori Rd. (© **04/476-4961;** www.mudcycles.co.nz), which is next to Wellington's Mountain Bike Park in Karori, offers a full fleet of rental touring and mountain bikes for children and adults. They also offer guided tours and instruction for all abilities.

SWIMMING The **Wellington Regional Aquatic Centre,** 62 Kilbirnie Crescent, Kilbirnie (© **04/387-8029**), has four heated pools: a lap pool, a learners' pool, and adjoining junior and toddler pools with an access ramp for people in wheelchairs. There are also diving facilities, Jacuzzis, saunas, a sun deck, a cafe, and a YMCA fitness center. The **Freyberg Pool,** 139 Oriental Parade (© **04/801-4530**), is an easy walk from most inner city accommodations.

TENNIS The **Wellington Renouf Tennis Centre,** 20 Brooklyn Rd., Central Park (© **04/384-6294;** www.wellingtontennis.org.nz), has 14 outdoor courts and 4 indoor courts. It's open Monday through Friday from 6am to 11pm, Saturday and Sunday from 8am to 11pm. A cafe and bar are on the premises.

WALKING There are endless walking opportunities in Wellington. The most obvious that spring to mind are a quiet amble through the **Botanic Garden** or around **Oriental Parade,** or a more taxing climb up any one of the many **Mount Victoria** tracks. The visitor center has a wide range of excellent brochures for self-guided tours including **Heritage Trail** tours, which give you the chance to learn and discover as you go; **Explore Wellington** tours (more than 10 of them), which detail various themed walks in different areas of the city; and **Five Lunchtime Walks,** which cover different parts of the inner city area in less than an hour.

SHOPPING

Wellington is such a compact city that it's easy for visitors to find their way around and to wander at ease. You can pick up the free guides, *The Fashion Map* and *The Arts Map,* at the visitor center. From the department and designer stores of Lambton Quay (nicknamed the Golden Mile) up Willis Street to the funkier side of town on Cuba Street, you'll find markets, alternative boutiques, secondhand stores, and great cafes. It's all easy and shopper-friendly. Store hours are usually Monday through Friday from 9am to 5:30pm, Saturday from 9am to 4:30pm, and Sunday from 10am to 2pm.

The always popular **Simply New Zealand,** 13 Grey St. (📞 **04/472-6817**), has a huge range of gifts, jewelry, and crafts, as well as wool knitwear, Maori carvings, and America's Cup souvenirs. **Te Papa Store ★★★**, Te Papa, Cable Street (📞 **04/381-7000**; www.tepapastore. co.nz), has one of the best selections of New Zealand arts, crafts, and souvenirs in the city. Everything is top quality and attractively laid out, and you don't pay local tax (GST) if you're mailing gifts overseas. **Ora ★**, 23 Allen St., Courtenay Place (📞 **04/384-4157**; www.ora.co.nz), open daily 9am to 4pm, features a big range of top-quality handmade New Zealand artworks in glass, fiber, ceramics, native timbers, and mixed media. They post goods overseas tax-free.

Other worthy places to browse top-notch arts, crafts, and jewelry are **Avid,** 48 Victoria St. (📞 **04/472-7703**; www. avidgallery.com); **Kura,** 19 Allen St. (📞 **04/802-4934**; www.kuragallery. co.nz); and **Vessel,** 87 Victoria St. (📞 **04/499-2321**). And for all things woolly, drive around the bays to **Sheepskin Warehouse,** Evans Bay Parade, Greta Point (📞 **04/386-3376**; fax 04/386-3379). New Zealand has the best technology in the world for sheepskin products, and if you doubt that, come here. An overseas shipping service is available and GST is deductible. For top-quality Maori art, both contemporary and traditional, step into **Iwi Art ★★**, 19 Tory St. (📞 **04/803-3253**; www.iwiart.co.nz).

The best place to start is **Lambton Quay,** which has three linked arcades, and **Capital on Quay,** at 250 Lambton Quay (📞 **04/473-8868**). There are boutiques, a heap of shoe stores, music shops, and excellent bookstores. It's also where you'll find Wellington's most famous department store, **Kirkcaldie & Stains** (📞 **04/472-5899;** www.kirkcaldies.co.nz), which has been offering traditional service and quality merchandise since 1863. Nearby, **Untouched World ★★★**, 147 Featherston St. (📞 **04/473-2596;** www.untouchedworld.com), showcases renowned lifestyle clothing in merino and possum fur.

The historic Bank of New Zealand building on Lambton Quay is now the **Old Bank Arcade & Chambers** (📞 **04/922-0600;** www.oldbank.co.nz), a retail arcade after the style of Sydney's Queen Victoria Arcade. It has attracted interest from top national and international retail stores and includes cafes, restaurants, and designer clothing stores.

As you move onto **Willis Street,** you'll find more fashion, books, and music; and **Quoil ★★**, 149 Willis St. (📞 **04/384-1499;** www.quoil.co.nz), a gallery representing New Zealand's top contemporary jewelers. Further along, **Aquamerino ★★**, 97 Willis St. (📞 **04/473-9106;** www.aquamerino.com), sells a beautiful range of New Zealand merino clothing for men and women. Turn down **Manners Street** and make your way into the weird and wonderful **Cuba Street** area, which gets more interesting the higher up the mall you go. If you want your future predicted, your sexual preferences catered to, your body pierced or tattooed, or if you're just craving a cup of damn good coffee, you're in the right area. For the finest New Zealand contemporary art, head for **Hamish McKay Gallery ★★★**, 1st floor, 39 Ghuznee St. (📞 **04/384-7140;** www.hamishmckaygallery.com); collectible designer toys are just along that street at **Pop-Ups ★★**, 57 Ghuznee St. (📞 **04/801-5105;** www.popups.co.nz).

Another good specialty-store area is the **Tinakori Road Village.** Much more upmarket than Cuba Street, it's not overly big, just a few smart, little gift stores, galleries, and the like. My favorite is **Millwood Gallery,** 291b Tinakori Rd., Thorndon (© **04/473-5178;** www.millwoodgallery.co.nz), an art-and-book boutique filled to the gills with divine papery offerings. It specializes in original works of art based on Wellington and has a range of cards and gift wraps. Antiques fans will love **Tinakori Antiques ★★,** 291a Tinakori Rd. (© **04/472-7043**), which has two small stores crammed with collectibles, furniture, and antique jewelry. I spent far too much time here. **Groom ★,** 306 Tinakori St. (© **04/472-5605**), will appeal to the men. This tiny little squeeze of a store is home to barber and stylist, ex–All Black Johni Rutene, who has covered the walls in rugby paraphernalia. Complete with an old-fashioned barber chair, it is one of the few barbershops offering hot-towel cutthroat shaves.

WELLINGTON AFTER DARK

This is one city where you won't run out of things to do after dark. Start by checking the current issues of *Capital Times* and *What's On,* both free and available at visitor centers and many cafes.

The Performing Arts

Wellington is home to the largest performing-arts festival in the country (see "Special Events," earlier in this chapter); it is also home to the National Orchestra and Opera, the Royal New Zealand Ballet, and four thriving professional theater companies. In addition, you'll find the National Dance and Drama Centre, the New Zealand School of Dance, and the New Zealand Drama School, all based in the capital.

The rejuvenated **Westpac St. James Theatre,** 77–87 Courtenay Place (© **04/ 802-4060;** www.stjames.co.nz), opened its doors in 1998 after a NZ$21-million refurbishment project; this fine Edwardian venue now combines a preserved heritage theater with state-of-the-art technology. Apart from staging top-quality musical shows, it is also now the permanent home of the Royal New Zealand Ballet Company.

The city has a healthy professional theater scene. The **Downstage Theatre,** in Hannah Playhouse, Courtenay Place and Cambridge Terrace (© **04/801-6946;** www.downstage.co.nz), presents first-rate theater in an award-winning structure. Downstage's year-round season presents its own productions and the best touring shows, including classics, contemporary drama, comedy, and dance, with an emphasis on quality New Zealand works. Tickets are NZ$40 to NZ$45 for most shows.

Circa Theatre, 1 Taranaki St. (© **04/801-7992;** www.circa.co.nz), sits grandly beside Te Papa. It produces quality and generally innovative productions. You can enjoy a preshow meal at its licensed cafe. Tickets are NZ$46 for adults and NZ$25 for under 25s. **Bats Theatre,** 1 Kent Terrace (© **04/801-4176;** www.bats.co.nz), is seen as the country's top developmental theater, presenting new and experimental plays and dance at great prices (NZ$12–NZ$20). **Embassy Theatre,** 10 Kent Terrace (© **04/384-7657;** www. deluxe.co.nz), was refurbished for the world premiere of *The Lord of the Rings: The Return of the King.* The combination of sumptuous 1920s decor with a giant screen and state-of-the-art digital sound, not to mention its cafe and bar, makes it well worth a visit. There are summer screenings of *The Lord of the Rings* every Sunday afternoon.

The Club & Bar Scene

It's simple: When it gets dark, the party starts, and again, the compact nature of the city is a blessing for those looking for a good time. There are late-night bars and dance venues aplenty, and if you want to bypass the quiet start and head straight for the action, then **Courtenay Place** it is. Not everyone will enjoy the large number of drunken youths in this area on Thursday, Friday, and Saturday nights, but there are enough bars in this part of town for all ages to find a comfortable niche, and anyone over 25 who has outgrown the vomiting-in-the-street trick need only look around for a place that suits his or her mood. Be warned though—the Wellington bar scene is ever-changing and venues listed here may have changed names and owners by the time you arrive. The best bars are also typically in tiny, tucked-away places, so ask the locals about the latest hot spots.

The closing time for bars and clubs varies wildly in New Zealand. It depends on whether you're in the provinces or a major city, whether it's summer or winter, and what type of liquor license the establishment holds. In a major city like Wellington, it is safe to assume that most stay open in summer until between midnight and 2am. Many have 24-hour licenses.

The "in" places for the older crowd (that's 30-plus) are always changing, but you'll be safe if you start with trendy **Zibibbo,** 25–29 Taranaki St. (℃ **04/385-6550**), which inhabits the old central police building. You can get great Spanish-Italian tapas here along with sophisticated nightlife. One of the coolest places to be seen at is the very posh **Arbitrageur ★★★**, 125 Featherston St. (℃ **04/499-5530**), where you'll find sophisticated club style, over 600 of the best wines, and an interior that will win over any wine purist's heart. It's open Monday through Thursday from 11:30am till late and on Saturdays from 5pm.

Matterhorn ★★★, 106 Cuba St. (℃ **04/384-3359**), serves great cocktails, and once the restaurant crowd is satisfied, it turns into a funky bar deserving of its accumulated awards. **Mighty Mighty ★**, Level 1, 104 Cuba St. (℃ **04/385-2890**), has gone retro with menus on old record covers and cocktails that will get your evening off to a good start. **Concrete Bar ★**, Level 1, Cable Car Lane, Lambton Quay (℃ **04/473-7427**), is a sophisticated joint with a great wine-and-beer list that's also a good spot to commence a night on the town. **Motel ★★**, Forrester's Lane (℃ **04/382-8585**), creates an exotic mood with a retro twist that includes sculptures and oriental lamps. It's very suave and runs adjacent to the ever-popular Chow restaurant. **Red Square ★★**, 28 Blair St. (℃ **04/802-4244**), has one of those sumptuous, moody interiors that instantly puts you in a party mood, helped greatly by a head-spinning vodka list. It attracts a mixed crowd—as does its downstairs counterpart, **Ponderosa,** 20 Blair St. (℃ **04/384-1064**), which, as the name suggests, has let loose with a cowboy-themed lounge bar. If you can overlook corny names like Stubborn Mule and Randy Ranger, you'll have a great time with their delicious cocktail list. **The Apartment ★★**, 25 Allen St. (℃ **04/385-9771**; www.theapartment. co.nz), is a chic spot modeled after a New York loft apartment. It comes complete with bookshelves, dining room, leather sofas, a terrace, and a bedroom—all done in the best of taste. Feeling romantic? **Hawthorn Lounge ★★★**, 82 Tory St. (℃ **04/890-3724**; www.hawthornlounge.co.nz), is an intimate bar with a 1920s private gentlemen's club vibe.

Molly Malones, Taranaki Street and Courtenay Place (℃ **04/384-2896**; www. mollymalones.co.nz), is the biggest and busiest Irish bar in town, with live music every weekend. Also in this area is the hugely popular **Coyote,** 63 Courtenay Place (℃ **04/385-6665**), which attracts a mixed and generally rowdy crowd.

There are also interesting bar and dance choices in the Cuba and Willis streets area, which tend to be a bit less concerned with fashion and making an appearance.

Beer Literacy

If you're a beer lover, Wellington will please you to no end. I'd start with **Tasting Room,** 2 Courtenay Place (📞 04/384-1159; www.thetastingroom. co.nz), which is New Zealand's 10th location of Monteith's Craft Beer Bar. They know all about creative beer and food matching. **Bodega,** 101 Ghuznee St. (📞 04/384-8212; www.bodega. co.nz), is Wellington's original ale house serving the city's only hand-drawn ales. It has 17 different tap beers and a massive selection of imports. They also host top New Zealand bands. **Mac's Brewery,** corner of Taranaki and Cable streets (📞 04/802-1956), has great harbor views where you can sit back and see why these beers are international award winners. Take one of their beer- and food-matching evenings or a brewery tour. The **Courtenay Arms,** 26–32 Allen St. (📞 04/385-6908), is a real English ale house with premium imported British ales on tap. And no beer selection would be complete without the **Malthouse** ★, 48 Courtenay Place (📞 04/802-5484; www.themalt house.co.nz), which has New Zealand's largest range of beers—over 150 local and international brews.

The Gay Scene

The visitor center has folders full of information related to the gay scene, including gay-friendly accommodations and nightspots other than those listed here. **S&M's (Scotty & Mal's),** 176 Cuba St. (📞 04/802-5335; www.scottyandmals.co.nz), is an intimate two-level gay cocktail lounge with a B&D (basement and dance) bar downstairs; and **Club Ivy,** 3rd floor, 13 Dixon St. (www.clubivy.wordpress.com), is a leading lesbian, gay, and bi club with a party atmosphere. There's a gay sauna at **Checkmate,** 15 Tory St. (📞 04/385-6556; www.checkmatesauna.co.nz). For more info, call **Gay Wellington** (📞 04/473-7878; www.gaywellington.org.nz). The line is open nightly from 7:30 to 10pm for information and support. **Gay Line Wellington** (www.gayline.gen.nz) is also a useful first stop. **Lesbian Line** (📞 04/499-5567) operates Tuesday, Thursday, and Saturday 7:30 to 10pm, offering information on accommodations, sporting events, and counseling services.

A SIDE TRIP TO WAIRARAPA ★★★

Don't be fooled by the quiet rural exterior and quaint, sleepy villages; there's a lot happening in the Wairarapa. This is the place of wine, warmth, and more wine. And I'm not talking hobby vineyards—Wairarapa is home to some of the world's finest boutique vineyards, and built around that draw card is the biggest array of boutique accommodations you'll find anywhere in New Zealand.

Just over an hour's drive from Wellington across the winding Rimutaka Hills (take care driving in winter), you'll find a spread of productive farmland hemmed in by the rugged Tararua Ranges to the west and the dramatic Pacific Ocean to the east.

Twenty years ago, Wellingtonians scarcely gave Wairarapa a second look; now it's one of their hottest weekend getaway spots. Most of the activity is centered on **Greytown,** which has become a haven of boutique stores and cafes; and in **Martinborough,** where Hong Kong businessman Mike Laven bought the old **Martinborough Hotel** (p. 296) and turned it on its head. It's now one of the premier accommodations in the area. Not content to rest on his laurels, our Mr. Laven simply picked up the old Station Hotel in **Masterton,** a little farther north, moved it to Martinborough, and turned it into a restored office, retail, and wine complex.

It's entrepreneurial action and foresight such as these that have seen Martinborough and its southern neighbors, **Featherston** and **Greytown,** really take off. Wharekauhau Country Estate at Palliser Bay is a stunning addition to the Small Luxury Hotels of the World group, and there are new shops, cafes, and lodgings opening all the time. The **Toast Martinborough Wine, Food & Music Festival** attracts over 9,000 fans every year, the Martinborough Craft Fair is an annual favorite, and there are numerous outdoor activities to keep you amused if you ever run out of wine to taste.

Essentials

GETTING THERE   From central Wellington, take the northern motorway, driving around the harbor toward Lower Hutt, and follow the signs to Wairarapa. Once on this route, you head over the Rimutaka Hills and arrive in Featherston, the southernmost village in Wairarapa, around 1½ hours later.

If you're entering the area from the north, it takes 3 hours from Napier and 1 hour from Palmerston North to reach Masterton. Flying to Martinborough from Wellington by helicopter takes just 15 minutes.

VISITOR INFORMATION   In Masterton, the **Masterton Visitor Centre,** corner of Dixon and Bruce streets (© **06/370-0900;** fax 06/378-8451; www.wairarapa nz.com), is open daily Monday to Friday 9am to 5pm, and weekends 10am to 4pm, with extended hours in summer. If you don't intend to drive the extra 30 minutes north from Featherston/Martinborough, check out the office at 18 Kitchener St., Martinborough (© **06/306-5010**). It's open the same hours.

Exploring the Area

About 27km (17 miles) north of Masterton on State Highway 2, **Pukaha Mount Bruce National Wildlife Centre ★★** (© **06/375-8004;** www.pukaha.org.nz) is New Zealand's main center for the captive breeding of endangered species. Wheelchair-accessible walkways wind through rainforest and aviaries where threatened birds such as the kiwi and stitchbird are making a comeback. Make your first stop the excellent audiovisual display, which will help you understand what the center is all about, and then pick up the free walkway guide. Make sure you see the live nest-cam film. Admission is NZ$20 for adults, NZ$6 for children 5 to 15, and NZ$50 for a family. It's open daily from 9am to 4:30pm (closed Dec 25); the monster eels are fed at 1:30pm and the kaka (native parrots) at 3pm.

The artistically minded might like to investigate **Aratoi-Wairarapa Museum of Art & History,** Bruce and Dixon streets, Masterton (© **06/370-0001;** www.aratoi. co.nz), which is open daily from 10am to 4:30pm, showcasing local talent.

Heading south toward Cape Palliser, look out for **Putangirua Pinnacles ★★★,** a world-class example of badlands erosion. The pinnacles were formed in the past 120,000 years by heavy rain eroding an ancient gravel deposit, and it's worth the 30-minute walk off the road to see these spectacular formations. Quite eerie, and great photographic material. Farther around the coast, you'll find the cute fishing village of **Ngawi** and the country's largest breeding area for **New Zealand fur seals.**

The **Hau Nui Wind Farm,** New Zealand's first commercial wind farm, is 21km (13 miles) southeast of Martinborough on White Rock Road. Huge turbines are spaced along a 540m (1,770-ft.) ridge and make a dramatic silhouette against the skyline. The site itself is not open to the public, but you can check out a viewing area with information about the project.

If walking is your thing, consider the 3-day **Tora Coastal Walk** (✆ **06/307-8115** or 06/307-8862; www.toracoastalwalk.co.nz), which takes you through native bush and river valleys, staying at a different hill-country farm each night. It costs NZ$415 per person, and includes accommodations and luggage cartage. It's open from October through April and bookings are essential.

Fine **gardens** abound in the Wairarapa. The visitor center's *Wairarapa Escape Planner* lists great gardens along with other attractions of the region. The *Garden Trails* brochure lists 10 South Wairarapa gardens. The daily **Wairarapa Garden Escape ★★** (✆ **0800/471-227** in NZ; www.tranzit.co.nz) is a good value; the tour takes you from Wellington or Lower Hutt by train to the Wairarapa, where you join a coach and visit two extraordinary gardens, the very formal Richmond (www.boxwood. co.nz) in Carterton (a Garden of National Significance), and the hillside garden of Assisi (www.assisigardens.co.nz). Lunch, wine tasting, and a wander though the village of Greytown are included. The package costs NZ$182 for adults (NZ$213 with Wellington hotel transfers), and NZ$115 for children 5 to 15 (NZ$138 with transfers).

THE WINERIES

The high sunshine hours and low autumn rainfall of the Martinborough region have been major factors in the international success of the small boutique wineries in this area. It is distinguished from other New Zealand wine areas by the high proportion of red-wine grape plantings and by its reputation for quality pinot noir. Most wineries are open for tastings while stocks permit, and some are open year-round. There are over 30 vineyards in the Martinborough area alone, and large tracts of grapes have also been planted at Gladstone and Masterton. The best time to visit is from late October to early March, when new wine stocks have been released. The best way to explore the area is to pick up a copy of the **Classic New Zealand Wine Trail Guide ★★** (www.classicwinetrail.co.nz) from an i-SITE Visitor Centre. It links five of New Zealand's best wine regions, including the Wairarapa, and adds in sights, shopping, and dining opportunities so you can get the most from the regions it covers. To find out more about winemaking in this region, go to www.nzwine.com. Conducted group tours to area wineries can be made only by prior arrangement. Contact the Martinborough visitor center (✆ **06/306-9043**), which can also supply the free brochure *Martinborough & Wairarapa Wine Trails.*

When it comes to selecting the best of the bunch, it's pretty subjective, but local opinion consistently swings in the direction of **Dry River Wines,** Puruatanga Road (✆ **06/306-9388;** fax 06/306-9275), a small low-tech winery specializing in the Alsace varietals pinot gris, Gewürztraminer, and Riesling, as well as chardonnay, pinot noir, and sauvignon blanc. The majority of its wines are sold by mail order within a few weeks of release, so it's unlikely you'll find the place open.

Ata Rangi Vineyard ★★, Puruatanga Road (✆ **06/306-9750;** www.atarangi. co.nz), maker of an internationally acclaimed pinot noir, has been operating since 1980. It has an excellent tasting room for sampling the flagship pinot noir along with sauvignon blanc, chardonnay, and a summer rosé.

Palliser ★★, Kitchener Street (✆ **06/306-9019;** www.palliser.co.nz), is a leading force in this area. It features a purpose-built winery and a large barrel hall, and it has an excellent reputation for its award-winning pinot noir, chardonnay, sauvignon blanc, and Riesling. Wines are produced under the Palliser Estate and Pencarrow labels. Palliser is open daily for cellar sales.

The **Paua World,** 54 Kent St., Carterton (© 06/379-4247; www.pauaworld. com), is an attraction in its own right. It gets over 50,000 visitors a year and has a huge range of jewelry and souvenirs at factory prices. It's open daily and there are factory tours and video presentations to enjoy. **Martinborough Cheese Shop,** 8 Kitchener St., Martinborough (© 06/306-8383), features specialty cheeses and local delicacies, including wines and olive oils, and is open daily from 10am to 5pm. **Saratoga Dairy Goats,** Caveland Road, Gladstone, Masterton (© 06/372-7074; www. saratoga.co.nz), produces handcrafted goat cheeses; while **Kingsmeade Cheese,** Olivers Road, Masterton (© 06/377-5252; www.kings meadecheese.co.nz) is the medal-winning maker of sheep's milk cheese. There are nearly 20 olive-oil producers in the Wairarapa; two worth visiting are **Olivo Olive Grove,** Hinakura Road, Martinborough (© 06/306-9074; www. olivo.co.nz), which has award-winning extra-virgin and infused olive oils, with tastings and sales most weekends; and **Juno Olives,** 1931 St. Hwy. 2, Greytown (© 06/304-8895; www.juno-olives. co.nz), which is open weekends for tours and sales, or by appointment.

Martinborough Vineyard, Princess Street (© 06/306-9955; www.martin borough-vineyard.co.nz), was one of the original four vineyards in the area and was set up by a group of six investors who bought 6.4 hectares (16 acres) in one of the few zones in New Zealand with similar climactic conditions to Burgundy. It's open daily from 11am to 5pm for tasting and is dedicated to producing pinot noir, chardonnay, Riesling, sauvignon blanc, and pinot gris. Its star is the award-winning pinot noir.

Te Kairanga, Martins Road (© 06/306-9122; www.tkwine.co.nz), open daily from 10am to 5pm, is one of the founding and most popular vineyards in this area. Established over 20 years ago, it now has six vineyards in the region, each with its own distinctive qualities, and it is a key venue in the annual Toast Martinborough celebrations. It produces a wide range of wines, including pinot noir, chardonnay, cabernet sauvignon, and sauvignon blanc.

Others worth visiting are the very pretty **Gladstone Vineyard** ★, Gladstone Road, RD2, Carterton (© 06/379-8563; www.gladstone.co.nz), which has weekend lunches from November to March; **Margrain Vineyard,** Ponatahi Road (© 06/306-9292; www.margrainvineyard.co.nz), with rather divine villa accommodations; and **Walnut Ridge Vineyard,** 159 Regent St. (©/fax 06/306-9323; www.walnutridge.co.nz).

Martinborough Wine Centre, 6 Kitchener St., Martinborough (© 06/306-9040; www.martinboroughwinecentre.co.nz), represents 30 of the region's 40 vineyards. If you're short on time, or visiting out of the main wine season, this is the perfect place to get a comprehensive overview. Tastings cost NZ$10 to NZ$15 per person. A delightful cafe/delicatessen and retail store are on-site. Every Sunday from 10am to 2pm, the center stages the **Martinborough Country Market**—the perfect place for wines, breads, organic produce, fish, local cheeses, preserves, and much more. The **Wairarapa Farmers' Market** is held every Saturday from 8:30am to 12:30pm under cover at Solway Showgrounds, Judds Road, Masterton. If you're interested in wine tours of this region, leave your car in Wellington and leap on the train for the **Tranzit Gourmet Wine Escape** ★★ (© 0800/471-227 in NZ; www.tranzit.co.nz). You'll connect with a coach tour in the Wairarapa and have tastings at four vineyards, a vineyard lunch, and a visit to the Martinborough Wine Centre for NZ$182 round-trip per person from Wellington and Hutt Valley (NZ$213 with Wellington hotel transfers). Tours run daily. For a smaller, more personal outing, join **Zest Food Tours** ★★★ (© **04/801-9198;** www.zestfoodtours.co.nz), for one of their excellent gourmet wine tours (NZ$245–NZ$380 per person), which takes you behind the scenes of top food producers.

MUSEUM MANIA

There's no shortage of museums in the Wairarapa. The **Fell Locomotive Museum,** State Highway 2 & Lyon Street, Featherston (© **06/308-9379;** www.fellmuseum. org.nz; open daily 10am–4pm), houses the only remaining Fell engine in the world. Admission is NZ$7 adults, NZ$4 children, NZ$15 family. Next door, the **Featherston Heritage Complex** (© **06/308-9517**), displays early settler memorabilia and Japanese POW camp history. It's open Thursday and Friday 10am to 1pm, weekends 10am to 4pm, or by arrangement. Admission is NZ$2 per adult.

 Shear Discovery, The National Museum of Sheep and Shearing, 12 Dixon St. Masterton (© **06/378-8008;** www.sheardiscovery.co.nz), is the place to find out about the Wairarapa's sheep farming history and the amazing success story of the Golden Shears shearing competition. It's open daily from 10am to 4pm and admission is NZ$8 for adults, $2 children ages 5 to 15, and NZ$15 for families. **Cobblestones Museum,** 169 Main St., Greytown (© **06/304-9687;** www.cobblestonesmuseum. org.nz), has historic displays and a blacksmith's shop. It's open daily from 9am to 4:30pm. Admission is NZ$6 for adults, NZ$4 for kids 5 to 15. **Martinborough Colonial Museum,** the Square, Martinborough (© **06/306-9736**), is open Saturday and Sunday from 2 to 4pm. Admission is by donation. **Mount Bruce Pioneer Museum,** 18km (11 miles) north of Masterton on State Highway 2 (© **06/372-5859;** h.christensen@xtra.co.nz), is Wairarapa's largest working museum with over 3,000 items on display. It's open daily from 9am to 5pm; admission is NZ$3 for adults, NZ$1 for children 5 to 12.

Where to Stay

You'll be spoiled for choice here. This region is one of the best in the country when it comes to terrific accommodations. There are over 100 self-contained cottages alone, most of them cute as buttons. There are endless numbers of homestays and several top-quality upmarket options as well. The visitor center has two excellent booklets, *A Taste of Greytown* and *Martinborough Accommodation.*

 In Greytown, you'll find four delightful rooms at **Westwood,** 82 West St. (www. westwood.greytown.co.nz; © **06/304-8510**), priced from NZ$250 to NZ$350. In addition, the lovely three-bedroom Cherry Cottage sits in Westwood's garden and sleeps six. **Parehua Country Estate** ★★, New York Street, Martinborough (www. parehua.co.nz; © **06/306-8405**), has 28 gorgeous new cottages and villas set on 2 hectares (5 acres) of parklike grounds. They have all the mod-cons and an outdoor pool, restaurant, bar, tennis courts, free Wi-Fi throughout the property, and rental bikes complete the picture. Rates are very reasonable, from NZ$300 for the simplest cottages to NZ$675 for a villa. Also in Martinborough, the **Peppers Martinborough Hotel** ★★, The Square (www.peppers.co.nz; © **06/306-9350**), is an old, restored beauty, a favorite weekend spot with Wellingtonians, and a fine place to base yourself for vineyard exploration. There are nine units in the charming main hotel building (my preference are the Riddiford and Weld) and seven luscious new (and bigger) rooms in the garden courtyard (opt for the Barton or Sheko). Amenities include a restaurant, two bars, Wi-Fi, and nearby golf. Rate range from NZ$320 to NZ$385.

The 15% GST is included in the rates below.

Wharekauhau Country Estate ★★★ Set amid 2,000 hectares (5,000 acres) of a working sheep station, this little piece of paradise sits in splendid isolation overlooking the rugged seas of Palliser Bay. It's highly rated by Andrew Harper (www.andrew harpertravel.com), among others, and you'll be paying top dollar for the sublime comforts of a cottage suite with all the best trimmings—big four-poster beds, dressing room, luxurious bathrooms with great views, and private verandas. It's a member of Small Luxury Hotels of the World and has won several New Zealand Tourism Awards. This is warmth, elegance, and style at its best. You'll be pleased you went the distance.

Western Lake Rd., Palliser Bay, RD3, Featherston. www.wharekauhau.co.nz. ℂ **06/307-7581.** Fax 06/307-7799. 18 units. NZ$2,172 cottage suites; NZ$4,613 2-bedroom Chateau Wellington; NZ$6,497 3-bedroom; NZ$1,772 Wharepapa 3-bedroom cottage. Cottage suite rates include breakfast, predinner drinks, canapés, and 4-course gourmet dinner. Off-peak rates and special deals. AE, DC, MC, V. Closed mid-July for 3 weeks. **Amenities:** Bar; babysitting; free use of bikes; concierge; gym; outdoor Jacuzzi; heated indoor pool; day spa; all-weather tennis court. *In room:* LCD TV, fridge, hair dryer, Internet, MP3 docking station, minibar.

Where to Eat

In Masterton, **Café Cecille ★**, Queen Elizabeth Park (ℂ **06/370-1166;** www.cafececille.co.nz), has a great reputation for service and lamb and beef dishes. It's open Monday through Friday 10am until late, and weekends 9am until late. **Entice Café ★★**, Bruce & Dixon streets (ℂ **06/377-3166;** www.entice.co.nz), serves delicious Fair Trade coffee and food with a Mediterranean flavor.

In Greytown, **Main Street Deli Café,** 88 Main St. (ℂ **06/304-9022**), is open daily for all meals and continues to attract a team of happy regulars. Across the road you'll find a fabulous array of baked goods and good coffee at the **French Baker ★★**, 81 Main St. (ℂ **06/304-9569**). **Vintage Tea Rooms ★**, 101 Main St. (ℂ **06/304-9073**), will take you back to the golden era of Devonshire and high teas. It's open daily from 10am to 4pm. **Salute,** 83 Main St. (ℂ **06/304-9825;** www.salute.net.nz), is always a reliable stop for a tasty lunch; in summer you can dine outside.

Just out of Featherston village, the **Tin Hut ★**, State Highway 2, Tauherenikau (ℂ **06/308-9697**), gets rave reviews from the locals for its excellent pub-style fare in a revamped interior—traditional Kiwi pub meets French Country—and barnyard animals will be a hit with the kids.

In Martinborough, the **Village Café,** the Wine Centre, Kitchener Street (ℂ **06/306-8814**), serves up tasty food and some of the region's best wine and cheeses. **Wendy Campbell's French Bistro ★★**, 3 Kitchener St. (ℂ **06/306-8863**), is a small, charming spot with a menu that changes daily. It's open Wednesday through Sunday from 6pm. **Est Wine Bar ★★**, 8 Memorial Sq. (ℂ **06/306-9665;** www.est.org.nz), is another culinary gem that shouldn't be missed. It's open Wednesday through Friday 11am until late. Try their rabbit flavored with thyme and juniper. The classy vineyard restaurant **Tirohana Estate ★★★**, Puruatanga Road, Martinborough (ℂ **06/306-9933;** www.tirohanaestate.com), is a place to spoil yourself, with its beautiful setting and first-rate service. It's open for lunch and dinner.

MARLBOROUGH & NELSON

So, here you are on the South Island—the Mainland—home to around a million people. (Over three million live on the North Island and two-thirds of them north of Taupo, so there will be days when you think you have the huge and spectacular South Island all to yourself.) There's less traffic here, but you'll be traveling greater distances between major towns, and when you arrive at a few places, you may well think you have stepped back in time.

The stunning southern landscape—big, majestic, unforgiving—is dominated by the central spine of the Southern Alps, and anyone who lives here has enormous respect for its grandeur. You'll soon see why.

If you cross over from Wellington on the Cook Strait ferry, your introduction to the south will be at Picton, which sits at the head of the beautiful Marlborough Sounds. Nearby is Blenheim, at the heart of Marlborough's famous winemaking province. To the west lies Nelson, the sunniest place in New Zealand and home to more vineyards, fine beaches, and the most accessible concentration of top artists and craftspeople in the country.

The greater Nelson province is geographically made up of five distinct areas, each with its own character: Nelson-Richmond, the urban heart; Motueka, the horticultural heartland; Abel Tasman National Park, a paradise of bush-wrapped beaches and crystal-clear waters; Golden Bay, heaven cast between two great national parks; and St. Arnaud–Murchison, an alpine-lakes area in the heart of Nelson Lakes National Park.

PICTON & BLENHEIM ★★

Picton: 146km (91 miles) E of Nelson; Blenheim: 117km (73 miles) SE of Nelson

Picton and Blenheim are the two main towns of Marlborough province, an area best known as New Zealand's largest and most spectacular wine region. Both townships are quiet and easygoing. Blenheim, the larger of the two, has a population of 30,200. Picton, a quaint waterfront village at the head of Queen Charlotte Sound, has a population of just 3,000, and its main claim to fame is that it's the arrival point for ferries from Wellington. Unfortunately, many travelers think that's the end of its attributes, when in fact it is also the stepping-off point for the unspoiled tranquil charms of the Marlborough Sounds. With over 1,500km (930 miles) of shoreline, the sounds—Queen Charlotte, Kenepuru, and Pelorus—are ideal for sailing, kayaking, fishing, and bush walking. You don't want to miss them.

Essentials

GETTING THERE & GETTING AROUND **By Plane** Air service to Picton from Wellington is provided by **Sounds Air** (✆ 0800/505-005 in NZ; www.sounds air.com). **Air New Zealand Link** (✆ 0800/737-000; www.airnewzealand.co.nz) flies into nearby Blenheim. The Picton Airport (also known as Koromiko Airport) is about a 10-minute drive from Picton's town center. The Blenheim Airport is 10km (6 miles) from its town center. **Marlborough Shuttle Services** (✆ 03/572-9910; www.marlboroughsoundsshuttles.co.nz) provides airport and ferry transport in both town.

By Train The TranzCoastal provides daily rail service between Picton and Christchurch. The trip takes about 5½ hours. Contact **Tranz Scenic** (✆ 0800/872-467 in NZ; www.tranzscenic.co.nz) for more information.

By Coach (Bus) Coach service into both Picton and Blenheim is provided by **InterCity** (✆ 09/623-1503). The trip from Christchurch takes 5 hours; from Nelson, 2 hours. Picton, and Kaikoura farther south, are both included in the routes of **Magic Travellers** (✆ 09/358-5600) and **Kiwi Experience** (✆ 09/366-9830).

By Car Most rental-car companies request that you turn in one car in Wellington (on the North Island) and pick up a new one in Picton. However, you can take cars and campers on the ferry should the need arise. If you're driving from Nelson, the trip takes about 2 hours; from Christchurch, 4 to 5 hours.

By Ferry For timetables and information on the **Interislander,** call ✆ 0800/802-802. For information on **Bluebridge** ferries, call ✆ 0800/844-844. See also "Orientation" in chapter 11.

By Water Taxi Picton doesn't have a local bus system, but water taxis from the **Cougar Line** (✆ 0800/504-090 in NZ, or 03/573-7925; www.cougarlinecruises. co.nz) provide regular service throughout Queen Charlotte Sound. **Endeavour Express** (✆ 03/573-5456; www.boatrides.co.nz) also has regular service; or call **West Bay Water Transport** (✆ 03/573-5597).

By Taxi Blenheim Taxis (✆ 0800/802-225 or 03/578-0225) serves Blenheim, Picton, and the Sounds. It has cars, 10-seater vans, and a wheelchair hoist available.

ORIENTATION It's difficult to get lost in Picton. The town faces Queen Charlotte Sound and the small shopping area is centered on High Street. London Quay runs along the foreshore, with the ferry terminal at one end and the town wharf at the other.

Blenheim is not quite so straightforward, despite its small size. Its layout has always puzzled me and no matter how many times I visit, I always go around in circles. Be sure to pick up a map at the visitor center!

VISITOR INFORMATION The **Picton i-SITE Visitor Centre,** the Foreshore (✆ 03/520-3113; fax 03/573-5021; www.lovemarlborough.co.nz), is in the same building as the **Department of Conservation** (the latter only in the building Oct–Apr), and is open daily 8:30am to 6pm in summer, 8:30am to 5pm in winter. The Blenheim office is at the Railway Station, Sinclair Street, State Highway 1 (✆ 03/577-8080; fax 03/577-8079). It's open December to March from 8:30am to 6pm Monday to Friday, and weekends from 9am to 5pm; March to November, it's open weekdays from 8:30am to 5pm, and weekends from 9am to 3pm.

Check the following websites for more information about the area: www.marlborough. co.nz, www.picton.co.nz, and www.marlborough4fun.co.nz (for events listings).

Marlborough, Nelson & Beyond

Exploring Picton & Blenheim
WET ADVENTURES: GETTING OUT ON THE WATER

It's not a question of *whether* you'll go out on the water in Marlborough Sounds, but rather *which* vessel you'll be on. The ferries from Wellington provide a good introductory view as they make their way toward Picton, but for a closer look you'll need to go out on a smaller, more specialized boat. The **Cougar Line,** London Quay, Waterfront, Picton (② **0800/504-090** in NZ, or 03/573-7925; www.cougarlinecruises.co.nz or www.queencharlottetrack.co.nz), has a range of cruise options in Queen Charlotte Sound. If your time is limited, take the 3-hour **Sounds Delivery Cruise,** which departs daily from Picton at 10am and returns at 1:30pm; it costs NZ$75 for adults, NZ$38 for children ages 5 to 15. This is a good way to fill in time if you're waiting for the ferry. Also offered are a twilight cruise during peak season and popular cruise-and-walk options to suit all levels of fitness. All-day tours cost NZ$75 to NZ$85 per person.

Another option is the 4-hour Queen Charlotte Sound **Magic Mail Run Cruise** operated by **Beachcomber Cruises,** London Quay, Picton (② **0800/624-526** in NZ, or 03/573-6175; www.mailboat.co.nz), for NZ$93 adults, NZ$47 for children 5 to 14. Or try the **Pelorus Mail Run** (② **03/574-1088;** www.mail-boat.co.nz), which departs Tuesday, Thursday, and Friday from Havelock at 9:30am and costs

NZ$130 for adults, free for children under 16. Tea and coffee are supplied, but bring your lunch. A courtesy coach is available to and from Picton.

Sea kayaking is one of the best ways to get intimate and up close to the Sounds. I had my first-ever kayaking experience here and now I'm hooked. Two recommended outfitters are **Sea Kayak Adventures,** Anakiwa Road, RD1, Picton (☏ **0800/262-5492** in NZ, or 03/574-2765; www.nzseakayaking.com), which has half-day guided trips from NZ$75 and 1-day freedom trips from NZ$85; and **Marlborough Sounds Adventure Company** ★★★, London Quay, Picton (☏ **0800/283-283** in NZ, or 03/573-6078; www.marlboroughsounds.co.nz). The latter company is the larger of the two and has more boats, more extensive trips, and the most central Picton base. Its most popular trip is the 1-day excursion for NZ$125 per person. For those who like sailing, **Compass Charters,** 20 Beach Rd., Waikawa Marina, Picton (☏ **0800/101-332** in NZ, or 03/573-8332; www.compass-charters.co.nz), is the South Island's largest charter company. They have budget to luxury-yacht and launch cruises—skippered or self-driven—priced according to the vessel and duration. Picton-based **Affinity Cruises** (☏ **0800/862-334** in NZ, or 03/572-7223; www. affinitycruises.co.nz) offers excellent 1-, 5-, or 7-day cruises with private cabins, including a lovely 1-night cruise (Sept–Oct) for NZ$450.

There's a treat in store for young and old alike at **Eco World Aquarium ★★**, 1 Dunbar Wharf, Picton (☎ **0800/800-081** in NZ, or 03/573-6030; www.eco worldnz.co.nz). Watch tiny, mysterious sea horses court and dance, see thousands of babies at various stages of growth, and find out about the mysteries of the male pregnancy. On top of that, there's a 6m (20-ft.) preserved giant squid—only one of two examples in the Southern Hemisphere. Kids can also get up close and personal with crayfish, sharks, stingrays, and the multitudes of fishes that thrive in New Zealand waters. Fish are fed at 11am and 2pm, and guided **Behind the Scenes** tours at offered at 11:30am, 2:30pm, and 3:30pm. Admission to the aquarium costs NZ$20 for adults, NZ$10 for children 4 to 15, and NZ$50 for a family pass; Behind the Scenes tours cost an extra NZ$10 per person. The aquarium is open daily from 10am to 8pm in summer (to 5:30pm in winter).

Bird-watchers will love the remote Chetwode and Outer Island Bird Tour run by **French Pass Sea Safaris ★★**, French Pass, Marlborough Sounds (☎ **03/576-5204;** www.seasafaris.co.nz), which takes you to a closed nature reserve (Feb–Apr only), to see a diverse mix of birds and marine mammals for NZ$175 per person.

Combination food, wine, and water lovers should opt for the **Marlborough Travel Greenshell Mussel Cruise ★★★** (☎ **0800/990-800** in NZ, or 03/577-9997; www.greenshellmusselcruise.co.nz). This terrific half-day outing takes you into the stunning Sounds environment, visiting a Greenshell mussel farm, where you'll be treated to a feast of yummy, freshly steamed mussels with a complimentary glass of Marlborough sauvignon blanc. The tour operates November through March, departing Havelock and Picton wharves at 1:30pm daily and from Portage Resort Hotel, Marlborough, at 3pm daily. It costs NZ$115 from Portage and Havelock and NZ$150 from Picton, and is worth every cent. Children travel for NZ$45.

Although passengers on any of these vessels may see dolphins, **Dolphin Watch Ecotours,** London Quay (☎ **0800/945-3543** in NZ, or 03/573-8040; www.nature tours.co.nz), makes these lovely creatures the focus of its naturalist tours; try the **Dolphin Swimming Ecotour** (NZ$160 for adults, NZ$100 for ages 8–15), or the **Dolphin Viewing Ecotour** (NZ$100 for adults, NZ$60 for children 5–15). Excellent bird-watcher's tours go for NZ$125 for adults, NZ$60 for children 5 to 15.

If you have fishing on your mind, contact Havelock-based **Captain Clay's Snapper Fishing Charters** (☎ **03/574-2911;** bluecottage@actrix.co.nz); fishing for two people costs NZ$250 for 3 hours from November through April. **Sounds Connection,** 10 London Quay, Picton (☎ **0800/742-866;** www.soundsconnection.co.nz), offers a half-day fishing adventure for NZ$95 per person, departing Picton at 1pm.

Culture buffs might enjoy a visit to the small but interesting **Marlborough Museum,** 26 Arthur Baker Place, Blenheim (☎ **03/578-1712;** www.marlborough museum.org.nz), which has excellent exhibits on the area's early pioneer days and the history of the local wine industry. It's open daily from 10am to 4pm (closed Dec 25), and admission is NZ$10 for adults and NZ$5 for children.

Another highlight is the **Omaka Aviation Heritage Centre ★★★**, 79 Aerodrome Rd., Blenheim (☎ **03/579-1305;** www.omaka.org.nz), where you'll find the brilliant Knights of the Sky exhibition. New Zealand's most respected cinematic and special-effects craftsmen at Weta Workshop have created a dramatic aviation theater in which original and full-scale replica WW1 aircraft, both static and working, are presented in all their glory. The collection is managed by the 14-18 Aviation Heritage Trust, which is chaired by film director Sir Peter Jackson, and includes several rare aircraft. Admission is NZ$25 for adults, NZ$10 for ages 5 to 15, and NZ$55 for a family. It's open 10am to 4pm daily. Every second year at Easter, the center hosts a **Classic Fighters Air Show.** The next show is in 2013.

THE QUEEN CHARLOTTE WALKWAY ★★★

If you're like me and love walking but hate carrying things, the Queen Charlotte Walkway is for you. It's a 1- to 4-day experience with amazing views and not a pack in sight. That's because kind people in boats do all the pack lifting and transferring of your goodies for you. Even better, you don't have to stay in cramped huts or tents, as there are smart lodgings along the way. There's lots more information about this walk in the "Tramping" section in chapter 4, but briefly, the 71km (44-mile) walking track passes through lush coastal forest, around coves and inlets, and along skyline ridges with breathtaking views of Queen Charlotte and Kenepuru sounds. If you've got time, try the excellent kayak/walk combos offered by **Wilderness Guides,** 3 Auckland St., Picton (✆ **0800/266-266** in NZ, or 03/573-5432; www.wildernessguidesnz.com), from NZ$240 per person day up to NZ$1,850 for a guided multiday experience. You can also tackle the track on mountain bikes. **Cycle Adventure Tours Downunder,** 1 Auckland St., Picton (✆ **03/573-8565;** www.cyclenz.com), has 1-day bike rentals from NZ$45 and 1- to 3-day guided tours from NZ$425, which includes transport, gear, and accommodations. The tour requires a reasonable level of fitness. The Picton and Blenheim i-SITE Visitor centers (p. 299) have an excellent brochure on the track, listing all transporters and accommodations, and you can find out more at www.qctrack.co.nz.

WINE, WINE & MORE WINE

It doesn't matter what time of year you visit Marlborough, because the weather is invariably balmy (with a few frosty winter mornings), and there's always wine to drink if all else fails. If you stand on any high point, you'll see grapevines spread across the rolling landscape in all directions as far as the eye can see—vines now cover approximately 23,000 hectares (57,000 acres). In just over 25 years, Marlborough has established itself as one of the world's premier wine-producing regions, responsible for over 63% of New Zealand's total wine production. There are about 160 wineries in the area and around 40 of those are open for cellar door visits; plus, many have restaurants, and some have galleries or crafts shops. Pick up the free *Marlborough Winemakers* map and the *Top of the South Wine Guide* from the visitor center before setting off, or check out www.winemarlborough.net.nz. You would also be wise to get a copy of *The Classic New Zealand Wine Trail* from visitor centers throughout the country. Following are a few wineries of note.

More than 30 years ago, **Montana Brancott Winery,** State Highway 1, Main Road South, Riverlands (✆ **03/577-5775;** www.montana.co.nz), planted the first vines in the region, and today it's New Zealand's largest winery. Tours leave Monday through Saturday from 10am to 3pm. The wine shop and the huge (and sometimes noisy) Montana Brancott Restaurant are open daily from 10:30am to 3pm.

Those with an eye for good wines will be familiar with **Cloudy Bay ★★★**, Jacksons Road, Blenheim (✆ **03/520-9147;** www.cloudybay.co.nz). Its name is well known internationally, and 75% of its acclaimed sauvignon blanc is exported. It also produces chardonnay, cabernet merlot, and a sparkling wine, Pelorus. It's open for tasting and sales daily from 10am to 5pm (closed Dec 25).

SLEEPING AMONG THE grapes

There are a growing number of vineyard accommodations for visitors to choose from. **Walnut Block Cottages** ★, 43 Blicks Lane, Blenheim (www.walnut blockcottages.co.nz; ☏ 03/577-9187), has two lovely, one-bedroom, self-contained cottages right beside vines, for just NZ$225 per night, which is a great value. Another option is **Straw Lodge** ★★, 17 Fareham Lane, Blenheim (www.strawlodge.co.nz; ☏ 03/572-9767), where three lovely private vineyard suites have their own courtyard and facilities. Rooms cost from NZ$335 to NZ$395 and the property has a Qualmark Enviro-Silver rating. **Vintners Retreat Resort** ★★★, 55 Rapaura Rd., Blenheim (www.vintnersretreat.co.nz; ☏ 03/572-7420), has a wide range of stylish one-, two-, and three-bedroom self-contained villas nestled among the vines, ranging in price from NZ$332 to NZ$495. At **St. Leonards Vineyard Cottages** ★★, 18 St. Leonards Rd., Blenheim (www.stleonards.co.nz; ☏ 03/577-8328), choose from five delightful self-contained cottages for the incredibly good value of NZ$115 to NZ$320.

Allan Scott Wines & Estates ★★, Jacksons Road, Blenheim (☏ 03/572-9054; www.allanscott.com), is just across the road and has a good vineyard restaurant called Twelve Trees. The winery produces chardonnay, sauvignon, and Riesling. The cellar is open for tasting daily from 9am to 4:30pm; the restaurant opens daily for lunch at noon. **Hunter's Wines,** Rapaura Road, Blenheim (☏ 03/572-8489; www.hunters. co.nz), is home to Jane Hunter, acclaimed as one of the five best women winemakers in the world. The winery is hugely popular with tour groups. The restaurant is open daily from 10:30am to 4:30pm; the wine shop, daily from 9:30am to 4:30pm.

Grove Mill ★★★, Waihopai Valley Road, Renwick (☏ 03/572-8200; www. grovemill.co.nz), is well worth a visit, especially if you're also an art lover. In addition to producing medal-winning chardonnay, Riesling, and cabernet sauvignon, its gallery features exhibitions of nationally recognized New Zealand artists. In 2006, it became the world's first carbon-neutral winery. It follows the carboNZero program and is a member of Sustainable Winegrowing New Zealand. It's open daily from 11am to 5pm. **Highfield Estate** ★★, Brookby Road, Blenheim (☏ 03/572-9244; www. highfield.co.nz), which produces classic varietal wines, has wine tastings, cellar door sales, and a restaurant with stunning views. It's open daily from 10am to 5pm.

Wairau River Wines ★★★, corner of Rapaura Road and State Highway 6, Blenheim (☏ 03/572-9800; www.wairauriverwines.com), has one of the best winery restaurants in the Marlborough region—a reliable brasserie with an innovative blackboard menu at reasonable prices. It's housed in a charming mud-brick building, has cellar door sales, and is open daily 10am to 5pm. **Mahi Wines** ★★, Terrace Road, Renwick (☏ 03/572-8859; www.mahiwine.co.nz), has a delightful cafe. French winemaker Daniel Le Brun established the vineyard in 1980, and with 12 generations of champagne making behind him, he's truly established in his new venture. It's open 10am to 4:30pm.

Johanneshof Cellars, State Highway 1, Koromiko (☏ 03/573-7035; www. johanneshof.co.nz), has spectacular underground wine cellars blasted into the hillside. It's open in summer Tuesday to Sunday from 10am to 4pm, and in winter, Tuesday to Friday 10am to 4pm.

WINERY TOURS   The **Sounds Connection ★★★**, 10 London Quay, Picton (✆ **0800/742-866** in NZ, or 03/573-8843; www.soundsconnection.co.nz), has half- and full-day tours from NZ$65 to NZ$150. Its groups are smaller than some larger companies, and you can choose the vineyards. If you want some exercise while you see the wineries, call **Wine Tours By Bike ★★★**, 191 Bells Rd., Blenheim (✆ **03/577-6954;** www.winetoursbybike.co.nz), which will take you on an explora- tion of its favorite cycling roads, scenic spots, vineyards, wineries, arts, crafts, and olive or fruit farms. Stop at a vineyard for lunch (extra cost) and soak up the quiet calm of this divine area. A tour of up to 4 hours costs NZ$45 per person; from 4 to 8 hours costs NZ$60 per person. You can find five leading Marlborough wineries rep- resented in one handy cellar door location at the **Wine Room ★★**, SH1, Grovetown, Blenheim (✆ **03/570-5490;** www.thewineroom.net.nz). It offers blind tastings, sells gourmet products like chocolate and olive oil, and will organize shipping of any wine you purchase.

Where to Stay

Book early if you want to stay in Picton, which is a busy place during the summer months. Blenheim has a larger range of accommodations, including many delightful self-contained cottages and vineyard stays (see "Sleeping Among the Grapes," above).

IN PICTON & THE SOUNDS

In addition to Picton township, there are quite a few lodgings waiting for you in the Marlborough Sounds. Prime among them is the very stylish **Bay of Many Coves Resort ★★★**, Arthur's Bay, Queen Charlotte Sound (www.bayofmanycoves.co.nz; ✆ **0800/579-9771** in NZ, or 03/579-9771), which has 11 one-, two-, and three- bedroom self-contained apartments priced from NZ$540 to NZ$975. It also has an excellent restaurant open to casual diners.

In Picton itself, **McCormick House ★★**, 21 Leicester St. (www.mccormick house.co.nz; ✆ **03/573-5253**), is hard to beat for character and charm. It has three beautiful rooms for NZ$350 to NZ$450 and hosts Carl and Jeanne Beaumont serve up delicious gourmet breakfasts. Their property has a Qualmark Enviro-Gold award for sustainability. The **Gables,** 20 Waikawa Rd. (www.thegables.co.nz; ✆ **03/573- 6772**), has three more modest rooms plus two cottage suites (NZ$140–NZ$175). For great-value backpacker accommodations, the **Villa Backpacker's Lodge,** 34 Auckland St., Picton (www.thevilla.co.nz; ✆ **03/573-6598**), is hard to beat. It has dorm beds for NZ$26 and double rooms for NZ$65 to NZ$75.

The Portage Resort Hotel ★ 📷   The Portage has been providing hospitality for more than 100 years, but in its latest revamped guise there's much to be recom- mended here. For a start, the Kenepuru Sounds setting is breathtaking. The rest of the world may as well not exist. All rooms—from backpacker style to deluxe suites— look out over the water. They're simple, fairly uninspired rooms and the bathrooms may be a little small in some cases, but this is offset by splendid public areas, a terrific restaurant (**Te Weka;** p. 306), and an unforgettable location that's just 10 minutes from Picton by water taxi.

Kenepuru Sound, Marlborough. www.portage.co.nz. ✆ **0800/762-442** in NZ, or 03/573-4309. Fax 03/573-4362. 41 units. NZ$245–NZ$400. Off-peak and long-stay rates. AE, DC, MC, V. **Amenities:** 2 restaurants; 2 bars; babysitting; bike rentals; children's program/adventure center; nearby 9-hole golf course; Jacuzzi; outdoor pool; watersports equipment rentals. *In room:* TV/DVD (in some), fridge, hair dryer, minibar on request.

IN BLENHEIM

If you're looking for a place with individuality and style, try **Hotel d'Urville ★★**, 52 Queen St. (www.durville.com; ✆ **03/577-9945**), which has 11 lovely themed rooms priced NZ$195 to NZ$290 right in the center of Blenheim township. Also centrally located, **Chateau Marlborough,** corner of High and Henry streets (www. marlboroughnz.com; ✆ **0800/752-275**), has 46 excellent motel rooms from NZ$260 to NZ$600. **The Peppertree ★★★**, SH1, Riverlands, Blenheim (www. thepeppertree.co.nz; ✆ **03/520-9200**), is an elegant, historic homestead where Werner and Heidi Pluss offer five beautiful rooms priced from NZ$595 to NZ$655. Rates include breakfast, coffee, cookies, and fruit at any time, and full use of all lodge facilities. Werner also has his own small vineyard, a tiny olive grove, a small farm, and organic gardens. The property has a Qualmark Enviro-Silver rating. **Uno Piu ★**, 75 Murphys Rd. (www.unopiu.co.nz; ✆ **03/578-2235**), offers lovely B&B homestead accommodations for NZ$430 plus a delightful, self-catering, two-bedroom mud-block cottage set in its own garden for NZ$470 (NZ$60 each extra person). You can also frolic in the home swimming pool.

Where to Eat

As well as the cafes and restaurants reviewed below, don't forget about all the winery restaurants. You'll find them listed on the free winery map from the visitor center.

IN PICTON

Picton eateries come and go, but one enduring favorite is **Le Café,** London Quay (✆ **03/573-5588**)—casual, friendly, reliable, and open daily. If you'd like a special dining experience, get a water taxi and head for Portage Resort's **Te Weka Restaurant ★★** (✆ **03/573-4309**), which serves divine New Zealand food—salmon, mussels, tuna, lamb, venison—and wine in a gorgeous bush-clad setting adjacent to their funky Retro Lounge Bar.

IN HAVELOCK

The highlight in Havelock is the delightful **Slip Inn Café Restaurant & Wine Bar ★★**, Havelock Marina (✆ **03/574-2345;** www.slipinn.co.nz), which is open daily from 8am until late. It offers unimpeded views over the marina and Pelorus Sound, as well as great value with seafood dishes and pizza priced around NZ$18 to NZ$22.

The Mussel Pot ★ SEAFOOD   The giant mussel shells on the restaurant roof are a dead giveaway: This is *the* place for the freshest, tastiest mussels you'll find anywhere. They're grown locally and treated with the utmost culinary care. Fresh steamers are served whole in their shell in special pots; fresh flats are grilled on the half shell and topped with something tasty; and the mussel chowder alone is worth the drive.

73 Main Rd., Havelock. ✆ **03/574-2824.** www.themusselpot.co.nz. Reservations required for dinner. Main courses NZ$18–NZ$32. MC, V. Summer daily 11am–9:30pm; winter daily 10:15am–9:30pm. At Havelock, St. Hwy. 6, 40 min. from Picton.

IN BLENHEIM

Hotel d'Urville Restaurant & Bar ★, 52 Queen St. (✆ **03/577-9945**), established itself early as a place for top, innovative cuisine and after a couple of jaded years, seems to have made a comeback. It offers an impressive local wine list (more than 60 selections) and is a good place for cocktails. Open daily for dinner 6:30 to 10pm; bookings are essential. **Bacchus ★★**, 3 Main St. (✆ **03/578-8099**), is a small, country Italian spot with warm, friendly service; it is widely considered to be the most reliable restaurant in town. They are open daily from 6pm. **Raupo Café ★★**,

If you feel like a drop of one of the world's most sought-after wines—Château de Valandraud—Hans and Therese Herzog of **Herzog Winery & Restaurant** ★★★, 81 Jeffries Rd., Blenheim (𝄞 **03/572-8770;** www. herzog.co.nz), can oblige. *Wine Spectator* has recognized Herzog for having one of the best wine lists in the world, and if you visit this little culinary paradise, you'll be reluctant to leave. Luckily you don't have to. As well as a divine Cellar Door & Bistro and a fine-dining restaurant with Michelin star-rated chefs, they also have a gorgeous little vineyard cottage for two restaurant guests at NZ$380 per night. Factor in an exciting range of cooking classes (from NZ$180 per person), and you'll think you've died and gone to heaven. Herzog Cellar Door is open weekdays 9am to 5pm; the bistro Tuesday to Sunday for lunch; the restaurant from 6:30pm Tuesday to Sunday (daily Dec–Mar). Restaurant main courses cost NZ$34 to NZ$54 and a three-course set menu is NZ$110; bistro mains run around NZ$28 to NZ$34.

6 Symons St. (𝄞 **03/577-8822;** www.raupocafe.co.nz), is another very good spot, especially for an alfresco breakfast or lunch overlooking the river. They're open daily from 7:30am until late.

For a coffee to jump-start your day, try **CPR @HQ,** 18–20 Wynen St. (𝄞 **03/579-5030;** www.cprcoffee.com), where they roast their own beans. Also check out **Figaro's,** 8 Scott St. (𝄞 **03/577-7277**), to find more excellent coffee along with great snacks, salads, and a menu that changes daily. It's open Monday to Friday 7:30am to 3:30pm, Saturday 9am to 1pm. Remember that some of the area's best restaurants are actually in the wineries (see above, especially the starred entries), although many are only open for lunch.

Heading South: En Route to Christchurch

If you're going south, the drive to Christchurch is approximately 4 hours. This is a perfect opportunity to stop off in Kaikoura or the winegrowing area of Waipara in North Canterbury. If you plan to do either, allow a whole day for the trip. For details on Kaikoura and its famous whale-watching excursions, see "Side Trips from Christchurch," in chapter 13.

Heading North: En Route to Nelson

The **Queen Charlotte Drive** offers wonderful views of the Marlborough Sounds, but it's a narrow, winding road that needs to be driven with great care. It's a drive worth doing, with several good lookout stops along the way. The road meets up with State Highway 6 at the little village of Havelock; you then continue east to Nelson. The whole trip should take about 2 hours.

NELSON, RICHMOND & MOTUEKA ★★★

144km (89 miles) W of Picton; 226km (140 miles) NE of Westport; 424km (263 miles) N of Christchurch

Nelson is the sunniest playground in New Zealand. Its 2,500 hours of annual sunshine, tranquil waters, gold-sand beaches, vineyards, and craft activities make it one of the most popular destinations in the country. And the good thing is, this applies to winter as well. While the rest of the country is lashed with foul winter chills, Nelson sits in a sheltered haven, blissfully unaware of everyone else's discomfort.

Perhaps this accounts for why the area is one of the last bastions of alternative lifestylers, especially in the Takaka–Golden Bay area. Immigrating Europeans and Americans have sought it out, too, so you'll find a variety of accents among the locals.

The combined population of Nelson City and nearby Richmond is about 45,000, and for the whole Nelson-Tasman region, 140,000. An hour's drive east is the small town of Motueka, population 7,500, and between the two is an area rich in tourist pickings. This is where you'll find most of the 300 full-time artists and craftspeople. It's thick with orchards, vineyards, galleries, quaint shops, and cafes, and a visit here should not be rushed. It's a laid-back province that quickly convinces you that laid-back is best. The region's tourism body, Nelson Tasman Tourism, is also right behind keeping it that way. It operates the Nelson Tasman Sustainable Tourism Charter to improve the environmental performance of all its members. You can find out who is working to protect this beautiful region by checking www.nelsonnz.com/sustainable.tourism.

Essentials

GETTING THERE   By Plane   Nelson City Airport is the fourth-busiest airport in New Zealand, with regular direct flights to and from Auckland, Wellington, Christchurch, and major provincial centers. It's serviced by **Air New Zealand** (✆ **0800/737-000;** www.airnewzealand.co.nz). **Super Shuttle** (✆ **0800/748-885** in NZ; www.supershuttle.co.nz) operates regularly between the airport and the city center for NZ$25 each way.

By Coach (Bus)   InterCity, 27 Bridge St., Nelson (✆ **03/548-1538;** www.intercity.co.nz or www.nelsoncoaches.co.nz), connects Nelson to Christchurch via Kaikoura/Marlborough or the Lewis Pass. Both **Kiwi Experience** (✆ **09/366-9830**) and the **Magic Travellers Network** (✆ **09/358-5600**) include Nelson on their schedules. There are several local bus companies that link all towns within the region. Details are available from the visitor center.

By Car   The scenic drive from Picton to Nelson, via Queen Charlotte Sound (narrow and winding), or State Highway 6 (more direct), takes approximately 2 hours without stops. (The scenic route takes about a half-hour longer than the State Highway.) If you're coming from the West Coast, the drive from Westport takes approximately 3½ hours; from Christchurch via Lewis Pass, about 5 hours, or via Kaikoura-Blenheim, 6 hours.

By Taxi   Taxis pick up passengers outside the Majestic Theatre on Trafalgar Street and on Bridge Street opposite the Suburban Bus Company. For pickup, call **Nelson City Taxis** (✆ **03/548-8225**), **Sun City Taxis** (✆ **03/548-2666**), or **Motueka Taxis** (✆ **03/528-7900**).

ORIENTATION   Two landmarks will keep you oriented in Nelson: Trafalgar Street (the main street) and Church Hill, owned by Christ Church Cathedral and surrounded by lush lawns. The steps leading up to the church are a local gathering point. If there is any trouble at all to be had in Nelson, you'll usually find it in this area after dark.

Most shops, cafes, and restaurants are at Trafalgar and Halifax streets, although you'll find a few eateries around the bay on the waterfront. The waterfront road leads to Richmond township, 14km (8½ miles) and about a 10-minute drive away.

Past Richmond, you turn right over the railway bridge and take the Coastal Highway (St. Hwy. 60) to Motueka township, a 1-hour drive. Motueka itself is a straightforward

Central Nelson

RESTAURANTS ◆

Boatshed Café **2**
Haroo Sushi **16**
Harry's Bar **18**
Hopgoods **7**
Ikko Sushi **15**
Lambretta's Café Bar **13**
Miyazu Japanese Restaurant **8**
Morrison Street Café **14**
Penguino Gelato Café **4**
Pizza Bar **5**
Suter Café **17**
Zatori Café de Chocolat **7**
Zumo Coffee House **3**

HOTELS ■

Baywick Inn **19**
Cathedral Inn **20**
Joya Villa & Garden
  Studios **23**
The Little Retreat **10**
Long Lookout Gardens **22**
Paradiso Backpackers **12**
Rutherford Hotel Nelson **8**
Shelbourne Villa **21**
Te Puna Wai Lodge **1**
39 Russell **1**
Warwick House **24**

ATTRACTIONS ●

Founder's Heritage Park **11**
Nelson Provincial Museum **6**
South Street Historic
  Precinct **9**
Suter Art Gallery **17**

ⓘ Information
✉ Post Office

NORTH ISLAND
Auckland
Nelson
SOUTH ISLAND
Wellington
Christchurch
Dunedin

0   1/5 mi
0   0.2 km

little town built around the main highway at the mouth of the Motueka River. On the way to Motueka, stop off at the delightful little village of Mapua—it's just 5 minutes off the main highway. The wharf area particularly is home to a number of excellent cafes, galleries, and attractions.

VISITOR INFORMATION   The **Nelson i-SITE Visitor Centre,** at 77 Trafalgar St. (② **0800/635-827** in NZ, or 03/548-2304; fax 03/546-7393; www.nelsonnz. com), is open Monday through Friday from 8:30am to 5pm, and 9am to 4pm on weekends and public holidays (closed Dec 25). It occupies a stylish complex that incorporates a large gift store and a display center. Make sure you watch the fabulous video of the region's attractions. Major bus lines also arrive and depart from here. The **Department of Conservation** counter at the visitor center is staffed only from October to Easter. The **Motueka i-SITE Visitor Centre** is on Wallace Street, Motueka (② **03/528-6543;** fax 03/528-6563; www.motuekaisite.co.nz). Pick up a copy of the free newspaper *Discover the Top of the South* at either visitor center. It details many local attractions.

[Fast FACTS] NELSON

The **post office** is at the corner of Halifax and Trafalgar streets, diagonally opposite the visitor center. There is handy **Internet access** at the visitor center, or at **Boots-Off Travellers Centre,** 53 Bridge St. (② **03/546-8789**).

SPECIAL EVENTS   Sadly, the **Montana World of Wearable Art Awards** (www.worldofwearableart.com) are no longer held in Nelson; they've transferred to Wellington in the interests of coping with larger audiences. (See "Special Events" in chapter 11.) The **Nelson Jazz Festival** (www.nelsonjazzclub.co.nz) runs from late December to early January. The **Nelson Arts Festival** (www.nelsonartsfestival.co. nz), in late October, celebrates the region's diverse creativity over 12 days. For details on the wide range of Nelson regional events, contact the visitor center or check www. nelsonfestivals.co.nz.

Exploring the Area

The **Nelson Sightseeing Double Decker Experience** is an excellent way to see Nelson's best attractions. Tickets and bus stops are available from the visitor center or from the bus driver: NZ$8 for adults, NZ$6 for children, NZ$25 for a family. The double-decker bus leaves from the visitor center at 11am and 1pm and a complete loop of the attractions takes about 2 hours. It operates Wednesday through Sunday all year and daily during summer school holidays (except Dec 25), from December through February.

NELSON'S TOP MUSEUMS & HISTORIC BUILDINGS

Nelson Provincial Museum ★★, Trafalgar and Hardy streets (② **03/548-9588;** www.nelsonmuseum.co.nz), relocated to its original 1842 site in 2005 and now the treasure-filled museum is welcoming in a new era of fascinating permanent displays and changing exhibitions. Look out for the fabulous silver collection, antique furniture, historical books, and Maori artifacts—not to mention the new stained-glass window featuring native birds and plants. Its research center in the former museum building in Isel Park, Stoke, houses one of the largest historical photographic collections in the country, and a comprehensive reference library on local history. The museum is open Monday to Friday 10am to 5pm (weekends and public holidays until 4:30pm); the Research Facility is open Tuesday through Saturday 12:30 to 4:30pm by appointment. Museum admission is by donation; the research facility is free. Some charges may apply to touring exhibitions.

In Stoke, a suburb of Nelson, you'll find the **Broadgreen Historic House ★**, 276 Nayland St. (© **03/547-0403;** www.broadgreenhistorichouse.co.nz), a restored two-story cob house built in the mid-1850s. This New Zealand Tourism Award winner has 11 rooms furnished to faithfully represent a family home of the period. It's open daily from 10:30am to 4:30pm; call for winter hours. Admission is NZ$8 for adults and NZ$4 for children 14 and under.

In central Nelson, it's worth visiting the **South Street Historic Precinct ★★**. Just off Nile Street West behind the Rutherford Hotel, this cute little street captures the feel of a past era. Sixteen working-class cottages built between 1863 and 1867 remain intact and are still inhabited. Nearby, on top of Church Hill, is **Nelson Cathedral,** 367 Trafalgar St. (© **03/548-1008;** www.nelsoncathedral.org). It's open daily free of charge to visitors, in summer from 8am to 6pm and in winter from 8am to 5pm. Built of local Takaka marble, the cathedral is known for its striking stained glass, carved features, and unique free-standing organ. Car and fashion buffs—jointly or separately—will enjoy the **World of Wearable Art & Classic Cars Museum ★★★**, Cadillac Way, off Quarantine Road (© **03/547-4573;** fax 03/547-0856; www.wowcars.co.nz), which presents about 100 collectible cars and motorbikes, as well as a stunning collection of over 600 past entries and winners of the internationally renowned World of Wearable Arts Awards. It's open daily from 10am to 5pm (closed Dec 25). Admission is NZ$22 for adults, NZ$8 for children ages 5 to 14; family discounts available. Also onsite are a cafe, and a gallery.

Across town, the **Founder's Heritage Park ★★**, 87 Atawhai Dr. (© **03/548-2649;** www.founderspark.co.nz), is a replica of a historic village containing many of the old buildings and artifacts of Nelson. Special attractions include Dr. Bush's Windmill, the Port Nelson Exhibition, vintage and horse-drawn vehicles, fire engines, and a working train. It's open daily from 10am to 4:30pm (closed Good Friday and Dec 25); admission is NZ$7 for adults and NZ$15 per family; children under 12 are free. Train rides run daily between December 26 and January 10, otherwise every

---

 Liquid Sunshine

Nelson olive oils are rapidly gaining recognition nationally and internationally as some of the best you'll taste anywhere. If you're a fan of dipping, drizzling, and pouring, give in to temptation and visit some of the following. *Note:* It pays to call first to make sure they're open for direct sales. **Moutere Grove**, 979 Central Rd., Upper Moutere (© 03/543-2232; www.mouteregrove. co.nz), has a free tour and organic olive oil tastings by appointment only. **Hau Plains Olive Oil,** 543 High St., Motueka (© 03/528-6391; www.hauplains.co. nz), is open most days for sales and tastings. Others to look out for are **Frog's End Estate,** Westdale Road, Richmond (© 03/544-0570; www. frogsendoliveoil.co.nz); **Tasman Bay Olives,** Horton Road, Tasman (© 03/540-2084; www.olivesnewzealand. com); and **Mount Heslington Olives,** 89 Mount Heslington Rd., Brightwater (© 03/542-3727; mt.heslington@clear. net.nz).

Sunday. Look out for the very good cafe and an interesting organic brewery complex on-site, and they stage a farmers' market from 3 to 6pm on Friday evenings.

Last, but definitely not least, is the **Suter Art Gallery ★★**, 208 Bridge St. (📞 **03/548-4699;** www.thesuter.org.nz), the region's public art museum. The collection includes works by 19th-century New Zealand artists with strong Nelson ties, such as Gully, Lindauer, and Van der Velden. There's an excellent crafts shop and a bush-clad cafe overlooking Queens Gardens. Open daily 10:30am to 4:30pm (closed Good Friday, Dec 25, and Jan 1); admission is NZ$3 adults, NZ$1 for students and kids.

THE MOUTERE HILLS WINERIES

Most of Nelson's 25 wineries are scattered along the rolling Moutere Hills and the alluvial Waimea Plains. The wines—Riesling, chardonnay, sauvignon blanc, Gewürztraminer, cabernet franc, merlot, cabernet sauvignon, and pinot noir—have intense fruit flavors, good acidic balance, and weight. Many wineries have tasting rooms and restaurants. For more on Nelson wineries, tap into the **Nelson Winemakers Association** website at www.nelsonwines.co.nz, or www.eatdrinknelson.co.nz.

The visitor center has a leaflet and a very clear map pinpointing the best of the area's wineries, or you can take a wine tour with **JJ's Quality Tours ★★**, 31A Stansell Ave., Nelson (📞 **0800/229-868** in NZ, or 📞/fax 03/546-5470; www.jjstours. co.nz). Prices start at NZ$89 for a half-day tour. JJ's also offers a tour of local breweries, or a mix of breweries and wineries. For a similar price (NZ$97), **Bay Tours,** Nelson (📞 **0800/229-868** in NZ, or 03/548-6486; www.baytoursnelson.co.nz), also offers an excellent range of gourmet wine tours that include either food or art stops. If you're short on time, hotfoot it straight to the **Regional Wine Centre ★★**, 67 Aranui Rd., Mapua (📞 **03/540-2526;** fax 03/540-2561), which features a showing of the region's best wines, olive oils, beers, and gourmet foods. It includes a wine and taste center, a cafe, and a restaurant. Or, in Nelson City itself, **Casa del Vino ★★**, 214 Hardy St. (📞 **03/548-0088;** www.casadelvino.co.nz), stocks a huge range of Nelson and New Zealand wines and holds regular wine tastings in summer. You can also pick up wine maps of the region here and take advantage of the worldwide shipping service. They're open Monday to Thursday 10am to 6:30pm and Friday and Saturday 10am to 7:30pm, except in December and January, when they're only open on Sundays 10am to 3pm.

One of the best-known producers is **Neudorf Vineyards ★★★**, 138 Neudorf Rd., Upper Moutere (📞 **03/543-2643;** www.neudorf.co.nz). Set in a picturesque vineyard, the winery offers prearranged tastings of its prizewinning chardonnay, Riesling, pinot noir, and sauvignon blanc. It's open Monday through Friday from 10am to 5pm all year and also weekends from October through April. **Seifried Estate Vineyard and Restaurant,** Main Road, Appleby, Richmond (📞 **03/544-1555;** www. seifried.co.nz), has a large restaurant and tasting room, open daily from 10am to 5pm. A winery tour and tasting is NZ$12 per person, by appointment, Monday through Saturday. Dinner is available in the restaurant Friday and Saturday evenings from 6pm; reservations are recommended.

Moutere Hills Vineyard ★★, Eggers Road, Upper Moutere (📞/fax **03/543-2288;** www.moutere hills.co.nz), serves beautifully presented light meals in its converted-wool-shed winery, along with Riesling, sauvignon blanc, and chardonnay. It's open October 24 to Easter, Tuesday through Sunday, from 11am to 6pm.

Waimea Estates, 22 Appleby Hwy., Hope (📞 **03/544-4963;** www.waimea estates.co.nz), produces all the main wine types, and their cafe and cellar door are open in summer daily 11am to 5pm; in winter, Wednesday to Sunday until 4pm.

To Market, to Market

You'll gain a terrific insight into local activities if you go to the **Nelson Market** ★★★, in Montgomery Square (📞 **03/546-6454**). It's held every Saturday from 8am to 1pm and offers fine crafts, fresh food and produce, and a whole heap of the unexpected. **Monty's Sunday Market** is held every Sunday from 8:30am to 1pm in the same place and features more bric-a-brac, clothing, and oddments. The **Motueka Sunday Market** ★, in the carpark behind the Motueka Visitor Centre in Wallace Street, Motueka (📞 **03/540-2709**), is held every Sunday from 8am to 1pm. Stalls here include fresh produce, clothing, crafts, and jewelry.

Woollaston Estates ★★★, School Road, Mahana (📞 **03/543-2817**; www. woollaston.co.nz), has a fabulous underground complex complete with a contemporary art gallery. They offer wine tasting and live music on the first Sunday of each month in summer. They're open daily, 11am until 4:30pm from mid-October through April. **Ruby Bay Vineyard** ★★, 271 Pomona Rd., Ruby Bay (📞 **03/540-3938**; www.rubybayvineyard.co.nz), has a luxurious lodge and cottage for rent (p. 319), and is open for wine tasting and sales from Thursday through Monday 11am to 4pm (reduced winter hours, or by appointment).

SHOPPING FOR ARTS & CRAFTS

The essence of Nelson province is found in its abundance of top-quality arts and crafts—by far the best concentration anywhere in New Zealand. There are over 300 practicing artists and 40 galleries and studios. Start by purchasing a copy of *Nelson Art Guide Book,* which is a terrific take-home, ring-bound volume available at the Nelson visitor center, which also distributes the free *Tourist Guide to Nelson Potters, Nelson Inner City Shopping Guide,* and *Nelson City Art Trail.* If you're driving to Motueka, pick up the free *Nelson's Coastal Way–Mapua & Coastal Villages,* a brochure that highlights top craftspeople, vineyards, and cafes. Also visit www.nelsonarts.org.nz.

    South Street Gallery, 10 Nile St. (📞/fax **03/548-8117**; www.nelsonpottery. co.nz), is well stocked with work by 25 top potters; it's open Monday through Friday from 9am to 5pm and weekends 10am until 4pm. **Jens Hansen Gold & Silversmith** ★★★, 320 Trafalgar Sq. (📞 **03/548-0640**; www.jenshansen.com), is a name associated with fine-quality New Zealand–made gold and silver jewelry—*and* the handmade rings and jewelry used in the *Lord of the Rings* trilogy. It's open Monday through Friday 9am until 5:30pm, Saturday 9am to 2pm, and Sunday 10am to 1pm. **RED** ★★, 1 Bridge St. (📞 **03/548-2170**; www.redartgallery.com), is a terrific place for contemporary fine art, jewelry, and New Zealand crafts. **Flame Daisy,** 324 Trafalgar Sq. (📞 **03/548-4475**; www.flamedaisy.com), is a glass art gallery, with a wide variety of items, many at cheaper prices than the gorgeous Höglund Art Glass (see below). It's open Monday through Friday 10am until 5pm, and weekends 10am to 4pm.

    Farther afield, potter **Steve Fullmer** ★★★, Baldwin Road, Tasman (📞 **03/526-6765**; fullmer.gallery@xtra.co.nz), is one of the country's best. His gallery is open daily 10am until 5pm in summer, and Wednesday through Sunday in winter. **Royce McGlashen Pottery** ★★★, 128 Ellis St., Brightwater (📞 **03/542-3585**; www. roycemcglashen.co.nz), is another high point. When it comes to color, some of the nicest pottery around is produced by **Katie Gold** ★★★, 1380 Main Rd., Upper Moutere (📞 **03/543-2544**; katie_gold@paradise.net.nz).

Cool Crafts

One of the loveliest little galleries around is the **Coolstore Gallery ★★★**, 7 Aranui Rd., Mapua (📞 **03/540-3778**; www.coolstoregallery.co.nz), located in a converted apple cool store on Mapua Wharf. It displays a wide range of contemporary art and crafts from the region's best artisans. It's open daily in summer from 11am to 5pm, and Wednesday through Sunday in winter from 11am to 4pm. Just down the road, you'll find it hard to suppress a smile at

Laughing Fish Studio, 24 Aranui Rd., Mapua (📞 **03/540-3940**; www.laughingfishstudio.co.nz), where large ladies cavort across everything from plates to wall works. And hat lovers will rejoice at **Serious Straws ★★**, 144 Aranui Rd., Mapua (📞 **03/540-3262**; www.seriousstraws.co.nz), which makes and imports a gorgeous range of fashionable and funky straw hats. If you can't make it to Mapua, they have a stall at Nelson's weekend markets.

If you like beautiful glass pieces, drive 20 minutes out of Nelson to **Höglund Art Glass ★★★**, 52 Lansdowne Rd., Richmond (📞 **03/544-6500;** www.hoglundartglass.com). Ola and Marie Höglund trained at Orrefors and Kosta Boda before emigrating from their native Sweden, and their skills have translated into stunning, colorful handblown glassware. Admission is free and you can watch the action in the studio by joining a guided studio tour (Dec 15–Apr 15; NZ$25 adults, free for kids 13 and under) that enlightens you to the history of glass and its processes; or you can make your own glass beads (NZ$75 per hour) or a paperweight (NZ$195 per person). And don't worry about having to cart your favorite piece home—they offer an international shipping service. It's open daily 10am to 5pm (closed Dec 25–26 and Good Friday).

ESPECIALLY FOR KIDS

Give the kids a chance to burn off some excess energy at **Nelson Fun Park** (📞 **03/548-6267**), adjacent to Tahunanui Beach, and just a 5-minute drive from Central City. They can unwind on the hydroslide, play miniature golf, or have fun on bumper boats. **Natureland Zoo** (📞 **03/548-6166;** www.naturelandzoo.co.nz) is also at Tahunanui Beach, and open daily from 9:30am to 4pm (last entry 3:45pm). Here, kids get to get up close to wallabies, meerkats, otters, monkeys, and exotic birds; it costs NZ$9 for adults, NZ$4.50 for children 2 to 14, and NZ$23 for families.

Touch the Sea Aquarium ★★, 8 Aranui Rd., Mapua (📞/fax **03/540-3557;** www.seatouchaquarium.co.nz), is a charming little aquarium on Mapua Wharf where kids get to put their hands in special tanks to discover the mysteries of sea urchins, starfish, and various shells and fish. It's worth the admission of NZ$8.50 for adults, NZ$5.50 for kids 3 to 15, and NZ$20 for families. Also onsite are a playroom and an excellent gift store.

 Six Times the Fun

If you want to try a bit of everything and save money at the same time, check out combo deals with the Nelson Visitor Centre. If you invest in several activities, you'll pay far less, which is a big consideration when you're traveling with a family.

OUTDOOR PURSUITS

For a complete overview of outdoor activities in the region, it's best to start at one of the visitor centers, which are packed with brochures. There are three national parks within easy driving distance; that alone raises dozens of outdoor possibilities.

BEACHES   Nelson has dozens of fabulous beaches. Close to the city, the best bet is **Tahuna Beach,** which offers excellent swimming. Farther afield, just past Motueka, you'll find the hugely popular **Kaiteriteri Beach ★★★**, a favorite with Christchurch holidaymakers.

BIKING   You can hire bikes from **Stewarts Avanti Plus,** 114 Hardy St., Nelson (© 03/548-1666; www.avantiplusnelson.co.nz), for NZ$40 to NZ$100 per day depending on the bike you choose. They can also tell you about biking events and local trails. **Biking Nelson ★★** (© 0800/224-532 in NZ; www.bikingnelson.co.nz) offers excellent guided cycling and mountain bike tours from NZ$60 to NZ$125 for guided rides, all equipment included. If you're staying in Nelson, they'll meet you outside Henry's Bar, 296 Trafalgar St., just down from the Cathedral.

CAVING   Lovers of dark underground spaces will enjoy exploring **Ngarua Caves,** Takaka Hill, Motueka (© 03/528-8093). These marble caves feature the skeletal remains of New Zealand's extinct flightless bird, the moa, and a 45-minute guided tour is offered on the hour from 10am to 4pm (closed July–Sept). Entry is NZ$15 for adults, NZ$7 for children ages 5 to 15. The caves are 70km (43 miles) from Nelson and 20km (12 miles) from Motueka. Find further cave exploration in Takaka (see "Exploring Golden Bay," later in this chapter).

FISHING   Bait up those hooks and get out there! The fish are awaiting in lakes, rivers, streams, and the ocean. There's good onshore fishing at Connolly's Quay on Rocks Road, the western end of Tahuna Beach, Boulder Bay, and Cable Bay. When it comes to stalking trout, call John Brunwin of **Fly Fishing New Zealand,** 97 Murphy St., Nelson (© 03/548-9145; www.flyfishnewzealand.com).

FLIGHTSEEING   When you get up in the air over this stunning province, you'll truly understand why so many people love it. **Pilot a Stunt Plane ★★**, Motueka Airfield, Motueka (© 0800/360-180 in NZ, or 03/528-8290; www.uflyextreme.co.nz), offers a range of scenic flight packages. One of the most thrilling is a 15-minute "hands-on" flight for NZ$299 per person. Helicopter fans can buzz into the skies with **Nelson Helicopters,** Tangmere Place, Nelson Airport (© 0800/450-350 in NZ, or 03/547-1177; www.nelsonhelicopters.co.nz). Try their Nelson Lakes scenic tour, or visit *The Lord of the Rings* filming sites.

FOUR-WHEEL-DRIVE ADVENTURES   Just 10 minutes from central Nelson, you can don your helmet, get on a 4×4 motorbike, and go for it over your choice of testing tracks. **Happy Valley Adventures ★★**, 194 Cable Bay Rd., Nelson (© 0800/157-300 in NZ, or 03/545-0304; www.happyvalleyadventures.co.nz), is the place to call. Prices range from NZ$85 to NZ$165 per rider (NZ$20 extra for pillion passengers). Or you can fly on a Skywire for over 3km (1¾ miles) for NZ$85 adults, NZ$55 children 16 and under.

GOLF   **Nelson Golf Club,** Bolt Road, Tahunanui, Nelson (© 03/548-5028; www.nelsongolf.co.nz), is an 18-hole course open daily. Greens fees are NZ$50 for nonaffiliated members. **Greenacres Golf Club,** Best Island, Richmond (© 03/544-6441; fax 03/544-8420), also has 18 holes and is open daily; nonmembers pay NZ$40.

KAYAKING   If you don't have time to kayak in the unforgettable Abel Tasman, at least take to the waters near Nelson with **Cable Bay Kayaks,** Cable Bay Road, Nelson (© 0508/222-532 in NZ, or 03/545-0332; www.cablebaykayaks.co.nz).

They specialize in half- and 1-day tours that take in bird colonies, caves, and coves for NZ$65 to NZ$145 per person.

MOUNTAIN BIKING   Natural High, 52 Rutherford St., Nelson (℃ **0800/444-144** in NZ, or 03/546-6936; www.cyclenewzealand.com), offers guided bike excursions, from a 2-hour tour of the city sights and waterfront to multiday South Island tours and off-road adventures.

ROCK CLIMBING   Vertical Limits Climbing & Adventure Centre, 34 Vanguard St. (℃ **0508/837-842** in NZ, or 03/545-7511; www.verticallimits.co.nz), is the largest indoor climbing center in New Zealand. It offers indoor rock climbing, rappelling, and guided climbing and caving adventures with qualified instructors. A shot at the climbing walls costs NZ$18 for adults, NZ$15 for students, and NZ$12 for children under 12. It's open Monday through Friday 10am to 9pm, weekends 10am to 6pm.

SKY DIVING   Skydive Abel Tasman, 16 College St., Motueka Airport (℃ **0800/422-899** in NZ, or 03/528-4091; www.skydive.co.nz), has free-fall tandem sky dives with instructors priced NZ$299 to NZ$399.

**WALKING   **Just about anywhere in Nelson is suited to walking. From a leisurely stroll to full multiday treks, you'll be in your element. For information on multiday walks, see "Tramping" in chapter 4. Also check out "Abel Tasman National Park & Golden Bay," later in this chapter.

For a charming city walk, find the Maitai River off Nile Street and follow the signposted walkway to the locals' favorite swimming spot—Girlie's Hole. Another good 45-minute walk traces Nelson's old water system up through the native bush to dams built in the 1870s. Go to Brook Motor Camp; there's a parking area by the dam, and the trail leads on from here. Within 5 minutes, you'll be in native bush and a quiet valley. There are steps and handrails on the trail.

If you'd like to walk with the birds, go along Motueka Sandspit and enjoy the views across Tasman Bay to D'Urville Island and Nelson City. This is an internationally important seabird habitat and is home to many varieties that come here to breed. (Please keep dogs away from the southern end of the spit.) It's part of the Motueka Walkway, which is detailed in a brochure available at the visitor center. Access the walkway from the end of Staples Street.

> **A Walk to Remember**
>
> A walk along **Boulder Bank**—the thin strip of land that reaches out from Nelson into the sea—is an unusual and exhilarating experience. Take water, sun protection, and a windbreaker for this 2½-hour, 8km (5-mile) walk, which begins and ends at Boulder Bank Drive.

WHITE-WATER ADVENTURES   Ultimate Descents New Zealand, Motueka (℃ **0800/748-377** in NZ, or 03/523-9899; www.rivers.co.nz), seems to have every possible white-water activity covered. It offers a wide range of outings by kayak, raft, or river bug (also known as a sled; this involves going through white water lying facedown on the sled), from Grade II to the savage Grade V on rivers throughout the greater Nelson province. Half-day to multiday rafting and kayaking trips for all ages cost from NZ$135 to NZ$575. There is a minimum age limit of 13.

Where to Stay

Nelson isn't short of beds, but if you're visiting over the December-to-January period, you'll be competing with thousands of New Zealanders who descend upon the area.

Book early! There is a wide range of accommodations—including lots of smart B&Bs and excellent backpacker offerings—and with one or two exceptions, most are incredibly well priced. The rates given below include 15% GST and free parking.

IN NELSON
Expensive

Te Puna Wai Lodge ★★   Consummate hosts James Taylor and multilingual Richard Hewitson attend to your every comfort. They offer two rooms and an apartment in a lovely 1857 home complete with antiques, art, and beautiful ocean views. Lower rooms open onto a balcony overlooking the sea and the attic suite offers huge picture windows. There's a small, narrow staircase winding up to the attic, but once there, you'll be in a world of your own with a glamorous bathroom.

24 Richardson St. www.tepunawai.co.nz. ✆ **03/548-7621.** 3 units. NZ$220 Wakatu room, NZ$325 Fifeshire suite; NZ$345 Haulashore apt. Rates include breakfast. Long-stay & off-peak rates. AE, MC, V. **Amenities:** Nearby golf course; massage by arrangement. *In room:* TV/DVD, fridge, hairdryer, Wi-Fi.

39 Russell ★★★ 📷   This sublime self-contained hillside cottage is where acclaimed artist Jane Evans has used her creative talents and good taste to create a place you won't want to leave. Folding doors and windows open to sea views and a divine courtyard; and with two guest rooms (both with bathrooms), it's an ideal stop for two couples. Suffused with color, original art, fabulous books, and a bulging pantry, it is one of the best-value B&B stays in the country. Jane does her part for the environment by utilizing solar energy and environmentally friendly cleaning products. Make sure you arrange a studio visit so you can see into Jane's creative world.

39 Russell St., Port Nelson. www.39russell.co.nz. ✆ **03/548-7621.** One 2-bedroom cottage. NZ$355; NZ$25 each extra person. Minimum 2-night stay. Rates include self-catered breakfast. Long-stay and off-peak rates. MC, V. From Haven Rd., turn onto Russell St. and go uphill, keeping to the steep left-hand road; halfway up is a private road—it's the first house on the left. No children 11 and under. **Amenities:** Nearby golf courses, Wi-Fi in lounge. *In room:* TV/DVD, hair dryer, full kitchen w/stocked pantry, minibar.

Moderate

Rutherford Hotel Nelson, Trafalgar Square (www.heritagehotels.co.nz; ✆ **0800/ 368-888** in NZ, or 03/548-2299), is a good, centrally located spot that always has good deals. Its 113 rooms are priced from NZ$205 to NZ$460. You'll also find seven B&B rooms in a large, character homestead behind the cathedral at **Cathedral Inn,** 369 Trafalgar St. (www.cathedralinn.co.nz; ✆ **03/548-7369**); they're priced from NZ$195 to NZ$310.

Baywick Inn ★ 🖋   Canadian Janet Southwick and her New Zealand husband Tim Bayley have been doing a fabulous job of hosting guests at terrific prices long enough to be considered experts. Upstairs rooms in their 1885 restored Victorian have plenty of space and character; the Parkdale has a huge step-down bathroom complete with claw-foot tub and shower, plus its own sunroom. A recent addition, an ecofriendly cottage in the garden, offers two more rooms (one up, one down) overlooking the stream and garden—ideal for families or two couples who like to be close to each other. Expect terrific breakfasts. All this just 5 minutes' walk from town.

51 Domett St., Nelson. www.baywicks.com. ✆ **03/545-6514.** Fax 03/545-6517. 5 units. NZ$165– NZ$250. Long-stay and off-peak rates. Rates include breakfast. MC, V. No children under 12. **Amenities:** Free use of bikes; nearby golf course. *In room:* A/C (some rooms), TV, fridge, hair dryer, Wi-Fi.

The Little Retreat ★★ 📷   This little gem is right in the heart of Nelson's historic South Street area, and owner Angela Higgins also owns the natural health center located directly beneath—just the place for a soothing shiatsu massage after a day of sightseeing. She leaves you entirely to yourself but not before you have experienced her terrific hospitality. The modern, open-plan apartment has a king-size bed, leather chairs, full kitchen and laundry, two private balconies, and a barbecue. Waking up to a hearty breakfast, eating out on the balcony, and watching the world go by are what a holiday is all about.

22 Nile St. W., Nelson. www.nelsongetaways.co.nz. © **03/545-1411** or 021/247-1891. Fax 03/545-1417. 1 unit. NZ$195–NZ$240. Rates include breakfast provisions. Long-stay and off-peak rates. AE, MC, V. **Amenities:** Babysitting; nearby golf; health center. *In room:* A/C, TV/DVD, hair dryer, kitchen, Wi-Fi.

Long Lookout Gardens ★★ 🎁 David and Yvonne Trathen are not wrong when they say that the hardest thing you'll ever have to do is leave Long Lookout Gardens. As a lover of old homes, I find it very easy to recommend this gorgeous 1864 homestead set in English-style gardens. The two suites are elaborate and luscious with rich silks and satins, and beautiful modern bathrooms are a big plus. It's hard to choose between the ground-floor Richmond and the first-floor Hunter-Brown suites. Both are exquisite. Breakfasts also get rave reviews.

60 Cleveland Terrace, Nelson. www.longlookoutgardens.co.nz. © **03/548-3617.** Fax 03/548-312. 2 units. NZ$325. Long-stay and off-peak rates. Rates include breakfast. MC, V. **Amenities:** Airport transfers; bike rentals; nearby golf course. *In room:* TV, fridge, hair dryer, Wi-Fi.

Shelbourne Villa ★★ Wayne and Val Ballantyne have converted their two-story 1929 villa into a pleasurable oasis offering four lovely room choices. I'd opt for the Loft if you like a modern look, plenty of space, and balcony views; like the Master Suite, it has its own fireplace and king-size bed. The downstairs Garden Suite is also very appealing and has a separate living room and kitchenette. Wherever you end up sleeping, you won't be disappointed. The property has a Qualmark Enviro-Gold rating and is a member of the Nelson Sustainable Tourism Charter.

21 Shelbourne St., Nelson. www.shelbournevilla.co.nz. © **03/545-9059.** Fax 03/546-7248. 4 units. NZ$295–NZ$435. Long-stay and off-peak rates. Rates include breakfast. AE, DC, MC, V. No children under 12. **Amenities:** Nearby golf course. *In room:* A/C, TV/DVD, fridge, hair dryer, kitchenette (Garden Suite), Wi-Fi in some areas.

Warwick House ★★ At this gigantic mansion you will get a feel for what life might have been like for the landed gentry who settled early Nelson. It's a spectacular heritage home that Nick and Jenny Ferrier have spent years converting into an elegant B&B. The Bayview Suite is the biggest and best room but all have an individual charm and character—and their own en-suite bathrooms. If you're traveling with a small family, or with friends, the lower ground apartment is a good option. The property has a Qualmark Enviro-Silver rating.

64 Brougham St. www.warwickhouse.co.nz. © **0800/022-233** in NZ, or 03/548-3164. 6 units. NZ$179–NZ$395. Long-stay & off-peak rates. Rates include breakfast. MC, V. No children under 8. **Amenities:** Bike rentals; nearby golf course; massage by arrangement; Wi-Fi in main reception areas. *In room:* TV, fridge, hair dryer.

Inexpensive

There are modest but comfortable self-contained and B&B rooms at **Joya Villa & Garden Studios,** 49 Brougham St. (www.joya.co.nz; © **03/539-1350**); four rooms go for NZ$95 to NZ$185.

Paradiso Backpackers ★ 🎁 You can expect a crowd at Paradiso—it's definitely the most popular Nelson backpacker stay. One look at its fabulous pool, its conservatory kitchen/dining room, and its quirky lounge set up in an old bus, and you realize why. Bedrooms might be pretty standard and boring, but they're comfortable, and with all the other luxuries on hand, who cares?

42 Weka St., Nelson. www.backpackernelson.co.nz. ✆ **0800/269-667** in NZ, or 03/545-7128. Fax 03/546-7533. 95 beds with shared bathrooms, 9 en suites, 10 apts. NZ$24 dorm; NZ$75 double; NZ$85–NZ$165 apt. Long-stay and off-peak rates. AE, MC, V. **Amenities:** Jacuzzi; outdoor heated pool; sauna. *In room:* A/C (apts. only), high-speed Internet.

IN TAHUNANUI-RICHMOND

Tahuna Beach Holiday Park, 70 Beach Rd., Tahunanui (www.tahunabeach.co.nz; ✆ 0800/500-501 in NZ, or 03/548-5159), is the largest motor camp in New Zealand, accommodating several thousand travelers a night during the summer months. It has motel units, tourist and standard cabins, and tent sites—not to mention a fabulous atmosphere. Just make sure you book early because this is a favorite camp for New Zealanders. For a more contemporary stay, you'll have every comfort at hand at **The Sands ★★**, 623 Rocks Rd., Tahunanui (www.thesandsnelson.co.nz; ✆ 0800/635-766 in NZ, or 03/539-6030). Modern one-, two- and three-bedroom apartments overlook pretty Tahunanui Beach, just 5 minutes from central Nelson; from NZ$175.

IN MOTUEKA/MAPUA
Very Expensive

Motueka township itself doesn't contain an abundance of nice accommodations, but outlying areas have rich pickings for those wanting a peaceful country stay. **Bronte Country Estate ★★**, Bronte Road East, near Mapua (✆ 03/540-2422; www.brontecountryestate.co.nz), is one such place, with two luxury suites (NZ$585) and three villas ranging from NZ$720 to NZ$1,230 (NZ$155 for each additional person). Private dinners cost NZ$200 per person.

Edenhouse ★★★ Set in 48 acres of private grounds and gardens in peaceful Orinoco Valley, this exclusive country retreat is the brainchild of Peter and Bobbie Martin, who have two top-quality suites in the main house, plus a roomy cottage suite. It's a winner in every way—it's spacious, luxurious, and private, with well-traveled hosts who know how to treat discerning guests. There are several vineyards close by and they're just 30 minutes from beautiful Abel Tasman National Park.

Orinoco Valley, Motueka. www.edenhouse.co.nz. ✆ **03/526-8174.** 3 units. NZ$1,050–NZ$1,290 bedroom suite; NZ$1,150–NZ$1,390 cottage suite. Off-peak rates. Rates include breakfast, dinner, pre-dinner drinks & wine. AE, DC, MC, V. **Amenities:** Membership for guests at nearby Monterey House Country Club & golf course; Jacuzzi; artist studio. *In room:* A/C, TV/DVD, fridge, hair dryer, free Wi-Fi.

Expensive

Ruby Bay Vineyard Lodge & Cottage ★★ Waking up in top-quality bed linens to vineyard views and a delicious big breakfast is the perfect way to start any holiday. There's a romantic, two-bedroom cottage here, plus two lodge suites; once you've settled in, you can explore the vineyard and try wine tasting in the Ruby Bay cellar. The fully equipped cottage, complete with laundry, is ideal for two couples. The lodge's guest lounge has a movie projection system.

271 Pomona Rd., Ruby Bay. www.rubybayvineyard.co.nz. ℂ **03/540-3938.** 3 units. NZ$395 cottage; NZ$450 lodge suites. Rates include breakfast. Long-stay & off-peak rates. MC, V. Closed June–Oct. No children under 12 in lodge suites. *In room:* TV/DVD, full kitchen & laundry in cottage, fridge, hair dryer.

Wairepo House ★★   In a fourth-generation apple and pear orchard, this big colonial homestead oozes romance. With nearly a hectare (2½ acres) of woodland gardens (including a giant chess set), this peaceful, rural oasis begs a lingering stay. Richard and Joyanne Easton will make sure it's everything you hoped for, starting with the fresh produce from their organic gardens and orchard that are used in their gourmet breakfasts. The big two-bedroom top-floor suite is the most spacious and has a double Jacuzzi, lounge, kitchen, and balcony. Others open onto the pool and garden.

22 Weka Rd., Mariri, Tasman. www.wairepohouse.co.nz. ℂ **03/526-6865.** Fax 03/526-6101. 4 units. NZ$460–NZ$660. NZ$55 per person for extra adults. Long-stay rates. Rates include breakfast, canapés, and pre-dinner drinks. MC, V. Closed Dec 24–Jan 12. **Amenities:** Airport transfers (charge applies); babysitting; nearby bike rentals; nearby golf course; outdoor heated pool; grass tennis court. *In room:* TV/CD, fridge, hair dryer, kitchenette (in 1 suite), minibar, Wi-Fi.

Moderate

A lovely discovery in this area is **Neudorf Hall** ★, 252 Neudorf Rd., Upper Moutere (www.neudorfhall.co.nz; ℂ **03/543-2252**), which is just a short stroll from nearby Neudorf Vineyard; two rooms are priced NZ$195 to NZ$315. **Nautilus Lodge Motel,** 67 High St., Motueka (www.nautiluslodge.co.nz; ℂ **0800/628-845** in NZ, or 03/528-4658), is a good motel with simple rooms (NZ$115–NZ$225).

Aporo Pondsiders ★★   Mike and Marian Day have come up with a gem of an idea—two supercute, self-contained, environmentally friendly cottages overhanging an ornamental pond in a peaceful rural environment. You'd be silly to miss them! Staggered for privacy, they have king-size beds and modern furnishings with a small kitchen, living room, and balcony overlooking the water. Pick up the binoculars and watch herons and shags, row in the dinghy, or walk in the woods. They have a Qualmark Enviro-Gold rating for environmental friendliness.

23 Permin Rd., Tasman. www.aporo.co.nz. ℂ **03/526-6858.** Fax 03/526-6258. 2 units. NZ$320. Long-stay rates. Rates include breakfast provisions. MC, V. 30-min. drive from Nelson, 10 min. from Motueka. **Amenities:** Babysitting; free use of bikes; nearby golf course. *In room:* TV/CD, hair dryer, kitchen, free Wi-Fi.

Where to Eat

Nelson is the seafood capital of New Zealand, so it isn't unreasonable to expect top seafood in the area's restaurants. Combine that with a wealth of horticultural produce, world-renowned wines, and a casual atmosphere, and the stage is set for some memorable dining. There's been a rush of new cafes—not all worth visiting—and you won't be short of an opportunity to dine well.

> **Top Tastes**
>
> Pick up a free copy of *Eat Drink Nelson* from the visitor center, or check www. eatdrinknelson.co.nz for all the best restaurants and boutique food producers in the region.

IN NELSON

For the best coffee in town, head for **Zumo Coffee House** ★★, 42 Rutherford St. (ℂ **03/548-7405;**

Mouthwatering Morsels

For the best and biggest range of ice cream in town, head for **Penguino Gelato Café ★★★**, 85 Montgomery Sq., Nelson (✆ 03/545-6450; www.penguino.co.nz), where you'll find 18 flavors made from traditional Italian recipes. Try the gelato, sorbet, sundaes, "bambinos" for children, and big four-flavor cone for the ambitious. They're open daily in summer, 11am to 6pm. Chocoholics should explore the sweet delights at **Zatori Café de Chocolat ★★★**, 270 Trafalgar St. (✆ 03/546-9202; www.zatori.co.nz). It's the perfect place for an indulgent morning or afternoon tea, or dessert after dinner. They're open Monday through Saturday 9am to late.

www.zumo.co.nz), open Monday through Friday 7am to 4pm, weekends 8am to 3pm. **Lambretta's Café Bar ★**, 204 Hardy St. (✆ 03/545-8555; www.lambrettas.co.nz), remains popular for light meals (especially their pizzas), and a good time. It's invariably packed with people enjoying pastas, pizzas, and seafood dishes daily from 8:30am until late. The Suter Art Gallery's **Suter Café ★★**, 208 Bridge St. (✆ 03/548-4040), looks out into the leafy environs of Queen's Gardens. They have delicious counter food, with lots of vegetarian, gluten-free, and dairy-free options. They're open daily from 9am to 4pm in summer (until 3:30pm in winter).

Excellent Japanese cuisine can be found at **Miyazu Japanese Restaurant ★★★**, Rutherford Hotel, Nelson (✆ 03/548-2299; www.heritagehotels.co.nz), where you can watch slick Japanese chefs preparing your meal in front of you. They're open Monday through Saturday from 6pm. For a quick sushi fix, don't miss **Haroo Sushi,** 50 Bridge St., Nelson (✆ 03/546-6123); and pizza fans can eat their fill at **Pizza Bar,** 105 Hardy St. (✆ 03/548-8990; www.pizzabar.co.nz).

Boatshed Café ★ SEAFOOD   The over-the-water setting of this busy Nelson landmark is a terrific feature, and while it continues to deliver good seafood meals in a memorable location, the service and staff's attitudes fluctuate a little more than is desirable. You can handpick your own wriggly crabs or lobster and have them delivered to the pot for the chef's attention, or select from a large seafood menu.

350 Wakefield Quay. ✆ **03/546-9783.** www.boatshedcafe.co.nz. Reservations required for dinner. Main courses NZ$24–NZ$34. AE, DC, MC, V. Daily 9am–late.

Harry's Bar ★★ PACIFIC/ASIAN   Locals seem very happy with Harry's and that's usually a good sign. Sited in old legal chambers, it has a reputation for serving consistently excellent meals with an emphasis on Asian flavors—crispy, red-braised duck and chili-salt squid are two favorites. The modern interior, built around glass and lighting effects, can distract you from the sometimes patchy service. It's lively, especially in the early evening when locals gather for pre-dinner drinks.

306 Hardy St. ✆ **03/539-0905.** Reservations recommended. Main courses NZ$22–NZ$34. AE, MC, V. Tues–Sat 5pm–late.

Hopgoods ★★★ MODERN NEW ZEALAND   Kevin Hopgood has worked with the Ruex brothers and Gordon Ramsey in London, and he brings a welcome style and professionalism to Nelson with this calm, contemporary addition to the main street. Expect a showcase of local produce at great prices and a hoard of returning locals.

> ## Raise Your Glass
>
> With a strong hop-growing history, it's not surprising that Nelson delivers on the beer front. Two breweries to visit are **Founders Organic Brewery** ★★★, Founders Historic Park, 87 Atawhai Dr., Nelson (✆ 03/548-4638; www.biobrew.co.nz), the country's first certified organic brewery complete with a cafe that serves great lunches; and **The Vic Brew Bar** ★★★, 281 Trafalgar St., Nelson (✆ 03/548-7631; www.macs.co.nz), where they serve a range of premium, award-winning beers. They're open daily from 11am until late.

284 Trafalgar St. ✆ **03/545-7191.** www.hopgoods.co.nz. Reservations essential. Main courses NZ$26–NZ$38. AE, MC, V. Tues–Sat 9am–late; Mon 5:30pm–late.

Ikko Sushi ★ CASUAL JAPANESE   Sushi and Japanese noodle fans will love this gem tucked-away in an alley. The interior is small and completely forgettable but the food is divine, the service fast and friendly. Fill up on satisfying teriyaki chicken don, or delicate tempura don for ridiculously reasonable prices. Teriyaki tofu will melt in your mouth.

Marble Arch Arcade, 167 Hardy St. ✆ **03/548-1591.** Main courses NZ$12–NZ$16. MC, V. Daily 11am–late.

Morrison Street Café ★★ CAFE   This popular award-winning spot has excellent coffee, a busy, friendly atmosphere, and some of the tastiest lunches in town. Their menu changes regularly but tasty salads, mussel laksa, and dishes like marinated lamb fillet with Indian spices are regulars. Table service can be erratic, but their food is worth the wait and there's always an interesting mix of people. Wheat- and gluten-free options are available and you can dine indoors or out.

244 Hardy St. ✆ **03/548-8110.** www.morrisonstreetcafe.co.nz. Main courses NZ$15–NZ$24. AE, DC, MC, V. Mon–Fri 7:30am–4pm, Sat 8:30am–4pm, Sun 9am–3pm. Closed Dec 25, Jan 1, Easter Friday & Easter Sunday.

IN RICHMOND

One of the popular casual favorites in the area is the **Honest Lawyer Country Pub** ★, 1 Point Rd., Monaco (✆ 03/547-8850; www.honestlawyer.co.nz), which is not actually in the country at all, but near Nelson Airport. It's a replica of a classic English pub, offering breakfast, lunch, and dinner daily from 7am till late. But by far the nicest Richmond eatery is **Bouterey's Restaurant** ★★★, 251 Queen St., Richmond (✆ 03/544-1114; www.boutereys.co.nz). It's open Monday to Saturday for dinner and features fresh and organic local produce whisked into edible delicacies by Michelin-trained owner/chef Matt Bouterey. Before coming to Nelson, Bouterey ran the famous Sugar Reef Restaurant in London and cooked for celebrities like Angelina Jolie and Michael Caine. His international menu will seduce you in seconds.

IN MOTUEKA/MAPUA

The **Naked Bun Patisserie** ★★, 66–68 Aranui Rd., Mapua (✆ **03/540-3656;** www.thenakedbun.co.nz), is a European-style patisserie where you'll get not only divine sweet things but also organic breads and savory snacks. It's open Monday through Friday from 7:30am to 4:30pm, weekends 8am to 4:30pm; dining is available indoors or out. See also "The Moutere Hills Wineries," earlier in this chapter, for more dining opportunities at some of the local wineries.

ABEL TASMAN NATIONAL PARK & GOLDEN BAY ★★★

Marahau, the southern gateway to the park: 67km (42 miles) NW of Nelson; Takaka, the gateway to Golden Bay: 109km (68 miles) NW of Nelson

Abel Tasman is New Zealand's smallest national park. It protects 23,000 hectares (57,000 acres) of easily accessible coastline, offering unbeatable gold-sand beaches and forested headlands. Marahau and Totaranui are the main gateways to the park, a 1½- and 2½-hour drive, respectively, from Nelson.

Farther north, Golden Bay sits peacefully beyond the twists and turns of Takaka Hill, opening out in a spread of forested parks and golden beaches. The scenery is breathtaking, and the area draws many visitors keen to hike the Abel Tasman's Coastal Track and Kahurangi's Heaphy Track. Today, it is a fertile mix of dairy farming and arty alternative lifestyles—a reflection of the number of people who've reached this corner of the world and found they didn't want to leave.

Essentials

GETTING THERE & GETTING AROUND **By Plane** **Capital Air** (℃ 0800/ 588-885; www.capitalair.co.nz) has scheduled flights between Wellington and Takaka, plus Heaphy Track and Abel Tasman National Park connections. The flight from Wellington to Golden Bay takes just 50 minutes. Several other small operators, including **Abel Tasman Air** (℃ 0800/304-560 in NZ; www.abeltasmanair.co.nz), also service this area.

By Coach (Bus) **Abel Tasman Coachlines,** 27 Bridge St., Nelson (℃ 03/548-0285 in Nelson or 528-8850 in Motueka; www.abeltasmantravel.co.nz), operates year-round daily service from Nelson to Kaiteriteri, Marahau, Totaranui, and Abel Tasman National Park. It also provides connecting service to Kahurangi National Park and the north entrance to the Heaphy Track. They offer a number of well-priced 1-day Abel Tasman packages. **KBus,** P.O. Box 1079, Blenheim (℃ 0508/458-835 in NZ, or 03/358-8355; www.kbus.co.nz), has scheduled service between Picton, Blenheim, Motueka, Nelson, Abel Tasman, Golden Bay, and Heaphy Track, plus service between Collingwood and Takaka.

By Shuttle **Trek Express** (℃ 0800/128-735 in NZ, or 03/540-2042; www. trekexpress.co.nz) operates a four-wheel-drive shuttle to Kahurangi Park and all other major hikes in the area.

By Car The trip from Nelson to Takaka via State Highway 60 takes about 2 hours and includes a long, steep, winding section crossing Takaka Hill. To reach Marahau, turn right at the bottom of Takaka Hill, just past Motueka (don't go over Takaka Hill), and drive through Kaiteriteri. The trip takes about 1½ hours.

VISITOR INFORMATION The **Department of Conservation,** 62 Commercial St., Takaka (℃ 03/525-8026; www.doc.govt.nz), provides information on the national parks and huts available on the tracks. It's open Monday through Friday from 8:30am to 4pm. The **Golden Bay i-SITE Visitor Centre,** Willow Street, Takaka (℃ 03/525-9136; www.nelsonnz.com), is open in summer daily from 9am to 5pm, and winter daily from 9am until 4pm (closed Dec 25). The **Farewell Spit Visitor Centre & Paddlecrab Kitchen,** RD1, Collingwood, Golden Bay (℃ 03/524-8454;

Exploring Abel Tasman National Park ★★★

Abel Tasman is the jewel among popular national parks. It's a sea kayaker's paradise, and it's great for swimming and fishing. The **Abel Tasman Coastal Track** is one of the Department of Conservation's eight identified Great Walks and the only coast track of its kind in the country. It can be done in 3 to 5 days, or combined with water taxis or sea kayaks for added interest. See p. 64 for more details.

Sea kayaking is probably the best way to see the area, and **Abel Tasman Kayaks ★★★**, Main Road, Marehau (© **0800/732-529** in NZ, or 03/527-8022; www.abeltasmankayaks.co.nz), pioneered the activity in this region. They're the largest kayaking company in the area and they operate all year, with a large base with secure car parking and hot showers. A range of guided trips are available and they'll give you an insight into the Maori and European history of the area. The most popular are the full-day guided excursions, which can include guided walks or swimming with seals, or both. Prices range from NZ$115 for short outings to NZ$599 for a 3-day kayak-camping (catered) tour, departing Monday, Wednesday, and Friday. You must be 14 and over for all tours. Prices include pickup and transport from Motueka. Return transport to Nelson costs NZ$35. **Kaiteriteri Kayaks ★★★**, Kaiteriteri Beachfront (© **0800/252-925** in NZ, or 03/527-8383; www.seakayak.co.nz), is smaller and only operates during summer. It's a great one for going to see the seal pups, who are at a very cute stage in January. Their trips range from NZ$30 to NZ$199 per person. Children's prices apply to some trips. *Note:* If you're being picked up from Nelson for any of these park excursions, you'll have to allow 1½ hours each way on a bus. You'll leave Nelson at 7:15am, 8:30am, or 3:40pm, returning 1:55pm, 5:15pm, 6pm, or 7:15pm. There's only one bus in from late April to October, leaving Nelson at 8:30am, returning at 6pm.

Wilsons Abel Tasman ★★★, 265 High St., Motueka (© **0800/223-582** in NZ, or 03/528-2027; www.abeltasman.co.nz), operates buses, launches, and beachfront lodges. It's an award-winning family-owned business run by the Wilson family, who pioneered tourism in the park in 1977. They arrange 1- to 5-day guided walks and sea-kayaking trips that include stays at their Torrent Bay Lodge and Meadowbank Homestead-Awaroa. All trips can be arranged as walking only, or walking/sea kayaking combinations, and skilled guides and chefs provide quality experiences and meals. During high season, a 1-day guided sea kayaking trip costs NZ$160 adults and NZ$110 children ages 12 to 14; the 3-day guided walk is NZ$1,350 for adults, NZ$945 for children 8 to 14; the 5-day guided kayak and walk trip costs NZ$2,030 for adults only (or children over 12 paying adult fee). Rates are lower from mid-April to mid-October. Scenic cruises are offered on the company's **Vista Cruises** aboard the catamaran *Abel Tasman Voyager,* which carries 140 passengers and makes three trips a day. The Southern Cruise and Walk package costs NZ$69 for adults, NZ$34 for ages 5 to 14 years; the Northern Cruise and Walk costs NZ$78 for adults, NZ$39 for kids.

Abel Tasman Aqua Taxi ★, Main Road, Marahau (© **0800/278-282** in NZ, or 03/527-8083; www.aquataxi.co.nz), has a 3-hour cruise that visits points of interest along the park beaches and the fur-seal colony on Tonga Island. The price ranges from NZ$75 to NZ$95. If you're short on time, do the cruise if nothing else, or you'll miss seeing this spectacular unspoiled coast. Another lovely way to experience the best of the Abel Tasman is to join **Abel Tasman Cruises** ★, Port Nelson (© **0508/488-066** in NZ; www.abeltasmancruises.co.nz), in Nelson, for their day trip to Awaroa. You see all the gorgeous golden sand beaches on the way and have a fabulous lunch at Awaroa Lodge before returning to Nelson on their fast catamaran. This costs NZ$245 per person and runs November through April.

For a terrific guided walk, look no further than **Kahurangi Guided Walks** ★★, Dodson Road, Takaka, Golden Bay (© **03/525-7177**; www.kahurangiwalks.co.nz). They offer 1-, 3-, or 5-day walking trips in the Abel Tasman and Kahurangi National Parks. There are excellent half-day trips for those on a tight schedule, for NZ$35 to NZ$75 per person. **Bush and Beyond Guided Walks** ★★, 35 School Rd., Motueka (© **03/528-9054;** www.bushandbeyond.co.nz), has day and multiday walks priced from NZ$195.

WHERE TO STAY

Kaiteriteri Beach has a wealth of accommodations, but you'll have to book months in advance. At Marahau Beach, backpackers and campers should check out the **Barn,** Harvey Road, Marahau (© **03/527-8043;** fax 03/527-8440), the closest lodgings to the park, with a shared dorm, double and twin rooms, and motor-home or tent sites from NZ$25 to NZ$75. **Marahau Beach Camp,** Franklin Street, Marahau (www.abeltasmanmarahaucamp.co.nz; ©/fax **03/527-8176**), also has backpacker and camping facilities. There are smarter rooms at the ecofriendly **Abel Tasman Ocean View Chalets,** 305 Sandy Bay Rd., Marahau (www.accommodationabeltasman.co.nz; © **03/527-8232**), with rates of NZ$145 to NZ$285 for their one- and two-bedroom chalets. They have a Qualmark Enviro-Silver rating and are members of the Nelson Sustainable Tourism Charter.

My pick for this area is ecofriendly **Awaroa Lodge** ★★★, Abel Tasman National Park (www.awaroalodge.co.nz; © **03/528-8758**), which has 26 modern rooms priced from NZ$415 to NZ$460. Tucked into the northern end of the park, Awaroa is a feature destination of the Abel Tasman Coastal Track, and has its own restaurant, which serves food grown in their amazing organic garden. It has won a New Zealand Tourism Innovation in Ecotourism award for its sound ecological practices, which include a sophisticated, sustainable waste-management system. There is no road access. You reach the lodge via foot, kayak, water taxi, catamaran, helicopter, or small, fixed-wing aircraft. Another ecofriendly choice is **Abel Tasman Marahau Lodge** ★ , Marahau Beach (www.abeltasmanmarahaulodge.co.nz; © **03/527-8250**), which has 12 smart studio units with en-suite bathrooms for NZ$170 to NZ$270. It's not the Hilton, but you do get great service, a magical setting, and incredible silence; and it has a Qualmark Enviro-Silver rating.

Exploring Golden Bay ★★★

The main town near Golden Bay is Takaka, which has an astoundingly small population of 1,100. Another 28km (17 miles) north is Collingwood, which is even smaller. While in Takaka, you can peek in at the **Golden Bay Museum & Gallery,** 69 Commercial St. (© **03/525-6268** or 03/525-9990), open daily in summer from 10am to 4pm (closed Sun in winter). Admission is by donation. You'll find several working artists in the area, and the free brochure *Arts of Golden Bay,* available from the visitor center (© **03/525-9136**), details the locations and visiting hours of some of the best.

Golden Bay is rich in natural attractions, and one of the best known is **Te Waiko-ropupu Springs ★★**, called Pupu Springs by the locals. Here you'll find rushing water claimed to be the clearest fresh water in the world. It's signposted just north of Takaka township.

Cave formations are also common; one of the most famous, **Harwood's Hole,** plummets an awesome 180m (600 ft.) straight down. The visitor center can supply you with details. There are three other cave systems worth investigating. **Ngarua Caves,** 20km (12 miles) from Motueka on Takaka Hill (✆ **03/528-8093**), are easily negotiated and feature stalactites aplenty and the skeletal remains of the extinct moa. Guided tours are given on the hour between 10am and 4pm from mid-September to June 7. Admission is NZ$15. **Te Anaroa & Rebecca Caves,** Rockville, Golden Bay (✆ **0800/832-283**), have easy access and the best glowworms. They're very beautiful, but some of the rooflines are low and narrow, which may put you off if you're claustrophobic. **Rawhiti Caves,** also in Golden Bay (✆ **0800/832-283**), is accessed via a 40-minute bush walk. You're greeted with a huge entrance and a steep descent. You need to be agile for this outing, and it's not recommended for children 4 and under. Te Anaroa & Rebecca Caves and Rawhiti Caves are administered by the Department of Conservation in Takaka, and both are free walks.

Local rock climbers know all about the many attributes of **Payne's Ford Scenic Reserve,** near Takaka. The limestone bluffs they favor dominate the area; a track through the reserve follows an old tramway line. You'll find excellent swimming holes in the nearby Takaka River.

All along the road from Takaka to Collingwood, you'll see signs pointing to the coast. Each beach is different, but much of the bay is shallow; swimming at high tide involves a lot less walking. Tata Beach is deeper.

Another 26km (16 miles) north of Collingwood is the base of **Farewell Spit,** a unique sand spit 35km (22 miles) long and nearly a half-mile wide. All along its length are sand dunes as high as seven- to eight-story buildings. The bird life here is amazing, as it is a migratory stopover for several species. **Farewell Spit Eco Tours ★★**, 6 Tasman St., Collingwood (✆ **0800/808-257** in NZ, or 03/524-8257; www.farewell spit.com), has a range of superb tours to Farewell Spit. Most popular is the Lighthouse trip, a 4½-hour excursion that costs NZ$120 for adults, NZ$50 children 15 and under. Special bird-watching trips can be arranged and cost from NZ$120 to NZ$145 for adults, NZ$50 to NZ$55 children 15 and under. Bring binoculars and a camera.

For information on the **Heaphy Track** and **Kahurangi National Park,** see "Tramping" in chapter 4. And pick up the two free guides *Bike Tasman* and *Walk Tasman* from any Nelson visitor center.

WHERE TO STAY

Sans Souci Inn ★, 11 Richmond Rd., Pohara Beach (www.sanssouciinn.co.nz; ✆/fax **03/525-8663**), is an ideal beach stay near Takaka if you're into simplicity and style. The seven-unit grass-roofed inn, run by a young Swiss couple with a strong interest in sustainable tourism, is a divine hideaway with a Japanese feel. Mediterranean floor tiles, low futon-style beds, and scented Lawson cypress ceilings give it a unique character. The San Souci use solar energy and recycle all waste. Six rooms share bathroom facilities. Doubles are NZ$110 to NZ$155 and a restaurant is on-site. If you'd like a big, self-contained holiday home, **Villa on the Bay ★**, Beachfront, Pohara Beach (www.villaonthebay.co.nz; ✆ **03/525-8465**), will be hard to beat. It has five lovely rooms, modern facilities throughout, and it comes with a car—all for NZ$790 to NZ$850 per night (minimum 2-night stay).

Farther north, **Collingwood Homestead ★★**, 15 Elizabeth St., Collingwood (www.collingwoodhomestead.co.nz; ✆ **03/524-8079**), is one of the best homestays in the region. It's hard to find fault with the personalized hospitality and two large bedrooms with modern bathrooms. The rate is NZ$265, which includes a wonderful breakfast. If you'd like to rent a holiday home in this region, contact **Golden Bay i-SITE,** Willow Street, Takaka (www.nelsonnz.com; ✆ **03/525-9136;** fax 03/525-9288). They manage over 60 holiday homes and can point you in the direction of a unique stay. But get in early, as New Zealand holidaymakers love this area too.

WHERE TO EAT

It's easy to recommend the **Wholemeal Café ★★**, 60 Commercial St., Takaka (✆ **03/525-9426**). It has the best food in the area, and you can't help feeling it's horrendously healthy as well as delicious. It's also a great place to pick up picnic fare. The cafe is open in summer daily from 7:30am to 9:30pm; after Easter, it's open Sunday through Tuesday 8:30am to 5pm, and Thursday through Saturday from 8:30am until late.

Near Collingwood, the **Old School Café & Bar,** 1115 Collingwood Puponga Main Rd., Pakawau (✆ **03/524-8457**), is an excellent pit stop (summer daily 10am–late; winter Wed–Sun 11am–late); and at Pohara, enjoy a wide choice of seafood and gourmet pizzas at **Penguin Café & Bar,** 818 Abel Tasman Dr. (✆ **03/525-6126**). It's open daily in summer from 9am.

CHRISTCHURCH & CANTERBURY

13

New Zealand's place in English history is visibly apparent in Christchurch's architecture and design. Dubbed "The Garden City," one-eighth of its land is dedicated to parks, reserves, and recreation. Life here revolves around enjoying the natural beauty, minimal rain, and plenty of long, sunny days. Although it's often considered the most conservative of New Zealand cities, don't let that fool you. There are world-class wineries nearby and the vast surrounding province of Canterbury, stretching from the Southern Alps to the Pacific Ocean, has legendary physical attractions. And over the next decade, as Christchurch builds a new heart following the earthquakes of 2010 and 2011, you can expect exciting developments.

Things To Do   Go **punting** on the Avon River that winds through the **Botanic Gardens.** For staggering views take a trip on **Christchurch Gondola** before discovering the city's pioneer history at **Ferrymead Heritage Park.** Take a day trip to the French-settled **Akaroa;** watch whales in **Kaikoura;** soak in hot thermal pools at **Hanmer;** or discover ancient Maori rock art in **Timaru**—each area presents its own version of provincial hospitality, rural escapism, and heart-stopping outdoor adventure.

Eating & Drinking   Start the day with a delicious eggs Benedict at **Brigittes Espresso** in Merivale, or a caffeine jolt at local favorite **Addington Coffee Co-Op.** Serious foodies head for **Pescatore** for sublime degustation flavors; and **Rotherhams of Riccarton** takes the best the region has to offer—lamb, beef, fresh fish, and cheeses—and serves them with European flair. Wash it all down with a glass of rich Pinot Noir from the nearby **Waipara Wine Region.**

Active Pursuits   Christchurch and Canterbury are an outdoor lover's paradise. On weekends, locals head to the **Port Hills** for walks, mountain biking, and picnics; or to the beaches for swimming, surfing, and sunbathing. Go trekking, rock climbing, or mountain climbing in the pristine landscapes and mountain air of **Arthur's Pass;** and in winter, choose from a dozen ski fields within an hour's drive of the city. Take a guided walk on a high-country farm, go rafting on a South Canterbury river, or horseback riding in the hills. Anything is possible.

Nightlife & Entertainment   Christchurch is about to enter a new age of development and cultural recovery—one that will build on its vibrant theater and bar scene. Take in a live show at **Court Theatre** in an old grain store in suburban Addington. Join rugby fans in one of the sports bars at **Ferrymead** or **Riccarton.** Relax in style in one of the alfresco bars in the upmarket suburb of **Merivale.** Or take in an evening Maori cultural performance at **Willowbank Wildlife Centre.**

ORIENTATION
Arriving

BY PLANE Christchurch has frequent air service from all major centers via Air New Zealand (© 0800/737-000; www.airnewzealand.co.nz) and Air New Zealand Link. **Christchurch International Airport** is 10km (6 miles) from Cathedral Square and it receives direct flights from several countries. It is currently half-way through a NZ$237-million upgrade. The first stage—a new, joint domestic and international check-in hall and first floor food court and retail space—opened in May 2011. New baggage claim areas and aircraft docking areas will be completed by September 2012. The project is slated for completion by 2013. The terminal features everything travelers will need, including boutique shopping, a large food hall, ATMs, currency exchange, help desks, Internet access (with 30 min. free Wi-Fi), car-rental counters, baggage wrapping and storage facilities, postal services, and a Time-Out Zone in the international terminal. The **Travel and Tourism Centre** (© 03/353-7774; www.christchurchairport.co.nz) can help with accommodation, adventure, and transport bookings at no charge. The **Christchurch i-SITE Visitor Centre** (© 03/353-7774; www.christchurchnz.com) also has an outlet at the airport. For further international airport details, check www.christchurchairport.co.nz.

Several shuttle companies operate between the airport and Central City. **Super Shuttle** (© 0800/748-885 in NZ; www.supershuttle.co.nz) runs daily 24 hours and charges NZ$18 to NZ$25. The **Red Bus Free City Shuttle Service** (© 0800/733-287 in NZ; www.redbus.co.nz) has bright yellow shuttle buses that depart from the airport every 15 minutes between 7am and 10pm. Its current city terminus locations are, at time of writing, at the Hospital (Parkside), on Hagley Avenue between St. Asaph Street and Riccarton Avenue; and at temporary stop locations on the south side of Bealey Avenue between Durham Street North and Montreal Street. Keep an eye on the Red Bus website for transportation updates during the city rebuild. For a 20-minute taxi ride from the airport, call **First Direct** (© 03/377-5555), **Gold Band** (© 0800/379-5795), or **Green Cabs** (© 0508/447-336). The fare to Central City should be NZ$40 to NZ$65.

BY TRAIN & COACH (BUS) Train service to and from Christchurch has been greatly reduced as railway companies consolidate their operations. The TranzAlpine (Greymouth), and the TranzCoastal (Picton) are the only two still running. For information, call **Tranz Scenic** at (© 0800/872-467 in NZ, or 03/341-2588; www.tranzscenic.co.nz). The **Christchurch Railway Station** is on Clarence Street, in Addington. Regular shuttles run from the station to the city.

InterCity (© 0800/468-372 in NZ, or 03/365-1113; www.intercity.co.nz) covers most of the South Island, offering service between Christchurch, Dunedin, Fox and Franz Josef Glaciers, Greymouth and the West Coast, Wanaka, Queenstown and Mount Cook, Invercargill, Timaru, Picton, and Kaikoura. At press time, InterCity buses were departing from 126 Bealey Ave. There is an airport drop-off for those traveling north (from Queenstown, for example) on InterCity's Great Sights and Newmans buses. Great Sights is taking people directly to the airport (approximately a 7:30pm drop off) and Newmans is taking passengers to the International Antarctic Centre, which is a short walk from the airport. If you prefer something cheaper,

Christchurch

CHRISTCHURCH—A shaken CITY

On September 4, 2010, at 4:35am, Christ-church residents were shaken awake by a violent 7.1 earthquake. The quake caused extensive physical damage but no lives were lost. That all changed 5 months later, when the city was struck by an even more devastating 6.3 quake at 12:51pm on February 22, 2011. The central city, the port town of Lyttelton, Sumner village, and several eastern residential suburbs suffered massive destruction, and 182 people died. The city business district was in complete lockdown for many months, but despite ongoing after-shocks, significant progress has been made to get the city back on its feet. Infrastructure, hotels, restaurants, night-life, and shops took a severe hit, but there are still plenty of options for visi-tors on the west side of the city; and many key attractions for the region lie well outside the city in Akaroa, Hanmer, Kaikoura, and South Canterbury, which were unaffected by the earthquakes.

There were over 6,000 businesses and 54,000 employees in the inner city prior to the quakes. Nearly 75% of those have now opened elsewhere. Around 1,000 inner city commercial buildings and 300 more in the suburbs, many of them architectural icons, will have been demolished by the time this book reaches the shelves. The city cordons are reducing all the time, as those demolitions are completed, and while pockets of the business district will remain off-limits, others will be open. Cashel Mall will open first and will act as a gateway to the rest of the city center. Re-locatable, expo-style structures will be placed in the mall for retailers and hospitality businesses, which are not able to open in their former premises. This will be in the area bounded by Oxford Terrace and Hereford, Colombo, and Lichfield streets. But Christchurch is constantly changing since the quakes and by the time you read this, more of

consider joining the younger, backpacking crowd and go with **Kiwi Experience** (© **09/369-9410;** www.kiwiexperience.com). Their service to Kaikoura is currently picking up from two Christchurch locations: the International Antarctic Centre, 38 Orchard Rd., near the airport (4pm); and the corner of Bealey Avenue and Papanui Road (2pm). Queenstown travelers will be dropped at the Antarctic Centre at approximately 4pm before the service continues to Kaikoura. Note these arrange-ments are likely to change, so check the website for updates.

BY CAR   If you're coming from the north, you'll drive in on State Highway 1 and enter the city through the northwest suburbs of Papanui and Merivale. It's 4 to 5 hours from Picton and 2½ hours from Kaikoura. From Dunedin, via Timaru and Ashburton, you'll also be on State Highway 1. It takes 5 hours from Dunedin, 2 from Timaru. From the southwest, via Lake Tekapo and Geraldine, travel on Highway 79 to Highway 77 and then Highway 73; this takes you to Mount Hutt and over the Rakaia River. If you're coming from the West Coast, you'll go over Arthur's Pass and enter Christchurch at Upper Riccarton. This trip takes 4 hours. Christchurch is 366km (227 miles) north of Dunedin, 350km (217 miles) south of Picton, and 254km (157 miles) southeast of Greymouth.

Visitor Information

The **Christchurch & Canterbury i-SITE Visitor Centre** is temporarily located in the foyer of the Chateau on the Park Hotel on the corner of Deans Avenue and the city will probably be open. If you are planning a visit here, it is vitally important that you check on the current status of the city and its infrastructure. A good source of information is **Christchurch i-SITE Visitor Centre,** at Christchurch Airport Domestic Terminal (✆ **03/353-7744;** www.christchurchnz.com). Their central city premises temporarily relocated to the foyer of **Chateau of the Park Hotel,** at the corner of Deans Avenue and Kilmarnock Street, Riccarton (✆ **03/379-9629** for the visitor center), but this may also change. Their website is the best first stop.

The shopping centers of Lyttelton over the Port Hills and the city commercial suburb of Sydenham will be the first to be rebuilt. About 60 of the city's 150 suburban centers, which range from large malls to small shopping blocks, were damaged in the February quake. In the meantime, much of the social and commercial business of the city is now conducted in the largely unaffected suburbs of Riccarton (west of Hagley Park), Merivale, Papanui (north of central city), and Ferrymead in the east, near Sumner. At time of writing, there were still 26 major city attractions and activities operating, plus 8 hotels, 10 lodges and apartment blocks, 105 motels, 17 holiday parks, 15 backpacker lodges, and 70 B&Bs in full operation, providing a total of 7,100 guest beds. There are another 11,500 guest beds available in the greater Canterbury region, so you don't need to worry about not having a place to stay. Earthquake damage is very localized and most of the region is unaffected, so there is no need to cancel your holiday. Just keep checking **www.christchurchnz. com** for constant updates. This particularly applies to public transport systems. Limited bus services resumed within weeks of the quakes and these will be extended by 2012.

Kilmarnock Street, Riccarton—a 15- to 20-minute walk through Hagley Park from the inner city (✆ **03/379-9629;** fax 03/377-2424; www.christchurchnz.com). It's open daily from 8:30am to 5pm (closed Dec 25). Keep an eye on their website for possible location changes. Useful websites are www.bethere.org.nz or www.whatson christchurch.co.nz.

Special Events

Christchurch is the festival capital of New Zealand—no matter when you visit, it's bound to coincide with a festival of some sort. The **World Buskers Festival ★★★** (✆ **03/377-2365;** www.worldbuskersfestival.com), from mid- to late January, is the largest street performance festival in the Southern Hemisphere. You'll be treated to jazz and comedy shows, as well as acts of juggling, contortionism, and more. In February, the city bursts into bloom with the **Festival of Flowers** (✆ **03/365-5403;** www.festivalofflowers.co.nz) and the **Ellerslie International Flower Show** (✆ **03/379-4561;** www.ellerslieflowershow.co.nz). The **Christchurch Arts Festival ★★★** (✆ **03/365-2223;** www.artsfestival.co.nz) is staged every 2 years in July and showcases international talent. The next one will be held in 2013. **Showtime Canterbury ★★,** featuring the **Canterbury A & P Show** (✆ **03/343-3033;** www.theshow.co.nz), is an absolute tradition in this part of the world. Staged the second week of November, it features thoroughbred and standard-bred racing.

City Layout

Cathedral Square (also known as the Square) is the center point around which the main roads are laid out in a grid system, surrounded by four main avenues—**Bealey, Moorhouse, Deans,** and **Fitzgerald.** The winding **Avon River** meanders 24km (15 miles) from the west of Christchurch, through the city and out to sea. The **Port Hills,** south of the city, are an ever-present landmark from which you can always get your bearings. Colombo Street is the main street running north–south to the Port Hills. Note, however, that since the earthquakes some central city roads will remain closed during repairs. Cordons are changing all the time, so be prepared for some re-routing.

Neighborhoods in Brief

Fendalton This is the heart of Christchurch conservatism and money—the southern equivalent of Auckland's Remuera. You'll find wonderful old homes and beautiful tree-lined streets, but its retail center is small, unimaginative, and easily bypassed altogether in favor of Merivale shopping. You'll find few accommodations in this area.

Merivale/Papanui Those among the moneyed set who consider themselves a little more contemporary throng to Merivale to shop and eat. Located between Papanui and the inner city, Merivale is an attractive suburb, close to the heart of things; it offers a good number of B&Bs along with "Motel Mile," which stretches south along Papanui Road from Merivale Mall to Bealey Avenue. Always safe, in all senses of the word, it is a pleasant place to be, and you can walk here from the heart of the city in about 30 minutes. Papanui is a little further north on Papanui Road. This is where you'll find the large shopping mall of Northlands and a few cafes and bars.

St. Albans This older suburb lies adjacent to Merivale to the east—some would call it the poor man's Merivale, but now that most of the old villas have been significantly renovated, real-estate prices are a little out of the "poor" league. There is no real retail heart here and just a few lodgings—predominantly at the Bealey Avenue end of the suburb, where there is another good selection of motels.

Inner City While the core of the central city was badly damaged in the 2010 and 2011 earthquakes, some businesses, attractions, cafes, and accommodations are operating in un-cordoned areas. More will come on stream as the city rebuild gets underway. If you can, stay in the area bounded by the four main avenues: Deans, Bealey, Moorhouse, and Fitzgerald, as it will put you in a good position to walk to most places.

Hagley Park/Botanic Gardens Theoretically still the inner city, this compact area just west of the central business district is easily defined by its proximity to Hagley Park and the Botanic Gardens. It is generally the area west of Montreal Street, along Park Avenue, and through to Deans Avenue on the west side of the park. You'll find excellent accommodations and some of the major attractions, such as the Canterbury Museum and the new Art Gallery. It's a 5- to 10-minute walk along Worcester Boulevard to the Square.

Riccarton/Ilam Riccarton is on the western side of Hagley Park, and since the earthquakes, it has become an important retail and entertainment center. It has a huge shopping mall, a proliferation of cheap Asian restaurants, plus general shopping, and lots of motels and cafes. The area between Riccarton and Fendalton is known as Ilam, and this is where you'll find Canterbury University tucked into a beautiful leafy enclave.

Sumner/Ferrymead Once a holiday spot for Christchurch residents, Sumner has long since become a suburb of the city itself. It's a delightful place about 15 to 30 minutes from the city depending on traffic. The neighborhood is characterized by steep hillsides dotted with prime real estate with stunning views of the city and coast, as well as by quaint holiday homes that still sit near the beach. It's easily accessed by bus. Unfortunately, the village was badly battered in the earthquakes and many of its shops, cafes, and restaurants have been seriously damaged or demolished. But it's still a great place to visit in summer, when young surfers gather on The Esplanade, and there's volleyball and beach fun aplenty.

On the way to Sumner, you pass the shopping area of Ferrymead, which, as a result of the quakes, has become the primary restaurant, bar, cafe, and shopping area for this part of the city.

Lyttelton This is a quaint port village over the Port Hills from Christchurch, a 20- to 30-minute drive away. Sadly, it too was severely damaged in the earthquakes and much of its main street has been demolished. The good news is that it is also one of the first suburban areas scheduled for rebuilding, so by the time this book reaches the shelves, it may well be up and running again. Regardless, it's still an interesting half-day trip to drive through the tunnel to see the South Island's largest port. The port was extensively damaged during the earthquakes and to keep it running, it is now being extended, using millions of tons of city earthquake rubble to reclaim land at the north end of port.

GETTING AROUND

BY PUBLIC BUS   Red Bus Limited (℃ 0800/733-287 in NZ, or 03/379-4260; www.redbus.co.nz) operates the majority of urban bus services, with others provided by **Leopard Coachlines** (℃ 03/373-8100; www.leopard.co.nz). Zoned fares range from NZ$3 to NZ$10. For information and details on all-day passes, contact **Bus Info** (℃ 03/366-8855; www.metroinfo.org.nz). Because of the earthquakes, the Bus Exchange on Lichfield Street is currently closed and many Metro services are not running along their normal schedules or routes. City roads continue to be reviewed and as the city enters the rebuild phase, more services will resume. For the latest updates on public transportation, visit www.metroinfo.org.nz.

Check out the advantages of a **Metrocard All Day Pass,** which costs NZ$10 for unlimited travel. Purchase it from your bus driver or from temporary city bus terminus locations on Hagley Avenue, near Christchurch Hospital and Bealey Avenue (btw. Montreal and Durham sts.), between 7:30am and 6pm daily. You can view the latest Metro routes on your smart phone anytime at www.metroinfo.co.nz/m. use the "i" button to select your route and the compass button to show your current location. At time of writing, phones supported are iOS on the iPhone, Android 2.2 native browser, and Blackberry Torch (6.0) native browser.

BY PRIVATE BUS   The **Best Attractions Bus** (℃ 0800/484-485; www.leisuretours.co.nz) offers transportation to the area's most popular attractions: The **Must See Four** goes to Willowbank Wildlife Reserve, the International Antarctic Centre, Air Force Museum, and Christchurch Tram. The tour takes 6 hours and costs NZ$150 per person, which includes all transportation and admission prices. The **Big Five** includes Willowbank, the Antarctic Centre, Christchurch Tram, a Lyttelton Harbour excursion with Christchurch Wildlife Cruises, and a ride on the Christchurch Gondola. It takes 8 hours and costs NZ$210 per person.

BY TRAMWAY   Christchurch's short but pleasant tramway (℃ 03/366-7830; www.welcomeaboard.co.nz) was in the process of being greatly extended when the February earthquake struck. Many lines were damaged and it may be some time before the full service resumes. The route may also change, depending on plans for the city rebuild. The core part of the route currently runs from Cathedral Square down Worcester Boulevard, crossing the Avon River to the Arts Centre. From here, it turns right to Rolleston Avenue and travels on to Armagh and New Regent streets and back to the Square. It operates from 9am to 9pm in summer and until 6pm in winter; one circuit takes 25 minutes and there are 11 stops along the route. Tickets, which can be purchased on the tram, are NZ$25 for adults, NZ$12 children ages 5 to 15, NZ$65 for a family, and you can hop on and off the tram as often as you like for 2 days. These prices are based on the extended service, so may vary in coming months.

BY TAXI   Taxi stands are scattered around the inner city and at all transport terminals. **First Direct** (☎ **03/377-5555**) has a reputation for the best prices. For taxis that can accommodate wheelchairs, call ☎ **03/379-9788. Blue Star Taxis** (☎ **03/379-9799;** www.bluestartaxis.org.nz) offer women traveling alone a reassuring door-to-door service. Just request the Woman Alone service when you ring and the driver will escort you, from pick-up to destination, and wait until you are safely inside.

BY CAR   If you want to see only the main central-city sights, you probably won't need a car; you can make the most of free shuttles and cheap tour buses for those farther-afield destinations. If you do have a car, driving in Christchurch is slightly trickier since the earthquakes, especially in the eastern suburbs, where there has been extensive damage. Full road repairs are expected to take 2 years, so be wary of signs, potholes, protrusions, and closures. Parking buildings are currently closed, except for the one under Christchurch Art Gallery on Gloucester Street. This will obviously change as the city rebuilds. You'll find free car parking in Hagley Park during the day; enter at the end of Armagh Street. If you're visiting the suburban shopping areas of Sydenham, Riccarton, Merivale, Northlands (Papanui), Ferrymead, or The Palms (Shirley), you'll find plenty of free parking.

BY BICYCLE   Christchurch is a biker's heaven—it's flat (except for the Port Hills), and motorists are used to a high volume of bicycle traffic. Cycle lanes are set aside in many areas, especially in the northwest suburbs, where there's quite a bit of university bike traffic. Note that the condition of roads after the earthquakes is greatly impaired in places, so keep your eyes open for unexpected potholes and rises in the road surface. For information on rentals, see "Outdoor Pursuits," later in this chapter.

ON FOOT   Most of the main central-city attractions are well placed for easy walking—especially in the Art Gallery/Museum/Botanic Gardens area.

[Fast FACTS] CHRISTCHURCH

Area Code   The telephone area code (STD) is **03.**

Currency Exchange   The best place for currency exchange currently is at Christchurch Airport, where Travelex has six stores providing service. Banks are open Monday through Friday from 9am to 4:30pm, and ATMs are located in all major suburban shopping malls.

Dentist   For urgent dental care call the **NZ Dental Association** (☎ **03/366-6644,** ext. 3002) to find an available after-hours dentist.

Doctors   For referrals, emergencies, or medical care, contact **After Hours Surgery,** Colombo Street and Bealey Avenue (☎ **03/365-7777**).

Emergencies   Dial ☎ **111** to call the police, report a fire, or request an ambulance.

Hospitals **Christchurch Hospital,** Oxford Terrace and Riccarton Avenue ((C) **03/364-0640**), has an Accident and Emergency Department.

Internet There are Internet services at Christchurch Airport, at city and suburban libraries, and many cafes.

Pharmacy **Urgent Pharmacy,** 931 Colombo St., at the corner of Bealey Avenue ((C) **03/366-4439**), should cover all your needs.

Post Office There is a **Post Shop** at The Palms Mall in Shirley and another at Merivale Mall on Papanui Rd.

Services for Travelers with Disabilities Contact **Disability Information Service,** 314 Worcester St. ((C) **03/366-6189;** fax 03/379-5939; dis@disinfo.co.nz), open Monday through Friday from 9am to 4:30pm.

WHERE TO STAY

Although a number of central city hotels are no longer operational, or their re-opening may be delayed because they're in a cordoned area, there are still over 7,000 beds available within greater Christchurch, may of them in the central suburbs of Riccarton, Merivale, and Papanui (see "City Layout," above). You're still within walking distance of the main attractions if you stay here. All rates quoted include the 15% GST and free off-street parking unless otherwise stated.

In the Inner City

MODERATE

The Heritage Christchurch ★★ At the Heritage you have the choice of charm and character from the colonial past in the Old Government Building (OGB), or contemporary indulgence in the large rooms of the adjacent Heritage Tower. In the tower, the split-level one-bedroom suites have a separate lounge, walk-in wardrobe, and mezzanine bedroom. The sought-after heritage suites in the OGB also feature mezzanine bedrooms, along with open dining areas, kitchens, and laundry facilities, making them ideal for long stays. The marvelous location puts you close to everything.

28–30 Cathedral Sq., Christchurch. www.heritagehotels.co.nz. (C) **0800/936-936** in NZ, or 03/377-9722. Fax 03/377-9881. 177 units. NZ$240 deluxe; NZ$270 executive; NZ$340–NZ$480 penthouse studio; NZ$295–NZ$490 suite. Long-stay and off-peak rates, and special deals. AE, DC, MC, V. Valet parking NZ$25. **Amenities:** Restaurant; bar; babysitting; concierge; nearby golf course; well-equipped gym and day spa; Jacuzzi; heated indoor lap pool; room service; sauna; Wi-Fi in lobby and 1st floor of Tower Building. *In room:* A/C (in some), TV w/pay movies, fridge, hair dryer, Internet, minibar.

The Marque Christchurch ★ 🍴 Located in Christchurch's tallest building, this apartment-style hotel in the heart of the city opened in 2010. Its rooms are fresh and modern, its beds are big, and there are wonderful views over the city. It's popular with business and leisure travelers alike and is well equipped with all the mod-cons to make your stay as comfortable and efficient as possible. It sits near historic New Regent Street and is just a block from Cathedral Square.

166 Gloucester St., Christchurch. www.marquehotels.com.au. (C) **0800/666-777** in NZ, or 03/943-3888. Fax 03/943-3880. 171 units. NZ$220 standard; NZ$240 deluxe; NZ$340 junior suite; NZ$440 1-bedroom suite; NZ$540 2-bedroom suite. Long-stay and off-peak rates and special deals. AE, MC, V. Valet parking NZ$15. **Amenities:** Restaurant; bar, nearby golf course; gym; free Wi-Fi in lobby; limited room service; sauna. *In room:* A/C, TV, high-speed Internet; fridge, hair dryer, minibar.

INNER CITY backpackers

Many of the inner city backpacker hotels are no longer operating, but there are still some properties worth checking out. Here are my picks for the best within walking distance of the inner city. **Chester Street Backpackers,** 148 Chester St. East (www.chesterst.co.nz; ☎ **03/377-1897**), has dorms from NZ$24 to NZ$28, twin rooms from NZ$26 to NZ$30, and double rooms from NZ$28 to NZ$32. The property also owns the delightful 1870s Entwhistle Cottage, which is ideal for families, or for those after a peaceful stay. It costs NZ$130 (NZ$25 each extra person) and requires a 2-night minimum stay. **Kiwi Basecamp** ★★★, 69 Bealey Ave. (www.kiwibasecamp.co.nz; ☎ **03/366-6770**), is a good spot close to temporary bus stops. Rates include breakfast and it has free airport transfers and free use of hotel bikes. Dorm rooms run NZ$22 to NZ$30 and double rooms are NZ$32 to NZ$36. **Jailhouse Accommodation** ★★★, 338 Lincoln Rd., Addington (www.jail.co.nz; ☎ **0800/524-546** in NZ, or 03/982-7777), is a unique stay in the old Addington prison, designed by one of Christchurch's foremost early architects, Benjamin Mountfort, and built in 1874. It's been fully refurbished, of course, and is highly rated by those who stay. Dorms here are priced from NZ$30, single rooms from NZ$75, doubles from NZ$80, and family rooms from NZ$160. All have shared facilities.

Near Hagley Park

EXPENSIVE

The George Christchurch ★★★ 🗡 The George is a member of the Small Luxury Hotels of the World group, and its attention to detail is hard to fault. Sleek, cool, and modern, it typifies the new breed of boutique hotels that focus energy on individual guest needs. The George has also annexed an old adjacent homestead, which is now the Residence; it has two luxury suites and one studio apartment, plus a formal dining room, lounge, and kitchen for those booking the whole property. Plus, the George is home to the wondrous **Pescatore** (p. 343). I can think of no better place in town to indulge yourself—you get everything you pay for. The hotel is active in recycling, reducing its carbon footprint, and conserving water and energy. It also supports numerous local, national, and international charities.

50 Park Terrace, Christchurch. www.thegeorge.com. ☎ **0800/100-220** in NZ, or 03/379-4560. Fax 03/666-747. 53 units in hotel; 3 units in the Residence. NZ$506 executive; NZ$552 premium executive; NZ$799 junior suite; NZ$799 Residence suite; NZ$1,093 Park suite. Residence rooms can be booked individually, or the entire property can be booked for exclusive use. Long-stay rates and special deals. AE, DC, MC, V. **Amenities:** 2 restaurants; bar; babysitting; free use of bikes; concierge; concierge-level rooms; nearby 9-hole golf course; 24-hr room service; Wi-Fi in lobby. *In room:* A/C, TV w/pay movies, fridge, hair dryer, minibar, Wi-Fi.

The Worcester of Christchurch ★★ 🗡 This superb B&B is the only one in Christchurch with its own gallery. Host Maree Ritchie has been an art dealer for more than 20 years and the home she shares with her husband, Tony Taylor, is filled with paintings, sculpture, and antiques. Rooms in the 115-year-old home are well appointed with fine furnishings, fresh flowers, and chocolates. The Worcester suite overlooks Worcester Boulevard and has its own dressing room, while the Godley suite has its own lounge. This gem of a Victorian house is directly across from the Arts

Centre; you couldn't wish for a better location—*and* it's earned a Qualmark Enviro-Gold environmental rating.

15 Worcester Blvd., Christchurch. www.worcester.co.nz. ✆ **0800/365-015** in NZ, or 03/365-0936. Fax 03/364-6299. 2 units. NZ$580; extra person NZ$185. Rates include breakfast and pre-dinner drinks. MC, V. No children 11 and under. Closed May–Oct. **Amenities:** Nearby golf course and tennis courts. *In room:* TV, fridge, hair dryer, Wi-Fi.

MODERATE

Chateau on the Park ★★   Set amid 2 hectares (5 acres) of pretty gardens on the Riccarton side of Hagley Park, this comfortable, mid-range property has been pleasing guests for over 35 years. Its ponds and lush greenery (they even have their own minivineyard) create a calm atmosphere. Rooms in the Hagley wing have the best pool and rose garden views; and suites have desks, sitting areas, and large bathrooms with separate showers and spa baths. It's a short walk to Riccarton shops and to the Botanic Gardens and museum.

Intersection of Deans Ave. and Kilmarnock St. www.chateau-park.co.nz. ✆ **0800/808-999** in NZ, or 03/348-8999. 193 units. NZ$185–NZ$575. Long-stay and special deals. AE, DC, MC, V. **Amenities:** 2 restaurants; bar, babysitting; concierge; nearby golf course; heated outdoor pool; putting green; 24-hr room service; nearby tennis courts. *In room:* A/C, TV, fridge, hair dryer, Internet, minibar.

**The Classic Villa ★★ **   This 1897 central city home is riddled with history. It's been a chaplain's house, student flats, and an old folk's home; now it's a stylish, boutique hotel right in the heart of the action, opposite the Arts Centre. Upstairs accommodations were added in 2004. These rooms are modern, lighter, and sunnier than the original downstairs rooms, but the downstairs rooms have much more architectural character. The large, shared downstairs dining and sitting rooms open onto a small private garden where you can enjoy a quiet drink after a day sightseeing. Despite its size, it has a strong feeling of home and is a little more personable than nearby Orari. They also have a Qualmark Enviro-Silver rating.

17 Worcester Blvd. www.theclassicvilla.co.nz. ✆ **03/377-7905.** Fax 03/377-0210. 12 units. NZ$289 Corporate; NZ$339 deluxe; NZ$389 super deluxe; NZ$489 2-room suite. Rates include breakfast. Long-stay, off-peak, and special deals. AE, DC, MC, V. No children under 12. **Amenities:** Bar; bike rentals; concierge; nearby golf course; nearby gym. *In room:* TV, hair dryer, Wi-Fi.

◉ A Rare Privilege

Otahuna Lodge ★★★, Rhodes Road, Tai Tapu, Christchurch (www.otahuna.co.nz; ✆ 03/329-6333), is my favorite place on earth! This magnificent 1895 mansion, 20 minutes out of the city, gives you an insight into the life of the Victorian landed gentry—a life of privilege and luxury that has been accentuated by the clever hands and good taste of its owners, Hall Cannon and Miles Refo. The seven magnificent suites are gigantic and get my pick for the best accommodations in Canterbury. It is one of the grandest homes in the region and the level of craftsmanship and architectural detail is awe inspiring. The meals are divine, and the rural setting and 12 hectares (30 acres) of gardens have much to offer. Stay at least 2 nights to make the most of it. The wholly inclusive rate for suites is NZ$1,265 to NZ$1,695, and for master suites NZ$1,850 to NZ$2,275. Every comfort is assured.

Orari Bed & Breakfast ★ ⬧   Directly across Montreal Street from the Christchurch Art Gallery and right in the heart of the cultural precinct, Orari gets top marks for perfect positioning. It's a fabulous, big old house built in 1893 and its splendid timbers have been beautifully restored. Rooms are clean-cut, spacious, and comfortable. All but two have en-suite bathrooms. Big, stylish living rooms and a yummy breakfast add to its charms. The addition of five modern, three-level apartments next door—perfect for two to three couples and long stays—makes this one of the best value options in this area.

Gloucester and Montreal sts. www.orari.co.nz. ⓒ **0800/267-274** in NZ, or 03/365-6569. Fax 03/365-2525. 15 units. NZ$160–NZ$245 B&B (includes breakfast); NZ$350–NZ$395 apt. Minimum 3-night stay in apts. Off-peak and long-stay rates. MC, V. **Amenities:** Nearby golf course and tennis courts; Wi-Fi. *In room:* TV, hair dryer, full kitchen (in apts.).

INEXPENSIVE

There are numerous reasonably priced and very good motels along Riccarton Road, Bealey Avenue, and Papanui Road. It's a competitive market so don't forget to ask about special deals. **Annabelle Court Motel,** 42 Riccarton Rd., Riccarton (www.annabellecourtmotel.co.nz; ⓒ **0800/775-577** in NZ, or 03/341-1189), has 18 quality studios and one- and two-bedroom apartments priced from NZ$115 to NZ$150. It's close to Riccarton shopping and restaurants and is just a 15-minute walk through Hagley Park to city attractions.

YMCA ★★ ⬧   Three words spring instantly to mind—value, location, and liveliness. There's a constant flow of traffic of all ages here, and the modern six-story building is perfectly situated just across from the Arts Centre and Botanic Gardens. The apartments have kitchenettes, while the deluxe units have bathrooms and TVs. Each person in a 5-, 6-, or 10-bunk room gets a locker with a key. Overall, this is probably the most upmarket of Christchurch's hostels.

12 Hereford St., Christchurch. www.ymcachch.org.nz. ⓒ **0508/962-224** in NZ, or 03/366-0689. Fax 03/365-1386. 42 dorm beds, 34 units with shared bathrooms, 25 units with private bathrooms. From NZ$28 dorm bed; NZ$65 standard room; NZ$95 deluxe room; NZ$160–NZ$180 apt. Long-stay and off-peak rates and special deals. AE, MC, V. **Amenities:** Cafe; dining room; babysitting; children's school holiday programs; nearby golf course; full-scale gym; discount on fitness classes and climbing wall; Internet; sauna; nearby tennis courts. *In room:* Fridge (in deluxe and apts.), hair dryer (in deluxe rooms), kitchen (in 2 apts.), no phone, Wi-Fi.

In Fendalton/Merivale/St. Albans

EXPENSIVE

The Charlotte Jane ★★   No stone is left unturned at this smart boutique hotel. Formerly a Victorian school for young ladies, the old mansion has been converted into a haven of period luxury, and if you like big rooms, you'll be in your element here. Bathrooms are equally huge, some with monster Jacuzzis. They have a sustainability program in place and as part of that, they source local wine and produce for their restaurant, which sits between the main homestead and Henderson House, which was added to the property to provide extra guest accommodations. It's just a 5-minute walk to Merivale and approximately 15 minutes to the city.

110 Papanui Rd., Merivale. www.charlotte-jane.co.nz. ⓒ **03/355-1028.** Fax 03/355-8222. 12 units in the Charlotte Jane; 2 units in Henderson House. NZ$515 deluxe; NZ$555 luxury room; NZ$660 luxury and honeymoon suite; NZ$815 2-bedroom suite. Off-peak rates available. Rates include gourmet breakfast. MC, V. **Amenities:** Restaurant; bar; bike rentals; concierge; nearby golf course. *In room:* TV/DVD, hair dryer, kitchen (in 2-bedroom town-house suite), minibar (in suites), Wi-Fi.

MODERATE

Motels abound in this area and most offer good deals. Two I'd recommend are **Randolph Motel & Apartments** ★, 79 Papanui Rd. (www.randolphmotel.co.nz; ✆ **0800/537-366**), which has spacious, well-appointed apartments just a 5-minute walk from Merivale Mall and about 15 minutes into the city center. Rooms are priced from NZ$150 to NZ$275. **Salerno Motel Apartments,** 148 Bealey Ave. (www.salernomotel.co.nz; ✆ **0800/287-253**), offers 17 modern suites and apartments priced from NZ$125 to NZ$285. It's about a 10-minute walk to the inner city from here.

Elm Tree House ★   Built in 1920, this lovely two-story home is just a few steps from Merivale Mall and numerous cafes and restaurants. Rooms are big—all with en-suite bathrooms, one with a bathtub—and the original wood paneling throughout gives it a warm, intimate old-world feeling. The Honeymoon and Franz Josef suites are the sunniest and nicest (upstairs), but I can't imagine anyone complaining about any of the accommodations here.

236 Papanui Rd., Merivale. www.elmtreehouse.co.nz. ✆ **03/355-9731.** Fax 03/355-9753. 5 units. NZ$395; NZ$80 each extra person. Long-stay and off-peak rates. Rates include breakfast and pre-dinner drinks. AE, MC, V. Children 11 and under by arrangement only. **Amenities:** Babysitting; nearby golf courses; nearby gym; Internet; nearby tennis courts. *In room:* TV, hair dryer, Wi-Fi.

INEXPENSIVE

Campers will find very nice, reasonably priced digs at **Christchurch Top 10 Holiday Park** ★, 39 Meadow St., Papanui (www.christchurchtop10.co.nz; ✆ **0800/396-323** in NZ, or 03352-9176). It's a 5-minute walk to Northlands Mall and a 10-minute drive into the city. Kids will love unwinding in the playground and indoor heated pool area, and there's also a games room and barbecues for guest use. Motel rooms are NZ$97 to NZ$165, self-contained family units are NZ$77 to NZ$135, bunk rooms are NZ$68 to NZ$70, and tent and powered sites are NZ$35 to NZ$50.

In Sumner

Sumner Bay Motel ★★, 26 Marriner St. (www.sumnermotel.co.nz; ✆ **03/326-5969**), has 12 modern apartments and studios right in the main street beside the movie theater and cafes. Prices range from NZ$160 to NZ$215. **Sumner Beach Villa,** 24 Nayland St. (www.sumnerbeachbilla.co.nz; ✆ **027/326-7766**), is a lovely, restored 1920s villa just 500m (150 ft.) from the beach. It has four very pleasant en-suite bedrooms for NZ$350 to NZ$375. **Abbott House B&B,** 104 Nayland St. (www.abbotthouse.co.nz; ✆ **03/326-6111**), is also close to the beach; it offers a studio with a kitchen for NZ$120 to NZ$150, and a suite for NZ$140 to NZ$150.

Near the Airport

If you've just landed in Christchurch and urgently need sleep, try **Copthorne Hotel Commodore** ★, 449 Memorial Ave. (www.commodore.net.nz; ✆ **0508/266-663** in NZ, or 03/358-8129), which has 135 rooms from NZ$250 for a premium room to NZ$315 for very good business rooms. **Clearview Lodge** ★★, 8 Clearwater Ave. (www.clearviewlodge.com; ✆ **03/359-5797**), is a large family home next to the Clearwater Golfing Resort (below). It has three big rooms and the whole place is set on 4 hectares (10 acres) of vineyards, olive groves, and gardens, with its own heated pool and spa. You'll pay NZ$355 to NZ$395 for a stay here, with breakfast included. Just 2 minutes from the airport, **Sudhima Hotel Christchurch,** at the corner of Memorial Avenue and Orchard Road (www.sudhimachristchurch.co.nz;

Imagine total silence, snowcapped mountain peaks, and an endless spread of perfect rolling green. This is what you get when you stay at **Terrace Downs High Country Resort ★★**, Coleridge Road, Rakaia Gorge, Canterbury (www.terracedowns.co.nz; ✆ **0800/465-373** in NZ, or 03/318-6943; fax 03/317-9372), which is located 45 minutes northwest of Christchurch. Complete with a new day spa and one of New Zealand's top 18-hole golf courses, it provides accommodations in stylish villas and chalets, beautifully crafted from local stone and timber. It's close to Mount Hutt ski fields and some of the best fishing

around. Rates range from NZ$395 to NZ$895. I found the terrace villas just perfect.

For something more modest and closer to Christchurch, visit Merrilies Rebbeck, who will welcome you at **Ballymoney Farmstay ★**, Wardstay Road, RD2, Christchurch (www.ballymoney.co.nz; ✆ **03/329-6706**; fax 03/329-6709), located in the very pretty Tai Tapu area, just 15 minutes from central Christchurch. She has two guest suites (NZ$250–NZ$300, breakfast included), a gorgeous garden, and a small farm filled with an amazing array of special animals. Look out for the stunning white peacock.

✆ **03/358-3139**), is a large hotel with a variety of rooms, a pool, barbecue area, and lots of special deals. Rooms average around NZ$145 to NZ$195.

Huntley Lodge ★★★ 🏨 The grand old homestead at the center of this property was built in 1876 and deserves every superlative it gets. It's opulent and elegant, and modern adjacent buildings have been inspired by that same attention to detail. Garden rooms, suites, and two-bedroom apartments all overlook the pool and gardens, and it's all tucked down a long, leafy driveway well away from traffic and crowds. Just the place to spend a few days recovering from the hardships of travel. It's just 5 minutes' drive from Riccarton shopping and about 10 minutes' from the airport.

67 Yaldhurst Rd., Upper Riccarton. www.huntleylodge.co.nz. ✆ **03/348-8435**. 14 units. NZ$684 garden room, NZ$798 garden suite; NZ$1,144 2-bedroom apartment. Rates include breakfast, aperitifs, and canapés. Long-stay, off-peak, and special deals. **Amenities:** Restaurant; bar; free airport/train transfers; babysitting; concierge; nearby golf course; outdoor pool; nearby tennis courts. *In room:* TV/DVD, fridge, hair dryer, minibar, Wi-Fi.

Peppers Clearwater Resort ★★ 🏊 Much nicer than other airport-hotel options, the Clearwater, which opened in 2003, has the advantage of a rural situation, not to mention 18-hole international golfing resort facilities—and all for a very pleasing price. Set amid 186 hectares (465 acres) of greenery, golf courses, and trout-filled lakes, it's a short drive to the airport and rooms are modern, chic, individual, and beautifully cantilevered out over the water. Guest rooms and suites are great value, and the larger terrace apartments are perfect for long stays, sharing with friends, or families.

Clearwater Ave., Harewood, Christchurch. www.peppers.co.nz. ✆ **0800/275-373** in NZ, or 03/360-1000. Fax 03/360-1001. 74 units. NZ$259 lakeside room; NZ$305 lake-view suite; NZ$365 lakefront and quay suite; NZ$500 lakeside villa; NZ$575 apt and terrace villa. Off-peak and special rates. AE, DC, MC, V. **Amenities:** Restaurant; bar and wine cellar; free airport transfers; babysitting; bike rentals; concierge; 18-hole championship golf course (home of Clearwater Classic Australasian PGA tournament); gym; room service; spa; 2 outdoor lit tennis courts; on-site freshwater fishing guide and lessons. *In room:* A/C, TV/VCR/DVD, fridge, hair dryer, minibar, Wi-Fi.

WHERE TO EAT

Don't let the damage to the inner city faze you—you will still eat very well in Christchurch. The region is renowned for its lamb, seafood, produce, and world-class wines, and many excellent restaurants are tucked away in the suburbs. Please note that increasing numbers of cafes and restaurants will resume business within the central business district, as cordons are removed and the city continues to rebuild.

Near Hagley Park

EXPENSIVE

Pescatore ★★★ PACIFIC RIM   Pescatore has an established reputation for innovative cuisine. It even boasts a mention in the *New York Times*. It has an elegant ambience equal to a superb menu offering—the star of which is the 10-course Evolution degustation menu featuring Canterbury lamb, Akaroa salmon, Golden Bay crab, and scallops. Pescatore is a pricey option, but it's popular with local foodies, and the chance to sit back and enjoy a myriad of tastes cleverly matched with award-winning wines is too good to pass up. The service is very attentive.

The George Hotel, Park Terrace. ✆ **03/371-0257.** www.thegeorge.com. Reservations required. Main courses NZ$39–NZ$45; degustation menu from NZ$120, with suggested wines from NZ$195. AE, DC, MC, V. Oct–May daily 6–10pm; June–Sept Wed–Sun 6–10pm.

MODERATE

Chinwag Eathai ★★ MODERN THAI   Expect a creative twist to traditional Thai favorites in this smart but relaxed spot. Food is healthy, beautiful, and packed with aroma and flavor. The menu is large and diverse and includes succulent treats like caramelized pork hock with chili sauce, wok-fried prawns with lemongrass, pork wontons, and red curry with duck and cherry tomatoes. You'll be spoiled for choice.

131 Victoria St. ✆ **03/366-4544.** www.chinwageathai.co.nz. Reservations recommended. Main courses NZ$20–NZ$32. AE, MC, V. Daily 4pm–late.

The Curator's House ★★★ SPANISH/MODERN NEW ZEALAND   Spanish chef Javier Garcia takes fresh, local specialties—lamb, beef, fish, salmon—and serves

---

Cafe Hits

There's a busy, creative vibe at **Black Betty's Café ★★**, 165 Madras St. (✆ **03/365-8522**). Located just across the road from the Christchurch Polytechnic, it attracts a mixed crowd of students, lecturers, artists, and the like. Food and coffee are both worth stopping for, and hearty breakfasts are their specialty. It's open Monday through Friday from 7am to 4:30pm and Saturdays from 8am to 4:30pm. On Victoria Street, make sure you take a side step near the clock tower and veer over to **Blax Espresso Bar ★★**, corner of Montreal and Victoria streets (✆ **03/366-**8982). It's all white and bright, and you need to arrive early to snare one of their delectable *pain au chocolat,* or their fought-over small cakes. Blax is open Monday through Saturday 7:30am to 4pm. **Under the Red Verandah ★★★**, 29 Tancred St., Linwood (✆ **03/381-1109;** www.utrv.co.nz), is a suburban treasure that's worth the hunt as the food here is truly divine. They do terrific weekend brunches and their cakes and savories are outstanding. They're open Monday through Friday from 7:30am to 4pm, weekends from 8:30am to 4pm.

Coriander's Indian Restaurant ★★★, Shop 13, 76 Edgeware Rd., Edgeware (℃ **03/366-7223;** www.corianders.co.nz), is located near St. Albans and Merivale and is a crowd favorite. Starting platters are a terrific introduction to a wide range of flavorsome, aromatic dishes; they include onion *bhaji*, mutton *seekh kebab*, and tandoori chicken. Lamb *kadai* and chicken *do payaza* are popular choices, and their succulent tandoori kebabs are winners. Open daily from 11:30am until late.

them with Spanish flair. He has his own vegetable garden beside the restaurant, and the old-world style of the former Botanic Gardens curator's house makes for an elegant setting. Enjoy his seafood and chicken paella, house-made chorizo, or a roast shoulder of spring Canterbury lamb served with fresh vegetables.

7 Rolleston Ave., Christchurch Botanic Gardens. ℃ **03/379-2252.** www.curatorshouse.co.nz. Reservations recommended. Main courses NZ$26–NZ$37. AE, DC, MC, V. Daily 11am–late. Closed Dec 25-26.

In Fendalton/Merivale

In heartland Merivale, located just behind the mall on Aikmans Road, you'll find a fistful of swanky eateries rubbing shoulders in a sunny, shared courtyard filled with grassy patches, potted trees, and grape vines. It becomes quite a party on a warm summer's day.

Brigittes Espresso Bar ★ ☺ CAFE Half the population of Merivale seems to enjoy weekend brunch at Brigittes, so make sure you book ahead. The homey interior looks out onto the street and opens up to a sheltered courtyard. You'll find all the usual breakfast options, including eggs Benedict and eggs Florentine, plus lunch and dinner choices such as honey-glazed chicken on salad greens served with lime-ginger soy dressing. The service can be half-hearted but the atmosphere is always good.

Aikmans Rd. and Papanui Rd. ℃ **03/355-6150.** www.brigettes.co.nz. Reservations recommended. Main courses NZ$16–NZ$36. AE, DC, MC, V. Mon 8am–5pm; Tues–Sat 8am–late; Sun 9am–5pm; public holidays 10am–late.

JDV ★★ MODERN NEW ZEALAND This is where fashionable black garb and gold jewelry are ranked as highly as the coconut-and-ginger duck curry with sticky rice cake, steamed bok choy, lychees, and charred lime. Beef filet or lamb rump with savoy cabbage and bacon is another tasty choice. Movers and shakers (along with the rich and slothful), gather here to pay homage to the chefs' penchant for unexpected flavor mixes and reliably delicious meals.

The Mall, Aikmans Rd. ℃ **03/964-3860.** www.jdv.co.nz. Reservations recommended. Main courses NZ$35–NZ$38. AE, DC, MC, V. Daily 9:30am–late.

Tutto Benne ★★ 🍴 ITALIAN Felice and Paulette Mannucci have run a succession of excellent eateries in Christchurch for over 3 decades. This latest effort is a little gem—it's one of my favorite Christchurch restaurants. At this pizzeria-meets-small-neighborhood-restaurant, the full menu gallops across 15 pizza types, pastas, risottos, and traditional dishes like veal saltimbocca with prosciutto, sage, and Marsala. And while you shouldn't overlook the Italian *cassata*, the tiramisu is to die for!

192 Papanui Rd. ℃ **03/355-4744.** www.tuttobene.co.nz. Reservations recommended. Main courses NZ$20–NZ$35. AE, DC, MC, V. Daily 5pm–late.

In Riccarton

EXPENSIVE

Rotherhams ★★★ INTERNATIONAL   This is a tucked-away culinary jewel in the midst of Riccarton retail heartland. It's most definitely worth searching out and savoring. You'll get some of the best meals in the most romantic ambience of almost any restaurant in the city. Service is attentive, presentation first class, flavors divine, and the wine list impressive. If you have something special to celebrate (and who needs a reason?), let Swiss owner/chef Martin Weiss spoil you to bits. Meals can be highly decorative and elaborate, and you get the choice of a 5- or 8-course degustation, a set menu, or a la carte.

42 Rotherham St. Riccarton. *℃* **03/341-5142.** www.rotherhamsofriccarton.co.nz. Reservations required. Main courses NZ$35–NZ$45. AE, DC, MC, V. Tues–Sat 6pm–late.

MODERATE

Drexels ★★ 🍴 BREAKFAST/DINER   This all-day breakfast restaurant is an institution but don't come here if you're not hungry—the meals are huge. You get all the breakfast favorites from omelets and bagels to waffles, Iowa pancakes, hash browns, enchiladas, and burritos. It's a favorite with locals recovering from a big night out and the atmosphere is always friendly and happy. This place is hugely popular so be sure to reserve in advance.

28 Rotherham St., Riccarton. *℃* **03/343-3403.** www.drexels.co.nz. Reservations required. Main courses NZ$10–NZ$20. AE, DC, MC, V. Mon–Fri 6:30am–2pm, Sat–Sun 7am–2pm.

INEXPENSIVE

Fo Guang Shan Teahouse ★★ 🍴 VEGETARIAN/VEGAN   Located in the architecturally designed Buddhist Community Centre, this small, sunny restaurant and cafe has a calm, Zen-like mood and heavenly food that you should definitely make time for. The menu is not exhaustive but they have a very good range of filling noodle and dumpling soups, and their spring rolls and wontons are popular choices. Coriander pancakes with chili sauce are another highlight. They have dairy-free choices but there are also a few meat dishes and plenty of sweet temptations for later.

Buddhist Community Centre, corner Riccarton Rd. & Harakeke St. *℃* **03/341-6276** or 03/341-6297. Main courses NZ$8–NZ$13. MC, V. Tues–Sun 10am–4pm (lunch from 11:30am).

In Addington/Sydenham

MODERATE

Milieu ★★ CAFE   Located in a new industrial business area south of Riccarton, this smart cafe is so popular you sometimes have to fight your way in through the front door. They have a wide range of delicious and inventive salads in their deli cabinets, and you'll also dine very well on hot smoked salmon salad, gourmet chicken

---

📎 **Gourmet Takeaway**

For the best gourmet takeout meals in Christchurch, go to **Traiteur of Merivale,** at the corner of Papanui and Aikmans roads (*℃* **03/355-7750**; www.traiteur. co.nz). Its menu changes weekly with several starters, mains, and desserts, plus pasta and salad options, all well priced.

If you're in the Riccarton area on a Saturday morning, hunt out the **Christchurch Farmers' Market ★★★** (✆ **03/348-6190**; www.christchurch farmersmarket.conz), which is held every Saturday from 9am to noon, at Riccarton House, 16 Kahu Rd. There are edible treats galore here, as local producers gather under the giant oak trees to sell their wares. Look for handmade chocolates, boutique cheeses, handcrafted breads, Dutch pastries, coffee, and a ton of fresh produce you can buy if you're cooking while traveling. Historic Riccarton House (✆ **03/341-1018**; www.riccartonhouse.co.nz) and the surrounding Deans Bush are attractions in their own right. The house and its fine restaurant, **Taste at Riccarton House,** are open to the public. The restaurant is open Wednesday through Sunday for lunch (11am–3pm) and dinner (starting at 6pm). You can also explore walking tracks through Deans Bush, where you can see kahikatea trees up to 600 years old.

burgers, and fettuccine dishes. It's as popular with the weekday business crowd as it is with weekend brunch lovers.

112 Wrights Rd., Addington. ✆ **03/962-9629.** Reservations recommended. Main courses NZ$15–NZ$22. AE, MC, V. Mon-Sat 7am-4pm (until 7:30pm Fri).

INEXPENSIVE

Addington Coffee Co-Op ★★ CAFE Mismatched furniture, bicycles, and Chinese lanterns hanging from exposed timber rafters give this suburban cafe a unique, funky character. Everyone from businessmen to students and housewives make their way here for excellent coffee, or the hearty house breakfast that includes a stack of potato rösti, bacon, tomatoes, poached eggs, and hollandaise sauce. Whether you're working on a computer, chatting with friends, or enjoying a light lunch, it has a busy, friendly vibe that encourages a return visit.

297 Lincoln Rd., Addington. ✆ **03/943-1662.** www.addingtoncoffee.org.nz. Main courses NZ$12–NZ$22. AE, MC, V. Mon-Fri 7:30am-4pm, Sat-Sun 9am-4pm.

Honey Pot Café ★ 🍴 CAFE Come here if you're in the mood for a big, wholesome breakfast. It has a warm, casual atmosphere, and if you can get through its "Full Breakky" of two eggs with house sausages, grilled tomatoes, bacon, fried mushrooms, onions, hash browns, and an espresso, you're doing better than me. The lunch and dinner menus offer pizzas, gourmet sandwiches, and desserts. If you're on a budget it can fill the gaps.

458 Colombo St., Sydenham. ✆ **03/366-5853.** www.honeypotcafe.co.nz. Main courses NZ$15–NZ$22. MC, V. Mon-Fri 7am-late; Sat-Sun 8am-late.

In Sumner/Ferrymead

A trip to Sumner wouldn't be complete without a visit to **Coffee Culture Ltd. ★★**, 28 Marriner St. (✆ **03/326-5900;** www.coffeeculture.co.nz). Desserts and coffee are their specialty. The **Cornershop Bistro ★**, 32 Nayland St. (✆ **03/326-6720;** www.cornershopbistro.co.nz), is an excellent neighborhood restaurant that's casual and competent, presenting everything from racks of lamb to fresh grouper filets.

@Tony's ★★ 🍴 JAPANESE TEPPAN YAKI Chefs here love to show off their slick *teppan yaki* skills, so sit at the food bar if you can find a place and watch them chop your food at the speed of lightning. They offer a wide variety of fresh sushi and sashimi in addition to delicate tempura choices. Prawn tempura melts in the mouth and any one of their *teppan yaki* dishes is also bound to please. Meat lovers will enjoy the *usu-yaki*—julienne vegetables wrapped in thin slices of *teppan* beef. Service is authentically Japanese, with sweet smiles and quiet manners. A second location is at 85 Riccarton Rd.

2 Waterman Place, Ferrymead (main shopping area). ✆ **03/348-5644.** www.teppanyaki.co.nz. Reservations required. Main courses NZ$15–NZ$35. AE, MC, V. Tues–Fri noon–2:30pm and 5:30–10pm, Sat 5:30–10pm, Sun 5:30–9pm.

Winnie Bagoes ★★ ☺ PIZZERIA   Winnie's is a Christchurch icon known for its great-value pizzas, lively atmosphere, and friendly service, and it's invariably packed to overflowing. Try to score a table, inside or out. On weekends there's often live music. They have gluten-free choices and takeaway options.

2 Waterman Place, Ferrymead (main shopping area). ✆ **03/376-4900.** www.winniebagoes.co.nz. Main courses NZ$15–NZ$25. AE, DC, MC, V. Daily 11:30am–11:30pm.

EXPLORING CHRISTCHURCH

Christchurch prides itself almost equally on its arts, sports, history, and gardens. There are a number of theaters and art galleries, along with several excellent museums, parks, and gardens to explore. Attractions and events are listed in the daily newspaper, *The Press,* and in the monthly *Tourist Times,* available free at the visitor center. Keep in mind that some attractions are still closed for repairs but you can view them from the outside. Local news or individual attraction websites will give you an up-to-date appraisal of their status.

The Top Attractions

Arts Centre ★ ☺   You can't go to Christchurch and not check out the Arts Centre. Originally home to Canterbury University College from 1873 to 1975, it has sadly closed to the public for earthquake repairs but you can still admire its beautiful Victorian Gothic architecture from the street. After the February earthquake, all but one of its many buildings were red-stickered and deemed unsafe, and it has been estimated that repairs could take between 10 and 15 years to complete. The famous Arts Centre Market has transferred to Ferrymead Heritage Park (p. 350).

 Berry, Berry Nice

Berry picking can be a fun excursion, especially with children. Here are two chances to pick fresh berries and then sit down in smart little on-farm cafes for a meal or coffee and berry-based treats. Take a drive through the pretty lanes of the Halswell area and find **Otahuna Berries Raspberry Café** ★, Rhodes Road, Tai Tapu (✆ 03/329-6687). It's about a 20-minute drive out of town. Head out toward Tai Tapu on the main highway to Akaroa, and you'll see it signposted down Rhodes Road on your left. Pig out on *the* most divine cakes when you get there. **Berryfields' Sweethearts Restaurant** ★, 161 Gardiners Rd., Harewood (✆ 03/359-5630), is in the opposite direction, near the airport. It's more of a restaurant experience and attracts a more mature crowd. Note that the cafes are open year-round, but the actual picking season is roughly December through March.

Bounded by Worcester Blvd., Rolleston Ave., Hereford St., and Montreal St. ℂ **03/363-2836.** www.artscentre.org.nz.

Canterbury Museum ★★ ☺

Perfectly placed on the edge of the Botanic Gardens within a stone's throw of the Arts Centre, the Canterbury Museum has something for everyone. Check out the excellent Antarctic display, a must-see before going out to the International Antarctic Centre. Also look for the superb Natural History Discovery Centre, where you can happily pull open drawers and inspect the contents of jars and cases. The quaint Victorian Canterbury street is interesting, and there's an excellent Maori section. Allow 2 hours.

Rolleston Ave. ℂ **03/366-5000.** Fax 03/366-5622. www.canterburymuseum.com. Free admission; Discovery Centre NZ$2; fees for special exhibits. Oct–Mar daily 9am–5:30pm; Apr–Sept daily 9am–5pm. Free guided tours Tues–Thurs 3:30–4:30pm (meet in museum foyer). Closed Dec 25.

Christchurch Art Gallery Te Puna o Waiwhetu ★★★

I love the flashiness of this sparkling architectural icon that has rapidly established itself as the place to go since its 2003 opening. Curving glass facades and spectacular outdoor sculpture aside, it has one of the largest permanent collections in New Zealand, and with eight new gallery spaces, there's plenty of room for both contemporary and historic displays. The collection of over 5,500 paintings, sculptures, prints, drawings, and crafts emphasizes work from the Canterbury region, but there are regular touring international and national shows as well. The gallery served as the Civil Defence headquarters for both earthquakes and was closed to the public during that period of national disaster. It has since re-opened to the public in its role as the province's primary art gallery. Don't overlook the book and gift shop. It has some terrific New Zealand–made goods—as does the in-house craft gallery, **Form.** A cafe/restaurant completes the picture, making this a must-visit attraction.

Worcester Blvd. and Montreal St. ℂ **03/941-7300.** Fax 03/941-7301. www.christchurchartgallery.org.nz. Free admission; fees for special exhibits. Daily 9:30am–5pm (Wed till 9pm). Free guided tours daily at 11am and 2pm, Wed at 6:30 and 7:30pm. Closed Dec 25. Underground parking; enter off Gloucester St.

Christchurch Botanic Gardens ★ ☺

The turquoise-and-yellow Peacock Fountain just inside the main gate on Rolleston Avenue is a handy marker that can't be missed. This is the best point of entry to the lush 23 hectares (57 acres) of deservedly world-renowned gardens. Even if you've never considered yourself the slightest bit green-thumbed, there's something magical about this place. Sweeping lawns, fragrant rose gardens, and some of the country's oldest exotic trees provide spectacular displays year-round. The Avon River and its huge duck population add interest. The kids can run loose, feed the ducks, and frolic in the playground. Don't miss the lush tropical greenhouse, or the heavenly scented rose gardens adjacent to it. I also love the little alpine garden area and the two ponds that border the rhododendron and azalea gardens.

Rolleston Ave. ℂ **03/941-8999.** www.ccc.govt.nz/parks. Free admission; Caterpillar garden tours NZ$20 adults, NZ$8 children 5–18. Grounds open daily 7am–1 hr. before sunset; conservatories daily 10:15am–4pm; information center Mon–Fri 9am–4pm, Sat–Sun 10:15am–4pm. Caterpillar garden tours every 30 min., daily from 10am–4pm (departing from both Canterbury Museum entrance and Gardens Kiosk).

Christchurch Cathedral ★

Christchurch's iconic Anglican Cathedral was severely damaged in both earthquakes and while early thought was that it could be restored over many years, engineers discovered it is far more damaged than first thought and a question mark hangs over its future. Construction of the original church was begun in 1864, just 14 years after the first settlers arrived, and was completed in 1904. Today, it's New Zealand's most famous Gothic Revival church and Christchurch's most important landmark. The cathedral is now out of bounds to the public but you can still view its damaged form from beyond the cordons.

Cathedral Sq. ℂ **03/366-0046.** www.christchurchcathedral.co.nz.

International Antarctic Centre ★★★ ☺ If you've always wanted to romp with penguins, stroke a leopard seal, climb aboard a snowmobile, explore a snow cave, and feel the icy wind chills of Antarctica, this is probably as close as you'll ever get. Everything about this attraction is of superb value and you'll get a particular thrill from the live penguin display. It takes more of a geographic/natural history approach than the Canterbury Museum's Antarctic exhibition, and if you see both, you'll have a healthy appreciation for life on the ice. Considered one of New Zealand's leading attractions, it gives you a feel for modern Antarctic life through sophisticated sound-and-light shows, a spine-tingling audiovisual presentation, and interactive exhibits. The center is suitable for visits of 30 minutes or half a day, but spending 1 to 2 hours is ideal. Two wheelchairs are available for use by the public.

The **Antarctic Hagglund Ride ★★** is the only one of its type in the world. Its 15-minute tour gives you a unique insight into the planning of Antarctic journeys. It's a big hit with kids.

38 Orchard Rd., adjacent to the Christchurch International Airport. ℂ **0508/736-4846** in NZ, or 03/353-7798. Fax 03/353-7799. www.iceberg.co.nz. All-day pass with unlimited Hagglund Rides and entry to 4D extreme Theatre NZ$65 adults, NZ$36 children 5–15, NZ$170 families; group rates available. Audio tour available in 6 languages for NZ$10. Oct–Mar daily 9am–7pm; Apr–Sept daily 9am–5:30pm. The center is a 15-min. drive from Central City and an 8-min. walk from the Christchurch Airport Terminal. The city/airport bus runs to the center every half-hour; the complimentary Super Shuttle runs from the airport to the center. Free parking.

Additional Attractions

Animal lovers who are short on time may have to choose between Orana Park and Willowbank Wildlife Reserve. Both are closer to the airport than to Central City, so either could make a good last-minute stop. Personally, I'm a big-cat fan, so I'd opt for Orana, where things African are to the fore. But if you want a guaranteed sighting of a kiwi before you leave New Zealand, go to Willowbank.

Orana Park ★★★ ☺ There's something quite magical about getting up close and personal with Rothschild giraffes. You can feed them and fondle their ears and they won't mind a bit, but don't try that with the park's lions, tigers, and cheetahs. Set in 80 attractively laid-out hectares (198 acres), the park is New Zealand's largest wildlife reserve. You'll see few fences and cages here—the emphasis is on a natural environment, which seems to agree with the cheetahs, the only successfully breeding ones in Australasia (over a dozen new cubs in the past 16 years). At 3:55pm daily, you can see them make a dash for their raw-meat supper, which is attached to a fast-moving lure. The main lion feeding time is 2:30pm daily. This is the only place in Christchurch to see a tuatara, and there's a nocturnal kiwi house as well, but the one at Willowbank is bigger and better. If you're in a hurry, take the park's 40-minute free shuttle circuit.

743 McLeans Island Rd. ℂ **03/359-7109.** Fax 03/359-4330. www.oranawildlifepark.co.nz. Admission NZ$26 adults, NZ$9 children 5–14, NZ$60 families; group rates available. MC, V. Daily 10am–5pm. Closed Dec 25. The park is a 20-min. drive from Central City and is well signposted from the airport. Free parking.

Willowbank Wildlife Reserve ★ ☺ Willowbank is a good place for children to get close to relatively tame animals of all sorts, but it doesn't have the impact of

Take the stunning scenic drive over the Port Hills to Lyttelton, and once you've explored the little village, leap aboard the **Diamond Harbour Ferry** (⒞ **03/366-8855**), located on Lyttelton Wharf. For the small sum of NZ$12 for adults and NZ$6 for children ages 5 to 16, you can travel across to the other side of the harbor and back. You can get off and explore the little village of Diamond Harbour but I think there's better value and more to see at **Quail Island**. A ferry run can drop you off on the island for 2 to 5 hours, depending on which ferry you take. This former quarantine station and leper colony was also used by Scott and Shackleton as home base for their Antarctic expeditions. It abounds with interesting walks and historic points of interest. Get dropped off by **Black Cat Cruises**, B Jetty, Port of Lyttelton (⒞ **0800/436-574; www.blackcat.co.nz**). The trip costs NZ$22 adults and NZ$12 for children 5 to 15.

Orana's exotic animals. It does, however, have the country's largest collection of kiwis, and you won't find any glass between you and the feathers. It takes a few minutes for your eyes to adjust to the dimly lit nocturnal house, but if you're patient and quiet, you will see a kiwi. This is guaranteed if you take a guided tour at 11:30am or 2:30pm. I'd recommend paying the extra for the Kiwi Breeding Tour—it's the best thing about Willowbank in my view. Night tours of the New Zealand Kiwi Experience are at 7:30, 8:30, and 9:30pm. Another very good feature is the Ko Tane Cultural Performance at 5:30 and 6:30pm, which is a fun introduction to things Maori.

60 Hussey Rd. ⒞ **03/359-6226.** Fax 03/359-6212. www.willowbank.co.nz or www.kotane.co.nz. Admission and Kiwi Tour NZ$29 adults, NZ$12 children 5–15, NZ$65 families. Ko Tane performance NZ$59 adults, NZ$30 children 5–15. Group discounts available. AE, DC, MC, V. Daily 9:30am–10pm. Take Harewood Rd. and turn right on Gardiners Rd.; turn right again on Hussey Rd. It's a 15-min. drive from the city.

Air Force Museum of New Zealand ☺   If you've got a hankering to indulge your passion for flight, this past winner of Best New Zealand Attraction is your place. Two hours will give you a good overview of flight simulators, the history hall, and displays of planes—everything from Spitfires and Skyhawks to Tiger Moths. There's an excellent 1-hour Restoration Tour, which takes you inside two hangars not normally open to visitors, where you get to see the restoration of an Airspeed Oxford, a Curtiss P-40 Kittyhawk, a Vickers Vildebeest MK III, and 13 other aircraft. They also have a special kids' tour that runs on weekends and during school holidays at 11:15am.

45 Harvard Ave., Wigram. ⒞ **03/343-9532.** Fax 03/343-9533. www.airforcemuseum.co.nz. Free admission. NZ$10 Restoration Tour, NZ$5 Children's Air Force experience and NZ$3 for accompanying adults, NZ$15 Discover Wigram Historic Walking tour. AE, MC, V. Daily 10am–5pm. Closed Dec 25. Located at Wigram Air Base, a 15-min. drive from the center, via Riccarton Rd. or Blenheim Rd., both of which merge into Main South Rd.

Ferrymead Heritage Park ☺   The 8-hectare (20-acre) historical park offers a look at life in early colonial Christchurch, with buildings, streets, fashions, and other paraphernalia of a bygone era. There's a schoolhouse, jail, houses, printery, church, and operating bakery, along with tram and train links between the two main areas of the park. This could be a stopover to or from the Mount Cavendish Gondola, which is also accessed off Bridle Path Road. Many stallholders from the city's famous weekend Arts Centre Market have shifted here since the earthquakes. Weekend admission to the park is therefore now free.

Ferrymead Park Dr., Ferrymead. (*© **03/384-1970.** Fax 03/384-1725. www.ferrymead.org.nz. Static day (no trains or tram running) admission NZ$12 adults, NZ$6 children 5–15, NZ$ 26 family. Expect to pay more when the trams and trains are operating. Tram runs Sat–Sun in school holidays; the steam train runs the 1st Sun of the month and sometimes more during holidays. Daily 10am–4:30pm. Closed Dec 25. Take Ferry Rd. east and take the 1st right after Heathcote Bridge.

Christchurch Gondola ★ ☺   The Christchurch Gondola may not have quite the same breathtaking impact as the Queenstown equivalent, but for unparalleled views westward over the city and the Canterbury Plains to the Southern Alps, and for the full sweep of Pegasus Bay and the Pacific Ocean all the way up to the Kaikoura Ranges, you can't beat it. Perched on the crater rim of an extinct volcano, 445m (1,460 ft.) above sea level, the gondola complex features the Time Tunnel Heritage Show, with a Canterbury video presentation and a walk-through exhibition.

If you want to take the Freedom Walk in the Port Hills, pay for the gondola ride up and then walk down any of the numerous hill tracks to Sumner Beach (allow 2 hr.), from which you can catch a bus back to the city, or to Lyttelton, also about 2 hours. Wear sturdy walking shoes—the tracks are steep and can be slippery. The **Mountain Bike Adventure Co.** (*© **0800/424-534;** www.cyclehire-tours.co.nz) is another option for your descent. Reservations are essential and can be made at the visitor center (*© **03/379-9629**).

10 Bridle Path Rd. (*© **03/384-0310.** Fax 03/384-0757. www.gondola.co.nz. Admission NZ$26 adults; NZ$12 children 5–15; NZ$60 families. Discounts for seniors and students. Oct–Apr daily 10am–midnight; winter daily noon–10pm. The lower terminal is 15 min. from the city center. Take Ferry Rd. and head east; take the 1st right over the Heathcote Bridge. Free parking.

Yaldhurst Museum ★   Transport and classic car lovers will enjoy this 40-year-old museum with its collection of over 400 vehicles, plus one of the country's largest collections of horse-drawn vehicles and associated memorabilia. From an 1810 American buggy, a unique 1860 Phaeton, an 1866 glass-sided hearse, fire engines, and carriages, there's something for vehicle fans of all sorts. Set in the grounds of an 1876 colonial homestead and run by Grant Cooper, great grandson of the original owner, it's a great value rural outing.

26 School Rd., Yaldhurst. (*© **03/342-7914.** Fax 03/342-7916. www.yaldhurstmuseum.co.nz. Admission NZ$15, NZ$5 children 5–14, NZ$30 families. Daily 10am–5pm. Closed Dec 25 and all of June. Near the airport and 20 min. from city center. Take St. Hwy. 73 and take 1st turn right past Yaldhurst Hotel.

Parks & Gardens

Christchurch isn't called the Garden City for nothing, and taking pride of place among them all are the **Botanic Gardens ★★★**, described under "The Top Attractions," earlier in this chapter.

Mona Vale ★, 63 Fendalton Rd. (*© **03/941-8999;** www.ccc.govt.nz/parks/gardencity), has 5.5 hectares (14 acres) of rolling lawns, rose gardens, and fountains,

---

A "Grand" Deal

Get three rides for the price of one with the **Christchurch Grand Tour** offered by **Christchurch Gondola** (*© **0800/242-486;** www.welcomeaboard.co.nz). This sightseeing tour of Christchurch includes tram tickets (when they resume operation), a gondola visit, and a ride upon a boat, Punting on the Avon (see "Boating," below). Pay NZ$129 for adults, NZ$79 for children ages 4 to 14, NZ$25 for kids under 4.

Exploring Christchurch

open to the public free of charge. Guided garden tours are held daily from November through March. The **Avon River** runs along the border of Mona Vale, and a punting excursion will give you a peek into some of the beautiful private gardens on the river. Unfortunately the beautiful Mona Vale homestead was severely damaged by the earthquakes and has been slated for demolition. The 2½-hour **Garden Drive,** described in the *Christchurch Scenic Drive Guide* brochure at the visitor center, includes both the Botanic Gardens and Mona Vale. Although much of the tour highlights architecture rather than actual gardens, it will give you a good look around the northwest suburbs, where there are many exquisite private home gardens.

Two other self-guided drives in the same brochure cover the **Port Hills Drive ★★★** and the **Avon River Drive,** which are not exactly garden tours, but will give you an excellent overview of the city and its natural landscape. The Port Hills Drive is especially worth doing for its spectacular views from Alps to ocean.

If you take the spectacular drive up Dyer's Pass Road and over the Port Hills to Governor's Bay, you'll find Barry Sligh at **Taunton Gardens ★★** (✆ **03/329-9746**). Barry is an enthusiastic plant breeder whose stunning 2 hectares (5 acres) of woodland gardens are open September to April Tuesday through Sunday for NZ$15.

The Wineries

Home to more than 80 wineries, the Canterbury region is now the fourth-largest winemaking area in the country. The combination of long hours of sunshine; stony, free-draining soils; low rainfall; extended autumns; and cool winters produces grapes with complex and developed flavors. The region is well suited to the production of red wines such as cabernet, merlot, and pinot noir. The main growing areas are Waipara, Christchurch, and Banks Peninsula.

For details on March's **Waipara Wine & Food Festival,** call ✆ **0800-166-071** in New Zealand or visit www.waiparawineandfood.co.nz.

The visitor center's brochure on the *Waipara Valley Wineries Wine Trail* has a map showing the main wineries. Or pick up a copy of the very informative *North Canterbury Food & Wine Trail ★* guide from Kaiapoi Visitor Information Centre ✆ **03/327-3134**; it details wineries, food suppliers, and farmers' markets. Here are a few suggestions to whet your appetite.

The **Mud House Winery & Cafe,** State Highway 1, Waipara (✆ **03/314-6900**; www.mudhousewineryandcafe.co.nz), planted their first vines in 1994 and pinot noir is their flagship. They're open daily from 10am to 5pm for tastings and they also have a large restaurant. **Daniel Schuster Wines ★**, 192 Reeces Rd., Omihi, North Canterbury (✆ **03/314-5901**; www.danielschusterwines.com), is one of my personal favorites. It's a few kilometers north of Waipara Valley in the Omihi area, and international wine consultant and owner Danny Schuster is well worth meeting. You can visit the tasting room and peruse wine for sale, or take a more comprehensive cellar tour and enjoy barrel tastings with the winemaker by prior arrangement. The vineyard produces pinot noir, chardonnay, and Riesling. Open daily 10am to 5pm.

Well Oiled

If you're in the Waipara Valley, make sure you visit **Athena Olive Groves,** 164 Mackenzies Rd. (✆ **03/314-6774**; www. athenaolives.co.nz), and try their fabulous range of extra-virgin and flavored olive oils, plus their pickled olives. Open daily from 10am until 5pm.

wine **TOURS**

Canterbury Wine Tours (✆ **0800/081-155;** www.waiparavalley.co.nz) offers a range of options from half-day Waipara Valley wine tours starting at NZ$65. Tours operate year-round and include tastings at three award-winning wineries. **Canterbury Leisure Tours** (✆ **0800/484-485** in NZ; www.leisuretours.co.nz) has a half-day tour of the Waipara region that explores four leading wineries and costs NZ$80 per person.

If you need transport from Christchurch to Waipara, take the **Hanmer Connection** shuttle (✆ **0800/377-378** in NZ) for NZ$25 one way. It leaves from the Christchurch visitor center, with hotel pickups by arrangement.

Rossendale Wines, 168 Old Tai Tapu Rd., Halswell (✆ **03/322-9684;** www.rossendale.co.nz), is located in the charming Tai Tapu Valley area, on the perimeter of Christchurch. It has an established tradition of good wine and good food. Wines available here including Riesling, Gewürztraminer, sauvignon blanc, merlot, and pinot noir. **Trents Estate Vineyard & Restaurant,** Trents Road, Templeton (✆ **03/349-6940;** www.trentsvineyard.co.nz), is a charming setting, built around a 125-year-old historic chicory kiln, which has been cleverly converted into a rustic restaurant. It is surrounded by pinot noir, chardonnay, and Riesling grapes. **Waipara Springs Winery & Restaurant ★,** State Highway 1, Waipara (✆/fax **03/314-6777;** www.waiparasprings.co.nz), is one of the oldest vineyards in the region, producing premium-quality sauvignon blanc, Riesling, chardonnay, cabernet sauvignon, and pinot noir grapes from its own 20 hectares (50 acres). It has won numerous medals, in New Zealand and overseas, including a Gold Medal for its 1996 cabernet sauvignon, a Silver Medal for the 1997 sauvignon blanc, and a Gold for its 1997 Riesling.

Pegasus Bay Winery & Restaurant ★★, 263 Stockgrove Rd., Amberley (✆ **03/314-6869;** www.pegasusbay.com), is a small vineyard and winery run by the Donaldson family, who have been seriously involved with wine for over 30 years. Specialties include sauvignon/semillon, chardonnay, merlot cabernet, pinot noir, and Riesling. Its 100-seat restaurant serves top-quality cuisine. Open daily: tasting room 10am to 5pm, restaurant noon to 4pm.

If you'd like to stay in the Waipara Wine Region, I highly recommend **Claremont Country Estate ★★★,** 828 Ram Paddock Rd., Waipara Gorge, Amberley (✆ **03/314-7559;** fax 03/314-7065; www.claremont-estate.com), which offers fantastic tours on its 960-hectare (2,400-acre) working station and nature reserve, complete with 65-million-year-old fossils. They have B&B rates from NZ$880 and lodge rates from NZ$1,120. Tours cost extra. A more moderately priced option—but also divine—is **Dry Paddocks Country Retreat ★★,** 325 Purchas Rd., Waipara Valley, Amberley (✆ **03/314-9639;** fax 03/314-9637; www.drypaddocks.co.nz), which has a beautiful, modern, self-contained cottage for NZ$295 to NZ$395. It's closer to Christchurch than Claremont.

Organized Tours

For a good overview of Akaroa and Banks Peninsula, call **Canterbury Trails** (✆ **03/337-1185;** www.canterburytrails.co.nz), which offers comprehensive day tours to the area that include a nature harbor cruise or an opportunity to swim with

Tucked away in suburban Christchurch sits the largest urban marae and carved ancestral house (Aoraki) in New Zealand. **Nga Hau E Wha National Marae,** 250 Pages Rd., Wainoni (🕾 **03/382-6628**), offers a variety of cultural experiences (day and night); you'll be impressed by the bounty of fine Maori carving on-site. This is the best place in the South Island to enjoy a traditional hangi experience.

dolphins. If mountain scenery is more your thing, consider the trip to Arthur's Pass National Park, which can also include a ride on the TranzAlpine train (one-way). Prices begin around NZ$280.

Unlimited New Zealand (🕾 **03/960-9119;** www.unlimitednz.co.nz) will get you out into the wide-open spaces of Arthur's Pass for a firsthand experience in Canterbury's magnificent high country. Their walk up Bealey Valley takes in several different ecosystems, right up to the sub-alpine zone. It's a full day out and you return to Christchurch on the TranzAlpine. You need warm, wet-weather gear and good boots, and it costs NZ$325 per person.

In the food and drink line, **Taste Canterbury ★** (🕾 **03/326-6753;** www.good things.co.nz) offers a terrific set of personalized gourmet food and wine tours of the greater Canterbury region. Mavis Airey is a knowledgeable guide and food writer, and her half-day tours cost NZ$140 per person for two (less if there are more of you), or NZ$240 per person for a full day. You'll get a lovely overview of rural Canterbury on the Akaroa and Ellesmere tours. I strongly recommend them—and all the goodies you get to sample and buy.

And for something entirely different again, allow a full day for the **TranzAlpine & High Country Explorer ★★** (🕾 **0800/863-975;** www.high-country.co.nz). You'll never forget this standout adventure. You'll board the TranzAlpine in Christchurch and travel to Arthur's Pass where you'll be picked up by a 4WD tussock buggy for the trip to Flock Hill Lodge and a hearty three-course lunch. Then it's a 22km (14-mile) safari into spectacular and otherwise inaccessible areas of Flock Hill sheep station. The last leg of the journey is an exhilarating jet-boat ride down the Waimakariri River to Woodstock sheep station for afternoon tea. A coach returns you to the city. It's a big day but one you'll love. Make sure you take warm clothes as the high country can be chilly, even in summer. This superb tour costs NZ$375 for adults, NZ$188 for children ages 4 to 14. Don't forget your camera: There's dynamite scenery along the way!

Canterbury Leisure Tours (🕾 **0800/484-485** in NZ, or 03/384-0999; www. leisuretours.co.nz) has a comprehensive selection of half- and full-day tours that cover everything from whale-watching in Kaikoura (see "Side Trips from Christchurch," later in this chapter) to wine trails, sheep-farm tours, horse trekking, Mount Cook, Hanmer Springs (see "Side Trips from Christchurch"), and more.

And if you *still* haven't gotten *The Lord of the Rings* out of your system—and believe me, plenty haven't—you're a sure thing for **Hassle-Free Tours'** adventures. Call 🕾 **0800/427-753** in New Zealand, or 03/385-5775, or visit the website at www.hasslefree.co.nz to find out about their 4WD excursions that deposit you in the thick of Edora, the capital city of the people of Rohan of the film trilogy. The cost is NZ$215 adults, NZ$150 children.

Adventure Canterbury (℃ 0800/847-455 in NZ; www.adventurecanterbury. co.nz) and **Tuatara Tours ★★** (℃ 0800/377-378; www.tuataratours.co.nz) are two more excellent companies offering a wide range of half-day, 1-day, and multiday tours into the wider Canterbury landscape. I can personally recommend Tuatara Tours' 3- to 4-day Akaroa Walk, which takes you into spectacular landscapes—make sure you're fit, as it involves a *lot* of uphill walking. Or try their much less taxing 4-day West Coast Trail, which is a truly beautiful introduction to things West Coast. The great thing about these tours is that, in addition to excellent guides, you only have to carry a small day pack, you eat well, and you sleep in comfortable beds.

OUTDOOR PURSUITS

BEACHES   Christchurch has three main beaches—Sumner, Taylor's Mistake, and New Brighton. Originally a quiet holiday suburb, **Sumner ★** is now favored by city dwellers on weekends. Its attractive beach is a magnet for swimmers, surfers, and volleyball players. There are plenty of good cafes, restaurants, and bars (see "Where to Eat," earlier in this chapter). Lots of families, lots of young people.

Taylor's Mistake is a surfer hangout with some quaint old holiday homes tucked into the cliffs. There's a good walk around the cliff tops from Taylor's Mistake to Boulder Bay. Directions are on a big board to the right of the parking area behind the surf club. The beach is over the hill from Sumner and is best accessed by car. Once past Scarborough Hill, there's no place else to go but down to Taylor's Mistake.

New Brighton is a good place to take the kids for fishing, safe swimming, and surfing. The long beach is ideal for long walks and its popular with surfers. All in all, a better family beach experience awaits at Sumner.

 AN unforgettable **TRAIN TRIP**

The **TranzAlpine ★★★** is rated as one of the five most spectacular train journeys in the world; you can't fail to be impressed by the scenery as you make your way from Christchurch in the east to Greymouth in the west. The train travels over the Canterbury Plains; through the heart of the Southern Alps; and through tunnels, beech forests, and massive river gorges to the West Coast. It's a must-do for anyone visiting the South Island.

The round-trip excursion costs NZ$150 to Arthur's Pass and NZ$199 to Greymouth, with cheaper rates for children—and cheaper specials if you book online. If you take the Arthur's Pass option, you'll have 5 hours for exploration there before the train returns, but there are many

excellent bush walks in the area and a couple of nice cafes (see "Side Trips from Christchurch," later in this chapter).

If you go to Greymouth, you'll have only 1 hour in the township before the train returns to Christchurch—not a lot of time to do much more than wander about. Check out the "Greymouth & Lake Brunner" section in chapter 14 for possible activities.

The train leaves from Christchurch's main railway station at 1 Clarence St., Addington. For reservations and further information, contact **Tranz Scenic** (℃ **0800/872-467** in NZ; www.tranz scenic.co.nz). Food is available on the buffet car, or you can bring your own picnic. The train makes six stops during the journey.

BIKING   Christchurch has a reputation as a cyclist's paradise because of its overall flat terrain. Bike lanes are marked off in several parts of the city, and parking lots provide bike racks. For rentals, contact **City Cycle Hire** (✆ **0800/343-848** in NZ, or 03/339-4020; www.cyclehire-tours.co.nz), which will deliver bikes to your accommodations. They have road and mountain bikes plus tandems, and all are supplied with locks and helmets. Half-day, 1-day, and long-term hires are available.

BOATING   Punting is a fun activity, especially since someone else is doing all the work. You'll spot the young men from **Punting on the Avon** (✆ **03/366-0337;** www.welcomeaboard.co.nz) in straw hats pushing their way up the Avon River at the junction of Oxford Terrace and Worcester Boulevard. You can reserve a ride at the visitor center and pay NZ$25 for adults and NZ$12 for children. You can also get tickets from the landing stage at Worcester bridge. Punts depart daily 9am to dusk.

If canoeing is your thing, rent one from **Antigua Boatsheds,** 2 Cambridge Terrace (✆ **03/366-6768;** www.boatsheds.co.nz), for NZ$12 per hour. It opens at 9am; the last boats go out at 5pm.

CLIMBING   Many of the favorite Port Hills rock climbing spots were destroyed or rendered unstable after the earthquakes, so make sure you check with local climbers before trying any climbing in the area. **Castle Hill** in Arthur's Pass has hundreds of climbs for mixed levels and is excellent for boulder climbing. Or head to the **YMCA Indoor Rock Climbing Wall,** 12 Hereford St. (✆ **03/366-0689;** www.ymcachch. org.nz), which is open daily from 8am to 10pm and costs NZ$12 for adults, NZ$8 for children; it's an extra NZ$5 for harness hire and NZ$5 for shoe hire.

DOLPHIN-WATCHING   Christchurch Wildlife Cruises, 17 Norwich Quay, Lyttelton (✆ **0800/436-574** in NZ, or 03/328-9078; www.blackcat.co.nz), has an afternoon dolphin-watching cruise, departing daily at 1:30pm all year. It costs NZ$67 to NZ$69 for adults and NZ$25 for children ages 5 to 15. They also operate dolphin-watching cruises in Akaroa (see "Side Trips from Christchurch," later in this chapter). You'll find free parking near the wharf. A free shuttle also connects with each cruise.

FISHING   Embark on a four-wheel-drive adventure into the backcountry landscapes of the Southern Alps to fish for brown and rainbow trout in the capable hands of guides from **Back Country New Zealand ★★★** (✆ **021/644-507;** fax 03/308-2665; www.backcountry.co.nz). They offer a wide range of fishing and hunting excursions starting at around NZ$650 per person.

GOLF   The Canterbury region boasts over 40 courses. **Russley Golf Club,** 428 Memorial Ave., near the airport (✆ **03/358-4748**), has reasonably flat, well-bunkered greens and is one of the premier courses in New Zealand. It is open by arrangement. Greens fees are around NZ$85. **Harewood Twin Courses,** 371 McLeans Island Rd. (✆ **03/359-8843;** www.harewoodgolf.co.nz), is the largest golf club in the South Island, with two 18-hole courses. Greens fees are NZ$30 to NZ$50. **Clearwater Resort,** Johns Road (✆ **03/360-1003;** www.clearwaternz.com), is a par-72 course and players will pay around NZ$135 for a round of golf. The **Terrace Downs Country Resort and Golf Club** (✆ **0800/465-373** in NZ, or 03/318-6943; www.terracedowns.co.nz), in Rakaia, a 50-minute drive from Christchurch, at the base of the Mount Hutt ski field and on the banks of the Rakaia Gorge, is a par-72 course with 70 bunkers, eight lakes, rolling fairways, and spectacular views; non-members pay around NZ$135. **Pegasus Golf Course,** Pegasus Town, North Canterbury (✆ **03/920-330;** www.pegasustown.com), has a new 18-hole golf course. Greens fees are NZ$90. **Christchurch Golf Club** (sometimes referred to as

Shirley), 45 Horseshoe Lake Rd. (☎ **03/385-2738**), was temporarily closed at time of writing for earthquake repairs.

HORSE-TREKKING Kate Tapley Horse Treks (☎ 03/329-0160; www.katetapley.co.nz) offers 2- and 3-hour treks, all-day riding adventures, and multiday treks at My Lyford in North Canterbury. Short riding sessions are based at Otahuna Lodge (p. 339) and run from 10am and 1:30pm daily. Prices start around NZ$90 per person.

HOT-AIR BALLOONING There is no other place in the world where it's possible to fly from the center of a city, in view of the ocean, toward snowcapped mountains. **Up, Up, and Away** (☎ 03/381-4600; www.ballooning.co.nz) charges around NZ$350 for adults and NZ$275 for children ages 5 to 11 for a special first-light experience. Free transport is provided from city locations.

JET-BOATING Several operators offer exhilarating spins up the Waimakariri River. The longest established is **Alpine Jet** (☎ 0800/263-626 in NZ, or 03/318-4881; www.alpinejet.co.nz). It's a little farther out of town than **Jet Thrills** (☎ 0800/847-455 in NZ; www.adventurecanterbury.com), a 15-minute drive away, but both give you something to squeal about. Prices are NZ$90 to NZ$385 per person.

MOUNTAIN BIKING The Port Hills are a favorite place for mountain biking. The **Mountain Bike Adventure Co.** (☎ 0800/424-534 in NZ) makes it possible to take the Christchurch Gondola to the top and then bike down one of the hill tracks or the road. The cost is NZ$65. The gondola operates daily October through April from 10am to midnight, in winter from noon to 10pm. Mountain-biking reservations can be made at the visitor center.

PARAGLIDING Nimbus Paragliding ★★ (☎ 0800/111-611 in NZ; www.nimbusparagliding.co.nz) was the early pioneer of Canterbury paragliding and has pilots who will assist you in leaping off one of three superb Port Hills sites. Four to ten minutes of flying will cost NZ$180 tandem. A paragliding school with 1- to 11-day courses is also available. Seriously addicted paragliders might consider the company's Adventure Tours, which include all flying equipment, campervans, and a New Zealand–wide itinerary covering the best flying sites. Prices start at NZ$240 per person. Check the website for more details.

SKY DIVING If you feel ready for that ultimate adrenaline rush, ring **Skydivingnz.com** (☎ 0800/697-593 in NZ; www.skydivingnz.com). You'll be attached to its highly experienced tandem instructor. Free-fall sky diving over Hagley Park costs NZ$335 to NZ$445. Courtesy transport is provided from the city.

WALKING The visitor center has several brochures detailing city walks. There is also a network of good walking tracks through the Port Hills that you can enjoy on your own, free of charge.

The more energetic will find the 4-day, 35km (22-mile) **Banks Peninsula Track ★★** worthwhile (see "Akaroa" under "Side Trips from Christchurch," later in this chapter); there's also the 3-day, 43km (27-mile) **Kaikoura Coast Track ★★**. **Arthur's Pass National Park,** 150km (93 miles) west of Christchurch, is another tramper's heaven (see "Side Trips from Christchurch," later in this chapter). Or call **Hiking New Zealand** (☎ 0800/697-232 in NZ; www.hikingnewzealand.com), which has a range of 50 superb multiday treks. It's based in Lyttelton but offers treks all over New Zealand. **Hiking Guys NZ** (☎ 03/960-9119; www.hikingguys.co.nz)

TAKING TO THE slopes

There are excellent ski fields within 2 hours of Christchurch. Closest among them are the five main fields of the Arthur's Pass area—Porter Heights, Mount Cheeseman, Broken River, Craigieburn Valley, and Temple Basin—all 1 to 1½ hours from the city. **Porter Heights** (✆ 03/318-4002; www.skiporters.co.nz) is the closest commercial field. It has the longest downhill drop in New Zealand, and although the facilities are pretty basic, it has a variety of terrain and stunning views. It's good for all skill levels. **Mount Cheeseman** (✆ 03/379-5315; www.mtcheeseman.com) is a club field and the second closest to Christchurch. It's good for all skiers and snowboarders, but it's not as big as the others. **Broken River** (✆ 03/318-7270; ski@brokenriver.co.nz) is another club field and a bit more rugged; it has rope tows only. **Craigieburn Valley** (✆ 03/365-2514; www.craigieburn.co.nz) is a club field 1¼ hours away, perfect for intermediate and advanced skiers. **Temple Basin** (✆ 03/377-7788; www.templebasin.co.nz), a club field beyond Arthur's Pass, has the most reliable snow in Canterbury facing the sun. It's a steep and enclosed field, and skiers say that if you can ski at Temple Basin, you can ski anywhere in the world. It's a snowboarder's paradise, too.

North Canterbury also has **Mount Lyford** (✆ 03/315-6178; www.mtlyford.co.nz), a privately owned commercial field 1 hour from Kaikoura and 1½ to 2 hours north of Christchurch; and **Mount Olympus** (✆ 03/318-5840; www.mtolympus.co.nz), a club field in the back of the Craigieburn range, set in a wide south-facing basin, that offers a variety of runs on uncrowded slopes.

Farther afield is **Mount Hutt Ski Area,** Main Road, Methven (✆ 03/302-8811; www.nzski.com). Right in the heart of the Southern Alps, Mount Hutt is recognized internationally as having the longest number of skiable days in Australasia. By car, it's 90 minutes south of Christchurch. Although it's the most developed ski area in Canterbury, Mount Hutt is very popular because it's well serviced by T-bars and chairlifts, and good shuttles are available. It's quite crowded here, and it isn't every skier's favorite. It doesn't have the same good fall line as Porter Heights, but it does have much better après-ski and on-field facilities. **Note:** It's important to read all signs here. If they say CLOSED, they mean it—it can get dangerous here because the weather closes in very quickly. It's a long haul up the mountain, and chains are necessary for a good part of the season. For a snow report, call ✆ **0900/99-SNO** [99-766].

Addicted skiers tell me you should never go anywhere in the Porter Heights range or Mount Hutt when Canterbury's infamous nor'west wind blows; apparently it's often raining in the mountains then and you'll be plagued by horrendous winds.

has a 1-day tour from Christchurch to Arthur's Pass that includes a TranzAlpine train trip plus a 3- to 4-hour guided walk in Arthur's Pass National Park. It costs NZ$350 for adults and NZ$240 for children 5 to 14.

WHITE-WATER RAFTING Rangitata Rafts (✆ 0800/251-251 in NZ, or 03/696-3735; www.rafts.co.nz) will take pleasure in introducing you to the Rangitata River's Grade V rapids. You'll start the adventure with a relaxed lunch rather than hard work. That comes later as you go through safety briefs, practical training, and a natural progression to the intense Grade IV and V section. End with hot showers and a barbecue. The cost is NZ$218 per person if you start in Christchurch (transport provided), or NZ$198 if you drive yourself to Peel Forest in South Canterbury.

SHOPPING

The Malls

The city has a number of suburban malls. **Westfield Riccarton** (© 03/348-4119; www.westfield.co.nz/riccarton) has more than 200 shops over two levels; the bus stops right outside the door. **Northlands Mall,** in Papanui (© 03/352-6535; www.northlands.co.nz), has 135 stores. The **Palms,** in Shirley (© 03/385-3067; www.thepalms.co.nz), has more than 110 stores, a big entertainment complex, and good bus services. The recently revamped **Merivale Mall** ★ (© 03/355-9692; www.merivalemall.co.nz) is smaller with around 40 stores, but features a pricier range of designer shops and boutiques. All malls are open daily.

The Markets

The **Arts Centre Market** offers a good range of quirky and quality items. Stallholders sell everything from hand-knitted, 100% New Zealand wool garments to jewelry, clothing, housewares, candles, toys, and handcrafted soaps. Because of the earthquakes this market is now staged at the Ferrymead Heritage Park (p. 350).

   Riccarton Rotary Market ★★ (© 03/339-0011; www.riccartonmarket.co.nz), which you'll find Sundays from 8am at Riccarton Racecourse, on Racecourse Road, Upper Riccarton, is supposedly New Zealand's biggest outdoor market and attracts over 300 vendors. Arrive early to get the best bargains. The goods are predominantly secondhand, but there are some good buys in sheepskin products and crafts. You'll need to sift through everything as there's a lot of junk, but it's a good cultural study.

City Shopping Spots

Christchurch's inner city shopping precincts have been severely impacted by the earthquakes. The suburb of Sydenham is due to be rebuilt first and some retailers are open in temporary premises in Cashel Mall. More will come onstream as the new city develops. Top-quality New Zealand arts, crafts, and jewelry can be found at **Form Gallery** ★★★, in the new Christchurch Art Gallery (© 03/377-1211; www.form.co.nz).

   J. Ballantyne & Co., at City Mall and Colombo Street (© 03/379-7400), is still considered *the* department store in Christchurch. It has been operating with distinctive style for over 100 years and its Contemporary Lounge is a good spot for top international clothing and accessories brands that can't be found elsewhere on the South Island.

CHRISTCHURCH AFTER DARK

Discover what's going on in Christchurch by checking the "Entertainment" section of Friday's *Press* or consulting the "What's On" section of the *Tourist Times*.

The Performing Arts

The **Court Theatre,** Bernard Street, Addington (off Lincoln Road; © 0800/333-100 in NZ, or 03/963-0870; www.courttheatre.co.nz), is the home of the best professional theater company in New Zealand. For the time being it has had to vacate its Arts Centre premises and has temporarily relocated to an old grain store in Addington, where it has created a purpose-built theatre, box office, and bar. Shows range from Shakespeare to contemporary American and British theater to the best New Zealand plays. Tickets for most shows are NZ$30 to NZ$42.

The Club & Bar Scene

The most visible evidence of Christchurch nightlife is now in the suburbs of Merivale, Riccarton, and Ferrymead.

In Merivale, **Aikmans ★★**, 154 Aikmans Rd. (✆ **03/355-2271**), is buzzing Thursday through Saturday nights, and it has a fabulous outdoor courtyard with fireplace and leather sofas. Adjacent **JDV,** Aikmans Road (✆ **03/964-3860**), has a gorgeous little martini bar that rocks until late, especially on Thursday nights; and **No. 4 ★★**, 4 Mansfield Ave. (✆ **03/355-3720**), attracts a wide age group looking for a good time—and in Merivale that tends to mean a clubby-style bar with free-flowing alcohol and lots of beautiful people doing things they might regret in the morning.

In Ferrymead, **Ferry Speight's Ale House,** 2a Waterman Place, Ferrymead (✆ **03/376-4071;** www.ferryalehouse.co.nz), is a popular brew-bar that draws a mixed crowd. They have big-screen TVs for watching major sporting events. There is also a **Speight's Ale House** at 263 Bealey Ave., Inner City (✆ **03/366-9958**); and another at Tower Junction, 55 Clarence St., Riccarton (✆ **03/348-6020**). **Winnie Bagoes** at Ferrymead (p. 347) is another popular night spot.

Movies

Currently, a number of the city's movie theaters are closed because of earthquake damage. But there are still regular sessions at the eight-theater **Readings Complex** at the **Palms** in Shirley (✆ **03/375-7080;** www.readingcinemas.co.nz); and at the **Hoyts Cinemas** (✆ **0508/446-987** in NZ; www.hoyts.co.nz) at **Westfield Riccarton** and **Northlands Malls** (see "Shopping," above, for mall locations.)

SIDE TRIPS FROM CHRISTCHURCH

Akaroa ★★★

There's a rather off-putting, winding hill road between Christchurch and Akaroa—but the scenery is wonderful and you shouldn't let a few steep twists and turns deter you from visiting this little French-inspired whimsy on the shores of Akaroa Harbour.

 Made in New Zealand

Head for Untouched World ★★★, 155 Roydvale Ave. (✆ **03/357-9399;** www.untouchedworld.com), where you'll find a stunning range of top-quality, New Zealand–made wool garments. It has a delightful setting with a top-end restaurant and native garden.

From the time you reach the breathtaking setting of the **Hilltop Café & Bar** (⟨℃ **03/325-1005**), a country pub overlooking Akaroa and the harbor, you'll be seduced by this dramatic volcanic landscape. Jean Langlois, an early French explorer, took word of it back to France, and in 1840, two ships and a handful of settlers arrived to colonize the site. They were too late—the British had beaten them to it when they signed the Treaty of Waitangi the year before. The French abandoned their plan, but the settlers stayed on, casting

The Gay Scene

Christchurch is a very "polite" city, and its gay scene is less overt than in the bigger cities. Check www.gaynz.com for information, event listings, and clubs.

about names such as Le Bons Bay, Duvauchelle, and French Farm. Today, you'll still find "rues" here, not streets.

In recent years, the community of about 1,000 residents has pulled up its promotional socks, and you'll find a growing number of excellent lodgings, restaurants, and shops. The Maori word *akaroa* means "long harbor," and that's exactly what dominates the village and its activities.

ESSENTIALS

GETTING THERE From Christchurch, follow State Highway 75 to Akaroa, passing through Halswell Village and Little River, up over the hills and down around Akaroa Harbour. Two shuttle companies operate regularly from Christchurch. Akaroa **French Connection** (℃ **0800/800-575** in NZ, or 03/366-4556; www.akaroabus. co.nz) has daily departures from Christchurch Visitor Centre and a complimentary pickup service from inner city accommodations. They charge NZ$49 round-trip. The **Akaroa Shuttle** (℃ **0800/500-929**; www.akaroashuttle.co.nz) charges NZ$45 per person round-trip (cash only) for the direct shuttle service. Both make the 1-hour trip daily, and both also offer scenic tours; reservations are essential.

VISITOR INFORMATION The **Akaroa Visitor Centre,** located in the old post office building, 80 Rue Lavaud (℃/fax **03/304-8600;** www.akaroa.com), is open daily in summer 9am to 5pm; and in winter, Monday to Friday 9am to 5pm, weekends 10am to 4pm.

EXPLORING THE TOWN & HARBOR

A small **museum,** made up of four historic buildings on Rue Lavaud (℃ **03/304-1013;** akaroa.museum@ccc.govt.nz; admission is NZ$4 adults, and NZ$8 families), has lively displays and good Maori collections. It's open daily from 10:30am to 4:30pm. The **Langlois-Eteveneaux Cottage** was partly prefabricated in France around 1846 and is probably the oldest in Canterbury. The **Old French Cemetery** was the first consecrated burial ground in Canterbury and is just off Rue Pompallier. The old **lighthouse,** which was in service from 1880 to 1980, is also interesting.

If you're artistically inclined, pick up the brochure for the self-guided **Akaroa & Bays Art Trail ★**, which leads to the homes and studios of 18 local artists and craftspeople. You'll need at least a day, as many of them are scattered farther afield in the surrounding bays. One of the most striking and unusual artist environments is the **Giant's House—Linton ★★★**, 68 Rue Balguerie (℃ **03/304-7501;** www.linton. co.nz), where sculptor Josie Martin has created one of the wackiest and most inspiring gardens you'll find anywhere. She's surrounded her gorgeous historic home (B&B accommodations available) with landscaped gardens and a myriad of amazing mosaic sculptures that are bound to delight. Children will love it, and it's bound to be one of your lasting Akaroa memories, too. The garden is open daily from noon to 4pm December to March, and from 2 to 4pm from April through November. Admission is NZ$15 for adults, NZ$7 for children, and there's a cafe on-site. For a sample of local village culture, visit **Akaroa Cinema & Café ★**, 4 Selwyn Ave. (*℃* **03/304-7678;** www.cinecafe.co.nz), which has two tiny theaters showing the latest foreign and art-house films. It's a great experience!

One thing every visitor should do is experience the harbor firsthand. **Pohatu Sea Kayaking ★★** (*℃* **03/304-8552;** www.pohatu.co.nz) offers excellent guided kayak tours in the Flea Bay Marine Reserve, which should yield views of lots of penguins. Your tour guide is one of the volunteers working on penguin conservation and protection, and the evening tours cost NZ$75 per person.

Akaroa Harbour Nature Cruises ★★   *The Cat* takes 90 people and offers great views throughout a 2-hour scenic cruise, which visits a salmon farm, a *paua* pearl farm, and bird-life sites. You have to be quite unlucky on this trip *not* to see the charming Hector's dolphins. The company's 3-hour dolphin-swimming trip gives you a chance to have a close encounter. See the section on sustainable tourism in chapter 2 for more information on swimming with dolphins.

Main Wharf. *℃* **0800/436-574** in NZ, or 03/304-7641. Fax 03/304-7643. www.blackcat.co.nz. Scenic nature cruise NZ$60 adults, NZ$30 children 5–15. YHA discounts available. May–Sept daily 1:30pm; Oct–Apr daily 11am and 1:30pm. Dolphin swimming NZ$130 adults, NZ$110 children 5–15. May–Sept daily noon; Oct–Apr 8:30am, 11:30am, 1:30pm, and 3:30pm. Parking at base of wharf and along the waterfront.

WALKING THE WALK

Consider this: 35km (22 miles) of unspoiled coastal farmland scenery; undisturbed colonies of fur seals, penguins, and dolphins; sheltered turquoise bays; the rustic comforts of trampers' huts; and enough moderate exertion to keep you honest. This is what you get with the **Banks Peninsula Track ★★** (*℃* **03/304-7612;** www.bankstrack.co.nz). The track twice climbs to 600m (1,970 ft.) and features rugged, exposed headlands, so a reasonable level of fitness is required. The season runs from October through April. The cost is NZ$230, and includes transport from Akaroa to the first hut, 4 nights' accommodations, track registration, and landowners' fees. The 2-day tramp, at NZ$150 per person, is recommended only for the very fit.

The **Southern Bays Track** (*℃*/fax **03/329-0007**) offers guided and unguided tramps over the southern coastlines, cliffs, valleys, bush, and peaks of Banks Peninsula, descending into the Little River village via the Okuti Valley. For those who like a challenge without the hassle, the guided walk, with packs carried by someone else, is a dream option. The season runs from mid-October to the end of May; call for pricing.

WHERE TO STAY

In addition to the properties listed below, I recommend these additional options. **Garthowen on the Waterfront,** 7 Beach Rd. (www.garthowen.co.nz; ☎ **03/304-7419**), is centrally located opposite the main beach and has four good-size bedrooms with en suites. **Chez la Mer Backpackers,** 50 Rue Lavaud (www.chezlamer.co.nz; ☎/fax **03/304-7024**), has shared bunkrooms for NZ$28 per person, and twins/doubles for NZ$70 to NZ$90. But if you truly want to get away from it all, stay at one of my favorite old country homes, **Rowandale Homestead ★★**, 894 Okains Bay, Banks Peninsular (www.rowandalehomestead.co.nz; ☎ **03/304-8615**). It's 20 minutes from Akaroa, and with rates of just NZ$165 to NZ$295 and some of the best food and hospitality in a unique setting, it's a must-stay in my view. Hostess Angela Thacker will spoil you with fresh, organic produce straight from her large garden. Beyond those recommended here, Akaroa now has umpteen lovely accommodations offerings.

Rates given include 12.5% GST.

Maison de la Mer ★★★ 🄾 Bruce and Carol Hyland's Devonport B&B, though now closed, was my favorite in all of New Zealand. Thankfully, their wonderful Akaroa venture has all that same romance, class, and hospitality transferred south. For privacy, opt for the Boathouse, a self-contained apartment set apart from the main house that has its own kitchen. Two luscious rooms in the main house have wide sea views. The Fleur de Lys has a private sunroom.

1 Rue Benoit, Akaroa. www.maisondelamer.co.nz. ☎ **03/304-8907.** Fax 03/304-8917. 3 units. NZ$400–NZ$450. Rates include breakfast. AE, MC, V. Closed July–Aug. No children 11 and under. **Amenities:** Free use of bikes; nearby golf course; Internet. *In room:* TV/DVD, fridge, hair dryer, kitchen (in the Boathouse), minibar, free Wi-Fi.

Wilderness House ★★ ⚘ This big two-storied home, set in a large garden, is just a short stroll from the heart of the village. It oozes old-world charm and, of the four rooms, I like the elegant botanically themed Nalder Room the best. Mind you, the claw-foot tub was a draw card in the Walker Room, and the private balcony and French Provincial style of the Shepherd Room were just as appealing. You even get to wander in a tiny private vineyard as part of the deal.

42 Rue Grehan, Akaroa. www.wildernesshouse.co.nz. ☎ **03/304-7517.** Fax 03/304-7518. 4 units. NZ$290. Long-stay and off-peak rates. Rates include breakfast. MC, V. No children 11 and under. **Amenities:** Nearby golf course. *In room:* Fridge, hair dryer, free Wi-Fi.

WHERE TO EAT

It always surprises me that good restaurants come and go with frightening regularity in Akaroa. I think it says something about the service and the winter downturn in

The Big Cheese

As you drop down from the hills into Barrys Bay on your drive to Akaroa, keep an eye out on the left for **Barry's Bay Cheese ★★★** (☎ **03/304-5809**; fax 03/304-5814), makers of mouthwatering traditional cheeses—everything from award-winning cheddars to Maas-dam, Gouda, Edam, and havarti, to name just a few. During the cheesemaking season (usually Oct–Apr), you can watch cheesemaking activities every other day, through the viewing gallery window. There's a shop, and I advise you to stock up! They're open daily.

SPECIAL delivery

One adventure that shouldn't be missed is the **Eastern Bays Scenic Mail Run ★★** (✆ **03/304-8526,** or call the visitor center; www.akaroa.com). Join mail carriers Robin and Jo, who make this 120km (74-mile), 4-hour journey around some hair-raising Banks Peninsula roads every day. They deliver mail, papers, and freight to the isolated farms and communities of the peninsula, and they'll take up to eight passengers along for the ride. They'll even stop to let you take photos—and believe me, you'll want to. The Mail Run departs from the visitor center Monday through Saturday at 9am. It costs NZ$60; reservations the day before travel are essential.

tourism. Of those that endure, **Ma Maison ★**, 2 Rue Jolie (✆ **03/304-7668;** www. mamaison.co.nz), is a good bet for a tasty meal without too many frills. Set away from the main street, it's a great place to look out over the water. The **Akaroa Bakery,** 51 Beach Rd. (✆ **03/304-7663**), open daily from 7:30am to 4pm, has specialty breads, sandwiches, pies, and cakes baked fresh daily—a great choice for picnic fare.

Bully Hayes Bar & Café MODERN NEW ZEALAND This one is right on the promenade—a modern spot that maximizes its waterfront location with lots of glass and a big terrace where you can enjoy a glass of Canterbury wine. The menu is concise and seafood is a strength. Their seafood chowder is a great lunchtime filler; at night you can enjoy mains like seared salmon filet, seafood risotto, or braised venison shank.

57 Beach Rd. ✆ **03/304-7533.** www.bullyhayes.co.nz. Reservations recommended. Main courses NZ$24–NZ$28. AE, DC, MC, V. Daily 8:30am–late. Closed Dec 25.

C'est La Vie Bistro/Café ★ FRENCH You'll pay city prices here and I'm not entirely sure they're always justified. The menu generally includes seafood specialties and treats such as quail wrapped in speck and sauce burgundy. The duck à l'orange is legendary. The bistro has an intimate interior with space for 24 in two seatings.

33 Rue Lavaud. ✆/fax **03/304-7314.** Reservations essential. Main courses NZ$28–NZ$38. MC, V. Daily 6pm–late. Closed July–Sept.

Arthur's Pass ★★

Arthur's Pass, named after Arthur Dudley Dobson, who discovered it in 1865, connects Canterbury and Westland. Nestled in the Southern Alps on State Highway 73, the pass has become a destination in its own right, and Arthur's Pass village (pop. minuscule) has a growing range of modest accommodations. The area has several ski fields (see "Taking to the Slopes," on p. 358) and many short walks; Arthur's Pass National Park is a favorite with trampers. If you like a dramatic landscape and weather conditions to match, this is the place for you.

ESSENTIALS

GETTING THERE From Christchurch, take State Highway 73 to Arthur's Pass National Park. The alpine village of Arthur's Pass is 2 hours from Christchurch and your halfway mark to the West Coast. You can also go by train on the TranzAlpine (see "An Unforgettable Train Trip" on p. 355) or by shuttle with **West Coast Shuttles** (✆ **03/768-0028;** www.westcoastshuttle.co.nz). Another option is a 1-day tour from Christchurch with **Travel Pioneer** (✆ **0800/808-070** in NZ) or **Peninsula &**

Alpine Tours (✆ 03/384-3576; fax 03/384-3971). The only daily afternoon service is provided by **Alpine Coaches** (✆ 0800/274-888 in NZ).

VISITOR INFORMATION   The **Arthur's Pass Visitor Centre,** State Highway 73 (Main Road), P.O. Box 51008, Arthur's Pass (✆ **03/318-9211;** fax 03/318-9093; www.doc.govt.nz), is a good place to start. The weather in this area can be extremely changeable—never underestimate the danger; people can die when they are ill-prepared and ignore warnings. The center staff will be able to advise you on all safety issues related to walking tracks. Open daily, except December 25.

WALKING ON THE WILD SIDE

Snow, avalanches, and over 4,000 millimeters (160 in.) of rain a year have their impact on the walking tracks here. Despite these changing conditions, the area has numerous 2- to 3-day tramps and many shorter walks that bring you up close to thundering waterfalls, wild rivers, dripping beech forests, and a wealth of bird life.

A lot of them are also tough going and require a degree of skill in personal navigation using maps and compasses. Make sure you're tackling something within the range of your ability, and no matter what the weather is like when you set off, *always* bring plenty of warm clothing. Pick up the Department of Conservation's two brochures, *Walks in Arthur's Pass National Park* and *Arthur's Pass Village Historic Walk,* at the visitor center.

Two short walks worth doing are **Devil's Punchbowl Waterfall** ★ and **Bridal Veil.** Each takes 1 to 1½ hours. The **historic village walk** ★ is a pretty 1½-hour wander that can be accomplished easily if you've stopped off at Arthur's Pass on the return TranzAlpine journey.

WHERE TO STAY

For the modest sum of NZ$120 to NZ$150, you can take a bed at **Arthur's Pass Chalet Restaurant & Accommodation,** Main Road (www.arthurspass.co.nz; ✆ 03/318-9236). Its 11 units are right in the heart of the little township.

Grasmere Lodge ★★★   A member of the Small Luxury Hotels of the World, this is the New Zealand equivalent of an English country-house hotel where an intimate number of guests receive the very best personal service. Owner Tom Butler makes sure your stay is first-rate. The original homestead is the center of lodge activities and modern, alpine-styled chalets spread around it. All of the spacious rooms offer every comfort and bathrooms are fabulous. I love the pool complex here; there's nothing better than floating in the middle of this magnificent landscape.

St. Hwy. 73, Cass. www.grasmere.co.nz. ✆ **03/318-8407.** Fax 03/318-8263. 13 units. NZ$1,400 lakeview room; NZ$1,843 mountain-view room; NZ$2,173 chalet and cottage suite. NZ$197 per person sur-

---

🎁 A Beach Diversion

On the way to or from Akaroa on State Highway 75, take a detour to **Lake Ellesmere.** It measures 287 sq. km (111 sq. miles), but it's only 2m (6½ ft.) deep at its deepest point and is home to thousands of Australian black swans and other birds. And for a dramatic seascape, don't miss **Birdling's Flat** ★★, in the same area. The seas are very dangerous on this stone-covered beach, so don't attempt swimming under any conditions. It's signposted off the main highway about 30 to 40 minutes from Christchurch.

HOT & steamy

Hanmer Springs Thermal Pools & Spa, 42 Amuri Ave. (② **0800/442-663** in NZ, or 03/315-0000; www.hanmer-springs.co.nz), has attracted visitors for over 125 years. The complex boasts nine open-air thermal pools, three sulfur pools, sauna and steam rooms with plunge pool, four private thermal suites, a 25m (16-ft.) heated freshwater pool, a family activity pool with two water slides, a gym, and therapeutic massage facilities. The water in the pools is maintained at a temperature between 90°F and 104°F (32°C–40°C). The Garden House Café overlooks the whole complex. The pools are open daily from 10am to 9pm. Adults pay NZ$14 admission; children pay NZ$7. Hanmer Springs is 1½ hours northeast of Christchurch. It's a picturesque drive, but be careful in winter, when icy conditions can make the roads dangerous. Take Highway 1 out of Christchurch and go 45 minutes to the left-hand Hanmer turnoff just over the Waipara River Bridge. It's well signposted the rest of the way. If you don't have a car, call the **Hanmer Connection** (② **0800/242-663** in NZ; www.atsnz.com), which operates daily between Christchurch and Hanmer. Bookings are essential. It costs NZ$33 one-way, NZ$60 same-day round-trip. They also offer package deals that include a swim at the pools.

The **Hanmer Springs i-SITE Visitor Centre,** 42 Amuri Ave. (② 03/315-7128; fax 03/315-7658; www.alpinepacific tourism.co.nz), is open daily from 10am to 5pm in winter and 9:30am to 5:30pm in summer.

For an overnight stay in Hanmer Springs, try the **Cheltenham House ★★**, 13 Cheltenham St. (www.cheltenham. co.nz; ② 03/315-7545). Len and Maree Earl have decades worth of local knowledge and an elegant 1930s home with six sunny, spacious bedrooms; central

charge Dec 25. Rates include breakfast, predinner canapés, 5-course dinner, and transport from TranzAlpine stop at Mount White Bridge. AE, MC, V. Located 120km (74 miles) from both Greymouth and Christchurch. Inquire in advance about acceptance of children 11 and under. **Amenities:** Restaurant; bar; free use of bikes; concierge; limited fitness equipment; heated outdoor pool; tennis court; canoes; Wi-Fi in main reception. *In room:* A/C, fridge, hair dryer, minibar.

Wilderness Lodge ★★   Nature lovers will want to stay at this wonderful high-country lodge, where hosts Gerry McSweeney, ecologist/conservationist extraordinaire, and his wife, Anne Saunders, have developed a very special experience. Although it's not nearly as luxurious as Grasmere, the lodge offers superior outdoor activities and informed, guided nature tours—all of which highlight environmental conservation practices on the property. All rooms overlook the Waimakariri valley and mountain peaks and there are four alpine lodges for a bit of extra pampering. I recommend a 2-night minimum stay to fully enjoy the property. It has a Qualmark Enviro-Gold rating for its excellent conservation and recycling measures, and it has its own hydro-power scheme.

St. Hwy. 73, Arthur's Pass. www.wildernesslodge.co.nz. ② **03/318-9246.** Fax 03/318-9245. 24 units, all with private bathroom. NZ$780–NZ$980. Surcharge for Dec 25 and 31 and Jan 1. Off-peak rates. Rates include breakfast, dinner, use of lodge facilities, and guided nature and farm activities. MC, V. **Amenities:** Restaurant; bar; babysitting by prior arrangement; room service on request; canoe trips; Wi-Fi in lounge. *In room:* Fridge, hair dryer.

Kaikoura ★★★

The seaside settlement of Kaikoura is located halfway between Christchurch and

Picton on the rugged east coast. Waves lap at its toes and huge mountains stretch heating and electric blankets will insulate you against those icy, 14°F (–10°C) winter mornings. The house is set in large gardens, a 2-minute stroll to the Hanmer Springs Thermal Pools and Spa, and only NZ$220 to NZ$260 a night. Another good B&B option is **Rippinvale Retreat ★**, 68 Rippingale Rd., Hanmer (www.rippinvale.co.nz; ✆ **0800/373-098** in NZ, or 03/315-7139), where John and Helen Beattie offer two beautiful full suites, each with its own sitting room and kitchen, each NZ$355. The **Heritage Hanmer Springs ★**, 1 Conical Hill Rd. (www.heritagehotels.co.nz; ✆ **0800/368-888** in NZ, or 03/315-0060), is another excellent choice, with 64 stylish rooms from NZ$235 to NZ$425.

For a host of excellent, fast-paced activities all centered in one place, contact **Thrillseekers Canyon Adventure Centre ★★**, 839 Main Rd., Hanmer Springs (✆ **03/315-7046;**

www.thrillseekerscanyon.co.nz), which is open daily 9am to 5:30pm offering everything from bungy jumping and jet-boating to river rafting and assorted combos. Walkers *must* investigate **Hanmer Forest ★★★**, which provides a web of pretty walkways through stunning collections of exotic trees. An excellent forest brochure at the visitor center outlines the best woodland, forest, and alpine walks. Make sure you take your camera!

Hanmer is now home to a host of excellent eateries. One I always enjoy is **Malabar ★★**, Alpine Pacific Centre, 5 Conical Hill Rd. (✆ **03/315-7745**), which has a delicious Asian-Indian menu. For the best coffee, go straight to **Powerhouse Café ★**, 8 Jack's Pass Rd. (✆ **03/315-5252**), or **Springs Deli Café ★**, 47 Amuri Ave. (✆ **03/315-7430**). The latter has a fabulous range of takeout picnic food.

away from its shoulders. It's a stunning combination that never fails to impress and these days the population of approximately 4,000 never misses a beat in capitalizing on natural attributes. Chief among them is the marine bounty—several breeds of whales, dolphins, seals, and thousands of seabirds. Once a sleepy hollow that virtually closed down in the winter, Kaikoura is now a thriving little town that is especially energetic and interesting during the tourist season. It was also the first local authority in the world to achieve Green Globe 21 certification, proving the town's commitment to reducing environmental impacts.

ESSENTIALS

GETTING THERE Traveling on State Highway 1, Kaikoura is an easy 2½-hour drive from Christchurch—unless you use this opportunity to stop over in the Waipara wine region, in which case you should allow a whole day. It is approximately 2 hours south of Blenheim. You can also go by train and the **TranzCoastal** (✆ **0800/872-467** in NZ; www.tranzscenic.co.nz) is certainly a lovely trip. As a round-trip day trip from Christchurch, it costs NZ$88 for adults and NZ$62 for children ages 2 to 14, but check online for cheaper fares. The train gives you around 5½ hours to explore Kaikoura or go whale-watching. It departs Christchurch at 7:30am and returns at 7pm. One-way fares are also available. **ATSNZ Hanmer Connection** (✆ **0800/242-663;** www.atsnz.com) provides a shuttle service to Kaikoura via Hanmer Springs on Tuesday, Thursday, and Saturday; **InterCity** (✆ **09/623-1503**) and **Newmans** (✆ **09/623-1504**) both pass through the township.

Wine on High

Make sure you don't drive past **Kaikoura Winery**, 140 St. Hwy. 1 ((℄ 03/319-7966; www.kaikourawinery.co.nz), perched high above the ocean on limestone cliffs, to the south of the town. It's worth a stop for some of the most scenic wine tasting you'll ever experience. The ocean views are wonderful and they have a very impressive underground cellar and a cafe. You're welcome to have a picnic there, and they have gourmet food available. It's open daily from 10am until 5:30pm and tours are held on the hour for NZ$15 per person. Wine tasting costs NZ$5.

VISITOR INFORMATION   The **Kaikoura i-SITE Visitor Centre** is located at the south end of the town's main carpark, West End ((℄ **03/319-5641;** www. kaikoura.co.nz or www.naturallykaikoura.co.nz). It has comprehensive displays of all the town's attractions and can organize transport.

SPECIAL EVENTS   Do your utmost to be here for the first week of October for **Seafest ★★★** in Takahanga Domain ((℄ **0800/473-2337;** www.seafest.co.nz), Kaikoura's crazy and delicious celebration of the ocean and its extravaganza of tastes.

WALKING THE WALK

The **Kaikoura Coast Track ★★**, Medina, 210 Conway Flat Rd., Cheviot ((℄ 03/319-2715; www.kaikouratrack.co.nz), begins almost an hour south of Kaikoura and takes you across a historic sheep station, up into tussock land, down into bush valleys, and along a beach beneath cliffs embedded with 8,000-year-old tree stumps and fossils. It's 3 days in country otherwise inaccessible to you, and for NZ$185 per person it's money very well spent. You sleep in farm cottages along the way and home-cooked meals can be provided.

   Kaikoura Wilderness Walk ★★★ ((℄ 0800/945-337 in NZ, or 03/319-6966; www.kaikourawilderness.co.nz) is a comfortable 2-day hiking experience over 17km (11 miles) in the Puhi Peaks Nature Reserve, a remote area that is home to rare wildlife. You'll overnight at Shearwater Lodge, which was built in 2004 on a precipitous location that has to be seen to be believed. The 2- to 3-day guided walk, all meals, and accommodations cost from NZ$795 to NZ$995 per person. Only available from October through April, this is a more mountainous, wilderness experience than the more farm-based Kaikoura Track. Both are well worth doing.

WHERE TO STAY

Nikau Lodge ★, corner of State Highway 1 and Deal Street, Kaikoura (www. nikaulodge.com; (℄ 03/319-6973), has six B&B rooms (five with en-suite bathrooms, one with a private bathroom), plus a two-bedroom cottage, for NZ$165 to NZ$225.

   All rates quoted below include the 12.5% GST and free off-street parking unless otherwise stated.

Hapuku Lodge ★★★ 🍴   You won't believe your eyes when you see the level of style and quality you get here for the oh-so-reasonable price. It is, without doubt, one of the smartest small contemporary lodges in the country and you'll love the deep, restful silence of nights spent in this out-of-town location. Handcrafted furniture; big, well-designed bathrooms; and generous beds all add up to a fantastic stay. If you want extra space and privacy, opt for the apartment above the olive mill. But my favorite spot is tucked up in one of the exquisite treehouses.

Hapuku Rd., just off St. Hwy. 1, Kaikoura. www.hapukulodge.com. ℂ **0800/521-568** in NZ, or 03/319-6559. Fax 03/319-6557. 14 units. NZ$394–NZ$462 lodge room; NZ$655–NZ$855 treehouse. NZ$75 each extra person. Off-peak rates and special rates. Rates include breakfast. AE, MC, V. Located 12km (7½ miles) north of Kaikoura township. **Amenities:** Restaurant; bar; airport transport to Kaikoura; free use of bikes; small gym; room service; Wi-Fi. *In room:* A/C (in treehouses), TV/DVD/CD, fridge, hair dryer, minibar, Wi-Fi.

Kincaid Lodge ★ Located 6km (3¾ miles) north of Kaikoura, this old farm homestead, built in 1903, now has a new life thanks to extensive renovations by owners Greg and Jessica Frost. It's a pretty property set in a peaceful garden well back from the main highway, with farm animals peering over the fence. If you prefer more privacy, take the self-contained two-bedroom cottage; but lodge rooms are spacious with nice bathrooms. You get better value at the much more stylish Hapuku Lodge up the road, but it's a lovely stay nonetheless and it's more intimate than Hapuku.

marine EXPERIENCES IN KAIKOURA

Whales and other marine mammals are the primary draw of Kaikoura, but be aware that you'll be fighting for a place with hundreds of others *and* that it's all weather dependent. **Whale Watch Kaikoura** ★★★ (ℂ **0800/655-121** in NZ, or 03/319-6767; www.whalewatch.co.nz) gives you a close encounter with the giant sperm whale. Book well ahead for this awesome adventure. It offers four 2½-hour tours daily on two types of vessels. The fare is NZ$145 for adults, NZ$60 for children ages 3 to 15 (not suitable for kids 2 and under). You may also spot dolphins, fur seals, and seabirds. If you're prone to seasickness, make sure you take the appropriate medication because even the sight and smell of others being sick around you is enough to upset the sternest gut. This is a slick, well-managed operation, the films and videos first-rate, but I found there was something slightly manic about it all and you spend most of the trip waiting to see a whale's tail from about 30m (100 ft.) away.

Wings Over Whales (ℂ **0800/226-629** in NZ, or 03/319-6580; www.whales.co.nz) offers an airborne perspective to whale-watching via a 30-minute flight (NZ$165 per person). If you're short on time, this is probably the best alternative.

Encounter Kaikoura ★★ (ℂ **0800/733-365** in NZ, or 03/319-6777; www.encounterkaikoura.co.nz) has tours for watching and/or swimming with dusky dolphins, the most playful and acrobatic of all the dolphins. The cost is NZ$165 for adults, NZ$150 for children 14 and under. Reserve well in advance. I'd also recommend their **Albatross Encounter** ★★, which gets you up close and personal with the area's astounding seabird population. Make sure you take your camera for this one. It costs NZ$110 for adults and NZ$55 for children ages 8 to 14. **Seal Swim Kaikoura** (ℂ **0800/732-579** in NZ, or 03/319-6182; www.sealswimkaikoura.co.nz) operates October through May and has seal swims priced from NZ$70 to NZ$90.

Kaikoura Kayaks ★★★ (ℂ **0800/452-456** in NZ, or 03/319-7118; www.kaikourakayaks.co.nz) provides one of the loveliest ways of getting a feel for the richness of Kaikoura's marine environment. You'll have fur seals diving around your kayak and seabirds diving down from above. This is what I'd be doing if I only had a day in Kaikoura. Half-day trips cost NZ$85 for adults, NZ$75 for kids 12 and under.

A Cultural Exchange

Maurice and Heather Manawatu of **Maori Tours Kaikoura ★★** (① **0800/866-267** in NZ, or 03/319-5567; www.maoritours.co.nz) will send you away with some of your loveliest New Zealand memories. They'll take you on a journey through Kaikoura's rich Maori history to ancient Maori sites, and you'll explore a beautiful stand of native bush, learning about the traditional uses of plants by Maori. Wear sensible walking shoes and take along a sense of humor and a willingness to participate. The 3- to 4-hour tour costs NZ$115 for adults, NZ$65 for children ages 5 to 15.

611 Main North Rd., Kaikoura. www.kincaidlodge.co.nz. ① **03/319-6851.** Fax 03/319-6801. 4 units. NZ$545. Long-stay rates. Rates include breakfast. MC, V. **Amenities:** Free use of bikes; nearby golf course; outdoor tennis court; watersports equipment; Wi-Fi in lounge. *In room:* TV/DVD, fridge, hair dryer.

WHERE TO EAT

New cafes and restaurants pop up in Kaikoura like mushrooms on a damp day, but they're variable in service and all-around quality, and there's a definite lack of anything really classy. For the size of the place, though, there are more than enough casual options to choose from. **Hislops Wholefoods Café ★**, 33 Beach Rd. (① **03/319-6971**), is an excellent cafe. It has an organic focus and the food is always great. **Encounter Kaikoura ★**, West End (① **03/319-6777**), is my preferred hit for a delicious lunch, or coffee and a snack. They have an excellent menu, fabulous counter food, and a busy, modern environment that teems with people of all nationalities. **Craypot Café ★**, West End (① 03/319-6027), is well placed on the main street opposite the carpark and it's a good relaxed spot for lunch. Service can be patchy but I always enjoy their seafood chowder. Another fun, casual choice is **Kaikoura Seafood Barbecue ★**, Jimmy Armers Beach, near the end of Fyffe Quay (① **027/433-9691**), which is a little-known treat for seafood lovers. They serve fresh scallops, mussels, whitebait, and crayfish for under NZ$25; and their stand and outdoor, umbrella-covered tables are open daily year-round from 10am until dark—unless it's raining.

En Route to the West Coast & the Glaciers

From Christchurch, take State Highway 73 through the magnificent landscape of Arthur's Pass National Park. In 2 hours, you'll get to the village of Arthur's Pass, your halfway point to the West Coast. You'll then pass over the new Otira Viaduct, which takes care of the worst and most dangerous part of the journey. Proceed with caution, though, especially when it's snowing. From Otira, it's another 1 to 1½ hours to Greymouth on the West Coast. If you're traveling straight down to Franz Josef and Fox glaciers, follow State Highway 6 all the way. You can expect the drive to the glaciers to take another 3 to 5 hours, depending on how often you stop.

WEST COAST & THE GLACIERS

This is a unique part of New Zealand, where people approach life with a laid-back attitude and a strong sense of community. It's a place of majestic landscapes, rich history, and colorful characters, and you'll be hard-pressed to find anything slick or superficial here.

Greenstone was the first treasure of these wild and beautiful shores, and it's still the best place in the country to purchase contemporary jade carvings. Gold and timber have also shaped the course of coast history, and both continue to figure prominently in what you'll experience here.

More than anything, though, the dramatic landscape draws visitors. Almost 80% of the West Coast land area is protected under the Department of Conservation, and five of the country's thirteen national parks are wholly or partially in this region. The rainforests of the West Coast are among the most diverse in New Zealand, and few places in the temperate world contain such a variety of vegetation. Naturally, these forests are well sustained by the West Coast's notoriously high rainfall, so bring a raincoat, lots of insect repellent, and a sense of humor—you'll need all three!

From its subtropical north to its rainforested south, the West Coast is diverse and always interesting. Where else in the world could you find an icy glacier just a few kilometers from a sandy beach?

WESTPORT ★ & KARAMEA ★★★

Westport: 101km (63 miles) N of Greymouth; 226km (140 miles) SW of Nelson

The drive to **Westport** (town pop. 4,000) is better than actually arriving here. This funny little township is slightly shabby and smells of coal. I think calling it the "Adventure Capital of the West Coast" is stretching it a bit, but the area's mild climate and coastal to subtropical mountain scenery do provide an ideal setting for such outdoor activities as whitewater rafting, jet-boating, horse trekking, caving, and rock climbing. For the not-so-adventurous, there are excellent sea and river fishing, gold panning, and a variety of scenic and historic walks.

Traveling 1½ hours north to **Karamea** is worth your time and effort. This little corner of paradise is snuggled into the warm northwest part of the South Island and is, in fact, much farther north than Wellington. It is the terminal point of the Heritage Highway, the gateway to the Kahurangi

The Long Road

The West Coast is the longest region in New Zealand—550km (340 miles)—which is roughly equivalent to driving from Auckland to Wellington. In many ways—certainly geographically—it is an epic journey and it is important that you don't underestimate driving times. Take care at all times and stop to enjoy the quaint townships and spectacular scenery along the way.

National Park—the beginning of a natural heaven. It's my favorite part of the West Coast—all those nikau palms are just so unexpected.

Essentials

GETTING THERE & GETTING AROUND **By Plane** **Air New Zealand Link** (☏ **0800/737-000** in NZ; www.airnewzealand.co.nz) flies daily to Westport from Wellington.

By Coach (Bus)   Westport is serviced daily by **InterCity** (☏ **09/623-1503**). Both **Magic Travellers** (☏ **09/358-5600**) and **Kiwi Experience** (☏ **09/366-9830**) also include Westport on their schedules.

To get from Westport to Karamea, go with either **Cunningham Passenger Services** (☏ **03/789-7177**), which charges NZ$30 per person one-way, NZ$14 for bikes; or **Karamea Express** (☏ **03/782-6757**), which charges NZ$30. Both make the trip Monday through Friday and connect with other bus services to Nelson, Greymouth, Hokitika, and Christchurch. **Drive Me Wild Hikers' Transport** (☏ **0800/945-369** in NZ, or 03/546-8876; www.drivemewild.co.nz) offers transport on both sides of Heaphy Track. From Karamea, they travel to Nelson via Westport and Motueka on the day you finish walking.

By Car   Westport can be reached on Highway 6 from Greymouth in the south in about 2 hours, or from Nelson via the Buller Gorge in approximately 3½ hours. All roads are good, but look out for single-lane bridges and those that share the bridge with trains—a unique West Coast feature.

Karamea is just 100km (60 miles) north of Westport, but you should allow 1½ to 2 hours for the trip, as at least 25km (15 miles) of it is steep and winding. It's a beautiful drive over the Karamea Bluff, descending into bush landscape and then along the coast. And look out for truck drivers who dominate the road!

VISITOR INFORMATION   The **Westport i-SITE Information Centre,** 1 Brougham St. (☏ **03/789-6658;** fax 03/789-6668; www.westport.org.nz), opposite the post office, is open in summer daily from 9am to 5pm, and in winter Monday through Friday from 9:30am to 4pm (closed Dec 25).

The **Karamea Information & Resource Centre,** Market Cross (☏ **03/782-6652;** fax 03/782-6654; www.karameainfo.co.nz), is opposite the Karamea Store in the tiny village of **Market Cross.** From November to April, it's open daily from 9am to 5pm; May to October, Monday through Friday from 9am to 5pm, Saturday 9am to 1pm. There is also a post office here along with a garage, crafts outlet, and cafe. Just beyond Market Cross are the Karamea Tavern, a supermarket, general store, the police station, motels, and the Last Resort (p. 377). Everything is within walking distance, but the entrance to the Heaphy Track and Kahurangi National Park is

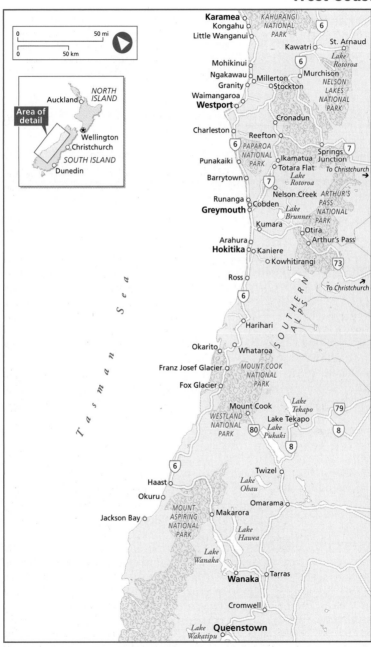

another 15km (9 miles) farther on at the end of State Highway 67. For more information, check www.westcoastnz.com.

Exploring Westport

Coal Town Museum, 165 Queen St. (☎/fax **03/789-8204**), gives you the chance to walk through a true-to-life coal mine, complete with sound effects from the deep bowels of the earth. Even if you're not lured here by these promises, you'll find an interesting repository of historical artifacts. Check out the displays of maritime and pioneering history. The museum is open daily, from 9am to 4:30pm October through April (until 5pm in Jan; closed Dec 25) and 10am to 4pm from May through September. Admission is NZ$13 for adults, NZ$5 for children ages 6 to 16, and NZ$30 for a family.

If you want an insight into the rugged history of the Westport area, try the local guides at **Outwest Tours** (☎ **0800/688-937** in NZ; www.outwest.co.nz), who will take you on personalized tours of old coal mining and off-the-beaten-track areas, like **Stockton Mine ★★**, New Zealand's largest coal mine, 750m (2,500 ft.) above sea level on the Stockton Plateau. You'll travel in 4×4 Unimog vehicles, traversing rivers and generally taking on everything in your path. It won't always be smooth, but it will be exciting.

OUTDOOR PURSUITS

ABSEILING (RAPPELLING) & ADVENTURE CAVING **Norwest Adventures Ltd. ★★**, The Charleston Hotel, SH6, Charleston (☎ **0800/116-686** in NZ, or 03/788-8168; www.caverafting.com), can introduce you to the mystery and intrigue of the underworld. The Adventure Caving trip costs NZ$330 per person and requires high levels of fitness for people ages 16 and over—don't try it if you get claustrophobic or are afraid of heights. The Glow Worm Cave Tour (NZ$105 adults, NZ$80 children 5–15, NZ$335 family) is the dry, passive version of the Underworld Rafting tour (below). You travel by Rainforest Train to the huge Nile River glowworm caves, where you get to see amazing stalactites and stalagmites. You need to be able to walk unassisted on uneven surfaces, and robust footwear and warm clothing are advised. The Underworld Rafting experience involves making your way by raft along underground stream passages and out into the Nile River rapids. Some consider it a tamer adventure than that offered by Wild West Adventure in Greymouth (p. 380). It's a 4- to 5-hour trip that costs NZ$165 per person.

ECORAFTING For multiday white-water rafting expeditions, check out **Eco-Rafting Adventures NZ ★★**, 108 Mawhera Quay, Greymouth (☎ **0508/669-675;** www.ecorafting.co.nz), for a range of adventure packages on different West Coast rivers priced from NZ$500 to NZ$2,000, depending on the river and length of the trip.

KAYAKING **Ultimate Descents,** 54 Fairfax St., Murchison (☎ **0800/748-377;** www.rivers.co.nz), offers three types of kayaks for all skill levels on Grade II to III rivers. You must be 13 years and over to participate in the 4½-hour trips. Trips range in price from NZ$130 for a half-day's rafting adventure to NZ$135 for a half-day kayaking.

SURFING Chief among the best beaches is **Tauranga Bay,** 15 minutes south of Westport.

SWIMMING   Two phrases sum up swimming on any of the West Coast beaches—
extreme care and *are you mad?* Undertows are common and an ever-present hazard on
beaches exposed to the westerly swell. Always seek local advice about safe areas. If
you're uncertain, *never* get wet!

SWING BRIDGE   If you haven't found enough ways to test your nerves already,
take a walk across New Zealand's longest swing bridge. **Buller Gorge Swingbridge
& Adventure Park ★**, State Highway 6, Buller Gorge (© **03/523-9809;** www.
bullergorge.co.nz), offers a heart-pumping distraction 1 hour from Westport.

WALKING   Tauranga Bay **★★★** is a popular place to explore beaches, coastline, and seal colonies. There is a good-quality short track through the area, specially
designed to accommodate wheelchairs. The seal-colony walk is 20 minutes round-
trip, and the **Cape Foulwind Walkway ★★★** is 1½ hours. A Department of Conservation's brochure with maps of both walks is available at the visitor center.

WHITE-WATER RAFTING   Call **Buller Adventure Tours ★★**, in Lower
Buller Gorge, SH6 (© **0800/697-286** in NZ, or 03/789-7286; www.adventuretours.
co.nz), which also offers jet-boating and horse-trekking tours. Eco- and white-water
rafting start at NZ$125, horse treks at NZ$85, and jet-boating at NZ$85.

WHERE TO STAY

If you're looking for classy, upmarket accommodations in Westport, stop now—you
won't find any. You will, however, find one or two smart, moderately priced options
that are bound to bring a satisfied smile to your face. Campers can head for **Westport Holiday Park & Motels,** 31–37 Domett St. (www.westportholidaypark.co.nz;
© **03/789-7043**), which has motel rooms, cabins, tent and caravan sites, and bunk
rooms in a native bush setting. Motel units range from NZ$115 to NZ$150, cabins
NZ$60 to NZ$95 and tent and powered sites from NZ$30 to NZ$38. **Chelsea Gateway Motor Lodge ★**, 330 Palmerston St. (www.chelseagateway.co.nz; © **0800/660-
033** in NZ, or 03/789-6835; fax 03/789-6379), is clean, comfortable, and reasonably
priced with 20 one-, two-, and three-bedroom units for NZ$135 to NZ$245. It also
has a Qualmark Enviro-Silver rating. **River View Lodge,** State Highway 6, Buller
Gorge Rd., Westport (www.rurallodge.co.nz; © **0800/184-656** in NZ, or 03/789-
6037), has four en-suite B&B rooms for NZ$225. Closed in July.

All rates quoted above include the 15% GST and free off-street parking unless
otherwise noted.

WHERE TO EAT

The notion of culinary excellence and innovation has yet to hit Westport, and if it's your
first West Coast destination, it will give you the chance to get used to the West Coast
dining style, which, at best, can be described as laid-back. **Yellow House Café ★**, 243
Palmerston St. (© **03/789-8765;** www.yellowhousecafe.co.nz), is a casual stop serving good pasta dishes and a range of mains like sage- and Parmesan-crusted pork ten-
derloin or pan-fried beef fillet with roasted mushrooms, plus good vegetarian choices.
It's open daily from noon to 9pm in summer; winter hours vary but are generally from
5 to 9pm daily. Everyone's favorite, The Bay House, has sadly shifted from its dramatic
Jackson's Bay location to become **The Town House ★★**, at Cobden and Palmerston
streets, Westport (© **03/789-7133;** www.thetownhouse.co.nz). It's the best dining in
Westport and is open Monday through Wednesday 10am to 10pm, Thursday and Friday 10am to 1am, Saturday 8am to 1pm, and Sunday 8am to 4pm.

Exploring Karamea ★★★

Caught between the wild Tasman Sea on one side and the bush-clad mountains of Kahurangi National Park on the other, Karamea (pop. 650) is a thin sliver of subtropical paradise. As the gateway to the Kahurangi, it offers a host of natural attractions, and it is here that Heaphy Track walkers arrive at the end of their 4- to 6-day tramp. Much of the coastline is wild and rugged, with rocky points and narrow beaches backed by steep cliffs. Nikau palms, rainforest, and dairy-farm pastures all flourish in the warm temperatures, and the limestone landscape contains many spectacular caves.

 Gas Up Before You Go

Before you leave Westport, heading to either Nelson or Greymouth, fill your car with petrol. There are no more petrol stations until you hit Murchison, or 87km (54 miles) south near Greymouth.

Tops on your list should be a visit to **Oparara Arch ★★★**, the biggest limestone arch of its type in the Southern Hemisphere. The drive to the arch takes approximately 1 hour through rainforest. If you're short on time, go straight to **Oparara Basin Guided Tours** (✆ 03/782-6652; www.oparara.co.nz). They take you into to the restricted **Honeycomb Cave area ★★★**, which was discovered in 1980. Now managed by the Department of Conservation, it's in pristine condition, complete with moa bones. Most people are completely blown away by the experience. The full 5-hour **Grand Eco Tour** includes an extensive tour of the basin and arches with the choice of either a Honeycomb Hill cave tour or a kayak trip. It costs NZ$240 per person. Shorter guided tours are available for NZ$95 for adults, NZ$45 for children under 12. *Please note:* These caves are protected and access is by guided tour only. You'll need warm clothing and a good degree of fitness; no walking sticks are allowed in the caves.

OUTDOOR PURSUITS

CANOEING   Hire a canoe from the **Last Resort** (✆ 03/782-6617; www.last resort.co.nz) for NZ$35; or **Karamea Motors** (✆ 03/782-6757). Paddle in the safe estuaries, but be aware of tidal changes and keep away from river mouths. The Last Resort also hires kayaks from NZ$25.

FISHING   There are over 320km (200 miles) of accessible heli-fishing on several backcountry rivers. The 40km (25 miles) of coastline are suitable for surf-casting, and the Karamea River is a trout fisherman's heaven. Trout licenses can be obtained from the **Karamea Hardware Store,** State Highway 67, Market Cross, on a daily, weekly, or annual basis.

The whitebait season is from September 1 to November 14. Whitebait are the young of three main species of migrating fish. They're considered a delicacy and found predominantly on the West Coast. Special rules and regulations apply for whitebaiters, so make sure you get a copy of them from the Department of Conservation or the Karamea Information & Resource Centre (p. 372).

MOUNTAIN BIKING   Mountain biking is prohibited in Kahurangi National Park, but if you'd like to ride in other areas, the **Last Resort** and **Karamea Motors** (see "Canoeing," above) have bikes for rent.

WALKING   There are two major hikes in this area—the famous **Heaphy Track ★★★**, which is suitable for trampers of all ages, and the **Wangapeka Track,** which is better suited to the well-equipped tramper. Both tracks take about 4 days, and both require hut ticket passes available from the Karamea Information & Resource Centre. Parts of the Wangapeka Track have been washed out by flooding, so always check first with the information center to make sure it is open. For more information on the Heaphy Track, see "Tramping" in chapter 4.

There are also many excellent short walks. For the **Nikau Loop Walk,** drive to the Kohaihai River mouth at the start of the Heaphy Track. The walk is suitable for all ages and takes 40 minutes. **Heaphy Hut Walk ★★★** gives you a 5-hour taste (round-trip) of the Heaphy Track. Guided walk companies operating in this area include **Kahurangi Guided Walks,** Dodson Road, Takaka, Golden Bay (*©* **03/525-7177;** www.heaphey-track.co.nz); and **Bush and Beyond Guided Treks,** 35 School Rd., Motueka (*©* **03/528-9054;** www.naturetreks.co.nz).

WHERE TO STAY

Karamea River Motels (www.karameamotels.co.nz; *©* **0800/527-263** in NZ, or 03/782-6955; fax 03/782-6944), 31 Bridge St., just over the Old Karamea Bridge, 500m (1,600 ft.) from the township, is ideal for families or travelers aiming to spend a few days in the area. Eight studio and one- and two-bedroom units are NZ$125 to NZ$165.

Last Resort ★★ 🎁 This grass-roofed complex may well surprise you. First opened as budget accommodations in 1991, they now offer another tier of comfort in en-suite units and three cottages. The latter are the biggest, with full cooking facilities and two bedrooms each. There is also a good restaurant and bar, following the same Mediterranean style and incorporating huge native timber beams from the forest floor.

71 Waverly St., P.O. Box 31, Karamea. www.lastresort.co.nz. *©* **0800/505-042** in NZ, or 03/782-6617. Fax 03/782-6820. 30 units. NZ$30–NZ$35 shared backpacker rooms; NZ$75 lodge room with shared bathroom; NZ$95–NZ$105 lodge room with en-suite bathroom; NZ$125 studio with en-suite bathroom; NZ$150 cottage. Long-stay and off-peak rates. AE, DC, MC, V. Less than 1km (½ mile) from local shops, 5km (3 miles) from beach. Bus service from door. **Amenities:** Restaurant; cafe; 2 bars; bike rentals; nearby golf course; miniature golf; Jacuzzi; watersports rentals. *In room:* TV, hair dryer, kitchen (in cottages), no phone in some units.

En Route to Greymouth: Punakaiki

The drive between Westport and Greymouth is simply stunning, with some of the best coastal views in the country. There are many walkways leading to a variety of natural attractions. Chief among them is the world-famous **Punakaiki Pancake Rocks and Blowholes ★★★**, the main feature of the 10-minute **Dolomite Walk** in the heart of the **Paparoa National Park.** These strange pancakelike limestone formations were pushed up from the ocean floor by seismic action 30 million years ago. For the best show, try to visit the rocks at high tide with a westerly swell running; water comes surging into the deep caverns below and can spout up to 9m (30 ft.) in the air. The rocks are 45km (28 miles) north of Greymouth on the coast section of State Highway 6. If you're on an InterCity coach, the bus will stop here to enable you to do the 20-minute round-trip walk. The track is wide, well maintained, easily negotiable, and there are opportunities for great photos. Expect crowds in mid-summer.

Across the road from the track entrance, you'll find a busy gathering of little cafes and crafts stores, along with the **Punakaiki-Paparoa National Park Visitor Centre,** SH6, Punakaiki (*©* **03/731-1895;** fax 03/731-1896; www.punakaiki.co.nz). The **Department of Conservation** (*©* **03/731-1895;** www.doc.govt.nz) is in the same building; it is open daily in summer 9am to 6pm, and in winter to 4:30pm (closed Dec. 25). **Punakaiki Crafts ★★** (©/fax **03/731-1813;** www.punakaiki. co.nz/crafts) is a cooperative with the best, most innovative arts and crafts on the coast. It's open daily from 8:30am to 6pm. There's an excellent espresso outlet here, too, but you may have to queue during peak tourist season.

There are plenty of other excellent short walks in the area. Both the **Truman Track ★★** and the **Punakaiki Cavern** are under 1 hour and suitable for the entire family. The Truman includes a stroll through coastal forest to a beach with caves and a waterfall. The **Pororari River Walk** is another beautiful walk. I did this as part of a guided walking tour run by Christchurch-based **Tuatara Tours** (www.tuataratours. co.nz). It's part of their excellent **West Coast Trail,** an easy 4-day experience that introduces you to some of the best highlights between Porter's and Arthur's Passes, and the West Coast from Greymouth to Punakaiki. You get to the Punakaiki area on day 3 of the tour, and for 2 days your guide will lead you through the Punakaiki Pancake Rocks Track, the Truman Track, the Fox River or Cave Creek Track (depending on weather), and the Pororari River Walk.

All of these afford you a terrific insight into the Paparoa National Park area, which is often overlooked in favor of the better known, longer tracks elsewhere in the South Island. It's an area filled with dramatic limestone cliffs, towering bluffs, and dense subtropical forest filled with coastal broadleaf plants, nikau palms, incredible tree ferns, and immense rata trees.

There is also rich bird life here, and if you go quietly, your guide will point out the friendly plump wood pigeons; tomtits; our favorite songbirds, the tui and the bellbird; and the friendly New Zealand robins that will hop right up to your feet. The tour is one I recommend constantly. Apart from the stunning scenery, you stay in comfortable accommodations along the way, and you only have to carry a day pack. It is rugged country though, so you need excellent hiking boots and a reasonable level of fitness.

Punakaiki Horse Treks (© **03/731-1839;** www.pancake-rocks.co.nz) offers a variety of activities from the third week of October through June that explore the rich park environment, including nature tours of the magnificent Punakaiki Valley in an eight-wheeled amphibious vehicle, and horse treks through bush and beach environments. The latter start at NZ$145 per person for a 2½-hour ride.

Punakaiki Canoes ★★, State Highway 6, Punakaiki (© **03/731-1870;** www. riverkayaking.co.nz), will take you upstream on the Pororari River, through a stunning gorge cut from limestone cliffs. It's suitable for all ages and experience levels and costs NZ$45 per person for half-day rental; guided trips start at NZ$85.

WHERE TO STAY

Many travelers now stop over in Punakaiki on the trip from Nelson to the West Coast. It's an excellent place for a rest before heading south to the glaciers, but accommodations options are fair to middling at best.

Punakaiki Resort, State Highway 6 (www.punakaiki-resort.co.nz; © **0800/624-646** in NZ, or 03/731-1168), opened in 2001 with bright rooms right on the beach. It's a stunning location, and while rooms are comfortable, I have found the service here to be less than impressive, especially in the restaurant. But it's the closest to the Pancake Rocks, and the prime location may make up for other flaws. The 61 rooms range in price from NZ$140 to NZ$350. **Paparoa Park Motel,** State Highway 6 (www.paparoa.co.nz; © **0800/727-276** in NZ, or 03/731-1883), is just a short distance south of the Pancake Rocks over the Punakaiki River. It has tidy native-timber studios and family units from NZ$120 to NZ$220.

You can find lovely rooms just north of Punakaiki, at **Birds Ferry Lodge & Ferry Man's Cottage ★★**, Birds Ferry Road (www.birdsferrylodge.co.nz; ✆ **0800/212-207** in NZ, or 03/429-1604). Andre and Alison Gygax have two en-suite rooms plus a self-contained cottage that sleeps up to six people. Rates range from NZ$275 to NZ$425, and include breakfast. The property has a Qualmark Enviro-Gold rating. The **Rocks Homestay ★**, 33 Hartmount Place (www.therockshomestay.com; ✆ **0800/272-164** in NZ, or 03/731-1141), is 3km (2 miles) north of Punakaiki; their three rooms cost from NZ$195 to NZ$220. Farther south, 29km (18 miles) from Punakaiki and 15km (9 miles) north of Greymouth, **Breakers Boutique Accommodation ★**, 9 Mile Creek, State Highway 6 (www.breakers.co.nz; ✆ **0800/350-590** in NZ, or 03/762-7743), has four en-suite rooms for NZ$215 to NZ$355, and a Qualmark Enviro-Silver rating. Request the Breakwater Room for fabulous views.

GREYMOUTH & LAKE BRUNNER

101km (63 miles) SW of Westport; 45km (28 miles) N of Hokitika; 290km (180 miles) SW of Nelson

I've always felt Greymouth was rather well named. Personally, it's never been a town to inspire a long stopover, despite the fact that it is centrally placed and has the best access to Nelson and Christchurch. It has had a bit of a face-lift recently, though, and in mid-summer it's a busy stopover for international visitors.

It is also part of a rich history. The Grey River was the landing place for Maori canoes on the hunt for greenstone, or *pounamu*—the jade that was Westland's most prized possession. Even today, the Grey River gap has great significance in Maori myth, and greenstone is just as prized as ever. The discovery of gold in the 1860s also left its mark on the area.

With a population of 10,000, Greymouth keeps busy with coal and timber exports. It is the largest town and the commercial heart of the West Coast, and most goods and services are available here—although some of them could do with a bit of a crank-up. If you're trying to decide whether to stay in Greymouth or travel another 45km (28 miles) to Hokitika, know that Greymouth has better food outlets, while Hokitika has a greater range of attractions, better accommodations, and tourist shopping.

Essentials

GETTING THERE & GETTING AROUND   By Plane   Daily flights between Christchurch and Hokitika are operated by **Air New Zealand** (✆ **0800/737-000** in NZ; www.airnewzealand.co.nz). A shuttle service carries visitors the extra 30 minutes by road to Greymouth.

By Train   The **Tranz Scenic** TranzAlpine route (✆ **0800/872-467** in NZ; www.tranzscenic.co.nz) runs daily between Christchurch and the Greymouth railway station on Mackay Street and will stop in Moana (at Lake Brunner) on request. This is New Zealand's best rail experience (see p. 355 for more details).

By Coach (Bus)   InterCity (✆ **09/623-1503,** or 03/768-7080) buses reach Greymouth from Queenstown, Fox Glacier, Franz Josef, Nelson, and Westport. Both **Kiwi Experience** (✆ **09/366-9830**) and **Magic Travellers** (✆ **09/358-5600**) include Greymouth on their routes. **West Coast Shuttle** (✆ **03/768-0028;** www.westcoastshuttle.co.nz) travels Greymouth to Christchurch and returns daily, with stops at Arthur's Pass and other small towns along the way.

By Car Greymouth is reached via Highway 6 from both the north and the south. Highway 7 brings travelers from the east coast via Lewis Pass, and Highway 73 takes you through Arthur's Pass National Park on the road from Christchurch. The trip from Nelson takes approximately 4 to 5 hours; from Christchurch, 4 hours.

VISITOR INFORMATION The **Greymouth i-SITE Visitors Centre,** in the Regent Theatre Building, at Herbert and Mackay streets ((☎ **0800/473-966** in NZ, or 03/768-5101; fax 03/768-0317; www.greydistrict.co.nz), is open in summer Monday through Friday 8:30am to 6pm, Saturday 9am to 5pm, Sunday and public holidays 10am to 5pm (closed Dec 25). It has reduced hours in winter, closing at 5:30pm Monday through Friday. It also serves as the Department of Conservation agency for the region.

Exploring Greymouth

If you're a history buff, you'll find that **Shantytown Heritage Park** ★★ ((☎ **0800/742-689** in NZ, or 03/762-6634; www.shantytown.co.nz) has been rather well done. Situated amid native bush, the replica West Coast gold-mining town includes over 30 historic buildings, and a collection of more than 10,000 historic objects, photographs, archives, and textiles. A steam train operates on a 20-minute bush track, and a stagecoach will rattle you over an old bush road. You can pan for gold, and the sawmill experience takes you through what appears to be an operating sawmill, complete with historical film footage. It's open daily from 8:30am to 5pm. Admission is NZ$29 for adults, NZ$13 for children 5 to 17, with family concessions (this includes a steam train ride and gold panning). To get here, drive 8km (5 miles) south of Greymouth to Paroa, make a left, and go another 3km (2 miles) inland.

For a summary of the region's artistic talents, head for **Left Bank Art Gallery** ★, 1 Tainui St. ((☎ **03/768-0038;** www.leftbankarts.org.nz), Monday through Friday from 11am to 4pm; and weekends 11am to 2pm. It has changing exhibitions (free admission), an excellent shop featuring the work of 70 West Coast artists, and the New Zealand Pounamu Jade Collection. It's closed weekends in winter.

If you prefer something a little more intoxicating, go to **Monteith's Brewery** ★★, 60 Herbert St. ((☎ **03/768-4149;** www.monteiths.co.nz), to book the NZ$30 brewery tour and tasting. Daily tours are given at 11:30am, 2pm, 4pm, and 6pm (closed Easter Friday and Saturday, Dec 25, and Jan 1).

OUTDOOR PURSUITS

CAVE RAFTING Wild West Adventures ((☎ **0508/286-877** in NZ, or 03/768-6649; www.fun-nz.com) has a 5-hour Dragon's Cave Rafting Trip for NZ$165

(NZ$245 with rappelling), taking you deep into a subterranean wonderland of lakes, glowworms, and waterfalls. They also offer kayaking and guided walk packages, bird-watching and photographic tours, and jade and gold-hunting adventures.

GOLF   **Greymouth Golf Club,** Golf Links Road, Kaiata (© **03/768-5332**), is 3km (1¾ miles) from town, has 18 holes. Greens fees are from NZ$30.

OFF-ROAD ADVENTURES   Five kilometers (3 miles) north of Greymouth, you can experience an off-road adventure with **On Yer Bike** (© **0800/669-372** in NZ, or 03/762-7438; www.onyerbike.co.nz) on either a four-wheeled bike or the amphibious eight-wheeled Argo. A 1-hour Enchanted Forest quad-bike ride costs NZ$115 for adults, NZ$90 children 12 to 15. One hour on a two-seater go-cart will set you back NZ$125 for the driver; a second adult passenger pays NZ$125, a passenger aged 3 to 15 pays NZ$70.

SURFING   The main breaks are on **Cobden** and **Blaketown** beaches, both sign-posted about 5 minutes north of central Greymouth, and farther north at **9-Mile Beach.**

WALKING   The **Point Elizabeth Walkway ★★** starts at Rapahoe and follows the coast south around the headland to the Cobden Beach road end. The track takes under 2 hours one-way. If the tide is low, return along the beach. Go in early evening to enjoy one of Greymouth's fabulous sunsets.

   Wild West Adventures (see "Cave Rafting," above) has details on 83 walks within **Te Ara Pounamu ★★★**, the Greenstone Pathway—a spectacular 720km (450-mile) route that has been followed for hundreds of years by Maori traders. Walks range from 30-minute wanders to multiday options; some are guided. **Walks & Drives** (© **03/768-4090**) has a wide range of guided walks from a few hours to several days anywhere on the West Coast or the greater South Island.

WHITE-WATER RAFTING   **Wild West Adventures** (see above) has a wide range of rafting packages that can include trail rides, helicopters, walking, or drinking champagne in natural hot pools surrounded by rainforest. There are three popular Hot Rock options. The 5-hour guided walk, raft, and hot pools trip costs NZ$280 per person. If you include a helicopter ride, the price rises to NZ$545.

ORGANIZED TOURS

Kea Heritage Tours, 152 Golf Links Rd. (© **0800/532-868** in NZ, or 03/768-9292; www.keatours.co.nz), has a number of half- and 1-day tours to the glaciers, Punakaiki, Shantytown, and Blackball. These range in price from NZ$75 per person to NZ$287 per person for the Twin Glaciers and Lake Matheson Tour.

   Off Beat Tours (© **0800/270-960** in NZ, or 03/731-1424; www.offbeattours. co.nz) goes all the way south to the glaciers and all the way north to Karamea and the spectacular Oparara Limestone Arches. Prices range from NZ$105 for a half-day tour to NZ$2,475 for the full-day glacier trip.

   For one of the best-value scenic flights, seek out **Air West Coast ★★★** at Greymouth Airport (© **03/738-0524;** www.airwestcoast.co.nz). The four-seater Cessna 172 takes you all the way down to Milford Sound. It's a full figure-eight trip that also covers the glaciers, Mount Cook, valleys, rivers, forests, and lakes. They also connect with cruise boats at Milford Sound and helicopter flights at Franz Josef to land on the snow. To fly to Mount Cook, the glaciers, Milford, and back to Christchurch (an advantage if you've traveled to Greymouth via the TranzAlpine and need to get back for connecting flights) costs NZ$890 per person (minimum two people). Keep in mind that you'll pay close to that for some of the scenic flights out of Queenstown that are shorter and cover far less territory. A shorter flight to Mount Cook and the glaciers will cost NZ$352 per person, minimum two people.

Where to Stay

Greymouth Seaside Top 10 Holiday Park, 2 Chesterfield St. (www.top10 greymouth.co.nz; © **0800/867-104** in NZ, or 03/768-6618), has tent and caravan sites, cabins, motel units, and a backpacker bunkhouse. Backpackers have some fun choices in the fish-themed **Neptunes,** 43 Gresson St. (www.neptunesbackpackers. net.nz; © **0800/003-768** in NZ, or 03/768-4425), which has a free Jacuzzi; the animal-themed **Noah's Ark Backpackers,** 16 Chapel St. (www.noahs.co.nz; © **0800/662-472** in NZ, or 03/768-4868); and **Global Village Backpackers,** 42–54 Cowper St. (www.globalvillagebackpackers.co.nz; © **03/768-7272**), which has a charming riverside setting and has been completely refurbished with new beds throughout.

All rates given here include the 15% GST and free off-street parking.

Kingsgate Hotel ★ 🍴 This is my choice for the best lodging in Greymouth, but don't get too excited, it's nothing special. It offers tidy, spacious guest rooms with everything you'll need on-site. The six-floor hotel tower contains 42 premium rooms, and seven family suites are available as well. The property is within walking distance of restaurants and attractions; it has a better in-house restaurant than Hotel Ashley. Many tour groups and business travelers frequent the place.

32 Mawhera Quay, P.O. Box 337, Greymouth. www.millenniumhotels.co.nz. © **0800/805-085** in NZ, or 03/768-5085. Fax 03/768-5844. 98 units. NZ$180–NZ$240. Off-peak rates. AE, DC, MC, V. **Amenities:** Restaurant; bar; small gym; nearby golf course; high-speed Internet; 24-hr room service; some Wi-Fi hot spots. *In room:* TV, fridge, hair dryer, minibar.

Rosewood Bed & Breakfast ★ This restored 1920s home is minutes from the town center. Four big bedrooms have en suites. The Mona room upstairs is the nicest and has the best bathroom, although the front room downstairs is very pleasant, with a window seat looking out into the garden. Overall, it's a pleasing, well-located stay.

20 High St., Greymouth. www.rosewoodnz.co.nz. © **0800/185-748** in NZ, or 03/768-4674. Fax 03/768-4694. 4 units. NZ$185–NZ$235. Long-stay & off-peak rates. Rates include breakfast. MC, V. **Amenities:** Free pick-up from TranzAlpine; nearby golf course. *In room:* TV, hair dryer, Wi-Fi.

Where to Eat

Apart from the eateries reviewed below, the restaurants at Quality Kings Hotel and Hotel Ashley also serve good meals. Both veer toward the more formal—or as formal as things get on the West Coast. For good coffee, Internet, and adventure atmosphere, try **dp: one café ★**, 108 Mawhera Quay (℃ **03/768-4005**), which is my pick for the best relaxed cafe environment. If you prefer a less-funky interior, you'll be happier at **Café 124 on Mackay,** 124 Mackay St. (℃ **03/768-7503**), which has reasonable all-day food, but the service is patchy at best. **Jones's Café & Bar,** 37 Tainui St. (℃ **03/768-6468**), is another nice coffee spot with an all-day blackboard menu. For evening and lunchtime dining, **The Coalface,** opposite Greymouth i-SITE, at Mackay and Boundary streets (℃ **03/768-9223**), is the town's newest addition. It has a separate bar, and a very good stone-grill menu. **Trawlers Seafood Restaurant,** 14–16 Tarapuhi St. (℃ **03/768-9254**), has the smartest restaurant interior and good meals, but the service is often hopeless. I'll say it again: Don't expect dining miracles on the West Coast. For pizza try **Friar Tuck Pizza,** 1 Marsden St. (℃ **03/768-066**), or **Bonzai Pizzeria,** 31 Mackay St. (℃ **03/768-4170**).

A Side Trip to Lake Brunner ★★

Lake Brunner and the little township of Moana, situated on its northern shore, lie 30 minutes east of Greymouth. It's a peaceful, scenic diversion serviced by both the TranzAlpine train and a daily shuttle bus—and, I regret to say, great clouds of greedy sand flies that you'll spend time swatting away. Access by road is via Arthur's Pass or Lewis Pass, which makes it a good stopover point if you're heading north or south.

The lake and surrounding rivers have some of the best trout fishing in the South Island. The prime time for fishing is between October and April. The Greymouth i-SITE Visitor Centre has a big list of guides and will point you in the right direction for the best spots. Just make sure you get a license first.

If you find the tranquil nature of this location appealing and you decide to stay over, you'll find a motel complex, a motor camp, and the old **Moana Hotel,** Ahau Street, Moana (www.moanahotelmotel.co.nz; ℃ **03/738-0388**), which offers inexpensive motel/hotel rooms and cabins. If you prefer a more upmarket option, stay at **Lake Brunner Lodge ★★**, Mitchells, RD1, Kumara, Westland (www.lakebrunner. co.nz; ℃/fax **03/738-0163**), on the unpopulated side of the lake. It has 11 rooms and has recently been upgraded. Rates run from NZ$320 to NZ$475, and a five-course dinner costs NZ$120 per person. It's looking very smart, and it's a great hit with fishermen.

Dining out is a little more limited. Your best option is **Stationhouse Café,** 40 Koe St., Moana (℃ **03/738-0158;** www.lakebrunner.net), where pastas, steaks, and roast lamb range from NZ$16 to NZ$30. It's a pretty setting overlooking tiny Moana Railway Station and the lake, but a trifle overpriced and you have to take the service as you find it. It's open daily from 9:30am (10:30am in winter) until late.

En Route to Hokitika

This 45km (28-mile), 30-minute drive south follows the coastline closely along mostly flat farmland. Nothing too inspiring, but there are hints of the Southern Alps that await when you turn away from the Tasman Sea farther south. About 30km (20 miles) from Greymouth, you'll cross the **Arahura River,** where Maori found huge supplies of greenstone.

HOKITIKA: GREENSTONE, GLOWWORMS & GOLD

45km (28 miles) S of Greymouth; 147km (91 miles) N of Franz Josef Glacier

As you drive into the quiet, rather forlorn-looking township of Hokitika, you'll find it hard to believe that it was once a boisterous "Goldfields Capital," where more than 35,000 miners and prospectors patronized more than 102 hotels and kept the dance halls roaring. As many as 80 boats would be docked at the wharves, many of them waiting to transport gold out of the area.

Sadly for Hokitika, the gold supply was finite; when the rush died, so did the wild, carefree days. The economy took a downward turn, and the livelihood of most of today's 3,500 residents is based on farming, forestry, and tourism. But the town is renowned for the Wildfoods Festival, held each March, and it is *the* place to buy crafts on the West Coast. During the summer months, it's probably the cheeriest and busiest of the West Coast towns. It has 1,850 sunshine hours annually and 2,783 millimeters (110 in.) of rainfall—keep your wet-weather gear handy if you're staying for any length of time.

Essentials

GETTING THERE By Plane There is air service via **Air New Zealand Link** (© 0800/737-000 in NZ; www.airnewzealand.co.nz) between Hokitika and Christchurch.

By Train Access to the nearest rail service is in Greymouth (see "Greymouth & Lake Brunner," earlier in this chapter).

By Coach (Bus) InterCity (© 09/623-1503) has daily departures from Hokitika to Nelson, Westport, Greymouth, and Fox Glacier. Both **Magic Travellers** (© 09/358-5600) and **Kiwi Experience** (© 09/366-9830) pass through Hokitika on their way from Greymouth to the glaciers.

By Car Hokitika is reached from the north and south via Highway 6.

VISITOR INFORMATION The **Hokitika i-SITE Visitor Centre,** Carnegie Building, Tancred and Hamilton streets, Hokitika (© 03/755-6166; fax 03/755-

 Wildfoods Festival

If you're in the area around the second Saturday in March, stop in Hokitika for the **Hokitika Wildfoods Festival** ★★★ (© 03/756-9048 or 756-9045; www. wildfoods.co.nz). On the easy side of things, you'll be able to sample wild pig, venison, wild herbs, honey, and fish from local waters; the much braver visitor might like to try possum pâté, wild goat, wriggling grubs, and the unmentionable parts of a variety of animals. The general motto here is close your eyes, swallow, and ask questions later! Admission is NZ$30 for adults, NZ$5 for children, and ticket numbers are limited to 17,000 each year. It's a crazy get-together that will give you a real insight into the quirky character of the West Coast. Not to be missed if you're in the area. *Note:* If you intend to visit during the festival, make sure you book several months ahead, as the town is filled to capacity that weekend.

Bright Lights: Spotting Glowworms for Free

When people talk about the bright lights of Hokitika, they don't mean a dazzling display of neon and inner city activity. It's much more likely that they're referring to the largest outdoor gathering of glowworms in New Zealand. Head north, to the edge of the town, and there, right on the edge of the main road (St. Hwy. 6), is a charm-ing, easily accessed dell that shines bright every evening. The glowworms thrive in the moist atmosphere of the wooded banks. Make sure it's properly dark before you visit, speak quietly, and don't turn on torches (flashlights), or these shy critters will vanish. It's free, quite magical, and well worth the effort of groping your way through darkness.

5011; www.hokitika.org), is open December through April daily from 8:30am to 6pm, May through November Monday through Friday from 8:30am to 5pm, and Saturday and Sunday from 10am to 4pm. Twenty-five minutes south of Hokitika, the **Ross Goldfields Information & Heritage Centre,** 4 Aylmer St., Ross (☎ **03/755-4077;** www.ross.org.nz), is open daily in summer from 9am to 4pm, and in winter from 9am to 3pm. Admission to the **History Museum** is NZ$2 for adults, free for kids. Gold panning costs NZ$11 per person, and gold pan hire is NZ$10 per day.

Note: If you're traveling farther south, Hokitika is the last stop for banks, ATMs, pharmacies, and major supermarkets until you reach Wanaka, 450km (279 miles) away. For more information on this area check www.hokitika.com and www.west landdc.govt.nz.

Exploring Hokitika

To gain insight into the history of this little town, pick up the *Hokitika Heritage Walk* brochure at the visitor center or the West Coast Historical Museum.

The **Hokitika Museum,** Tancred and Hamilton streets (☎ **03/755-6898;** www.hokitikamuseum.co.nz), features reconstructions and artifacts of the 19th-century "alluvial placer" gold-mining era on the West Coast. Wood and slab dwellings display household furnishings. A typical bar, horse-drawn vehicles, mining tools, and pictorial records of the harbor's maritime history are among the wealth of items you'll see. Gold panning is an all-weather attraction in the miner's hut. The museum is open daily from 9:30am to 5pm in summer with reduced winter hours. Admission is NZ$5 for adults, children under 15 are free.

If you're traveling with kids, the **National Kiwi Centre ★**, 64 Tancred St. (☎ **03/755-5251;** www.thenationalkiwicentre.co.nz), is worth a visit. The stars here are the 63 rather repulsive, but nonetheless fascinating, giant eels. The eldest is over 80 years old, and some weigh up to 25 kilograms (55 lb.). Try to visit during their feeding (10am, noon, 3pm), and try a spot of hand-feeding. It also features Australasia's largest tropical aquarium, with an indoor lake, giant trout, birds, reptiles, and, of course, the kiwi. It is open daily from 9am to 5pm (9:30am–4:30pm in winter). Admission is NZ$19 for adults, NZ$11 for children ages 5 to 14, and NZ$48 for families.

West Coast history is riddled with stories about *pounamu,* which is the Maori word for the dark green jade, or greenstone, that is found exclusively in the South Island and especially along the West Coast. Find out about its importance to the local Ngati Waewae people and to the Ngai Tahu tribe generally, at **Te Waipounamu Maori**

Heritage Centre ★★, 39 Weld St. (② 03/755-8304; www.maoriheritage.co.nz). They have excellent displays of local stone (no imports here!) and carved pieces and they'll give you a rundown of local Maori history and the different types of stone favored by Maori. Admission is free.

Take to the water on a Scenic Waterways **Paddle Boat Cruise** ★, Main Road South (② 03/755-7239 or 755-6166; www.paddleboatcruises.com). A dreamy tour down tranquil Mahinapua Creek is just the thing to do on a leisurely afternoon (Jan–Apr daily at 2pm). Keep a look out for the beautiful white herons that may be in residence. The 1½-hour cruises cost NZ$30 for adults, NZ$15 for kids (ages 5–12). The morning cruises departs at 9am and the evening cruise (NZ$35 adults, NZ$20 children) departs at 7pm. Make reservations in advance at the visitor center.

Exploring Lake Kaniere Scenic Reserve ★★★

This beautiful nature reserve, centered on one of the South Island's largest lakes, is just 18km (11 miles) from Hokitika. If you don't have time to stay and explore, there's a lovely 58km (36-mile) circular scenic drive past the lake and back through Kakatahi Valley farmlands.

Lingering, however, will be rewarded by vistas of the lake ringed by unspoiled forests with a backdrop of distant mountains. You'll find an information kiosk and toilets at the landing, where the road first comes to the water's edge. There are picnic tables, fireplaces, and toilets at Sunny Bight. This is also the starting point for two walks: the **Kahikatea Forest Walk** ★, a 10-minute stroll through the forest; and the **Lake Kaniere Walkway** ★★, a 3½-hour trek that features beaches, rainforest, and bird life. Drive on further to the tiny Lake Kaniere holiday settlement to continue the circular route. The nearby, pristine **Hokitika Gorge Scenic Reserve** is well worth visiting. You'll be amazed by the turquoise blue water and the beautiful bush surrounds. Well-defined walking paths and bridges have been built to give you the best photographic views. Pick up advance information and local maps for the walks and the gorge at the visitor center in Hokitika.

Shopping

In peak season, shopping takes on the nature and dimensions of a sport in Hokitika, as the human contents of buses spill out into the vicinity of Tancred Street. All of the following stores are open daily (usually 10am–5pm). At the **Gold Room,** 37 Tancred St. (② 03/755-8362; www.thegoldroom.co.nz), you'll see gold in every form—from raw nuggets and flakes to top-quality crafted jewelry. **Hokitika Craft Gallery,** 25 Tancred St. (② 03/755-7800; www.hokitikacraftgallery.co.nz), features the work of 19 of the West Coast's top artisans under one roof. Look out for contemporary works in fiber, wood, pottery, jade, leather, wool, glass, and bone. My pick is the furniture by top craftsman Marc Zuckerman. **Hokitika Glass Studio,** 28 Tancred St. (② 03/755-7775; www.hokitikaglass.co.nz), is home to more glass penguins than the average person could cope with; but beyond that, there are some stunning glassworks here. Bowls, platters, and gorgeous perfume bottles are my picks. **House of Wood,** 29 Tancred St. (② 03/755-6061), has the best range of handcrafted wooden items. Browse the creative boxes, lovely bowls, and wooden toys. You can also watch wood-turners at work in the studio. **Mountain Jade,** 43 Weld St. (② 03/755-8007; www.mountainjade.co.nz), generally has up to seven carvers at work, and a big selection of excellent-quality jewelry is for sale. Free educational tours are offered daily at 10:30am, 1pm, and 2:30pm. **Westland Greenstone,** 34 Tancred St. (② 03/755-8713), is a good place to see greenstone and *paua* jewelry being made. The showroom has a wide range of the finished products at factory prices.

Where to Stay

Campers will find a good deal at the **Hokitika Holiday Park,** 242 Stafford St. (www.hokitika.com/holidaypark; ✆ **0800/465-436** in NZ, or 03/755-8172). It has tent and caravan sites (NZ$22–NZ$30), cabins (NZ$38–NZ$85), and motel rooms (NZ$90–NZ$100). **Mountain Jade Backpackers,** 41 Weld St. (✆ **0800/838-301** in NZ, or 03/755-8007; fax 03/755-7804), has roomy dorms with beds from NZ$25. **Beachfront Hotel ★,** 111 Revell St. (www.beachfronthotel.co.nz; ✆ **0800/400-344** in NZ, or 03/755-8344; fax 03/755-8258), offers 53 rooms from NZ$205 to NZ$335. I'd opt for the newer Ocean View rooms, which are more modern and better equipped than the older Driftwood rooms. They are also just a few steps from the beach. Further south, between Hokitika and Franz Josef, you'll find **Paramata Lodge ★★**, Bold Head Road (www.paramatalodge.co.nz; ✆ **027/367-2699**), where three beautiful, modern suites look out on untouched native bush and a remote, sandy beach. They're incredibly good value at NZ$325 to NZ$375.

All rates include 15% GST.

Rimu Lodge ★★ 🔥   Peter and Helen Walls have built a real gem on the top of a spur, overlooking bush-clad slopes and the Hokitika River. You'll be hard-pressed to find a more serene and tranquil setting, or better views. Four big suites (two up, two down) will bring an instant smile to your face. They're modern, spacious, and gorgeous. The two upstairs rooms have bigger bathrooms.

33 Seddons Terrace Rd., Hokitika. www.rimulodge.co.nz. ✆ **03/755-5255.** Fax 03/755-5237. 4 units. NZ$295–NZ$375. MC, V. Off-peak rates. Rates include breakfast. Drive south over the Hokitika River Bridge and turn left on Arthurstown Rd.; travel 4km (2½ miles) to a T-junction and turn right; pass Rimu Hotel on the right, go uphill, and Seddons Terrace Rd. is the 1st on your left. No children 11 and under. **Amenities:** Free airport transfers; nearby golf course. *In room:* Hair dryer, fridge, free Wi-Fi.

Teichelmann's Bed & Breakfast ★ 🔥   Brian Ward and Frances Flanagan transformed this iconic Hokitika B&B, making it lighter, brighter, and lovelier. The upstairs Wilson room—creamy and luscious—is my favorite. The sun pours in, and the room has a king-size and larger-than-normal single beds plus a private bathroom. Four other rooms have en suites. If you're lucky, you might be able to nab the cute garden suite with its big Jacuzzi. Overall a terrific stay for the price.

20 Hamilton St., Hokitika. www.teichelmanns.co.nz. ✆ **03/755-8232.** Fax 03/755-8239. 6 units. NZ$225–NZ$260. Off-peak rates. Rates include breakfast. MC, V. Directly opposite the visitor center. No children 9 and under. **Amenities:** Nearby golf course. *In room:* Hair dryer, Wi-Fi.

Where to Eat

Pounamu Kai, 23 Weld St. (✆ **03/755-8581**), serves light lunches, including vegetarian, vegan, and gluten-free fare and some of the best coffee in Hokitika. **Ocean View Restaurant,** in the Beachfront Hotel, 111 Revell St. (✆ **03/755-8344**), is a great spot for balcony dining overlooking the beach. They serve breakfast, lunch, and dinner, and are open from 7am until late; and **Stumpers Bar and Café ★★**, corner of Weld and Revell streets (✆ **0800/788-673;** www.stumpers.co.nz), gets the most local votes for the most consistently good meals. It's open daily from 7am until late.

    Café de Paris ★, 19 Tancred St. (✆ **03/755-8933**), seems like it has been around forever. It provides reasonably good meals; the French owner has always

Okarito is also the only place in the South Island where you can venture into bush at night in the hope of spotting kiwi in their natural habitat. **Okarito Kiwi Tours,** The Strand, Okarito ((✆ **03/753-4330;** www.okarito

kiwitours.co.nz), offers a low-impact, ecominded jaunt into the night bush for NZ$75 per person. Numbers are limited to eight and the tour takes 2 to 3 hours, leaving just before sunset.

swung his menu in favor of things European. When service is not patchy, you'll dine well. They're open daily, 7:30am till late. For tasty treats to eat in or takeaway, visit **Hokitika Cheese & Deli ★**, 84 Revell St. ((✆ **03/755-5432**). They stock an excellent range of imported and local cheeses, fresh and cured meats, and delicious cabinet food for light lunches or picnics; and are open daily from 7:30am. **Eats Café,** 105 Revell St. ((✆ **03/755-8612**), is another good spot for a quick lunch or takeaway picnic fare. They serve all-day breakfasts, gourmet pizza, and a variety of baked goods.

En Route to Franz Josef & Fox Glaciers

There are no banks or ATMs in either glacier village, so remember to get money before going south—you won't be able to do so again until you get to Wanaka, some 450km (280 miles) away. Credit cards are accepted in most places, though. If you're driving nonstop to Wanaka, allow 6 to 7 hours. The drive to Franz Josef from Hokitika takes about 2 hours.

If you're in the **Whataroa** area (35km/22 miles north of Franz Josef) during the November-to-February nesting season of the *kotuku* (white heron), book one of the **White Heron Sanctuary Tours ★★★** ((✆ **0800/523-456** in NZ, or 03/753-4120; www.whiteherontours.co.nz). Entry to the country's only white-heron nesting colony is by permit and starts with a 20-minute jet-boat ride. You then walk through native rainforest accompanied by a guide. The excursion costs NZ$120 for adults, NZ$55 for children 12 and under.

A little farther west, **Okarito Lagoon,** 10km (6 miles) off State Highway 6, is a beautiful spot where **Okarito Nature Tours ★★** ((✆ **03/753-4014;** www.okarito.co.nz) can introduce you to the wonders of New Zealand's largest unmodified wetland—home to over 70 species of birds including the Great White Heron and the Royal Spoonbill. Guided kayak tours have fabulous photo opportunities and are priced from NZ$80 per person. Kayak rental is NZ$45 per person for 2 hours, NZ$65 per person for a full day.

FRANZ JOSEF & FOX GLACIERS ★★★

Franz Josef: 188km (117 miles) S of Greymouth; 24km (15 miles) N of Fox Glacier

It seems improbable that you could find a glacier on a South Pacific island and ice in a temperate rainforest, but that's New Zealand for you—full of surprises. Nowhere else in the world outside arctic regions will you find glaciers just 300m (1,000 ft.) above sea level and just 12km (7½ miles) from the sea.

The two glaciers are just a small part of the 115,000-hectare (284,000-acre) **Westland National Park,** an impressive area of high mountains, glacial lakes, and rushing rivers. The park is popular for tramping, mountain climbing, fishing, canoeing, hunting, and horse trekking. In 1990, the combined Mount Cook/Westland National Parks, Fiordland National Park, Mount Aspiring National Park, and all the significant adjacent natural areas were incorporated into a single vast **Southwest New Zealand World Heritage Area (Te Wahipounamu),** which contains about 10% of New Zealand's total land area, or 2.6 million hectares (6.4 million acres). The World Heritage Highway traverses the northern third of this region and is largely confined to the West Coast side of the Main Divide.

So what are the differences between Franz Josef and Fox glaciers and their townships? Fox Glacier is longer, with better helicopter and walking options; Franz Josef village has a better visitor center and is busier overall, with superior food and lodging options. Just a short distance apart, the drive should nonetheless be undertaken with care.

Essentials

GETTING THERE   By Coach (Bus)   InterCity (✆ 09/623-1503) provides regular transport to the glaciers from north and south. Both **Magic Travellers** (✆ 09/358-5600) and **Kiwi Experience** (✆ 09/366-9830) include the glaciers on their itineraries as well.

By Car   The World Heritage Highway (St. Hwy. 6) follows the coast from Whataroa to Franz Josef Glacier to Fox Glacier to Haast and over the Haast Pass. The Department of Conservation's *World Heritage Highway Guide* suggests places to stop along the way. Roads in this area should always be treated with respect, especially in wet or icy conditions.

GETTING AROUND   I'd be surprised if you can't walk the full length of either village in just 10 minutes. Bike rentals are available in both, and you can travel between the two via InterCity coach.

VISITOR INFORMATION   The **Westland National Park Visitor Centre and i-SITE,** State Highway 6 (✆ 03/752-0796; www.doc.govt.nz), is in the center of the village. Their displays, literature, and activities are essential to a full appreciation of the area; they're open daily in summer 8:30am to 6pm, in winter 8:30am to 5pm. For additional information check www.glaciercountry.co.nz.

Exploring the Glaciers

Ask at the visitor center about the schedule for nature lectures, slide presentations, and guided walks—and see the excellent *Flowing West* movie at the **Alpine Adventure Centre,** Main Street, Franz Josef (✆ 03/752-0793), or at **Fox Heli Services,** Alpine Guides Building, Fox Glacier (✆ 03/751-0866). It runs daily continuously from 10:30am and it will take your breath away.

The visitor center administers the alpine and tramping huts available for overnight hikers, and keeps track of trampers and climbers as well—it is essential to check conditions and register your intentions before setting out. The center's displays give a complete rundown on the formation of glaciers, the movement of ice, the mountains, the history of the region, and more.

Sightseeing at the glaciers can be as costly or as inexpensive as your budget dictates. Several options can put a rather unfriendly hole in your budget, but these are among the most spectacular travel experiences in the world and are therefore worth every cent. If you'd rather, there are plenty of self-guided walks in the area, many of which give good views of the glaciers.

The silence of any fine morning in glacier country is ruptured by the frenetic buzz of **helicopters,** but it's one of the best ways to see and appreciate the natural splendor of this area. Equally amazing are the **guided glacier walk** or the **heli-hike,** which combines both.

The choice of what to do may not turn out to be as agonizing as you think—the weather could very easily decide for you. To say that the weather here is unpredictable is an understatement, and even when it appears fine and sunny on the ground, conditions up on the glacier may preclude a helicopter landing. If your time is short, take the first flight available lest you miss out.

Several operators offer glacier hikes. The **Helicopter Line ★★★** (© 0800/807-767 in NZ, 03/752-0767 in Franz Josef, or 751-0767 in Fox Glacier; www.helicopter.co.nz) is the biggest heli-tourism operator in New Zealand. Its most popular trip is the 30-minute twin glacier option with snow landing for NZ$275. Mention you saw them in Frommer's and you'll get a 10% discount when booking direct. **Glacier Helicopters** (© 0800/800-732 in NZ, 03/752-0755 in Franz Josef, or 751-0803 in Fox Glacier; www.glacierhelicopters.co.nz) has a 30-minute twin glacier trip with an 8- to 10-minute névé landing (atop the glacier) from NZ$270. They also give Frommer's readers a 10% discount when booking direct. **Fox and Franz Josef Heliservices** (© 0800/800-793 in NZ, 03/751-0866 in Fox Glacier, or 752-0793 in Franz Josef; www.scenic-flights.co.nz) also offers a comprehensive range of flights, with a 30-minute flight including a snow landing going for NZ$260; children 5 to 15 are half price. Remember that flight routes and snow landings are always weather dependent and at the pilot's discretion.

Another option that everyone raves about is the **heli-hike ★★★**, which you can do with either the Helicopter Line (see above for contact information) or **Fox Glacier Guiding ★★★** 44 Main Rd., Fox Glacier (© 0800/111-600 in NZ, or 03/751-0825; www.foxguides.co.nz). If you have deep pockets and love adventure, set NZ$399 aside for Fox Glacier Guiding's Flying Fox Helihike. They fly you to a high glacier level to spend 3½ hours exploring spectacular ice formations. The helicopter then returns to pick you up. It's suitable for all fitness levels, but does require some agility.

Less taxing options, like guided glacier walks, are good for families and the less fit. Fox Glacier Guiding (see above) has both half- and full-day options on Fox Glacier. An expert guide will lead the way, chipping steps in the ice for you; you'll go up into the icefall, walk among the crevasses, and listen to the deep-throated grumble of the moving glacier. Hobnailed boots, waterproof parkas, heavy socks, and a walking stick are provided. The Fox Trot Half Day Walk costs NZ$109 for adults, NZ$89 for children (16 and under), or NZ$299 for a family.

Franz Josef Glacier Guides, 6 Main Rd., Franz Josef (© 0800/484-337 in NZ, or 03/752-0763; www.franzjosefglacier.com), offers half-day hikes from NZ$125 for adults and NZ$100 for children 6 to 16; a full-day glacier adventure NZ$180 for adults and NZ$145 for children; glacier valley ecotours from NZ$67 for adults, NZ$52 for kids (no children 5 and under); and heli-hike options from NZ$405. It also has a slower, more informative half-day walk for the less agile.

Last but not least, **Mount Cook Ski Planes ★★** (*©* **0800/368-000** in NZ, 03/752-0714 on the West Coast, or 03/430-8034 at Mount Cook; www.mtcook skiplanes.com) offers a fabulous-value specialist experience. This is New Zealand's only fixed-wing glacier landing, and when you land up on the snow and the engines are switched off, you're in total silence. This makes for a very different experience compared to a helicopter glacier landing. The twin glacier excursion takes 30 minutes and costs NZ$350 for adults, NZ$260 children 5 to 15. The 50-minute Glacier Magic trip costs NZ$435 for adults and NZ$330 for children. This one will give you fantastic close-up views of Aoraki/Mount Cook and Mount Tasman, from both the eastern and western sides of the Southern Alps.

Beyond the Glaciers: What to See & Do

Skydive NZ ★★★ (*©* **0800/751-0080** in NZ, or 03/751-0080; www.skydivingnz. co.nz) takes you up around the side of Mount Cook and over some of the most awesome scenery in the country. Then lucky you gets to jump 2,700m (8,900 ft.) for NZ$300.

Glacier Country Lake Tours ★, 64 Cron St., Franz Josef (*©* **0800/525-386** in NZ, or 03/752-0244; www.ecocruise.co.nz), takes cruises on nearby, mirrorlike Lake Mapourika. Bird-watchers will love this one, as the lake edge is home to some of New Zealand's rarest species. Photographic opportunities abound here, so make sure you have your camera ready. The scenery is beautiful. They operate daily at 9:30am, 11:30am, 1pm, and 3pm all year, with additional cruises at 5pm and 7pm from October through March. The ecocruise costs around NZ$105 for adults, NZ$55 children (4–12), and NZ$2455 for a family.

The West Coast's wet weather is great news for rafters; if you want to see how brave you really are, join **Eco Rafting Adventures ★★**, 15 Stewart St., Ross, north of Franz Josef (*©* **0508/669-675** in NZ, or 03/755-4254; www.ecorafting.co.nz), for an unforgettable day on otherwise inaccessible Grade IV and V rivers. You'll get there by helicopter, and multiday hike and raft options cost NZ$250 to NZ$1,500. They have a fun family rafting and floating adventure for NZ$160 for adults, NZ$130 for children 5 to 15. It's your best chance to get into an untouched wilderness.

Walkers and trampers should stop by either visitor center to collect Department of Conservation material on the numerous tracks in the area. The **Copland Track ★★** is a popular overnight round-trip that provides a glimpse of Westland's spectacular scenery, with the natural hot pools at Welcome Flat an added attraction. Rainfall in the area is high, so come well equipped and always sign in (and out) before undertaking any hike.

Another walk takes you to a **seal colony at Gillespies Beach ★★★**, a 21km (13-mile) drive from Fox village. Take Cook Flat Road–Lake Matheson Road from the village and follow the signs to the beach. The last 11km (7 miles) of the road are unpaved. Allow 3 hours round-trip.

If all this exercise seems positively tedious, why not take a quiet after-dark amble to Fox's mini **glowworm dell?** Wait until it's very dark, and keep quiet. There is a short track just off the main road opposite the BP gas station. There is a small charge for adults, but children enter free. The ultimate way to relax after all this adventure, though, is to soak in divine hot pools at the **Glacier Hot Pools ★★★**, Cron Street,

lake matheson & LAKE MAPOURIKA

Lake Matheson, 5km (3 miles) from Fox Glacier township, shows up on all the postcards, but what the pretty pictures don't show is the wonderful **Lake Matheson Walk ★★**, an easy track around the lake that takes about 1½ hours. You'll enjoy great views of Mount Cook (on the right) and Mount Tasman (to the left), and if you go to the lake before dusk, you can watch the mountains turn pink in the sunset—along with plenty of other sightseers doing exactly the same thing. When the lake and air are still, you'll be able to get one of those famous photographs of the mountains perfectly reflected in the water. **Café Lake Matheson** is at the parking area where the walk starts; it's open daily from 7am to 5pm.

Lake Mapourika, 9km (5½ miles) north of Franz Josef, is the largest lake in Westland National Park and deserves attention for its arresting reflections and setting. You can swim and fish, or opt for a peaceful cruise (see Glacier Country Lake Tours under "Beyond the Glaciers: What to See & Do," above).

Franz Josef (*℮* **0800/044-044** in NZ, or 03/752-0099; www.glacierhotpools.co.nz), set in native rainforest. They have three lovely fern-enclosed public pools, three private pools, and lovely massage facilities; they're open from noon to 10pm (closed Dec 25). Admission to the public pool (for an unlimited duration) is NZ$23 for adults and NZ$17 for children (16 and under). Private pools (for 45 min.) cost NZ$45 per person. Massage rates range from NZ$85 (30 min.) to NZ$185 (1½ hr.).

Where to Stay

During peak season, accommodations are woefully short in these parts. You'll be competing for rooms with lots of tour groups. On top of that, some hotels are overpriced for what they offer. My best advice is to book well ahead or travel outside the summer months; otherwise, you may find yourself staying as far away from the glaciers as Greymouth. You can experience the glaciers without staying overnight in Fox or Franz Josef townships, but the advantage of sleeping here is being close enough to jump on flights when there's a break in the weather.

IN FRANZ JOSEF

The **Franz Josef Top 10 Holiday Park,** Main Road (www.mountainview.co.nz; *℮* **0800/467-897** in NZ, or 03/752-0735), has tent and powered sites, cabins, a lodge, tourist cabins, and flats. **Rainforest Retreat & Backpackers ★**, 46 Cron St. (www.rainforestretreat.co.nz; *℮* **0800/873-346** in NZ, or 03/752-0220), is nestled in native rainforest and provides some lovely, reasonably priced options for travelers on a budget. Another smart new option for a few more dollars is **Glenfern Villas ★**, State Highway 6 (www.glenfern.co.nz; *℮* **0800/453-633** in NZ, or 03/752-0054), where you'll find very comfortable one- and two-bedroom villas with fully equipped kitchens priced from NZ$150 to NZ$266. Plus, they're just a short walk to village shops and cafes. Good, hotel-style B&B digs are at **Franz Josef Glacier Country Retreat,** State Highway 6, Lake Mapourika (www.glacier-retreat.co.nz; *℮* **0800/372-695**), which has 12 rooms for NZ$445, and two suites priced NZ$625 to NZ$650.

The rates provided here include 15% GST and free off-street parking.

Holly Homestead ★★ Gerard and Bernie Oudemans have renovated and extended their gracious 1926 homestead to include five very nice guest rooms with en suites. The superior rooms with king-size beds are more spacious; and the suite has a private lounge. An upstairs deck is perfect for taking in those wonderful southern sunsets, and an overall mood of warmth and hospitality prevails. It's just a few minutes north of the township.

St. Hwy. 6. www.hollyhomestead.co.nz. ✆ **03/752-0299.** Fax 03/752-0298. 4 units. NZ$265–NZ$430. Off-peak rates. Rates include full breakfast. MC, V. No children 11 and under. *In room:* TV, fridge (in suite), hair dryer, Wi-Fi.

Punga Grove Motor Lodge ★★ 🍃 This gorgeous spot surrounded by huge tree ferns and rainforest is also a great value. The seven rainforest studios built in 2003 are the best of all. They have big Jacuzzis and leather furnishings, and look directly into the forest. Among the original units, the two-bedroom suite is especially appealing, with a big kitchen. Four other units have two levels with rooms looking directly into the treetops. They're shady, inviting, and well situated for long stays. The complex is in a quiet location, 150m (500 ft.) from shops and restaurants and just across the road from the Glacier Hot Pools.

40 Cron St., Franz Josef. www.pungagrove.co.nz. ✆ **0800/437-269** in NZ, or 03/752-0001. Fax 03/752-0002. 20 units. NZ$190 standard studio; NZ$250 executive studio; NZ$205 1-bedroom suite; NZ$275 2-bedroom suite. NZ$25 each extra person. Off-peak rates. AE, DC, MC, V. Turn off St. Hwy. 6 to Cowan St., then left to Cron St. Children 11 and under in family units only. **Amenities:** Internet. *In room:* TV, fridge, hair dryer, kitchenette.

Te Waonui Forest Retreat ★★★ 🏨 This hotel, opened in 2009, is located right beside the Glacier Hot Pools (above) and outclasses most other accommodations in the area. The NZ$25-million, ecofriendly, sustainable property has an all-timber construction that blends seamlessly into the native forest and all rooms have restful, natural views. Rooms are simple and uncluttered. The twin rooms have two big beds and all rooms have bright, fresh, big bathrooms. It's an easy walk to the village.

3 Wallace St., Franz Josef. www.tewaonui.co.nz. ✆ **0800/696-963** in NZ, or 03/752-0555. Fax 03/752-0550. 100 units. NZ$769. NZ$179 each extra person. Long-stay & off-peak rates available. Rates include 5-course degustation dinner and breakfast. AE, DC, MC, V. **Amenities:** Restaurant; bar; concierge; Wi-Fi in main reception area. *In room:* A/C, TV, fridge, hair dryer, minibar.

IN FOX GLACIER

Heartland Hotel Glacier Country, State Highway 6 (www.scenichotelgroup. co.nz; ✆ **0800/696-963** in NZ, or 03/751-0847), is the baby of the Scenic Hotel Group. You can expect modest accommodations at affordable prices, often well below the rack rates of NZ$327. Built in the late 1960s, it's right in the heart of the village and is the smaller and older of the two Scenic Hotel Group hotels in Fox Glacier. You'll find new motel rooms at the **Westhaven** (www.thewesthaven.co.nz; ✆ **0800/369-452** in NZ, or 03/751-0084), right in the heart of the action.

Distinction Te Weheka ★ These central accommodations opened in two stages in 2001 and 2002, and provide one of the nicer stays in Fox Glacier. Rooms are spacious with king-size or twin beds and they have balcony views toward the village. Bathrooms are also a decent size and have a bathtub as well as a shower. An upstairs guest lounge and library are for relaxing and there's a sunny dining room for breakfast.

St. Hwy. 6, Fox Glacier. www.distinctionfoxglacier.co.nz. © **0800/313-414** in NZ, or 03/751-0730. Fax 03/751-0731. 20 units. NZ$395. Long-stay & off-peak rates. Rates include breakfast. AE, DC, MC, V. **Amenities:** Bar; babysitting; Internet in lounge. *In room:* Fridge, hair dryer.

Where to Eat
IN FRANZ JOSEF

If you've decided to do your own cooking, head for **Fern Grove Food Centre,** Main Road (© **03/752-0177**), especially for fresh bread and Mrs. Mac's famous meat pies; it's open daily, 7:45am until late. My choice for the best coffee, though, goes to **Full of Beans Café ★**, Main Road (© **03/752-0139**). It's open daily from 7am, and in addition to home-baked cabinet food, they'll also serve you home-style roast meals. Don't expect anything posh, but if you like good organic, free-trade coffee, this is the place. Another good coffee stop is **Aviators Café,** Alpine Adventure Centre, Main Road (© **03/752-0134**), which has the best breakfast in town, and serves beef hot pot, braised lamb shanks, and fish of the day among other menu offerings from 7:30am to 8:30pm daily in summer (until 4pm in winter).

The **Blue Ice Restaurant & Bar ★**, Main Road (© **03/752-0707**), serves pizza, is fully licensed, and gets raves for the best cafe atmosphere in glacier country. It turns into a party venue as the night wears on. **Beeches Café & Bar,** Main Road (© **03/752-0721**), is a more expensive option with reasonably good food, a big wine list, and all-day service. **The Landing ★**, Main Road (© **03/752-0229**), is a popular sports bar serving pizza, snacks, and platters. It's nothing fancy, but service is good (mostly) and it's a good value-for-money option; it's open daily in summer 10am till late, and in winter 4 to 10pm.

IN FOX GLACIER

The **Fox Glacier General Store ★**, Main Road (© **03/751-0829**), sells everything from foodstuffs and hot meat pies to camping supplies, hardware, and boots. It's open daily from 8am till late. **Hobnail Café ★**, Main Road (© **03/751-0005**), right next to the Alpine Guides booking office, has a constant traffic of eager adventurers. It's open for breakfast, lunch, and all-day snacks, and the simple timber-tabled interior is always bustling and sunny. It's open daily from 7:30am to 4pm.

Café Neve ★★, Main Road (© **03/751-0110**), has a terrific range of pizzas along with delicious counter food and dinner dishes such as venison *osso buco* served on a Kumara (sweet potato) mash with steamed vegetables. Another choice is the traditional West Coast whitebait omelet with fresh herbs. It's open from 8am till late and is definitely one of the nicest options. **Matheson Cafe ★**, Lake Matheson Road (© **03/751-0878**), has a fabulous aspect beside the lake, a nice "woody" interior, and great-value light meals. Take a walk around the lake first to work up an appetite. They're open daily from 7:30am until late in summer (from 8am with reduced hours in winter).

Cook Saddle Café and Saloon, Main Road (© **03/751-0700**), is a Tex-Mex favorite with backpackers. It has good ambience in true eclectic West Coast style—a trophy head here, an animal skin there. Venison burgers, Boss Hogg ribs, and Texas T-bone all speak of a slightly displaced sense of geography, but if a full stomach and a good night are your intention, then you've come to the right place. The **Plateau Café & Bar,** corner of Sullivan Street and State Highway 6 (© **03/751-0058**), is a nice spot in the Glowworm Forest Building, open for lunch and dinner daily with homemade baking all day.

En Route to Haast

Just 1 hour south of Fox Glacier (62km/38 miles) is the **Salmon Farm Café,** State Highway 6, South Westland (✆ **03/751-0837**). The menu is predictably "fishy," with both fresh and smoked salmon dishes in abundance. It's open daily from 8am to 4pm, with shorter winter hours. It's a popular stop for tour buses, so try to avoid the main lunch hour or you'll face a long queue. The food here is still fine, but the place is definitely looking a little shabby from the outside and could do with a makeover.

Farther south, the magnificent vistas from the **Knight's Point View Point** are worth a stop to take in sandy coves, bush-clad hillsides, rocky headlands, and ocean views.

Haast itself is 121km (75 miles) south of Fox Glacier. The **South Westland World Heritage Visitor Centre** is at the junction of State Highway 6 and Jackson Bay Road (✆ **03/750-0809;** fax 03/750-0832; www.doc.govt.nz). The center has excellent exhibits on coastal highlights and is open daily from 9am to 4:30pm, May through September (closed 12:30–1pm), and 9am to 6pm October through April (closed Dec 25). The *Edge of Wilderness* movie costs NZ$3 per person.

If you feel like getting some fresh air in your lungs before the long journey further south, join the crew at **Haast River Safari ★★★**, the Red Barn, Haast Junction, SH6 (✆ **03/750-0101;** www.haastriver.co.nz), for a breathtaking exploration of the remote Haast River. The 90-minute tour costs NZ$139 for adults, NZ$99 for children 13 to 16, and NZ$59 for children 5 to 12. It's a leisurely, informative trip (rather than a high-speed adrenalin kick) designed to give you a rare peek into the wilderness backcountry.

En Route to Wanaka

The highway between Haast and Wanaka is magnificent, moss-covered, and often misty. It follows the course of the Haast River for much of the way. High peaks rise up on either side of the road. The route took 40 years to build and is 563m (1,847 ft.) above sea level. The Department of Conservation has created many walks along the way. Traveling nonstop, the trip to Wanaka should take 2 to 3 hours. Be prepared to make camera stops along the way of stunning waterfalls and river views.

En Route to Queenstown

Highway 6 is good traveling all the way to Wanaka. From there, the trip to Queenstown will take around 1½ hours. You drive around the edge of Lake Dunstan, which was formed behind the Clyde Dam. Bypassing Cromwell township, you then travel through the stone fruit orchards of the Cromwell area. After passing through the Kawarau River Gorge, you come into Gibbston Valley and on into Queenstown.

If you're a competent driver, you could also go to Queenstown via the Crown Range. It's unsuitable for caravans and can be slippery and icy in winter, but the views from the top are stunning, and it's 30 minutes shorter than State Highway 6. If you are crossing the Crown Range in winter, it is now a legal requirement to carry chains. If you don't have them, expect a NZ$200 fine. They are available for hire from most gas stations in the Wanaka/Queenstown area.

QUEENSTOWN & ENVIRONS

Queenstown and the southwestern section of the South Island hold some of New Zealand's greatest natural beauty. At its heart, the Fiordland National Park is but a small portion of Te Wahipounamu, the South West New Zealand World Heritage Area—2.6 million hectares (6.4 million acres) that make up about 10% of New Zealand's total landmass. The area gives a whole new meaning to the word "wilderness," and in one tiny corner, the hip and hedonistic alpine resort of **Queenstown** acts as the gateway.

Things to Do   Step out into this vast paradise on one of the world-famous tracks—the **Milford, Routeburn,** or the **Hollyford.** Explore the dramatic lake and landscapes of nearby **Wanaka;** or cruise across **Milford Sound** described by Rudyard Kipling as the eighth wonder of the world. Adrenalin junkies can bungy in three different **A. J. Hackett** locations, **jet-boat** up the **Shotover River** or remote reaches of the **Dart River,** or paraglide off **Queenstown Hill.** Keen photographers have a snap-worthy view in any direction; and winter skiers will be in heaven with five major ski and snowboarding fields to choose from.

Eating & Drinking   Start the night with a cocktail at the oh-so classy **Eichardt's House Bar;** discover the tucked-away culinary heaven that is **The Bunker;** or dine on the finest New Zealand meats at **Botswana Butchery.** Visit one of the hundred or so **Central Otago vineyards** for lunch and wine tasting; or let the helicopter team at **Over the Top** whisk you to the top of a remote mountain for a champagne picnic. There's something for every foodie's fancy in Queenstown.

Shopping   Stock up on fine New Zealand–made **woolen clothing,** try on **leather jackets** in Queenstown and Wanaka, or select contemporary **New Zealand jewelry** to take home. Wander the brick lanes for duty-free goods; or spend a morning ambling along the historic main street of nearby **Arrowtown,** where you can buy gold and top-quality outdoor and leisurewear.

Nightlife & Entertainment   **Queenstown** puts the life into nightlife, especially during the winter ski season when it turns into a cosmopolitan "party central." Take a bet at one of two casinos, or dance the night away in a chic club. There are classy wine bars for unwinding with a glass of

Central Otago pinot noir and brew bars where you can enjoy a well-earned local ale overlooking **Lake Wanaka** or **Lake Wakatipu** in Queenstown.

WANAKA: GATEWAY TO MOUNT ASPIRING NATIONAL PARK ★★

145km (90 miles) S of Haast; 117km (73 miles) N of Queenstown

Either you warm to Wanaka (pop. 7,000), or you don't. It's often seen as a very quiet, less self-important version of Queenstown, or to put it another way, Queenstown, circa 25 years ago. Often overlooked by visitors on the move between the West Coast and Queenstown, Wanaka is the perfect place to spend a couple of days recharging. There has been a huge amount of growth in the town in the last 10 years, with much-needed new accommodations, restaurants, shops, and tourism operators opening for business.

And one last key thing to remember about Wanaka, which is often overlooked in favor of Queenstown in relation to Milford Sound: If you plan to fly to Milford, keep in mind that if you fly from Wanaka instead of Queenstown, you will get a longer flight over a different route—one that takes in great swaths of the Mount Aspiring National Park, not seen on the Queenstown flights.

Lake Wanaka Tourism is another of the six members of the government's Environmentally Sustainable Tourism Project. Sustainable Wanaka has over 65 registered charter members in accommodations, retail, transportation, and activity businesses. Check www.sustainablewanaka.co.nz for charter member listings.

Essentials

GETTING THERE   By Plane   Air New Zealand (✆ **0800/737-000** in NZ; www.airnewzealand.co.nz) provides daily service from Christchurch. **Aspiring Air** (✆ **0800/100-943** in NZ, or 03/443-7943; www.aspiringair.com) has three flights a day from Queenstown.

By Coach (Bus)   InterCity (✆ **09/623-1503**) provides coach service linking Wanaka to the West Coast, Christchurch, Dunedin, Mount Cook, Queenstown, Te Anau, and Milford Sound. **Kiwi Experience** (✆ **09/366-9830**) and **Magic Travellers** (✆ **09/358-5600**) both include Wanaka on their routes. **Wanaka Connexions** (✆ **0800/244-844** in NZ, or 03/477-2224; www.time2.co.nz) runs between Wanaka and Queenstown several times a day, and also has a daily service to Invercargill, Dunedin, and Christchurch.

By Car   Wanaka is reached via the Haast Pass from the West Coast. It's a 4-hour drive from the glaciers. State Highway 6 connects it to Cromwell and Queenstown, 1½ hours to the south. State Highway 89, the Cardrona Road over the Crown Range, is a more direct and impressive route that takes around 1 hour (if you stop to admire the views). Once narrow, winding, and treacherous, it's now fully paved and is, in fact, the highest tar-sealed road in Australasia. Keep in mind that if you travel the Crown Range Road in winter, you are now legally required to carry chains (available for hire from service stations). If you're caught without them, you'll get a NZ$200 fine. Wanaka is a 5-hour drive from Christchurch and 3½ hours from both Dunedin and Te Anau.

Lake Wanaka

0 —————— 1/2 mi
0 —————— 1/2 km

Lake   Wanaka

Eely Point Rec. Res.
Eely Point Rd.
17
Winders St.
Beacon Point Rd.
Matai Rd.
Totara Terr.
Kings Dr.
Aubrey Rd.
Plantation Rd.
Anderson Rd.
Lakeside Rd.
Lismore Rec. Res.
Lismore St.
Hedditch St.
84
18
14
Roys   Bay
17 **12**
15 **16**
Stratford Terr.
Ballantyne Rd.
Ardmore St.
9 **10** **12**
13
Hewick St.
Pembroke Park
Brownston St.
8
Dungarvon St.
19
Bills Wy.
1
2 **3**
Roys Bay Rec. Res.
Sargood Dr.
Old Station Ave.
Wanaka - Mount Aspiring Rd.
Stonebrook Dr.
Wanaka Recreation Reserve
Upton St.
McDougal St.
Warren St.
Roche St.
Tenby St.
Golf Course Rd.
7
Cem.
Meadowstone Dr.
Stone St.
Faulks Terr.
Studholme Rd.
6
5
Cardrona Valley Rd.
Orchard Rd.
4

HOTELS ■
Edgewater Resort **2**
Glendhu Bay Lakeside Holiday
 Park **1**
Lime Tree Lodge **19**
Maple Lodge **18**
Minaret Lodge **17**
Mountain Range **6**
Riverrun **18**
Te Wanaka Lodge **15**
Waiorau Homestead **4**
Wanaka Cottages **5**
Wanaka Top 10 Holiday Park **1**
Whare Kea Lodge **1**
YHA Wanaka Purple Cow **8**

RESTAURANTS ◆
Ardmore Street Food
 Company **9**
Botswana Butchery **16**
Café Gusto **14**
The Cow **16**
Kai Whakapai Café & Bar **10**
The Landing **14**
Relishes Café **12**
Ritual Espresso **13**
Sapphire **7**
Sargoods Restaurant **3**
Sasanoki Japanese Kitchen **11**

NORTH ISLAND
Auckland
SOUTH ISLAND
Wellington
Christchurch
Wanaka
Dunedin

15

QUEENSTOWN & ENVIRONS | Wanaka & Mount Aspiring National Park

VISITOR INFORMATION The **Lake Wanaka i-SITE Visitor Centre,** 100 Ardmore Rd., is in the log cabin on the lakefront (✆ **03/443-1233;** fax 03/443-1290; www.lakewanaka.co.nz). It's open daily May to mid-September from 8:30am to 5pm, mid-September through April from 8:30am to 6pm (closed Dec 25). The **Department of Conservation (DOC),** Ardmore Street and Ballantyne Road (✆ **03/443-7660;** fax 03/443-8777; www.doc.govt.nz), provides information on Mount Aspiring National Park and all DOC tracks in the area. The visitor center is open November through mid-April daily from 8am to 5pm, and in winter Monday through Friday from 8:30am to 5pm, Saturday from 9:30am to 4pm (closed Sun and noon–12:30pm daily).

[FastFACTS] WANAKA

The fastest and cheapest Internet access is offered by **Dub Dub Dub,** corner of Helwick and Brownston streets (✆ **03/443-7078**). **Wanaka Internet,** upstairs, 3 Helwick St. (✆ **03/443-7429;** www.wanakainternet.co.nz), is another very good option. For medical matters, go to **Wanaka Medical Centre,** 21 Russell St. (✆ **03/443-7811**). The **Post Office,** Ardmore Street, as you drive into Wanaka (✆ **03/443-8211**), is open 8:30am to 5pm, Monday through Friday.

SPECIAL EVENTS Wanaka Rodeo (✆ 03/443-7736) is held in early January. **Rippon Open-Air Music Festival** (✆ **03/443-1833;** www.ripponfestival.co.nz) is a biennial open-air music festival in a vineyard in early February; the next festivals are in 2012 and 2014. April's **Warbirds Over Wanaka International Air Show** (www.warbirdsoverwanaka.com) combines classic vintage and veteran aircraft, machinery, fire engines, and tractors with dynamic Air Force displays and aerobatic teams in the natural amphitheater of the Upper Clutha Basin. It's one of the top four Warbirds Air Shows in the world and is held every second Easter in even-numbered years. The next show is Easter 2012 (Apr 6–8). The biennial **Festival of Colour** (www.festivalofcolour.co.nz), held in autumn in odd-numbered years, promises 5 days of intense arts, dance, theater, and music. The next festival will be held April 16–21, 2013. There are also numerous ski festivals during winter; the visitor center has details.

Exploring Wanaka

There's fun to be had at **Stuart Landsborough's Puzzling World** ★★, on State Highway 89, 2km (1¼ miles) from Wanaka (✆ **03/443-7489;** www.puzzlingworld.co.nz). Since 1973, Stuart Landsborough (aka Professor Puzzle) has drawn thousands of visitors to the confusing passageways of his elaborate Great Maze. The crazy Tilted House and Leaning Clock Tower will further test your perceptions. Admission to both the Great Maze and the Illusion Rooms is NZ$15 for adults and NZ$10 for children ages 5 to 15; it's open daily from 8:30am to 5:30pm (until 6pm in summer). Allow 1 to 2 hours for your visit.

At time of writing, the New Zealand Fighter Pilots' Museum, home to the largest collection of flyable World War II fighter planes in the Southern Hemisphere, was in the middle of a NZ$10-million redevelopment program. What emerged in late 2011 was the outstanding Warbirds & Wheels ★★★ (✆ 0800/927-247; www.warbirdsandwheels.nz), which maintains the fine collection of warbirds aircraft, and also features classic cars, a retro diner, and more. The museum is open 9am to 50m daily (closed Dec 25); admission is NZ$20 adults; NZ$15 seniors and students; NZ$5 ages 5 to 15; and NZ$45 for families.

Get real local flavor at **Cinema Para-diso ★★★**, 1 Ardmore St. (☏ 03/443-1505; www.paradiso.net.nz), Wanaka's only movie theater, and the wackiest place in town. Seats take the form of old sofas and cushions in the aisles, and a Morris Minor car has been installed for a drive-in feel. You'll get a personalized, off-the-wall introduction from the owner, and there's a 30-minute intermission for quick cafe meals—and yes, they will hold the movie until you're finished eating. Showtimes are at 6 and 8:30pm daily; admission is NZ$15 for adults, NZ$10 for children.

Take a break at **Wanaka Beerworks ★**, State Highway 6 (☏ **0800/273-9754** in NZ, or 03/443-1865; www.wanakabeerworks.co.nz), which is wedged between two museums. This little boutique brewery with a cozy bar and tasting room is open daily from 9am until 4pm; tours and tastings are offered daily at 2pm.

Rippon Vineyard ★★★, Mount Aspiring Road (☏ **03/443-8084**; www.rippon.co.nz), was established by Rolfe and Lois Mills, pioneer grape-growers in Central Otago, and their vineyard location overlooking Lake Wanaka is simply stunning. It's open daily for free tastings and sales (Dec–Apr 11:30am–5pm and July–Nov 1:30–5:30pm).

Organized Tours

Camera buffs will enjoy an outing with photographer and naturalist Gilbert van Reenen of **Clean Green Phototours,** 641 Ballantyne Rd., Wanaka (☏ **03/443-7951;** www.cleangreen.co.nz), who will tailor a photographic expedition to suit your interests. You'll pay from NZ$350 per person for a 2-hour tour for up to three people. For some of the most dramatic landscapes and photographic opportunities, join **Ridgeline Adventures ★★**, Wanaka (☏ **0800/234-000** in NZ; www.ridgelinenz.com), which will take you up into the high country surrounding Lake Wanaka. Their Nature Tour will cost NZ$350 for adults and NZ$220 for kids ages 5 to 15. You'll be taken into the hills by 4WD transport and there's a short walk before you enjoy the views, good coffee, and tasty treats. Wine lovers can explore some of Central Otago's premier wineries with **Wanaka Wine Tours** (☏ **027/534-8388**; www.wanaka winetours.com); a full-day tour visits a number of wineries and includes a winery lunch. It runs daily from 10am to 4:30pm and costs NZ$235 per person.

Outdoor Pursuits

CANYONING Contact **Deep Canyon** (☏ **03/443-7922;** www.deepcanyon.co.nz), pioneers of the sport in New Zealand. You'll get a tobogganing, rappelling, and swimming adventure guaranteed to thrill. The 7½-hour Niger Stream adventure costs NZ$240 and includes lunch. Deep Canyon operates November through April and offers a range of day trips, including an introduction to rock climbing, which costs NZ$210 for a full day, NZ$125 for half-day.

CLIMBING There's a lot of excellent, stable climbing in the area. **Wanaka Rock Climbing,** 7 Apollo Place St. (☏ **03/443-6411;** www.wanakarock.co.nz), can introduce you to all the best places. You'll pay from NZ$120 for a range of options.

ECORAFTING This is an easy adventure for less active people. It's all about learning as you paddle, and guides will enlighten you about flora and fauna along the way. From September to April, **Pioneer Rafting** ★★ (✆ **03/443-1246;** www.ecoraft.co.nz) conducts half- and full-day excursions down the Upper Clutha. This is not white-water rafting, and the trip is suitable for all ages. A half-day trip costs NZ$135 for adults and NZ$75 for children ages 5 to 15 (no kids age 4 and under).

FISHING   Opportunities abound in the Wanaka area, with plenty of guides operating on the rivers and lakes. **Lakeland Adventures** (✆ **0508/525-352** in NZ, or 03/443-7495; www.lakelandadventures.co.nz) charges from NZ$330 for guided trout fishing for three people. **Southern Lakes Fishing Safaris** (✆/fax **03/443-9121;** www.southernlakesfishing.co.nz) specializes in fly-fishing for all levels of experience and charges from NZ$675 for a full day for one to two people. **Eco Wanaka Adventures** (✆ **0800/926-326** in NZ, or 03/443-2869; www.ecowanaka.co.nz), offers a 3-hour boat fishing excursion from 9am (NZ$195 for adults; NZ$125 for children under 15).

FLYING   **Aspiring Air** (✆ **0800/100-943** in NZ, or 03/443-7943; www.nz-flights.com) offers a variety of scenic flights in the Mount Aspiring area from NZ$185 per person. Their Milford Sound flight with included boat cruise costs NZ$445 for adults and NZ$300 for children ages 3 to 13. **Alpine Helicopters** (✆ **03/443-4000;** www.alpineheli.co.nz) can give you a scenic flight over Wanaka for NZ$185 per person; and **Aspiring Helicopters,** Cattle Flat Station (✆ **03/443-7152;** www.aspiringhelicopters.co.nz), has a 50-minute Mount Aspiring and Glacier trip with snow landing for NZ$420. **Southern Alps Air,** 48 Helwick St. (✆ **0800/345-666** in NZ), has an excellent range of options from short flights at NZ$99 to a Milford Sound flight-and-cruise option for NZ$450 for adults and NZ$275 for children 5 to 15. All passengers get a window seat for superb views over glaciers, snowcapped mountains, rivers, forests, and national parks.

GOLF   **Wanaka Golf Club,** Ballantyne Road (✆ **03/443-7888;** www.wanakagolf.co.nz), is a challenging 18-hole course with astounding views. There is a well-stocked pro shop and it costs NZ$60 for 18 holes or NZ$40 for 9 holes.

JET-BOATING   The best jet-boating is with **Wilkin River Jets** ★★★, State Highway 6, Makarora (✆/fax **03/443-8351;** www.wilkinriverjets.co.nz), between Fox Glacier and Wanaka. Locals say it's better than the much-lauded Dart River experience at Glenorchy, near Queenstown. Priced at NZ$98 for 1 hour, it's also cheaper and offers a mix of thrill riding and the softer approach, so you get a good feel for this remote region. They also offer combo packages that include a helicopter flight, bush walk, and river jet from NZ$359 per person. **Wanaka River Journeys** ★★ (✆ **0800/544-555** in NZ, or 03/443-4416; www.wanakariverjourneys.co.nz) explores the braided Matukituki River and includes a wilderness walk into native beech forest to a waterfall. You have the option of being met at the top of the river by helicopter for a flight into Mount Aspiring's magnificent glacial areas. The river journey with a wilderness walk is NZ$255 for adults, NZ$165 for children 15 and under; the jet/heli combo is NZ$585 for adults, NZ$355 children 15 and under.

KAYAKING   **Alpine Kayak Guides,** 119 Main Rd., Luggate (✆ **03/443-9023;** www.alpinekayaks.co.nz), offers half- and full-day trips on three rivers, ranging in difficulty from beginner to experienced. Trips last 5 to 8 hours and run daily from November to April. Costs start at NZ$155 for adults, NZ$95 for children 14 and over, and include equipment, lessons, and lunch. For NZ$15 an hour, you can rent single or double kayaks for a lake paddle from **Lakeland Adventures** (✆ **03/443-7495**).

MOUNTAIN BIKING   The Department of Conservation's leaflet on bike trails in the Wanaka area is available from its office at Ardmore Street and Ballantyne Road

(📞 **03/443-7660**). Mountain bikes can be rented from **Racer's Edge/Mountain Bikes Unlimited,** 99 Ardmore St. (📞 **03/443-7882;** www.racersedge.co.nz), for NZ$65 for adults per day; kids' bikes start at NZ$30 per day. Good bikes are also available from **Lakeland Adventures** (📞 **03/443-7495**), next door to the information center, for NZ$15 per hour, or NZ$30 for a half-day; and there are excellent (and easy) biking tracks around the lake.

QUAD BIKES For rugged outdoor fun, **Cardrona Adventure Park ★** (📞 **0800/102-122** in NZ, or 03/443-6363; www.adventurepark.co.nz) offers tours on four-wheel all-terrain quad bikes priced from NZ$185 for a 2-hour tour. You must be at least 16 and have a driver's license. They also have a crazy range of monster trucks that you can ride in or drive, plus go-karts and shorter quad bike rides.

SKIING **Cardrona Ski Field** is 40 minutes from Wanaka on State Highway 89. The more challenging **Treble Cone Ski Field** is also 40 minutes away. In addition, you'll find cross-country skiing and heli-skiing in the Harris Mountains. And for Nordic skiing, head to the **Waiorau Snow Farm,** in the Cardrona Valley. For further information on all ski fields in this area, see chapter 4.

WALKING Walking opportunities in Mount Aspiring National Park vary from easy strolls through lowland forest to tramps on mountain tracks that may take several days. Brochures and information can be obtained from the Department of Conservation office. **Eco Wanaka Adventures ★★**, 5 Rimu Lane (📞 **0800/926-326** in NZ, or 03/443-2869; www.ecowanaka.co.nz), has a full-day guided Rob Roy Glacier Valley Trek priced from NZ$255 for adults and NZ$175 for children 15 and under. At **Diamond Lake,** 20 minutes from town, you'll find the Diamond Lake and Rocky Mountain Track, which takes 1½ hours from the carpark to the summit. For a more remote walk, call **Siberia Experience ★★★** (📞 **0800/345-666** in NZ, or 03/443-4385; www.siberiaexperience.co.nz), which offers a combo of scenic flight, jet boat, and a 3-hour walk in remote beech forests for NZ$347 for adults, NZ$285 for children ages 3 to 13. Their guided experiences are unique and some of the best in the region. Just make sure you take plenty of insect repellent to keep the notoriously greedy sand flies at bay! Fit, adventurous travelers might like to be tested by a remote wilderness experience with **Wild Walks ★★**, Level 1, 99 Ardmore St. (📞 **03/443-9422;** www.wildwalks.co.nz). Their specialist mountain guides take just five people maximum into remote backcountry locations. Their 3-day Mt. Aspiring Discovery costs from NZ$940 per person; or if you're very fit, you can tackle New Zealand's longest guided trekking adventure, the 8-day Gillespie–Rabbit Pass Traverse for NZ$2,450 per person.

But if all you really want is a light amble, follow my footsteps around the lovely, tree-covered tracks of the lake. Start at the information center and simply follow your nose. Even if you don't exert yourself, it will leave your conscience clear for dinner.

Where to Stay

If you're looking for accommodations with style and character, you'll definitely find them in the Wanaka area. There has been a lot of development in the township itself, especially around the lake edge. Quality lodges and bed-and-breakfasts are increasing in numbers, and you won't be short of a good stop here, but you will need to book well ahead if you're planning to stay between November and March. Wanaka is a favorite playground for New Zealanders.

All rates quoted include the 15% GST and free off-street parking unless otherwise noted.

VERY EXPENSIVE

Whare Kea Lodge ★★★ 🎁 Tucked away from the public eye, Whare Kea offers style and luxury at its most sublime. Walk through the door and you'll be overwhelmed by one of the most remarkable residential views in the country. This monster of a house has huge bedrooms with verandas, deep bathtubs, dual-sided showers, and top-quality furnishings. A classy hideaway for those who like to indulge. As an added bonus, they have a fabulous alpine chalet in the heart of the Southern Alps, accessible only by helicopter. The chalet accommodates six, but all facilities are shared with a qualified mountain guide and staff member; access is weather dependent. The property also boasts a Relais & Châteaux Environmental Award.

494 Mount Aspiring Rd., Wanaka. www.wharekealodge.com. 🕻 **03/443-1400.** 6 units, 1 chalet. NZ$1,610 deluxe; NZ$1,955 master suite; NZ$6,500–NZ$7,500 chalet. Lodge rates include breakfast, dinner, and use of all facilities; chalet rates include helicopter and mountain guide. AE, DC, MC, V. Follow signs on Mount Aspiring Rd., 5 min. west of Wanaka township. No children 13 and under. Closed June. **Amenities:** Bar; charged airport transfers; bike rentals; nearby golf course; limited room service; Jacuzzi. *In room:* TV, fridge, hair dryer, minibar, Wi-Fi.

EXPENSIVE

Wanaka Cottages ★★, 11 Orchard Rd. (www.wanakacottages.co.nz; 🕻 **0800/292-6252** in NZ), offer a luxurious four-bedroom house and a two-bedroom cottage in a new residential suburb for NZ$525 and NZ$395, respectively. They're a short drive from the township and just a block from the golf course. **Lime Tree Lodge ★★★**, Ballantyne Road, RD2, Wanaka (www.limetreelodge.co.nz; 🕻 **03/443-7305**), is a gorgeous spot with six beautiful suites that range in price from NZ$495 to NZ$695. It's set on 4 hectares (10 acres) just outside of Wanaka, and you'll be spoiled rotten here with gorgeous meals based on organic garden produce (dinner NZ$150 per person). They are charter members of Sustainable Wanaka.

Minaret Lodge ★★ 🎁 Open since 2002, this smart B&B is full of surprises (and that includes a *Lord of the Rings* room) and exceeds all expectations. The dining and living room facilities are contained within a stylishly renovated home in a peaceful residential neighborhood, and three purpose-built chalets are set in a .8-hectare (2-acre) garden with an attractive spa and sauna complex a short stroll across the lawn. Chalet beds are big and bathrooms are well appointed—the suite chalet is the biggest and includes a tastefully finished lounge and en-suite bathroom with both tub and shower. There is a greater sense of privacy here than at other similarly priced B&B options in Wanaka. The property plays an active role in sustainable tourism and is a charter member of Sustainable Wanaka.

34 Eely Point Rd., Wanaka. www.minaretlodge.co.nz. 🕻 **03/443-1856.** Fax 03/443-1856. 5 units. NZ$395–NZ$565. Rates include pre-dinner drinks and full gourmet breakfast. Long-stay & off-peak rates. AE, MC, V. **Amenities:** Free transfers from Wanaka Airport; babysitting; free use of bikes; nearby golf course; Jacuzzi; sauna; all-weather tennis court. *In room:* TV/DVD/CD, fridge, hair dryer, minibar, Wi-Fi.

Riverrun ★★★ 🌱 When you see the facilities at the environmentally aware Riverrun, you'll know you've got one of the best lodge deals in the country. John Pawson and Meg Taylor have built with imagination and flair: Everything smacks of originality and every room is arranged with comfort in mind. You'll find generous beds, fine linens, and superb marble bathrooms. John and Meg are outdoors types who love mountaineering and climbing, and John also tends their 170-hectare (420-acre) mixed farm that borders the Clutha River; they will make certain you have everything you need, and for yet one more incentive—Meg is a superb chef.

Halliday Rd., RD2, Wanaka. www.riverrun.co.nz. © **03/443-9049.** Fax 03/443-8454. 5 units. NZ$380–NZ$525. Dinner by arrangement. Long-stay rates and winter packages during ski season. AE, MC, V. 6-min. drive east of central Wanaka. Turn off St. Hwy. 6 to Halliday Rd.; continue to stone gates and drive through to Riverrun. No children 8 and under. **Amenities:** Bar; free use of bikes; outdoor Jacuzzi. *In room:* TV/DVD, fridge, hair dryer, Wi-Fi.

MODERATE

Te Wanaka Lodge, 23 Brownston St. (www.tewanaka.co.nz; © **03/443-9224**), is a small boutique hotel with 13 rooms and lots of charm. Rooms are a great value at NZ$215 to NZ$245, and if you get in quick, you might be able to score the garden cottage for a little more privacy.

Edgewater Resort ★★ 🏊 Situated right on the shores of Lake Wanaka, this Green Globe affiliate and Sustainable Wanaka charter member property is a favorite with New Zealanders who like resort-style accommodations. There's a welcoming atmosphere here and style tends toward that of a high-country fishing lodge. All the one- or two-bedroom suites, which have been extensively upgraded recently, offer balconies or terraces. In short, it's a friendly, comfortable 25-year-old development that has aged well and oozes Kiwi atmosphere, and its Sargoods Restaurant (p. 406) can't be beat for international cuisine. If you're after space and value, go for the one-bedroom suites, which have bigger bathrooms with double tubs.

Sargood Dr., P.O. Box 61, Wanaka. www.edgewater.co.nz. © **0800/108-311** in NZ, or 03/443-8311. Fax 03/443-8323. 104 units. NZ$245–NZ$525. Package deals, long-stay, and off-peak rates. AE, DC, MC, V. 20-min. stroll to town center. **Amenities:** 2 restaurants; bar; free transfers from Wanaka Airport (book when making reservations); babysitting; bike rentals; children's playground; concierge; nearby golf course and 9-hole putting green on-site; 2 Jacuzzi; limited room service; sauna; 2 all-weather tennis courts; kayaks hire. *In room:* LCD TV, hair dryer, kitchens or kitchenettes, minibar on request, Wi-Fi.

Maple Lodge ★★ 🏊 Paul and Bernadette Raymont's purpose-built, Qualmark Enviro-Gold-rated lodge is set amid a 2.8-hectare (7-acre) maple tree plantation 4 minutes from Wanaka. Seven modern suites open onto private balconies or patios; and heated floors, de-misting mirrors, great views, and big beds are indicative of the attention to detail. All rooms are in a separate wing of the house, and a large guest lounge and library is the meeting spot for pre-dinner drinks and afternoon tea. This is a great-value that definitely deserves a 2-night stay minimum. They are also charter members of Sustainable Wanaka.

56 Halliday Rd., Wanaka. www.maplelodgewanaka.co.nz. © **03/443-6275.** 7 units. NZ$295–NZ$335. Off-peak rates. AE, MC, V. **Amenities:** Free Wanaka airport transfers; nearby golf course; Jacuzzi. *In room:* A/C, TV/DVD/CD, hair dryer, Wi-Fi (in suites).

Mountain Range ★ If you want breathtaking views of three mountain ranges, peace and quiet, and spacious rooms with beautiful bathrooms, Mountain Range delivers. Mel and Stuart Pinfold are terrific young hosts, and they go out of their way to make you comfortable. They're newer to the game than Wanaka Springs (and their rooms are bigger), but there's a sense of understated service and comfort that makes them one of my favorite Wanaka spots. Ask for the McKerrow room if you want a giant bathtub, or the loft room for coziness and great views. They have a Qualmark Enviro-Bronze rating for environmental friendliness.

Heritage Park, Cardrona Valley Rd., Wanaka. www.mountainrange.co.nz. © **03/443-7400.** Fax 03/443-7450. 7 units. NZ$320–NZ$355. Long-stay, off-peak, and special deals. Rates include breakfast. MC, V. Just off Cardona Valley Rd., 2km (1¼ miles) outside Wanaka. No children 10 and under. May close

May–June. **Amenities:** Free transfers from Wanaka Airport; free use of bikes; nearby golf course; outdoor Jacuzzi. *In room:* TV/DVD, hair dryer, free Wi-Fi.

Waiorau Homestead ★★ 🏠 This gorgeous old homestead, tucked into an idyllic rural setting near Cardrona Alpine Resort, has had a modern makeover that attends to every traveler's needs. Blyth Adams (a chef) and Anne Lockhart offer four large, beautifully appointed guest rooms (three with en-suite bathroom; one with access to a private bathroom). The room with the private bathroom is the largest; and the separate smaller room right beside the swimming pool is the most fun. They are 20 minutes from Wanaka, but once you get here you won't want to leave anyway—especially once you sit down to one of Blyth's meals. It's farther out than Riverrun or Maple Lodge and has a more intimate B&B atmosphere.

2127B Cardona Valley Rd., Wanaka. www.waiorauhomestead.co.nz. ☏ **03/443-2225.** 4 units. NZ$320–NZ$350. Extra person NZ$70. Long-stay and off-peak rates. Dinner by arrangement. MC, V. Take Cardona Valley Rd. from Wanaka. Approx. 20 min. on, turn left into Snow Farm Rd. Turn right immediately and follow yellow signs. The homestead driveway is 300m (984 ft.) ahead on your left, just before the farm buildings. **Amenities:** Transfers to Queenstown and Wanaka airports (fee); babysitting; free use of bikes; outdoor Jacuzzi; outdoor heated pool. *In room:* TV/DVD/CD, hair dryer, Wi-Fi.

Wanaka Springs ★ Wanaka Springs is a purpose-built lodge on a quiet residential street. Rooms here envelop you in warmth and rich color, and garden views (with decks) add a restful quality. Bathrooms are big and modern, and the main living spaces are lovely. At the end of a hard day, there's nothing better than relaxing in their eight-seater Jacuzzi in the garden. They're a member of Sustainable Wanaka and have a Qualmark Enviro-Silver rating. They also give NZ$1 of every booking to the Te Kakano Aotearoa Trust, which is developing a native nursery for community and reforestation projects.

21 Warren St. www.wanakasprings.com. ☏ **03/443-8421.** Fax 03/443-8429. 8 units. NZ$328–NZ$364. Rates include breakfast. Long-stay & off-peak rates. AE, DC, MC, V. May be closed in May or June; call or check website. **Amenities:** Free transfers from Wanaka airport; free use of bikes; nearby golf course; outdoor Jacuzzi. *In room:* TV, DVD (in some), hair dryer, Wi-Fi.

INEXPENSIVE

The **YHA Wanaka Purple Cow,** 94 Brownston St. (www.yha.co.nz; ☏ **0800/772-277** in NZ, or 03/443-1880), is frequented by budget-minded travelers from throughout the world. It's just a step or two from town and has dorm beds from NZ$18 to NZ$28 per person and doubles from NZ$78 to NZ$84. Campers will find excellent facilities at **Wanaka Top 10 Holiday Park ★★**, 217 Mount Aspiring Rd., Wanaka (www.wanakatop10.co.nz; ☏ **0508/926-252** in NZ), which has a parklike setting that's just a 20-minute walk from the town center. There's a swimming pool and spotless communal facilities. Motel units cost NZ$115 to NZ$165, self-contained cabins are NZ$60 to NZ$140, and powered sites go for NZ$45. **Glendhu Bay Lakeside Holiday Park ★★**, 1127 Mt. Aspiring Rd. (☏ **03/443-7243;** www.glendhubay motorcamp.co.nz), is further around the lake (about a 15-min. drive), but it has unsurpassed views of the lake and mountains and is right on the lakefront. It's much cheaper at NZ$20 for a basic cabin and NZ$16 for tents and powered sites, but it fills fast with Kiwi holidaymakers in summer, so book early.

Where to Eat

There are plenty of places to eat in Wanaka. **Sargoods Restaurant ★**, Edgewater Resort (☏ **03/443-8311**), serves remarkably good international cuisine from an a la carte menu with main courses priced from NZ$32. You'll find excellent picnic foods (and light meals) at **Ardmore Street Food Company** ★, 155 Ardmore St. (℃ **03/443-2230**); and you'll always get great pizzas, pasta, and atmosphere at **The Cow,** Post Office Lane (℃ **03/443-4269**), which is open daily from noon to midnight. **Post Office Lane** ★★, off Ardmore Street near the Post Office (www.good group.co.nz), is a small, well-designed cluster of bars and restaurants that is worth seeking out if you want to socialize with locals and international travelers alike. They all open onto a big courtyard complex with a roaring fire and outdoor tables. This is where you'll find **Botswana Butchery** ★★★, upstairs (℃ **03/443-6745;** www. goodgroup.co.nz), which specializes in specialty meat cuts cooked to perfection. Take a fat wallet, because it's the most expensive in town. It has a sister restaurant in Queenstown. **Sasanoki Japanese Kitchen,** Unit E, Pembroke Mall, 139 Ardmore St. (℃ **03/443-6474**), is a great place for a light Japanese lunch or dinner. They're open Monday through Friday from 11:30am to 9pm and Saturday from 5 to 9pm. **Ritual Espresso,** 18 Helwick St. (℃ **03/443-6662**), is open Monday 8am to 5pm and Tuesday through Sunday 9am to 5pm for very good coffee.

Café Gusto MODERN NEW ZEALAND   Right next to Lakeside Apartments, Gusto draws you in with bright yellow furniture on a sunny patio overlooking the lake. It has delicious lunch and casual evening dining selections: Moroccan lamb salad, pumpkin and spinach risotto, curries, and delicious soups, to name a few. It's colorful, bright, and popular with locals and visitors alike.

1 Lakeside Dr. ℃ **03/443-6639.** Main courses NZ$18–NZ$25. AE, MC, V. Daily 8am–late.

Kai Whakapai Café & Bar ★ 🖋 NEW ZEALAND/CAFE   The most visible and definitely the most popular of Wanaka's casual cafes, this one is oozing with smiles and good food at sensible prices. Quite apart from the divine pizzas, burgers, croissants, and fresh pastas, much of it with a vegetarian slant, this place comes alive as a bar in the early evening. And it's open nice and early for coffee. It could do with a spruce-up inside, but otherwise it's one of my favorites.

Lakefront. ℃ **03/443-7795.** Main courses NZ$12–NZ$24. AE, DC, MC, V. Daily 7am–late.

The Landing ★★ PACIFIC RIM   Always broad in its focus, Pacific Rim cuisine comes peppered with a few international touches at this extremely popular award-winning Wanaka restaurant. This is where you can savor braised lamb shoulder stuffed with olives, scallop and vanilla risotto, or a tangy Thai salad. Casual by day and moody by night, with a menu that combines a wealth of interesting flavors, it has the best wine list in Wanaka and reliable, professional service.

Level 1, 80 Ardmore St. ℃ **03/443-5099.** www.thelandinglakewanaka.co.nz. Reservations recommended. Main courses NZ$25–NZ$38. AE, MC, V. Daily 4pm–late.

Relishes Café ★★ INTERNATIONAL   Relishes has been a top spot for years and I've had some of my nicest fish meals here. If you need proof of popularity, people are turned away in droves for lack of space. It's a simple, country-style interior, nothing flashy, but the baked blue cod served with hazelnut and lemon butter left a memorable impression. It's one of the most consistent places in town and many prefer its relaxed atmosphere and friendliness over the much-touted Botswana Butchery.

1/99 Ardmore St. ℃ **03/443-9018.** Reservations highly recommended. Main courses NZ$20–NZ$32. AE, MC, V. Daily 8am–late (dinner from 6pm).

Sapphire ★★ MODERN NEW ZEALAND   Meals here focus on the very best of Central Otago produce and the region's fine wines. There's a lovely rustic, European feeling to the restaurant itself and you can choose between intimate dinners inside, or terrace dining with stunning views over the town. The seasonal menu changes regularly but you can expect taste treats like wild Fiordland venison with mushrooms and juniper jus, or aged Angus beef with watercress mash.

76 Golf Course Rd. ✆ **03/443-1105.** www.sapphirerestaurant.co.nz. Reservations recommended. Main courses NZ$35–NZ$38. AE, MC, V. Daily 5pm–late.

MOUNT COOK ★

263km (163 miles) NE of Queenstown; 331km (205 miles) SW of Christchurch

Mount Cook Village is known throughout the world for its alpine beauty and remoteness. It sits within the 70,000 hectares (173,000 acres) of **Mount Cook National Park,** some 753m (2,470 ft.) above sea level and surrounded by 140 peaks over 2,100m (6,888 ft.) high, 22 of which are over 3,000m (9,840 ft.). Most famous of all is **Aoraki–Mount Cook,** which rises 3,695m (12,120 ft.) into the sky. *Aoraki* means "cloud piercer" in Maori. A third of the park is permanent snow and ice, and the **Tasman Glacier,** at 29km (18 miles) long and 3km (2 miles) wide, is the longest known glacier outside arctic regions. More difficult to get onto than Fox or Franz Josef glaciers, it's still accessible for exhilarating downhill skiing.

Essentials

GETTING THERE   There is a daily **InterCity** (✆ 09/623-1503) link between Mount Cook and Christchurch, Queenstown, and Timaru. The **Cook Connection,** Twizel (✆ **0800/266-526** in NZ; www.cookconnect.co.nz), offers daily trips from Lake Tekapo and Twizel to Mount Cook from September through May between 7:30am and 9pm. The return trip from Tekapo to Mount Cook costs NZ$60 (NZ$45 from Twizel); kids ages 5 to 15 get a 20% discount, and they carry bikes for NZ$10 each. By car, Mount Cook is reached via State Highway 80 and great care should be taken on all roads in the area during autumn and winter when surfaces become icy and slippery. Twizel is 45 minutes from Mount Cook World Heritage Park and is the base for a number of tourism businesses operating in the Mount Cook area.

ORIENTATION   A T-intersection at the end of the highway marks the entrance to Mount Cook Village. Turn left and you'll pass Glencoe Lodge, a modern motor hotel, the youth hostel, Alpine Guides Mountain Shop, and finally the Aoraki–Mount Cook National Park Visitor Centre. Turn right at the intersection and you'll pass Mount Cook Chalets before reaching the peak-roofed, internationally famous Hermitage Hotel, which now includes a modest grocery store and post office.

VISITOR INFORMATION   The **Aoraki–Mount Cook National Park Visitor Centre,** 1 Larch Grove, Mount Cook Village (✆ 03/435-1186; fax 03/435-1080; www.doc.govt.nz), is open daily in summer from 8:30am to 6pm and in winter until 5pm (closed Dec 25). Department of Conservation officers can give you the latest information on weather, track, and road conditions. Trampers and mountaineers must check in and sign the intentions register before entering the park. Officers can also fill you in on high-altitude huts, hut passes, picnic grounds, and recommended walks in the area. The center is well worth a visit as it has excellent displays detailing the natural and human history of the national park.

The **Lake Pukaki Visitor Centre,** State Highway 8, Pukaki (✆ **03/435-3280;** fax 03/435-3283; www.mtcooknz.com), is another good resource. **Alpine Guides,** Main Road, Mount Cook (✆ **03/435-1834;** fax 03/435-1898; www.alpineguides. co.nz or www.heliskiing.co.nz), can also provide a wealth of information on alpine activities, schedules, and fees. For information on Mount Cook ski areas, connect to www.nzski.com and www.mtcooknz.com.

Exploring the Area

Clearly, the mountains are the main attraction here. Before you get out onto the ice and snow, make your way to the **Sir Edmund Hillary Alpine Centre ★★★**, the Hermitage Hotel (✆ **0800/686-800** in NZ, or 03/435-1809; www.hillarycentre. co.nz), which showcases the Mount Cook area. It features a very moving 3-D movie, New Zealand's first full dome, a digital planetarium, a museum, and gallery that documents the pioneering heart of the region and Sir Edmund's long association with the Mount Cook region. The Explorer Pass for museum admission is NZ$27 for adults, NZ$14 for children ages 4 to 14, and NZ$54 for families. It gives access to all theater shows over a 24-hour period. The Hillary Centre's **Big Sky Star Gazing ★★★** attraction begins with an introduction in the full dome digital Theatre Planetarium before visitors are taken to an outdoor stargazing site for spectacular views of the southern sky, as seen through the naked eye, high-powered binoculars, and state-of-the-art telescopes. It costs NZ$50 for adults, NZ$25 for children ages 4 to 14.

 Be Prepared

If you're driving up to Mount Cook Village during winter, make sure you have antifreeze fluid in your car radiator.

The Mount Cook area is also the access point for the beautiful **Tasman Glacier.** If you missed the scenic glacier flights at Fox and Franz Josef, you'll have another chance here. Go with award-winning **Air Safaris ★★** (✆ **0800/806-880** in NZ, or 03/680-6880; www.airsafaris.co.nz). Its 50-minute Grand Traverse leaves from Lake Tekapo and flies over the McKenzie Basin and lakes, around Mount Cook, over 12 major glaciers, across the Main Divide to the Westland World Heritage National Parks, to the West Coast Glaciers, and back to Lake Tekapo. This stunning flight costs NZ$325 for adults and NZ$215 for children ages 3 to 13. **Mount Cook Ski Planes,** Mount Cook Airport, St. Hwy. 80 (✆ **0800/800-702** in NZ, or 03/430-8034; www.mtcookskiplanes.com), is the only company licensed to land scenic flights on Tasman Glacier and in Mount Cook National Park. Their unforgettable fixed-wing Glacier Highlights flights take you the length of Tasman Glacier before landing on the glacier to take in this pristine alpine environment. It costs NZ$405 for adults and NZ$295 for children 3 to 14.

The **Helicopter Line,** Glentanner Park, Mt. Cook (✆ **0800/650-651** in NZ, or 03/435-1801; www.helicopter.co.nz), has several tours, such as the Alpine Wonderland, a 45-minute flight which covers Mount Cook, the Main Divide, and Tasman Glacier for NZ$450 per person. This includes a glacier landing. Mention Frommer's for a 10% discount when booking direct. All helicopter operations in the Mount Cook area are based at Glentanner Helicopter Base, 15 minutes from Mount Cook Village. All fixed-wing craft operate from Mount Cook Airport.

Skiers will head for the Tasman Glacier during the June-to-October season, but know in advance that skiing here is neither cheap nor for novices. Skiing on the

Night Skies

The skies above Lake Tekapo are renowned as some of the clearest in the world. That's why the top of Mount John is dotted with assorted international observatories. Visit this unique and fascinating spot for extraordinary night skies (and breathtaking daytime views) with **Earth & Sky Observatory ★★★**, Mount John, Tekapo (**☎ 03/680-6960**; www.earthandsky.co.nz). Their 35-minute day tour leaving from Astro Café (p. 412) on Mt. John costs NZ$40 for adults, NZ$25 for children ages 5 to 15. The 2-hour night tour costs NZ$90 for adults and NZ$55 for children ages 5 to 15. Either should be on your must-do list. Allow 15 minutes to drive to the top of Mt. John from Tekapo, or 1 hour to walk to the summit. The right-hand turn-off is well signposted, just south of Tekapo township.

glaciers involves two runs of about 11km (7 miles) each, with ski planes returning you to the top after the first run and flying you out at the end of the day. The glacier is perfect for intermediate-grade skiers; it's a long distance, but not steep. The full-day excursion costs from NZ$850 and can be booked through **Alpine Guides** (**☎ 03/435-1834;** www.alpineguides.co.nz), which also rents ski and climbing equipment and can organize guides to take you **mountain climbing** as well. Their 6- to 10-day guided ascents and mountain experience courses cost from NZ$2,025 to NZ$5,050. **Harris Mountain Heliski,** Glentanner Park, Mt. Cook (**☎ 03/435-1801;** www.heliski.co.nz), operates daily from June to October, taking adventurous skiers into remote, exclusive ski terrain for about NZ$795.

If you prefer something a little less expensive, park conservation offices can furnish a map of easy walks, which take anywhere from half an hour to half a day—you'll be able to commune with Mother Nature to your heart's content.

Glacier Explorers ★★★, Mount Cook Village (**☎ 0800/686-800;** www.glacierexplorers.com), can take you on an unbelievable 3-hour boat ride on Tasman Glacier Lake for NZ$140 for adults and NZ$70 for children ages 4 to 14. These tours only operate from mid-August through May (providing the lake is not frozen), and they include a 15-minute drive followed by a 30-minute walk to the lake. It's the only tour of its kind in New Zealand and one of only three in the world that takes you so close to a glacier face by boat.

Walkers and mountaineers should contact **Aspiring Guides ★★★** (**☎ 03/443-9422;** www.aspiringguides.com), which offers guided ascents of both Mt. Cook and Mt. Aspiring (from NZ$1,795 per person), plus 7-day mountaineering instruction courses (from NZ$2,250 per person), ice-climbing, and ski-touring (from NZ$750 per person).

Another fun way to experience the Tasman Glacier is by **Tasman Valley 4WD & Argo Tours ★★**, Mt. Cook Village (**☎ 0800/686-800** in NZ, or 03/435-1809; www.mountcooktours.co.nz). Their eight-wheel, all-terrain vehicle operates daily all year (weather permitting), and takes you close to the Tasman Glacier and its gigantic moraine walls. The vehicle stops at several vantage points so you can get those once-in-a-lifetime photographs. The tour costs NZ$75 for adults, NZ$38 for kids 4 to 14.

Where to Stay & Eat

Almost all of the accommodations in Mount Cook Village are owned by the same company, so you'll have minimal bargaining power. Still, call before you arrive as there are daily specials, especially at the ecofriendly and recently refurbished (2011) **Hermitage Hotel, Motels & Chalets ★★**, Terrace Road (www.hermitage.co.nz; ✆ **0800/686-800** in NZ, or 03/435-1809). This old-faithful complex is an uneven mix of older motel units, chalets, and new and old hotel rooms, but recent renovations have made it more cohesive; and the on-site restaurants have greatly improved. Hotel rates range from NZ$215 to NZ$575; motel rooms are NZ$189 to NZ$269; and chalets are NZ$269—but don't forget those specials. This is one hotel where I would be prepared to spend extra for views, because they are simply breathtaking. In addition, the hotel has a Qualmark Enviro-Gold rating and takes part in local native planting programs and a gene conservation program for native flora in the area.

Built in 2005, the **Aoraki/Mount Cook Alpine Lodge ★**, 101 Bowen Dr., Mount Cook (www.aorakialpinelodge.co.nz; ✆ **0800/680-680** in NZ, or 03/435-1860), was a much-needed, independent addition to the village accommodations scene. Its 16 rooms have lovely views and are much more reasonably priced at NZ$159 to NZ$245. Some larger family rooms have bunks and can sleep four. There's also a fully equipped self-catering kitchen and a terrific communal dining and lounge area for the people of all ages and nationalities who stay here. It has a lively, family atmosphere.

The **Mount Cook YHA Hostel,** Bowen Drive and Kitchener Avenue (www.yha. co.nz; ✆ **0800/278-299** in NZ, or 03/435-1820), has 70 beds in 17 rooms, including 6 twins and 2 doubles. The cost is NZ$32 per dorm bed, NZ$95 to NZ$156 for a twin or a double. It has the best shop in the village, plus a sauna, video library, TV lounge, luggage lockers, and a ski drying room. Reservations are essential from November to April. New in 2010, **Mount Cook Backpacker Lodge,** Mt. Cook Village (www.mountcookbackpackers.co.nz; ✆ **0800/100-512** in NZ, or 03/435-1653), has 80 quad dorm beds (NZ$35), 21 double rooms (NZ$125), and six private units (NZ$170).

Camping and **caravanning** are permitted in Mount Cook National Park at designated sites; water and toilets are available. If you use these facilities, remember that fires are prohibited within park boundaries. Check with the park visitor center for locations and conditions. Hikers and mountaineers have the use of 12 huts in the park, which have bunks and emergency radios. Only the Mueller Hut is within easy reach of the casual tramper. The others are at high altitudes and you need to be an experienced expert climber to reach them. The fee for overnight use of the huts is NZ$25 to NZ$40 per person, and arrangements must be made at the National Park Visitor Centre.

Rather than staying in Mount Cook Village itself, you might prefer to spend the night in one of the surrounding towns: Twizel, Fairlie, Tekapo, Omarama, and Kurow are all within a 2-hour drive and have motels, B&Bs, and homestays aplenty. Best among them is **Peppers Bluewater Resort ★★**, State Highway 8, Tekapo (www. peppers.co.nz/bluewater; ✆ **0800/680-570**), which offers 142 very reasonably priced new rooms and villas, from NZ$240 to around NZ$400. And if you stay in Tekapo, don't miss a visit to the new **Alpine Springs Spa & Winter Park ★★★**, 6 Lakeside Dr., Tekapo (✆ **0800/235-3823** in NZ; www.alpinesprings.co.nz), which features delicious hot pools, a day spa, an ice rink, snow tubing, and curling. They have skates for hire. Admission to the hot pools area is NZ$18 for adults, NZ$10 for children 3 to 12, and NZ$55 to NZ$65 for a family. Look out for combo deals that include some variation of pool, ice skating, and snow tubing; finish off with a relaxing massage or sauna. They're open from 10am to 8:30pm.

Panorama Restaurant, Hermitage Hotel, Mt. Cook (© **03/435-1809**), is well named. It has the best views in the country and a very good a la carte menu, but it's also on the pricey side and a favorite of tour parties. The hotel is also home to the **Alpine Restaurant** (for buffet) and the more casual **Sir Edmund Hillary Café & Bar. Old Mountaineers' Café, Bar & Restaurant** (© **03/345-1890**), next to the DOC Visitor Centre, is a popular rustic cafe with a big fire that's open daily 10am until late. It serves big breakfasts, good coffee, pizzas, and other light fare. In Tekapo, Mt. John's **Astro Café** (© **03/680-6960;** www.earthandsky.co.nz), is a must-visit. If the weather is clear, there are incredible 360-degree views of the Mackenzie Basin, including Aoraki/Mt. Cook, which will take your breath away. The cafe is fully glazed (including a glass ceiling) and serves salads, quiche, all-day breakfasts, and coffee. It's open daily from 9am to 6pm in summer (10am–5pm in winter).

En Route to Queenstown

State Highway 6 is good traveling all the way from Wanaka to Queenstown; the trip takes around 1½ hours. You'll drive around the edge of Lake Dunstan, which was formed behind the Clyde Dam. Bypassing Cromwell township, you then travel through the stone fruit orchards of the Cromwell area. As an introduction to the rapidly expanding wine industry in this area, stop at the **Big Picture ★★**, corner Sandflat Road & State Highway 6, Cromwell (© **03/445-4052;** www.bigpicture wine.com). It has an excellent interactive wine film and tasting auditorium, a good cafe and restaurant, and a tasty selection of goodies from the area's wineries and boutique culinary producers. It's past the Cromwell turnoff on the left and open daily from 9am until 8pm. After passing through the winding Kawarau River Gorge, you come into Gibbston Valley—awash with vineyards—and on into Queenstown.

You could also go to Queenstown via the Crown Range. You'll be rewarded by spectacular views and a slightly shorter travel time than on the State Highway 6 route.

QUEENSTOWN ★★★

404km (250 miles) SW of Franz Josef; 263km (163 miles) SW of Mount Cook; 117km (73 miles) S of Wanaka; 172km (107 miles) NE of Te Anau

Queenstown has over one million visitors a year and you don't have to be a genius to figure out why. We've all heard the endless hype about it being the adventure capital of the world, and there are certainly enough crazy activities here to challenge the strongest, but Queenstown offers much more. Don't be put off by comments that it's touristy, un-Kiwi, crowded, and overrated. Sure, the streets are dominated by booking offices, but Queenstown has excellent shopping, restaurants, cafes, and clubs as well. And in many adrenalin-seeking ways, it encapsulates much of what New Zealand is about.

Famed for its international winter ski profile, Queenstown is also a brilliant spring, summer, and fall destination. This is when you get the best of its scenic beauty, easy walks, and endless opportunities to relax. Thrill seeking may be touted as the major attraction, but you can just as easily go fishing, golfing, gold panning, wine tasting, or boating. One thing is certain: You won't run out of things to do.

It seems as though the whole world suddenly wants to live in Queenstown, and the town has experienced a phenomenal growth in development in the last 10 years. The inner commercial area has several new retail, office, and restaurant complexes, with

Central Queenstown

HOTELS ■
A Boutique Hotel—
  Queenstown House **17**
Arrowfield Apartments **1**
Arrowtown House
  Boutique Hotel **1**
Arrowtown Lodge **1**
Brown's Boutique Hotel **9**
Chalet Queenstown **20**
Crowne Plaza Queenstown **10**
The Dairy Private Luxury Hotel **8**
Eichardt's Private Hotel **14**
Garden Court Suites
  & Apartments **19**
Heritage Queenstown **13**
Hilton Queenstown **21**
Historic Stone House **18**
Kawarau Hotel, Managed
  by Hilton **21**
Matakauri Lodge **13**
Millbrook Resort **1**
Pencarrow **21**
Pinewood Lodge **2**
Queenstown Park Hotel **7**
Queenstown Top 10 Holiday Park
  Creeksyde **3**
The Rees Hotel & Luxury
  Apartments **21**
Remarkables Lodge **21**
Scenic Suites Queenstown **31**
Sofitel Queenstown **23**
White Shadows Country Inn **1**

ATTRACTIONS ●
Department of
  Conservation **24**
Kiwi & Birdlife Park **6**
Skyline Queenstown **5**
Steamer Wharf &
  TSS *Earnslaw* **11**

RESTAURANTS ◆
Bella Cucina **22**
Boardwalk Seafood
  Restaurant **12**
Botswana Butchery **15**
The Bunker **28**
The Cow **28**
Eichardt's House Bar **14**
Fergburger **25**
Fishbone Bar & Grill **27**
Gantley's Restaurant **1**
Joe's Garage **29**
Left Bank Café **23**
Skyline Queenstown
  Restaurant **4**
Tatler **30**
True South **21**
Wai Waterfront
  Restaurant **12**
Vesta **16**
Vudu Café **26**

more under construction. Residential expansion is also obvious, although the current worldwide economic recession has stalled a number of major developments, including the new town of Five Mile, which was being developed near the airport at Frankton.

Essentials

GETTING THERE & GETTING AROUND   **By Plane**   Queenstown is well serviced by **Air New Zealand National** and **Air New Zealand Link** (℃ 0800/737-000 in NZ; www.airnewzealand.co.nz) from such cities as Christchurch, Auckland, Wellington, and Rotorua. Air New Zealand also has a weekly flight from Sydney year-round and a weekly flight from Brisbane during ski season. The Air New Zealand Travel Centre is at 41 Shotover St., Queenstown (℃ 03/441-1900). **Qantas** (℃ 0800/808-767 in NZ; www.qantas.com) also has a weekly flight direct from Sydney and Brisbane in winter. **Jetstar** (℃ 0800/800-995 in NZ; www.jetstar.com) also flies into Queenstown. **Pacific Blue** (℃ 0800/670-000; www.flypacificblue.com) has flights between Queenstown, Auckland, and Sydney year-round and from Sydney, Melbourne, and Brisbane in winter. Visit www.queenstownairport.co.nz for more flight details.

Super Shuttle (℃ 03/442-3639; www.supershuttle.co.nz) will take you downtown for NZ$20 per person; the **Connectabus** (℃ 03/441-4471; www.connect abus.com) goes between the airport, Queenstown, Arrowtown, major attractions, hotels, shopping centers, and Millbrook Resort. A Day Pass costs NZ$17 for adults, NZ$12 for kids 14 and under; buses run from 6am to midnight. A **taxi** (℃ 03/442-7788) to the town center costs NZ$25 to NZ$35 depending on your final destination.

By Coach (Bus)   **InterCity** (℃ 09/623-1503) runs between Queenstown and Christchurch, Dunedin, Fox Glacier, Franz Josef, Invercargill, Milford Sound, Mount Cook, Te Anau, and Wanaka. The InterCity depot is at the visitor center, Camp and Shotover streets (℃ 03/442-2800). **Kiwi Experience** (℃ 09/366-9830), **Magic Travellers** (℃ 09/358-5600), and **Backpackers Express** (℃ 03/442-9939) all service Queenstown as well.

The **Original Arrowtown Bus** (℃ 03/442-1900; www.arrowtownbus.co.nz) provides transportation between Queenstown and Arrowtown. Queenstown pickup is outside O'Connell's Centre on Camp Street at 9:45am, 11am, 1pm, 3:15pm, and 5:15pm; in Arrowtown catch the bus behind the museum on Ramshaw Lane at 8:30am, 10:30am, noon, 2pm, and 4:30pm. The round-trip costs NZ$25, and they make two photo stops along the way.

By Car   Allow 6 hours from Christchurch, 3½ hours from Dunedin, 5½ hours from Franz Josef, 2½ hours from Te Anau, 5 hours from Milford Sound, and 2½ hours from Invercargill. All roads leading into town are excellent. All major rental-car companies have offices in Queenstown.

By Taxi   Call **Queenstown Taxis** (℃ 03/442-7788) or **Alpine Taxis** (℃ 03/442-6666). Fares from the town center to most accommodations are between NZ$5 and NZ$15.

ORIENTATION   Queenstown is a compact town, with most shops, restaurants, and amenities within easy walking distance. There is no public bus system, but the Connectabus (see above) provides excellent all-day service. The central shopping area is bordered by Marine Parade on the lakefront, Camp Street to the north of that, and Shotover Street, which runs into Lake Esplanade. Focus on Beach Street, Rees Street, and The Mall for shopping. That said, there's a new shopping area at Remarkables Park, near Queenstown Airport. It's open daily and has 700 free parking spaces. If you have a car, keep in mind that parking in Queenstown is limited and expensive. Save yourself much time and frustration and head straight for the new carpark on Man Street (beside the Sofitel), from where everything is within easy walking distance.

The historic village of Arrowtown is 20km (12 miles) to the northeast. A calm counterbalance to the frenetic pace of Queenstown, Arrowtown is one of New Zealand's last little frontier towns. Glenorchy, now billed as the "Gateway to Paradise," is a 45-minute drive around the west arm of Lake Wakatipu.

VISITOR INFORMATION The **Queenstown i-SITE Visitor Centre,** Clocktower Centre, Shotover and Camp streets (© **0800/668-888** in NZ, or 03/442-4100; fax 03/442-8907; www.queenstown-vacation.com), is open in summer daily from 7am to 7pm, and from Easter to the end of October from 7am to 6pm. It sells stamps; sends faxes and e-mail; exchanges currency; and makes reservations for accommodations, transport, and activities. The **Real Journeys Queenstown Visitor Centre** is on the Steamer Wharf, Beach Street (© **0800/656-503** in NZ, or 03/442-7500; fax 03/442-7504; www.realjourneys.co.nz). The **Department of Conservation Information Centre,** 37 Shotover St. (© **03/442-7933**), is the place to go for information on walking trails and national parks.

While at the visitor center, pick up a copy of the *Queenstown Today & Tonight* brochure. For a critical lowdown on what to do, get *iTAG* and the *Backpackers' Guide to Queenstown.* Also look for the two free tourist papers, *The Mountain Scene* and *Qt Visitor Information.*

Get an online introduction to the area at www.newzealand-vacation.com, www. queenstown-nz.co.nz, www.queenstownadventure.com, www.queenstownvisitor guides.com, www.arrowtownnz.com, and www.centralotagonz.com.

SPECIAL EVENTS The visitor center can provide details on a vigorous program of special events held in the area throughout the year. Here's a small sampling of what you can expect.

In January, riders from all over the South Island participate in the famous **Glenorchy Races,** which include bareback riding and attract thousands of spectators. The **Queenstown Jazz Festival** (© **03/441-2453;** www.asbjazzfest.co.nz) presents 10 days of top jazz. The **Arrowtown Autumn Festival** (© **027/210-1570;** www. arrowtownautumnfestival.org.nz) runs the week after Easter. The festival celebrated its 25th anniversary in 2009, and it features market days and street entertainment celebrating the gold-mining era. The **Queenstown American Express Winter Festival** (© **0800/337-8482;** www.winterfestival.co.nz) is the perfect excuse for 9 days of unadulterated madness and mayhem in July. It features a big opening ceremony and Mardi Gras, ski events, and street entertainment, and just about anything goes. The **Spring Carnival** (© **03/442-4615;** www.nzski.com), held in mid-September at the Remarkables Ski Resort, presents a feast of snow-related sports and social activities.

[FastFACTS] QUEENSTOWN

American Express The office is at 59 Beach St. (📞 **03/442-7730**).

Area Code The telephone area code (STD) for Queenstown is **03.**

Currency Exchange Try **Thomas Cook,** 34 Camp St. (📞 **03/442-6403**), or **BNZ Bureau de Change,** 11–13 Rees St. (📞 **03/442-5810**).

Dentists For 24-hour service, call 📞 **03/442-7274,** 442-8580, or 442-2711.

Doctors The **Queenstown Medical Centre** is at 9 Isle St. (📞 **03/441-0500**).

Emergencies For police, fire, or ambulance services, dial 📞 **111.**

Internet Access **Internet Outpost,** 27 Shotover St. (📞 **03/441-3018;** www.internet-outpost.com), open daily from 8:30am to 11:30pm, charges NZ$6 per hour. **Budget Communications,** above McDonald's in O'Connell's Mall (📞 **03/441-1562**), is open daily from 9am until 11pm and charges from NZ$3 per hour.

Pharmacy **Bradley's Pharmacy,** 19 Rees St. (📞 **03/442-8338**), is open daily from 8am to 10pm. After hours, call 📞 **03/442-9140.**

Post Office The post office is on Ballarat Street (📞 **03/442-8238**). It's open Monday through Friday from 7:30am to 4pm.

Exploring the Area

IN QUEENSTOWN

There is no better place to appraise Queenstown than from your perch aboard one of the gondolas of the **Skyline Queenstown ★★★** (📞 **03/441-0101;** www.skyline. co.nz), which takes you up to **Bob's Peak.** The view is well worth the effort. You can stay for lunch or dinner at the buffet restaurant or cafe (see "Where to Eat," later in this chapter). The gondola operates daily from 9am until the restaurant closes around midnight. The round-trip fare is NZ$25 for adults, NZ$14 for children ages 5 to 14, and NZ$64 for a family. The complex includes a very good souvenir shop and a nearly 1km (½-mile) luge for the brave-hearted. From the top of the gondola you can then take a free chairlift another 100m (330 ft.) higher for even better views, and then walk the short distance down to the complex to enjoy the 30-minute Maori cultural performance by Kiwi Haka. The combo ticket for both the gondola and the performance costs NZ$59 for adults, NZ$32 for children, and NZ$148 for a family. Haka performances run daily at 5:15pm, 6pm, 7:15pm and 8pm. Numerous other combos include restaurant meals and luge rides, for a variety of prices.

The **Kiwi & Birdlife Park ★**, Brecon Street (📞 **03/442-8059;** www.kiwibird. co.nz), is in tranquil 3-hectare (8-acre) surroundings near the base of the gondola. Allow 30 to 40 minutes to see the bird life and reptiles close at hand. Along with daily conservation shows (11am and 3pm), they have several rare birds that can't be seen anywhere else. Daily kiwi feeding sessions are at 10am, noon, 1:30, and 4:30pm. You can also watch Maori dance performances at 11am and 3pm at the early Maori hunting village within the park. Admission (including shows) is NZ$38 for adults and NZ$19 for children 5 to 15. The park is open daily, from 9am to 6pm in summer (until 5pm in winter).

Goldfields Mining Centre, in Kawarau Gorge (📞 **03/445-1038;** www. goldfieldsmining.co.nz), is open daily from 9am to 5pm. The gold fields of this region were among the richest in the world in the early 19th century, and Goldfields is the official gold-mining demonstration site. It's a 40-minute drive through the Kawarau

fun stuff, ESPECIALLY FOR KIDS

Many Queenstown adventures have high minimum age requirements, but these fun, family-friendly activities don't:

Family Adventures ★★★, 4 Brecon St. (☎ **03/442-8836;** www.family adventures.co.nz), which encourages families to take part in its scenic four-wheel-drive excursion into Skipper's Canyon to see old mining relics and jet boats in action, before embarking on a 1½-hour gentle rafting tour down the safest section of the Shotover River. The cost is from NZ$170 for adults and NZ$115 for children ages 3 to 16 (no kids 2 and under allowed).

Caddyshack City ★, 25 Brecon St. (☎ **03/442-6642**), is an indoor miniature-golf experience that makes for lots of laughs. Open daily from 10am to 8pm, it costs NZ$19 for adults, NZ$12 for children 5 to 14, and NZ$55 for families. Kids 4 and under cannot play, but strollers are provided.

Off-Road Adventures Kids Quads, 61a Shotover St. (☎ **03/442-7858;** ww.off road.co.nz), has a family tour for NZ$189 a person, complete with kid-size quads; and **Strike Bowl Queenstown,** Coronet Alpine Hotel, 161 Arthurs Point Rd. (☎ **03/409-2135;** www.strikebowl.co. nz), has child-sized bowling equipment; before 5pm it costs just NZ$14 for adults and NZ$10 for children (includes shoes).

Kiwi & Birdlife Park ★ (see above) gives kids a good introduction to conservation and New Zealand bird life. The **Skyline Luge** ★★★ (see "Outdoor Pursuits," later in this chapter) is great fun for all ages, as is Real Journey's **Walter Peak Farm Excursion** ★★ (see "Lake Cruises," below), which includes a steamship cruise and a farmyard tour where children can help feed the animals.

The **Underwater Observatory,** Main Pier (☎ **03/442-8538**), will also amuse the kids. Fish are fed each day and eels should also make an appearance. Admission is NZ$5 for adults, NZ$3 for children, and a mere NZ$10 for a family pass, which probably makes it Queenstown's cheapest attraction. Take some NZ$1 coins for the fish feeding machine, which attracts some huge specimens.

You'll find a kids' playground with swings, slides, and a climbing frame at the **Main Beach, The Esplanade.** Toilets and a barbecue area are also available for use. **Outside Sports Queenstown,** 36–38 Shotover St. (☎ **03/450-2118;** www.outsidesports.co.nz), has bikes for all the family to hire. Adults bikes cost NZ$30 for a half-day and kids' bikes cost NZ$20 per half-day. If you're traveling with kids, pick up the free guide *Kidz Go!* at visitor centers.

Gorge on the way to Cromwell, so if you're on your way to Wanaka or Dunedin, stop in. You have to walk over a narrow but stable bridge that crosses high above the river; and if you've got a fear of heights like me, you might shake in your boots a bit. But if I can do it, so can you. A self-guided tour costs NZ$20 for adults and NZ$8 for children 5 to 15 and includes gold-panning.

If you have an interest in the arts, take the self-drive **Wakatipu Arts Trail,** which takes you through the pretty back roads between Queenstown and Arrowtown, visiting eight well-known artists and craftspeople. Pick up the brochure from the visitor center and allow at least a morning to appreciate fine watercolors, oils, wood art, and jewelry.

If you're not in the mood for paid adventures, there is always plenty to see by wandering around the compact center of Queenstown itself. You can sit on the little beach and have a picnic; on Saturdays you can visit the **Queenstown Art & Craft Market** at Earnslaw Park, which runs near Steamer Wharf from 9am to 4:30pm; and you can explore the **Steamer Wharf complex** itself. Designed by a local architect, Michael Wyatt, Steamer Wharf is home to restaurants, cafes, and the TSS *Earnslaw* (see below), one of the last remaining coal-fired passenger-carrying vessels operating in the Southern Hemisphere. It's always fun to take a seat on the wharf and watch the *Earnslaw* and other boats coming and going.

IN NEARBY ARROWTOWN

For an enjoyable outing and a less hectic pace, drive out to the once-thriving gold-mining town of Arrowtown. It sprang up on the banks of the Arrow River when gold was discovered here in 1862. Many of the quaint original buildings remain, along with stunning avenues of trees planted in 1867. In autumn, the whole town glows with colorful foliage. To get a better understanding of the town's history, go to the **Lakes District Museum ★**, 49 Buckingham St. (✆ **03/442-1824;** www. museumqueenstown.com). Admission is NZ$7 for adults, NZ$1 for children ages 5 to 14, and NZ$14 per family; it's open daily from 8:30am to 5pm.

Although there is no longer a Chinese community in Arrowtown, you can take a stroll in the restored **Chinese Camp,** on Bush Creek at the northern end of town. The camp was once occupied by the Chinese gold-mining community in the late 19th century. Look out for **Ah Lum's General Store** and the tiny dwellings tucked under rocky outcrops.

Other places to explore include the **Royal Oak Hotel,** 47 Buckingham St. (✆ **03/442-1700**), one of the oldest licensed hotels in Central Otago, where you can still enjoy a drink and a hearty round of pub food; the **Old Gaol,** on Cardigan Street; and **St. John's Presbyterian Church,** which dates back to 1873, at Durham and Berkshire streets. Overall, Arrowtown is very pretty, but in peak tourist season it's about as "touristy" as touristy gets. It's much better in autumn when the crowds have dissipated and the leaves are falling. If you have time on your hands, catch a movie at **Dorothy Brown's Boutique Cinema ★★**, 144 Buckingham St. (✆ **03/442-1964;** www.dorothybrowns.com), which is a fabulous little den of art-house movies with a bar, bookstore, and lounge. It's open 11am to 11pm; reservations are recommended.

Organized Tours

Start with the sedate **Queenstown-Arrowtown Double Decker Bus Tour ★★** (✆ **03/441-4471;** www.doubledeckerbus.co.nz), which gives a bird's-eye view of the Wakatipu Basin without leaving the ground. It includes a 1-hour stop in Arrowtown; you can also leave the bus there in the morning and go back to Queenstown on the afternoon return trip. It costs NZ$48 for adults and NZ$25 for children 14 and under and departs daily from the top of Camp Street at 9:30am and 1:30pm, returning at 1 and 5pm. Allow 3 hours and purchase tickets from the visitor center, or on the bus.

For information on **Wine Trail** tours, see "The Wineries," below.

Trilogy Trail (✆ **0800/676-264** in NZ, or 03/442-2207; www.trilogytrail.com) is operated by people who were involved in the making of *The Lord of the Rings* trilogy, and they'll give you an insight into Middle Earth, visiting filming locations by air or road. Tours run from 2½ to 5 hours. A 4WD tour costs NZ$148 for adults, NZ$75 for children 5 to 15. A flying/land tour runs from NZ$350 to NZ$1,250 for adults, NZ$175 to NZ$665 for children 13 and under.

Nomad Safaris ★★ (✆ **0800/688-222** in NZ, or 03/442-6699; www.nomad safaris.co.nz) has exclusive rights to guide in the old mining towns of Macetown and

A SIDE TRIP TO SKIPPERS canyon ★★

Skippers Canyon, 22km (13 miles) from Queenstown, at the head of the Shotover River, was made famous by the discovery of gold there in 1862; within 4 months of that first find, over 10,000 miners were in the canyon. A settlement quickly sprang up to accommodate the miners, and at one time there were four hotels there. Today, among the few reminders of that bustling era are an old schoolhouse and the incredibly narrow, winding road that was carved out of the rock faces by Chinese laborers. It can be a hair-raising journey, and I'd think twice about doing it on your own steam. Instead, I recommend you join one of the experienced tour operators who know this iconic route well.

Of the operators taking four-wheel-drive tours into Skippers Canyon,

Queenstown Heritage Tours ★★★ (*℃* 03/409-0949; www.qht.co.nz) is one of the best. The half-day tour is limited to four to six people and culminates in a delicious picnic on the edge of the cliff. The cost is from NZ$160 for adults and NZ$80 for children 5 to 15. Nomad Safaris (*℃* 0800/688-222; www.nomadsafaris.co.nz) offers a 4-hour 4WD safari into the canyon for NZ$165 for adults and NZ$80 for children ages 4 to 14. You can also go into the canyon with Skippers Canyon Jet (*℃* 0800/226-966), for NZ$119 for adults and NZ$79 for children 3 to 15; some operators include a little gold panning in their excursion.

Sefferstown, taking you through spectacular Otago scenery along the way. They also offer two 4WD "Safari of the Rings" tours, visiting *Lord of the Rings* filming locations. Several of their drivers were extras in the film trilogy, and all have an in-depth knowledge of Tolkien's work that is bound to satisfy the most dedicated fans; their experience for *Rings* tours is by far the best. For the most landscape diversity, take the Wakatipu Basin tour; for the most film locations and more remote scenery, take the Glenorchy tour. Both are 4 hours long and cost NZ$165 for adults, NZ$80 for children 4 to 14.

If, like me, you're not given to throwing yourselves off high places for the hell of it, take the excellent Secrets of the Bungy Tour ★★, Kawarau Bungy Centre (*℃* 0800/286-495 in NZ, or 03/442-4007; www.bungy.co.nz), which gives you a 45-minute behind-the-scenes insight into this iconic New Zealand activity. Pricing for the Secrets of Bungy tour (self-drive to the bungy site) is adults NZ$20, children NZ$15, NZ$50 for a family. If you would like to be picked up in central Queenstown and transported to the site, ask for prices that include transport.

If you want to tour in style, contact Limousine Line (*℃* 03/442-2040; www.limousineline.co.nz). Its knowledgeable drivers give clients a unique, personal experience based on their interests and time constraints.

LAKE CRUISES

If you need a moment of serenity, get aboard the 1912 vintage steamship TSS *Earnslaw* and cruise across Lake Wakatipu in style. Affectionately known as the "Lady of the Lake," the *Earnslaw* was built to service the remote farming communities around Lake Wakatipu. She could carry 1,500 sheep and 30 cattle on her decks. Today, she carries up to 350 passengers on daily scheduled excursions and makes around 2,000 trips per year. The vessel has had combustion fans fitted on both main steam boilers to optimize her coal-burning efficiency and reduce emissions. Some of the older decking was also replaced. In 2012, the steamship's entire forward deck section will be replaced, once the correct timber has been sourced, cured, and prepared. For that period (May to early June 2012), a launch will act as substitute vessel. The TSS *Earnslaw* also turns 100 in October 2012 and there will be a week of celebrations, including a re-enactment of the first voyage. Keep an eye on the website for details.

The **TSS *Earnslaw*** departs on 1½-hour cruises to Walter Peak up to six times a day, year-round (with a reduced winter schedule). Cost is NZ$50 for adults and NZ$22 for children ages 5 to 14. Passengers with more time can disembark at Walter Peak on the 3½-hour farm excursion, which includes a country-style morning or afternoon tea (NZ$72 adults, NZ$22 children ages 5–14). Alternatively, from October to mid-April, you can take a 40-minute horse trek across the foothills, enjoy a delicious Walter Peak barbecue, learn about the area's history on a Heritage Excursion, or splurge on the evening dining excursion, which features a three-course carvery buffet and a shortened farmyard tour. Contact **Real Journeys,** Steamer Wharf (**②** **0800/656-503** in NZ, or 03/442-7500; www.realjourneys.co.nz).

Sail Queenstown ★★★, Steamer Wharf (**②** **03/442-7517**), gives you the chance to sail on former America's Cup vessel, *NZL 14*, which was skippered by Russell Coutts. You can sit back and enjoy the ride, or act as part of the crew. No former experience is needed and you'll pay NZ$150 for the pleasure (children NZ$110). Allow 2 hours for high-level excitement. Daily sails are at 11am and 2pm.

The Wineries

There's new gold in this picturesque valley—liquid gold, in the form of prizewinning wine! Central Otago's rugged hillsides are clad in lush vineyards that produce some of the country's most distinctive wines. Pinot noir (85% of the total plantings), chardonnay, sauvignon blanc, pinot gris, and Riesling varieties are well suited to the hot summer days and cool nights. Since 1990, Central Otago pinot noir has topped its class five times in national wine competitions. Pick up the free brochure *The Central Otago Wine Map,* which locates the major wineries. Study it carefully and choose the wineries that best suit your preferences. It's by far the best, most concise overview of the entire wine industry in this region.

New vineyards are coming on stream all the time as the region's 686 hectares (1,694 acres)—and expanding—mature, and many are developing new winery and restaurant complexes. There are now more than 70 vineyards in the region. The Queenstown and Wanaka visitor centers can provide a comprehensive map and brochure of the Central Otago wine industry to make your self-drive exploration more satisfying and straightforward. For more information check **www.otagowine.com** or **www.cowa.org.nz**.

Start your wine exploration at the very classy **Amisfield Winery** ★★★, 10 Lake Hayes Rd. (**②** **03/442-0556**; www.amisfield.co.nz), where you'll find one of the best restaurants in the region, along with an underground barrel hall and cellar door. They're just 10 minutes from Queenstown and are producers of pinot noir, aromatic whites, and *méthode traditionelle* wines. **Chard Farm Vineyard** ★, State Highway 6, just past the Kawarau bungy bridge, 20 minutes from Queenstown (**②** **03/442-6110**; www.chard farm.co.nz), is one of the most spectacularly situated vineyards in the country. Straddling a narrow ledge between rugged mountains and the Kawarau River Gorge, it's reached via a narrow, unpaved road 100m (330 ft.) above the river. Available wines include chardonnay, pinot noir, Riesling, sauvignon blanc, pinot gris, and Gewürztraminer.

The Wine Tours

Queenstown Wine Trail ★★ (📞 0800/ 827-8464 in NZ, or 03/441-3990; www. queenstownwinetrail.co.nz) offers a 5-hour tour with an informed commentary and tastings at four wineries. This includes a winery lunch and a visit to a cheesery. Tour prices start at NZ$129 per person and operate all year. If this tour is booked, try **Appellation Central Wine Tours ★★** (📞 03/442-0246; www.appelationcentral.co.nz), which will take you to the rapidly expanding Bannockburn and Cromwell vineyard regions, where you'll explore many of the best new vineyards. It has two daily

options, one including lunch in the historic town of Clyde. Prices range from NZ$165 to NZ$215 per person. If you don't have time to get to the vineyards at all, visit **Wine Tastes New Zealand Wine Experience,** 14 Beach St., Queenstown (📞 03/409-2226; www. winetastes.com), which carries a selection of over 700 of New Zealand's best wines, over 80 of them available to taste by the glass. They're right in the center of town and are open daily from 10am to 10pm. They can also arrange to ship your purchases home.

GVW Winery ★★, State Highway 6, 25 minutes from Queenstown (📞 03/442-6910; www.gibbstonvalleynz.com), is a popular lunch stop. It's the most visited winery in Australasia, with not only great food but also a divine setting. As pioneers of winemaking in Central Otago, Gibbston has set high standards. Many of its wines are stored in the climatically controlled wine cave, which was blasted out of a rocky outcrop behind the restaurant. Connoisseurs will enjoy the tour through the caves and the tasting of four wines. There is also a large gift store and delicatessen on-site, and next door, **Gibbston Valley Cheesery ★★** (📞 03/441-1388; www.gvcheese. co.nz) makes and sells top-quality regional cheeses.

Just down the road you'll find **Peregrine ★★★** (📞 03/442-4000; www. peregrinewines.co.nz). Named after the falcon now found only in the Central Otago region, Peregrine is a relatively new player on the scene. Success has come early, though, and its 1998 sauvignon blanc won New Zealand, Australian, and United Kingdom trophies. The opening of its new architecturally designed restaurant complex, with a distinctive curved wing-shaped roof, has cemented it as one of the most stylish wineries to visit. They produce good pinot noir, pinot gris, Riesling, sauvignon blanc, chardonnay, and rosé.

You won't regret a trip into the Bannockburn area, either. Drive through the Kawarau Gorge and just before Cromwell, you'll see Bannockburn signposted to your right. This is where you'll find **Mt. Difficulty Wines ★★**, Felton Road, Bannockburn (📞 03/445-3445; www.mtdifficulty.co.nz), which produces excellent pinot noir, Riesling, chardonnay, sauvignon blanc, pinot gris, and merlot. They also have a very pleasant cafe open for lunch at noon.

You could easily spend a whole day in the Bannockburn area alone, as there are dozens of wineries here. If you're on a tight schedule, though, and want to maximize your time, I suggest you take a wine tour. The two outlined below are the best.

Side Trips to Milford Sound ★★★

If you don't have time to make the long drive to Milford Sound, there are numerous operators offering trips from Queenstown. Flying is money well invested, as the long

1-day coach trips can be exhausting and you'll spend most of your time on a bus. If you are planning to drive yourself, I definitely recommend spending a night at Te Anau before undertaking the journey to Milford Sound. That way, your Milford trip can be taken at a leisurely pace, and you can stop along the way to enjoy the scenery. Otherwise it can be an arduous journey.

There are numerous suppliers of fixed-wing scenic flights from Queenstown to Milford. You'll get a 10% discount if you mention Frommer's to either **Air Fiordland,** Queenstown Airport (✆ **0800/103-404;** www.airfiordland.com), or **Milford Sound Scenic Flights,** Queenstown Airport (✆ **0800/207-206;** www.milford flights.co.nz). They're similarly priced, offering flights and inclusive boat cruise options for around NZ$440 to NZ$475 for adults and NZ$286 to NZ$309 for children. Their longer fly/cruise/coach options are a little cheaper and will give you the opportunity for an on-the-ground look at this remarkable landscape. But if you're short on time and you can afford to fly both ways, it's definitely the way to go. You'll see many hidden valleys and lakes never seen from the road, and the flight only takes around 35 minutes from Queenstown to Milford.

If flying and driving are not options, don't despair. **Great Sights** (✆ **0800/744-487;** www.greatsights.co.nz) and **Real Journeys** (✆ **0800/656-503;** www.real journeys.co.nz) both offer coach trips from Queenstown. Allow at least 12 hours for a trip of this nature, of which approximately 10 hours will be spent on the bus. A better option is to coach in and fly out, which saves time and lets you see the landscape from two different perspectives, but if the weather closes in—and it often does—you'll end up coaching both ways.

Real Journeys also offers coach and Milford Sound cruises from Queenstown; they range from NZ$198 to NZ$226 for adults and NZ$99 to NZ$113 for children 5 to 14. The vessel is designed along the lines of a traditional trading scow and there's an onboard nature guide. A coach/day cruise/fly package is offered year-round from Queenstown and costs NZ$578 to NZ$606 for adults, NZ$346 to NZ$360 for ages 5 to 14. You can book Real Journey excursions at the visitor center at Steamer Wharf (✆ **03/442-7500;** fax 03/442-7504). It has excellent coaches, comfortable cruising vessels, informed drivers, and interpretation in eight languages, including English.

Outdoor Pursuits
IN QUEENSTOWN
There's no doubt Queenstown has more crazy, boundary-testing activities per square mile than anywhere else in New Zealand.

BIKING **Outside Sports,** 36 Shotover St. (✆ **03/441-0074;** www.outsidesports. co.nz), rents road and mountain bikes. It also supplies mountain-bike trail maps. Rentals range from NZ$50 to NZ$120 per day. Serious mountain bikers should consider the guided tours provided by **Gravity Action** (✆ **03/442-5277;** www.queenstown adventure.co.nz/gravity-action.htm), which is operated by **Vertigo Bikes,** 4 Brecon St. (✆ **03/442-8378;** www.vertigobikes.co.nz). Vertigo also operates a downhill mountain bike rental stall at the top of the Skyline Gondola, daily from 10am to 8pm. Bikes can be hired from NZ$69 for a half-day and from NZ$99 for a full day.

BUNGY JUMPING There are three bungy-jumping sites in Queenstown. So what's the difference between them? **A. J. Hackett Bungy ★★★** (✆ **0800/286-4958** in NZ, or 03/442-4007; www.bungy.co.nz) now operates them all.

Kawarau Suspension Bridge, at 43m (140 ft.) high, was the world's first commercial bungy operation, and since it was the "original," it seems to hold a special

For an unforgettable adventure, call up experienced Queenstown helicopter pilot Louisa "Choppy" Patterson at **Over the Top ★★★**, the Blue Hangar, Tex Smith Lane, Queenstown Airport (📞 **0800/123-359** in NZ, or 03/442-2233; www.flynz.co.nz). Something of a legend in these parts, Choppy knows all the magic picnic spots thousands of feet up in the mountains. She can land you there, leave you with a champagne lunch in total solitude, and return later to drop you back into civilization. This truly memorable excursion will start at around NZ$755 for two people, depending on where you decide to fly. Don't miss this unique chance for adventure! As well as investing in quieter aircraft, Over the Top partnered with the Department of Conservation and the University of Otago to sponsor two ecoprojects donating helicopter time to help ensure this unique World Heritage area remains pristine. The company also offers a wide range of other scenic flights and snow landings, flights to wineries, ski fields, and fly-fishing expeditions.

place in jumpers' hearts. It's great for water touches in the Kawarau River and is 23km (14 miles) from Queenstown. The full package, including jump, T-shirt, video, photos, and transport, costs NZ$180 for adults, NZ$130 for children ages 10 to 15. Allow 1 to 3 hours. At the top of Bob's Peak, the **Ledge** is 47m (155 ft.). This is what you might call an urban bungy experience that has two angles—the Wild Side and the Mild Side. You can also jump at night. You'll pay NZ$180 for the jump (NZ$130 kids 10–15), a T-shirt, and the gondola ride; allow 1 hour. The **Ledge Sky Swing** also operates here and costs NZ$130 for adults and NZ$90 for children ages 10 to 15. The **Nevis Highwire Bungy ★★★** is Hackett's big daddy of bungy. At 134m (440 ft.) over the Kawarau River, it is the tallest bungy site in New Zealand. The full package here costs NZ$260 for adults and NZ$210 for students with ID; minimum age is 13. The **Nevis Arc** is the latest addition to this thrill seekers' heaven. It's right beside Nevis Bungy. You'll walk across a 70m (230-ft.) suspension bridge to the launchpad, and then decide which way you're going to free fall 160m (525 ft.) through the air above Doolan's Creek Gorge. This crazy adventure will cost you NZ$180 for adults, NZ$120 for children ages 10 to 15; minimum age is 10.

Don't forget to check out the A. J. Hackett combos, which offer several thrills at a reduced cost.

CANYONING   Canyoning is an energetic sport where participants make their way through river canyons using a number of adventure skills including rappelling, walking, climbing, jumping, and swimming. **Canyoning NZ** (📞 **03/441-3003;** www.canyoning.co.nz) does a half-day Queenstown trip for NZ$185 (minimum age 10); and a full-day Routeburn canyoning trip for NZ$240 per person. Allow 3 hours, 1½ of them wet. They also offer a heli-canyon combo, and operate daily from mid-October through to mid-April.

FISHING   The visitor center can advise you on several recognized trout-fishing operators with prices ranging from NZ$85 per hour to NZ$800 or more for a full-day excursion. **Queenstown Fishing Charters** (📞 **03/441-1330;** www.queenstowncharters.co.nz) and **Stu Dever Fishing Charters** (📞 **03/442-6371;** www.fishing-queenstown.co.nz) both offer trips from 2 hours to a full day. Both

15

QUEENSTOWN & ENVIRONS

Queenstown

charge around NZ$125 for 2 hours, NZ$165 for 3 hours, and NZ$225 for 4 hours. Or try **Over The Top Fly Fishing** (ⓒ **0800/123-359** in NZ, or 03/442-2233; www.flynz.co.nz) for a truly out-of-the-way guided heli-fly-fishing experience.

GOLF   The ultimate in Queenstown golf is **Millbrook Resort ★★★**, Arrowtown (ⓒ **0800/800-604** in NZ, or 03/441-7010; www.millbrook.co.nz), where you'll pay NZ$70 to NZ$165 for the par-72, Bob Charles–designed course. Carts, equipment, instruction, and a free shuttle from Queenstown are available. The 18-hole **Queenstown Golf Club,** Kelvin Heights (ⓒ **03/442-9169;** www.queenstowngolf.co.nz), is a full-service course with NZ$75 to NZ$90 greens fees and NZ$65 for club rental.

HORSE TREKKING   There are a number of horse-trekking operators who charge from NZ$55 to NZ$125 for a tour. **Moonlight Stables** (ⓒ **03/442-1229;** www.moonlightcountry.co.nz) is on the 325-hectare (800-acre) Doonholme Farm, 15 minutes from Queenstown. Well-mannered horses and experienced guides offer full- or half-day treks through spectacular landscapes and deer farms. **Shotover Stables** (ⓒ **03/442-9708**) is just 6 minutes out of town at Arthur's Point.

HOT-AIR BALLOONING   **Sunrise Balloons ★★** (ⓒ **0800/468-247** in NZ, or 03/442-0781; www.ballooningnz.com) will give you a memorable experience floating silently over the Wakatipu Basin at dawn. The price—NZ$395 for adults, NZ$295 for children ages 4 to 12—includes a champagne breakfast after landing.

JET-BOATING   **Shotover Jet ★★★** (ⓒ **0800/746-868** in NZ, or 03/442-5591; www.shotoverjet.com) is perhaps the best-known operator and the biggest adrenaline rush. You'll pay from NZ$119 for adults and NZ$69 for kids ages 5 to 15 to blast through narrow rocky canyons in as little as 10 centimeters (4 in.) of water for 30 minutes. **Kawarau Jet** (ⓒ **0800/529-272** in NZ, or 03/409-0000; www.kjet.co.nz) departs from the main town pier and skates across Lake Wakatipu to the Kawarau and Shotover rivers. The 45- to 60-minute trip costs NZ$99 for adults, NZ$55 for kids 5 to 15, and NZ$257 for a family (see "Money-Saving Combos," below, for other options).

LUGE   The **Skyline Luge ★★★** (ⓒ **03/441-0101;** www.skyline.co.nz) is nearly 1km (½ mile) of downhill fun. Various packages are on offer, including several rides and gondola transport. The gondola- and single-luge ride costs NZ$33 for adults and NZ$23 for children. Multi-ride deals are also available. It operates daily from 10am to 9pm in summer (5pm in winter); purchase tickets at the Skyline Gondola terminals.

HANG GLIDING/PARAGLIDING   **Queenstown Paragliding School** (ⓒ **0800/727-245** in NZ; www.extremeair.co.nz) will give you a day's course in the basics from NZ$235. There are approximately 15 **tandem gliding** operators, most working above the gondola on Bob's Peak; prices are NZ$195 to NZ$275 for an introductory tandem flight.

RIVER BOARDING/RIVER SURFING   If you thought surfing was restricted to the ocean, forget it. Now you can cling to a specially designed boogie board, don a helmet, and go for it down churning river rapids. **Serious Fun River Surfing** (ⓒ **0800/737-468** in NZ, or 03/442-5262; www.riversurfing.co.nz) goes down a 7km (4-mile) stretch of the Kawarau River for NZ$175. You'll progress from flat water to Grade IV rapids with instruction as you go along. No experience is necessary, but confidence in the water is. Trips are conducted from October to May from 8am to 8pm. An extra guide is provided for children under 12.

SKIING   From late June to September, the international ski crowd flocks to Queenstown to enjoy the accessible slopes of **Coronet Peak;** the least-crowded slopes of the **Remarkables;** the best family fields at **Cardrona;** and the most challenging slopes at **Treble Cone.** For the ultimate rush, try a day of heli-skiing or heli-boarding with **Harris Mountains Heliski** (✆ 03/442-6722; www.heliski.co.nz), **Heli-Guides** (✆ 03/442-7733; www.flynz.co.nz), or **Glacier Southern Lakes Heliski** (✆ 03/442-3016; www.heli-flights.co.nz). For more information on skiing and snowboarding in the area, see chapter 4.

SKY DIVING   For NZ$269 to NZ$429, **NZONE** (✆ 03/442-5867; www.nzone.biz) will fly you over awesome scenery and then drop you out to fall at speeds of up to 200kmph (124 mph).

WALKING   Three well-known multiday walks start in the Queenstown vicinity. See "Tramping" in chapter 4 for information on the **Routeburn,** the **Greenstone Valley,** and the **Grand Traverse Tracks.** Each starts near the little township of Glenorchy, at the far end of Lake Wakatipu, 47km (29 miles) from Queenstown. It's also possible to sample these great walks by going in several hours and back out again on the same day. Alternatively, you can do the **Routeburn Encounter Guided Day Walk ★★** (✆ 0800/768-832 in NZ, or 03/442-8200; www.ultimatehikes.co.nz) from November to April, with transport from Queenstown provided. The track rises 230m (755 ft.) over 6.5km (4 miles) and is suitable for reasonably active people. Take warm and waterproof clothing and good boots. It costs NZ$1,350 to NZ$1,495 for adults and NZ$1,100 to NZ$1,245 for children 10 to 15. **Ultimate Hikes,** The Station Building, Duke St., Queenstown (✆ 0800/659-255 in NZ, or 03/450-1940; www.ultimatehikes.co.nz), offers a similar 1-day guided walk on the Milford Track, plus multiday guided options. A guided walk on **Hollyford Track** (✆ 0800/832-226 in NZ, or 03/442-3000; www.hollyfordtrack.com) includes a unique perspective on the Maori history of the area. Guided walks are available October through April for NZ$1,695 for adults and NZ$1,295 for children ages 10 and up.

The **Department of Conservation Information Centre,** 37 Shotover St. (✆ 03/442-7935), open daily from 8am to 8pm, can furnish details on short walks around Queenstown as well as those farther afield. There are at least 10 walks of 1 to 8 hours' length in and around town. One of the most testing is the 2- to 3-hour, uphill **Queenstown Hill Track,** which starts and finishes on Belfast Terrace. You'll be rewarded by great views and photo opportunities if you make it to the top. There are also several excellent walks around **Lake Wakatipu,** including the pleasant and easy **Bobs Cove Track and Nature Trail ★★,** which starts 14km (9 miles) from Queenstown on the road to Glenorchy. **Guided Walks of New Zealand ★★★** (✆ 0800/455-712 in NZ, or 03/442-7126; www.nzwalks.com) specializes in treks with nature interpretation. They offer half- and full-day options for a maximum of seven people, costing from NZ$110 to NZ$435 per person.

Pleasant walks and trails are scattered in and around **Arrowtown.** Pick up the Department of Conservation brochure, which details all these walks, their conditions, and fitness requirements. For weather forecast information, call **Metphone** (✆ 0900/99-903 in NZ; www.metservice.co.nz).

WHITE-WATER RAFTING   The Shotover and Kawarau rivers are top spots for white-water rafting. The Kawarau trips are generally better for those who are rafting for the first time. The Shotover trips are much more challenging and are usually accompanied by safety kayaks. **Challenge Rafting ★★** (✆ 0800/442-7318 in

If you want to try a variety of activities, look into money-saving combos. Most booking agents around Queenstown can fill you in on all the details and several adventure operators have their own combinations. The **Shotover High Five ★★** combines the Shotover Jet with a helicopter ride, luge, and gondola ride. **Queenstown Combos** (📞 0800/423-836 in NZ, or 03/ 442-7318; www.combos.co.nz) has about 14 different packages and can make reservations for you. Prices start at NZ$257. Mention Frommer's and get a 10% discount if you book direct. **Extreme Combos** (📞 03/442-8517; www.nzraft.com) offers a range of raft-ing-based combos that include bungy, helicopter rides, sky diving, and jet boats.

NZ; www.raft.co.nz), has half- and full-day rafting trips from NZ$175. Mention Frommer's and you'll get a 10% discount when booking direct. **Queenstown Rafting** (📞 0800/723-846 in NZ; www.rafting.co.nz) operates similar trips priced from NZ$195. They also have a multiday rafting trip in the Landsborough Valley for NZ$1,495. **Extreme Green Rafting ★★★** (📞 03/442-8517; www.nzraft.com) is a smaller operator with more competitive prices. It also has an Upper Shotover Scenic option, which includes a flight or drive to the top of the river. This full-day outing is a passive rather than high-adrenaline activity, suitable for all ages and levels of fitness. It's also priced at NZ$195.

IN NEARBY GLENORCHY

Glenorchy is a tiny village surrounded by rugged high country, mountains, glacier-fed lakes, and ancient beech forests—*The Lord of the Rings* country, in fact. Much of the filming was done in this remote area. It's also the latest hot spot in southern tourism. Just 40 minutes away, it's now a base for several tour operators, all of which offer transport from Queenstown.

FUNYAKING Sitting in an inflatable Canadian-style canoe and floating down-stream at 8kmph (5 mph), enjoying the scenery, is my idea of a sensible adventure. With **Funyaks ★★★** (📞 03/442-9992; www.dartriversafaris.com) you'll jet-boat up the Dart River for 75 minutes (or you can go by 4WD vehicle, if you prefer), then canoe back down to Glenorchy in stable inflatable canoes. No need for daredevil confidence—it's a family trip guaranteed to please everyone. The price—NZ$289 for adults, NZ$189 for children ages 3 to 15, and NZ$767 for a family—includes trans-port, guides, and lunch.

HORSE TREKKING Dart Stables ★ (📞 0800/474-3464 in NZ, or 03/442-5688; www.dartstables.com) has exclusive riding territory in the high country of the 200-hectare (500-acre) Wyuna Station and sole rights to trek through Department of Conservation areas. Treks are available for all abilities and range from 2 hours to overnight excursions. Shorter treks range in price from NZ$135 to NZ$315 per per-son while an overnight adventure with 2 days riding and all food and accommodations included costs NZ$615 to NZ$635.

JET-BOATING Dart River Jet Safaris ★★★ (📞 0800/327-8538 in NZ, or 03/442-9992; www.dartriverjetsafaris.com) provides one of the best jet-boating expe-riences in New Zealand. Its Wilderness Safari combines jet-boating with walks in ancient forests and visits to *Lord of the Rings* sites at Paradise. It departs Glenorchy daily at 9am and 1pm (Queenstown 8am and noon). Allow 6 hours in total and expect to pay NZ$219 for adults, NZ$119 for children 3 to 15, and NZ$557 for a family.

WALKING   Glenorchy is the departure point for the **Routeburn,** the **Greenstone and Caples,** and the **Rees and Dart** tracks, all of which are internationally renowned. Get information at the **Department of Conservation,** Glenorchy Visitor Centre (✆ **03/442-9937;** www.glenorchyinfocentre.co.nz). See also "Tramping" in chapter 4.

Shopping

Queenstown has an excellent range of New Zealand–made goods, from sheepskin products, leather, and outdoor wear to fine crafts, pure wool hand-knits, and jewelry. Most shops are open daily to 10pm, and many offer overseas packaging and postal services. In addition to the main township, don't forget to check out **Remarkables Park Town Centre** (www.remarkablesparktowncentre.co.nz), which has a range of national retailers and boutique stores, banks, supermarkets, cafes, and restaurants. It's open daily (most stores open 9am–6pm), and is well signposted off Kawarau Road (St. Hwy. 6), near Queenstown Airport. Pick up the free *Queenstown Dining & Shopping Guide* at the visitor center.

Nearby Arrowtown also makes for a lovely shopping outing. Its short main street is filled with heritage buildings bulging at the seams with great quality New Zealand fashion and leisure wear, gold, jade, art, and assorted specialty stores. Standout stores here are fashion and New Zealand leisurewear suppliers **Woolpress Arrowtown,** 40 Buckingham St. (✆ **03/442-0033;** www.thewoolpress.com), and **Te Huia,** 38 Buckingham St. (✆ **03/442-1355;** www.tehuianz.com).

In Queenstown, **O'Connells Shopping Centre,** Camp and Beach streets (✆ **03/442-7760**), has 25 stores offering everything from food and fashion to knitwear, jewelry, and contemporary art. If you missed **Canterbury New Zealand** (✆ **03/442-4020**) in other major centers, you'll find it here.

Bonz Gallery, upstairs in **Bonz New Zealand** ★, 8–10 The Mall (✆ **03/442-5398;** www.bonz.com.au), is a top outlet for original designs in 100% merino wool hand-knit sweaters and jackets. **Goldfields Jade and Opal,** top of The Mall (✆ **03/442-9356**), and the **Opal Centre,** Beach and Rees streets (✆ **03/442-8239;** www.opalsnz.com), have the finest collections of investment opal jewelry.

For one of the biggest selections of sheepskins, woolen jerseys, leisurewear, jewelry, wooden carvings, confectionery, and local honeys and jams, go to **DF Souvenirs,** 32 The Mall (✆ **03/442-5275**). Another good source of all of the above is the **Mountaineer Shop,** Beach and Rees streets (✆ **03/442-7460**). And if you have a sweet tooth, don't miss the **British Lolly Shop,** Church Lane (✆ **03/441-2274;** www.thebritishlollyshop.com), which seems an awfully long way from home to me, but some among you may be glad of that. You'll find another very cute little gift store at **Vesta** ★, Williams Cottage, 19 Marine Parade (✆ **03/442-5687**), which is hardly bigger than a doll's house, yet manages to present some excellent New Zealand art, design work, and a tiny cafe.

Untouched World ★★★, The Mall (✆ **03/442-4992;** www.untouchedworld.com/default.aspx), is a fabulous source of exclusive men's and women's apparel—especially Merinomink garments that combine 100% New Zealand merino wool with possum fur for pure luxury. If you'd like to take home a special memento of your time in New Zealand, visit **Toi o Tahuna Fine Art Gallery** ★★★, Church Lane,

Queenstown (✆ **03/409-0787;** www.toi.co.nz), which has a great range of original art, sculpture, ceramics, glass, and jade.

Where to Stay

There are now over 20,000 guest beds in this small town, ranging from backpackers to new apartments, international-class hotels, and luxury lodges, yet still they keep coming. Even with multiple new additions, it still pays to book well in advance. If you're looking for something extra special, refer to the Queenstown luxury concierge company, **Touch of Spice Private Villa Collection ★★★** (www.touchofspice. co.nz; ✆ **03/450-0855**), listed in chapter 17, "Planning Your Trip to New Zealand." They provide a luxury concierge service for their Private Villa Collection—everything from rustic cottages to country lodges and luxury penthouses. **Hilton Queenstown** is a new, 178-room lakeside property with a heated swimming pool, a health club, and a spa. Next door is the **Kawarau Hotel Managed by Hilton,** which has 98 1-bedroom, apartment-style rooms plus a restaurant and lounge. Both opened in 2011 and are in Kawarau Village, Peninsula Road, Queenstown (www.hilton.com/queenstown; ✆ **03/450-9400**). Rates below include 15% GST and free off-street parking unless otherwise noted.

IN QUEENSTOWN
Very Expensive

Eichardt's Private Hotel ★★★ 🏨   Voted the Best Small Hotel in the World by Andrew Harper (www.andrewharpertravel.com) in 2003, Eichardt's takes on the best of any luxury accommodations in New Zealand and comes up trumps. It's small, but first class in every respect. The large rooms have luxurious bathrooms, and you'll get all the modern conveniences in an exquisite interior that draws on the original building's history. Service is detailed, interior design mouthwatering, and its central location a bonus. Just be sure to pack earplugs as noise in this central location can sometimes be an issue. And check out their modern Lakefront Cottage with four two-bedroom suites, just down the street.

Marine Parade, Queenstown. www.eichardts.com. ✆ **03/441-0450.** Fax 03/441-0440. 9 units. NZ$1,449 lakefront family; NZ$1,190 lakefront suite; NZ$1,640 mountain view; NZ$1,895 lake view. NZ$260 each extra person; NZ$260 per person Christmas/New Year supplement. Long-stay and off-peak rates. Rates include breakfast and cocktails. AE, DC, MC, V. **Amenities:** Restaurant; bar; airport transfers available; babysitting; bike rentals; concierge; 5 nearby golf courses; room service. *In room:* A/C, TV/DVD/CD, fridge, hair dryer, kitchenette in lakefront cottage suites, minibar, Wi-Fi.

Sofitel Queenstown ★★★   This is New Zealand's first Sofitel hotel—and with bigger rooms, wired concierge, and espresso machines in every room, it's setting a new standard for service. Rooms are classic yet sensual, bathrooms are orchid-filled and complete with LCD screens over the bathtub. It's right in the center of town surrounded by new shops and restaurants. It's a sophisticated stay for the discerning traveler and even classier after a NZ$2-million upgrade in 2010 and 2011. I recommend its wonderful Parisian-style eatery (**Left Bank Café;** p. 437), and its luxurious day spa gives you just one more reason to treat yourself! The property has a Qualmark Enviro-Gold rating.

8 Duke St., Queenstown. www.sofitel.co.nz. ✆ **03/450-0045.** Fax 03/450-0046. 82 units. NZ$389–NZ$649 superior; NZ$539–NZ$799 executive; NZ$689–NZ$949 suite; NZ$2,000–NZ$2,500 penthouse. Long-stay, off-peak, and special packages. AE, DC, MC, V. Valet parking NZ$20 per day. **Amenities:** Restaurant; cafe, bar; airport transport; nearby bike rentals; Les Clefs d'Or Concierge; executive-level rooms; nearby golf course; gym; Jacuzzi (in penthouses); 24-hr. room service; infrared

Body Business

When the stress of being a tourist gets the better of you, turn your attention to one of Queenstown's best pampering services. Among them, **Body Sanctum Day Spa** ★★, Level 1, 10 Athol St. (✆ 03/442-4336; www.bodysanctum. co.nz), comes most highly recommended. Men and women alike can feel the benefits of aromatherapy, sports massage, shiatsu, reflexology, and a variety of beauty therapy services. You can also unwind at the **Millbrook Resort Day Spa** ★★★, Malaghan Road (✆ 03/441-7000; fax 03/441-7007); it's the biggest and classiest, and offers a full range of wet and dry massage therapies, a hair salon, facials, beauty treatments, manicures, and pedicures—all set within the restful acres of Millbrook.

Aspects Day Spa, 53 Shotover St. (✆ 03/442-7389; www.aspectsdayspa. co.nz), can rejuvenate the weariest traveler with a range of massage therapies, body wraps, Jacuzzis, and manicures. **Hush Spa** ★★, Level 2, the Junction, corner of Gorge and Robins roads (✆ 03/409-0901; www.hushspa.co.nz), will soothe you with exotic body therapies, massage rituals, and facial treatments. **Le Spa at Sofitel** ★★, Sofitel Hotel (✆ 03/450-0045; www. lespaqueenstown.co.nz), is the best equipped and the most glamorous of the Queenstown day spas. Its classy spa suites and gorgeous French products take personal indulgence to new heights.

room; steam room; day spa and beauty treatments. *In room:* A/C, TV/DVD/CD, fridge, hair dryer, kitchen (in penthouses), minibar, Wi-Fi.

Expensive

A Boutique Hotel—Queenstown House ★ In addition to remodeling this unique stay into something between a small boutique hotel and a B&B, owner Louise Kiely gave it a big revamp in 2010. The property has seven delightful rooms in the main house and seven new villa suites in an adjacent building. Each has its own special charm but for the best views, go for the larger Baron Room. Apartment suites in the new block are much bigger and have their own decks, large sitting rooms, and a modern kitchen. Louise has personality-plus and encourages guests to meet for pre-dinner drinks in the cozy living room. A delicious breakfast is served in the dining room overlooking the lake and township, which is only a short walk downhill.

69 Hallenstein St., Queenstown. www.queenstownhouse.co.nz. ✆ **03/442-9043.** Fax 03/442-8755. 15 units. NZ$250–NZ$395 in main house; NZ$395–NZ$595 villa. Long-stay and off-peak rates, special deals. Rates include breakfast and pre-dinner drinks. AE, DC, MC, V. **Amenities:** Babysitting; nearby golf course. *In room:* TV/DVD, fridge (in some), hair dryer, kitchen (in suites), Wi-Fi.

The Dairy Private Luxury Hotel ★ Once a 1920s general store, the Dairy has grown beyond a simple B&B and is now a small, boutique hotel. Bedrooms are beautifully decorated and there are excellent social spaces, including a roaring fire and reading room. You'll be spoiled with delicious afternoon tea scones. Always a well-loved spot just a stroll from town, it has a stronger hosting presence than Brown's and Queenstown House, but the latter both have bigger rooms. The premier rooms here have the best views. The property has a Qualmark Enviro-Silver rating.

10 Isle St., Queenstown. www.thedairy.co.nz. ✆ **03/442-5164.** Fax 03/442-5166. 13 units. NZ$465–NZ$495. Long-stay and off-peak rates. Rates include breakfast. AE, MC, V. Limited off-street parking.

It's a 150m (490-ft.) uphill walk from town center. No children under 12. **Amenities:** Bar; bike rentals; airport transfers (fee); Jacuzzi. *In room:* TV, hair dryer, high-speed Internet.

Pencarrow ★★ 🏆   Bill and Kari Moers' outstanding service and value put them in a class of their own when it comes to B&Bs; in fact, they rival many more expensive options in their attention to detail and the warmth of their welcome. Factor in four fabulous big rooms and a collection of Persian rugs to die for—not to mention great views and an unforgettable breakfast—and you'll see why I rate this as one of the best B&B stays in the country.

678 Frankton Rd., Queenstown. www.pencarrow.net. ✆ **03/442-8938.** Fax 03/442-8974. 4 units. NZ$595 suite. Long-stay rates. Rates include breakfast. AE, DC, MC, V. Turn off Frankton Rd. btw. the Remarkables and Greenstone apartment complexes and head straight up the central (and steep) gravel driveway. No children 12 and under. **Amenities:** Nearby golf course (free use of clubs available); small fitness room; Jacuzzi. *In room:* A/C (in 2 upstairs rooms), TV/VCR, fridge, hair dryer, kitchen (in 1 suite), minibar, free Wi-Fi.

Queenstown Park Hotel ★★   This small, boutique hotel has an understated glamour that will appeal to those who like a sleek, contemporary stay. Rooms are generous and have terrific views to the mountains and gondola in one direction and over the lake and township in the other. Glass-walled bathrooms are large. Service is first rate and the property has a Qualmark Enviro-Silver rating.

21 Robins Rd., Queenstown. www.queenstownparkhotel.co.nz. ✆ **03/441-8441.** Fax 03/441-8451. 19 units. NZ$450–NZ$590; Tower Suite NZ$795. Long-stay and off-peak rates. Rates include pre-dinner drinks and canapés. AE, DC, MC, V. **Amenities:** Breakfast restaurant; babysitting on request; concierge. *In room:* A/C, TV/DVD, fridge, hair dryer, kitchenette, minibar, Wi-Fi.

Moderate

Brown's Boutique Hotel 🏆   You'll be right at home at Brown's if you want a good-value stay with character and friendly, knowledgeable local hosts. The hillside, Tuscan-style property with great views offers spacious rooms with big bathrooms and luxurious beds. Size-wise, it's on a par with the Dairy and Queenstown House, although being purpose-built, it has a more distinct small hotel character. There are five guest rooms on two levels, with generous living areas and patios on the ground floor. Town is just a 4-minute walk downhill.

26 Isle St., Queenstown. www.brownshotel.co.nz. ✆ **03/441-2050.** Fax 03/441-2060. 10 units. NZ$325–NZ$345. Long-stay and off-peak rates. Rates include breakfast. AE, DC, MC, V. **Amenities:** Nearby golf course. *In room:* TV/DVD, fridge, hair dryer, free Wi-Fi.

Chalet Queenstown ★ 🏨   This Swiss-style chalet was completely revamped in 2009 and now offers warm, stylish rooms with big beds, luxurious feather duvets, private bathrooms, and glorious balcony views across Lake Wakatipu. Guests have a comfortable lounge and a peaceful courtyard for relaxing. A hearty breakfast is served and the property is just a 5-minute walk to the central shopping area via the walking track around the lake. It's very good value all round.

1 Dublin St., Queenstown. www.chaletqueenstown.co.nz. ✆ **0800/222-457** in NZ, or 03/442-7117. Fax 03/442-7508. 7 units. N$195–NZ$270. Long-stay and off-peak rates. Rates include breakfast. AE, MC, V. **Amenities:** Airport transfers (charge applies); babysitting on request; nearby bike rentals; nearby golf courses. *In Room:* TV, fridge, hair dryer, Wi-Fi.

Crowne Plaza Queenstown ★★   After a NZ$12-million upgrade in 2006–07, this central hotel has moved several notches higher in the style and service stakes. All of its 139 rooms were completely refurbished and its chic, innovative lobby, bars, and recommended restaurant (Three-Sixty) make a fabulous first impression. Rooms here are lake view, mountain view, or courtyard view, and they're priced accordingly. In reality, they're all exactly the same—pleasantly decorated in crisp white and earth-toned color schemes, with good bathrooms and excellent desks. I love the sleek, contemporary look of this place, and it's in a great spot within walking distance of all downtown shopping. The property has a Qualmark Enviro-Silver rating.

Beach St., Queenstown. www.crowneplazaqueenstown.co.nz. ℂ **0800/154-181** in NZ, or 03/441-0095. Fax 03/442-8895. 139 units. NZ$169–NZ$350 standard; NZ$250–NZ$675 suite. Long-stay, off-peak, and special deals. AE, DC, MC, V. Valet parking NZ$15 per day. **Amenities:** Restaurant; 2 bars; babysitting; concierge; nearby golf courses; 24-hr room service; sauna; Wi-Fi in public areas. *In room:* A/C, TV/DVD, fridge, hair dryer, minibar.

Garden Court Suites & Apartments ★ ✦

This is where you'll find a combination of motel units and contemporary apartments at a reasonable price in a good location. Existing motel studios are on a terraced slope, away from the road, so there's no traffic noise. Among these, the two-bedroom apartments are the best value, with a cozy living area, kitchen, and bathroom downstairs, and two bedrooms and a second toilet upstairs. If you want style and comfort, you won't find much to complain about in the new apartment block. Its bathrooms are simply great—well lit, spacious, and with combination tub/showers. Fourteen new one-bedroom apartments overlook the lake and are the quietest.

41 Frankton Rd., Queenstown. www.gardencourt.co.nz. ℂ **0800/427-336** in NZ, or 03/442-9713. Fax 03/442-6468. 54 units. NZ$192 studio suite; NZ$232–NZ$253 1-bedroom apt; NZ$304–NZ$392 2-bedroom apt. Extra person NZ$36. Off-peak rates. AE, DC, MC, V. .5km (¼ mile) from town center, opposite Millennium Hotel; on Shopper Bus route. **Amenities:** Breakfast restaurant; bike rentals; nearby golf course; Jacuzzi. *In room:* TV/VCR, fridge, hair dryer, kitchen (in studio suites and apts.), Wi-Fi.

Heritage Queenstown ★★★

This is a big hotel with an intimate boutique feel, idyllically set in an alpine forest and offering traditional hotel-style rooms as well as apartment-style suites with kitchen and laundry facilities. Accommodations are in three wings, with uncovered walkways between them and the main lodge (umbrellas are provided). The staff is incredibly friendly, the property is quiet, and you'll quickly get that home-away-from-home feel. Twenty large, stylish new villas came on stream in 2003, and these are terrific value for families and long-stayers. The property is Green Globe benchmarked and has a Qualmark Enviro-Gold rating.

91 Fernhill Rd., Queenstown. www.heritagehotels.co.nz. ℂ **0800/424-988** in NZ, or 03/450-1500. Fax 03/442-4989. 211 units. NZ$245–NZ$299 deluxe; NZ$330–NZ$550 suite; from NZ$620–NZ$699 villa. NZ$80 surcharge on lake-view rooms. Long-stay, off-peak, and special deals. AE, DC, MC, V. Drive through town and go up the hill at the Fernhill roundabout; 20-min. walk to town. **Amenities:** Restaurant; bar; babysitting; concierge; small exercise room; Jacuzzi; indoor/outdoor heated pool; room service; sauna; spa; Wi-Fi in reception and restaurant. *In room:* A/C, TV/DVD, fridge, hair dryer, high-speed Internet, kitchenette (in suites), minibar.

Historic Stone House ★ ✦

This charming, historic stone house, built in 1874, has a long history as an accommodation now; in the hands of Alex McMillan and John Oaten it has been converted into three stylish, self-catering apartments. Sink into luxurious beds a world away from the action, yet only a short walk to restaurants and shops. Open fires in winter give the guest lounge a cozy, home-away-from-home feel.

47 Hallenstein St., Queenstown. www.historicstonehouse.co.nz. ℂ **0800/222-457** in NZ, or 03/442-9812. Fax 03/442-7508. 3 units. NZ$199–NZ$225 1-bedroom apt; NZ$295–NZ$495 3-bedroom apt. Long-stay and off-peak rates. AE, MC, V. **Amenities:** Babysitting on request; nearby bike rentals; nearby golf courses. *In room:* TV/DVD, kitchenettes in all, fridge, hair dryer, Wi-Fi.

The Rees Hotel & Luxury Apartments ★★★ This modern, ecofriendly combination of hotel-style rooms and fabulous one- to four-bedroom apartments is terraced down the banks of Lake Wakatipu midway between the airport and the town. Rooms have a wonderful sense of privacy and staggering views, and there's a first-class restaurant (**True South;** p. 436), and exceptionally friendly service. You'll love the extra touches like the library of rare books, a wine cellar featuring New Zealand's best collection of Bordeaux wines, the gallery of original paintings, and an overall sense of being safely in the capable hands of someone who really knows how to look after you.

377 Frankton Rd., Queenstown. www.therees.co.nz. ✆ **03/450-1100.** Fax 03/409-2852. 150 units. NZ$245–NZ$325 Lake View Hotel room w/breakfast; NZ$325–NZ$425 1-bedroom apt; NZ$445–NZ$650 2-bedroom apt; NZ$595–NZ$855 3-bedroom apt. Long-stay and off-peak rates and special deals. AE, DC, MC, V. **Amenities:** Restaurant; bar; airport transfers (NZ$25 per person); babysitting; bike rentals; concierge; nearby golf courses; gymnasium; room service. *In room:* TV/DVD, fridge, hair dryer, Wi-Fi, kitchen (in apts.).

Scenic Suites Queenstown 🍴 Bright, new, contemporary—with big living areas, good-size bathrooms, and lovely kitchens—the apartments here are roomy and they have proximity to town on their side. Great value, great views. Scenic Suites shares reception and gym facilities with its sister property, the adjacent Heartland Hotel Queenstown (✆ **0800/696-963**), which also has good value, but older rooms.

27 Stanley St., Queenstown. www.scenichotelgroup.co.nz. ✆ **0800/696-963** in NZ, or 03/442-4718. Fax 03/442-4715. 84 units. NZ$370 superior room; NZ$450 1-bedroom suite; NZ$688 2-bedroom suite. Long-stay, off-peak, and special deals. AE, DC, MC, V. Shopper Bus stops nearby. **Amenities:** Restaurant; bar; nearby golf course; room service; Wi-Fi in reception. *In room:* TV, fridge, hair dryer, kitchen (suites only), minibar.

Inexpensive

Queenstown Top 10 Holiday Park Creeksyde, 54 Robins Rd. (www.camp.co.nz; ✆ **03/442-9447**), is definitely the Mercedes of campgrounds, situated in what was once a nursery—so there are trees and plants aplenty, plus room for 90 campervans, all with power outlets and water (solar heating) and waste hookups. There are also completely self-contained units and budget-priced lodge rooms. They have a Green Globe Gold certificate, and it's within a 5-minute walk of town. Rates are NZ$48 to NZ$55 for powered sites; NZ$62 to NZ$70 for lodge rooms; NZ$120 to NZ$226 for holiday units; and NZ$125 to NZ$234 for motel rooms. **YHA Queenstown Lakefront ★**, 88–90 Lake Esplanade, Queenstown (www.yha.co.nz; ✆ **0800/278-299** in NZ, or 03/442-8413), has 147 beds—dorm beds from NZ$30 to NZ$32 and doubles from NZ$57 to NZ$175.

Pinewood Lodge ★ 🍴 Rob and Roz Greig have created one of the best budget options on the South Island. The series of little houses dots a tree-covered hillside, and new complexes, housing a dorm area, kitchens, and lounges, rival many pricier operations. There's a real family feel about this place, the perfect choice if you want quality budget digs and a sociable atmosphere.

48 Hamilton Rd., Queenstown. www.pinewood.co.nz. ✆ **0800/746-3966** in NZ, or 03/442-8273. Fax 03/442-9470. 105 units. From NZ$28 dorm bed; NZ$60–NZ$90 double/twin; NZ$80–NZ$95 standard; NZ$100–NZ$120 en-suite unit. Extra person NZ$20. MC, V. **Amenities:** Children's playground; Jacuzzi. *In room:* TV (in some), no phone, kitchenette (in some), Wi-Fi.

JUST OUT OF TOWN
Very Expensive

Matakauri Lodge ★★★ It's very easy to fall in love with Matakauri. You only need to lie in your huge bathtub overlooking Lake Wakatipu to be seduced. Now owned by the Robertson family, it is the sister property to The Lodge at Kauri Cliffs and The Farm at Cape Kidnappers, and you can expect that same high level of service and attention to detail. All suites have breathtaking mountain and lake views and there's an intimacy and seclusion here that's absent from many larger properties. It has a certain x-factor that the similarly scaled Remarkables Lodge doesn't have.

Farrycroft Row, off Glenorchy Rd., Queenstown. www.matakaurilodge.com. © **03/441-1008.** Fax 03/441-2180. 11 units. NZ$1,369–NZ$2,737. Off-peak rates. Rates include pre-dinner drinks, canapés, gourmet dinner, full breakfast, complimentary minibar. AE, DC, MC, V. 5km (3 miles), a 7-min drive out of Queenstown on the road to Glenorchy. **Amenities:** Restaurant/dining room; bar; airport transfers NZ$105 each way; babysitting from NZ$35 per hour (min 3-hr. charge); free use of bikes; concierge; nearby golf courses; gym; Jacuzzi; day spa; limited room service; sauna; outdoor heated pool. *In room:* A/C, TV/DVD, fridge, hair dryer, minibar, free Wi-Fi.

Remarkables Lodge ★★ 🗡 Brian Savage and Colleen Ryan sailed around the world chartering their yacht for 10 years, and then bought Remarkables Lodge, which they have infused with new life and style. With a big extension and a total makeover, this lovely rural property is quiet and understated. Standouts here are the friendly staff, the fabulous meals, and some of the best beds I've slept in. They also offer some terrific, exclusive tours—Cascade Hut, for instance—that you won't want to miss. They have a Qualmark Enviro-Gold rating and are Green Globe benchmarked.

595 Kingston Rd., Queenstown. www.remarkables.co.nz. © **03/442-2720.** Fax 03/442-2730. 7 units. NZ$1,090–NZ$1,425. Long-stay, off-peak, and special deals. Rates include breakfast, afternoon tea, pre-dinner drinks and canapés, and 4-course dinner. AE, MC, V. Located 10 min. south of Queenstown, a few minutes after the entrance to Remarkables Ski Field. **Amenities:** Bar; free airport transfers; free use of bikes at nearby Jack's Point; nearby golf course (Jack's Point greens fees included in tariff); small fitness room; Jacuzzi; outdoor pool; room service; sauna; asphalt tennis court. *In room:* TV/DVD, fridge, hair dryer, free minibar, free Wi-Fi.

NEAR ARROWTOWN
Very Expensive

Millbrook Resort ★★★ 🗡 You'll love the minivillage feel to this rural resort—and its dramatic location. I can't fault the quantity and quality of facilities here. It has luxury accommodations and international-caliber golf at unbeatable rates, plus the best giant bathtubs. Opened in 1992, this award-winning resort is a destination in itself. The pricier cottages and villas are ideal for families or friends traveling together, while the generously sized village inn rooms offer the best value. Every comfort is attended to with 2m-wide (7-ft.) beds, fireplaces, and walk-in wardrobes. All this overlooks one of the best championship golf courses in the country. There are good walks between restaurants, spa facilities, and your room. One of the best-value stays you'll find.

Malaghans Rd., Arrowtown, Private Bag, Queenstown. www.millbrook.co.nz. © **0800/800-604** in NZ, or 03/441-7000. 170 units. NZ$435 village inn; NZ$485 villa suite; NZ$685 hotel villa; NZ$625 cottage; NZ$900–NZ$1,675 Fairway Home. Rates include breakfast. Special deals available. AE, DC, MC, V. 20 min. from Queenstown and 3 min. from Arrowtown. **Amenities:** 3 restaurants; bar; babysitting; bike rentals; children's programs; concierge; 18-hole golf course designed by Bob Charles, pro shop, driving and putting greens; extensive gym; 2 Jacuzzis and 1 Japanese hot pool; heated indoor pool; room service; saunas; day spa; 3 tennis courts (1 all-weather, 2 grass). *In room:* TV/DVD, fridge, hair dryer, high-speed Internet, kitchen (in some), minibar.

White Shadows Country Inn ★★ 📷 Set on 4 hectares (10 acres) of terraced gardens, lawns, and ponds, this romantic hideaway opened in 1999. Since then, hosts William Bailey and Michael Harris have impressed hundreds of international guests. Two guest suites are in a separate, secluded stone cottage with its own private courtyard. Rooms are plush and en-suite bathrooms have glass roofs. Wood beams, stone fireplaces, fine linens, and gourmet breakfasts are just a few of the reasons you should stay here.

58 Hunter Rd., RD1, Queenstown. www.whiteshadows.co.nz. ℂ **03/442-0871.** Fax 03/442-0872. 2 units. NZ$695 suite. 2-night minimum stay. Rates include breakfast, pre-dinner drinks, and hors d'oeuvres. AE, MC, V. Closed May to mid-Oct. No children 12 and under. **Amenities:** Free airport transfers; free use of bikes; several nearby golf courses; outdoor Jacuzzi. *In room:* A/C, TV/DVD, fridge, hair dryer, free minibar, free Wi-Fi.

Expensive

Arrowtown House Boutique Hotel ★★ I have followed Steve and Jeanette Brough to their third highly successful lodging. Like the two previous, this one is quite delicious, and Steve and Jeanette are the best and friendliest hosts you'll find. They've traveled extensively themselves, and they've applied that experience to providing first-rate rooms in a modern building beside the main lodge. All have balconies or patios, and you'll never know anyone else is around. It's just a 5-minute walk into town. They're both superb cooks, too, so expect a breakfast to remember.

10 Caernarvon St., Arrowtown. www.arrowtownhouse.com. ℂ **03/441-6008.** Fax 03/441-6015. 5 units. NZ$489 standard suite; NZ$544 superior suite. Long-stay and off-peak rates. Rates include gourmet breakfast, pre-dinner drinks, and canapés. MC, V. As you drive into Arrowtown, turn left into Caernarvon St. by the small church. **Amenities:** Bar; airport transfers (NZ$55); babysitting; nearby golf courses. *In room:* TV, fridge, hair dryer, minibar, free Wi-Fi.

Moderate

Arrowfield Apartments ★★★, 115 Essex Ave., Butel Park, Arrowtown (www.arrowfield.co.nz; ℂ **03/442-0012**), has 22 modern, self-contained one-, two-, and three-bedroom apartments, and guests have the use of an indoor lap pool, gym, and tennis courts. The apartments are beautifully appointed and are ideal for families or couples traveling together. They're priced from NZ$175 to NZ$550 per apartment.

Inexpensive

Arrowtown Lodge ★, 7 Anglesea St., Arrowtown (www.arrowtownlodge.co.nz; ℂ **0800/258-802** in NZ, or 03/442-1101; fax 03/442-1108), has four semidetached cottages that replicate something of Arrowtown's gold-rush heritage. You'll get charm and 21st-century comfort here for the very reasonable rate of NZ$120 to NZ$200.

IN NEARBY GLENORCHY

There's a bit of everything in Glenorchy, from cheap backpacker properties to a high-end lodge. **Glenorchy Hotel,** Mull Street, Glenorchy (www.glenorchynz.com; ℂ **03/442-9902;** fax 03/442-9912), is a classic Kiwi country-style hotel with nine rooms and backpacker accommodations; **Glenorchy Holiday Park & Backpackers,** 2 Oban St., Glenorchy (glenpark@queenstown.co.nz; ℂ **03/442-7171**), has the usual campground facilities, plus lodge rooms and cabins; and gorgeous little **Kinloch Lodge ★**, 862 Kinloch Rd., Glenorchy (www.kinlochlodge.co.nz; ℂ **03/442-4900**), located between the Greenstone and Routeburn tracks, offers bunks (from NZ$33 per person) and private rooms with shared facilities (NZ$85–NZ$298), in a setting you'll always remember. Drive 45 minutes out to Glenorchy, then take a 3-minute boat ride across the lake to the low-cost comforts of this outback gem.

Very Expensive

Blanket Bay ★★★ This is luxury at its most sublime. Opened in 1999, this Small Luxury Hotels of the World member is set on sprawling grounds on the bush-clad fringes of Lake Wakatipu. At the heart of the lodge is a 9m-high (30-ft.) great room

Winning Wines

Gantley's Restaurant, 172 Arthur's Point Rd., Arthur's Point (📞 **03/442-8999;** www.gantleys.co.nz), has an extensive wine list with over 250 selections, showcasing some of the most outstanding wines produced in New Zealand. One of only a few New Zealand restaurants to win an Award of Excellence from *Wine* *Spectator* magazine for "having one of the most outstanding restaurant wine lists in the world," Gantley's is favored for its romantic interior and superior wine selections. Main courses range from NZ$35 to NZ$45, and they're open daily from 6pm; they offer courtesy transport from Queenstown.

with a massive log fireplace and antique wooden floors. No expense has been spared in the construction of the spacious guest rooms. All beds are king-size, and all bathrooms have double sinks and separate showers and tubs. High-fidelity sound systems and private balconies are in every room. Designed as an exclusive haven, Blanket Bay promises a lot—and delivers. A big bonus here is the award-winning cuisine.

Rapid No. 4191 Glenorchy Rd., Glenorchy. www.blanketbay.com. 📞 **03/441-0115.** Fax 03/442-9441. 13 units. NZ$1,590 lodge room; NZ$2,350 suite; NZ$2,950 stateroom. Extra person NZ$375. Off-peak rates. Rates include breakfast, pre-dinner cocktails, and dinner. AE, DC, MC, V. Closed June. Near Glenorchy, a 45-min. drive from Queenstown. Water and helipad access and limousine transport can be arranged. No children 13 and under. **Amenities:** 3 dining rooms; 2 bars; airport transfers (NZ$205 each way); free use of bikes; concierge; well-equipped gym; Jacuzzi; heated outdoor pool; 24-hr. room service; 2 steam rooms; free watersports equipment. *In room:* A/C, TV/DVD, fridge, hair dryer, minibar, free Wi-Fi.

Where to Eat

Queenstown is filled with an ever-changing array of good cafes and restaurants. The **Skyline Queenstown Restaurant** (📞 **03/441-0101;** www.skyline.co.nz) is as much an experience as a meal. Enjoy lavish lunch and evening buffets accompanied by spectacular views. A buffet dinner including gondola ride is NZ$76 for adults (NZ$36 children 5–14) and lunch is NZ$51 (NZ$26 for children). The restaurant is huge and tour groups are seated in a separate area. You can include a *haka* performance for NZ$110 for adults, NZ$54 children ages 5 to 14, and NZ$282 for a family. Bookings are essential.

IN QUEENSTOWN
Expensive
Boardwalk Seafood Restaurant ★ SEAFOOD   After 15 years in operation, but now with a new owner, this upstairs spot has a new lease on life. It's always been recognized for its excellent seafood—in partnership with New Zealand beef and lamb—and that hasn't changed. The big seafood platters are always popular, daily fish specials are innovatively presented, and the roasted rack of lamb wins fans every time. Despite the competition from new fine-dining players, award-winning Boardwalk is always mentioned in top recommendations.

Steamer Wharf, Beach St. 📞 **03/442-5630.** www.boardwalk.net.nz. Reservations recommended. Main courses NZ$40. AE, DC, MC, V. Daily 6pm–late.

Botswana Butchery ★★ CONTEMPORARY NEW ZEALAND/EURO-PEAN   Chef Leungo Lippe's kitchen is in an opulent, upmarket little restaurant in a historic cottage on the waterfront. It's a meat-eater's heaven where they specialize in fine beef cuts, wild game, and organic foods. All meat cuts are aged and are served

Every city has them—those luscious little culinary secrets that locals like to keep for themselves. **The Bunker ★★★**, Cow Lane (✆ **03/441-8030; www.thebunker.co.nz**), is a sublime dining experience but don't think that just because I've given you the address, you're going to be able to find it easily. It hides behind a very unassuming door and just assumes that people who are hungry and passionate enough will find it. You won't regret the hunt. It's a tiny restaurant with a huge reputation for classy haute cuisine, an intimate atmosphere, and an impressive collection of single malt whiskeys. Venison, lamb, scampi, quail, and duck all take their place on an innovative menu that most definitely will make a hole in your wallet. It's open from 5pm until 5am, by which time you'll probably be bankrupt but hugely satisfied. Reservations are essential, and main courses range from NZ$44 to NZ$50.

either wood-grilled or pan-seared to your liking. Expect to pay extra for even a leaf of greenery to add to already expensive plates. It's a lovely atmosphere, though, and decorative touches like meat cleavers for door handles make it interesting.

Marine Parade. ✆ **03/442-6994.** www.botswanabutchery.co.nz. Reservations recommended. Main courses NZ$34–NZ$80, vegetables NZ$6–NZ$15 extra. AE, DC, MC, V. Daily noon–late.

Eichardt's House Bar ★★★ 🎁 CONTEMPORARY NEW ZEALAND For a sublime lunch experience (or just coffee and cake), treat yourself to the oh-so-classy environs of Eichardt's House Bar, in the private hotel building on the ground floor. Just five tables add to the air of exclusivity, so be in quick. New Zealand crab and scallop cake, wild pork pies, Moroccan chicken, and delicious vegetarian dishes have all been featured on this top menu. Small, but big on atmosphere, it's a must. It's also a great cocktail spot at night, before or after dinner.

Ground Floor, Eichardt's Private Hotel, Marine Parade. ✆ **03/442-0450.** www.eichardtshotel.co.nz. Reservations recommended. Main courses NZ$26–NZ$34. AE, DC, MC, V. Lunch daily noon–2pm. Bar daily 11am–11pm.

True South ★★ CONTEMPORARY EUROPEAN I like a restaurant that offers you lots of choices, and here at True South you can take your pick from a truly memorable 10-course degustation menu, two-or three-course set menus, or a la carte, all of which include delectable treats like poached blue cod with fennel, gnocchi, and ratatouille; or wild venison braised and roasted with red cabbage and chocolate. It's an adventurous menu and visually stunning, and I for one think that "food as theater" is a very important component of dining out.

The Rees Hotel, 377 Frankton Rd. ✆ **03/450-1100.** www.truesouthdiningroom.co.nz. Reservations essential. Main courses NZ$32–NZ$38; 10-course degustation menu NZ$85; 2-course set menu NZ$45; 3-course set menu NZ$55. AE, DC, MC, V. Daily 6pm–late.

Moderate

Bella Cucina ★★ ITALIAN COUNTRY This little gem was opened by the people who brought us Wai Waterfront (see below), and it's quickly established itself as a local favorite. They have great wood-fired pizzas, and pasta is made on-site each day. Factor in seafood and slow-cooked meat dishes—all at very affordable prices—and you have a winner. The menu changes daily, based on available fresh ingredients, and the mood is relaxed and intimate.

6 Brecon St. ☎ **03/442-6762.** www.bellacucina.co.nz. Reservations recommended. Main courses NZ$18–NZ$31. AE, DC, MC, V. Daily 11am–11pm.

The Cow ★ PIZZERIA   A big fire roars in this dark little den of delicious, great-value tastes. It's all wood, moody, and very, very popular. It's less authentically Italian than Bella Cucina, but it invariably has a great atmosphere. If your budget has taken a beating, this is a great place to fill up on treats like pepperoni pizza, Bolognese with fresh green salad, or homemade soups and crusty bread. It's a good family stop, too.

Cow Lane. ☎ **03/442-8588.** www.goodgroup.co.nz. No reservations. Main courses NZ$18–NZ$32. AE, MC, V. Daily noon–late.

Fishbone Bar & Grill ★★ SEAFOOD   If I could have a restaurant in my back-yard, it would be this one. It's wacky and colorful, the decorative fish-filled interior is a joy, and the seafood meals rate among the best I've had. Fresh fish is sourced daily and the South Island salmon smoked over Canadian sycamore wood chips is an eternal favorite. The blue cod dishes are also reliably good; and for a well-priced fill-up, you can't pass up their seafood chowder.

7 Beach St. ☎ **03/442-6768.** www.fishbonequeenstown.co.nz. Reservations recommended. Main courses NZ$20–NZ$32. AE, DC, MC, V. Daily 5pm–late.

Left Bank Café ★★★ ☺ PARISIAN-STYLE CAFE   Enjoy Parisian style without ever leaving Queenstown in this new addition to the Sofitel hotel. Named after that hallowed French haunt of artists, writers, and philosophers, it's part open French kitchen and part Parisian tea room with a menu that skips from modern New Zealand cuisine to traditional French fare like daily baked pastries, crepes, and waffles. It's filled with art posters from the 1930s through 1950s and mosaic floor tiles were shipped in from France. Romaine salad, pear and blue cheese tart, and Akaroa salmon risotto with parmesan are good lunch selections, and there's a special menu for kids.

Sofitel Queenstown, 8 Duke St. ☎ **03/450-0045.** www.sofitelqueenstown.com. Reservations recommended. Main courses NZ$12–NZ$20. AE, DC, MC, V. Daily 6am–4pm.

Tatler ★ INTERNATIONAL   This is one of the justifiably favored restaurants in Queenstown. The dark-timbered interior sets up an instant atmosphere and meals are consistently well flavored and tasty. I can't always say the same about the service—like most New Zealand restaurants, it has peaks and troughs—but I always enjoy a meal here. Whether it's slow-roasted tuna steak, Southland rack of lamb with field mushrooms, or a big hearty breakfast, Tatler is a sure thing. I go there every time I'm in Queenstown.

5 The Mall. ☎ **03/442-8372.** www.tatler.co.nz. Reservations recommended for dinner. Main courses NZ$28–NZ$38. AE, MC, V. Daily 10am–late.

Wai Waterfront Restaurant ★ MODERN NEW ZEALAND   Wai (Maori for "water") was a winner from the beginning. Its heavy focus on fresh seafood and oysters is well complemented by the water lapping directly outside its doors, and summer outdoor tables give it a festive feel. If you like fresh oysters, you'll be in seventh heaven (when they're in season, that is), and you should try them with lime sorbet and vodka, or baked in an herb Parmesan crust. Beyond that, venison, beef, lamb, duck, and ostrich also feature on an exciting menu; or you can treat yourself to the nine-course degustation menu.

Steamer Wharf, Ground floor, Beach St. 📞 **03/442-5969.** www.wai.net.nz. Reservations required,
especially for a waterfront table. Main courses NZ$38–NZ$45; NZ$135 degustation menu. AE, DC, MC,
V. Daily noon–late.

Inexpensive

If you're after a great-value feed without the fuss, get thee to **Fergburger ★★★**, 42
Shotover St., Queenstown (📞 **03/441-1232;** www.fergburger.com), where a Mr. Big
Stuff burger (NZ$16) means a quarter-pound of prime New Zealand beef topped
with melted Edam cheese, streaky American bacon, and barbecue sauce. This will
satisfy the biggest appetite and yes, they do have smaller burgers.

Joe's Garage ★ 🍴 CAFE   Although trendily hard to find, you *must* seek out Joe's
because in my mind, it is the best coffee provider in QT. It's a case of American
roadie-style cafe meeting Queenstown hip—and strangely, it works. It's virtually
unadorned but for the buzzy atmosphere and chatty locals. Sit up at the counter while
you wait for a strong espresso, bacon and bun, panini, or burger. This is my favorite
Queenstown cafe; I just can't keep away from it. Look out for their Arrowtown cafe
on Arrow Lane—it's just as good.

Searle Lane. 📞 **03/442-5282.** Most menu items under NZ$20. AE, MC, V. Daily 7am–5pm.

Vesta 🍴 CAFE   For a truly unique coffee experience mixed with history, contemporary design, and quirky retail opportunity, head for Vesta. This tiny espresso bar
(with snacks and light meals) is tucked into the back of Queenstown's oldest house
(1864), and modern art and design appear against a backdrop of the original, peeling
1800s floral wallpapers. Don't miss it and be prepared to loosen your wallet on goodies to take home.

Williams Cottage, Marine Parade. 📞 **03/442-5687.** Menu items NZ$5–NZ$20. AE, MC, V. Daily 9am–
5pm.

Vudu Café ★ CAFE   Vudu Café is one that has endured for years, so it must be
doing something right. I know the divine almond croissant I had there recently certainly guaranteed a return visit from me. It's small and it can be hard to get a seat
(another good sign), but keep persisting, because they make excellent coffee and have
delicious prepared food. It always has a buzzy atmosphere and they offer organic
options.

23 Beach St. 📞 **03/442-5357.** Menu items NZ$5–NZ$20. AE, MC, V. Daily 8am–late.

IN NEARBY ARROWTOWN

Amisfield Winery & Bistro ★★★ MODERN NEW ZEALAND   I've never heard
a bad word about Amisfield Bistro. It's been *the* lunch spot of choice ever since it opened
a few years ago. Just about as classy—and somewhat bigger—than Eichardt's, it features
a daily changing menu based on local, fresh, and organic ingredients. Corn-fed chicken

with garlic butter and watercress; Serrano ham, steamed asparagus, and poached egg; or seared salmon with cumin, couscous, tomato, and yogurt are just some of the temptations on offer. And don't pass up their spectacular wine-tasting room.

10 Lake Hayes Rd. (btw. Queenstown and Arrowtown). ℭ 03/442-0556. www.amisfield.co.nz. Reservations recommended. Main courses NZ$18–NZ$30. AE, DC, MC, V. Tues–Sun 11:30am–8pm (last reservations at 6pm).

Pesto ✦ ITALIAN/PIZZA   Baby sister to Saffron (see below), Pesto offers a copper-clad casual setting in which to bite into some of the most succulent pizzas in this part of the world. Pasta with anchovies, tomato, Italian sausage, spinach, and lemon chili oil will also tempt. All ages gather in the sunny courtyard and the super-cool interior.

18 Buckingham St. ℭ **03/442-0885.** Reservations recommended. NZ$22–NZ$28. AE, DC, MC, V. Daily 5pm–late.

Postmaster's House ★★ CONTEMPORARY NEW ZEALAND/EUROPEAN   This is another feather in Arrowtown's rather surprising culinary cap. Who would have expected this tiny village to dish up another top eatery after Saffron? Come here to enjoy a restored historic building, an elegant interior, and delicious meals that might include pan-roasted white veal; lamb rack; prime beef-eye filet with béarnaise, merlot, and mushroom jus; or a simple-yet-delicious crispy roast duck salad with fennel. Sink back in your leather chair with a glass of the region's best wine and resign yourself to indulgence.

Buckingham St., Arrowtown. ℭ **03/442-0991.** Reservations essential. Main courses NZ$28–NZ$38. AE, DC, MC, V. Daily 11:30am–late.

Saffron ★★★ 🏨 MODERN NEW ZEALAND   When you're named in *Condé Nast Traveler's* list of the 100 Best Tables in the World (2001), you've got a lot to live up to, but Saffron seems to have managed the stress rather well. It's still considered one of the most serious fine-food places in the region. Book ahead, because people are coming from miles around to enjoy Bollinger by the fireside before meals such as Thai duck and lemon-grass curry with two rices.

18 Buckingham St. ℭ **03/442-0131.** www.saffronrestaurant.co.nz. Reservations required. Main courses NZ$29–NZ$40. AE, DC, MC, V. Daily noon–late.

> ### For Chocolate Lovers
>
> **Patagonia Chocolates ★★★**, Lakeside, 50 Beach St., Queenstown (ℭ **03/442-9066**), and also at Ramshaw Lane, Arrowtown (ℭ **03/409-8584;** www.patagoniachocolates.com), are must-stop/must-eat destinations. They're open daily from 8am to 10pm.

IN NEARBY GLENORCHY

Glenorchy is a bit lean on dining options, but you won't starve. **Glenorchy Hotel** (ℭ **03/442-9902**) has a terrace cafe and restaurant with a la carte, stone grill, and bistro dining; and **Glenorchy Café** (ℭ **03/442-9958**) can fill the gaps with snacks and light meals in a casual atmosphere. **Kinloch Lodge ★** (ℭ **03/442-4900**) has the best menu, with the likes of Mediterranean baked lamb, seared grouper, or homemade meatballs.

Queenstown After Dark

Midwinter in Queenstown is a night owl's paradise. There's plenty happening all year, of course, but once the town fills up with international visitors, anything can, and often does, happen.

Queenstown now has two casinos. **SKYCITY Queenstown Casino,** 16–24 Beach St. (☎ **03/441-0400;** www.skycityqueenstown.co.nz), has over 80 gaming machines and the usual table games such as roulette, blackjack, and baccarat. Also here are **Wild Thyme Bar & Restaurant** and live entertainment on Friday and Saturday nights. It's open daily from noon to 4am and they have a free courtesy shuttle. **Lasseters Wharf Casino,** Steamer Wharf (☎ **03/441-1495;** www. lasseterswharfcasino.co.nz), is a boutique operation with much the same on offer in the way of games. It's open daily from 11am to 3am. In both cases, you must be 20 and over and smartly dressed to enter.

Those of you who like a sense of discovery in your nightlife may want to hunt for "the B bars"—a cluster of nightspots all beginning with the letter B. **The Bunker** ★★★, Cow Lane (☎ **03/441-8030;** www.thebunker.co.nz), is favored by a monied crowd and plays on no advertising, no signs, and the fact that it's hard to find. (It will also make a handsome hole in your wallet.) In addition to being a first-rate restaurant (p. 436), it is a moody cocktail bar. Equally obscure is **Bardeaux** ★★, Eureka Arcade, off The Mall or Searle Lane (☎ **03/442-8284;** www.goodgroup. co.nz), a sophisticated late-night wine and cocktail bar, with a huge range of local pinot noir and champagne, and a big selection of whiskey. **Barup,** next to Bardeaux and upstairs from Minibar (☎ **03/442-7707**), is an exclusive Swiss chalet–type of wine and cocktail bar where locals of mixed ages head for a good time. **Barmuda,** Searle Lane (☎ **03/442-7300;** www.goodgroup.co.nz), has a big cocktail list and a gorgeous private lounge to enjoy it in. **MiniBar** ★★, Eureka Lane (☎ **03/441-3212;** www. goodgroup.co.nz), is, as the name suggests, tiny, but it has over 100 premium beers and a whole lot of atmosphere. **Buffalo Club,** 8 Brecon St. (☎ **03/442-4144**), is all about DJs, live music, and late nights. And **12 Bar,** 178 Earl St. (☎ **03/409-2162;** www.12bar.co.nz), is popular with both the gay and straight crowd. It has a big cocktail list and a dance floor.

If you prefer something a little more sedate, then head for **Lombardi,** Hotel St. Moritz, 10–18 Brunswick St. (☎ **03/442-4990**), which is a classy cocktail and tapas bar, set apart from the town center bedlam. It's all class and cocktails at **Eichardt's House Bar** ★★★, Marine Parade (☎ **03/441-0442**), which is bound to be a favorite; pricey, but fabulous. And for a night with a difference you can freeze your tail off in the name of a good time at **Minus 5,** Steamer Wharf (☎ **03/442-6050**), in the company of hand-sculpted ice and their famous vodka cocktails. Big coats and woolly gloves are provided.

Those with wild times on their mind head for **Chico's Restaurant & Bar,** on The Mall (☎ **03/442-8439**). It has great food, live entertainment, and dancing from 10:30pm until late. The **Edge Niteclub,** Camp and Main streets (☎ **03/442-4144**), and the **World,** Shotover Street (☎ **03/442-6757**), are part of the recognized backpacker scene. **Shooters Bar,** 10 Brecon St. (☎ **03/442-4144**), is dominated by pool tables and a football crowd. The **Dux de Lux** ★, 14 Church St. (☎ **03/442-9688;** www.thedux.co.nz), draws big crowds with its specialty beers and great atmosphere, and next door is the ever-popular **Monty's Bar** ★★, 12 Church St. (☎ **03/441-1081;** www.montysbar.co.nz), which offers a full range of Monteith's beers. Not far away, the **Pig & Whistle Pub** ★, 19 Ballarat St. (☎ **03/442-9055**), has had a serious makeover and, as an English-themed pub, is doing a roaring trade. They also have excellent pub meals at reasonable prices. **Speight's Ale House,** at the corner of Stanley and Ballarat streets (☎ **03/441-3065**), occupies the old council chambers and serves up the full range of Speight's beer, brewed in Dunedin since 1880.

QUEENSTOWN & ENVIRONS

Moviegoers will enjoy a more subdued night out at **Dorothy Brown's Boutique Cinema & Bar ★★★**, Buckingham St., Arrowtown (𝄐 **03/442-1964;** www.dorothybrowns.com), where you can relax in big seats with a glass of wine and a cheese board, and enjoy an art-house movie.

En Route to Te Anau

Te Anau is a 172km (107-mile) drive from Queenstown on excellent roads. Follow State Highway 6 through **Kingston** at the south end of Lake Wakatipu, and on through the tiny township of **Athol.** Then turn west onto State Highway 94 over the summit of **Gorge Hill,** along the **Mararoa River,** and through sheep and cattle country to **Te Anau,** nestled beside the largest lake on the South Island.

TE ANAU ★★

172km (107 miles) SW of Queenstown; 116km (72 miles) S of Milford Sound; 157km (97 miles) NW of Invercargill

Te Anau is the hub of Fiordland National Park, a magnificent 1.2-million-hectare (3-million-acre) World Heritage Site filled with scenic wonders, serenity, mystery, and some of the best walking tracks in the world. The little resort township is built around the foreshore of Lake Te Anau, the largest of the South Island lakes. It has a permanent population of about 4,000, which swells to over 10,000 in summer. If you're coming to explore Fiordland's waterfalls, virgin forests, mountains, rivers, and lonely fiords, this is the place to base yourself.

Lake Te Anau is a wonder in itself. Its eastern shoreline, where the township is located, is virtually treeless, with about 76 centimeters (30 in.) of annual rainfall, while its western banks are covered in dense forest nurtured by more than 254 centimeters (100 in.) of rain each year. What attracts visitors to New Zealand's second-largest lake are the opportunity for watersports and the proximity to Milford Sound, 116km (72 miles) away. The sound, which is actually a fiord, reaches 23km (14 miles) in from the Tasman Sea, flanked by sheer granite peaks and traced by playful waterfalls. Its waters and surrounding land have been kept in as nearly a primeval state as humans could possibly manage without leaving them totally untouched. In fine weather or pouring rain, Milford Sound exudes a powerful sense of nature's pristine harmony and beauty.

Milford Sound may be the most famous and accessible of the fiords, but Doubtful Sound is the deepest and, according to some, the most beautiful. Even farther south, Dusky Sound may well qualify as the most remote and mysterious of the famous trio.

Fittingly, as one of the most pristine regions in New Zealand, Destination Fiordland (with Venture Southland) is one of the six regions participating in the government initiative, the Environmentally Sustainable Tourism project. As in the other five participating regions, the Southland/Fiordland project encourages tourism operators to focus on energy efficiency, waste reduction, recycling, water quality, and conservation. You can check charter members at www.southlandnz.com or www.fiordland.org.nz.

Essentials

GETTING THERE By Plane   Air services to Te Anau and Fiordland are provided by **Air Fiordland Ltd.** (𝄐 **0800/107-505** in NZ, or 03/249-6720; fax 03/249-6721; www.airfiordland.com). Charter flights are also available.

For an excellent cinematic introduction to the greater Fiordland region—much of which you will never lay eyes on otherwise—make sure you see *Fiordland on Film - Ata Whenua* ★★★, a stunning and unforgettable cinematic journey. See it at **Fiordland Cinema, 7 The Lane, Te Anau** (✆ **03/249-9089**; www.fiordlandcinema.co.nz); screening times are on the hour 9am to 9pm in summer and 4 to 7pm in winter (closed Dec 25). It costs NZ$10 for adults, NZ$5 children 5 to 15.

By Coach (Bus) Daily coach service runs between Te Anau and Christchurch, Dunedin, and Invercargill via **InterCity** (✆ **09/623-1503**). Daily service also runs to Te Anau and Milford Sound from Queenstown. And numerous shuttle bus companies make daily trips, too. Information is available at the visitor centers in Queenstown, Invercargill, and Te Anau.

By Car From Queenstown, take State Highway 6, then State Highway 94 (see "En Route to Te Anau," above, for details).

ORIENTATION Te Anau's main street is State Highway 94, called Milford Road within the township, with the post office, restaurants, grocery stores, and most shops. The majority of hotels and motels are on Lakefront Drive, which stretches attractively around the lake. The township is tiny and very easy to negotiate on foot or by car.

VISITOR INFORMATION The **Fiordland i-SITE Visitor Centre,** Lakefront Drive, Te Anau (✆ **03/249-8900;** fax 03/249-7022; fiordland-isite@realjourneys. co.nz), sits at the lake end of Milford Road. It shares the same office as **Real Journeys** (✆ **0800/656-501** in NZ, or 03/249-7416; www.realjourneys.co.nz). Hours are daily from 8:30am to 6pm in summer and 8:30am to 5pm in winter. The **Fiordland National Park Visitor Centre,** Lakefront Drive, Te Anau (✆ **03/249-7924;** fax 03/249-8515; www.doc.govt.nz), is a must for anyone contemplating doing either short walks around Te Anau or the well-known multiday tramps—Hollyford, Routeburn, Milford, Kepler, and Caples. It's open daily in summer from 8:30am to 6pm, and in winter until 4:30pm. It operates 8:30am to 1pm on December 25. For more information, go to www.fiordland.org.nz or www.fiordlandnz.com.

SPECIAL EVENTS The **DOC Fiordland Summer Nature Programme** (✆ **03/249-7921**) presents a wide range of adventures in the national park during the summer months, and encourages people to explore some of the park's lesser known beauties. Details are available from the National Park Visitor Centre. The **Kepler Challenge** and the **Luxmore Grunt** (✆ **03/249-9596;** www.keplerchallenge.co.nz) are tough international ultra-marathon races held in December each year.

Exploring Te Anau & the Sounds

Milford and Doubtful sounds are the primary draws of this area, and in Te Anau you'll discover a number of options for exploring one or both. You can drive, fly, or take a coach to Milford Sound from Te Anau (see "Milford Sound" below), and you can fly over or take a scenic cruise through Doubtful Sound.

You'll quickly discover that people in Te Anau are reluctant to recommend one sound or one excursion above another, so explore the choices carefully. Consider your available time and the amount of money you want to spend. My advice would be to drive to Milford and, if you can, overnight on one of the boats; then, if you're still keen

Skippers Range

MOUNT ASPIRING
NATIONAL PARK

HUMBOLDT MTNS.

Martins Bay

Lake McKerrow

Historic Suspension Bridge   Skippers

Coronet Peak

Hollyford Track

RICHARDSON MTNS.

Speargrass Flat

Hollyford Camp

Routeburn Shelter

Lower Hollyford Rd.

Glenorchy

Queenstown

Milford Sound

DARRAN MTNS.

Milford Sound

Mitre Peak

Sandfly Point

The "Divide Shelter"
Lake Howden

Homer Tunnel

Caples Track

AILSA MTNS.

Greenstone Track

Fernhill

Launch Cruises

Walter Peak Stn.

Elfin Bay

Lake Wakatipu

WICK MTNS.

Lake Ada

Sutherland Falls

Milford Track

Clinton River

EARL MTNS.

94

LIVINGSTONE MTNS.

Walter Peak

FRANKLIN MTNS.

STUART MTNS.

Mavora Lakes Rd.

FIORDLAND

NATIONAL

PARK

Launch Cruises   Te Anau Downs

Lake Te Anau

Mt. Nicholas Rd.

Te Ana-Au Caves

94

MURCHISON MTNS.

Te Anau

Kakapo Rd.

94

The Key

94

KEPLER MTNS.

Lake Te Anau Control Gates

Kepler Track

95

Launch Cruises
Lake Manapouri

Manapouri

NORTH ISLAND

Auckland

Wellington

Area of detail

Christchurch

SOUTH ISLAND

Dunedin

West Arm Power Station

Wilmot Pass

- - - Trail
■ Point of Interest
■ Trailhead/
   Trail End

0   15 mi
0   15 km

15

QUEENSTOWN & ENVIRONS | Te Anau

to see Doubtful and Dusky sounds, take the 40-minute flight. Not only does this take just a fraction of the cruise time, but you also get a thrilling perspective of otherwise inaccessible areas. Either way, don't try to see everything in 1 day. It is definitely worth staying in this area for 2 to 3 days if you can.

Air Fiordland, Manapouri Airport, Te Anau (℡ **0800/107-505** in NZ, or 03/249-6720; www.airfiordland.com), has several Milford Sound flight packages, some combining cruise options, plus an excellent 40-minute flight over Doubtful Sound.

Southern Lakes Helicopters, 79 Lakefront Drive (℡ **0508/249-7167** in NZ, or 03/249-7167; www.southernlakeshelicopters.co.nz), has a 50-minute flight over Doubtful Sound that passes soaring peaks and waterfalls. The highlight is the flight into Campbell's Kingdom, which is accessible only by helicopter. Call for prices of all their flights. **Fiordland Helicopters,** Te Anau Airport (℡ **03/249-7575;** www.fiordlandhelicopters.co.nz), offers trips that range from 15 minutes to 1½ hours. It's a little cheaper than Southern Lakes, but it's based farther out of town.

If a full-day bus tour (from Te Anau) is more your style, join the Milford Sound Day Tour run by **Great Sights** (℡ **0800/744-487** in NZ; www.greatsights.co.nz). It runs daily, departing 10:15am from Te Anau Travel Centre and returning at 5:15pm. It costs NZ$153 for adults and NZ$75 for children ages 5 to 14. You can include lunch for an extra NZ$15 to NZ$30 per person. You'll travel in a glass-topped coach, which gives you great views on the road to Milford Sound. Once there you board the boat for a 1 ¾-hour cruise of the sound. Another good option is the popular **Milford Sound Barbecue Bus ★★** (℡ **0800/421-045;** www.milford.net.nz), which departs from either Queenstown or Te Anau. It's a smaller group tour and includes a classic barbecue lunch in spectacular Hollyford Valley rather than on the cruise boats. It links with the 2pm Milford Sound cruise, which is the off-peak and therefore less crowded time; and if you like you can fly back to Queenstown. From Te Anau to Milford and back to Te Anau, it costs NZ$155 for adults and NZ$95 for children ages 4 to 14.

DOUBTFUL SOUND ★★★

Doubtful Sound makes an idyllic day excursion from Lake Manapouri. At 21m (69 ft.), it's the deepest of the fiords. Filled with ancient rainforest, cascading waterfalls, towering peaks, and abundant wildlife, it's an unforgettable experience. An air of complete silence, broken only by birdcall, adds to the mystery.

Doubtful Sound is 10 times bigger than Milford, and although it can't boast Mitre Peak, its still waters mirror 1,200m (3,900-ft.) **Commander Peak.** Another difference between the two sounds is that you always know Milford is close to civilization because of the buzz of aircraft going to and from the airstrip and the multitude of buses that make their way there on a daily basis. Doubtful is much more remote.

There's no way to get to Doubtful Sound on your own. Real Journeys (see "Visitor Information," above) transports visitors from Manapouri, then takes a launch trip to the West Arm, followed by a 20km (12-mile) coach trip to Deep Cove in Doubtful Sound. The coach takes you up and over Wilmot Pass, 662m (2,171 ft.) above sea level, stopping on the way to visit **Manapouri Power Station,** where you spiral 225 eerie meters (750 ft.) downward to view the seven immense underground turbines. A second launch then takes you out into the sound, and if you're lucky, you'll spot the resident pod of 60 or more dolphins, fur seals, and rare crested penguins. You'll get close enough to waterfalls to feel the spray, and you'll be able to savor total silence when the captain shuts off the engine.

A Sound Difference

Real Journey's Doubtful Sound cruise is a longer cruise than the Milford Sound option and much more remote. You'll see far fewer people at Doubtful—and given that there are around 100 buses a day going into Milford, that says a lot. Milford Sound is more dramatic and awe-inspiring, but Doubtful is a lot more untouched and remote. You're also far more likely to see wildlife at Doubtful—not that the dolphins are on the payroll! The cruise has English-only commentary and two styles of picnic lunches are available for purchase.

Real Journey's Doubtful Sound day excursions use a modern, purpose-built catamaran, *Patea Explorer*. It carries 150 passengers over two decks and departs daily from Manapouri with connecting coaches from Queenstown or Te Anau. Visitors can self-drive from Queenstown in 2½ hours and from Te Anau in 40 minutes. Reservations are essential. From Manapouri, the Wilderness trip costs NZ$198 to NZ$265 for adults (price depends on time and season), NZ$65 for children ages 5 to 14. From Te Anau, add about NZ$25, and about NZ$75 from Queenstown. Preordered picnic lunches start at NZ$17. From September to May, Real Journeys offers overnight cruises on the *Fiordland Navigator*. Prices vary depending on the season, starting at NZ$473 for an off-peak cruise from Manapouri; children's fares start at NZ$237.

THE MILFORD TRACK & OTHER WALKS

Most dedicated trampers consider the famous **Milford Track ★★★** among the finest anywhere in the world. Four days are required to walk the 54km (33 miles) from Glad Jetty at Lake Te Anau's northern end to Sandfly Point on the western bank of Milford Sound. If you're short on time, you could join the **Real Journeys Milford Track Day Walk** (② 0800/656-501; www.realjourneys.co.nz), which includes a Lake Te Anau cruise, coach transfers, lunch, and a nature guide. It operates November through April. The minimum age is 10 years and the excursion costs NZ$195 for adults and NZ$127 for children. The 3-day **Hollyford Track Guided Walk ★★★** (② 0800/832-226 in NZ, or 03/442-3000; www.hollyfordtrack.com) takes you through spectacular landscapes with local wilderness guides, who give you an insight into the rich Maori and pioneer history of the region. You stay in cozy, purpose-built lodges, complete with roaring fires. It operates October through May and costs from NZ$1,695 for adults and NZ$1,295 for children ages 10 to 14. Other popular walks in this area are the **Routeburn** and the **Kepler.** For more information, see "Tramping" in chapter 4.

OTHER OUTDOOR PURSUITS

FISHING   Fiordland offers unsurpassed opportunities for wilderness trophy trout fishing. The best fishing is in the Eglinton Valley. Ian Murray of **Fish 'n' Trips** (② 03/249-7656; www.fiordland-flyfishing.co.nz) clearly has a sense of humor. If you want a guided wilderness fishing experience, call him. He charges NZ$350 to NZ$375 for a half-day trip and NZ$600 to NZ$650 for a full day. **Fiordland Guides ★★**, 472 Te Anau-Milford Hwy. (② 03/249-7832; www.fiordlandguides.co.nz), can take you on a terrific fishing trip for NZ$800 per day for two people. The price includes a guide, picnic lunch, and fishing tackle.

The **Te Anau Glowworm Caves** ★★ excursion on Lake Te Anau is operated by **Real Journeys,** Lakefront Drive, Te Anau (© **0800/656-501** in NZ, or 03/249-7416; www.realjourneys.co.nz). This adventure runs year-round and includes an underground boat ride into the glowworm grotto. The geologically young caves (only about 15,000 years old) have 200m (660 ft.) of passages, which are still being formed by water cascading down the cave tiers at a rate of 55,000 gallons per minute. On the second level of the water bed, you'll see the glowworm grotto. A major upgrade of the caves excursion was completed in 2006. One major element was the addition of a multimillion-dollar catamaran for accessing the caves across Lake Te Anau. If you want to make the most of the 15km (10-mile) scenic lake cruise, take the daylight option (NZ$70 for adults, NZ$22 for children ages 5–14). Alternatively, evening options provide an interesting nocturnal experience from October to April.

HORSEBACK RIDING   Pay NZ$95 per person (minimum age 10) for a 3½-hour horse trek through beautiful landscapes of a 700-acre working deer, sheep, and cattle farm with **High Ride Adventures,** 245 Dale Rd. (© **0508/444-4743** in NZ, or 03/280-0552; www.highride.co.nz), or NZ$80 for 2 hours (minimum age 6). They have a variety of horses to suit all levels of experience. The 2-hour tour departs at 1pm and the longer tour departs at 9am and 4pm.

KAYAKING   **Fiordland Wilderness Experiences,** Sandy Brown Road, Te Anau (© **03/249-7700;** www.seakayakfiordland.co.nz), offers guided sea-kayaking options ranging in length from 1 to 6 days (Sept–May). The tour goes to Milford, Dusky, and Doubtful sounds and Lake Manapouri. See the section on "Milford Sound," below, for further kayaking options. Kayakers must be 16 and over. A 1-day guided kayak trip in Milford Sound costs NZ$165 per person.

Where to Stay

Reserve well ahead for visits between Christmas and February. Once the peak season is over, you can expect to get some incredibly good deals. There are numerous motel complexes along the waterfront, and backpackers are well served in Te Anau. One of the nicest is **Te Anau Lakefront Backpackers,** 48–50 Lakefront Dr. (www.teanau backpackers.co.nz; © **0800/200-074** in NZ, or 03/249-7713), where dorm beds cost from NZ$25 to NZ$30 and doubles cost NZ$75 to NZ$95. The lovely **Fiordland Lodge** ★★★, 472 Te Anau-Milford Hwy., Te Anau (www.fiordlandlodge.co.nz; © **03/249-7832**), is at the other end of the spectrum—a rural lodge that sits on a tussock-covered ridge overlooking Lake Te Anau. Think stylish treehouse and you won't be far wrong. Take one of the smart lodge rooms for in-house comforts, or opt for the privacy and romance of one of the two quaintest little log cabins. Rates are NZ$940 for a lodge room, NZ$1,140 executive suite, and NZ$740 for a log cabin. There's a restaurant and bar on premise.

   Blue Ridge Bed and Breakfast ★★, 13–15 Melland Place (www.blueridge.net. nz; © **03/249-7740;** fax 03/249-7340), has four sunny rooms with mountain views, en-suite bathrooms, big beds, and kitchenettes. Breakfast is included for the very reasonable tariff of NZ$275 to NZ$325. The old-world charms of **Te Anau Lodge** ★★, 52 Howden St. (www.teanaulodge.com; © **03/249-7477**), are also worthy of your attention. Originally a convent, this grand old building has been relocated to a new garden and restored to offer eight rooms—seven with en-suite bathrooms, for NZ$255 to NZ$375. New in 2007, the **Dock Bay Lodge ★★**, 192 William Stephen Rd., Te Anau (www.dockbaylodge.co.nz; ℂ **0800/258-522** in NZ, or 03/249-7709), offers five big, modern suites right beside Te Anau Golf Course, for NZ$375 to NZ$590—definitely the nicest rooms in Te Anau township.

Where to Eat

The dining scene is slowly improving, but there's still room for innovation and snappier service. Just remember that if you come here out of the main tourist season, several eateries close for the winter months. Apart from the listings below, try **La Toscana ★**, 108 Town Centre (ℂ **03/249-7756;** www.latoscana.co.nz), one of the town's better culinary bets. It's open from 5:30pm. The terms laid-back, casual, and friendly were invented for **The Fat Duck Café & Restaurant ★**, 124 Town Centre, Te Anau (ℂ **03/249-8480**), where they cater to everyone, including the kids. Don't expect anything fancy, but big servings of blue cod, beef filet, or salmon will certainly fortify you after a hard day in the national parks. Good for breakfast, too. Open daily in summer (10am–late); Wednesday to Sunday winter (10am–late). **The Redcliff Café ★★**, 12 Mokonui St. (ℂ **03/249-7431**), set in a cute old cottage refitted with a contemporary bar and moody little dining rooms, offers a lively atmosphere and great eats, ranging from Fiordland venison to orange roughy grilled with a chili-and-coriander-herb crust. Vegetarians and vegans are well taken care of. Open daily in summer (3pm–3am); call for winter hours. **Sandfly Café ★★**, 9 The Lane (ℂ **03/249-9529**), is my favorite Te Anau cafe—quirky, charming, and friendly. People of all ages and walks of life congregate here for the excellent coffee, tasty salads, soups, and hot panini. Open daily 8am to 6pm with reduced hours in winter.

En Route to Dunedin

If you've already visited Milford Sound and are planning to travel to Dunedin from Te Anau, the drive will take about 4½ hours over good roads. Take State Highway 94 across Gorge Hill into Lumsden, across the Waimea Plains to the milling center of Gore, through farmlands to Clinton, and across rolling downs to Balclutha. From there, take State Highway 1 north along the coast past Milton and Lookout Point, where you'll get your first look at Dunedin.

MILFORD SOUND ★★★

119km (74 miles) NE of Te Anau; 286km (177 miles) NW of Queenstown

No matter when you visit or what the weather is like, your memories of Milford Sound are bound to be special. Its 14 nautical miles leading to the Tasman Sea are lined with mountain peaks that rise sharply out of the water to heights of 1,800m (5,900 ft.). Forster's fur seals laze on rocky shelves, and dolphins play in water that reaches depths of 600m (2,000 ft.). The sound's entrance is so hidden when viewed from the sea that Captain Cook sailed right by without noticing it when he charted the waters some 200 years ago.

It rains a lot in Milford Sound, and that's an understatement. And while I'm on negatives, it can't be stressed enough that weather in this area is extremely changeable, even in summer, so come prepared. As many have found, reading about the cold and rain in midsummer is one thing, experiencing it quite another. Over 927 centimeters

(365 in.) fall annually, so be prepared to get wet. The sound is a mystical, moody place when it rains. You may not glimpse the mountaintops or Mitre Peak through the mist, but you'll see hundreds of waterfalls cascading down spectacular cliff faces. In dry conditions, there are only three or four permanent waterfalls in the sound.

In summer, coaches pour in at a rate of 100 per day for the launch cruises—that's up to 5,000 people joining you for a look at this special place. If you're prepared to overlook this rather cramped state of affairs, you'll be rewarded with grand, unforgettable landscapes.

The Milford Road

The road to Milford Sound is world-famous. Although it can be completed in 2 hours, allow at least 3 so you can stop to look at the many natural attractions along the way. Highway 94 from Te Anau leads north along the lake, with islands and wooded distant shores on your left. The drive is often a slow one, especially in wet conditions, as you make your way through steep gorges and between walls of solid rock and moss-covered inclines. I would discourage anyone from taking a motor home on this road as it is narrow, steep, and winding with a lot of bus traffic—and if that doesn't put you off, the dark, narrow tunnel will. The road is usually very busy in summer and there can be delays, especially at Homer Tunnel. **Remember:** There are no fuel stops between Te Anau and Milford, so make sure your tank is full. This is *not* a road you want to be "marooned" on—in any season. During the winter months, all drivers on Milford Road are required by law to carry chains for their vehicles. Road conditions can be checked on www.milfordroad.co.nz, or by calling ✆ **0800/444-449** in New Zealand, or check www.transit.govt.nz/projects/milfordroad.

Heed the Warnings

During the winter months, take the NO STOPPING—AVALANCHE ZONE signs along the Milford Road very seriously. No matter how much you want to stop and take a photograph, don't—it could cost you your life.

Be sure to stop for pictures at the **Mirror Lakes.** The road winds down the **Eglinton** and **Hollyford valleys,** through the astoundingly narrow and steep **Homer Tunnel,** and down into the majestic **Cleddau Valley,** to Milford Sound. Before you go, stop by the **Fiordland National Park Visitor Centre,** Lakefront Drive, Te Anau (✆ **03/249-7921;** fax 03/249-7613; www.doc.govt.nz), for information on Fiordland National Park. Ask specifically for the pamphlet *The Road To Milford* (NZ$6), which describes each mile of the journey. It's not a bad idea to go armed with sand fly repellent, too.

Homer Tunnel, about 100km (65 miles) into the journey, is a major engineering marvel: a 1.2km (¾-mile) passageway first proposed in 1889, begun in 1935, and finally opened in 1940. It wasn't until 1954 before a connecting road was completed and the first private automobile drove through. There's no lighting in the tunnel and it's very narrow. Drive with extreme care!

About 6km (3¾ miles) past the tunnel, stop and walk to the **Chasm.** The pleasant 15-minute round-trip goes through mossy undergrowth and beech forest to see a rather wonderful feat of natural erosion on the **Cleddau River.**

Exploring the Sound

To be fully appreciated, Milford Sound must be seen from the deck of one of the cruise vessels. **Real Journeys,** Lakefront Drive, Te Anau (✆ **0800/656-502** in NZ, or 03/249-7416; www.realjourneys.co.nz), operates a bewildering array of cruises—both daytime and overnight options. Prices differ depending on whether you join the activity in Queenstown, in Te Anau, or at Milford Sound, and whether you have coach, car, fixed-wing, or helicopter connections. A popular day option is the **Coach and Nature (or Scenic) Cruise,** which departs Queenstown daily at 7:30am and returns at 8:30pm; the cost is NZ$235 for adults, NZ$120 for kids ages 5 to 14 (the Scenic Cruise costs slightly less). If you go coach both ways, don't expect to be back in Queenstown until around 8pm, but also be aware that flights in and out of Milford are completely dependent on the weather and you may have to bus it if your flight is canceled. If you choose to fly one-way you will pay close to twice the above prices. The scenic cruises tend to have more tour groups on board.

You can overnight on Milford Sound in Real Journey's *Milford Mariner* (Sept–May), which features 30 en-suite cabins and includes kayaking and trips in tender vessels, a three-course buffet, and breakfast; rates are from NZ$495 for adults, NZ$248 for children. The *Milford Wanderer* sleeps 61 in quad-share bunk-style compartments, with shared bathroom facilities; quad-share rooms are NZ$260 for adults, NZ$130 for kids; twin share cabins with shared bathroom are NZ$$325 for adults, NZ$165 for kids. Coach connections are available from Te Anau and Queenstown at extra cost.

Southern Discoveries (℃ **0800/264-536** in NZ, or 03/441-1137; www.southerndiscoveries.co.nz) has been a tradition here since 1957. It has four boats operating day cruises only. The Encounter Nature Cruise is priced from NZ$75 for adults and NZ$15 for children 4 to 14; a Scenic Cruise is priced from NZ$65 for adults and NZ$15 for children. Preordered picnic lunch options are available and Great Sights coaches from Queenstown and Te Anau connect with all cruises.

Both of the above cruise companies will take you to **Milford Deep Underwater Observatory ★★** (℃ **0800/264-536** in NZ, or 03/441-1137; www.discovermilfordsound.co.nz), where you'll descend over 10m (33 ft.) beneath the fiord surface to observe the vibrant underwater community. It costs NZ$40 extra above your cruise price for adults, NZ$20 extra for kids. **Mitre Peak Cruises** (℃ **0800/744-633** in NZ, or 03/443-8787; www.mitrepeak.com) operates two small vessels for more personalized 2-hour cruises. They travel farther out than the other boats—all the way to the Tasman Sea, past St. Annes Point Lighthouse. Their prices are NZ$65 to NZ$75. **Kiwi Discovery,** 37 Camp St., Queenstown (℃ **0800/505-504** in NZ, or 03/442-7340; www.kiwidiscovery.com), offers a year-round day coach trip to Milford Sound for NZ$165 per person, with discounts for kids and families.

Walking is another marvelous activity in this area if you have the time. The Fiordland National Park Visitor Centre in Te Anau (see "Te Anau," earlier in this chapter) will furnish you with details on guided outings that climb into the peaks, meander along the shore, or take you close to waterfalls. One to consider is the much-praised **Trips 'n' Tramps** (℃ **0800/305-807** in NZ, or 03/249-7081; www.tripsandtramps.com), which has a 1-day walk on the Milford Track as part of a small group of 12 for NZ$175 per person.

Kayaking may be the most popular activity here after the cruises. Your best bet is **Rosco's Milford Sound Sea Kayaks,** 72 Town Centre, Te Anau (℃ **0800/476-726** in NZ, or 03/249-8500; www.roscosmilfordkayaks.com). These easygoing excursions offer an extraordinary way to experience the sound. You don't have to be super-fit or have previous kayaking experience. One of the most popular is the Milford Track Paddle 'n Walk trip, which departs daily at 2:30pm and returns by 7:30pm. This costs

QUEENSTOWN & ENVIRONS

Milford Sound

NZ$199 per person and includes an easy walk through pristine rainforest. Early risers might like to get the best of the day on the Sunriser Classic trip for NZ$130 per person. For people traveling out of peak tourist season, keep in mind that Rosco offers several excellent winter kayaking options. **Adventure Kayak & Cruise** ★, 33 Waiau St., Manapouri (✆ **0800/324-966** in NZ, or 03/249-6626; www.fiordlandadventure. co.nz), offers a stunning guided day tour on Doubtful Sound for NZ$239 per person. The minimum age is 14.

Where to Stay

The historic Mitre Peak Lodge provides accommodations only to members of guided Milford Track parties. The hotel dates from 1891, when Elizabeth Sutherland (wife of the sound's first settler) established a 12-room boardinghouse to accommodate seamen who called into the sound. The **Milford Sound Lodge,** St. Hwy. 94 (Private Bag, Te Anau), Milford Sound (www.milfordlodge.com; ✆ **03/249-8071**), is the only land-based lodge in Milford Sound and it is basic, no-frills, and generally filled with young backpackers, but the complex is set in splendid surroundings and was refurbished in 2007. Four riverside chalets allowing a little more privacy are the best option here. Rates are NZ$30 dorm bed, NZ$80 to NZ$90 double, and NZ$255 to NZ$275 chalet; campervan and tent sites available.

DUNEDIN, SOUTHLAND & STEWART ISLAND

D unedin, the "capital" of Otago province; Southland; Invercargill; and Stewart Island have generally been lumped together as the south of the south; if visitors tend to overlook any part of the country, it would be this one.

This is unfortunate because the area offers some of the most diverse and fascinating flora and fauna; some of the quaintest "real New Zealand" townships; and probably one of the least harried travel experiences of all.

Southland extends as far northwest as Lake Manapouri and as far east as Balclutha. It is the country's coolest and rainiest region, yet the even spread of its rainfall is the very foundation of its economy—the production of grass and grass seed, which in turn supports large numbers of sheep and dairy farms. Southland also has the longest daylight hours in New Zealand, and the Percy Burn Viaduct (near Tuatapere) is believed to be the largest wooden rail viaduct remaining in the world.

The area's coastline saw early settlement by Maori sealers and whalers. Today, the region's fishing industry is a major force—its contributions include those succulent Bluff oysters and crayfish (rock lobsters) you've devoured in your New Zealand travels.

Invercargill is a convenient central base for exploring the deep south. It lies an easy 2-hour drive from Fiordland and 2½ hours from Dunedin, via State Highway 1. It is the central focus of Southland—the only place in New Zealand where Scottish heritage has left a distinctive accent among the people, which you'll notice in the way many people roll the letter *r*. It is a place of incredible friendliness and hospitality, and the only spot in the world where people can see living tuatara, the only lizard left from the dinosaur age.

Stewart Island, the third-largest island of New Zealand, is an area of raucous birdcall, lush native vegetation, and unchanged Kiwi habits—which goes for both the human and the ornithological species. It is a rare treat and I haven't heard of one person who has regretted making the effort to get there.

Stewart Island and Southland both come under the umbrella of the Venture Southland/Destination Fiordland Sustainable Tourism Charter and participating tourism operators are listed at www.southlandnz.com.

DUNEDIN ★★

283km (175 miles) S of Queenstown; 366km (227 miles) S of Christchurch; 220km (136 miles) N of Invercargill

Dunedin is a southern gem—sometimes gray, bleak, and freezing in winter, but a gem nevertheless. I love the place for its dramatic scenery, its fine historic buildings, and most of all, for the immediacy of its funky university life, which lends an alternative air to what is inherently a strongly Scottish Presbyterian base.

With a population of about 125,000 (one-fifth of them university students), Dunedin is New Zealand's fourth-largest city and the second largest in the South Island. The city itself is vital, and you'll quickly notice that the streets are filled with young people. It's the main business center for Otago province, and nearby Otago Peninsula is home to several internationally recognized reserves, where some of the world's rarest wildlife can be viewed year-round in their natural habitats.

The splendor of many of its grand city buildings reflects Dunedin's economic and cultural preeminence in Victorian New Zealand, and today it has a justly deserved reputation as one of the best-preserved Victorian and Edwardian cities in the Southern Hemisphere. The original 344 Scottish settlers, who arrived in the area in March 1848, would be proud if they could witness the outcome of their early endeavors.

Things can be, and often are, a little different down here. Where else could you find a kilt shop in New Zealand, plus a thriving population of alternative musicians, fashion designers and artists, a castle, New Zealand's only whiskey distillery, a haggis maker, a colony of albatrosses, a traditional Chinese garden, some of the best student pubs in the country, and a chocolate factory? It's a slightly disconcerting mix that will charm the socks off you.

Essentials

GETTING THERE **By Plane** **Air New Zealand** (www.airnewzealand.co.nz) has flights between Dunedin and Sydney, Melbourne, and Brisbane. **Air New Zealand,** at the corner of The Octagon and Princes Street (© **0800/737-000** in NZ, or 03/479-6594; www.airnewzealand.co.nz), provides service between Dunedin and Auckland, Wellington, and Rotorua in the North Island, and Christchurch and Invercargill in the South Island. **Pacific Blue** (www.flypacificblue.com) flies between Dunedin and Christchurch daily. **Stewart Island Flights** (© **03/218-9129;** www.stewartislandflights.com) has flights to and from Stewart Island on Monday, Wednesday, Friday, and Sunday.

The Dunedin airport (www.dnairport.co.nz) is inconveniently placed 40 minutes out of the city, and taxis charge approximately NZ$60 for the trip into town. You'd be well advised to take one of the shuttles that run to the city at regular intervals. The **Dunedin Taxis Airport Shuttle** (© **0800/505-010** or 03/477-7777; www.dunedintaxis.co.nz) charges around NZ$25 to NZ$30 to most parts of Central City. **City Taxis** (© **0800/771771** in NZ, or 03/477-1771; www.citytaxis.co.nz) offers a fixed-fare service from the airport if you are staying at a city hotel; the rate is NZ$70, which covers one to four people in the taxi.

By Coach (Bus) InterCity (☎ 09/623-1503) provides coach service between Dunedin and Christchurch, Invercargill, Picton, Queenstown, Te Anau, and Timaru. The bus terminal is at 205 St. Andrew St. (☎ 03/477-8860). **Bottom Bus,** The Octagon (☎ 0800/304-333 in NZ, or 03/477-9083; www.travelheadfirst.com/bottom-bus), has a range of Southern tours including the 5-day In a Stew trip, which begins and ends anywhere you like in this region and costs NZ$625. It includes a Milford Sound cruise and travel to Stewart Island. It offers discounts to travelers with YHA, VIP, and BBH backpacker cards.

By Car Dunedin can be reached via state highways 1 and 87. It is 366km (227 miles) and approximately a 5-hour drive south of Christchurch; 220km (136 miles) and approximately 3 to 4 hours northeast of Invercargill; and 4 hours from Queenstown, inland through Central Otago. The Southern Scenic Route from Invercargill is another possibility; this route passes through the forested coastal Catlins area and is well worth the slight diversion from State Highway 1.

ORIENTATION All good cities have a heart, and Dunedin is no exception. Rather than a square, though, it has a tree-lined octagon, which acts as a central meeting place. This is where you'll find the visitor center, bus terminals, the main art gallery, and a host of cafes and bars. It boasts a statue of Scotland's beloved poet Robert Burns (whose nephew was Dunedin's first pastor), grassy areas under trees, and a giant chessboard. The Octagon divides the city's main street into George Street to the north and Princes Street to the south. A popular shopping area is located in the George Street section (see "Shopping," later in this section). The city center is at the head of Otago Harbour, and is encircled by a 200-hectare (500-acre) strip of land, the Green Belt.

GETTING AROUND **By Bus** The **GoBus** service is run by the **Otago Regional Council** (☎ 0800/474-082 in NZ, or 03/474-0287; www.orc.govt.nz). Most city buses leave from the vicinity of The Octagon. Your best bet is to get bus timetables from the visitor center on The Octagon or check www.orc.govt.nz. There is frequent service during the week, but it's a little spotty on weekends. The fares are by zone and range from NZ$2 to NZ$6.50 per section, but you get 10% off every trip if you purchase a GoCard from the driver. These cost NZ$5 and require a minimum loading of NZ$10. They can be regularly topped up and can also be used on Queenstown's Connectabus service.

By Taxi Taxi stands can be found at The Octagon, at all terminals, and near the Chief Post Office. Or call **Dunedin Taxis** (☎ 03/477-7777) or **City Taxis** (☎ 03/477-1771).

By Car Once you familiarize yourself with the one-way systems and the interrupted street pattern around the Octagon, Dunedin is easy to negotiate. Most central streets have metered parking, and there's a municipal parking building near City Hall and a carpark in the Meridian Shopping Centre. If you'd like to drive yourself in style, contact **Executive Car Rentals,** 331A King Edward St. (☎ 0800/567-000 in NZ, or 03/455-9060; www.executivecar-rentals.co.nz), which specializes in European car rentals, from BMWs to Mercedes

Scottish Roots

Dunedin is the ancient Gaelic name of Edinburgh in Scotland, and Otago University, the oldest in New Zealand, was modeled after Glasgow University.

HOTELS ■

The Brothers Boutique
  Hotel **13**
526 George Street **6**
Fletcher Lodge **28**
Glendinning House **2**
Hazel House **33**
Hilltop on High Street **29**
Larnach Lodge **34**
Living Space **11**
Manor House Backpackers **30**
Motel on York **10**
Nisbet Cottage **34**
Quest Dunedin **12**
Scenic Hotel Dunedin City **22**
Scenic Hotel Southern
  Cross **26**
St. Clair Beach Resort **33**
Tower House **3**

ⓘ Information   ┼┼ Railroad

RESTAURANTS ◆

Bacchus **20**
Etrusco **15**
Everyday Gourmet Ltd. **7**
Governor's Café **8**
The Jitsu **18**
Mazagram Espresso Bar **14**
Nectar **27**
Nova **16**
Otago Farmers Market **21**
Pier 24 **32**
Plato **31**
Speight's Ale House **23**
Strictly Coffee **19**
Swell Café **32**
Table Se7en **9**

ATTRACTIONS ●

Dunedin Botanic Gardens **1**
Dunedin Chinese Garden **25**
Dunedin Public Art Gallery **17**
Otago Museum **5**
Otago Settlers Museum **24**
The Theomin Gallery – Olveston **4**

from NZ$125 to NZ$339 per day. GPS devices, children's car seats, and snow chains are optional extras.

VISITOR INFORMATION The **Dunedin i-SITE Visitor Centre,** 48 The Octagon (✆ **03/474-3300;** fax 03/474-3311; www.dunedinnz.com or www. dunedin.govt.nz), is set in the magnificently restored Municipal Chambers. It's open Monday through Friday from 8:30am to 5pm, weekends and holidays from 9am to 5:30pm. In summer, the office remains open daily until 6pm.

SPECIAL EVENTS Dunedin has an all-year program of festivals and events. To find out about them, check at the visitor center.

The **Dunedin Summer Festival** in February and March presents themed weekends, exhibitions, outdoor concerts, family activities, and sporting and cultural events. At the same time is the **id Dunedin Fashion Show** (✆ **03/477-1092;** www.id-dunedinfashion.com), where the city's many designers showcase their work on the Dunedin Railway Platform in front of international media. In May, the **Regent Theatre 24-Hour Book Sale ★** (✆ **03/477-6481**) offers up over 300,000 volumes in the country's largest sale of secondhand books. It all started as a way to raise funds for the theater's restoration, and it's become a successful, established event filled with fun, live entertainment, and great bargains. In July, the **Dunedin Cadbury Chocolate Carnival** (www.chocolatecarnival.co.nz) is held during the winter school holidays. Chocolate-themed events are held throughout the city. In the third week of October, **Dunedin Rhododendron Festival** celebrates the exotic beauty of Dunedin's most famous flower. A happy combination of soil and climate makes the city one of the finest rhododendron-growing areas in the world. More information about Rhododendron Week and its private garden tours is available by calling ✆ **03/474-3300** or visiting www.rhododunedin.co.nz.

[Fast FACTS] DUNEDIN

Area Code The telephone area code (STD) for Dunedin is **03.**

Automobile Association The **AA** is at 450 Moray Place (✆ **03/477-5945,** or 025/386-122 after hours; fax 03/477-9760), and is open Monday through Friday from 8:30am to 5pm. If your car breaks down, phone ✆ **0800/500-222.**

Dentists Raymond J. George, Level 7, at The Octagon and George Street (✆ **03/477-7993**), provides 24-hour service. The **After Hours Emergency Dentist** can be reached at ✆ **03/477-7230.**

Doctors Go to the **Travellers Medical & Vaccination Centre,** 169 Eglinton Rd., Mornington (✆ **03/453-6121**); or **Dunedin Urgent Doctors,** 95 Hanover St., Dunedin (✆ **03/479-2900**).

Emergencies For police, fire, or ambulance service, dial ✆ **111.**

Internet Access **A1 Internet Café,** Level 1, 149 George St. (✆ **03/477-5832**), is open from 10am until late. The visitor center also offers Internet service.

Post Office The Chief Post Office is at 243 Princes St. (✆ **03/477-3517**); there's another at 233 Moray Place (✆ **03/474-0932**).

Restrooms There good public restrooms on Municipal Lane on the Upper Octagon, between the visitor center and the public library. Open Monday through Saturday from 8:30am to 8:30pm and Sunday from 9am to 5pm.

Exploring Dunedin

Swing by the visitor center to watch the half-hour video *Dunedin Discovered,* which will give you an overview of the region. Also pick up a sightseeing map and look for the *Walk the City* brochure (NZ$3). There are terrific scenic drives around the city and on the peninsula, and the visitor center has plenty of maps and brochures to show you where to go and what to look out for along the way. One of your first stops should also be the Otago Museum (see below). Its gallery, "Southern Land, Southern People," will bring more meaning to your visit.

TAKING IN THE VIEWS

There are three good lookout points from which to view the city and its environs: **Mount Cargill Lookout,** 8km (5 miles) from the city center (turn left at the end of George St., then left on Pine Hill Rd. to its end, and then right onto Cowan Rd., which climbs to the summit); **Centennial Lookout,** or Signal Hill (turn onto Signal Hill Rd. from Opoho Rd., then drive 3km/1¾ miles to the end of Signal Hill Rd.); and **Bracken's Lookout** (at the top of the Botanic Gardens), which was named after poet Thomas Bracken, who wrote the words to New Zealand's national anthem.

MUSEUMS, GALLERIES & HISTORIC HOMES

Otago Museum ★★★ ☺ Established in 1868, this is New Zealand's fourth-largest museum with over 1.7-million items; most people are surprised by the depth of its large ethnographic, natural-history, and decorative-arts collections. It also has the best Pacific and Southern Maori collections in the country.

After a recent multimillion-dollar upgrade, it now has a new and improved foyer, cafe, and shop, a new special-exhibitions gallery, a stylish atrium, a new 6-minute introductory video (the best way to begin your visit), and a stunning gallery called **"Southern Land, Southern People" ★★**, which tells the human and natural-history story of the southern region. Allow an hour for this section and to get the best from it take a guided tour, which can be booked in advance.

Visitors can meet the extinct giant moa in a gallery that includes the museum's world-class collection of complete moa skeletons and one of the few complete moa eggs in the world; and fans of old-style museums should not miss the new **Animal Attic ★**, which replicates the Victorian timbered gallery of the museum as it was in 1868. It's my favorite museum space—unforgettable for its visual impact and zany collections of stuffed animals (which kids will love), birds, and New Zealand spiders. And don't overlook the fun factor of **Discovery World,** one of those terrific places for children where you end up playing yourself. The live butterfly experience is also a wonderful treat. Allow 2 hours for a good look around.

419 Great King St. ☎ **03/474-7474.** Fax 03/477-5993. www.otagomuseum.govt.nz and www.discoveryworld.co.nz. Free admission to museum; admission to Discovery World Tropical Forest NZ$10 adults, NZ$5 children 2–15, family NZ$21–NZ$25. Southern Land Tour NZ$10 per person. Daily 10am–5pm. Closed Dec 25.

Otago Settlers Museum ★★ This is Otago's museum of social history, tracing the stories of those who have made the region home—from the original Maori inhabitants to the sturdy Scottish pioneers, the rough-and-ready gold miners to the business entrepreneurs who followed them. Exhibitions are comprehensive, presenting even the most detailed engineering and scientific facts in a readily accessible manner. There are also exhibits on the Ngai Tahu Maori communities of Otago, an ever-popular transport collection (engine buffs will be in heaven), and a Penny Farthing cycle you can actually ride. A new gallery features the 19th-century settlers' shipboard experience, which includes a mock-up of the steerage of a sailing ship. Allow an hour for a quick overview. *Note:* The museum is closed until late 2012 for a NZ$38-million redevelopment. Please call or check the website before your visit.

31 Queens Gardens. © **03/477-5052.** Fax 03/474-2727. www.otago.settlers.museum. Free admission. Daily 10am–5pm. Closed Good Friday and Dec 25.

Dunedin Public Art Gallery ★★ When the Dunedin Public Art Gallery opened in 1996, art lovers throughout the country celebrated. The new space is one of the best in New Zealand and has received acclaim for both its architecture and its collection—one of the best in Australasia. There are significant holdings of European art, Japanese prints, and French Impressionist works (including the only Monet in a New Zealand public collection), along with a comprehensive collection of contemporary and early New Zealand art, and a gallery dedicated to the works of painter Frances Hodgkins. The shop stocks a good range of art-related products and the gallery offers free Wi-Fi to visitors.

30 The Octagon. © **03/474-3240.** Fax 03/474-3250. www.dunedin.art.museum. Free admission; charges for special exhibitions. Daily 10am–5pm. Special tours available by arrangement. Closed Good Friday and Dec 25.

The Theomin Gallery—Olveston ★★★ 🎁 Olveston is one of New Zealand's best-known stately homes and if, like me, you have a passion for grand old homes, it should definitely be on your agenda. Designed by London architect Sir Ernest George, the 35-room, Jacobean-style mansion was built between 1904 and 1906 by the much-traveled and very prosperous Theomin family. It sits on an acre of tree-sheltered grounds, and since it was bequeathed to Dunedin in 1966, it has been carefully maintained in virtually its original state. David Theomin had a passion for Eastern decorative arts, and he filled his home with bronze, cloisonné, ivory, ceramics, jade, and over 250 paintings. On top of its unique interior finery, the house itself is a work of art and pays homage to the skills of 19th-century craftsmen. Those with reservations are given preference; house viewing is by 1-hour guided tour only. Reservations are required for the 2-hour painting tours.

42 Royal Terrace. © **03/477-3320.** Fax 03/479-2094. www.olveston.co.nz. Admission NZ$17 adults, NZ$8 children ages 5–15. Guided tours daily at 9:30 and 10:45am, noon, 1:30, 2:45, and 4pm. Closed Dec 25.

OTHER HIGHLIGHTS

Forgive me for not walking up **Baldwin Street,** which, according to the *Guinness Book of World Records,* is the world's steepest street. I couldn't face the 270 steps that take you to the top, or the footpath and its impossible gradient. Just minutes from the city center, this little street tricks you with a gentle beginning. It then rears dramatically skyward to come to a dead end on the hillside. If you're hale and hearty and have something to prove, this could be a good test, and I believe the views from the top are worth it. And if you want a certificate to prove to your friends back home that you had what it takes, then stop by the **World's Steepest Street Tourist Shop,** 282 North Rd. (© **03/473-0923**). To get to Baldwin Street, take the Normandy bus to North Road; Baldwin is the 10th street on the right past the Botanic Gardens. And remember, if you drive to the top, there's only a very tight turnaround space and only one way out—down the way you came!

Dunedin's **Railway Station** warrants more than a cursory glance. This marvelous old Flemish Renaissance–style structure was designed by George A. Troup and built

Chocolate Heaven

Chocolate lovers and fans of *Charlie & the Chocolate Factory,* rejoice! The famous **Cadbury World,** 280 Cumberland St. (✆ **03/467-7967;** www.cadburyworld.co.nz), is open. This unique, interactive chocolate-themed center offers daily guided tours of New Zealand's most famous—and favorite—chocolate factory every half-hour from 9am until 3:15pm. Immerse yourself in the process and sample treats along the way. A full tour takes about 75 minutes, but be aware that many of the most interesting processes are "secret" and you don't get to see them. I found that a little disappointing, and I suspect younger children may be less enchanted by the mechanical focus. It costs NZ$18 for adults, NZ$12 for children ages 5 to 15, and NZ$48 for families. A retail outlet here also offers special "tour only" prices, but you can't shop here unless you do take the tour.

between 1904 and 1906. Troup won the Institution of British Architects Award for his efforts and was later knighted. Built of Kokonga basalt with Oamaru limestone facings, the station's most prominent feature is its large square clock tower. Equally impressive are the Aberdeen granite pillars supporting arches of the colonnade across the front, the red Marseilles tiles on the roof, and the colorful mosaic floor (more than 725,000 Royal Doulton porcelain squares) in the massive foyer depicting a "Puffing Billy" engine. Look for the replica of Dunedin's coat of arms and the stained-glass windows above the balcony. This is where you'll find the **New Zealand Sports Hall of Fame,** 1st floor, Main Railway Station (✆ **03/477-7775;** www.nzhalloffame.net. nz), which gives you an overview of New Zealand's great sporting moments. It's open daily from 10am to 4pm. Admission is NZ$5 per person.

The **Dunedin Gasworks Museum** ★★, 20 Braemar St., South Dunedin (✆ **03/455-5062;** www.gasworksmuseum.org.nz), is an unexpected find. The gasworks opened in 1863 and today it is one of only three gasworks museums in the world. You'll find interesting displays of old, steam-pumping engines and an appraisal of the city's early industrial heritage. It's open the first and third Sunday of every month, plus every Tuesday, from noon to 4pm; visits by appointment at other times. Admission is NZ$5 for adults and NZ$8 for a family.

PARKS & GARDENS

The 28-hectare (69-acre) **Dunedin Botanic Gardens** (✆ **03/477-4000;** www.dunedin.govt.nz/facilities/botanic-garden) were the first to be established in New Zealand, in 1869. At the northern end of Castle Street, they feature the world-renowned Rhododendron Dell. Nestled into native bush with magnolia, cherry, and maples, the Dell features over 3,000 rhododendron plants and has spectacular masses of blooms from October to December. You can also see the comprehensive native-plant collection, an Edwardian conservatory garden, rock gardens, and rose gardens. The gardens are open daily from dawn to dusk, free of charge. A kiosk restaurant offers light snacks and morning and afternoon teas; a shop and information center are also on the grounds. All three are open daily from 10am to 4pm. Pick up the free gardens map from the visitor center.

For information on Dunedin's famous October **Rhododendron Festival,** go to www.rhododunedin.co.nz.

Tours of **Speight's Brewery Heritage Centre ★★**, 200 Rattray St. (© 03/477-7697; www.speights.co.nz), cost NZ$23 for adults, NZ$10 for children ages 5 to 15, and NZ$48 for a family. For that you'll spend about 1½ hours looking at the brewing processes of this "Pride of the South," with tastings and a sample of the product at the end. Speight's has been favoring us with its fine ales since 1876, and the tour gives a good overview of the industry. Make sure you see the stunning Otago video presentation at the end—it made my little Kiwi heart burst with pride. Tours are limited to 25 people and run daily at 10am, 11:45am, and 2pm, with an extra 7pm tour Monday through Thursday. Ask about a combo deal that includes a Cadbury World chocolate factory tour.

A new addition to the Dunedin garden scene is the magnificent and somewhat unexpected **Dunedin Chinese Garden ★★★**, corner of Rattray and Cumberland streets, Dunedin (© **03/477-4000** or 03/477-3248; www.dunedinchinesegarden. com), which opened in 2008 and is said to be one of only three truly authentic Chinese gardens outside of China. The garden was created with authentic materials by Chinese craftsmen and artisans in Dunedin's sister city, Shanghai. The garden was then dismantled, shipped to New Zealand, and reconstructed on the current site under the supervision of the Chinese craftsmen. It was the brainchild of the Dunedin Chinese Garden Trust, supported by the local Chinese community, many of whom have roots back to the Chinese gold miners of the 1860s Otago gold rush. The garden is open daily from 10am to 5pm, with an evening viewing from 7 to 9pm on Wednesdays. Admission is NZ$9 for adults; children 13 and under enter free. A 1-hour guided tour costs NZ$20 per person and is run daily at 2pm.

Exploring Otago Peninsula

Otago Peninsula is simply spectacular, especially on a clear day. It has some of the finest views of the southern coastline and is one of New Zealand's most renowned ecotourism areas, with several excellent wildlife centers. You can book tours of the peninsula through the visitor center, or pick up the free *Visitors' Guide to the Otago Peninsula,* which features a comprehensive map of attractions, arts and crafts, accommodations, and restaurants. The 33km (20-mile) peninsula curves around one side of Otago Harbour. It's an easy road, although some portions are unpaved, and it takes you past quaint coastal boatsheds and quiet settlements. The listings below cover Otago's highlights. As most tourism operations based on or visiting this area depend on the welfare of the peninsula's wildlife, you'll find most take a conscientious approach to environmentally safe viewing practices.

Royal Albatross Centre ★★★ It seems a cruel irony that a magnificent bird such as the royal albatross, which can stay in the air for weeks on end, should make such an ungainly landing when it finally decides to come down to earth. But we can be thankful that it has chosen to do so at Taiaroa Head, the only mainland colony of albatrosses in the world. One-hour tours will show you the birds only; 90-minute tours add the tunnel complex of the old Fort Taiaroa and the last working example of an Armstrong Disappearing Gun. The best times to visit are January and February, when the chicks are hatching; in late afternoon, you'll see courtship displays. After

6:30pm, the sea breezes come up, and juveniles come in from the sea. It's important to remember, though, that this is wildlife and there are no guarantees. Sometimes you can see birds as close as 3.5m (12 ft.) away, sometimes much farther. But with binoculars and a telephoto camera lens, you're bound to get good results. During the mating season, the main observatory is closed, and viewing is from an alternative spot a little farther away. It's a 2-minute walk up a path to the observatory; mobile carts are available for visitors with disabilities. A souvenir shop, cafeteria, and wildlife displays are on the grounds.

Taiaroa Head. © **03/478-0499.** Fax 03/478-0575. www.albatross.org.nz. Free admission to Albatross Centre. Daily 1-hr. Albatross Tour, from NZ$45 adults, NZ$25 children 5–14; daily 90-min. Unique Albatross Tour NZ$50 adults, NZ$25 children 5–14; Fort Taiaroa Tour, NZ$25 adults, NZ$15 children 5–14. Center daily 9am–7pm. Closed Dec 25. Tour reservations required; call visitor center on The Octagon or the Albatross Centre directly.

Penguin Place ★★★ When you consider that every yellow-eyed penguin has 200 feathers per square inch, you realize there's likely to be a whole lot of preening going on in the heart of this excellent conservation project. The 1½-hour tour begins with an informative talk and slide presentation; you're then driven 5 minutes across farmland to an extensive network of tunnels and hides that took 8 years to build. Here you'll be able to watch the world's rarest penguins at close quarters without disturbing them. Fifteen years ago, there were 8 breeding pairs; today, there are over 35 pairs in the colony, which represents 20% of New Zealand's mainland yellow-eyed population. You'll need sensible walking shoes, as there's at least 500m (1,600 ft.) of walking involved, much of it uphill and steep. But you'll be rewarded with fabulous coastal views, colonies of fur seals, possibly Hooker sea lions if you're lucky, and incredible, swirling tangles of sea kelp—all fantastic photographic opportunities, but no flashes are allowed near the penguins.

Pakihau Rd. © **03/478-0286.** Fax 03/478-0257. www.penguinplace.co.nz. Admission from NZ$55 adults, NZ$30 children 5–14. MC, V. Tours given Nov to mid-Mar 10:15am–7:45pm; reservations required. Tours depart from the McGrouther Farm on Harrington Point Rd. It is well signposted and just 5 min. before the Royal Albatross Centre.

Larnach Castle ★★ Larnach Castle may be small by European standards, but it's clear William Larnach had more than a simple bungalow in mind when he set about constructing this marvelous edifice in 1871. No doubt keen to impress his French heiress wife, he hired 200 workmen for 3 years just to build the shell; a host of European master craftsmen took another 12 years to complete the interior. The carved foyer ceiling alone took three craftsmen 6½ years to finish. The Georgian hanging staircase is the only one in the Southern Hemisphere, and it fits comfortably with the best of everything that Larnach incorporated.

Larnach came to New Zealand from Australia in the late 1860s to set up the first Bank of Otago. He later became a Member of Parliament, but with three marriages behind him and a family history dotted with scandal and misfortune, he committed suicide in the Parliament Buildings in Wellington. (His first two wives both died at the age of 38, and his third dealt him a fatal emotional blow by dallying with the son from his first marriage.) After his death, the crown used the castle as a mental hospital. For nearly 40 years, it has been the home of Margaret Barker and her family, who have committed themselves to its restoration. Pick up the self-guiding pamphlet at the reception area and wander as you wish. If you'd like to stay in the castle lodge or stables, see "Where to Stay," below.

145 Camp Rd., off Highcliff Rd. © **03/476-1616.** Fax 03/476-1574. www.larnachcastle.co.nz. Admission to castle and grounds NZ$27 adults, NZ$10 children; grounds only NZ$13 adults, NZ$4 children. Daily

If you're traveling with kids—or even if you're not—don't miss the **New Zealand Marine Studies Centre & Westpac Aquarium ★★**, Portobello, Otago Peninsula (✆ 03/479-5826; www.marine.ac.nz). I can't keep my hands out of things, so I delighted in being able to delve into marine tanks—although it goes without saying that you should first see who's living in there. After all, there's no point in losing a finger to a lobster. You can help feed the sea critters every Wednesday and Saturday from 2 to 3pm; or take one of the daily guided tours at 10:30am. The center is open daily from 10am to 4:30pm. A self-guided visit costs NZ$13 for adults, NZ$6 children 5 to 15, and NZ$25 for a family; the guided tour is NZ$22 for adults, NZ$11 for children, and NZ$49 for a family. If you're heading out to view the albatrosses, it's on your way. Be aware that it's a narrow, unsealed road through farmland to the aquarium (slippery when wet) and when you get there, there is a sudden, very steep descent into a small car park. The views for photographs are well worth the effort.

9am–5pm. Closed Dec 25. Take Portobello Rd. 3km (2 miles) north of Glenfalloch Woodland Garden and follow the signs inland.

Organized Tours

Dunedin is blessed with a number of excellent tour operators who provide enjoyable sightseeing the easy way. You'll find a profusion of pamphlets at the visitor center on The Octagon. During summer months, it pays to reserve early.

If you have food and wine on your mind, you should definitely hook up with **Zest Food Tours ★★★** (✆ 0800/937-886; www.zestfoodtours.co.nz), which will take you on a walking tour of the city, introducing you to the many gourmet tastes of the area. And if you join them on a Saturday, you'll also get a tour of the Otago Farmers' Market, which is held at the spectacular Dunedin Railway Station. Book your tour at the Dunedin i-SITE Visitor Centre and pay around NZ$185 per person.

Take the hedonistic approach to touring with **Top Hat Limousines** (✆ 03/455-9060; www.tophat.co.nz). They can tailor-make a tour to suit your needs anywhere in the South Island; their standard hourly rate is NZ$145. **Classic Jaguar Limousines** (✆ 03/488-5961; www.classicjaguar.co.nz) offers a very good 5-hour **Dunedin City Heritage Tour** for NZ$200 per person, or a tour of the city's heritage homes for NZ$210. It's also a very stylish way to travel to Oamaru to see the Moeraki Boulders and the Blue Penguin Colony (p. 474). Kids ages 6 to 12 travel at half-price.

Many of the operators are geared toward peninsula exploration. Outdoor types will find pleasure in the sea-kayak, rafting, walking, and mountain bike tours offered by **Wild Earth Adventures ★★★** (✆ 03/489-1951; www.wildearth.co.nz). Its **Ocean Discovery Kayak Tour** takes you along wild beaches and soaring sea cliffs to the albatross colony and offers amazing photographic opportunities. It costs NZ$125 per person.

Also popular is **Elm Wildlife Tours ★★★** (✆ 0800/356-563 in NZ, or 03/454-4121; www.elmwildlifetours.co.nz). Twice voted New Zealand's best wildlife tour, it gives you a sound insight into the habits of various penguin species, fur seals, and sea lions. Viewing hides give you a close encounter and options range from NZ$99 to NZ$213. You'll need good walking shoes as you'll be walking on coastal hillsides. Most tours are 6 to 8 hours long. They are closed from December 25 to 31.

COACH (BUS) TOURS

Citibus Newton Tours, Princes Street and Transport Place (© **03/477-5577;** www. newtons.co.nz), conducts excellent tours of varying duration, from the comfort of a double-decker bus, all with guides providing valuable insight into the area's highlights, along with the occasional anecdote to liven things up. All tours may be booked directly with Citibus Newton, online, or at the Dunedin i-SITE Visitor Centre. Pickups from your lodging can be arranged. The **First City ★★** tour departs five times per day from the visitor center. The fare is NZ$20 per adult, NZ$10 per child 14 and under. The company's **Wildlife Tour of Otago Peninsula** includes Larnach Castle; other wildlife tours include either the Albatross Centre or Penguin Place. Tours depart daily from the visitor center at 2:30pm and cost NZ$95 for adults, NZ$48 for children.

CRUISING THE PENINSULA

A number of cruise options can show you the wildlife delights of Otago Peninsula. The visitor center has a comprehensive selection of brochures and a helpful staff to help you sort out your priorities.

Locals are quick to tell you about the fantastic value offered through the family-owned and -operated **Monarch Wildlife Cruises ★★★**, Wharf and Fryatt streets (© **0800/666-272** in NZ, or 03/477-4276; www.wildlife.co.nz). Established in 1983 by owners with degrees in biology and a wealth of experience on research vessels, Monarch won the New Zealand Tourism Awards Natural Heritage category in 1994 and the Ecotourism category in 1997. Crewmembers are experienced Department of Conservation officers or have degrees in zoology, so there's not much you won't be able to find out about albatrosses, New Zealand fur seals, yellow-eyed penguins, and other species you're likely to see. If you're short on time, opt for the 1-hour albatross cruise from Wellers Rock, which costs NZ$49 for adults, NZ$22 for children ages 5 to 15. It departs from Wellers Rock at 10:30am, noon, 2pm, 3:15pm, and 4:30pm in summer and at 2:30pm in winter. (Remember that Wellers Rock is a 45-min. drive from Central City.) Monarch also has full harbor cruises from Dunedin lasting just over 5 hours. Dress warmly and take your camera; if you're unsure about which option to take, note that the most popular is the cruise-and-bus trip, which includes a guided tour of Penguin Place—it gives you a taste of everything. Half-day tours cost NZ$90 to NZ$140, and full-day options from NZ$235 to NZ$275.

Outdoor Pursuits

BEACHES New Zealanders don't often utter the two words "Dunedin" and "beaches" in the same breath, but the truth is, there are at least eight or nine

 Dunedin's Unique Tours

If you think ghosts don't exist, Andrew Smith's **Hair Raiser Ghost Walk ★★** (© **03/477-2258;** www.hairraisertours. com) might convince you otherwise. Get behind the city's beautiful architecture and discover the truth behind many famous ghost sightings, the wandering habits of the supernatural, and The Octagon fires. Based on fact,

not fiction, the tour is not for the faint-hearted and there's no guarantee of a good night's sleep afterward. No garlic or crucifixes allowed. Tours leave from outside the visitor center daily April through September at 6pm, and October through March at 8pm; they cost NZ$30 for adults, NZ$15 for children 12 and under. No credit cards.

EXPERIENCING THE HEARTLAND: CENTRAL OTAGO rail trail

Get off the beaten track to see the dramatic landscapes and quaint villages of central Otago by following the **Central Otago Rail Trail ★★★** (**ⓒ 03/474-6909**). Opened to the public in 2000, this 150km (93-mile) trail between Middlemarch and Clyde—great for cycling, walking, or horseback riding—follows the old railway line that took 16 years to build between 1891 and 1907. The trail can be started and finished at either Middlemarch or Clyde and you should allow 4 days to complete it, cycling for around 4 hours a day over gravel surfaces. There are no very steep climbs but a good level of fitness and some cycling experience makes for a much better experience. If you're walking, you'll need to be fit and you should allow 6 days. You'll pass through tunnels (take a torch), over viaducts, and through surreal rocky landscapes, stopping each night at one of the many excellent accommodation spots along the way, which must be booked well in advance. Informative panels dot the trail, detailing the history and geography of the region; and pubs, cafes, and grocery stores in some small villages can be found along the way. Make sure you take cash as ATMs are few and far between. You can find out all you need to know about the trail, bike hire, accommodation, and transport at www.otagocentralrailtrail.co.nz. There is also an excellent brochure available from the Dunedin i-SITE Visitor Centre.

magnificent, unspoiled, white-sand beaches within an easy drive of Dunedin. You may not always want to swim in the coolish waters, but from a scenic point of view, they're worth a visit. **St. Kilda** and **St. Clair** are probably the best known, made famous by a dedicated band of wet-suited surfers. A short drive north to the Port Chalmers area reveals **Long Beach, Aromoana,** and **Purakanui,** and on Otago Peninsula, **Pilot's Beach** (near the Albatross Centre), **Victory Beach, Sandfly Bay,** and **Seal Point** are all generally deserted and beautiful. Closer to town you have **Tunnel Beach,** which is accessed through private property and a tunnel. Ask the staff at the visitor center for driving instructions. You'll find great walks on **Brighton Beach,** a 20-minute drive south of Dunedin.

BIKING   Dunedin may be hilly, but there are great cycling opportunities, especially out on the peninsula. Rent a bike from **Browns,** 110 Crawford St. (**ⓒ 03/477-7259**). If you're more into fat tires, the visitor center's excellent brochure *Mountain Bike Rides in Dunedin* outlines all the best tracks. Visit www.cyclingotago.co.nz for even more information.

FISHING   Nearby Port Chalmers is known for its stellar salmon and trout fishing from October to April. If you want to try your hand at shark fishing, deep-sea fishing, saltwater, or light-tackle sport fishing, call **Otago Harbour Salmon Fishing Charters,** 7 Henderson St., Mornington (**ⓒ 03/453-6614**), or inquire at the Dunedin visitor center for other options. **Wannabe Fishin'** (**ⓒ 03/415-7146**; wbfishing@xtra.co.nz) knows all the best local spots for trout fishing and hunting.

GOLF   The **Otago Golf Club Balmacewen Course** (**ⓒ 03/467-2096**; www.otagogolfclub.co.nz) has been operating since 1896. It's an 18-hole championship course with a fully stocked pro shop. Members pay NZ$45, nonmembers pay NZ$75.

St. Clair Golf Club (© 03/487-7076; www.stclairgolf.co.nz) is also popular; greens fees are NZ$55 per person.

SEA KAYAKING Otago Harbour is the perfect playground for sea kayakers. You can explore the spectacular sea cliffs teeming with wildlife, or turn your hand to a surf landing on an isolated beach. Contact **Wild Earth Adventures** (see above in "Organized Tours") for the best outings.

SURFING Head for **St. Clair** and **St. Kilda** beaches on The Esplanade. This is the center of Dunedin's surfer activity.

SWIMMING If the ocean seems too daunting, head for **Moana Pool,** 60 Littlebourne Road and Stuart Street (© 03/471-9780). It has a terrific leisure pool, lap pool, and diving pool, and the water slides are fully enclosed tubes; you can opt for a slow or fast descent. Other watery options include scuba instruction, aqua-fitness classes, underwater hockey, and water polo. Or laze around in the cafe while the kids run wild in the play area. Admission is NZ$5 adults and NZ$3 children for a casual swim. There are discount cards for multiple swims and there is a gym onsite.

 A TRAIN TRIP TO taieri gorge

The **Taieri Gorge Railway** ★★★ (© 03/477-4449; www.taieri.co.nz) is more than a small jaunt on a train—it is an award-winning journey through history and spectacular scenery that is otherwise inaccessible to the public. No matter what time of the year, you'll be impressed with both the scenic beauty and the sheer engineering feat of the railway's construction. The 75km (47 miles) of rail includes 12 tunnels, and the magnificent **Wingatui Viaduct,** which took 42 years to build, beginning in 1879. Make sure you get *Your Guide to the Taieri Gorge* when you board the train, so you can follow your progress through to the tiny township of Middlemarch, the final stopping point—a funny little backwater of a place where bachelors need hard-to-find wives. Once here, you can get off and, if you're not interested in finding the bachelors, you can link up to a coach to Queenstown; mountain bike, walk, or horseback ride—which will take you several days; or stay on the train for the return trip.

From October through April, the Dunedin–Middlemarch round-trip train runs Friday and Sunday morning,

leaving Dunedin Railway Station at 9:30am; it takes a 45-minute stop at Middlemarch, and returns to Dunedin at 3:25pm. (Reduced hours in winter; call or check the website for details.) It costs NZ$97 round-trip for adults. Students get a 20% discount; one child (ages 3–17) per adult rides free, additional children pay NZ$22 each. The shorter 4-hour trip to Pukerangi (19km/12 miles short of Middlemarch) runs daily at 2:30pm, returning 6:30pm, and costs NZ$84. Both trips include at least two photo stops, excellent ongoing commentary, and a buffet car for snacks and drinks. An adults-only car and a wheelchair-accessible carriage (book in advance) are available. For a coastal train experience, leap aboard the **Seasider,** which departs on selected Wednesdays and Saturdays in the summer season. I haven't tried this one yet, but I'm assured that the wild coastline on the trip north to Palmerston makes it more than worthwhile. You can make it a round-trip, or link with a gold-mine tour. It costs NZ$80 round-trip for adults, NZ$25 children ages 3 to 17.

St. Clair Hot Salt Water Pool, at St. Clair Beach (☎ 03/471-9780), is a 25m (80-ft.) outdoor pool right beside the ocean and, if your bones are aching from too much walking, a soak in the therapeutic waters will do you a world of good. The pool's seawater is heated to a pleasing 82°F (28°C) and you can hear waves crashing on the nearby shore. It's open from late October through March Monday through Friday from 6am until 7pm, weekends 7am to 7pm. Admission is NZ$6 for adults, NZ$3 for children 5 to 15, and NZ$12 for a family. Ask about their pool parties, which include fun activities, games, and a barbecue.

Where to Stay

Dunedin provides the usual range of lodgings, from backpacker hostels to motels to fine hotels. But what I love most about the area is its fine choice of heritage home-stays and B&Bs, many of which are in exquisite Victorian-style buildings. At certain times of the year, midrange options are heavily booked because of university activities, so make your reservations early. Rates given below include the 15% GST and free off-street parking.

IN TOWN
Expensive

Fletcher Lodge ★★★   This house is a stunning example of Dunedin's unique architecture. Built by one of New Zealand's leading industrialists in 1924, it features impressive detailing such as the Wedgwood ceiling and frieze in the music room and stained-glass inserts in almost every window. Keith and Ewa Rozecki-Pollard carried out major refurbishments in 2003; and they've more recently added two large suites in adjacent dwellings that are linked to the main house by boardwalks. All guest rooms contain desks and sofas, plus luxurious touches such as under-floor heating in the tiled bathrooms and sumptuous bedding that begs you to sleep in. Fletcher Lodge welcomes a wide range of overseas visitors, ambassadors, diplomats, and business-people. Definitely a place for the discerning traveler, but now it's more of a small boutique hotel than a B&B.

276 High St., Dunedin. www.fletcherlodge.co.nz. ☎ **0800/843-563** in NZ, or 03/477-5552. Fax 03/474-5551. 10 units. NZ$335 standard; NZ$480 premium; NZ$595 deluxe; NZ$650 apt. NZ$50 each extra person. Long-stay rates. Rates include breakfast. AE, DC, MC, V. No children 11 and under. **Amenities:** Bar; 4 nearby golf courses; Jacuzzi. *In room:* A/C, TV, hair dryer, kitchenette (in apt), Wi-Fi (small fee).

Scenic Hotel Southern Cross ★★★ 🏄   This moderately sized hotel has always been seen as the city's best, and after an NZ$8-million revamp in 2008, it has cemented that reputation. It has the advantage of being centrally located; and rooms, in three wings and across a range of prices, are very good value. I'm also happy to report that, after testing beds all over New Zealand, I've decided the Southern Cross has the best beds in the country. Rooms in the Exchange Wing are the newest—they were added in 2000—and the four corner rooms in that wing are the largest. The premium apartment, with two bedrooms and two bathrooms, is perhaps the best value of all. The Dunedin Casino is located within the same building, and the property has a Qualmark Enviro-Silver rating.

Corner of Princes and High sts., Dunedin. www.scenichotelgroup.co.nz. ☎ **0800/696-963** in NZ. 178 units. NZ$288 standard; NZ$351 superior; NZ$437 junior suite and premium apt; NZ$546 executive suite. Long-stay, off-peak, and special deals. AE, DC, MC, V. Valet parking NZ$15. **Amenities:** 3 restaurants; 2 bars; babysitting on request; concierge; nearby golf course; gym; 24-hr. room service. *In room:* TV/DVD, fridge, hair dryer, high-speed Internet, minibar.

Moderate

If you're looking for a smart motel close to town, **Motel on York ★**, 47 York Place (www.motelonyork.co.nz; ✆ **0800/006-666** in NZ, or 03/477-6120), should do the trick. Just two streets off The Octagon, its 24 nonsmoking units offer all the comforts of a good little boutique hotel for NZ$155 to NZ$255. You'll also find very reasonably priced, modern apartments in the heart of the city at **Quest Dunedin,** 333 Cumberland St. (www.questdunedin.co.nz; ✆ **0800/470-1725** in NZ, or 03/470-1725), where 42 apartments go for NZ$135 to NZ$265. Check the website for special online deals and note that it's located on a north-running one-way street.

The Brothers Boutique Hotel ★ ✍

Formerly a Christian brothers' residence, this stately brick building has been converted into an oasis of warmth and comfort. Rooms are not lavish—there's a fitting conventlike feel to them—but they all have en-suite bathrooms and breathtaking views across the city and harbor. It's riddled with charm and history and just a 5- to 10-minute downhill walk to the city. Request a balcony room for the best views.

295 Rattray St., Dunedin. www.brothershotel.co.nz. ✆ **0800/477-004** in NZ, or 03/477-0043. 15 units. NZ$180–NZ$185 standard; NZ$210–NZ$255 superior balcony; NZ$320–NZ$350 chapel. Rates include breakfast. Off-peak and special deals. AE, MC, V. No children under 12. Car park is off Brown and Bishops Rd. Drive up Rattray St., turn left into Brown St, left again into Elm Row, then left into Bishop Rd. **Amenities:** Broadband Internet. *In room:* TV, hair dryer, shared fridge, shared minibar, Wi-Fi.

Glendinning House ★★

Jocelyn Robinson and Sandy Black's fabulous big house entices from the minute you walk in. The air is filled with the delicious smells of baking and there's an instant feeling of home about the place. Jocelyn is a former caterer, so expect a fantastic breakfast (and dinner if you give her 48-hr. notice). The two upstairs rooms are huge and both open on to a big balcony. My pick here is the two-bedroom Blue Suite, which has an en-suite bathroom (shower only). The Yellow Room has a private bathroom across the landing with both bath tub and shower.

222 Highgate Rd., Roslyn, Dunedin. www.glendinninghouse.co.nz. ✆ **03/477-8262.** 2 units. NZ$380–NZ$440; NZ$105 each additional adult in suite; NZ$75 per child. Rates include breakfast, pre-dinner drinks, and canapés. MC, V. **Amenities:** Babysitting by prior arrangement; 3 nearby golf courses. *In room:* TV/DVD, hair dryer, free Wi-Fi.

Hilltop on High Street ★★ ✍

Rodney McDonald and Craig Sherson have taken a landmark, historic home and turned it into an oasis of peace and privacy overlooking the city and harbor. It's an elegant mix of Edwardian architecture and modern chic, with beautiful plaster ceilings, colored leadlight glass, and your own modern kitchen if you feel like cooking. Rooms are large—two have their own balcony and en-suite bathroom—and it's all a short walk downhill to the city.

433 High St., Dunedin. www.hilltoponhighst.co.nz. ✆ **03/477-1053.** 4 units. NZ$190–NZ$225. Rates include breakfast. MC, V. **Amenities:** Nearby golf courses. *In room:* TV, fridge, hair dryer, free Wi-Fi.

Scenic Hotel Dunedin City ★

Located just 1 block off the Octagon, this small, modern hotel is perfectly placed for exploring the city's attractions and architecture. You can opt for city or harbor views and rooms are spacious and fresh. Eleven new air-conditioned rooms on the 8th floor are the best value. The property has a Qualmark Enviro-Silver environmental rating.

Corner Princes and Dowling sts., Dunedin. www.scenichotelgroup.co.nz. (✆ **0800/696-963** in NZ, or 03/470-1470. Fax 03/470-1477. 110 units. NZ$291 standard; NZ$317 superior; NZ$397–NZ$593 executive (8th flr); NZ$899 executive 2-bedroom suite. Long-stay, off-peak, special deals. AE, DC, MC, V. Valet parking NZ$10. **Amenities:** Restaurant; bar; babysitting on request; nearby golf courses; small gym; limited room service; Wi-Fi in main reception areas. *In room:* A/C (8th-floor rooms), TV, fridge, hair dryer, minibar.

Inexpensive

There are modest B&B digs at **Tower House,** 9 City Rd., Roslyn (www.thetower house.co.nz; (✆ **03/477-5678**), where the price is from NZ$110 to NZ$150. Backpackers, meanwhile, will be well taken care of at **Manor House Backpackers,** 28 Manor Place (www.manorhousebackpackers.co.nz; (✆ **0800/477-0484** in NZ, or 03/477-0484), where dorm beds go for NZ$30 per person. There are also excellent, new, budget accommodations at **Living Space ★**, 192 Castle St., Dunedin (www.livingspace.net; (✆ **0508/454-846** in NZ, or 03/951-5000), which offers the nicest budget rooms in the city. Hotel rooms are NZ$99 to NZ$109; studios NZ$109 to NZ$129; and premiums NZ$144 to NZ$155. Another well-priced central city stay at **526 George Street,** 526 George St., Dunedin (www.hotel526.co.nz; (✆ **0800/779-779** in NZ, or 03/477-1261), which offers 14 very tidy rooms in a beautiful old home, formerly a surgeon's residence, for NZ$120 to NZ$190.

AT ST. CLAIR BEACH

There are very stylish bed-and-breakfast lodgings at the classic 1900s villa, **Hazel House ★★**, 50 Hazel Ave, Hazelhurst (www.hazelhouse.co.nz; (✆ **03/487-6550**), which is a short drive from St. Clair Beach. Brent and Sandy Ward have two rooms in their beautifully restored home for NZ$165 to NZ$175.

St. Clair Beach Resort ★★★ 🏨 Come here to relax in large, modern, well-appointed, restful rooms overlooking Dunedin's famous, wild surf beach. Balcony rooms decorated in soft sand and sea tones are the best. They overlook the ocean, which is generally peppered with black-suited surfers frolicking in the waves like seals. There's a delightful holiday atmosphere to this little beach suburb and once you've dined in the in-house signature restaurant, **Pier 24** (p. 471), you won't want to leave.

24 The Esplanade, St Clair, Dunedin. www.stclairbeachresort.com. (✆ **03/456-0555.** 26 units. NZ$195–NZ$400. Long-stay and special deals. AE, MC, V. No children under 12. **Amenities:** Restaurant; bar; airport transfers NZ$85; bike rentals; concierge; 3 nearby golf courses; Internet in reception areas; massage; limited room service; free use of nearby heated outdoor pools. *In room:* TV, kitchenette (some rooms); fridge, hair dryer.

ON OTAGO PENINSULA

There are certainly enough things to see on the peninsula to justify an overnight stay. At ecofriendly **Nisbet Cottage ★★**, 6A Elliffe Place, Shiel Hill (www.natureguides otago.co.nz; (✆ **03/454-5169**), hosts and nature guides Ralf and Hildegard Lubcke can advise you on the area's natural history and unique bird life. They specialize in nature-based accommodations packages that enlighten visitors to conservation issues and practices, in which you tie up 2 or more nights' stay with guided wildlife tours of Dunedin, Otago Peninsula, and the Catlins. There are two lovely suites with en-suite bathrooms and stunning views over Dunedin Harbor. Two-night tour packages start around NZ$645 and include breakfast, tour, and picnic lunch. Their Sunrise Penguin Walk is a great experience but you need to be fit for the 4-hour tour, which sees you climbing giant, steep, sand dunes and walking the length of a beach at dawn.

Larnach Lodge ★ Larnach Castle (see "Exploring Otago Peninsula," earlier in this chapter) provides an imposing backdrop to the lodge's 12 spacious, themed rooms, which all have magnificent views. (There are no lodgings in the castle itself.) The Gold Rush Room features a king-size bed made from an old cart found on the castle grounds, complete with four huge wheels and the driver's seat and brakes attached to the end. There's a hint of the Wild West about it that doesn't quite fit the elegance of the rest of the lodge and castle. That aside, beds are comfortable and bathrooms are generous. If you want to enjoy dinner in the castle's formal dining room, book by 5pm. They've now added modern luxurious rooms at Camp Estate, next door to the castle property. Overall, an excellent place to base yourself for peninsula exploration, but a bit far out if you want town action.

Larnach Castle, 145 Camp Rd., Otago Peninsula. www.larnachcastle.co.nz. ℂ **03/476-1616.** Fax 03/476-1574. 17 units. NZ$265 standard; NZ$285 premium; NZ$380 Camp Estate rooms. Rates include breakfast. MC, V. No children 14 and under. **Amenities:** Dining room; nearby golf course. *In room:* TV, fridge, hair dryer, Wi-Fi.

Where to Eat

As a university town, Dunedin is home to many establishments that cater to students. Restaurants are therefore less stratified than in other New Zealand cities, and you'll find everyone—students, businesspeople, families, elderly couples—dining happily together in most places. There are plenty of budget options and quirkily named cafes and bars.

IN TOWN
Expensive

Bacchus ★★ CONTEMPORARY NEW ZEALAND This upstairs restaurant looks out over the Octagon. Try and get a window seat if you can as the city life is a pleasant distraction while you wait between courses. It's a sophisticated spot, a favorite with lunching businessmen, and just the place to relax in leather chairs to enjoy lamb rump with mint pesto crust, or rare tuna steak on artichoke hearts.

12 The Octagon, 1st floor. ℂ **03/474-0824.** www.bacchuswinebarrestaurant.co.nz. Reservations recommended. Main courses NZ$33–NZ$39. AE, MC, V. Mon–Fri noon–late, Sat 6pm–late.

Plato ★★ INTERNATIONAL/SEAFOOD Located in an old seafarers' hostel near the wharves, Plato is a consistent winner in local cuisine awards. There's a big emphasis on fish; dishes like pan-fried salmon on fennel gnocchi, Thai seafood curry, or slow-braised duck leg make it a popular choice. Take a cab, as it's easy to get lost in the wharf area.

2 Birch St., Inner Harbour Warehouse Area ℂ **03/477-4235.** www.platocafe.co.nz. Reservations recommended. Main courses NZ$30–NZ$34. AE, MC, V. Mon–Sat 6pm–late, Sun 11am–9pm.

Table Se7en ★ INTERNATIONAL There's a slither of big-city style in this upstairs eatery that looks over the main shopping street. You can relax at the bar before tucking into meals like venison tenderloins, *manuka*-smoked beef filet, duck confit, or twice-baked pork belly on roasted root vegetables. It's an informal spot with a nice atmosphere.

Level 1, corner of Hanover and George sts. ℂ **03/477-6877.** www.tableseven.co.nz. Reservations recommended. Main courses NZ$32–NZ$37. AE, MC, V. Mon–Sat noon–3pm and dinner 6pm–late.

Moderate
Etrusco ★ ITALIAN PIZZERIA/SPAGHETTERIA Located on the first floor of the historic Savoy building, this large wooden-floored restaurant is invariably packed

Fresh is Best

The **Otago Farmers Market** (✆ 03/489-3622; www.otagofarmersmarket.org.nz) is staged every Saturday from 8am to 12:30pm in the north car park of the Dunedin Railway Station, off Anzac Avenue. It's one of the best and most vibrant farmers' markets in the country, with over 65 stalls bulging at the seams with fresh fruit, vegetables, flowers, locally farmed beef and lamb, local boutique cheeses, handcrafted breads and baked treats, plants, and nuts. There are coffee vendors, cooking demonstrations, live music, and much more. It's well worth getting out of bed early for this one—rain, hail, or shine, it provides an insight into local community life. Make sure you take cash.

with customers enjoying good-value meals. There's a big range of authentic pasta dishes and thin crust pizzas oozing with delicious toppings, and in the unlikely event that you're still hungry, there are Italian breads, antipasti, and wonderful homemade *dolci* (desserts). It can get a bit rowdy, so don't expect intimate conversations.

8A Moray Place, Dunedin. ✆ **03/477-3737.** www.etrusco.co.nz. Reservations essential. Main courses NZ$19–NZ$24. AE, MC, V. Daily 5:30pm–late.

Mazagram Espresso Bar ★ 🍴 ESPRESSO BAR   One of my favorite Dunedin haunts, this is a must-visit treat if you're a coffee connoisseur. You'll find yourself crammed into a tiny roastery with just four little marble tables (though there are more tables outside). Mazagram supplies most of Dunedin's leading cafes. It does a mean brew and can also tempt you with a sweet to accompany your coffee.

Upper Moray Place. ✆ **03/477-9959.** Cakes NZ$6–NZ$12. No credit cards. Mon–Fri 8am–6pm; Sat 10am–2pm.

Nova ★★ ITALIAN/ASIAN   No trip to Dunedin is complete without a visit to trendy Nova. Step down off The Octagon into this smart, city-style cafe oozing ambience, and you'll find everything from delicious breakfast classics such as bagels and panettone to an easy mix of Italian and Asian dinner dishes. Seafood gumbo is a favorite—thick, spicy soup of seafood, bacon, and sausage served with toasted rye— or select from warm Vietnamese chicken salad with crispy noodles, risotto of the day, steamed mussels, or Thai green vegetable curry, among others. Everyone comes to Nova, especially tourists and locals of an artistic bent, stepping in from the adjacent Public Art Gallery.

Dunedin Public Art Gallery, 29 The Octagon. ✆ **03/479-0808.** Reservations recommended. Main courses NZ$18–NZ$25. AE, DC, MC, V. Mon–Fri 7am–11pm; Sat–Sun 8:30am–11pm.

Speight's Ale House BREWPUB   This is the perfect spot to unwind after you've done the Speight's Brewery tour (p. 460). Tuck into hearty grilled Otago lamb with crispy potatoes, or chicken breast pocketed with soft cheese and cashew nuts, wrapped in bacon and served with kumara mash and black cherry sauce. A berry meringue mountain layered with berries and cream seems the only logical conclusion.

200 Rattray St., Dunedin. ✆ **07/477-7697.** www.thealehouse.co.nz. Reservations recommended. Main courses NZ$18–NZ$30. MC, V. Daily 11:30am–9pm.

Strictly Coffee ★ CAFE   I almost got a chill up my spine when I discovered this cute, hidden-away place down a back alley. It's just my sort of place—slightly disheveled in a shabby-chic kind of way, unpretentious, friendly, and known to anyone who's anyone. On top of that, you get excellent coffee, fresh from their own roastery that you can huddle beside if you feel so inclined; sweet, savory treats; and good magazines. They've also wised up to the fact that opening early saves caffeine-deprived lives! And now they have a second location in the alley off George Street, opposite the Meridian Centre.

23 Bath St. ℂ **03/479-0017.** www.strictlycoffee.co.nz. Cafe food NZ$6–NZ$15. AE, MC, V. Mon–Fri 8am–5pm.

Inexpensive

For a firsthand taste of university social life, head for the **Governor's Café,** 438 George St. (ℂ **03/477-6871**), open daily from 8am to midnight, where the food is cheap, plentiful, and tasty. You'll find numerous reasonably priced ethnic restaurants, sushi bars, and cheap Japanese restaurants in central Dunedin, so you're never short of a good meal at a reasonable price; and all the usual fast food outlets have a presence too. **The Jitsu,** 133 Lower Stuart St. (ℂ **03/470-1155**), is one of my favorite Japanese spots. You can get a filling meal of sushi and tempura for as little as NZ$13. They're open daily from noon until 5pm.

Nectar CAFE   This bright, busy cafe spread out over three levels in the old Exchange building is a good place to stop for lunch between adventures and shopping. Or start the day with free-range eggs on grilled ciabatta. Locals recommend the coffee here and the lunch menu has a tasty selection of soups, nachos, corn fritters, and risotto dishes. If it's a sunny day, find a seat in the outdoor courtyard.

286 Princes St. ℂ **03/477-8676.** www.nectarespresso.co.nz. Main courses NZ$9–NZ$16. AE, MC, V. Mon–Tues 7am–3:30pm, Wed–Fri 7am–late, Sat–Sun 8:30am–3:30pm.

AT ST. CLAIR BEACH

Pier 24 ★★★ MODERN NEW ZEALAND   Serious foodies will swoon over meals prepared by award-winning Dunedin chef Michael Coughlin. This classy, semi-formal, glasshouse-like restaurant with waterfront views is all about culinary adventure. Pan-roasted lamb rump with chocolate nib and fennel rub, orange candied parsnip, rosemary potatoes, marmalade, and 85% bitter chocolate glaze is a good example. Make sure you're hungry as this menu is bursting with temptation.

St. Clair Beach Resort, 24 The Esplanade, St. Clair Beach. ℂ **03/456-0555.** www.stclairbeachresort. com. Reservations recommended. Main courses NZ$34–NZ$38. AE, DC, MC, V. Daily 7am–late.

🎁 Gourmet Gifts

Everyday Gourmet Ltd. ★★★, 446 George St. (ℂ **03/477-2045**), provides instant gourmet satisfaction and the chance to find that perfect, unusual gift for friends and family back home. Quite apart from the delicious counter food and light meals on offer, there are shelves bulging with products from near and far. I've decided it's easier to give in to temptation than to resist.

You'll find New Zealand–made items that will surprise and delight: the country's best olive oils, sauces, honey, preserves, chocolates, and cheeses, all presented in attractive gift packs. While you try to decide what to buy, enjoy the terrific coffee. It's open Monday through Friday from 9am to 6pm, Saturday from 10am to 3pm.

Swell Café ★ CAFE   Stop here for lunch or light refreshments overlooking the waves. Whether it's coffee and cake or sautéed prawns and squid served with asparagus, you'll get the best local produce crafted into flavorsome goodies. There's an outdoor courtyard for balmy summer days, or a casual interior to relax in.

8 The Esplanade, St Clair Beach. ℭ **03/455-9500.** www.swellcafe.co.nz. Main courses NZ$11–NZ$22. AE, DC, MC, V. Daily 8am–late.

Shopping

Dunedin offers excellent shopping, with most stores open Monday through Thursday from 9am to 5:30pm, Friday from 9am to 7pm, and Saturday and Sunday from 10am to 4pm.

A good place to park your car and start browsing is the new **Meridian Shopping Centre,** George Street (ℭ 03/477-1129), which has over 40 specialty stores and an international food court. For a Kiwi memento to take home, check out the **New Zealand Shop** (ℭ 03/477-3379; www.upic.co.nz), in the civic center, next door to the visitor center on the Octagon. It's open Monday to Thursday 9am to 5:30pm, Friday 9am to 6pm, Saturday 9:30am to 4:30pm, and Sunday 10am to 4pm—they will even open just for you if you call ahead. It'll pack and ship your order overseas, too.

If you want something with a "bonny wee Scottish" flavor, head for the **Scottish Shop,** 17 George St. (ℭ 03/477-9965; www.scottishshop.co.nz). It has a wide range of tartan and heraldic goods, right down to tartan ties. **Helean Kiltmakers,** 8 Hocken St., Kenmure (ℭ 03/453-0233), continues the theme with made-to-measure kilts.

Hides, 185 George St. (ℭ 03/477-8927), has top-quality Dunedin-made sheepskin and leather jackets, while **Glen's Leather & Accessories,** 192 Castle St. (ℭ 03/477-3655), offers good-value lambskin and leather products. **Kathmandu Ltd.,** 144 Great King St. (ℭ 03/474-5178), will see you right for all your outdoor gear.

For top-quality, one-of-a-kind New Zealand designer jewelry, you can't do better than **Lure ★★★,** 130 Lower Stuart St. (ℭ 03/477-5559). This gallery exhibits the works of leading New Zealand jewelers and exquisitely detailed pieces displayed in pull-out drawers beg to be purchased! For top-quality New Zealand designware, furniture, lighting, and contemporary art, visit **White Room ★★★,** 25 Moray Place (ℭ 03/477-7875; www.whiteroomdesign.co.nz), which has beautiful, handcrafted works from top New Zealand designers and artists. It's open Monday through Friday from 11:30am to 5pm and Saturday from 11am to 3pm.

The award-winning **University Book Shop,** 378 Great King St. (ℭ 03/477-6976; www.unibooks.co.nz), offers just about anything you're likely to want to read. It's just across the road from the Otago Museum and open Monday through Friday from 8:30am to 5:30pm, Saturday from 9:30am to 1:30pm, and Sunday 11am to 3pm. Secondhand bookshop lovers won't want to leave **Raven Books ★★★,** 389 Princes St., Dunedin (ℭ 03/474-5562). It's a glorious, old-style emporium filled with collectible, antiquarian, and general secondhand books, plus New Zealand small press and art books. They're open Monday through Friday 10am to 5pm, and Saturday 10am to 3pm. **Milford Galleries,** 18 Dowling St. (ℭ 03/477-7727), is the best dealer showing contemporary New Zealand art.

Dunedin After Dark

Dunedin's nightlife ranges from its legendary university swill holes where drunken, animal-like behavior is de rigueur to smart, upmarket wine bars and a boutique

Hunt for the *pièce de résistance* of Dunedin bars, the very suave, very hard-to-find gem **Pequeño ★★★**, Lower Ground Floor (they really mean "underground"), Savoy Building, 50 Princes St. (✆ **03/477-7830**). Alternatively, if you can find a friendly local to direct you, you can access it from a steep, dark alley off Upper Moray Place.

I was taken here by Andrew of Hair Raiser Ghost Walk, so it stands to reason he would pick the darkest, seediest entry. Once inside, though, it is a salubrious and classy little den—all fur, leather, and artistic Dunedin types out for a good time. Definitely a place for grown-ups, and they have a terrific wine and cocktails list.

casino. There are also two good theaters, a multiscreen movie theater, and several cafes that double as live-music venues.

THE PERFORMING ARTS The **Fortune Theatre,** Stuart Street and Upper Moray Place (✆ **03/477-8323;** www.fortunetheatre.co.nz), plays a major part in the cultural life of Dunedin with a wide range of performances, from Shakespeare to contemporary New Zealand works. The theater is in a historic late-1800s building. Its season runs from February to December. Tickets generally cost around NZ$35 for adults and NZ$25 for students.

The **Regent Theatre,** on the Lower Octagon (✆ **03/477-8597;** fax 03/477-4726), hosts a range of national and international performances. Check the local paper for the current schedule of concerts. Also look out for the Dunedin Sinfonia concert series brochure at the visitor center. Ticket prices vary.

THE BAR, CAFE & PUB SCENE We can thank the student population for much of the color in Dunedin's after-dark scene. Their favorite hangouts include **ReFuel Bar,** 21 Frederick St. (✆ **03/477-2575**), where the Lounge and Fusion bars provide a changing array of nightly entertainment.

The **Bennu Café & Bar,** 12 Moray Place (✆ **03/474-5055**), and the **Ra Bar,** 21 The Octagon (✆ **03/477-6080**), are currently deemed to be the happening spots for good food and a lively bar atmosphere for anyone over 25. The **Craic Irish Tavern,** 24 The Octagon (✆ **03/479-0781**), pours Irish beers and whiskeys for you to enjoy in front of the fire.

Bacchus Winebar, upstairs at 12 The Octagon (✆ **03/474-0824**), is a nice enough place overlooking The Octagon. It never really takes off in terms of a wild night out—it's more of a sedate place to savor good company and good wine in a smoke-free environment.

MOVIES There are six big screens at the **Hoyts 6 Cinema,** 33 The Octagon (✆ **03/477-7019**). It has a cafe and bar and plenty of parking at the rear. There is also a **Rialto 3** theater complex now on Upper Moray Place. The **Metro Cinema,** Moray Place, shows artsy movies.

En Route to Invercargill

You could drive from Dunedin to Invercargill in roughly 2½ to 3 hours via State Highway 1, passing through the small Southland townships of Balclutha, Gore, and Edendale. This pleasant drive will take you past farmland and mile after mile of grazing sheep.

A SIDE TRIP TO historic OAMARU

Oamaru is a small town with the largest collection of **Victorian heritage buildings** in the country. If you're interested in architecture, it is a must-see. Built in locally hewn, creamy-white limestone, many of the hefty, ornate buildings, complete with enormous Corinthian columns, will make you think of ancient Greece. It's located 115km (71 miles) north of Dunedin (about a 1½-hour drive), and your first stop should be the **Oamaru i-SITE Visitor Centre,** intersection of Itchen and Thames streets (© 03/434-1656; www.visitoamaru.co.nz). Pick up the free *Historic Oamaru* brochure, which details 30 key buildings—many of them located in the restored **Victorian Oamaru Historic Precinct** (www.victorianoamaru.co.nz), which starts just around the corner from the visitor center in the Tees and Tyne Street area. Many of the buildings there now house artists, craftsmen, cafes, and pubs. One of the most fascinating is **Michael O'Brien Bookbinder ★★★**, 7 Tyne St. (© 03/434-9277); O'Brien is a renowned craftsman making beautiful books by traditional hand-bound methods. He even lives a Victorian lifestyle and dresses in period costume. **Forrester Art Gallery ★★**, 9 Thames St. (© 03/433-0853; www.forrestergallery.

com), is also worth a look, located on the town's main street and housed in the former Bank of New South Wales.

Wildlife enthusiasts also have a treat in store because Oamaru is home to a large colony of the world's smallest penguin, the Little Blue. You can find the **Oamaru Blue Penguin Colony ★★★**, Waterfront Road, Oamaru (© 03/433-1195; www.penguins.co.nz), by walking through the historic precinct on Tyne Street and then veering left onto Waterfront Road. It's an easy 5- to 10-minute walk, or a short drive to their visitor center, where you have to pay for daytime Behind the Scenes Tours (NZ$15 adults, NZ$5 children 5–15, NZ$35 family), or for the Evening Viewing, when you get to see the nocturnal blue penguins come ashore (NZ$25 adults, NZ$15 children, NZ$65 family). The center is open daily year-round from 9:30am until about an hour after dusk. For evening viewing, be sure to arrive 30 minutes before sunset.

It's well worth staying a night in Oamaru and you'll find very pleasant, moderately priced accommodation at **Highfield Mews ★**, 244 Thames St. (© 03/434-3437; www.highfieldmews.co.nz), where new motel rooms go for NZ$130 to NZ$220. If you want to treat

But if you want to see natural New Zealand, take the **Southern Scenic Route ★★★** via the **Catlins ★★★**, to explore a rich, unspoiled coastline. Spend a leisurely 7 hours getting from Dunedin to Invercargill (or stay overnight in one of the area's unassuming bed and breakfasts), taking as many side routes as you can. You won't regret a second of it. The region contains the most significant area of native forest on the east coast of New Zealand, and walking tracks will take you through tall podocarps such as rimu and totara.

Keep in mind, though, that rain falls in this area 214 days a year, so chances are you're going to get wet. However, a lot of the rainfalls occur overnight and won't disrupt your sightseeing. Be sure to pick up the visitor center's brochure on the Southern Scenic Route (St. Hwy. 92), so you can make informed decisions about the stops you make. It is also important to note that some of the roads are unpaved, and if you're unfamiliar with this sort of driving, knock 20kmph (12 mph) off your speed, concentrate, keep in the road grooves, and don't overreact if you skid.

yourself to an upmarket stay in one of Oamaru's most extraordinary heritage homesteads, make your way to the very beautiful **Pen-y-bryn Lodge** ★★★, 41 Towey St., Oamaru (📞 **03/434-7939;** www.penybryn.co.nz), where multilingual and multitalented Americans James Glucksman and James Boussy are your inspiring hosts. Rooms here are NZ$625 (including breakfast, pre-dinner drinks, and canapés) or NZ$875 if you include a 4-course dinner.

There are growing numbers of good cafes in the town. **Portside Restaurant** ★★, Waterfront Rd. (📞 **03/434-34000**), opposite the Blue Penguin Centre, is a lovely spot for hanging out over the harbor, for lunch or dinner. They're open Thursday through Tuesday from 11am until late. **Whitestone Cheese Café** ★, corner Humber and Torridge streets (north end of town; 📞 **03/434-8098;** www. whitestonecheese.co.nz), has a terrific cafe and a deli bulging with their award-winning boutique cheeses, and delicious lunch choices from soups and savory dishes to indulgent cakes with coffee. They're open daily 9am to 5pm.

If you're heading back to Dunedin, make sure you stop at the famous **Moeraki Boulders,** 36km (23 miles) south of Oamaru. These strange, perfectly round boulders, formed 65 million years ago, are strewn along the beach like giant eggs. They're well signposted and it's easiest to access them from **Moeraki Boulders Café,** State Highway 1 (📞 **03/439-4827;** www.moeraki boulders.co.nz). You could have breakfast or coffee there and then drive south a few hundred yards and turn left to the small fishing village of Moeraki (about 3km/2 miles away), where you'll find the multi–award-winning lunch restaurant **Fleur's Place** ★★★, 169 Haven St., Moeraki (📞 **03/439-4480;** www.fleurs place.com), at the end of the wharf. The fresh fish are well worth the trip. The restaurant is open Wednesday through Sunday from 10:30am.

If you're driving north from Oamaru, stop 12km (8 miles) further on, at the award-winning **Riverstone Kitchen** ★★★, 1431 State Hwy. 1 (📞 **03/431-3505;** www.riverstone kitchen.co.nz). In addition to having a large playground where kids can let off steam, their food has gained a near-legendary reputation in a very short time. They're open Thursday through Monday from 9am to 5pm; dinner is served Thursday through Sunday from 6pm.

Leaving Dunedin, your first diversion should be to the wildlife-rich area of **Nugget Point** ★, signposted just south of Balclutha. Gloriously undisturbed coastline awaits, and from here all the way to Waikawa, you'll find a rich vein of scenic opportunity. Chief among them will be **Purakaunui Falls,** accessed by a 20-minute round-trip walk through beech and podocarp forest; the pretty, deserted beaches and fossils outcrops at **Papatowai** ★★★; picture-perfect **Lake Wilkie,** which is just a 30-minute return walk from the highway; and the spectacular curve of **Tautuku Bay,** 2km (1¼ miles) south of Papatowai. If you see nothing else, the hilltop view of this bay alone makes the trip worthwhile; as well as **Cathedral Caves** ★, an 80-minute round-trip walk along the beach at low tide only.

Farther south, you'll find one of the world's finest fossil forests, which can be viewed at low tide at **Curio Bay.** This sea-washed rock terrace dates back 160 million years and is the original floor of a Jurassic subtropical forest of kauri trees, conifers, and other trees growing at a time when grasses had not evolved. At low tide, you can easily make out the stumps and fallen logs that were petrified after being buried in volcanic ash, then raised when the sea level changed.

Another worthwhile stop is **Slope Point.** As the name suggests, the strong winds here are responsible for the rather strange, bent-over form of the trees. Wear warm clothing, as the winds lash in off Foveaux Strait. This is the southernmost point of the South Island, and if you're here on a fine day, you'll be pleased with the views.

The Southern Scenic Route continues on to Te Anau—a total trip of 440km (275 miles) from Dunedin. The Catlins side of the journey is by far the most interesting leg, and it's easy to see why this area is one of the new frontiers of New Zealand tourism. There's a range of moderately priced motels, B&Bs, and backpacker accommodations along the way if you decide to stop over. There are brochures for many of these at the **Catlins Information Centre and Owaka Museum,** 10 Campbell St., Owaka (✆ **03/415-8371;** www.cluthacountry.co.nz), open Monday through Friday 9:30am to 1pm and 1:30 to 4:30pm, weekends 10am to 4pm. For more details on the route, call ✆ **0800/723-642** in New Zealand, or 03/214-9733, or visit www.southland.org.nz.

INVERCARGILL ★

190km (118 miles) S of Queenstown; 217km (135 miles) SW of Dunedin

Asked to name seven great things about Invercargill, most people hesitate and scratch their heads. The 53,000 residents of this southernmost city would be justifiably indignant. They'll quickly tell you that people from Invercargill are among the friendliest in the country, that the city has the best seafood, and that it makes a perfect base for exploring some of the country's finest scenery in Fiordland, the Catlins, and Stewart Island. Nor should we overlook the fact that Southland is the capital of country music in New Zealand; that it offers the lowest education fees in New Zealand; and it was the location for the hit movie *The World's Fastest Indian,* the story of Invercargill motorcycle legend Burt Munro.

Originally settled by Scottish immigrants, the city's prosperity has been founded on the lush grasslands of Southland, and today several million sheep and cattle graze the flat pastures that surround it. Invercargill is the province's major service center, with more than 1,000 motel and hotel beds.

This once swampy bogland first attracted Europeans keen to establish a flax-milling industry. It was surveyed in 1856 by New Zealand's first surveyor general, J. Thomson, who wisely mapped out the main streets (named after Scottish rivers) 40m (130 ft.) in width, still giving the city its distinctive spacious character. Southlanders continue to be seen as a hardy, practical, gregarious lot, and they'll make sure your stay here is a memorable one.

Essentials

GETTING THERE & GETTING AROUND   By Plane   Air New Zealand (✆ **0800/737-000** in NZ; www.airnewzealand.co.nz) has service between Invercargill and Auckland and Wellington on the North Island, and Christchurch and Dunedin on the South Island. **Stewart Island Flights** (✆ **03/218-9129;** www. stewartislandflights.com) has daily scheduled flights to Stewart Island. The airport is 2.5km (1½ miles) from the city center. **Spitfire Shuttles** (✆ **03/249-7654;** www. spitfire.co.nz) provides transport to and from the city. For more information, go to www.invercargillairport.co.nz. A cab to the city will cost around NZ$15.

To Milford Sound

To Queenstown

Lake Te Anau

Te Anau

94

FIORDLAND

NATIONAL

PARK

Five Rivers

Mossburn

OTAGO

6

8

Lumsden

6   94

Dipton

Riversdale

90

8

To Dunedin →

1

Lake Mahinerangi

Nightcaps

Gore

Waipahi

Milton

1

Te Waewae Bay

Winton

96

Mataura

Balclutha

1

Macarewa

Windham

1

Riverton

Invercargill

Waimahaka

Nugget Point

See detail inset

1

Foveaux Strait

Otara

Waikawa

Chaslands Mistake

PACIFIC OCEAN

Bluff

Ruapuke Island

Curio Bay

Codfish Island

Mason Bay

Oban

Halfmoon Bay

Mt. Allen

FRASER PEAKS

STEWART ISLAND

0   20 mi

0   20 km

NORTH ISLAND

Auckland

SOUTH ISLAND

Wellington

Christchurch

Dunedin

Area of detail

Invercargill

Victoria Ave.   QUEENS PARK

Southland Museum and Art Gallery

Gala St.

Leet St.   Water Tower

Bond St.

Mersey St.

6

Kelvin St.

Deveron St.

Yarrow St.

Spey St.

Doon St.

Queens Dr.

MacMaster St.

Leven St.

Dee St.

Don St.

Esk St.

Jed St.

Railway Station

The Crescent

Tay St.

1

Otepuni Creek

Wood St.

Forth St.

Tyne St.

Otepuni Gardens

St. Mary's Basilica

Eye St.

To ← Airport

Mersey St.

Tweed St.

Ness St.

Bond St.

Annan St.

Liddel St.

Clyde St.

Nith St.

Conon St.

Teviot St.

Ettrick St.

Elles Rd.

Princes St.

Bowmont St.

Ythan St.

Crinan St.

ⓘ Information

Post Office

1

Earn St.

Balmoral Dr.

0   0.5 mi

0   0.5 km

Dalrymple St.

Grace St.

By Coach (Bus)   InterCity (📞 09/623-1503) has coach service between Invercargill and Christchurch, Dunedin, Queenstown, Te Anau, and Timaru. The bus depot is also on Leven Street. Look out for the **Freebie,** a free local shuttle service connecting inner city businesses; it runs Monday through Saturday, every 15 minutes between 10am and 2:30pm. For information on connecting bus routes, call 📞 **03/218-7108.**

By Car   Invercargill can be reached on State Highway 6 from Queenstown or State Highway 1 from Dunedin. See the information on the Southern Scenic Route under "En Route to Invercargill," above. The **Automobile Association** office is at 47–51 Gala St. (📞 **0800/500-444**).

By Taxi   Call **Blue Star Taxis Ingill Ltd.,** Tay and Jed streets (📞 **03/217-7777;** www.blustartaxis.co.nz).

ORIENTATION   Invercargill's streets are laid out in grid patterns. The main thoroughfares are Tay Street (an extension of St. Hwy. 1) and Dee Street (an extension of St. Hwy. 6). Many of the principal shops and office buildings are found at their intersection. Queens Park is an 80-hectare (200-acre) green oasis in the center of town.

VISITOR INFORMATION   The **Invercargill i-SITE Visitor Centre,** in the Southland Museum and Art Gallery, 108 Gala St. (📞 **03/211-0895;** fax 03/218-4415; www.i-site.org.nz/otago-southland#invercargill), is open daily October through April 8am to 6pm, and in winter 8am to 5pm (closed Dec 25). The **Department of Conservation,** State Insurance Building, Seventh Floor, 33 Don St. (📞 **03/214-4589;** fax 03/214-4486; www.doc.govt.nz), is open Monday through Friday from 8am to 5pm (6pm in summer). For more information on this area, check www.invercargill.org.nz or www.southlandnz.com.

[FastFACTS] INVERCARGILL

The **Central Post Office** is at 1 Don St. **Southland Hospital,** Kew Road (📞 **03/218-1949**), has 24-hour emergency care. You can get prescriptions filled at **UFS Dispensary,** 76 Tay St. (📞 **03/218-9393**), or, for after-hours service, 90 Kelvin St. (📞 **03/218-4893**). For information on **major events** check www.southlandnz.com.

Exploring the Area
MUSEUMS, GALLERIES & ARCHITECTURE

It's hard to miss the big white pyramid of the **Southland Museum and Art Gallery ★★**, 108 Gala St. (📞 **03/219-9069;** www.southlandmuseum.com), near the main entrance to Queens Park. A wide range of exhibits brings the region to life. The biggest attraction of all, the **Tuatarium ★★★**, should not be missed. Here you'll find the fascinating tuatara—strange prickly reptiles that are descendants of the dinosaurs and now exceptionally rare. The museum breeding program is the only one in the world. As tuatara are nocturnal, they may be hard to spot during the day. The highlight is Henry, now over 100 years old, who, along with the successfully breeding Albert and his concubines, Mildred and Lucy, may show his face. Another excellent museum attraction is the comprehensive audiovisual program on New Zealand's **Sub-Antarctic Islands ★★**, an area of international importance because they have some of the world's last remaining areas of vegetation unmodified by humans. The museum is open Monday through Friday from 9am to 5pm; Saturday, Sunday, and holidays from 10am to 5pm. Admission is free but a charge may apply to some exhibits.

Anderson Park Art Gallery, 91 McIvor Rd., Waikiwi, Invercargill (© **03/215-7432**) is housed in a fine Georgian-style residence set on 24 hectares (59 acres) of landscaped gardens. You'll find this architectural delight 7km (4⅓ miles) north of the city, just a short drive east along McIvor Road, which runs off North Road. It's open daily from 10:30am to 5pm. Admission is free, except during exhibitions.

Speaking of things old, *Invercargill Heritage Trail* is an excellent brochure produced by the New Zealand Historic Places Trust and available at the visitor center. It highlights 18 of the city's finest architectural specimens, including St. Mary's Basilica, on Tyne Street, and the town's famous 43m (139-ft.) red-brick Romanesque water tower. There is a similar brochure for nearby Bluff; and the *Invercargill City Spirit Walk* brochure details a 1-hour walk through the inner city, following history in sculptures, landmarks, and information panels.

PARKS & GARDENS

The main entrance to **Queens Park** is near Southland Museum and Art Gallery. This cool green 80-hectare (200-acre) oasis is a perfect place to wander and it features some beautiful trees. You'll find formal rose gardens, a rhododendron walk, an iris garden, a Japanese garden, a wildlife sanctuary, a walk-through bird aviary, duck ponds, a winter garden, tennis courts, and an 18-hole golf course. The aviary has a good parrot collection and is best visited in early morning or late afternoon, when the birds are most active.

Maple Glen Gardens and Nursery, in nearby rural Wyndham (© **03/206-4983;** www.mapleglen.co.nz), is a remarkable private garden and exotic bird haven that every gardener should see. It's open daily from 9am to 5pm. A guided walk costs NZ$8 per person.

A SIDE TRIP TO BLUFF

If time permits, take a drive to Bluff to find **Tiwai Smelter Tours,** NZ Aluminium Smelters Ltd. (© **03/218-5494**). This free tour is much more interesting than you might think and is available weekdays at 10am, with only three tours per week. Bookings are essential; there are special clothing requirements for safety reasons. Children 11 and under will not be admitted. **Bluff's Maritime Museum,** 241 Foreshore Rd. (© **03/212-7534;** bluffmuseum@xtra.co.nz), is open 10am to 4:30pm Monday through Friday and from 1 to 5pm on weekends, and presents good coverage of Southland's maritime history. Admission is NZ$2 for adults, NZ$1 kids ages 5 to 15. If you visit during oyster season, try and attend the annual **Bluff Oyster & Southland Seafood Festival** ★★★ (www.bluffoysterfest.co.nz), which is held in late April at the Bluff Events Centre on Gore Road. More information on this tiny town can be found at www.bluff.co.nz. Bluff is 27km (17 miles) south of Invercargill. In Invercargill, get on Dee Street, which becomes State Highway 1; the drive will take about 30 minutes.

Organized Tours

If you haven't already explored the Catlins area (see "En Route to Invercargill," above), join the **Catlins Coaster** (© **03/477-9083;** www.travelheadfirst.com/catlins-coaster), which offers a full-day Catlins tour, exploring wildlife and natural attractions for around NZ$175. **Lynette Jack Scenic Sights** (©/fax **03/215-7741**

If you're looking for an interesting country drive out of Invercargill, go to **Cosy Nook ★★**, a delightful fishing settlement on one of the world's wildest coastlines. Near Riverton, it's well signposted from State Highway 99. You'll find cute old fishing boats and cottages and creative signage. **Riverton Rocks Beach** is also a treat, with gorgeous little green pebbles all over the place. It's about a 45-minute drive from Invercargill. Just over the hill to the southwest, you'll find **Colac Bay**—one big horseshoe swoop of surfing heaven, with a cluster of little cottages on the foreshore.

or 027/433-8370) has tours from 2 hours to a full day that explore not only the Catlins, but also Bluff, Riverton, and Western Southland. Her prices range from NZ$94 to NZ$350 per person depending on the destination and duration. To sightsee in total comfort, contact **Ambassador Limousines** (📞 **03/217-4504** or 025/339-889; www.ambassadorlimos.co.nz). Both **Southeast Air** (📞 **03/214-5522;** fax 03/214-5520) and **Southern Wings Air Charter** (📞 **03/218-6171;** www.southernwings. co.nz) offer chartered scenic flights around Southland.

Outdoor Pursuits

BEACHES   Oreti Beach, 9.5km (6 miles) west of Invercargill, out past the airport, is safe for swimming. This broad expanse of sand stretches from Omaui at the southern end right around to Riverton. There are surf patrols in attendance during summer.

BIKING   Single and tandem bikes can be hired from **Wensley's Cycles,** Tay and Nith streets (📞 **03/218-6206;** fax 03/218-6368).

FISHING   There are numerous fishing opportunities in Southland, many within 30 minutes of Invercargill. The famous **Mataura River** offers some of the best trout fishing in the world. The season in most areas opens October 1 and goes to April 30. There are exceptions, so check the regulation guide available at the visitor center. The team at **Outdoor World,** 27 Tay St. (📞 **03/214-2052**), can advise you on the best spots and the best tackle. **Alan Wilson** (📞/fax **03/217-3687;** www.southland flyfishing.co.nz) can help with wilderness and heli-fishing.

WALKING   There are numerous fine walks within an hour's drive of Invercargill. You can read about them in the Department of Conservation's excellent brochure *Day Walks from Invercargill,* available at the visitor center. **Sandy Point Domain,** 7km (4⅓ miles) west of the city, has attractive walking tracks through totara forest and sand dunes. The **Foveaux Walkway** in Bluff is a 2-hour walk around Bluff's rugged coastline. The track begins at Ocean Beach Road and ends at Stirling Point, or vice versa. The 30-minute **Glory Track** starts at Stirling Point and finishes at Gunpit Road. A little farther afield, the **Tuatapere Humpridge Track ★★**, 31 Orawia Rd., Tuatapere (📞 **0800/486-774** in NZ, or 03/226-6739; www.humpridgetrack.co.nz), is fast gaining a reputation as an excellent 3-day walk for those of moderate to high fitness levels. Tuatapere is 86km (53 miles) from Invercargill and 100km (60 miles) from Te Anau on the Southern Scenic Route. The Freedom Walk costs NZ$130 for adults, NZ$65 for children 10 to 14. The guided walk costs NZ$1,395 for adults, NZ$1,245 for children 10 to 14. The Humpridge Track is not suitable for kids under 14.

WINDSURFING   The best area for windsurfing is at **Awarua Bay.** Gear rental is available at **Anderson Wind and Surfing,** 204 Spey St. (© **03/214-4283**).

Where to Stay

Most of the 1,000 or so beds available in Invercargill are in the budget and moderately priced range, with little to offer in the bed-and-breakfast or expensive bracket. One thing the area can boast, though, is its wide range of home- and farmstay options scattered throughout the surrounding farmland, and plenty of reasonable motels. Pick up the visitor center's brochure detailing home- and farmstays. The rates given below include the 15% GST and free off-street parking.

EXPENSIVE

The Lodge at Tikana ★★★   You'll have to be in quick to secure the comforts of this gorgeous rural stay 30 minutes from Invercargill. Sadly, it's single-party bookings only (up to four guests), but if you're one of the lucky ones, you'll love this custombuilt den on a working farm. Beautiful beds, great meals, and all the mod-cons make this one of the best Southland stays I've discovered. The property also has a Qualmark Enviro-Gold rating and is a member of the Southland Sustainable Tourism Charter.

374 Livingstone Rd., Browns, Winton. www.tikana.co.nz. ©/fax **03/236-4117.** 2-bedroom lodge. NZ$1,955; extra person NZ$828. Rates include breakfast, predinner drinks, gourmet dinner. Minimum 2-night stay. AE, DC, MC, V. No children 11 and under. **Amenities:** Bar; babysitting; nearby golf course; room service; spa treatments; grass tennis court; Wi-Fi in main lodge. *In room:* TV/DVD/CD, stocked fridge, hair dryer, kitchenette, minibar.

MODERATE

Beersheba Boutique Accommodation, 58 Milton Park Rd., Invercargill (www.beersheba.co.nz; © **03/216-3677**), is a nice, new B&B offering two good rooms in the main house (NZ$250–NZ$270), plus a self-contained one-bedroom cottage in a private garden setting (NZ$290). The whole property sits within a 1.6 hectare (4-acre) landscaped garden with ponds and an abundance of bird life. For apartment-style lodging, you can't beat the modern studios and one- and two-bedroom apartments at **Quest Invercargill ★★**, 10 Dee St. (www.questinvercargill.co.nz; © **0800/101-801** in NZ, or 03/211-3966), in the refurbished historic post office building in the heart of the city. Tariffs range from NZ$139 to NZ$246. They offer great online deals and parking is free.

Ascot Park Hotel ★★   This is deemed Invercargill's top spot, and although it's a bit too far out of town (4km/2½ miles) to be convenient, it does have silence on its side—unlike the Kelvin Hotel (see below). The four deluxe units are a good pick if you like heaps of space. The suites are perfect for two couples or a family. The motel units come complete with kitchens. An additional 20 apartments and studios were added in 2010 and these are the best rooms. The property has a Qualmark Enviro-Gold rating.

Tay St. and Racecourse Rd., Invercargill. www.ascotparkhotel.co.nz. © **0800/272-687** in NZ, or 03/217-6195. Fax 03/217-7002. 116 units. Hotel rooms from NZ$187 superior; apartments from NZ$225; NZ$125 motel unit. Extra person NZ$25. Long-stay and off-peak rates. Special deals. AE, DC, MC, V. **Amenities:** Restaurant; 2 bars; free airport transport; free use of bikes; children's play area; concierge; nearby golf course; small exercise room; free Internet in reception; Jacuzzi; heated indoor pool; 24-hr room service; sauna. *In room:* TV, fridge, hair dryer, kitchenette (in motels & apts.), minibar, Wi-Fi.

Kelvin Hotel ★ This well-priced hotel is pretty much a standard facility, but rooms are all fresh and light. Bathrooms are small but smart, all with combination tub/showers. Room no. 601 is the corner honeymoon suite, with great views over the city. This is a hard-to-beat central-city location, but, unfortunately, it can be noisy, especially on weekends, so pack earplugs.

Kelvin and Esk sts., Invercargill. www.kelvinhotel.co.nz. ☎ **0800/802-829** in NZ, or 03/218-2829. Fax 03/218-2827. 61 units. NZ$155 deluxe; NZ$205 suite. Extra person NZ$25. Packages and long-stay rates negotiable. AE, DC, MC, V. **Amenities:** Restaurant; 2 bars; nearby golf course; nearby gym; free Internet in reception area; 24-hr room service. *In room:* TV, fridge, hair dryer, minibar, Wi-Fi.

INEXPENSIVE

Backpackers will find comfortable beds at **Living Space ★★**, 15 Tay St. (www.livingspace.net; ☎ **0508/454-846** in NZ, or 03/211-3800), with its colorful selection of studios (from NZ$99) and two- to three-bedroom apartments (NZ$129–NZ$149).

Where to Eat

It's only been in recent years that Invercargill has come up to snuff on the dining scene. Restaurants are still few and far between given the size of the town, but there are some good eateries. **HMS Kings Restaurant,** 80 Tay St. (☎ **03/218-3433**), is consistently favored by locals for its seafood, although service can be erratic; and **148 on Elles,** 148 Elles St. (☎ **03/216-1000**), is recommended. **Soprano's Pizzeria ★★**, 33 Tay St. (☎ **03/218-3464**), has a lively atmosphere and tasty pizzas if you just feel like a quick bite. Of all the eateries here though, the one I'm most inclined to is **Rocks Café ★★** , Courtville Place, 101 Dee St. (☎ **03/218-7597**), which is tucked away off the main beat and is the most likely to deliver a reliable, tasty meal. The always zany **Zookeepers Café ★★** (look for the large elephant on the roof), 50 Tay St. (☎ **03/218-3373**), is one of the most popular places in town. Crumbed Stewart Island blue cod with Kumara fries, minced lamb kabobs, rib-eye steak, pastas, and salads are typical options. Come here for the mood more than the food. Open daily 10am to late.

Invercargill After Dark

The **Lone Star,** Dee and Leet streets (☎ **03/214-6225**), draws a crowd of mixed ages. **Speight's Ale House,** 38 Dee St. (☎ **03/214-5333;** www.speights alehouseinv.co.nz), is a good spot to try Dunedin-brewed ales. It's always lively, especially during sports matches; and you can get a hearty meal here too. **Level One Bar,** Kelvin Hotel, Kelvin and Esk streets (☎ **03/218-2829;** www.kelvinhotel.co.nz), is a little more upmarket and definitely quieter. Suffice to say, Invercargill is not a place you seek out for its pulsating night life.

STEWART ISLAND ★★

30km (19 miles) SW of Bluff, across the Foveaux Strait

Anyone who tries to visit Stewart Island in a day won't be giving this near-perfect place a chance. It is almost a cliché to call it one of New Zealand's best-kept secrets, but given that so few people are aware of its unspoiled tranquillity, it probably deserves this label more than any other place in the country.

New Zealand's third island is far bigger than most people imagine, and almost without exception, first-time visitors are surprised by its temperate climate and the range of activities it provides. Roughly triangular in shape, it is 65km (40 miles) long

If you're taking the ferry, it is important to remember that Foveaux Strait is one of the most unpredictable passages in the world, and the water can be extremely rough. If you're prone to seasickness, come prepared and ask staff for comfortable sailing tips. They also sell homeopathic remedies at the check-in counter. It may be a short trip (1 hr.), but can be notoriously uncomfortable. Many people like to fly one-way and take the ferry the other. This gives you two perspectives, and eliminates a difficult water crossing if the weather is not fine.

and 40km (25 miles) at its widest point, and with an area of 1,680 sq. km (655 sq. miles), it is about the size of Singapore or Fiji. Only 1% of the island is inhabited—the rest is given over to natural native bush, exquisite white-sand beaches, bird sanctuaries, and rugged mountains. All this makes it a naturalist's and tramper's paradise, and the perfect place for a remote yet accessible holiday. You need to be here only a few hours before the rest of the world melts away and you find yourself adopting the unhurried, laid-back approach of the locals.

The main fishing village of Oban is your landing point, and this is where the population of approximately 390 bases itself. Most permanent residents are involved in the commercial fishing or tourism industries, and a surprisingly small number of other smart New Zealanders have invested in holiday homes, or cribs, here.

Originally called *Te Punga o Te Waka a Maui* by the Maori, which translates as "The Anchorstone of Maui's Canoe," it is more commonly known by the Maori name Rakiura, which means "Land of Glowing Skies," referring to the vivid colors of dawn and the twilight skies.

Today, the island community jealously guards the amazing natural heritage that surrounds it. This is natural New Zealand the way it used to be—truly picturesque and serene, a place where native birds will land within inches of your teacup, a place you should not overlook.

Essentials

GETTING THERE **By Plane** Air transport to Stewart Island is provided by **Stewart Island Flights** (✆ **03/218-9129;** www.stewartislandflights.com), which is based at Invercargill Airport. You get breathtaking views of the island from the nine-seat Britten-Norman aircraft, which takes approximately 20 minutes to cross Foveaux Strait. Shuttle buses then deliver you to your accommodations in Oban. The round-trip fare is NZ$185 for adults and NZ$105 for children 15 and under. Stewart Island Flights can also help you plan and book your entire Stewart Island holiday; and they have a number of day-trip specials that include a bus tour, walks, and short water-taxi trips. These are ideal if you're short on time but desperate to see something of the island. The five options are priced around NZ$300 for adults and NZ$150 for children.

By Boat The passenger-only ferry, operated by **Stewart Island Experience,** will have you on Stewart Island in an hour. It departs Bluff ferry terminal September through April daily from 8:30am until 4pm and from May through August 9:30am to 5pm. There's connecting bus service from Invercargill to Bluff; secure car parking (extra cost) is available near the Bluff ferry terminal. The round-trip fare is NZ$126 for adults and NZ$64 for children ages 5 to 14. There are very good, reliable coach connections that pick you up from your Invercargill or Bluff accommodations 1 hour before the ferry departure. Inquire at the time of ferry booking and expect to pay NZ$20 for adults and NZ$10 for children ages 5 to 14 for the coach trip. For inquiries and reservations, call ℂ **0800/000-511** in NZ, or 03/212-7660, or visit www.stewartislandexperience.co.nz.

GETTING AROUND   Most things on the island are within walking distance, although a number of the accommodations lie farther out. To reach them, and some of the divine beaches, means a good up- and downhill walk. A shuttle/minibus operates around the island like a taxi service; and you can rent cars (NZ$65 for a half-day), mountain bikes (NZ$36 a day), and scooters (NZ$45 per 2 hr.), from both the **Stewart Island Visitor Terminal,** on the wharf (ℂ 03/219-0034; www.stewartisland experience.co.nz), and the **Stewart Island Flights Depot,** Elgin Terrace (ℂ **03/219-1090;** www.stewartislandflights.com). The **i-SITE visitor center** (see below) can also provide details and rates on these options. Charter boats and water taxis can be arranged for sightseers, hunters, divers, trampers, and fishermen. Make reservations at the **Stewart Island Visitor Terminal** (ℂ 03/219-0034; www.stewartislandexperience.co.nz). If you prefer, reservations can be made directly with the operators; go to the i-SITE visitor center for information and brochures.

VISITOR INFORMATION   The ferry will deposit you on the wharf at Oban within a few hundred meters from the center of the small village.

The **Stewart Island i-SITE Visitor Information Centre** is at 12 Elgin Terrace (ℂ **03/219-1400;** fax 03/219-1401; www.stewartisland.co.nz). It's open daily; summer hours are 9am to 7pm, and winter hours are 9:30am to 6:30pm. The **Rakiura National Park Visitor Centre** is in the DOC building on Main Road (ℂ **03/219-0009;** fax 03/219-0003; www.doc.govt.nz). All trampers must report here for walking-track and hut passes. The staff members here are extremely well informed about all aspects of tramping and exploring the island; since some of the tracks are challenging, it pays to ask their advice. Also take a look at the 4-minute tramping video, which gives you an idea of what you're in for. They're open daily in summer from 8am to 5pm, and in winter from 8:30am to 4:30pm (closed Dec 25).

[FastFACTS] STEWART ISLAND

There is no full banking service available on the island. Credit cards are accepted by most businesses, but foreign traveler's checks and cash can be difficult to change, so it pays to arrive with New Zealand dollars.

Exploring the Island

Most visitors are drawn to Stewart Island's unspoiled beauty and unique lifestyle. Nowhere else in New Zealand will you find such ready access to fern-filled native forests and astonishing bird life (see "Walking & Tramping," below).

For those coming to simply unwind, there are lots of quirky activities that must be experienced. The **Rakiura Museum,** Ayr Street, Half Moon Bay (ℂ **03/219-1049;** fax 03/219-1126), will give you a glimpse at the island's past, featuring photographs and exhibits tracing the island's history through sailing, whaling, tin mining, sawmilling, and fishing. It also has shell and Maori artifact displays. It's open Monday through Saturday from 10am to 1:30pm, Sunday from noon to 2pm, with extended hours during the summer holidays. Admission is NZ$5. The **Fernery,** 29 Golden Bay

Rd. (☎/fax **03/219-1453**), is a recommended crafts shop and **Glowing Sky Studio Shop,** Town Centre (☎ **03/219-1528;** www.glowingsky.co.nz), stocks some lovely merino wool garments. The **Rakiura Gallery ★**, 10 Main Rd. (☎ **03/219-1429**), is your best bet for work by local artists.

WALKING & TRAMPING

Stewart Island offers unparalleled walking and tramping opportunities. Trampers will go through undisturbed native vegetation and see hundreds of birds. It is important to remember that rain falls on Stewart Island about 275 days of the year, so bring good waterproof clothing. The weather is very changeable, often swinging from rain to warm sun in the space of an hour. Track surfaces are varied and include long sections of boardwalk, which protects the native vegetation. Some tracks also include long stretches of deep mud, so wear sturdy boots. Contact the DOC for more information.

Anyone staying in huts on Stewart Island must pay hut fees. You need to purchase a **Great Walks Pass,** hut tickets, or an annual hut pass from the DOC (see "Visitor Information," above). Comfortable huts are conveniently spaced along the tracks (ranging in size from 6 to 24 bunks), but they're packed in summer. There's a 2-night maximum stay in any one hut, and you can use tents as well. You will be fined a surcharge if you are found using the huts without a Great Walks Pass.

The **Rakiura Track ★★★** is one of the DOC's eight identified Great Walks of New Zealand. The 36km (22-mile) track requires a moderate fitness level and can be comfortably hiked in 3 days, year-round. The circuit follows the open coast, climbs over a 300m (980-ft.) forested ridge, and traverses the sheltered shores of Paterson Inlet. Huts cost NZ$15 per person per night, campsites NZ$5 per person per night.

The **North West Circuit ★★** requires a much greater level of fitness and is recommended for experienced trampers, who need to be completely self-sufficient and prepared for 7 hours of tramping a day for 10 days. This track has long stretches of mud and is dangerous once snow falls. It takes in the northern third of the island and the island's highest peak, Mount Anglem (980m/3,200 ft.). A North West Circuit Pass costs NZ$50 and allows 1 night in each hut on the North West Circuit Track, including the Great Walks huts at Port William and North Arm. Backcountry hut tickets (NZ$5 per night), or a Backcountry Pass (NZ$90), may be used on the North West and the Southern Circuit Tracks, but separate passes must be purchased for the Great Walks huts (NZ$15 per night).

The **Southern Circuit,** which can be added to the above or done separately, is more of a wilderness experience that requires 6 to 7 days of tramping. It requires a much higher level of fitness and some orientation skills.

Stewart Island Day Walks range from 15 minutes to 7 hours and spread out in a number of directions from Oban. They include comfortable walks to Observation Rock, Golden Bay, Lonneckers Bay, Lee Bay, and Ringaringa Beach (a great spot for shell hounds when the tide is right), and longer walks to Maori Beach (7-hr. round-trip) and Garden Mound (5-hr. round-trip).

Ulva Island ★★★ is one of the best soft-core walking experiences of all. The Department of Conservation recognizes Ulva Island as the "Showcase Project" for its Southland Conservancy, and you can see the results of successful pest-eradication and endangered-species enhancement projects at close quarters. Catch a water taxi to the island (NZ$25) per person round-trip for two or more people from Golden Bay, which is a 20-minute walk over the hill from Oban. It's a short boat trip to somewhere close to paradise—a protected place where you can see rare birds and plants up close without harming them. The island has an 11km (6¾-mile) coastline, and there are walks from 20 minutes to 3 hours. You can spend several hours on the island—and if you're a keen photographer or naturalist, you'll want to—and arrange your return pickup with the water taxi when you land. For information on organized walking treks, see "Other Outdoor Pursuits," below.

OTHER OUTDOOR PURSUITS

GOLF   Don't miss New Zealand's only registered 6-hole golf course at **Ringaringa Heights,** overlooking Ringaringa Beach. Greens fees are NZ$10 for two people, which may well make it the cheapest golf course in the world. Club rentals are available at **Stewart Island Flight Depot** (✆ 03/219-1090) for NZ$5.

HUNTING   The elusive American whitetail deer was liberated on Stewart Island in the early 1900s and now provides sport for the energetic hunter. Hunting parties may spend up to 2 weeks camped in isolated places during the winter "roar." Contact **Southern Isle Charters** (✆ 03/219-1133; lhhansen@xtra.co.nz) to join a party.

KAYAKING   **Ruggedy Range Wilderness Experience ★★** (✆ 03/219-1066; www.ruggedyrange.com) offers six area coastal and river kayaking adventures, including multi-activity options, priced from NZ$175 to NZ$950 per person.

SKIN DIVING & FISHING   You'll immediately notice how clear the seawater is around Stewart Island, making it ideal for diving. Join Richard Squires of **Lo Loma** (✆ 03/219-1141; www.loloma.co.nz) for half- or full-day fishing and diving charters. Herbie Hansen of **Southern Isle Charters** (✆ 03/219-1133) offers diving and fishing charters. Fishermen should pick up the Department of Conservation leaflet called *New Regulations for Fishing in Paterson Inlet, Stewart Island.*

WALKING   Three companies offer excellent trekking options in various parts of Stewart Island. **Ruggedy Range Wilderness Experience** (✆ 03/219-1066; www.ruggedyrange.com) has trips to Ulva Island for NZ$110 to NZ$190, a kiwi-spotting adventure in Mason Bay for NZ$435 to NZ$835, and a 1-day coastal highlights hike on the Rakiura Great Walk for NZ$210 per person. **Ulva's Guided Walks ★★★** (✆ 03/219-1216; www.ulva.co.nz) has half-day guided walks on Ulva Island for NZ$110, which includes the water-taxi fare. Ulva has a terrific sense of humor and an incredible local knowledge, and she'll give you a rare insight into the birds and Maori history of the area. She also offers a half-day Port William guided walk for NZ$120. **Kiwi Wilderness Walks** (✆ 021/359-592; www.nzwalk.com) has 5-day walks that depart from Riverton (near Invercargill) for Mason Bay on Stewart Island, including sea kayaking and kiwi spotting, from NZ$1,500 per person.

Organized Tours

Most of the following tours are subject to weather conditions and all have minimum-number requirements.

   Stewart Island Experience ★★★ (✆ 0800/000-511 in NZ, or 03/219-1134; www.stewartislandexperience.co.nz), has an excellent adventure in an underwater submersible that enables you to see diverse fish species, sponges, sea quirts, and shellfish as you drift through crystal-clear water and kelp forests. It departs from the Stewart Island Visitor Terminal daily at 11:30am and 1:30pm all year, with an extra sailing at 4pm from November through March. It costs NZ$35 for adults, NZ$20 for kids ages 5 to 14. **Village & Bays Tours** (✆ 0800/000-511 in NZ, or

The nightlife on Stewart Island is a bit different from that on the mainland, and one of the strangest fellows you'll meet on your starlit adventures will be *Apteryx australis lawryi,* the Stewart Island brown kiwi. This bristly, brown flightless critter is a distinct subspecies of the brown kiwi found throughout New Zealand. It has larger legs and a longer beak, and females are generally bigger than males.

Everything you hear about this being the only place in New Zealand where you're likely to see a kiwi in the wild is true. They're often seen, day and night, foraging for sand hoppers among the kelp on the Stewart Island beaches. Just ask Phillip and Diane Smith—they're the experts at this kiwi-spotting game. Every second night, they gather up a bunch of curious, and hopefully fit, tourists and take them to the remote sandy beaches to find kiwis.

A shy creature at heart, the kiwi attracts a lot of attention, and in the interests of conservation, the Smiths limit their night tours to just 15 passengers (book ahead). The evening starts with a twilight cruise on the 16m (52-ft.) MV *Wildfire,* leaving from Half Moon Bay Wharf. After a 35-minute boat trip to

Glory Bay, you'll make your way to the jetty (with a ladder, not steps!) and, after a short bush walk, you'll spend the evening (or 3–4 hr. of it) prowling the length of Ocean Beach, looking for the ungainly bird that has won the hearts of so many. If you're lucky, you'll see its plump, feathered backside plodding along the sand as it absent-mindedly looks for its evening meal.

You can expect some rare nights out in New Zealand, but this one is sure to surpass the lot. You may never have envisioned yourself as a bird-spotter, crouching in the darkness on some strange southern coastline, but when you see this rare bird playing hard to get—plodding, darting, hiding, reappearing—you'll know you have experienced something unique. It could well be the best date you have in New Zealand—and you'll pay NZ$110 for the pleasure.

So gather your sturdy footwear, warm clothing, and torch (flashlight) and contact **Bravo Adventure Cruises ★**, P.O. Box 104, Stewart Island (✆/fax **03/219-1144**). The trip is subject to weather conditions; not recommended for kids under 15.

03/219-0034), gives a 1½-hour tour of Oban village and the surrounding bays. It allows for photo stops and short walks along the way (NZ$42 for adults, NZ$20 for kids 5–14).

I'd also recommend the pelagic seabird excursion offered by **Aurora Charters** (✆ **03/219-1126**). Leap aboard their modern catamaran, and they'll give you up-close encounters with seabirds and mammals. Don't forget your camera, and if you have a day to spare take their cruise to **Port Pegasus ★★★** (price on inquiry). It's the dramatic southern part of the island that you'll not otherwise see.

One wonderful way to experience the island from several perspectives is to indulge in the **Coast to Coast ★★** option with **Stewart Island Flights,** Invercargill (✆ **03/218-9129**), and **Seaview Water Taxis,** Stewart Island (✆ **03/219-1014**). This trip involves a flight to the magnificent **Mason's Bay** and a landing on its 13km (8-mile) stretch of unspoiled white-sand beach, a 4-hour bush walk to **Freshwater Landing,** and a return boat ride. The excursion is very dependent on tides, and you should be prepared for an unexpected night out if the weather gets rough. It costs NZ$205 for adults and NZ$145 for children. And if you're a helicopter fan like me, you'll adore an outing with Zane Smith of **Rakiura Helicopter Services ★★★**, Fern Gully heliport, 151 Main Rd. (*℃* **03/219-1155,** or 027/221-9217; rakiheli@ xtra.co.nz). He's a sixth-generation islander and there isn't a part of the island he hasn't explored. He knows the place like the back of his hand. This will be the highlight of your trip.

Where to Stay

If there is one negative thing to be said about Stewart Island, it must be about the overall standard of accommodations, which is nothing special (and the backpacker operations are fairly grim), but there is a good range of holiday homes available for rent. Remember that summer accommodations are often booked months in advance. **Bay Motel ★**, 9 Dundee St., Half Moon Bay (www.baymotel.co.nz; *℃* **03/219-1119**), is one I would recommend. It has 12 modern units (NZ$165–NZ$185), plus two two-bedroom apartments (NZ$200). Opt for the newer, quieter, motel rooms (NZ$85–NZ$155) over the older hotel rooms at **South Sea Hotel,** Elgin Terrace (www.stewart-island.co.nz; *℃* **03/219-1059**), which has the advantage of being right on the waterfront in the heart of the village.

Port of Call ★★ 🥄 If you've managed to beat out other desperate tourists, you can put your feet up and relax—which is the way of things on Stewart Island. Hosts Ian and Philippa Wilson run a thriving tourism business on the island, and if you combine their local knowledge with the comfort of their modern guest rooms and their self-contained studio, you have a great little operation. There's outdoor charm in large decks, barbecue areas, and courtyards. They also have a self-contained cottage surrounded by native bush, 5 minutes from the waterfront.

Leask Bay Rd., Stewart Island. www.portofcall.co.nz. *℃* **03/219-1394.** Fax 03/219-1394. 3 units. NZ$320 main house; NZ$180–NZ$250 self-catering studio; from NZ$200 Turner Cottage. Long-stay and off-peak rates. House rate includes breakfast. MC, V. No children 11 and under. **Amenities:** Free airport transport; nearby golf course. *In room:* TV/DVD, fridge, hair dryer, kitchen (in studio and cottage).

Stewart Island Lodge ★★★ I'm thrilled to say that this secluded spot is now in the capable hands of Stewart Island Experiences and has improved tenfold as a result. Set in native bush (at the top of a steep walk), just above the village, it has great views and five smart rooms with en suites and king-size beds. All open on to balconies and guests have the use of a private lounge in the main lodge. As part of Queenstown-based Real Journeys' operations the property has a Qualmark Enviro-Silver rating and is a member of the Southland Sustainable Tourism Charter.

14 Nichol Rd., Oban. *℃* **03/219-1085.** www.stewartislandlodge.co.nz. 5 units. NZ$390. Off-peak rates. Rates include breakfast and hosted predinner drinks with appetizers. AE, DC, MC, V. **Amenities:** Free airport transfers; nearby golf course; Internet. *In room:* Fridge, hair dryer.

Where to Eat

Dining out on Stewart Island barely warrants a separate section. **Church Hill Café & Restaurant ★★**, 36 Kamahi Rd. (*℃* **03/219-1323;** www.churchhillrestaurant. com), beside the Presbyterian Manse on the hill overlooking Oban, is not quite as consistent as we might like, but overall you'll probably get your best island meal here, especially seafood dishes. It's open daily 10am to late. The cheaper **Wharfside Cafe,** upstairs at the wharf (*℃* **03/219-1470**), is nothing fancy, but you'll be right in the island fishing atmosphere and you get good sea views. I always find it a good spot to relax while you wait for ferries or boat cruises. It's open from 10am until late, or from 7am for breakfast during the summer months. The seasonal **KaiKart Takeaways** is a mobile caravan on Ayr Street, beside the museum and school (✆ **03/219-1225; www.kaikartstewartisland.com**). It's open daily from noon to 2pm and 5pm until late during summer, providing excellent-value fish and chips, hamburgers, and assorted takeaways. Their blue cod snacks are definitely worth trying. Look out for **Bean Around Mobile Espresso** (✆ **03/219-1234**) for the best coffee. As the name suggests, they're mobile, so when you see them, grab that coffee! **Just Café,** 6 Main Rd., Oban (✆ **03/219-1422**), is otherwise the best source of coffee. They serve delicious counter food and juices too, and they have an Internet service as well.

PLANNING YOUR TRIP TO NEW ZEALAND

With so much to see and do, it's easy to feel over-whelmed and unsure about where to start your New Zealand holiday. I'm here to help—and in the pages that follow, you'll find all the nitty-gritty you need for organizing your South Seas excursion.

GETTING THERE

The cost of getting to New Zealand is likely to be your single biggest cash outlay, so it makes sense to shop around. Remember to check out those recommended agents and hot travel offers listed for your country of origin on the Tourism New Zealand website, **www.newzealand.com**. Also go to Air New Zealand's website at **www.airnewzealand.com** for special deals.

By Plane

From the West Coast of the United States, you can fly to New Zealand nonstop overnight; a direct flight from Singapore takes 10 hours; and a flight from eastern Australia is around 3 hours. Auckland (AKL), Wellington (WLG), and Christchurch (CHC) are all serviced by major domestic and international terminals. There are also much smaller international terminals at Hamilton (HLZ) and Dunedin (DUD); and most cities have domestic terminals. Auckland Airport is the major hub for most airlines coming in to New Zealand, followed by Christchurch and then Wellington. If you intend to spend most of your time in the South Island, it makes sense to fly into Christchurch, but depending on your airline, you may have to fly into Auckland and then transfer to domestic flights to Christchurch, Dunedin, or Queenstown.

At least 20 foreign airlines fly into Auckland. The main ones providing service from the **United States** are Air New Zealand, Qantas, and British Airways.

Canada is serviced primarily by Air New Zealand and Air Pacific, while **Europe** and the United Kingdom are serviced by Air New Zealand, British Airways, and Qantas. For travel from **Asia,** options include Singapore Airlines, Korean Air, Japan Airlines, Malaysian Airlines, Cathay Pacific, and Thai Airways. Dubai-based Emirates Airline now flies into New Zealand as well. There are also code-sharing arrangements with Lufthansa, American Airlines, United Airlines, and several others.

The timing of your trip can have a tremendous impact on your airline costs. New Zealand's **peak season** is December through February; the **shoulder season** includes March and September through November; and the **low season** begins in April and runs through August.

To find out which airlines travel to New Zealand, please see "Airline, Hotel & Car Rental Websites," p. 517.

By Boat

About a hundred cruises a year visit New Zealand and while the global economic downturn has impacted these numbers, New Zealand remains a popular cruise destination with over one-third of passengers coming from the United States.

Most cruises coming to New Zealand also visit Australia and are typically 12 to 16 days in duration. New Zealand cruise ports include Auckland, Tauranga, Napier, Wellington, Lyttelton (near Christchurch), Dunedin, and Milford Sound. You can fly to Australia or New Zealand to join a cruise, or you can take a segment on a world cruise that includes New Zealand.

At least a dozen international cruise lines include New Zealand on their itineraries. Among the main ones are Cunard (© 800/7-CUNARD [7-286273]; www.cunard. com), Silversea (© 877/276-6816; www.silversea.com), Holland America Line (© 877/932-4259; www.hollandamerica.com), Crystal Cruises (© 888/722-0021; www.crystalcruises.com), Regent Seven Sea Cruises (© 877/505-5370; www.rssc. com), Princess Cruises (© 800/PRINCESS [774-6237]; www.princess.com), P&O Cruises (© 0845/678-0014; www.pocruises.com), Fred.Olsen Cruise Lines (© 44/ 01473-746175; www.fredolsencruises.com), and Oceania Cruises (© 800/531-5619; www.oceaniacruises.com).

GETTING AROUND
By Plane

A year seldom passes without some slight upheaval in New Zealand's domestic air scene. **Air New Zealand** (© **0800/737-000** in NZ, or 09/357-3000; www.air newzealand.co.nz), along with its **Air New Zealand Link,** now dominates the airways, with **Qantas New Zealand** (© **0800/808-767** in NZ, or 09/357-8900; www. nz.qantas.com.au) servicing the main centers. British-owned Virgin Australia's transTasman flights operate under the name **Pacific Blue** (© **0800/670-000;** www. flypacificblue.com), with domestic flights between Auckland, Brisbane, Hamilton, Wellington, Christchurch, and Dunedin. **Jetstar** (© **0800/800-995;** www.jetstar. com) is another recent addition to the domestic airways, offering service between Auckland, Wellington, Christchurch, and Queenstown. Other smaller airlines fly internal routes, and you'll come across other aircraft willing to fly chartered routes.

If your time is limited, Air New Zealand (© **800/262-1234** in the U.S., or www. airnewzealand.com) is a good source of special deals. They regularly offer packages and deals of the month, but these must be purchased outside of New Zealand.

Once you're inside the country, **Air New Zealand's grabaseat Deals** are a fantastic option, although you need to be spending quite some time in New Zealand, as they're usually for travel 2 or 3 months in advance. They are posted online daily, and because they're restricted and at such amazing prices, they're snapped up fast.

By Car

I think the roads in New Zealand are pretty good, but I've heard many Americans say they're terrible and that New Zealanders are aggressive drivers. As for traffic on New Zealand roads, especially in the South Island, it's minimal compared to that found in Northern Hemisphere cities. Unfortunately, I do have to agree with the bit about aggressive drivers. The biggest dangers are excessive speed and foolhardy overtaking, so be careful of both. The New Zealand police have taken a much stronger stance against speeding in recent years, so expect many more speed cameras, more police on the roads, and much higher fines for speeding.

When driving between destinations, do not underestimate travel times. Distances may seem short in kilometer terms but roads are very often winding and sometimes narrow. Time and again I hear of international visitors driving from, say, Nelson to Queenstown in 1 day, or Auckland to Wellington in 1 day. It's certainly possible, but the idea is ludicrous. If you're that short on time, you'd be better off flying between destinations because you're not doing yourselves or the country any justice. Progress can be slower than you expect.

Note that petrol prices in New Zealand are currently fluctuating greatly. At time of writing, they ranged from NZ$2.10 per liter for 91 octane, NZ$2.27 for 95/96 octane, NZ$2.40 for 98 octane, and NZ$1.50 to NZ$1.60 per liter for diesel. For a good overview of current petrol prices in New Zealand, check **www.pricewatch.co.nz**.

Multilane motorways surround most of the larger cities, but most roads are dual carriageways. There are some single-lane and unsealed roads in remote areas, and these should be approached cautiously—as should all roads during the winter months when rain and ice can create treacherous surfaces.

Statistics show that in 2003, 632 drivers in New Zealand with foreign licenses were involved in nonfatal accidents and 23 in fatal crashes. Police at the scene of 85 of the nonfatal and three of the fatal crashes believed that the fact the driver was foreign was a factor in the accident. So, the message is to keep your wits about you and don't underestimate the danger just because fewer cars are on the roads. Pay particular attention on State Highway 1, north of Auckland and between Auckland and Hamilton, where statistics show a higher volume of crashes. Other hotspots are State Highway 2 to the Bay of Plenty and the Napier-Taupo highway. In the South Island, the most crashes occur on State Highway 1 between Nelson and Christchurch and Christchurch and Dunedin.

Car parking in Auckland, Wellington, and Christchurch can be expensive and hard to find. All cities have numerous car-parking buildings, though, and these are indicated in each chapter. Street parking is metered. You pay in coins, or by using a credit card or via your mobile phone. Instructions are marked clearly on each meter. If you exceed metered times, expect to be fined heavily in the major cities. Fines usually start at NZ$40 and go up from there the longer you overstay your limit.

New Zealand roads are not tolled, with one exception—the Northern Gateway Toll Road, a new stretch of the Northern Motorway, which bypasses the town of Orewa, north of Auckland. This is a more direct route between Auckland and Northland, but as it only cuts around 10 minutes off your journey and the automated payment of tolls has been causing headaches ever since it was instigated, I would strongly advise you

Mapping a Path

You'll receive a set of maps when you collect your rental car; if you're a member of the Automobile Association in the United States, Australia, Britain, or other European countries, you'll have reciprocal privileges with the New Zealand AA. One of the best maps of the country is issued by the **New Zealand Automobile Association,** 99 Albert St., Auckland (✆ **09/966-8800;** www.aa.co.nz); 205 Hills Rd., Shirley, Christchurch (✆ **03/386-1090**); or 343 Lambton Quay, Wellington (✆ **04/931-9999**). AA sells other detailed maps as well, plus "strip maps" of your itinerary and comprehensive guidebooks of accommodations (some of which give discounts to AA members). Be sure to bring your membership card from home. **Wises Mapping,** 604 Great South Rd., Ellerslie, Auckland (✆ **800/823-225;** www.wises. co.nz), also produces an excellent map, available at newsstands and bookshops throughout New Zealand.

simply turn off the motorway and continue on the old route through pretty, seaside Orewa. The exit for this free route on the Hibiscus Coast Highway via Orewa is clearly marked on signs above the motorway.

For those who wish to continue on the toll road, you will pay NZ$2 for a car or light commercial vehicle and NZ$4 for a heavy vehicle (exceeding about 7,700 lb. or 3.5 metric tons). Motorcycles are free. There is no additional charge for towing a trailer or caravan. The fully Electronic Toll Collection (ETC) system means tolls are collected without the need for vehicles to slow, stop, or change lanes to pay a toll; and you can pay at your convenience, either by setting up an account, via a toll-free phone number, or at one of the self-service kiosks. As a visitor to New Zealand, though, you'll be an occasional user, so you can buy single, return, or multiple trip tickets via the website www.landtransport.govt.nz/tollroad, at a service kiosk located along the road, or by calling the toll-free number ✆ **0800/402-020** between 8am and 6pm. The road is electronically patrolled and failure to pay the toll will result in fines. Again, I strongly suggest turning off the motorway and proceeding through Orewa. The way is well marked with signs.

If you plan to drive, consider joining the **New Zealand Automobile Association** (AA) while you're here. In New Zealand, call ✆ **0800/500-444** or visit www.aa. co.nz; they have offices around the country and can give you all the details about driving in New Zealand, plus maps, that you need. AA offers excellent breakdown services and advice to drivers. If you belong to a similar organization in your home country, membership is free, so don't forget to bring along your membership card.

DRIVING RULES & REQUIREMENTS

You must be at least 21 to 25 years old to rent a car in New Zealand, and you must have a driver's license that you've held for at least 1 year from the United States, Australia, Canada, or the United Kingdom (or an international driving permit). Recent law changes mean all drivers, including visitors, must carry their license or permit at all times.

Remember to drive on the left and wear seat belts at all times. The speed limit for the open road is 100kph (62mph); on the outskirts of many towns it is 80kph (50mph); and within towns and city boundaries it is 50kph (31mph). Rigid speeding laws are now in place and you face heavy fines if you exceed limits. New Zealand has also tightened up its drunk-driving laws, and if you are stopped in a random police check for compulsory breath testing for alcohol, you must take the test.

CAR RENTALS

Every major city has numerous rental-car companies, and international companies like Avis, Budget, and Hertz hire a wide range of vehicles. Most offer good deals that can be prebooked before you leave home. However, it pays to shop around and compare not only the prices, but also the cars. Some companies offer cheap deals, but their cars may be well over 10 years old. Most companies also require that you take out accident insurance with an insurance company authorized by them, and you generally need to be 25 to be able to rent a car in New Zealand.

Maui Rentals (© 800/351-2323 in the U.S.; www.maui-rentals.com) has vehicles that are either brand-new or less than a year old. Daily rates range from NZ$150 to NZ$400, depending on the size of the car and the time of year. The price includes the goods and service tax (GST) and unlimited mileage, but insurance runs about NZ$30 extra per day. Because Maui has offices in Auckland and Christchurch, there's no extra charge for one-way trips. They also rent a range of extras like a GPS, which goes for NZ$9 per day—a very good investment, I think. Contact the local offices at 36 Richard Pearce Dr., Mangere, Auckland (© 09/255-0620; fax 09/255-0629), or 530–544 Memorial Ave., Christchurch (© 0800/651-080 in NZ, or 03/358-4159; www.maui.co.nz). Both provide courtesy airport shuttle service.

Auto Rentals Kiwi Travel, New Brighton, Christchurch (© 0800/736-893 in NZ, or 800/905-8071 in U.S.; www.autorentals.co.nz), is an established chain offering a modern fleet of cars for budget-minded travelers. They offer sedans, station wagons, and minibuses at competitive rates. They are also an accredited TranzRail booking agency and can help with interisland ferry and train bookings, accommodations, and further vehicle rentals.

Affordable Rental Cars, 48 Carr Rd., Mount Roskill, Auckland (© 0800/454-443 in NZ, or 09/630-1567; fax 09/630-3692; www.car-rental.co.nz), has daily rates on unlimited-mileage vehicles from NZ$35 to NZ$95, depending on the vehicle and time of travel. Prices include GST and insurance.

If you want to spoil yourself, try **Classic Car Touring New Zealand,** 181 Hobson St., Auckland (© 021/702-623 in NZ; www.classiccartouring.co.nz), specializing in self-drive classic cars for NZ$350 to NZ$750 per day, depending on the vehicle; or **Smartcars Luxury Car Hire,** 110 Nelson St., Auckland (© 0800/458-987 in NZ, or 09/307-3553; www.smartcars.co.nz), offering the very latest convertibles and 4×4s from Europe.

You can also rent in advance from the following: **Avis** (© 800/230-4898 in the U.S.; www.avis.com), **Budget** (© 800/527-0700 in the U.S.; www.budget.com), **Hertz** (© 800/654-3131 in the U.S.; www.hertz.com), and **Thrifty** (© 800/847-4389 in the U.S.; www.thrifty.com). Daily costs average about NZ$100 to NZ$150.

Alternatives to Renting a Car

If you'll be in New Zealand for an extended period of time, it may be worthwhile to investigate the guaranteed tourist buyback plan offered by **North Harbour Hyundai,** 175 Wairau Rd., Takapuna (© 09/444-7777; fax 09/444-7099; www.hyundainz.co.nz). This Auckland dealership sells used Toyotas, Nissans, Hondas, and similar cars to visitors with a written agreement to purchase them back after a

Some kind and ever-so-thoughtful person—and I think it might be someone at **Jasons Publishing** (www.jasons.com)—had the good sense to create seven marvelous highway route planners. They include The Twin Coast Discovery Highway, covering Northland and Auckland; The Pacific Coast Highway, covering Auckland, Coromandel, coastal Bay of Plenty, Eastland, and Hawke's Bay; and the Classic New Zealand Wine Trail. These free maps detail the best features of each trip, places to stay and eat, and adventures to sample along the way. They're available at visitor centers throughout the country.

stipulated time period. Cars come with a nationwide warranty; the owner pays for the insurance. For an example of what to expect, **Wheels,** 376 Lincoln Rd., Christchurch (© **03/366-4855;** www.newzealandrentalcar.co.nz), has sold buyback vehicles for NZ$5,000 and bought them back for approximately NZ$3,000 after 3 months of use. (*Note:* This is only an example of a possible scenario.)

If you're staying in hostels, you'll often find car-share schemes advertised on notice boards. If you want to arrange a carpool officially, check **www.carpoolnz.org**. It puts people who need a ride in touch with those willing to give them one. The system operates throughout the country, and the person getting the ride pays a small commission and something toward gas costs, which usually works out to be about half the cost of a bus ticket.

By RV or Motor Home

If you want ultimate freedom, consider renting what we call a campervan. Both **Maui Rentals** (© **800/351-2323** in the U.S., or 0800/651-080 in NZ) and **Newmans** (© **09/302-1582** in Auckland) offer minivans and motor homes. Maui rents two-berth, four-berth, and six-berth vehicles, and you'll find their rates and special deals on their website. **Britz New Zealand** (© **0800/831-900** in NZ; www.britz.com) also has a range of excellent vehicles at good rates.

If you fancy yourself in something superfunky, opt for New Zealand's most distinctive campervans, individually painted by top New Zealand artists. You can get these from **Escape Rentals** (© **0800/216-171;** www.escaperentals.co.nz), which has depots in Auckland, Wellington, and Christchurch. They offer competitive rates and unlimited free kilometers, but don't for a minute think you'll escape attention. **Spaceships** (© **0800/772-237** in NZ; www.spaceships.tv) has great little cars that convert to mini campervans, and are much easier to drive than their bigger brother. Spaceships has depots in Auckland, Wellington, and Christchurch.

The minimum age required to drive a campervan rental in New Zealand is usually 21, but for some it may be as high as 23 to 25 years. There may also be restrictions for drivers over 75 years. Campervans also incur higher insurance charges. Make sure you at least have windscreen and tire insurance.

By Motorcycle

If you enjoy the thrill of speed and the wind in your hair, you can rent motorcycles or purchase tour packages with or without guides. Just bring your full motorcycle license or international driving permit and call **New Zealand Motorcycle Rentals and Tours,**

72 Barry's Point Rd., Takapuna, Auckland (© **09/486-2472;** www.nzbike.com), which has a wide range of BMW, Honda, Harley-Davidson, and Yamaha bikes. They're official New Zealand Tourism Award winners, and all their gear is in top condition.

Adventure New Zealand Motorcycle Tours & Rentals, 29 Bolt Rd., Nelson (© **03/548-5787;** www.gotournz.com), offers a range of deluxe tours with top-class bikes and upmarket accommodations for the 35 to 65 set. **Towanda Women, Christchurch** (© **03/314-9097;** www.towanda.org), specializes in guided New Zealand–wide motorcycle tours for women only.

By Bicycle

New Zealand's mild summer climate and varied landscape make it an ideal cycling destination. Many companies run tours or rent bicycles. Start with **Adventure Biking Natural High,** 58 McDonald Rd., Lincoln (© **03/982-2966;** www.bicycle rentals.co.nz), which offers a range of rental cycles, plus a buyback option that allows you to sell your bike for 50% of its cost at the end of your tour. **City Cycle Hire,** 73 Wrights Rd., Christchurch (© **03/377-5952;** www.cyclehire-tours.co.nz), has a 5-day adventure on the Central Otago Rail Trail. **Adventure South,** P.O. Box 33–153, Christchurch (© **03/942-1222;** www.remarkableadventuresnz.co.nz or www.advsouth.co.nz), offers a wide range of guided tours in the South Island.

By Taxi

Taxi stands are located at all airport and transport terminals and on major shopping streets of cities and towns. You cannot hail a taxi on the street within a quarter-mile of a stand. Taxis are on call 24 hours a day, although there's an additional charge if you call for one. Drivers don't expect a tip just to transport you, but if they handle a lot of luggage or perform other special services, it's perfectly acceptable to add a little extra. Be aware that many taxi drivers in Auckland, Wellington, and Christchurch are recent immigrants and don't always have a comprehensive grasp of English. See regional chapters for specific taxi companies throughout New Zealand.

By Interisland Ferry

Crossing Cook Strait on one of the ferry services will give you a chance to see both islands from the water, as well as the serene Marlborough Sounds. Two ferry companies operate on the Strait, which can be boarded in either Wellington or Picton.

The **Interislander** ferry system (© **0800/802-802** in NZ; www.interislander. co.nz) operates every day with three vessels—*Arahura, Kaitaki,* and *Aratere*—that offer a tourism experience in their own right, not just a practical means of getting across the water. You can choose from six daily departure times; the crossing takes 3 hours. The ferries have licensed bar and cafe areas, TV lounges, shops, and play areas, and the newer *Kaitaki,* the biggest ferry in New Zealand, has two movie theaters and room for 1,600 passengers. Interislander ferries have three fare types. **Easy Change** fares are the most flexible and can be canceled right up to check-in without cancellation fees. **Saver Change** fares are the midrange fares that incur a 50% fee if canceled. **Web Saver** fares are the cheapest way to travel, but once booked they're nonrefundable. They are available all year but numbers are limited, so book early. **Overseas bookings** can be made by international customers online, or by calling © **64/4-498-3302;** from outside of New Zealand you can book only Easy Change fares. Web Saver and Saver Change fares can be booked only within New Zealand, and they sell out quickly during peak season.

If you're traveling by train or InterCity Coach, ask about the cost-effective through-fares, which are subject to availability.

Bicycles and sports gear can be taken on the ferry for a small additional cost, as can campervans or motor homes—though these travel at a premium fare. *Note:* If you plan to transport any kind of vehicle (including bikes) by ferry, you need a confirmed reservation.

Bluebridge Cook Strait Ferry (© 0800/844-844 in NZ; www.bluebridge.co.nz) sails four times daily between Wellington and Picton. It operates two vessels, *Santa Regina* and *Straitsman*, which feature lounges, cafe and bar facilities, outdoor decks, free big-screen movies, and shops. Fare bookings are transferable until 24 hours before travel subject to availability, but they're nonrefundable.

Regardless of which ferry you select, keep in mind that Cook Strait is a notoriously changeable stretch of water, and high swells can affect those prone to seasickness. Bad weather may also affect scheduled departures.

By Coach (Bus)

Coaches offer a cost-effective way of getting around New Zealand; as a bonus, you don't have to worry about driving on the left or studying maps. Most provide excellent commentary and stop frequently for refreshments en route, but smoking is not permitted. There are three major services in New Zealand (all owned by the same company). **InterCity** operates three-star coaches on New Zealand's most comprehensive coach network, visiting 600 towns and cities, with over 170 services daily; **Newmans** is a standard route option throughout the country, except on the South Island's West Coast, where it operates as a tourist service and a code-share with Great Sights; and **Great Sights,** New Zealand's premier daily sightseeing operator, which provides the most extensive sightseeing network nationwide. *Reminder:* Book coach journeys in advance during peak travel periods (summer and holidays).

InterCity (© 09/583-5780 in Auckland and 03/377-0951 in Christchurch; www.intercity.co.nz) offers discounts to students, seniors (60 and over), and YHA members and VIP (Backpackers) cardholders. Check out their **Flexi-Pass,** which allows travelers to buy blocks of travel time up to 40% cheaper than standard fares on all InterCity and Newmans journeys. The Flexi-Pass gives you total freedom to explore the country with an hours-based pass that can be topped up like a prepaid phone card. Set your own itinerary and travel when and where you like. You can lock in discounts on every seat, every service, nationwide, every day; and the more hours you buy, the cheaper it becomes. The pass is valid for a year and can be used on the Interislander and on selected tours and dolphin-watching cruises in the Bay of Islands. Passes start at NZ$168 for 15 hours of travel. For more information, check out www.flexipass.co.nz.

InterCity and **Newmans** (© 09/583-5780; www.newmanscoach.co.nz) coaches are also included in the **Travelpass New Zealand** deal, which brings together an extensive range of "hop on and off" fixed itinerary passes based on the most popular touring routes throughout the country. It allows you to travel with New Zealand's largest coach, train, air, and ferry network. There are a number of different deals. For instance, the Aotearoa Adventurer gives you 14 days travel (minimum) throughout New Zealand for NZ$1,283; a Kiwi Explorer gives you 9 days travel (minimum) for

NZ$682. Among the North Island Passes on offer, the Discovery package gives 4 days travel (minimum) for NZ$279 and includes visits to Auckland, Rotorua, Napier, Taupo, and Wellington. In the South, the **West Coast Pass** costs from NZ$154 to NZ$180 depending on departure point and is good for 3 months on the route from Nelson to Queenstown. For information, contact **Travelpass New Zealand** (© **0800/339-966** in NZ, or 09/638-5780; fax 09/638-5774; www.travelpass.co.nz).

Great Sights, 102 Hobson St., Auckland (© **0800/744-487** in NZ, or 09/583-5790; www.greatsights.co.nz), offers a wide range of day, overnight, and multiday tours throughout New Zealand, utilizing a modern fleet of luxury coaches with complimentary hotel pickups. Experienced drivers offer informative commentary, and modern, low-emission luxury vehicles are equipped with air-conditioning, reclining seats, and onboard restrooms. They offer over 40 daily sightseeing trips across the country, including the Bay of Islands, Auckland Sights, Waitomo Caves, Rotorua, Mount Cook, Christchurch Sights, Milford Sound, and the West Coast Glaciers.

ALTERNATIVE BUSES & SHUTTLES

For the young and/or adventurous, **Kiwi Experience,** 85 Beach Rd., Auckland (© **09/336-4286;** www.kiwiexperience.com), and the **Magic Travellers Network,** 120 Albert St., Auckland (© **09/358-5600;** www.magicbus.co.nz), provide something that's between a standard coach and a tour.

Popular with backpackers, these coaches travel over a half-dozen established routes, and passengers can get off whenever they like and pick up the next coach days or weeks later. The coaches make stops at scenic points along the way for bush walking, swimming, and sometimes even a barbecue. Prices vary according to the route, but typically are from around NZ$790 to cover both islands in 14 days. Passes are valid for 12 months with Magic Travellers and 12 months with Kiwi Experience.

Flying Kiwi Expeditions, 4B Forests Rd., Stoke, Nelson (© **03/547-0171;** www.flyingkiwi.com), is another fun-packed flexible alternative to the well-beaten tourist trail. Ten different options combine travel and outdoor activities, priced according to the number of activities included. For other zany southern alternatives try **Travel HeadFirst Bottom Bus,** P.O. Box 434, Dunedin (© **03/477-9083;** www.travelheadfirst.com/bottom-bus), which offers fully guided bus tours exploring the very south of New Zealand.

Shuttle transport is another alternative. Numerous companies on both islands run minibus shuttles between cities. Some of them are listed in the regional chapters, and you can also get details from area visitor centers. **Atomic Shuttles,** Christchurch (© **03/349-0697;** www.atomictravel.co.nz), offers service between 30 South Island stops.

By Train

Tranz Scenic (© **0800/872-467** in NZ; www.tranzscenic.co.nz) operates three long-distance train routes through rugged landscapes—the Overlander, which runs Auckland to Wellington; the TranzCoastal, Christchurch to Picton; and the TranzAlpine, Christchurch to Greymouth. The trains are modern and comfortable, heated or air-conditioned, and ventilated. Service has greatly improved under new management, and views of spectacular landscapes are assured. Tranz Scenic offers discounts for students, YHA members, Backpacker cardholders, and those 55 and over. It also has a limited number of Saver Fares and Super Saver Fares during off-peak times.

Also ask about the **Scenic Rail Pass** (© 0800/872-467 in NZ; www.tranzscenic. co.nz), which enables you to discover New Zealand by train at your own pace and includes one ferry crossing (7-day Tranz Scenic Rail Pass costs NZ$420; a 14-day pass costs $530).

The train routes and their fares are as follows:

○ **Auckland–Wellington:** The Overlander has reclining seats and a licensed buffet car that serves drinks and food. A Super Saver fare costs NZ$125; if you miss out on one of those, check online for other good specials. You get informative commentary as you pass through many scenic highlights. Hostesses and stewards supply newspapers, magazines, and beverage service.

○ **Christchurch–Picton:** The TranzCoastal passes through dramatic landscapes for 5½ hours; the economy one-way fare is NZ$88 and you can choose to stop off in Kaikoura for a spot of whale-watching. There is also an excellent value standard through-fare available for NZ$150, which takes you from Wellington to Christchurch (or vice versa) and includes an Interislander ferry fare.

○ **Christchurch–Greymouth:** The TranzAlpine is the best of the lot. It goes through the unforgettable landscape of Arthur's Pass National Park, depositing you 4½ hours later in Greymouth. The standard return fare is NZ$250, but look out for specials online. Day excursions are also available on these routes.

TIPS ON ACCOMMODATIONS

Unfortunately, there's nothing standard about accommodations rates here; what you get for NZ$150 can be much better than something for two or three times the price. My advice: Ask around, visit websites for photographs, and don't assume that all places in the same price range offer the same standard of accommodations. (They probably do in the Expensive range, but certainly not in the Moderate and Inexpensive categories.)

New Zealand tourism's official mark of quality, **Qualmark** (www.qualmark.co.nz), has now been applied to all accommodations types and tourism businesses. This means they have been independently assessed as professional and trustworthy and graded one star (acceptable), two stars (good), three stars (very good), four stars (excellent), and five stars (exceptional, among the best in New Zealand). Each business has undergone a rigorous assessment and licensing process to receive the Qualmark designation.

However, you should realize that—according to this Qualmark system—a three-star hotel is not the same as a three-star B&B or a three-star lodge, and that a five-star B&B is not the same as a five-star hotel. Each category of accommodations is assessed on different criteria.

It is also worth noting that many accommodations operators have little faith in this rating system because it's voluntary and not all properties have been assessed. There is particular discontent at the top end of the market, where operators are disillusioned that star ratings are being applied to businesses that are already self-regulated.

If you would like more information when you arrive in New Zealand, pick up the free **Qualmark Accommodation Guide** from information centers (or order it at www.qualmark.co.nz); it lists all participating hotels, motels, B&Bs, backpackers, campgrounds, and tourism businesses.

Note that New Zealand now has an across-the-board legal ban on smoking in public buildings. That includes hotels and restaurants. Therefore, you should assume that accommodations listed throughout this guide have adopted a nonsmoking policy. It is also a legal requirement that all public buildings have access for travelers with disabilities. You should therefore assume that properties reviewed in this guide offer rooms with access for travelers with disabilities, although in the case of B&Bs it will pay to double-check before booking.

There is a multitude of lodging options available in New Zealand—here's a run-down on what you'll find. Price ranges are based on the following scale: **Inexpensive** (up to NZ$150); **Moderate** (NZ$151–NZ$300); **Expensive** (NZ$301–NZ$650); and **Very Expensive** (NZ$651 and up).

HOTELS   A hotel generally provides a licensed bar and restaurant, and guest rooms do not usually have cooking facilities. In New Zealand, "hotel" refers to modern tourist hotels, including the big international chains and older public-licensed hotels generally found in provincial areas. The latter are completely different from the former.

The country hotel, or pub, offers inexpensive to moderate accommodations of a modest nature. It's often noisy and old-fashioned with shared bathrooms down the hall. There are definitely exceptions, with upgrading a big trend in popular tourist areas. One way or another, they're usually rich in character.

Modern hotels come in all price levels. Several big international chains have two or three grades of hotels, and you can get exceptionally good deals if you book with the same chain throughout the country. In major tourist centers such as Queenstown, competition is fierce and good prices can be found. In major corporate destinations such as Auckland and Wellington, rates will be considerably higher during the week, with weekends bringing superb specials.

APARTMENTS   In the last several years, apartment-style accommodations have sprouted up in New Zealand like mushrooms on a damp day. Some have been added to existing hotels but most are free-standing complexes. If you'd like to stay in a modern apartment I suggest you contact one of the following first-class operators. **Touch of Spice,** Queenstown (www.touchofspice.co.nz; © **03/442-8672**), has been rated by *Condé Nast Traveler* as 1 of only 49 villa rental agents worldwide best qualified to match its readers with suitable holiday properties. This meticulous concierge and luxury lifestyle specialist offers a range of 30 luxury properties from inner-city apartments to country hideaways and private island retreats—all featuring modern furnishings and five-star quality, and full staff if required. **New Zealand Apartments** (www.nzapartments.co.nz; © **0800/692-727**) has a catalog of 48 stylish apartments in 33 locations nationwide. Most are under 10 years old and go for unbelievably good prices. They're serviced on demand and all have on-site managers to welcome you.

MOTELS & MOTOR INNS   A motel unit is self-contained and usually has cooking facilities, a bathroom, and one or two bedrooms. A motor inn often has a restaurant on the premises. Don't assume that New Zealand motels are the same as those you find in, say, the United States. There has been a major shake-up of standards in the motel industry, and many motels and motor inns are superior to some hotels. Look for the Qualmark sign of quality, which is prominently displayed on signs and promotional material. If you aim for four- and five-star properties I'm sure you'll be happy. **New Zealand Luxury Motels** (www.nzluxurymotels.co.nz; © **0800/692-727**) can save you a lot of time. They have 23 top-end motels nationwide on their books—15 of them built in the last few years to the highest specifications.

BED & BREAKFASTS   As the name suggests, B&B rates include bed and breakfast, but it's often difficult to tell the difference between a bed-and-breakfast, a homestay, a farmstay, a guesthouse, a lodge, and a boutique hotel. B&B operators seem to be using a plethora of terms to describe much the same thing. Suffice it to say, in all of the above, that the key advantage is interaction with New Zealanders.

Homestays and bed-and-breakfasts are pretty much the same thing, but the variation in quality within both can be disconcerting—you'll find both the ludicrously cheap and the ludicrously expensive, and price is not necessarily an indicator of what you'll get. **Homestays** tend to be more family oriented and modest, especially in rural areas and provincial towns. Be prepared to simply get a bed in a family home. **B&Bs,** on the other hand, can be as down-market or as upmarket as you're prepared to pay; some rival the best hotels for quality.

I strongly advise you to check websites, or wait until you're in New Zealand to purchase one of the numerous B&B guides. Look for *The New Zealand Bed & Breakfast Book,* which illustrates every property in color. *Heritage & Character Inns of New Zealand* (www.heritageinns.co.nz) is another good source; it details about 90 of the country's best B&Bs in heritage homes. Ask for brochures at visitor centers.

You can safely assume that **farmstays** are located on farms. They present an ideal opportunity to get a feel for New Zealand's rural life. Several organizations will put you in touch with a reliable farmstay; two of them are **Accommodation New Zealand** (www.accommodation-new-zealand.co.nz; ✆ **09/444-4895** or 03/487-8420), and **Hospitality Plus,** the New Zealand Home & Farmstay Company (www.hospitalityplus.co.nz; ✆ **03/693-7463;** fax 03/693-7462).

Guesthouses generally offer good value: modest rooms at modest prices. You can check out a selection of them with **New Zealand's Federation of Bed & Breakfast Hotels,** Inc., 52 Armagh St., Christchurch (www.nzbnbhotels.com; ✆ **03/358-6928;** fax 03/355-0291).

COUNTRY LODGES   Many establishments call themselves "lodges" when, strictly speaking, they don't meet lodge criteria as defined by the New Zealand Lodge Association. In the truest sense, country lodges in New Zealand are small and highly individual, with 4 to 20 bedrooms. They're fully licensed and have an all-inclusive tariff. They generally offer the very best of everything, including fine dining (three- to five-course dinners). The unspoken factors are the degree of exclusivity that exceeds B&Bs and the degree of personalized service and pampering that exceeds most hotels. For information, go to **www.lodgesofnz.co.nz**. A luxury accommodations category was also added to the Qualmark program in 2003.

HOLIDAY HOMES   When they're not being used by their owners, holiday homes can be rented by the night or for longer periods. Known as **baches** in the North Island and **cribs** in the South Island, they are a good value for independent travelers. You can buy *Baches & Holiday Homes to Rent,* which details over 500 properties, from bookstores or the **Automobile Association,** 99 Albert St., Auckland (✆ **09/966-8800**); 343 Lambton Quay, Wellington (✆ **04/931-9999**); or 205 Hills Rd., Shirley, Christchurch (✆ **03/386-1090**). For a wider variety—cozy cottages to super-luxury homes—contact **New Zealand Vacation Homes** (www.nzvacationhomes.co.nz), which lists self-catering properties throughout the country. In the Auckland area, pick

En Suites

In New Zealand, the term *en-suite bathroom* refers to a bathroom incorporated within the bedroom. A *private bathroom* refers to a bathroom outside the bedroom, which is used exclusively by the guests of one room. A *shared bathroom* is a communal bathroom used by all guests in the establishment. Many accommodations within New Zealand have en-suite bathrooms, but it still pays to request them in B&Bs and backpacker establishments, many of which still have shared or private bathrooms.

up a copy of the free brochure *Bach Escapes* from visitor centers, produced by the **Auckland Regional Council** (www.arc.govt.nz/bachescapes).

HOSTELS   Hostels are generally frequented by backpackers, but most welcome people of all ages and have single and double rooms as well as dorms. They have shared facilities (some have en-suite bathrooms) and communal lounges and kitchens; some have cafes and/or bars.

You can get more information by contacting the following: **YHA New Zealand National Reservations Centre** (✆ 03/379-9808; fax 03/379-4415; www.yha. co.nz), which has hostels open 24 hours a day that do not impose curfews or duties; **Budget Backpacker Hostels New Zealand** (✆ 03/379-3014; www.bbh.co.nz) lists over 300 hostels around the country; and **VIP Backpacker Resorts of New Zealand** (✆ 09/827-6016; fax 09/827-6013; www.vip.co.nz) is supported by over 60 hostels. **Nomads** (✆ 0800/666-237; www.nomadsworld.com) offers hostel accommodations at 16 sites.

MOTOR CAMPS & HOLIDAY PARKS   These properties have communal kitchens, toilets, showers, and laundries, and a variety of accommodations from campsites and cabins to flats and backpacker-style lodges. They are very popular with New Zealand holidaymakers during the summer months, so make sure you book ahead. They make an ideal base if you are traveling by motor home. Two organizations to contacts are **Top 10 Holiday Parks** (www.top10.co.nz; ✆ 0800/867-836 in NZ; fax 03/377-9950) and **Holiday Accommodation Parks New Zealand** (www. holidayparks.co.nz; ✆ 04/298-3283).

FAST FACTS: NEW ZEALAND

Area Codes   The area code for New Zealand is **64.** Within New Zealand, the following area codes should be added if dialing from outside each of the areas: Auckland and Northland, **09;** Coromandel Peninsula, Waikato, Bay of Plenty, Rotorua, Taupo, **07;** Tongariro National Park, Gisborne, Hawke's Bay, Taranaki, Wanganui, Wairarapa, **06;** Wellington, **04;** and the whole of the South Island, **03.**

Business Hours   Banks are open Monday through Friday from 9am to 4:30pm. Shops are usually open Monday through Thursday from 9am (sometimes 8am) to 5:30pm, and until 9pm on either Thursday or Friday. Increasingly, shops are open all day Saturday; many shops are also open all day Sunday, with others closing between noon and 4pm.

Car Rental   See "Getting There by Car," earlier in this chapter.

Cellphones   See "Mobile Phones," later in this section.

Crime   See "Safety," later in this section.

Customs   **What You Can Bring into New Zealand**   *Do not* bring any fruit or plants into New Zealand. Because of the importance of agriculture and horticulture to the economy, animal products, fruit, plant material, and foodstuffs that may contain plant or animal pests and diseases will not be allowed into the country. Heavy fines may be imposed on people caught carrying these prohibited materials. If in doubt, place all questionable items, especially fruit, into the marked bins before approaching the immigration area upon arrival at a New Zealand airport.

Firearms and weapons, unless a permit is obtained from the New Zealand police upon arrival at the airport, are not allowed. *Note:* This includes firearms intended for sporting purposes. Other prohibited items include ivory, in any form; tortoise- or turtleshell jewelry and ornaments; medicines that incorporate musk, rhinoceros, or tiger derivatives; carvings or anything made from whalebone or bone from any other marine animal; and cat skins or coats. Certain drugs (diuretics, tranquilizers, depressants, stimulants, cardiac drugs, and sleeping pills) may not be allowed unless they are covered by a doctor's prescription. Pirated copyright goods and objectionable (indecent) articles such as DVDs and publications are also prohibited. No live animals are allowed without going through the legal quarantine requirements.

Customs duties are not assessed on personal items you bring into the country and plan to take with you. New Zealand's duty-free allowances are 200 cigarettes or 250 grams (about 8 oz.) of tobacco or 50 cigars; 4.5 liters of wine or beer (equivalent to six 750ml bottles); three bottles of spirits or liquor (each containing no more than 1,125ml/ about 2½ pints); and goods totaling NZ$700 that were purchased for your own use or for a gift. Make sure you have receipts available for inspection. If you plan to take in anything beyond those limits, contact the embassy or consulate office nearest you *before* you arrive or check **www.customs.govt.nz**.

What You Can Bring Home   Returning **United States** citizens who have been away for 48 hours or more are allowed to bring back, once every 30 days, $800 worth of merchandise duty-free. You'll be charged a flat rate of 4% duty on the next $1,000 worth of purchases. Be sure to have your receipts handy. On mailed gifts, the duty-free limit is $200. You cannot bring fresh foodstuffs into the United States; tinned foods, however, are allowed. For more information, contact the **U.S. Customs Service,** 1300 Pennsylvania Ave., NW, Washington, DC 20229 (© **877/287-8867**), and request the free pamphlet *Know Before You Go.* It's also available online at www.customs.gov.

Canada allows its citizens a C$750 exemption, and you're allowed to bring back duty-free one carton of cigarettes, one can of tobacco, 40 imperial ounces of liquor, and 50 cigars. In addition, you're allowed to mail gifts to Canada valued at less than C$60 a day, provided they're unsolicited and don't contain alcohol or tobacco (write on the package "Unsolicited gift, under $60 value"). All valuables should be declared on the Y-38 form before departure from Canada, including serial numbers of valuables you already own, such as expensive foreign cameras. *Note:* The C$750 exemption can be used only once a year and only after an absence of 7 days. For a summary of Canadian rules, write for the booklet *I Declare,* issued by the **Canada Customs and Revenue Agency** (© **800/461-9999** in Canada, or 204/983-3500; www.ccra-adrc.gc.ca).

U.K. citizens returning from **a non-E.U. country** have a Customs allowance of 200 cigarettes; 50 cigars; 250 grams of smoking tobacco; 2 liters of still table wine; 1 liter of spirits or strong liquor (over 22% volume); 2 liters of fortified wine, sparkling wine, or other liquor; 60cc (ml) perfume; 250cc (ml) of toilet water; and £145 worth of all other goods, including gifts and souvenirs. People 16 and under cannot have the tobacco or alcohol allowance. For more information, contact HM Customs & Excise at ℰ **0845/010-9000** (from outside the U.K., 020/8929-0152), or consult their website at www.hmce.gov.uk.

The duty-free allowance in **Australia** is A$400 or, for those 17 and under, A$200. Citizens age 18 and older can bring in 250 cigarettes or 250 grams of loose tobacco, and 1,125 milliliters of alcohol. If you're returning with valuables you already own, such as foreign-made cameras, you should file form B263. A helpful brochure available from Australian consulates or Customs offices is *Know Before You Go.* For more information, call the **Australian Customs Service** at ℰ **1300/363-263,** or log on to www.customs.gov.au.

Disabled Travelers New Zealand is a relatively good destination for visitors with disabilities. Since 1975, every public building and major renovated structure in the country has been required by law to provide reasonable and adequate access for those with disabilities. In addition, accommodations with five or more units are required to provide at least one room for guests with disabilities. For general information, contact the **New Zealand Disability Resource Centre,** 14 Erson Ave., Royal Oak, Auckland (ℰ **09/625-8069;** www.disabilityresource.org.nz).

If you're traveling by air in New Zealand, you'll be relieved to know our airline staff is very considerate. You will always be taken onto the aircraft ahead of other passengers and you'll be last off.

If you have a disabled parking pass, bring it with you. You can contact the New Zealand Disability Resource Centre (above) well ahead of your travel time to organize a New Zealand pass, but bringing your own is a good backstop. Every town center and shopping mall has designated disabled parking spaces, so you're unlikely to encounter parking problems, even in peak tourist season.

Doctors If you need to visit a doctor, your hotel or accommodation provider can put you in touch with local services. Emergency doctors are also listed in the Fast Facts section of each destination chapter. If your condition is severe and urgent, go straight to the nearest hospital Accident & Emergency (A&E) department, or call an ambulance. Be aware though, that New Zealand A&E departments are usually extremely busy and under-staffed and you may have to wait several hours. Unless your life is under threat, it is always best to consult an emergency doctor first.

Drinking Laws The minimum drinking age is 18 in pubs and proof of age may be required, so make sure you carry some form of photo ID. Children are allowed in pubs with their parents, but they cannot be served alcohol. Beer and wine can be purchased from most supermarkets and from liquor stores. Wine can also be purchased from specialty wine shops and wineries. The closing time for hotels and bars varies—some have longer liquor licenses than others. In the main centers, most close between midnight and 2am, but some close at 3 or 4am. Some areas also observe complete liquor bans. Please take note of the signs and warnings or you will be arrested and fined heavily. Do not carry open containers of alcohol in your car or any public area that isn't zoned for alcohol consumption. The police can fine you on the spot. Don't even think about driving while intoxicated, or you'll be fined heavily. New Zealand Police often stage random drug and alcohol testing on roads of major cities to stop drink-driving. You must stop on request and you will have to take a breath test.

Driving Rules See "Getting Around," earlier in this chapter.

Electricity The voltage is 230 volts in New Zealand, and plugs are of the flat, three-pronged variety (with the top two prongs angled). If you bring a hair dryer, it should be a dual-voltage one, and you'll need an adapter plug. Most motels and some B&Bs have built-in wall transformers for 110-volt, two-prong razors, but if you're going to be staying in hostels, cabins, homestays, or guesthouses, bring dual-voltage appliances.

Embassies & Consulates   In Wellington, the capital city, you'll find the United States Embassy, the Canadian High Commission, and the British High Commission (see "Fast Facts: Wellington," in chapter 11). In Auckland, you'll find consulates for the United States, Canada, Ireland, and the United Kingdom (see "Fast Facts: Auckland," in chapter 5).

Emergencies   Dial ℭ **111** to contact the police, call an ambulance, or report a fire.

Family Travel   New Zealand offers some of the most exciting vacation opportunities for families with kids. Hiking, swimming, sailing, and whale-watching are only a few of the activities children of all ages can enjoy. A day at the beach may well end up being one of their best memories, and you won't have to pay a cent for the pleasure. All cities and towns also have free parks, walkways, and children's playgrounds; and if you're here in summer, swimming pool complexes in most towns make for a fun, inexpensive day out for all the family.

Make sure you ask at all visitor centers for advice on the best kids' attractions, although I have marked most in each chapter. Also ask about specific summer holiday festivals and kids' activities. Many of these are short-term, one-off events that could be the very thing to ease the family stresses that come with traveling with children.

Older, more adventurous kids will no doubt love caving, rafting, kayaking, and bungy jumping, although some activities do have minimum age limits, especially in Queenstown. Most sightseeing attractions admit children at half-price, and family prices are usually available.

Although many of the better B&Bs and upmarket lodges do not accommodate children, motels and farmstays are ideal for families. Both are usually cheaper, motel rooms are regularly equipped with cooking facilities, and children will enjoy roaming the fields and helping out on a working farm.

To locate accommodations, restaurants, and attractions that are particularly kid friendly, refer to the "Kids" icon throughout this guide.

Gasoline   See "Getting There By Car," earlier in this chapter.

Health   **Before You Go**   Vaccinations are not required to enter New Zealand. Health insurance is strongly advised because New Zealand's public and private medical/hospital facilities are not free to visitors, except as a result of accident. Make sure your health insurance covers you when you're out of the country; if it doesn't, get temporary medical coverage for the duration of your trip. Be sure to carry your identification card in your wallet.

Contact the **International Association for Medical Assistance to Travelers (IAMAT)** (ℭ **716/754-4883** or, in Canada, 416/652-0137; www.iamat.org) for tips on travel and health concerns in the countries you're visiting, and for lists of local, English-speaking doctors. The United States **Centers for Disease Control and Prevention** (ℭ **800/311-3435;** www.cdc.gov) provides up-to-date information on health hazards by region or country and offers tips on food safety. **Travel Health Online** (www.tripprep.com), sponsored by a consortium of travel medicine practitioners, may also offer helpful advice on traveling abroad. You can find listings of reliable medical clinics overseas at the **International Society of Travel Medicine** (www.istm.org).

As mentioned in "Medical Requirements," later in this chapter, it is advisable to bring any of your current prescription drug requirements with you—but be sure to carry a prescription note from your doctor. Pack **prescription medications** in your carry-on luggage, and carry them in their original containers, with pharmacy labels—otherwise they won't make it through airport security. Carry the generic name of prescription medicines, in case a local pharmacist is unfamiliar with the brand name. It is not necessary to pack anti-diarrheal and/or anti-emetic products as these are available over-the-counter in New Zealand pharmacies—as are most generic prescription drugs for common problems like headaches, coughs, fevers, and influenza.

Following are some ailments to be aware of:

○ **Bugs, Bites & Other Wildlife Concerns**   You've heard that New Zealand is a relatively safe place? Believe it! We have no snakes, no alligators or crocodiles, no wild animals of note, no scorpions. The worst we can offer you is our poisonous **katipo spider,** but because you're about as likely to see one of those, much less be bitten, as you are to encounter a bison in the main street of Auckland, I wouldn't start panicking just yet.

But knowledge is power, so here are the spidery details. The New Zealand katipo—*Latrodectus katipo* and *L. atritus* (yes, there are two species)—favors sparsely vegetated sand dunes and driftwood above the high-tide mark on sandy beaches. *L. katipo* is distinguished by the coloration of the adult female: black with a red stripe on the abdomen. The mature male is about one-sixth the size of the female and is predominantly white with a series of orange-red triangles and black lines on the abdomen. *L. atritus* is completely black.

Both species are poisonous, but they are rarely seen. And given that New Zealand is a nation of beach-lovers, it is comforting to know that there have only been two recorded fatalities, both in the 1800s—largely unconvincing evidence of toxic spiders. If, in the unlikely event that you are bitten by something black while on the beach, try to have the presence of mind to capture the offender and then take yourself off to the nearest hospital.

Heading inland, especially in the deep south around Fiordland, Te Anau, and up the South Island's West Coast, the biggest irritation will be **sand flies.** They may be tiny, but they have the power to drive you absolutely crazy. Take gallons of strong insect repellent, and keep dousing yourself in it. If you still get bitten, try not to scratch and ladle on plenty of antihistamine to prevent swelling. The good news is that not everybody suffers. I'm one of the lucky ones—sand flies don't seem to like my blood. You'll just have to hope you're as unattractive to them as I am.

○ **Environmental Hazards**   The ocean holds its fair share of dangers. Most popular New Zealand beaches are patrolled by lifeguards, and you should always swim between the flags. Ask if you're unsure, because many beaches have **dangerous currents and holes.** In more remote areas, beaches are not patrolled, and you should exercise common sense before entering the waves. This particularly applies to the hazardous west coast beaches of the whole country. You'll notice most New Zealanders swim on the much safer east coast beaches and seldom on any west coast beaches. I would strongly advise against swimming on any west coast beaches unless they have lifesaving patrols on duty. Never swim alone anywhere.

On the subject of beaches, it's important to point out the danger of **sharks.** *Always* check with the locals as to the possibility of sharks in the ocean. As we all know, the threat of being attacked can never be underestimated.

As with beaches, **mountain and bush safety** *should* be a matter of common sense, but you would be amazed at how many people think they know better than the locals, setting off on a bush walk with no warm clothing (just because the sun is shining at the beginning is no guarantee that it will be farther on), no extra water, and no precautionary measures taken whatsoever. Hypothermia, exposure, and excessive sunburn are very real dangers in New Zealand, and you take your life in your hands if you ignore warnings. Every year we read the news reports of some international visitors who have ignored the warning and ventured into the mountains ill-prepared, and have never returned. Some have never been found.

Take very particular note of rain warnings if you're going into the mountains. Most New Zealand rivers rise very quickly, especially in the South Island, and many people have drowned trying to cross swiftly flowing, flooded rivers.

Dietary Distress The only thing to look out for in the bush is the possibility of *Giardia,* a waterborne parasite that causes diarrhea. Always boil water when you're hiking. Closer to civilization, do take particular care in summer that all food is kept cool, especially chicken, eggs, and meat products. I'm sad to report that studies have shown that New Zealand has the highest incidence of *Campylobacter* in the developed world. Over 75,000 New Zealanders get stomach upsets as a result of these bacteria every year, so take care. Like *Salmonella* (also relatively common here), it is usually associated with poor hygiene and contaminated food products. Always eat fresh food, make sure all chicken is thoroughly cooked, and always wash your hands before eating. Food poisoning is usually indicated by symptoms like diarrhea, abdominal cramps, fever, nausea, vomiting, headaches, and muscle aches. Most people recover without treatment in a few days, but if symptoms persist, you should see a doctor.

What to Do if You Get Sick Away From Home Almost all New Zealand cities and many smaller towns have a general hospital or emergency medical facilities, and the standard of medical care in New Zealand is excellent. Obviously, the bigger the city, the better the facilities, with Auckland, Hamilton, Wellington, Christchurch, and Dunedin having the most, the biggest, and the best facilities. As a visitor you will pay for any hospital or medical care, unless you are admitted via an accident situation. Most cities also have a 24-hour doctor and pharmacy facility for filling urgent prescriptions. I list **emergency numbers** under "Fast Facts" in each chapter.

Very few health insurance plans pay for medical evacuation back to the U.S. (which can cost $10,000 and up). A number of companies offer medical evacuation services anywhere in the world. If you're ever hospitalized more than 150 miles from home, **MedjetAssist** (© **800/527-7478;** www.medjetassistance.com) will pick you up and fly you to the hospital of your choice virtually anywhere in the world in a medically equipped and staffed aircraft 24 hours day, 7 days a week. Annual memberships are $225 individual, $350 family; you can also purchase short-term memberships.

U.K. nationals will need a **European Health Insurance Card (EHIC)** to receive free or reduced-costs health benefits during a visit to a European Economic Area (EEA) country (European Union countries plus Iceland, Liechtenstein, and Norway) or Switzerland. The European Health Insurance Card replaces the E111 form, which is no longer valid. For advice, ask at your local post office or see www.dh.gov.uk/travellers.

Before leaving home, find out what medical services your health insurance covers. To protect yourself, consider buying medical travel insurance (see "Insurance," below).

Insurance   Purchase travel insurance before you come to New Zealand, so that you'll be covered for any unexpected medical expenses and lost belongings. For information on traveler's insurance, trip cancellation insurance, and medical insurance while traveling, please visit www.frommers.com/planning.

Internet & Wi-Fi   Without Your Own Computer   To find cybercafes in New Zealand, check **www.cybercaptive.com** and **www.cybercafe.com**.

Aside from formal cybercafes, most **youth hostels** have at least one computer you can use for Internet access. Most **public libraries** in New Zealand offer Internet access free, or for a small charge, as do many **i-SITE visitor centers.** All cities and most larger towns have retail Internet providers, and these can be easily found by asking at the visitor center. Avoid **hotel business centers,** unless access to them is included in your rates; otherwise, you'll find yourself paying an additional charge to use it. Most major airports now have **Internet kiosks** scattered throughout their gates.

With Your Own Computer   More and more hotels, resorts, airports, cafes, and retailers are going **Wi-Fi** (wireless fidelity) and becoming "hot spots" that offer free high-speed Wi-Fi access or charge a fee for usage. Most upscale accommodations and many B&Bs in New Zealand offer a free high-speed or Wi-Fi service, but for those that charge for the service, the rates can be excessive (say, NZ$35 for a 24-hour period). From my own experience, check hotel Internet fees before signing on. If you only want to check your e-mail, you're better off paying a mere NZ$5 to NZ$6 for an hour's computer use at a retail Internet provider. Most towns on the main tourist beat have at least two or three such retailers, and information centers will point you in the right direction.

Most laptops sold today have built-in wireless capability. To find public Wi-Fi hot spots at your destination, go to **www.jiwire.com**; its Global Wi-Fi Finder holds the world's largest directory of public wireless hot spots. The New Zealand Yellow Pages telephone directories also list wireless and Internet hot spots under "Internet Service." There are also some New Zealand listings at www.laptopfriendlycafes.com.

Wherever you go, bring a **connection kit** of the right power and phone adapters (the voltage is 230 volts in New Zealand, and plugs are the three-prong type), a spare phone cord, and a spare Ethernet network cable. Connectivity is often poor in more remote provincial areas.

Language   English is spoken by all New Zealanders. You'll hear Maori spoken on some TV and radio programs and in some Maori settlements. As New Zealand is officially a bicultural country, you'll also hear Maori words spoken in daily conversation. See "Maori Language & Culture," in chapter 2, New Zealand in Depth.

Legal Aid   While driving, if you are pulled over for a minor infraction (such as speeding), never attempt to pay the fine directly to a police officer; this could be construed as attempted bribery, a much more serious crime. Pay fines by mail, or directly into the hands of the clerk of the court. If accused of a more serious offense, say and do nothing before consulting a lawyer. International visitors should call their embassy or consulate.

New Zealand's **Ministry of Foreign Affairs & Trade,** 195 Lambton Quay, Wellington (© **04/439-8000;** www.mfat.govt.nz), can assist with initial advice if you find yourself in trouble. If you need help, know that you don't have to be a New Zealand citizen, or living here permanently, to qualify for free legal aid. If you've been charged with a criminal offense—drink-driving, assault, theft, bribery, fraud, sexual or drug offenses, arson, or murder—but can't afford a lawyer, your legal fees may be paid by Criminal Legal Aid, which covers all lawyers' costs. Check **Legal Services Agency** (www.lsa.govt.nz), which has 11 regional offices: Auckland, Waitakere and Manukau (both within Auckland), Whangarei, Hamilton, Rotorua, New Plymouth, Napier, Wellington, Christchurch, and Dunedin.

LGBT Travelers   Gay and lesbian travelers will feel at ease in New Zealand, especially in Auckland and Wellington. Some provincial areas have a slightly narrower view of life and gay travelers may get some derogatory comments, but overall there's no threat to safety. For information, go to the **New Zealand Gay and Lesbian Tourism Association** website at www.iglta.org, or write to them at P.O. Box 24-558, Wellington 6015, NZ (© **04/917-9184;** fax 04/917-9176). Other New Zealand gay and lesbian websites include www.gaynz.com, **Pink Pages New Zealand** (www.pinkpagesnewzealand.com), **Queer Resources Aotearoa** (www.qrd.org.nz), and **Gay Queenstown** (www.gayqueenstown. com). The **International Gay and Lesbian Travel Association (IGLTA)** (© **800/448-8550** or 954/776-2626; www.iglta.org) is the trade association for the gay and lesbian travel industry, and offers an online directory of gay- and lesbian-friendly travel businesses and tour operators. See also "Safety," below.

Mail   New Zealand post offices will receive mail and hold it for you for 1 month. Have the parcel addressed to you c/o Poste Restante at the Chief Post Office of the town you'll be visiting. It costs NZ$3 to send an airmail letter to the United States, Canada, United Kingdom, or Europe. Overseas postcards cost NZ$2. The postal service is very reliable. Send items Fast Post within New Zealand for a faster airmail service. Parcels and documents can also be sent by tracked post for extra security. Courier and tracked courier services both within New Zealand and to overseas destinations are faster and more secure, but tracked airmail packages are cheaper and just as secure. You can follow the progress of all tracked items on the New Zealand Post website, www.nzpost.co.nz.

Medical Requirements   Unless you are arriving from an area known to be suffering from an epidemic, inoculations or vaccinations are not required to enter New Zealand. If you are currently taking any prescription medicines for recognized medical conditions, it is wise to bring the dosage you'll require with you. Keep all drugs in original bottles and bring a cover letter from your doctor to show airport security staff if required. If you require needles, they'll be fine in the aircraft hold but if you need them during your flight you will need to make special arrangements. Also see "Health."

Mobile Phones   The three letters that define much of the world's **wireless capabilities** are GSM (Global System for Mobiles), a big, seamless network that makes for easy cross-border cellphone use throughout Europe and dozens of other countries worldwide. In the U.S., T-Mobile, AT&T Wireless, and Cingular use this quasi-universal system; in Canada, Microcell and some Rogers customers are GSM; and all Europeans and most Australians and New Zealanders use GSM.

If your cellphone is on a GSM system, and you have a world-capable phone such as many (but not all) Sony Ericsson, Motorola, or Samsung models, you can make and receive calls across civilized areas on much of the globe, from Andorra to Uganda. Unfortunately, per-minute charges can be high. New Zealanders, it should be noted, currently pay some of the highest cellphone usage charges in the world.

In New Zealand, the two main telecommunications providers are Telecom, which operates on an 800 megahertz frequency, and Vodafone, which operates on a 900 megahertz frequency. If your own cellphone is able to operate within either of those frequencies, your best-value option is to bring it with you and purchase a local SIM card when you get here.

You'll get good cellphone coverage in most urban areas in New Zealand, but be prepared for "black holes" where there is no coverage at all. These areas are usually off the beaten track and are too numerous to list. Thankfully, you seldom have to travel far before coverage resumes. The West Coast, Arthur's Pass, parts of Eastland, and parts of the far south are notorious for weaker coverage.

True wilderness adventurers should consider renting a **satellite phone.** Per-minute call charges can be even cheaper than roaming charges with a regular cellphone, but the phone itself is more expensive (up to $150 a week), and depending on the service you choose, people calling you may incur high long-distance charges.

Cellphone rental is not always cheap, and there is only one cellphone rental provider within New Zealand—Vodafone—so you can't shop around. If you wish to rent a cellphone for your trip, you need to call at the Vodafone Rental shop at either Auckland International Airport or Christchurch International Airport. The base rental rate for less than 1 week is NZ$8 per day. For more than 1 week it's NZ$4 per day, or NZ$30 per week. On top of that you pay a call rate of NZ90¢ per minute anytime, anywhere within New Zealand. International calls will cost more. You can check details at www.vodarent.co.nz.

Two good wireless rental companies outside of New Zealand are **InTouch USA** (© 800/872-7626; www.intouchglobal.com) and **RoadPost** (© 888/290-1606 or 905/272-5665; www.roadpost.com). Give them your itinerary, and they'll tell you what wireless products you need. InTouch will also, for free, advise you on whether your existing phone will work overseas; simply call © 703/222-7161 between 9am and 4pm EST, or go to www.intouch global.com/travel.htm.

Money & Costs

THE VALUE OF THE NEW ZEALAND DOLLAR VS. OTHER POPULAR CURRENCIES

NZ$	US$	UK£	Aus$	Can$	Euro €
1.00	0.82	0.52	0.80	0.80	0.60

Frommer's lists exact prices in the local currency. The currency conversions quoted above were correct at press time. However, rates fluctuate, so before departing consult a currency exchange website such as www.oanda.com/currency/converter to check up-to-the-minute rates.

It's always advisable to bring money in a variety of forms on your New Zealand vacation: a mix of cash, credit cards, and traveler's checks. You should also exchange enough petty cash to cover airport incidentals, tipping, and transportation to your hotel before you leave home, or withdraw money upon arrival at an airport ATM.

Most travelers find New Zealand to be very reasonably priced in most things—ludicrously so in some cases, I'm sure. Certainly anyone converting from British pounds or American or Canadian dollars is going to get great value across-the-board.

The **New Zealand dollar** (NZ$) is based on the decimal system, and there are 100 cents in the dollar. There are coin denominations of 10, 20, and 50 cents and $1 and $2, as well as bank notes in $5, $10, $20, $50, and $100 amounts.

ATMs ATMs are common throughout New Zealand. You'll find them inside and outside all banks, in major shopping centers, in supermarkets and gas stations. Some smaller towns in remote locations—on Stewart Island or Great Barrier Island for instance, or in some parts of the South Island's West Coast—don't have ATMs at all, but you'll find that noted in each appropriate chapter.

Most likely, your **ATM card** is compatible with New Zealand systems. The machines generally accept four-digit PINs, but it always pays to check with your bank beforehand. Also check with your bank about fees for using your card internationally. The Bank of New Zealand accepts ATM cards in the **Cirrus** system (© 800/424-7787; www.mastercard.com); other banks accept cards in the **PLUS** system (© 800/843-7587; www.visa.com).

WHAT THINGS COST IN NEW ZEALAND	NZ$
Taxi from the airport to downtown Auckland	50–90
Double room, moderate	350–600
Double room, inexpensive	150–250
Three-course dinner for one without wine, moderate	70–80
Bottle of beer	3.50–7
Cup of coffee	3.50–4.50
1 gallon/1 liter of premium gas	2.10–2.40
Admission to most museums	Free or by donation
Admission to most national parks	Free

Credit Cards   Most New Zealand businesses take MasterCard and Visa. American Express, Diners Club, Bankcard, and Japan Credit Bank are also widely accepted in major tourist centers, but less so in smaller towns.

You can withdraw cash advances from your credit cards at banks or ATMs, but high fees make credit card cash advances a pricey way to get cash. Keep in mind that you'll pay interest from the moment of your withdrawal, even if you pay your monthly bills on time. Also, note that many banks now assess a 1% to 3% "foreign transaction fee" on **all** charges you incur abroad (whether it's in local currency or your native currency).

Beware of hidden credit-card fees while traveling. Check with your credit or debit card issuer to see what fees, if any, will be charged for overseas transactions. Recent reform legislation in the U.S., for example, has curbed some exploitative lending practices. But many banks have responded by increasing fees in other areas, including fees for customers who use credit and debit cards while out of the country—even if those charges were made in U.S. dollars. Fees can amount to 3% or more of the purchase price. Check with your bank before departing to avoid any surprise charges on your statement. For help with currency conversions, tip calculations, and more, download Frommer's convenient Travel Tools app for your mobile device. Go to www.frommers.com/go/mobile and click on the Travel Tools icon.

Newspapers & Magazines   All New Zealand newspapers are printed in English. In Auckland the main daily is the *New Zealand Herald* (www.nzherald.co.nz); in Wellington, *The Dominion* (www.stuff.co.nz/dompost); and for the South Island, *The Christchurch Press* (www.stuff.co.nz/the-press). The major weekend newspaper is the *Sunday Star Times* (www.stuff.co.nz/sunday-star-times). Most dairies, supermarkets, corner stores, bookstores, and petrol stations sell newspapers. Hotels and most other accommodation providers also offer their guests a newspaper delivery service. New Zealand produces numerous specialized and general lifestyle magazines, which can be found in bookstores and supermarkets.

Packing   Regardless of the season, New Zealand weather can be very changeable. Even in summer, you will need to pack warm clothing and something weatherproof. This particularly applies if you are going walking, tramping, or mountaineering. Very few places have formal dress codes in New Zealand, requiring the use of jackets—perhaps just one or two of the luxury lodges; but in most cases, smart casual is perfectly acceptable. Many people do dress up if they are visiting high-end restaurants and bars, but this is optional. Some clubs, restaurants, and bars do not permit jeans. For more helpful information on packing for your trip, download our convenient Travel Tools app for your mobile device. Go to www.frommers.com/go/mobile and click on the Travel Tools icon.

Passports A **passport** is required for all entering visitors, and it must be valid for at least 3 months beyond your departure date from New Zealand. If you lose yours, visit the nearest consulate of your native country as soon as possible for a replacement.

For Residents of the United States: Whether you're applying in person or by mail, you can download passport applications from the U.S. State Department website at http://travel.state.gov/. For general information, call the **National Passport Agency** (☏ 202/647-0518). To find your regional passport office, either check the U.S. State Department website or call the **National Passport Information Center** (☏ 900/225-5674); the fee is 55¢ per minute for automated information and $1.50 per minute for operator-assisted calls.

For Residents of Canada: Passport applications are available at travel agencies throughout Canada or from the central **Passport Office,** Department of Foreign Affairs and International Trade, Ottawa, ON K1A 0G3 (☏ 800/567-6868; www.ppt.gc.ca).

For Residents of the United Kingdom: To pick up an application for a standard 10-year passport (5-year passport for children under 16), visit your nearest passport office, major post office, or travel agency, or contact the **United Kingdom Passport Service** at ☏ 0870/521-0410 or search its website at www.ukpa.gov.uk.

For Residents of Ireland: You can apply for a 10-year passport at the **Passport Office,** Setanta Centre, Molesworth Street, Dublin 2 (☏ 01/671-1633; www.irlgov.ie/iveagh). Those under age 18 and over 65 must apply for a 3-year passport. You can also apply at 1A South Mall, Cork (☏ 021/272-525), or at most main post offices.

For Residents of Australia: You can get an application from your local post office or any branch of Passports Australia, but you must schedule an interview at the passport office to present your application materials. Call the **Australian Passport Information Service** at ☏ 131-232, or visit www.passports.gov.au.

Petrol See "Getting Around by Car," earlier in this chapter.

Police The emergency number for New Zealand Police is 111; for non-emergencies, ring the local police number listed in Fast Facts in individual chapters, or check the local phone directory. Police drive white vehicles with bright blue and orange markings. In addition to dealing with general crime, they also have the power to stop vehicles for speeding, traffic infringements, or for alcohol breath testing. Some also drive unmarked cars, so don't even think about breaking speed limits just because you can't see a white police vehicle.

Safety New Zealand is generally a very safe destination, one of the safest in the world. Still, exercise the same care that you would in any major city. People-oriented dangers—theft, assault, murder—should be mentioned, but it's important to remember that violent crimes in most countries, especially in New Zealand, occur between acquaintances. As a traveler, it's unlikely you'll be a victim. If you're hitchhiking, however, that may be another matter.

On the subject of theft, it should be noted that many travelers are lulled into a false sense of security, leaving cars unlocked and valuables clearly visible. Always park your car in a well-populated area whenever possible; lock it and cover your luggage with a blanket or a coat. *Never* leave handbags or cameras in cars. The simple rule should be, if you can't do without it, don't leave it in the car, locked or otherwise.

The downtown areas of New Zealand's major cities, especially Auckland, Wellington, and Christchurch, are now well covered by closed-circuit cameras, which are monitored by police. This has significantly helped to reduce crime. It is still advisable to exercise caution, especially on Thursday, Friday, and Saturday nights, when social drinking sometimes gets out of hand.

There is a significant youth drinking problem in New Zealand, and this tends to manifest itself in areas with a large concentration of bars—Wellington's Courtenay Place and Christchurch's Oxford Strip are two good examples. That doesn't necessarily make these areas dangerous—far from it—but it is a good idea to be more vigilant and to stay away from any fights that might break out.

When it comes to traveling in the countryside, you should always be as cautious as you would be anywhere else. New Zealanders are generally friendly and welcoming, but if you're going to encounter any gender or racial bigotry, it is more likely to be in smaller rural communities. The risk is small, though. New Zealand is a bicultural country with increasing numbers of immigrants residing here.

Female travelers should never hitchhike alone or at night. Despite the wider population being tolerant of solo female travelers, there are always some unsavory characters who view this as an opportunity for theft, assault, rape, or worse. Don't put yourself in a vulnerable position. New Zealand men generally are fine, but there is a macho undercurrent in our society, especially when rugby and alcohol are part of the equation. Always take care in social environments, and if you are a single female traveling alone, don't drink too much, or you'll be easy prey.

Senior Travel   Discounts for those 60 and over are increasingly available in New Zealand, so be sure to inquire when making reservations for accommodations and attractions. Don't forget to carry photo identification. Those 60 and over are entitled to a 20% discount on InterCity coaches and Tranz Scenic trains. Newmans Coaches offers a 20% discount to anyone 60 and over. Good websites are **Grey Power** (www.greypower.co.nz) and **Age Concern** (www.ageconcern.co.nz).

Smoking   Smoking is illegal in all public buildings in New Zealand, from hotels and offices to restaurants and bars. Many bars and restaurants now provide an outdoor area for smoking customers, but it is increasingly frowned upon.

Single Travelers   New Zealand is a perfectly safe place for traveling solo, although I assume that everyone will act with common sense in terms of personal safety and late-night wanderings. (And of course, you won't want to take off on a long trek into the mountains on your own.) Some accommodations charge significantly less for one person than for two. All rates listed in this book are for doubles, so be sure to ask about single rates if you intend to travel alone.

On package vacations, single travelers are often hit with a "single supplement" to the base price. To avoid it, you can agree to room with other single travelers or find a compatible roommate before you go, from a roommate-locator agency.

Many reputable tour companies offer singles-only trips. **Singles Travel International** (⌀ **877/765-6874;** www.singlestravelintl.com) offers singles-only escorted tours to New Zealand.

New Zealand operators like **Kiwi Experience** (www.kiwiexperience.com) and the **Magic Travellers** network (www.magicbus.co.nz) have changed the face of singles travel in New Zealand. Their hop-on-and-hop-off bus tours of New Zealand are geared specifically toward backpacker culture, loads of fun, spontaneity, and great deals. Mostly filled with travelers in their 20s and 30s, they're a terrific way to meet people and make new friends as you travel—and isn't that half the fun of travel?

For a small-group experience, **Let's Trek Australia** (www.letstrekaustralia.com) is a partnership of small group and singles adventure specialists working together throughout

Australia and New Zealand. **Relaxing Journeys** (www.relaxingjourneys.co.nz) specializes in small, escorted tours—including self-drive tours, cruises, and coach trips—for independent travelers. You can also find information and useful tips at www.independenttraveler. com and www.solotravel.org.

Student Travel The **International Student Travel Confederation (ISTC)** (www.istc. org) was formed in 1949 to make travel around the world more affordable for students. Check out its website for comprehensive travel services information and details on how to get an **International Student Identity Card (ISIC),** which qualifies students for substantial savings on rail passes, plane tickets, entrance fees, and more. It also provides students with basic health and life insurance and a 24-hour help line. The card is valid for a maximum of 18 months. You can apply for the card online or in person at **STA Travel** (𝄞 **800/781-4040** in North America; www.statravel.com), the biggest student travel agency in the world; check out the website to locate STA Travel offices worldwide. The New Zealand headquarters is at 10 High St., Auckland (𝄞 **09/309-0458**). The ISIC card is also accepted by many New Zealand tourism operators including hotels, bars, transport providers, theaters, major attractions, and tour companies. The ISIC website lists New Zealand operators offering discounts.

If you're no longer a student but are still 25 and under, you can get an **International Youth Travel Card (IYTC)** from the same people, which entitles you to some discounts. **Travel CUTS** (𝄞 **800/592-2887;** www.travelcuts.com) offers similar services for both Canadians and U.S. residents. Irish students can try **USIT** (𝄞 **01/602-1904;** www.usit.ie), an Ireland-based specialist in youth travel.

Taxes There is a national 15% **Goods and Services Tax (GST)** that's applicable to everything. A **departure tax** of NZ$25 is assessed and can be paid by credit card or in cash in New Zealand currency.

Telephones To call New Zealand from another country:

1. Dial the international access code: 011 from the U.S.; 00 from the U.K. or Ireland; or 0011 from Australia.
2. Dial the country code, **64.**
3. Dial the area code (for example, 03, 09, or 06, but without the zero) known as **STD (subscriber toll dialing),** and then the number.

To call long distance within New Zealand: First dial the STD—**09** for Auckland and Northland, **07** for the Thames Valley, **06** for the east coast and Wanganui, **04** for Wellington, or **03** for the South Island—and then the local number. (If you're calling from outside New Zealand, omit the zero.) There are three main kinds of public telephones in New Zealand: card phones, credit card phones, and coin phones. Magnetic strip **phone cards** for public phones can be purchased from supermarkets, post offices, dairies, and service stations.

To make international calls: To make international calls from New Zealand, first dial 𝄞 00 and then the country code (U.S. or Canada 1, U.K. 44, Ireland 353, Australia 61). Next dial the area code and number.

The most economical way to make international phone calls from New Zealand is to charge them to an international calling card (available free from your long-distance company at home). All calls, even international ones, can be made from public phone booths. (Long-distance calls made from your hotel or motel often have hefty surcharges added.) You can also call home using **Country Direct** numbers. They are **000-911** for the U.S.; **000-944** for British Telecom (operator); **000-912** for British Telecom (automatic); **000-940** for UK Mercury; **000-919** for Canada; **000-996** for Australia-Optus; and **000-961** for Australia-Telstra.

For directory assistance within New Zealand: Dial ✆ **018.** For operator assistance within New Zealand, dial ✆ **010.**

For international operator assistance: If you need operator assistance in making a call, dial ✆ **0170;** for directory assistance for an international call, dial ✆ **0172.**

Remember that calling a 1-800 or toll-free number in your country from New Zealand is not toll-free. In fact, it costs the same as an overseas call.

Time   New Zealand is located just west of the international date line, and its standard time is 12 hours ahead of Greenwich Mean Time. Thus, when it's noon in New Zealand, it's 7:30am in Singapore, 9am in Tokyo, 10am in Sydney; and—all the previous day—4pm in San Francisco, 7pm in New York, and midnight in London. In New Zealand, daylight saving time starts the first weekend in October and ends in mid-March. For help with time translations, and more, download our convenient Travel Tools app for your mobile device. Go to www.frommers.com/go/mobile and click on the Travel Tools icon.

Tipping   Most New Zealanders don't tip waitstaff unless they've received extraordinary service—and then only 5% to 10%. Taxi drivers and porters are rarely tipped in this country. For help with tip calculations, currency conversions, and more, download our convenient Travel Tools app for your mobile device. Go to www.frommers.com/go/mobile and click on the Travel Tools icon.

Toilets   There are "public conveniences" strategically located in all cities and many towns. Local **Plunket Rooms** come with a "Mother's Room," where you can change your child's diapers. The Plunket Society is a state-subsidized organization that provides free baby care to all New Zealand families. You'll also find well signposted public toilets on the street in most towns and cities. They can also be found in hotel lobbies, bars, restaurants, museums, department stores, railway and bus stations, and service stations. Large hotels and fast-food restaurants are often the best bet for clean facilities. Restaurants and bars in resorts or heavily visited areas may reserve their restrooms for patrons.

VAT   See "Taxes" earlier in this section.

Visas   **Visas** are not required for stays shorter than 3 months (as long as you don't plan to study, work, or undergo medical treatment) if you're a citizen of one of the following countries: Andorra, Argentina, Austria, Bahrain, Belgium, Brazil, Brunei, Canada, Chile, Cyprus, Czech Republic, Denmark, Estonia, Finland, France, Germany, Greece, Hong Kong (if you're traveling with a Special Administrative passport or if you hold a British national passport), Hungary, Iceland, Ireland, Israel, Italy, Japan, Korea (South), Kuwait, Latvia, Liechtenstein, Lithuania, Luxembourg, Malaysia, Malta, Mexico, Monaco, the Netherlands, Norway, Oman, Poland, Portugal (Portuguese passport holders must have the right to live permanently in Portugal), Qatar, San Marino, Saudi Arabia, Singapore, Slovak Republic, Slovenia, South Africa, Spain, Sweden, Switzerland, United Arab Emirates, United States, Uruguay, and Vatican City. British citizens are allowed a 6-month stay without a visa.

If you're planning to visit for longer than is stated above, or if your country of origin is not listed, contact the nearest New Zealand embassy, consulate, or High Commission for information on the appropriate visa and an application. If you'd like to work or live in New Zealand, you can inquire at an embassy or consulate, or write to the **New Zealand Immigration Service,** P.O. Box 27-149, Wellington, NZ (www.immigration.govt.nz).

Before entering New Zealand you must have a confirmed round-trip or outward-bound ticket; enough money for your designated stay (NZ$1,000 per person per month; credit cards are accepted); and the necessary documents to enter the country from which you came or the next country on your itinerary.

Visitor Information   To get started, contact the nearest **Tourism New Zealand office** for a complimentary copy of its *New Zealand Vacation Planner.* Their offices can be found in the **United States** at 501 Santa Monica Blvd., Ste. 300, Santa Monica, CA 90401 (© **866/639-9325** in the U.S., or 310/395-7480); in **Canada** at 888 Dunsmuir St., Ste. 1200, Vancouver, BC V6C 3K4 (© **800/888-5494** in Canada, or 604/684-2117); in **Australia** at Level 8, 35 Pitt St., Sydney, NSW 2000 (© **02/9247-5222**); in **England** at New Zealand House, Haymarket, SW1Y 4TQ, London (© **020/7930-1662**); in **Germany** at Rossmarkt 11, 60311 Frankfurt am Main (© **069/9712-1110**); and in **Hong Kong** at Unit 1601 Vicwood Plaza, 199 Des Voeux Rd. (© **852/2526-0141**).

The official Tourism New Zealand website is **www.newzealand.com**, which provides comprehensive details for every aspect of your trip and is a must-visit. Click on your home country to see the latest deals, with contact information for travel agents. Other good sites include **New Zealand on the Web** (www.nz.com), which has hundreds of great links; for up-to-the-minute ski information, check **www.nzski.com**.

When you arrive in New Zealand, you'll find 80 official **i-SITE Visitor Centres** (www.i-site.org) scattered around the country. Friendly staff members can book accommodations, activities, and tours; provide maps; and sell stamps and phone cards. Each chapter in this book lists the appropriate information centers, and you can pick up a list of i-SITE locations at Auckland and Christchurch international airports.

Water   New Zealand tap water is pollution-free and safe to drink. In the bush, you should boil, filter, or chemically treat water from rivers and lakes to avoid contracting *Giardia* (a waterborne parasite that causes diarrhea).

Wi-Fi   See "Internet & Wi-Fi," earlier in this section.

Women Travelers   See "Safety" and "Single Travelers."

AIRLINE, HOTEL & CAR RENTAL WEBSITES

AIRLINE WEBSITES

Air New Zealand
www.airnewzealand.com

Air Tahiti Nui
www.airtahitinui-usa.com

American Airlines
www.aa.com

British Airways
www.british-airways.com

Cathay Pacific
www.cathaypacific.com

Emirates Airlines
www.emirates.com

Japan Airlines
www.jal.co.jp/en

Jetstar
www.jetstar.com

Korean Air
www.koreanair.com

Lan Airlines
www.lanchile.com

Lufthansa
www.lufthansa.com

Malaysian Airlines
www.malaysiaairlines.com

Qantas
www.qantas.com.au

Royal Brunei Airlines
www.bruneiair.com

Singapore Airlines
www.singaporeair.com

Thai Airways
www.thaiair.com

United Airlines
www.united.com

Virgin Blue
www.virginblue.com.au

MAJOR HOTEL & MOTEL CHAINS

Accor Hotels
www.accor.com

Crowne Plaza Hotels
www.ichotelsgroup.com/
crowneplaza

Hilton Hotels
www.hilton.com

Holiday Inn
www.holidayinn.com

Hyatt
www.hyatt.com

InterContinental Hotels & Resorts
www.ichotelsgroup.com

Scenic Hotels Group
www.scenichotels.co.nz

Westin Hotels
www.starwoodhotels.com/westin

CAR RENTAL AGENCIES

Avis
www.avis.com

Budget
www.budget.com

Hertz
www.hertz.com

Payless
www.paylesscarrental.com

Thrifty
www.thrifty.com

17

PLANNING YOUR TRIP TO NEW ZEALAND | Airline, Hotel & Car Rental Websites

KIWI TERMS & PHRASES

Who would have thought the English language could be so confusing? New Zealand may seem like an easy place to negotiate, but it has developed some very distinctive language characteristics. Here's a guide to help you negotiate everyday colloquialisms.

For tips on the Maori language, see p. 38 and 40.

KIWI/YANKEE TERMS

Air-conditioning Refers to both heating and cooling the air

All Blacks New Zealand rugby team

Bach North Island term for vacation house (plural: baches)

Bath Bathtub

Bathroom Where one bathes; bath

Biro Ballpoint pen

Biscuits/bickies Cookies

Bludge Borrow

Bonnet Hood of car

Boot Trunk of car

Bro Slang for "brother"; a friendly term used widely

Bush Forest

Chemist shop Drugstore

Chilly bin Styrofoam cooler (U.S.), esky (Aus.)

Coach Long-distance bus

Cocky Farmer

College High school

Cot Crib (place where a baby or toddler sleeps)

Crib South Island term for holiday house

Cuppa Cup of tea

Cyclone Hurricane

Dairy Convenience store

Dish As in "a bit of a dish"; a good-looking woman

Do As in "a bit of a do"; a party

Doona/Duvet Comforter, quilt (Aus.)

En suite In-room bathroom

Fanny Female genitalia; you'll shock Kiwis if you call the thing you wear around your waist a "fanny pack"

Flannel Face cloth

Footpath Sidewalk

Gallops Thoroughbred horse racing

Get stuck in Get started

Gidday Hello

Grizzle Complain

Grog   Booze

Gumboots   Waterproof rubber boots (U.S.), Wellingtons (Britain)

Hire   Rent

Homely   Homey

Hooker   Front-row rugby player

Hotties   Hot-water bottles

Housie   Bingo

Jandals   Thongs (Aus.), flip-flops (U.S./Britain)

Jersey   Pullover sweater (U.S.), jumper (Aus.)

Judder bars   Speed bumps (U.S.), sleeping policeman (Britain)

Jug   Electric kettle or a pitcher

Kiwi   Person from New Zealand; native bird of New Zealand

Knickers   Underwear, undies

Knock up   Wake up

Lift   Elevator

Loo   Toilet

Lounge   Living room

LSZ   Low-speed zone

Mate   Friend

Mossie   Mosquito

Nappy   Diaper

Pakeha   Anyone of European descent

Private facilities   Private bathroom

Pushchair   Baby stroller

Queue   Line, to wait in line

Rates   Property taxes

Return ticket   Round-trip ticket

Rug   Blanket

Serviette   Napkin

Shout   Treat someone (usually refers to a meal or a drink), buy a round

Single bed   Twin bed

Singlet   Sleeveless undershirt

Sister   Nurse

Smoko   Morning or afternoon break

Strides   Trousers

Ta   Thank you

Thongs   Brief underwear (not the Australian term for *jandals*—see above)

To call   To visit

Togs   Swimsuit (U.S.), cozzie (Aus.)

To ring   To phone

Track   Trail

Tramping   Hiking

Trots   Harness racing; in New Zealand the word also means diarrhea

Uplift   Pick up

Varsity   University, college

Yank   American

MENU TERMS

Afghans   Popular Kiwi cookies made with cornflakes and cocoa

ANZAC biscuits   Cookies named for the Australia New Zealand Army Corps; they contain rolled oats and golden syrup

Bangers   Sausages

Beetroot   Beets

Biscuits   Cookies

Blue vein   Bleu cheese

Capsicum   Green or red bell pepper

Chips   French-fried potatoes

Chook   Chicken

Courgette   Zucchini

Devonshire tea   Morning or afternoon tea, plus scones with cream and jam

Dinner   The main meal of the day; can be the meal eaten in the middle of the day

Entree   Appetizer

Grilled   Broiled

Hogget   Year-old lamb

Iceblock Popsicle

Jelly Gelatin dessert

Kumara Kiwi sweet potato

Lemonade 7-Up

Lollies Candy

Main course Entree

Marmite New Zealand–made yeast spread

Mash Mashed potatoes

Meat pie A two-crust pie filled with stewed, cubed, or ground meat (usually beef) and gravy

Milk shake Flavored milk

Milo A hot drink similar to Ovaltine

Pavlova Popular meringue dessert named after prima ballerina Anna Pavlova, served with whipped cream and fruit

Pikelets Small pancakes served at teatime

Pipis Clams

Pudding Dessert in general, not necessarily pudding

Roast dinner Roast beef or leg of lamb served with potatoes and other vegetables that have been cooked with the meat

Rock melon Cantaloupe

Saveloy A type of wiener

Scone A biscuit served at teatime

Silverbeet Swiss chard

Silverside A superior cut of corned beef

Snarlers Sausages

Takeaway Takeout

Tamarillos Tree tomatoes

Tea The national beverage; also a light evening meal, supper; see also "Dinner," above

Thick shake Milkshake

Tomato sauce Ketchup

Vegemite Australian-made yeast spread

Water biscuit Cracker

Weet-Bix A breakfast cereal similar to shredded wheat

Whitebait Very tiny fish, served whole without being cleaned

White tea Tea with milk

Index

G

H